A HISTORY OF SOVIET RUSSIA

A HISTORY OF SOVIET RUSSIA

by E. H. Carr

in fourteen volumes

*with R. W. Davies

FOUNDATIONS OF A PLANNED ECONOMY 1926-1929

BY

E. H. CARR

Fellow of Trinity College, Cambridge

AND

R. W. DAVIES

Director of the Centre for Russian and East European Studies
University of Birmingham

VOLUME ONE—PART II

M

First published 1969
Reprinted 1970, 1978

Published by
THE MACMILLAN PRESS LTD
London and Basingstoke
Associated companies in Delhi
Dublin Hong Kong Johannesburg Lagos
Melbourne New York Singapore Tokyo

Printed in Hong Kong by
CHINA TRANSLATION AND PRINTING SERVICES

British Library Cataloguing in Publication Data

Carr, Edward Hallett
    Foundations of a planned economy, 1926–1929
    Vol. 1. [Part] 2. — (Carr, Edward Hallett. History
    of Soviet Russia; 10)
    1. Russia — Social conditions — 1917–
    I. Title   II. Davies, Robert William
    309.1′47′0842   HN523

    ISBN 0-333-24571-7
    ISBN 0-333-24216-5   Boxed set

TABLE OF APPROXIMATE EQUIVALENTS

1 arshin = 2 ft. 4 in.
1 chervonets (gold) (10 rubles) at par = 1·06 £ sterling (gold)
or $5·15 (gold).
1 desyatin = 1·09 hectares = 2·70 acres.
1 hectare = 2·47 acres.
1 pud = 16·38 kilograms = 36·11 lb.
1 tsentner = 0·10 metric ton.[1]
1 vedro = 12·30 litres = 21·65 Imperial pints.
1 verst = 1·07 kilometres = 0·66 mile.

[1] Metric tons are used throughout this volume.

2 K

C : *Labour*

*

CHAPTER 17

THE LABOUR FORCE

(a) Workers in Industry, Building and Transport

THE Soviet Union between 1926 and 1929 continued to present the seemingly paradoxical phenomenon of a simultaneous increase in the number of employed and of unemployed workers. While the number of employed persons in agriculture (not including, of course, the mass of peasants who were not wage-earners) remained stationary, the number of workers in census industry increased by 23 per cent, and the number of building workers more than doubled.[1] The reservoir which fed this enlarged labour force was the surplus rural population. Russian industry had never entirely severed its links with the countryside ; and the seasonal employment of peasants in the cities had been a familiar phenomenon before the revolution.[2] In the middle nineteen-twenties, when the pressure of an increasing population again began to be felt in the countryside, and opportunities of temporary employment in the cities, especially in the building industry, presented themselves on an expanding scale, the seasonal flow of peasants to the cities was resumed. This migration was initially and by intention seasonal : the migrant returned to help in the harvest, or when jobs fell off in the town.[3] But the seasonal sometimes became permanent and statisticians

---

[1] See Table No. 21, p. 955 below ; in Soviet terminology, " industry " means factory and workshop industry, and does not include building or transport.

[2] For figures for 1906–1910 see G. von Mende, *Studien zur Kolonisation in der Sovetunion* (1933), p. 42.

[3] For a detailed analysis of migration of this kind from the Kostroma province in 1926–1927 see *Na Agrarnom Fronte*, No. 6-7, 1928, pp. 133-143. At the fifteenth party congress in December 1927, 100,000 peasants from Kaluga province were said to have worked in the cities in the past summer, and to have brought back with them an average of 150-200 rubles each ; the province of Tambov was so overpopulated that 500,000 peasants had to look for earnings from industry ; from Ryazan 220,000 peasants had gone to Moscow, Leningrad and other cities for seasonal work (*Pyatnadtsatyi S"ezd VKP(B)*, ii (1962),

had difficulty in distinguishing between the two. A round number of a million peasants were said to have settled in the towns in the three years from 1923–1924 to 1925–1926.[1] Thereafter, with the progressive increase in the tempo of industrialization, the tide became a flood. Permanent migrants from country to town numbered 945,000 in 1926, 1,062,000 in 1928 and 1,392,000 in 1929.[2] Rural population continued to grow, and urban population, reinforced by the constant influx of labour from the countryside, grew still more rapidly.[3] It was on any reckoning a major shift of population and a decisive factor in the process of industrialization. The compilers of the first five-year plan in 1928 assumed that the peak of the movement had been reached ; in projecting an increase in the number of employed persons from 11·4 to 14·8 millions (basic variant) or 15·8 millions (optimum variant) during the currency of the plan, they observed that this represented an annual increment of 6 per cent as against an annual increment of 11-12 per cent for the past five years.[4] From 1929 onwards, the reduced birth-rate of the years of war and revolution was expected to make itself felt in a reduced rate of expansion of the industrial labour force.[5] In the event, the inexhaustible reserves of labour

---

1094, 1254, 1266). Peasants were estimated to have earned 120-140 million rubles in industrial wages in the period from August to October 1926, and 300 millions in the same period of 1927 (*Na Agrarnom Fronte*, No. 4, 1928, p. iv). " Seasonal " work was legally defined as work limited by climatic or other conditions to not more than six months in the year (*Sobranie Uzakonenii, 1926*, No. 40, art. 290), " temporary " work as work for less than two months, or four months in case of temporary replacement of a permanent worker (*Sobranie Uzakonenii, 1927*, No. 9, art. 80).

[1] *Kontrol'nye Tsifry Narodnogo Khozyaistva na 1926–1927 god* (1926), p. 286.

[2] *Kontrol'nye Tsifry Narodnogo Khozyaistva SSSR na 1928–1929 god* (1929), p. 215 ; *Sotsialisticheskoe Stroitel'stvo SSSR* (1936), p. 545.

[3] The following were the totals (in millions) of rural and urban population in this period :

	December 17, 1926	January 1, 1928	January 1, 1929
Urban	26·3	27·6	29·0
Rural	120·7	123·0	125·3
Total	147·0	150·6	154·3

(*Sdvigi v Sel'skom Khozyaistve SSSR* (2nd ed., 1931), p. 9.)

[4] *Pyatiletnii Plan Narodno-Khozyaistvennogo Stroitel'stva SSSR* (1929), i, 92-93 ; for more detailed figures see *ibid.* ii, ii, 165.

[5] *Kontrol'nye Tsifry po Trudu na 1928–29 god* (1929), p. 14.

in the Russian countryside made this factor of little or no importance.

This was to a substantial extent a new labour force. The nucleus of industrial workers surviving from the period before the revolution had been decimated and dispersed in the civil war, and never fully reconstituted.[1] Of miners employed in 1929 61·6 per cent, of metal workers 40 per cent, and of textile workers 36·1 per cent, were of peasant origin.[2] The proportion of workers in industry who retained holdings of land showed a steady though unspectacular decline from 1905 to 1925, and then began to climb again with the fresh influx of workers from the countryside. Of workers entering the Donbass mines between 1926 and 1929 37·4 per cent still held land in 1929, of metal workers entering industry in Moscow and in the Ukraine in the same period 28·4 and 27·3 per cent respectively; percentages in other industries were lower.[3] Of workers who were party members 10·7 per cent retained links with the countryside ; the proportion was highest among building workers, lowest among skilled factory workers.[4] But everywhere peasants and members of peasants' families formed an important element in the unskilled labour force in mines and factories and in the building industry. Of workers sent to permanent jobs by the labour exchanges of the RSFSR in 1926, 34 per cent came from the countryside.[5] The influx of new recruits introduced a certain division between two categories of workers. An observer at one of the Yugostal works noted that, where one worker might be a genuine member of the " factory

[1] For the weakness of the proletariat in the early days of NEP see *Socialism in One Country, 1924–1926*, Vol. 1, pp. 100-103. Much information on the composition of the factory proletariat in Leningrad from 1921 to 1928 is collected in *Istoriya SSSR*, No. 5, 1959, pp. 33-38. The proportion of pre-1917 workers and their children was higher here than elsewhere ; but here too the influence of " new workers " after 1925 was responsible for a decline in discipline.

[2] *Sostav Fabrichno-Zavodskogo Proletariata SSSR* (1930), pp. 10, 12, 14.

[3] *Ibid.* pp. 20, 22, 42.

[4] A. Bubnov, *VKP(B)* (1931), p. 618 ; *Sotsial'nyi i Natsional'nyi Sostav VKP(B)* (1928), p. 68. The proportion of worker party members holding land was about half that of non-party workers (*Sostav Fabrichno-Zavodskogo Proletariata SSSR* (1930), p. 102).

[5] L. Rogachevskaya, *Iz Istorii Rabochego Klassa SSSR* (1959), p. 55 ; the percentage was unevenly distributed, rising to from 40 to 50 in provincial towns and falling to from 7 to 12 in Moscow and Leningrad.

proletariat ", another might be a rural employer of hired labour who had moved to the town from the countryside. "Two such workers, though working side by side in the same enterprise, are surely bearers and representatives of *two different social groups* " ; such conditions imported " an unhealthy attitude into the working class ".[1] Bukharin in a moment of frankness spoke of " a certain differentiation in the working class itself ".[2]

The concomitant phenomenon of rising unemployment continued in an aggravated form throughout this period. The number of unemployed registered at the labour exchanges was recorded by Narkomtrud (in thousands) as follows :

	Total	Members of Trade Unions	Non-members of Trade Unions
1925–1926	1017·2	485·0	532
1926–1927	1241·5	686·6	555
1927–1928	1289·8	866·7	423 [3]

These figures understated both the absolute number of unemployed and the rise in unemployment. The statistics of the labour exchanges were seriously incomplete ; in some regions exchanges scarcely existed. From 1926–1927 onwards the registration of certain categories of unemployed, especially migrants from the countryside, was deliberately curtailed. In March 1927, in order to curb the peasant influx into the labour market, a decree was issued to restrict registration at labour exchanges to " real unemployed ", defined as those who could prove previous employment for a certain length of time, together with children of workers and employees.[4] Of registered unemployed rather less than one-

---

[1] *Puti Industrializatsii*, No. 7, 1929, p. 16.

[2] *VIII Vsesoyuznyi S"ezd VLKSM* (1928), p. 37 ; Bukharin had admitted to a German workers' delegation in August 1926 that " only in the abstract is the proletariat unitary, in reality it is not " (*Bukharins Antwort an Sozialdemokratische Arbeiter* (1926), p. 21 ; the interview was briefly reported in *Pravda*, August 12, 1926). For an earlier comment by Bukharin on the " proletarianized peasant mass " see *Socialism in One Country, 1924–1926*, Vol. 1, p. 411.

[3] *Kontrol'nye Tsifry Narodnogo Khozyaistva SSSR na 1928–1929 god* (1929), p. 156.

[4] *Sobranie Zakonov, 1927*, No. 13, art. 132. According to *Ekonomicheskoe Obozrenie*, No. 9, 1929, p. 131, the effect of the decree was " to divide the unemployed into two groups " — those who had lost their jobs, including seasonal workers, and those who had never had jobs. The proportion of

third had never had paid employment.[1] Alternative figures prepared by the trade unions of unemployed members of trade unions were always higher than the Narkomtrud figures for the total number of unemployed, showing for example 1,667,000 unemployed members of trade unions on January 1, 1927. The percentages of unemployment among trade union members at this date were highest for workers in water transport (44 per cent), builders (37·9 per cent), sugar workers (32·4 per cent), agricultural and timber workers (27·1 per cent) and food workers (25·7 per cent); all these were to a greater or less extent seasonal occupations. On the other hand, only 9·4 per cent of metal workers were unemployed, only 6·7 per cent of miners and only 5·7 per cent of textile workers. The over-all proportion of all trade union members unemployed was 17·3 per cent.[2] But no figures fully reflected the number of aspirants to a place on the labour market recently arrived from the countryside. Tomsky spoke at the fifteenth party conference of October 1926 of " hundreds of thousands " of peasants attracted to the towns for the brief building season, and registered there as unemployed for the rest of the year ; [3] and in the same month the trade union central council issued an instruction to admit to trade union membership only those who had already worked for wages.[4] A disquieting feature was the particularly heavy incidence of unemployment in the younger age-groups ; in 1928 43·6 per cent of all registered

---

migrants from the countryside in the total number of registered unemployed was said to have declined from 13·7 per cent in 1925–1926 to 10 per cent in 1927–1928 (Kontrol'nye Tsifry Narodnogo Khozyaistva SSSR na 1928–1929 god (1929), p. 156); for earlier variations in the policy of registration see Socialism in One Country, 1924–1926, Vol. 1, p. 364.

[1] Obzor Deyatel'nosti NKT SSSR za 1927–1928 gg. (1928), p. 59 ; this proportion seems to have remained fairly constant throughout the period. The statement in Sed'moi S"ezd Professional'nykh Soyuzov SSSR (1927), p. 348, that 50 per cent of those registered had never worked for wages was a typical exaggeration.

[2] Article by Tomsky in Pravda, November 29, 1927, Diskussionnyi Listok, No. 8 ; these figures should be compared with much lower figures of unemployment given by Tomsky a year earlier to the fifteenth party conference — 17 per cent for builders, 15 per cent for agricultural workers, less than 5 per cent for the major unions (XV Konferentsiya Vsesoyuznoi Kommunisticheskoi Partii (B) (1927), p. 288). The opposition counter-theses of November 1927 (see p. 34 above) put the total of unemployed at 2,000,000.

[3] XV Konferentsiya Vsesoyuznoi Kommunisticheskoi Partii (B) (1927), p. 287.

[4] Trud, October 26, 1926.

Q 2

unemployed were said to be between the ages of 18 and 24, and
30·8 per cent between 24 and 29.[1] The paradox underlying this
situation was frequently remarked :

> Among the unemployed a very significant place is occupied
> by young physically capable workers, whereas a significant place
> among the employed is taken by older workers.[2]

Unemployment became during this period an increasingly
acute preoccupation of the authorities. Pyatakov at the session of
the party central committee in July 1926 called unemployment
" the index of an absence of equilibrium in the whole national
economy ", and declared that it refuted the claim that the economy
was advancing " without crises ".[3] In the next eighteen months
the opposition continually harped on this theme. Smilga wrote
that unemployment was a dangerous phenomenon, since " the
discontent of the unemployed links the discontent of the countryside with the discontent of the town ".[4] A resolution adopted by
the presidium of the trade union central council after a long discussion on September 29, 1926, was little more than a confession
of helplessness.[5] Tomsky, at the fifteenth party conference of
October 1926 emphatically attributed unemployment to two
causes — rural over-population and the seasonal character of
casual labour in the towns. In England, he remarked, the builder
worked all the year round, in the Soviet Union only in the summer
months.[6] In the Russian countryside in winter, he added a few
weeks later at the seventh trade union congress, " tens of millions
of people suffer from unemployment " ; when the summer work
was done, " they lie down on the stove, and go on lying ". It
would be dangerous to call this " rural unemployment ".[7] Strumi-

[1] *Vos'moi S"ezd Professional'nykh Soyuzov SSSR* (1929), p. 323.
[2] *Ekonomicheskoe Obozrenie*, No. 9, 1929, p. 136.
[3] *Bol'shevik*, No. 14, July 31, 1927, p. 27.
[4] Trotsky archives, T 1744.
[5] *Trud*, September 30, 1926 ; for the text of the resolution see *ibid.* October
7, 1926.
[6] *XV Konferentsiya Vsesoyuznoi Kommunisticheskoi Partii (B)* (1927),
p. 287.
[7] *Sed'moi S"ezd Professional'nykh Soyuzov SSSR* (1927), p. 232 ; Lenin,
in one of his early writings, referred to " the winter unemployment of our
peasantry ", and derived it " not so much from capitalism as from an insufficient
development of capitalism, i.e. from a backward economy, which is unable
to provide alternative employment " (*Sochineniya*, iii, 247).

lin once remarked that the only thing which distinguished an unemployed worker from a poor peasant was that the latter was not
registered at a labour exchange and had a tiny plot of land.[1] It
was above all the poor peasants who constituted the reserve army
of labour. This diagnosis led the trade unions to concentrate
almost exclusively on unemployment in heavy industry, mining
and other industries where the old trade union tradition was
strong, and where employment was regular ; unemployment elsewhere was a casual and seasonal phenomenon, not curable in
current conditions.[2] Bukharin, whose view was more humane,
though perhaps less practical, than the professional attitude of the
trade unions, spoke in January 1927 of " the army of the unemployed ", and refused to forget " that we have an immense
mass of unemployed, that many workers have no roof over their
heads " ; [3] and Kirov called unemployment a " huge ulcer on our
economic organism ".[4] " We must not ", wrote a commentator
at this time, " be in a hurry to drive from the countryside those
whom we cannot place in our factories ".[5] A decree of June 29,
1927, attempted to set up machinery to regulate the flow of
peasants to the towns as seasonal workers, and to provide information on the state of the labour market.[6] A foreign visitor at this
time witnessed disturbances at the Ryazan railway station when
the police tried to send back to the country " rural elements
arriving in a vain search for work in Moscow ".[7]

But, whatever attempts were made to explain away the phenomenon of mass unemployment, and to depreciate its economic
importance, the existence of large-scale unemployment even
among industrial workers could not be denied or ignored. Of
methods to mitigate the evil, the first to be tried was public works,
mainly building, which could readily absorb unskilled workers.
But this demanded too much capital outlay and was gradually
abandoned.[8] More popular were " collectives " of unemployed

[1] *Planovoe Khozyaistvo*, No. 8, 1929, p. 56.
[2] For earlier trade union attitudes to unemployment see *Socialism in One
Country, 1924–1926*, Vol. 1, pp. 365-367.
[3] For this speech see pp. 12-13 above.   [4] *Pravda*, January 29, 1927.
[5] *Na Agrarnom Fronte*, No. 11-12, 1926, p. 146.
[6] *Sobranie Zakonov, 1927*, No. 41, art. 410.
[7] A. Ciliga, *Au Pays du Grand Mensonge* (1938), p. 35.
[8] *Kontrol'nye Tsifry po Trudu na 1928–29 god* (1929), p. 20 ; Larin, a
notorious eccentric, had proposed at the fourth Union Congress of Soviets in

workers ; these included producer, trading and labour collectives, the first two consisting of artisans engaged in the manufacture and distribution of simple articles produced either for other industries or for the market, the third of gangs of unskilled workers organized as *artels* for collective employment. Over 130,000 unemployed found work in this way in 1928.[1] Direct relief in the form of free food and lodging was attempted only on a very limited scale, and soon abandoned to local authorities or voluntary organizations.[2] The social insurance fund covered only a small proportion of the unemployed, and at inadequate rates.[3]

These were at best only mitigating devices. The essential, though remote, aim was to restore the unemployed to regular employment through the processes of the " labour market " — a term still in current use at this time. The labour exchanges remained the main governmental agencies for dealing with unemployment. After 1923 the industrial managers had broken through the legal monopoly of the engagement of labour enjoyed by the exchanges under the labour code of 1922 ; and it was formally abandoned in January 1925.[4] But this change, which conferred on managers an unrestricted legal right to hire and fire, had always been resisted by the trade unions. Now that the principle of planning had been introduced into the economy, a new argument was provided for the use of the exchanges, which were government agencies, to control and direct labour. The Ukrainian party conference of October 1926 blamed the trade unions for tolerating the habit of engaging workers " at the factory gates " — a practice which " makes impossible the regulation of the urban labour market " ; [5] and the fifteenth party conference which im-

---

April 1927 a scheme of public works to employ a million unskilled workers (*SSSR : 4 S"ezd Sovetov* (1927), p. 372).

[1] See *Obzor Deyatel'nosti NKT SSSR za 1927–1928 gg.* (1928), pp. 63-67, for an account of these collectives. Building workers on large sites were commonly engaged not as individuals, but in *artels*, some of which constituted small religious communities (commonly Baptists) ; Dnieprostroi claimed to be the first large building site on which the *artel* system was broken down (Arzhanov and Mikhalevich, *Dneprostroi k XVI S"ezdu VKP(B)* (1930), pp. 38-41 ; I. Nekrasova, *Leninskii Plan Elektrifikatsii* (1960), p. 103).

[2] *Obzor Deyatel'nosti NKT SSSR za 1927–1928 gg.* (1928), p. 69.

[3] See p. 606 below.   [4] See *The Interregnum, 1923–1924*, pp. 63-64.

[5] *Kommunisticheskaya Partiya Ukrainy v Rezolyutsiyakh* (1958), p. 366 ; at the ensuing Ukrainian trade union congress a delegate accused the economic organs of engaging labour direct " from the village ", and alleged that in Soviet

mediately followed it condemned "patronage and nepotism (kumovstvo) " in the engagement and dismissal of workers.[1] At the seventh trade union congress, Shmidt, the People's Commissar for Labour, dropped the demand for a legal obligation to engage labour through the exchanges, but proposed that the collective agreements should contain a clause binding economic organs to engage 90 per cent of their labour in that way. Though Shmidt invoked the need to impart " a planned character " to the hiring of labour, the principal motive appeared to be to protect members of trade unions ; he spoke indignantly of cases in which factories had dismissed 1500 or 2000 workers, and replaced them a week later by new arrivals from the country.[2] The resolution passed by the congress, which went further than Shmidt's proposals, required that " all enterprises and institutions " should submit their labour requirements in good time to the local labour exchange, and that " all operations for the hiring of the labour force should be concentrated exclusively on the labour exchanges ".[3]

Two powerful forces thus worked together to re-establish the labour exchanges as effective organs. The trade unions saw in them agencies which would make it possible to secure for their members a monopoly, or at any rate priority, in the filling of vacancies, and to exclude the mass of new migrants from the countryside. The planners saw in them convenient and necessary instruments for the control and direction of labour to meet the requirements of a planned economy. The short-lived experiment in a quasi-free labour market which had been tried between 1924–1926 had broken down. After 1926 the labour exchanges partially recovered their importance as central agencies for the hiring of labour. According to figures given by Shmidt at the end of 1927, the proportion of workers engaged through labour exchanges in

---

trading organs "patronage has in many places built a secure nest for itself " (*Stenograficheskii Otchet 3⁹⁰ Vseukrainskogo S"ezda Profsoyuzov* (1927), pp. 257-258).   [1] *KPSS v Rezolyutsiyakh* (1954), ii, 324.
[2] *Sed'moi S"ezd Professional'nykh Soyuzov SSSR* (1927), p. 350. A delegate of Vserabotzemles described the way in which economic organs in the Ural region obtained seasonal labour for forestry and building ; private agents were employed who were paid 50 kopeks for every man recruited ; the workers were despatched in dirty and unheated railway wagons (*ibid.* p. 416). According to a writer in *Trud*, December 1, 1926, managers preferred to employ peasants who " are less demanding than urban workers and have greater physical endurance ".
[3] *Sed'moi S"ezd Professional'nykh Soyuzov SSSR* (1927), p. 752.

the principal towns rose from 27·4 per cent in January–March 1926 to 70·6 per cent in April–June 1927 ; the proportion was naturally highest in Moscow and Leningrad.[1] At the eighth trade union congress a year later, it was alleged that in many places factory workers were still " hired at the gates ". Members of trade unions could not find employment, while non-unionists — even " people of an alien stratum " — were engaged. The old complaint of bogus registrations of unemployed was again heard.[2] But Dogadov, in his report on the work of the trade unions, claimed that, whereas two years earlier the economic organs had filled only 30-40 per cent of their labour requirements through the exchanges, the proportion had now increased to 70-80 per cent. A spokesman of Narkomtrud stated that the number of workers engaged through the labour exchanges rose from 2,000,000 in 1925–1926 to 3,600,000 in 1926–1927 and 5,000,000 in 1927–1928. Success was also claimed in organizing seasonal labour ; in these two years the labour exchanges had been able to fill more than 95 per cent of vacancies notified to them in the building industry.[3]

The current pessimistic attitude to unemployment was based on the assumption that expansion of industry on a scale large enough to absorb the apparently unlimited surplus of labour was a utopian dream. " A considerable part of the peasants ", Rykov observed at the fifteenth party conference in October 1926, " who find no employment for their labour in agriculture, can earn a living in the towns only if industry grows." [4] A few weeks later the People's Commissar for Labour of the Ukrainian SSR told the third Ukrainian trade union congress that the thesis of the opposition that " the struggle against unemployment can be carried on through super-industrialization" was "unrealistic", and would merely lead to a " one-sided development of productive

[1] *Pravda*, November 17, 1927, *Diskussionnyi Listok*, No. 7.
[2] *Vos'moi S"ezd Professional'nykh Soyuzov SSSR* (1929), pp. 325-326, 340-341, 344.
[3] *Vos'moi S"ezd Professional'nykh Soyuzov SSSR* (1929), pp. 66, 324-325 ; for the growing numbers of workers engaged through the labour exchanges see tables in *Obzor Deyatel'nosti NKT SSSR za 1927–1928 gg.* (1928), pp. 35, 37, and for a list of enterprises with which labour exchanges had entered into agreements for the supply of labour *ibid.* p. 36.
[4] *XV Konferentsiya Vsesoyuznoi Kommunisticheskoi Partii (B)* (1927), p. 123.

forces".[1] In April 1927 at the fourth Union Congress of Soviets Rykov declared that the million unemployed included only 200,000 industrial workers, and cautiously confined prospects of full employment to this select minority :

> Unemployment of industrial workers is a temporary phenomenon, since in many regions the skilled labour force is even now insufficient. As industry expands (and our prospects in this direction are not bad), unemployment in these groups will be overcome.[2]

The resolution of the congress, however, only repeated the familiar panaceas — intensification of agriculture and development of rural industries, migration and public works.[3] When Kuibyshev addressed the TsIK of the USSR six months later, he explained that, under the optimum variant of the draft five-year plan, unemployment could be expected to fall from 1,268,000 in 1926–1927 to 848,000 in 1931–1932. But this most active protagonist of planning and industrialization held out no prospect of a total cure : " unemployment will not be overcome in this five-year period even on the most favourable programme of development of the national economy ".[4]

Such prominent features of the early stages of the industrialization drive as the " régime of economy " and " rationalization " campaigns [5] tended on a short view to swell the ranks of the unemployed. Trotsky, in his abortive proposals to the party central committee in July 1926, called for a commission to safeguard " the vital interests of the workers " under the régime of economy, and invited STO to draw up plans to deal with unemployment.[6]

---

[1] *Stenograficheskii Otchet 3⁰⁰ Vseukrainskogo S"ezda Profsoyuzov* (1927), p. 257 ; the verdict was endorsed by critical observers abroad : " To dream of absorbing this gigantic human flood in industry and other urban occupations is completely out of the question " (*Sotsialisticheskii Vestnik* (Berlin), No. 24 (142), December 20, 1926, p. 6).

[2] *SSSR : 4 S"ezd Sovetov* (1927), p. 213.

[3] *S"ezdy Sovetov v Dokumentakh*, iii (1960), 125.

[4] *2 Sessiya Tsentral'nogo Ispolnitel'nogo Komiteta Soyuza SSR 4 Sozyva* (n.d. [1927]), p. 264 ; this gloomy forecast was repeated by Rykov at the fifteenth party congress two months later (*Pyatnadtsatyi S"ezd VKP(B)*, ii (1962), 874).   [5] For these campaigns see pp. 334-337, 340-344 above.

[6] Trotsky archives, T 887 ; owing to the régime of economy, the industrial labour force declined slightly between March and September 1926, but thereafter rose again steadily (*SSSR : Ot S"ezda k S"ezdu (Mai 1925 g.–Aprel' 1927 g.)* (1927), p. 30).

When the slogan of the " régime of economy " had been replaced
by " rationalization ", the same point was repeated in the " declaration of the 83 " in May 1927 :

> The rationalization of industry has an accidental, unco-
> ordinated, unsystematic character, and results in thrusting more
> and more groups of workers into the ranks of the unemployed.[1]

When Larin at the fourth Union Congress of Soviets in April 1927
expressed the fear that rationalization would only swell the ranks
of the unemployed,[2] Kuibyshev made a somewhat embarrassed
reply. " Rationalization of production ", he explained, " inevitably brings about a reduction in the amount of labour power
required to produce the same output " ; otherwise it would not
be rationalization. On the other hand, " the working class as a
whole is interested in rationalization ", even though " individual
groups of workers may suffer from rationalization, thanks to reduction in a given enterprise ". Hope for the future must rest on the
plan :

> We must construct the plan in such a way that the total
> number of the working class in the country increases, notwith-
> standing the carrying out of rationalization.[3]

In discussions in party cells in Moscow after the session of the
party central committee in July 1928 similar fears were expressed
that the trend towards mechanization of agriculture would increase unemployment.[4]

It was the impact of planning which by slow degrees began to
dissolve this ingrained pessimism. The compilers of the Gosplan
control figures for 1927–1928 remarked that, whereas the control
figures for labour in previous years had been concerned mainly
with wages and productivity, it was now necessary " to link the
technical demands of the reconstruction period in the development
of our economy with the maximum possible utilization of our
labour power ", and that the drawing of the surplus rural population into normal economic life must become one of the most

---

[1] For this declaration see pp. 24-25 above.
[2] *SSSR : 4 S"ezd Sovetov* (1927), pp. 368-369.
[3] *Ibid.* pp. 389-390 ; for the converse effect of unemployment in discouraging rationalization and mechanization see pp. 415-416 above.
[4] Trotsky archives, T 2167 ; for this report see p. 83, note 3 above.

important tasks of the reconstruction period.[1] The fifteenth
party congress in December 1927, which issued the first formal
directives for a five-year plan, foresaw as one of the corollaries of a
planned and industrialized economy " the absorption of ' superfluous ' working hands on the basis of an uninterrupted rise in the
productive forces of the country " ; [2] and an article published at
this time hailed the construction of new projects like Dnieprostroi,
the Turksib railway and the Volga–Don canal as " a powerful
regulator in our struggle with unemployment ".[3] " Relative
agrarian over-population ", observed a commentator at this time,
was " nothing but the insufficient development of large-scale
industry ".[4] A decree of March 26, 1928 — the first of its kind —
on the employment of prisoners in penal settlements on construction work [5] was the first symptom of a state of affairs in which
shortage of labour would be a more serious danger than the unemployment of " superfluous " labour power. A new statute of
Narkomtrud promulgated on September 26, 1928, named as its
first function " the regulation of the labour market " and " the
struggle against unemployment " ; [6] and the spokesman of Narkomtrud at the eighth trade union congress in December 1928
unhesitatingly called unemployment " the central question in the
work of Narkomtrud ".[7]

[1] *Kontrol'nye Tsifry Narodnogo Khozyaistva SSSR na 1927–1928 god* (1928),
p. 207.
[2] *KPSS v Rezolyutsiyakh* (1954), ii, 456 ; this optimism was not, however,
shared either by Kuibyshev or by Rykov (see p. 463 above).
[3] *Pravda*, December 2, 1927, *Diskussionnyi Listok*, No. 11. Of the building force recruited for Dnieprostroi, 24 per cent were peasants and 74 per cent
former industrial workers, but 58 per cent had been unemployed for at least
three months before joining (Arzhanov and Mikhalevich, *Dneprostroi k XVI
S"ezdu VKP(B)* (1930), pp. 34-35). According to *Bol'shaya Sovetskaya
Entsiklopediya*, xxxii (1935), col. 773, a majority of the workers at Dnieprostroi
" came from the peasantry, and did not know what a collective is, what labour
discipline is ".   [4] *Ekonomicheskoe Obozrenie*, No. 9, 1928, p. 97.
[5] The decree was not included in the official collection of decrees, and its
text has not been available ; but what were apparently its main provisions were
recapitulated in theses presented to the sixth congress of judicial workers of the
RSFSR in October 1928, and published in *Ezhenedel'nik Sovetskoi Yustitsii*,
No. 46-47, December 12-19, 1928, and in a further decree of the RSFSR of
March 23, 1929 (*Sobranie Uzakonenii*, 1929, No. 37, art. 388) complaining of
delays in putting some of them into effect. The decree of March 26, 1928, will
be further discussed in a subsequent volume.
[6] *Sobranie Zakonov, 1928*, No. 62, art. 563.
[7] *Vos'moi S"ezd Professional'nykh Soyuzov SSSR* (1929), p. 322.

No vision had, however, yet been vouchsafed of the magnitude of the impending industrial expansion or of the calls on labour which it would involve ; and the rare recorded speculations on the subject were regarded even by their authors as utopian and unrealistic. Strumilin, who spoke at the Communist Academy in May 1926 of the absorption of three million workers by the five-year plan, and of a potential labour shortage in 1932,[1] admitted a year later that investment in industry under the plan would not suffice to cure unemployment.[2] Varga explained to the sixth congress of Comintern in the summer of 1928 that unemployment in the Soviet Union was a different phenomenon from unemployment in capitalist countries, where it was a necessary part of the economic structure :

> In the Soviet Union unemployment exists only because the economy is poor. If we could provide all the unemployed with means of production, there would never need to be unemployment in the Soviet Union.[3]

But this hope still seemed inconceivably remote. In many circles it was believed that the projected reduction in industrial costs, coupled with a rise in wages, could not be achieved without some reduction in the labour force. Grinko, a vice-president of Gosplan, referred to this as a possible, though " not proven ", contingency " in certain branches of industry ".[4] The Gosplan control figures for 1928–1929 allowed for a rise of 11 per cent in the forthcoming year in the total number of unemployed and of 15 per cent in the number of unemployed members of trade unions. The total labour force was to rise by no more than 2·8 per cent (against 3·6 in 1927–1928) ; this included a 20 per cent rise in building labour, an " insignificant rise " in factory labour, and an " almost stable "

[1] *Torgovo-Promyshlennaya Gazeta*, May 16, 1926.
[2] S. Strumilin, *Ocherki Sovetskoi Ekonomiki* (1928) p. 437. The first Gosplan draft of the five-year plan in March 1926 assumed an increase of a million in the industrial labour force in four years (*Problemy Planirovaniya (Itogi i Perspektivy)* (1926), p. 6) ; in the second draft a year later, the increase had been scaled down to 350,000-400,000 in five years (*Perspektivy Razvertyvaniya Narodnogo Khozyaistva SSSR na 1926/27–1930/31 gg.* (1927), p. 12). For these drafts see pp. 851-852, 855-856 below.
[3] *Sechster Kongress der Kommunistischen Internationale*, iii (1928), 519.
[4] G. Krzhizhanovsky and others, *Osnovnye Problemy Kontrol'nykh Tsifr Narodnogo Khozyaistva na 1928/29 god* (1929), pp. 71-72.

(in fact, slightly reduced) number of transport workers.[1]   In December 1928 Tomsky, at the eighth trade union congress, attributed " *unemployment*, with which we cope badly ", to " objective conditions " which could not be changed.[2]   The congress was still animated by the old restrictive spirit, and passed a resolution calling for " a more cautious attitude " towards the admission to the unions of seasonal, temporary and rural handicraft workers, and more care for unemployed members of the unions.[3]   The first five-year plan in its final form frankly regarded unemployment as " an incontestable fact which must be taken account of ", and budgeted for a reduction in the number of unemployed from 1,133,000 in 1927–1928 to 835,000 (basic variant) or 511,000 (optimum variant) five years later.[4]   Even these figures were regarded in many quarters as unrealistic.   A writer in the party journal, while defending the Gosplan figures, admitted that " it is difficult to believe in so substantial a reduction in unemployment in a single five-year period, at a time when we have hitherto had a growth of unemployment from year to year ".[5]   It seemed impossible at this time to imagine that 1930 would already be a time of acute labour shortage, and that by the end of that year unemployment would have been virtually eliminated from the economy.

Increasing anxiety was aroused during this period by the problem of labour turnover.   The common verdict which attributed this phenomenon to the restlessness and discontent of the workers

---

[1] *Kontrol'nye Tsifry Narodnogo Khozyaistva SSSR na 1928–1929 god* (1929), pp. 47, 452–453.

[2] *Vos'moi S"ezd Professional'nykh Soyuzov SSSR* (1929), p. 25.

[3] *Ibid.* p. 511.

[4] *Pyatiletnii Plan Narodno-Khozyaistvennogo Stroitel'stva SSSR* (1929), i, 91 ; ii, ii, 197 ; for an earlier estimate see p. 463 above.

[5] *Bol'shevik*, No. 11, June 15, 1929, p. 45.   An article in *Ekonomicheskoe Obozrenie*, No. 9, 1929, pp. 88-100, considered that the Gosplan estimate reflected " harmful optimism ", and concluded that " we cannot avoid unemployment in a certain degree, thanks to the rationalization and mechanization which we are carrying out ".   The article was published as a discussion article with an editorial criticism of " the author's general *pessimistic attitude* in questions of the struggle with unemployment " ; but the counter-article which appeared two months later relied primarily not on industrialization as the cure for unemployment, but on " the influence which the projected agrarian reconstruction will have on agrarian over-population " (*ibid.* No. 11, 1929, p. 55).

was not entirely just. In a period when labour was both inefficient
and super-abundant, factory managers were prone to change it
easily and often. Uglanov at the fifteenth party conference in
October 1926 related a case in which a factory manager had
recently discharged 300 workers and engaged 380 new ones.[1]
Shmidt, who complained at the seventh trade union congress a
month later of a mass dismissal of workers, connected the rapid
turnover of labour with " the strict discipline which we have
recently introduced ".[2] Melnichansky more seriously called for
study of this " curious and interesting phenomenon " of a constant
" hiring and firing, coming and going of workers " in the factories :
in some enterprises the labour force changed *one-and-a-half times*
in the course of the year.[3] So long as this process affected mainly
unskilled workers, and supplies of such labour were ample for all
needs, no remedy was found, and more concern was felt about the
difficulty of moving labour from place to place than about its
apparent unwillingness to remain long in the same job. The
eighth trade union congress in December 1928 did not discuss the
question, but perfunctorily recorded in one of its resolutions that
" a study of labour turnover should be carried out " in connexion
with " the improvement of planning and the organization of the
seasonal labour market ".[4]

The year 1928 seems to have been the first for which reliable
and systematic statistics of labour turnover were available.[5] Taking
the monthly average for that year, 8·4 per cent of the total labour
force was engaged, and 7·7 per cent dismissed every month; in 1929
these figures had increased to 10·2 and 9·6 per cent respectively, so
that the " average " worker remained in his job for less than a year.
Annual figures of those engaged and dismissed in percentages of

---

[1] *XV Konferentsiya Vsesoyuznoi Kommunisticheskoi Partii (B)* (1927), p.
382 ; the offence was aggravated by the fact that those discharged were
apparently members of the trade union and a majority of those newly engaged
were not.

[2] *Sed'moi S"ezd Professional'nykh Soyuzov SSSR* (1927), pp. 350-354 ;
for Shmidt's complaint see p. 461 above.

[3] *Sed'moi S"ezd Professional'nykh Soyuzov SSSR* (1927), p. 667.

[4] *Vos'moi S"ezd Professional'nykh Soyuzov SSSR* (1929), p. 558.

[5] Figures from 1923 onwards are given in *Trud v SSSR* (1936), p. 95, but
their reliability for the earlier years is uncertain : figures for particular industries (*ibid.* pp. 109, 116, 123, 137, 145, 155, 187) show wide variations, but in
general confirm the conclusions stated below.

the total labour force were as follows :

	1928	1929	1930
Engagements	101	122	176
Dismissals	92	115	152

The average figures concealed wide discrepancies. The turnover was greater in capital goods industries than in consumer goods industries, and was greatest of all in iron- and coal-mining ; the building industry, which worked mainly on casual labour, and transport, where labour was apparently more stable, were not included in the statistics.[1] Sensational figures were quoted from particular industries. Donugol had a labour turnover of 270 per cent in 1925–1926,[2] Yugostal of 200 per cent in six months of 1926–1927.[3] The annual turnover of workers on Dnieprostroi exceeded 100 per cent.[4] On the other hand textile factories were said to have a turnover of from 18 to 35 per cent ; only one was reported with a turnover of 100 per cent.[5] Average figures concealed the sharp divergence between the large group of unskilled, highly mobile workers who moved from job to job, and the basic cadre of workers who remained permanently at their posts.[6] Everywhere turnover varied inversely to qualification, being lowest among the most highly skilled and *vice versa*. By the same token, it was most prevalent among the lowest paid workers, and could be regarded as a specific product of low wages.[7] The situation in the trade unions, which included all skilled workers and excluded a high proportion of the casual and unskilled, was far better than the average. A census conducted in April–May 1929 in the three largest industrial unions — the metal workers, miners, and textile workers — revealed that only 8·2 per cent of workers had been engaged during the past year, though higher percentages were shown for coal-mining (14·8) and for iron-mining (12·9), and

---

[1] *Sotsialisticheskoe Stroitel'stvo SSSR* (1934), pp. 340-343; *ibid.* (1936), p. 531.   [2] *Torgovo-Promyshlennaya Gazeta*, August 2, 1927.

[3] *Ibid.* July 2, 1927.

[4] Arzhanov and Mikhalevich, *Dneprostroi k XVI S"ezdu VKP(B)* (1930), p. 21.   [5] *Torgovo-Promyshlennaya Gazeta*, September 27, 1928.

[6] *Torgovo-Promyshlennaya Gazeta*, April 11, 1928.

[7] *Ekonomicheskoe Obozrenie*, No. 10, 1929, p. 148.

labour turnover in all branches was higher in the Donbass and
Ural regions than elsewhere. The average record of service of
those working in 1929 was 11·3 years in the metal industries, 13·6
in textiles, and 9·3 in mining (including oil-extraction, which was
from this point of view a stable industry).[1] Krzhizhanovsky at the
fifth Union Congress of Soviets in May 1929 alleged that the
problem of turnover now extended not only to labour, but to technical personnel.[2] But it was not till 1930, when unemployment
ended, and the problem was aggravated by the competition of
different enterprises for scarce labour, that the matter was seriously
taken in hand.

(b) Women Workers

The friction over the employment of women in industry which
had marked the period from 1924 to 1926 [3] did not immediately
abate. The number of employed women enrolled in trade unions
rose steadily from 2,413,300 in October–December 1926 to
2,833,300 in April–June 1928 and 3,304,000 in 1929.[4] Throughout this period the proportion of women in the total labour force
remained constant at between 28 and 29 per cent. It fell in mining
and in the metallurgical industries. But, since these were rapidly
expanding industries, the proportional fall was accompanied by a
numerical increase ; and in most other industries the proportion,
as well as the number, of women rose.[5] Opportunity, combined
with dire necessity, drove women into the factories. Tomsky
found an explanation of the process in " our new conditions of
life " : the woman preferred " to work in the factory rather than
to toil and moil in the kitchen ".[6] In general, party and government desired the introduction of women into industrial employment, so far as possible, on equal terms with men. Protective
legislation still applied, at any rate in theory, to women workers ;
as late as April 1928 a party resolution drew attention to the employment of women underground in the Donbass mines as a viola-

[1] *Sostav Fabrichno-Zavodskogo Proletariata SSSR* (1930), pp. 8, 42, 44, 48,
52.   [2] *SSSR : 5 S"ezd Sovetov* (1929), No. 14, p. 8.
[3] See *Socialism in One Country, 1924–1926*, Vol. 1, pp. 367-369.
[4] *Pervye Shagi Industrializatsii SSSR 1926–1927 gg.* (1959), p. 223 ; *Trud
v SSSR* (1936), p. 25.
[5] *Obzor Deyatel'nosti NKT SSSR za 1927–1928 gg.* (1928), pp. 155-156.
[6] *XV Konferentsiya Vsesoyuznoi Kommunisticheskoi Partii (B)* (1927), p. 287.

tion of the labour code.[1] The trade unions, though they could not contest the principle, disliked the competition of female labour, especially when unemployment became a serious problem ; and managers, irked by the legal restrictions on employment of women, preferred male labour. Unconfessed discrimination against women prevailed everywhere. At the seventh trade union congress in December 1926, one woman delegate noted that only 7 per cent of the delegates were women ; another complained that, when women became literate, employers no longer wanted them ; a third drew attention to the small proportion of women workers promoted to responsible positions on the railways. Shmidt pointed out that, in spite of the preponderance of female labour in some industries, only 5 per cent of the personnel of the labour inspectorate were women ; [2] this was not surprising, since under art. 177 of the labour code of 1923 the inspectors were appointed by the trade unions and merely confirmed by Narkomtrud. It was only in the winter of 1927–1928, when the first effects of the drive for intensive industrialization began to be felt, that the introduction of the seven-hour day and the three-shift system, applying primarily to the textile industry where female labour was predominant, once more focused attention on the problems of women in employment.[3]

The first five-year plan drafted in the autumn of 1928 for the first time specifically posited an increase in female labour as part of the process of industrialization. The proportion of women in the labour force was to be raised from 27 per cent in 1927–1928 to 32·5 per cent in 1932–1933 ; and, since the plan provided for the largest expansion in heavy industries in which relatively few women had hitherto worked, it was noted that the projected increase in the employment of women would make it necessary to " widen the scope of female labour ".[4] The eighth trade union congress in December 1928 paid more attention to the question than its predecessor two years earlier. A woman member of the

[1] KPSS v Rezolyutsiyakh (1954), ii, 508.
[2] Sed'moi S"ezd Professional'nykh Soyuzov SSSR (1927), pp. 141, 197-198, 209, 343-344 ; the position had not improved two years later, when out of 1276 inspectors only 42 were women (Vos'moi S"ezd Professional'nykh Soyuzov SSSR (1929), p. 358).   [3] See pp. 501-504 below.
[4] Pyatiletnii Plan Narodno-Khozyaistvennogo Stroitel'stva SSSR (1929), ii, ii, 180.

central committee of the textile workers' union noted that of 700,000 women workers 480,000 were employed in the textile industry ; she argued that a woman's real working day was not 7 or 8, but 14 or 15, hours, and pleaded for more crèches, baths and wash-houses in the factories.[1] Though Tomsky and other trade union leaders again remained silent on the subject, the principal spokesman of Narkomtrud touched on unemployment among women. Using trade union figures, which as usual understated the magnitude of the problem, he claimed that the proportion of women among the unemployed had fallen from 46 per cent (at what date was not stated) to 41·2 per cent ; of unemployed women more than 60 per cent were unskilled, and about 25 per cent non-manual workers. To train more women as skilled manual workers seemed the main desideratum.[2] A woman official of Narkomtrud claimed that successes had been achieved " in respect both of protecting female labour and of establishing it in industry ", but protested against neglect of the prohibition on night work for pregnant and nursing women.[3] One resolution of the congress drew emphatic attention to the obligatory character of the regulations "*on not admitting pregnant and nursing women to night work* " ; another mentioned the need to increase the number of women inspectors.[4] But any general pronouncement on the increased employment of women in industry was avoided ; the higher rate of unemployment among women, and the lower rate of women's wages, were symptomatic of the discrimination against them. The deterioration of the situation between the summer of 1928 and the summer of 1929 was shown by the figures of unemployed registered at the labour exchanges (in thousands) :

	June 1, 1928	June 1, 1929
Total of Unemployed	1571	1633
Including		
Women	614·1	741·4
Juveniles	205·4	277·4

Total unemployment had increased during the year by 4 per cent, the number of unemployed women by 20·7 per cent and of

[1] *Vos'moi S"ezd Professional'nykh Soyuzov SSSR* (1929), pp. 77-78.
[2] *Ibid.* p. 323.   [3] *Ibid.* p. 358.   [4] *Ibid.* pp. 525, 557.

juveniles by 35·1 per cent. In 1928 51 per cent of the registered
unemployed had been women and juveniles, in 1929 64 per cent.[1]
In cotton-spinning the daily wages of men in 1929 ranged from
4·19 rubles for the most skilled to 1·89 for the unskilled with an
average of 2·97 ; for women the corresponding figures were 3·27,
1·77 and 2·28 rubles.[2] It was, however, a sign of the times when,
early in 1929, the party central committee took cognizance of the
need to train women for industry. A resolution of February 22,
1929, aimed at establishing a minimum proportion of places
for girls in VTUZy (20 per cent) and in factory schools (10 per
cent) ; party and trade union organizations had, it was observed,
hitherto paid "very little attention" to the matter.[3] The
programme of industrialization, with its insatiable demands for
labour, was soon to give urgent priority to the recruitment
of women into industry.

(c) Juvenile Workers

The employment of juveniles in industry had been a subject of
controversy ever since 1924.[4] After 1926, with increased population pressures [5] and rising unemployment, the controversy began
to take sharper forms. Unemployment among young workers was
a crying evil,[6] though only a small percentage of the youths
registered at the labour exchanges had ever worked. The managers were reluctant to employ juveniles who were protected by
legislative restrictions, including the limitation of their working
day to six hours. The trade unions, in a period of mass unemployment, saw no reason to encourage the competition of
juveniles for scarce jobs, and were at best interested only in placing
the children of their own members. Difficulties also occurred
over the provision in the labour code that juveniles, though

---

[1] *Ekonomicheskoe Obozrenie*, No. 9, 1929, p. 90.
[2] *Sostav Fabrichno-Zavodskogo Proletariata SSSR* (1930), p. 64.
[3] *Izvestiya Tsentral'nogo Komiteta VKP(B)*, No. 7 (266), March 20, 1929,
p. 15 ; for the VTUZy see pp. 591-592 below.
[4] See *Socialism in One Country, 1924–1926*, Vol. 1, pp. 370-372.
[5] According to labour exchange statistics, 400,000 juveniles in towns
reached working age every year (L. Rogachevskaya, *Iz Istorii Rabochego Klassa
SSSR* (1959), p. 57, note 125).
[6] *Professional'nye Soyuzy SSSR, 1926–1928: Otchet k VIII S"ezdu* (1928),
p. 125.

working only six hours, should be paid the full rate for the eight-hour day, the assumption being that the extra two hours were spent in the factory school. This was resented both by managements and by adult workers, and seems to have been widely evaded, since the discrepancy in wage payments was larger than could be accounted for by the fact that juveniles were naturally placed in the lowest grades.[1]

In these conditions, both managers and trade unions adopted a lukewarm attitude to juvenile labour, and connived at, or tolerated, failure to fill the so-called " ironclad minimum " (bronya) — the obligatory percentage of jobs reserved for juveniles in industry.[2] The average minimum required by law was 7 per cent (different percentages were fixed for different industries) ; the average percentage attained in 1926 was 5·7.[3] Managers sometimes professed to have complied with the minimum by including young workers between the ages of 18 and 23 (the latter being the maximum age for membership of the Komsomol) ; in some places 30 to 40 per cent of the minimum was said to be made up in this way.[4] The party and government declaration of August 16, 1926, referred to " the curtailment of the legal minimum for juveniles " as one of the current abuses of the régime of economy.[5] A census taken in 1929 showed that of those who had entered the metal industry before 1917 69·1 per cent had entered before the age of 16 ; of those entering between 1918 and 1925 and between 1926 and 1928 the corresponding proportions were 45·9 per cent and 33·7 per cent respectively.[6] The conditions of employment of juveniles were a main source of the constant friction between the trade

[1] The average wage of juveniles was 40·3 per cent of that of adults in 1926 and 41·6 per cent in 1927 (*Professional'nye Soyuzy SSSR, 1926–1928: Otchet k VIII S"ezdu* (1928), p. 120).

[2] See *Socialism in One Country, 1924–1926*, Vol. 1, pp. 369-371.

[3] *Sed'moi S"ezd Professional'nykh Soyuzov SSSR* (1927), p. 182 ; *Oppozitsiya i Komsomol* (1927), p. 10, recorded the following percentages : January 1923 — 6·5 ; January 1924 — 5·5 ; July 1924 — 4·8 ; January 1925 — 5·1 ; July 1925 — 5·0 ; January 1926 — 5·6 ; July 1926 — 5·4 ; January 1927 — 5·4. In the printing trade the minimum was apparently as high as 13 per cent ; a manager demanded its reduction to 8-9 per cent (*Predpriyatie*, No. 7, 1926, p. 40).

[4] *Professional'nye Soyuzy SSSR, 1924–1926: Otchet k VII S"ezdu* (1926), pp. 124-125.   [5] For this declaration see pp. 335-336 above.

[6] *Sostav Fabrichno-Zavodskogo Proletariata SSSR* (1930), p. 34 ; similar figures were quoted for other industries.

unions and the Komsomol. A delegate at the seventh Komsomol congress in March 1926 referred to relations with the trade unions as " contentious " ; the trade unions were said to cold-shoulder the Komsomol representative on the trade union central council.[1]

Even sharper controversy arose over the question of training. A network of factory schools was established under a department of the People's Commissariat of Education (Narkompros), known as Glavprofobr, in which vocational training was combined with party indoctrination.[2] The number of such schools rose from 782 with 69,000 trainees in 1924–1925 to 799 with 85,000 trainees in 1926–1927.[3] But in a period of rapid industrial expansion these figures were not impressive ; [4] and the schools catered mainly for the children of workers, who occupied 76·7 per cent of the places in 1926–1927.[5] Meanwhile the Central Institute of Labour (TsIT), not content with the theoretical study of methods of raising productivity, also set up vocational schools, which were suspect in party and trade union circles as an attempt, under the guise of the " scientific organization of labour ", to introduce Taylorism and other capitalist techniques into Soviet industry.[6] These methods of training enjoyed the support of Vesenkha and of the managers, who were accused of seeking to sabotage the factory schools.[7] Both the trade unions and the Komsomol were ardent advocates of the factory school and sceptical of the methods of TsIT. But, whereas the trade unions sought to confine places in the limited number of factory schools to children of workers, and especially of skilled workers, the Komsomol protested loudly against this discrimination, and wished the system of factory

---

[1] *VII S"ezd Vsesoyuznogo Leninskogo Kommunisticheskogo Soyuza Molodezhi* (1926), pp. 353-354.

[2] For some account of the development of the factory schools from 1921 to 1926 see *Voprosy Istorii*, No. 12, 1963, pp. 199-203.

[3] *Kontrol'nye Tsifry Narodnogo Khozyaistva SSSR na 1927–1928 god* (1928), p. 576.

[4] The Gosplan control figures for 1926–1927 estimated that of 64,000 skilled workers entering industry in that year only 15,000 would have graduated from the factory schools (*Kontrol'nye Tsifry Narodnogo Khozyaistva na 1926–1927 god* (1926), p. 91) ; according to *Kontrol'nye Tsifry Narodnogo Khozyaistva SSSR na 1928–1929 god* (1929), p. 458, 14,300 completed courses in the factory schools in 1926–1927 and 18,600 (including those in transport schools) in 1927–1928.   [5] L. Rogachevskaya, *Iz Istorii Rabochego Klassa SSSR* (1959), p. 56.

[6] See *Socialism in One Country, 1924–1926*, Vol. 1, pp. 383-384.

[7] *Oppozitsiya i Komsomol* (1927), pp. 100-101.

schools to be extended to all young workers. A resolution of the party central committee of March 11, 1926, made the best of both worlds by recommending " short-term courses and courses according to the method of TsIT for mass training " side by side with the factory schools, and spoke with guarded approval of " the method of TsIT for the accelerated training of skilled labour power ".[1] The Komsomol, at its seventh congress in the same month, fell tentatively into line. Its resolution firmly declared that the aim must be to produce " skilled, class-conscious and cultured workers ", and that " narrow specialization " was not enough. But it drew approving attention to the work of TsIT and suggested that factory schools might borrow some of its methods.[2] A decree of the party central committee of June 8, 1926, required that admission to factory schools should be confined to workers and peasants and their children. But in April 1927 the proportion of workers and peasants in the schools was actually said to have declined.[3]

These controversies were extensively aired both in the respective organs of the trade unions and of the Komsomol, *Trud* and *Komsomol'skaya Pravda*, and at the representative congresses and conferences of the period. At the fifteenth party conference in October 1926, Tomsky, at the end of a long report on the tasks of the trade unions referred cursorily to " unemployment among the young . . . and especially unemployment among the children of workers ", and drifted away into a long digression about hooliganism.[4] Two Komsomol delegates sharply attacked both the methods of Gastev, the director of TsIT, and the unsatisfactory attitude of

---

[1] *Direktivy KPSS i Sovetskogo Pravitel'stva po Khozyaistvennym Voprosam*, i (1957), 568-569 ; according to Kuibyshev a year later, TsIT claimed to be able to turn out a skilled worker in three months at a cost of 150 rubles, while a course at the factory school lasted a year and cost 800 rubles (2 *Sessiya Tsentral'-nogo Ispolnitel'nogo Komiteta Soyuza SSR 4 Sozyva* (n.d. [1927]), p. 247). The cost of factory schools in 1928–1929 was 35·7 million rubles and of TsIT 5·4 millions (*Pyatiletnii Plan Narodno-Khozyaistvennogo Stroitel'stva SSSR* (1929), ii, ii, 246) ; the annual output of workers from the factory schools was only about two-and-a-half times that of TsIT (*ibid.* i, 77).

[2] *VLKSM v Rezolyutsiyakh* (1929), pp. 244, 248 ; note was taken at this time of a gradual disappearance of the " semi-artisan " type of skilled worker and the need to develop standardized skills on a mass scale (*Oppozitsiya i Komsomol* (1927), pp. 102-103).

[3] *Spravochnik Partiinogo Rabotnika*, vi (1928), i, 694-696, 696-697 ; see also p. 591 below.

[4] *XV Konferentsiya Vsesoyuznoi Kommunisticheskoi Partii (B)* (1927), p. 288.

the trade unions to the training of young workers, and raised the issues of wages and the age of admission to the unions.[1] Tomsky in his reply defended the *status quo*, not without some jibes at the self-importance of the young ; and the section of the conference resolution significantly headed " Unemployment and the Children of Workers " confined itself to general injunctions to facilitate the employment of the children of workers, and to observe strictly the ironclad minimum.[2] At the seventh trade union congress in December 1926 the spokesman of Vesenkha made a thinly veiled attack on the whole policy of the minimum, arguing that it should not apply to unskilled workers or to youths under the age of eighteen ; [3] and on March 24, 1927, the party central committee, in its decree on rationalization in industry, announced a somewhat embarrassed concession to the trade unions and the managers on the ironclad minimum. This was to be brought, from October 1, 1927, into " maximum conformity with the practical requirements of industry ", and confined to skilled workers ; preference was to be given to the children of workers. On the other hand, this concession was not to exempt enterprises at present employing less than the obligatory minimum of juveniles from making up the numbers.[4] At the fifth Komsomol conference, which opened on the very day of the party ruling, Chaplin, the secretary of the Komsomol central committee, explained that rationalization involved " certain difficulties in questions of juvenile labour ", and that " in the name of rationalization we shall have to make some sort of concession ".[5] The resolution of the conference dutifully

---

[1] *Ibid.* pp. 328-331, 348-352, 391 ; one of the issues was a trade union proposal to introduce a separate wage-scale for trainees (see p. 536 below), which was suspect as an attempt to depress their wages, and had been rejected by the seventh Komsomol congress in March 1926 (*VLKSM v Rezolyutsiyakh* (1929), p. 249). For the age of admission to unions see p. 550 below.

[2] *XV Konferentsiya Vsesoyuznoi Kommunisticheskoi Partii (B)* (1927), pp. 411-413 ; *KPSS v Rezolyutsiyakh* (1954), ii, 324-325.

[3] *Sed'moi S"ezd Professional'nykh Soyuzov SSSR* (1927), pp. 368-369 ; in the building industry the minimum was regularly interpreted as a proportion of skilled workers only, thus virtually eliminating it from that industry (*Professional'nye Soyuzy SSSR : Otchet k VII S"ezdu* (1926), p. 191).

[4] *Direktivy KPSS i Sovetskogo Pravitel'stva po Khozyaistvennym Voprosam,* i (1957), 671 ; for this decree see pp. 341-342 above.

[5] *Komsomol'skaya Pravda*, March 27, 1927 ; a stenographic record of the conference was published, but has not been available. The official attitude was defended in the pamphlet *Oppozitsiya i Komsomol* (1927), pp. 45-50, 91-110.

rehearsed, in almost identical terms, the party proposal for the revision of the ironclad minimum ; [1] and in April 1927 the fourth Union Congress of Soviets obediently, and apparently without discussion, instructed the government " to establish norms for the ironclad minimum of juveniles in conformity with the practical requirements of industry, the effective percentage of the minimum being calculated in relation only to skilled workers ".[2] The opposition, now at the height of its activity, was particularly eager to make capital out of labour troubles ; " he is no Komsomolman ", ran a current opposition slogan, " who does not fight against a revision of the minimum ".[3] At the crisis of the struggle with the opposition, the party leaders sought to keep these contentious issues in the background.

The defeat of the opposition relaxed the need for an unbroken party front ; the drive for industrialization made all questions relating to the recruitment of labour more urgent and compelling. Trouble boiled up again on the issue of training. Gastev, the director of TsIT, published an article in *Pravda*, in which he propounded a " new culture of work ". What he called " a calculated engineer's approach " to labour was now " permissible and possible ", and he emphasized the importance of rigid training :

> The time has gone beyond recall when one could speak of the freedom of the worker in regard to the machine, and still more in regard to the enterprise as a whole. . . . Manœuvres and motions at the bench, the concentration of attention, the movement of the hands, the position of the body, these elementary aspects of behaviour become the cornerstone. Here is the key to the new culture of work, the key to the serious cultural revolution.[4]

When the eighth Komsomol congress met in May 1928, the theses presented to it by TsIT argued that the young peasant, being physically stronger than the young proletarian, was more suitable to train for heavy industrial work : " the wager on the urban

[1] *VLKSM v Rezolyutsiyakh* (1929), p. 291.
[2] *S"ezdy Sovetov v Dokumentakh*, iii (1960), 125.
[3] *Komsomol'skaya Pravda*, July 9, 1927.
[4] *Pravda*, February 10, 1928.

working youth . . . may be out of date ".[1] Chaplin, speaking
for the Komsomol, fiercely attacked Gastev's " anti-Marxist
platform ", which " merely expresses in concentrated form numerous tendencies prevalent among our managers and even, unfortunately, among our trade unionists ". For TsIT the worker was
" an adjunct of the machine, not a creator of socialist production " ;
and Gastev " in his understanding of the new worker is undistinguishable from Ford ". Chaplin made an impassioned defence
of the factory schools, whose methods of training Gastev had
described as " a guild-handicraft survival ".[2] Gastev, evidently
unwilling to engage in controversy before an unsympathetic audience, made a mild reply, pointing out that he was at one with the
Komsomol in his opposition to the restrictive attitudes of the trade
unions, and claimed the support of the party central committee in
its temporizing resolution of March 11, 1926 ;[3] and the resolution
on the preparation of cadres for the five-year plan, called for two
types of courses at the factory schools — two-year courses to train
" workers with mass qualifications ", and three-year or four-year
courses for skilled workers — and suggested that the cost should
be reduced " by rationalization of the methods of practical and
theoretical instruction, in particular by using the procedures of
TsIT ".[4] This official attempt at conciliation between the Komsomol and TsIT, however, did nothing to abate the mutual re-
criminations between Komsomol and trade unions carried on in
the columns of Komsomol'skaya Pravda and Trud throughout the
summer of 1928. The party central committee at its session of
November 1928, evidently anxious to heal the breach between the
factory school system and TsIT, prescribed that Vesenkha,
Glavprofobr and Narkomtrud should " organize their work for
the instruction of learners in production and for the re-training of
workers in such a way as to embody the new techniques of rationalization on the basis of the scientific achievements of TsIT ".[5] But

[1] The theses have not been available, but were quoted in VIII Vsesoyuznyi
S"ezd VLKSM (1928), p. 56, and in Shestnadtsataya Konferentsiya VKP(B)
(1962), p. 212 ; they were originally published in the monthly journal of
TsIT (ibid. p. 796, note 150).
[2] VIII Vsesoyuznyi S"ezd VLKSM (1928), pp. 54-59.
[3] Ibid. pp. 225-229 ; for this resolution see p. 476 above.
[4] VLKSM v Rezolyutsiyakh (1929), pp. 314, 323-324.
[5] VKP(B) v Rezolyutsiyakh (1941), ii, 305 ; the resolution was omitted from
later editions.

by this time Tomsky's association with Right opposition had made the trade unions particularly vulnerable ; and the disputes over the minimum for juveniles and the training of labour had become items in a general campaign against the trade unions, of which the Komsomol was the spearhead.[1]

When the eighth trade union congress opened on December 10, 1928, passions were already inflamed ;[2] and they mounted still higher when, on the third day of the congress, Zhdanov, in a harsh and uncompromising speech, put forward the demands of the Komsomol central committee in regard to the juvenile worker. He protested against the reduction of the ironclad minimum by a figure of 70,000 ; against the continuous rise in juvenile unemployment, which increased from 137,000 on January 1, 1927, to 213,000 on July 1, 1928 ; against the exclusion of young workers from trade union sanatoria and rest homes ; and against the attempt to confine the factory schools to the children of skilled workers. On all these points he acidly accused the trade union leaders of ignoring the views of the Komsomol and the interests of the young.[3] In the subsequent debate the discussion of the problems of juvenile labour generated more heat than light. Another Komsomol delegate denounced the campaign " to replace factory schools by short-term courses of TsIT ".[4] Gastev, having apparently made his peace with the trade unions, mildly defended himself against Komsomol attacks, remarking that the principles of TsIT won general acceptance, but that their practical application provoked " consternation ".[5] Later, in the debate on the report of Narkomtrud, another spokesman of the Komsomol resumed the tale of abuses. In spite of the legal prohibition on night work for juveniles, 10 per cent of all juveniles in industry, and 46 per cent of those employed in factories working the seven-hour day, were on night work. Juveniles, with the permission of the factory inspectors, worked a full seven- or eight-hour day on the plea that otherwise they would not be engaged and the quota would not be filled. Trade unions insisted on the direct engagement of

---

[1] See pp. 552-553 below.
[2] For a general account of the congress see pp. 556-560 below.
[3] Vos'moi S"ezd Professional'nykh Soyuzov SSSR (1929), pp. 110-113; for the setting of the speech see pp. 556-557 below.
[4] Vos'moi S"ezd Professional'nykh Soyuzov SSSR (1929), p. 145.
[5] Ibid. pp. 176-177 ; for an encomium of Gastev by Tomsky see ibid. p. 192.

children of their members and by-passed the labour exchanges.[1]
The resolutions of the congress contributed nothing to the settlement of these controversies.

The Komsomol had served its purpose as a spearhead of the
assault on Tomsky's authority in the trade unions. After his
downfall, the problems of juvenile labour receded into the background. It was claimed that the introduction of the three-shift
system had reduced unemployment among juveniles.[2] At the
sixteenth party conference in April 1929, one delegate attempted to
reopen the question of training, alleging that the Komsomol had
rightly and properly " struggled against an attempt to contaminate
the cadres of the proletariat with technically uneducated, technically illiterate, workers ". The method of TsIT was to turn out
not educated workers, but " mechanically trained workers " without theoretical background ; this was a " capitalist, Fordian
approach ".[3] But the heat had gone out of these debates ; and
nobody was eager to take up the challenge. The question did
not figure in the resolutions of the conference. It began to be
noticed at this time that, as a legacy of the period of war and
revolution, the proportion of youths in the population must soon
significantly decline. In 1927 the proportion of the age-group
15-17 was 6·6 per cent and of the age-group 18-24 16·7 per cent ;
by 1933 these percentages would be 4 and 13·7 respectively.[4] But
what changed — rather than solved — the whole problem of
juvenile labour was the advance of planned industrialization and
the ending of unemployment. Once competition for scarce jobs
had been eliminated, the need to press young workers on reluctant
managers and half-hearted trade unions disappeared. Once the
need had become urgent to train as many young workers as
possible in the shortest possible time, the struggle between different
institutions engaged in the process lost its sharpness or took
different forms. The factory schools and TsIT now appeared to
offer complementary rather than competitive systems of training ;
according to the estimates of the first five-year plan, the annual
output of the former would rise from 27,000 in 1928–1929 to

[1] *Ibid.* pp. 349-350.   [2] *Bol'shevik*, No. 8, April 30, 1929, pp. 46-47.
[3] *Shestnadtsataya Konferentsiya VKP(B)* (1962), pp. 212-214.
[4] *Pyatiletnii Plan Narodno-Khozyaistvennogo Stroitel'stva SSSR* (1929), ii,
ii, 164.

R

62,800 in 1932–1933 and of the latter from 11,500 to 32,500.[1]
Here as elsewhere, the landscape of a planned economy brought
new problems of its own, and made the problems of the later
nineteen-twenties obsolete and irrelevant.

(d) State Employees

State employees formed a separate category of the labour force,
and their wages and salaries were regulated under a different
system from those of workers.[2] They included administrative
and judicial officials, state employees at all levels, and all police
(the armed forces were in yet another category) ; all officials and
employees in social and cultural institutions ; and the headquarters staffs of all economic and commercial organizations, including transport. Thus the staffs of industrial trusts were state
employees ; directors and managerial staffs of factories were not.
The number of persons employed in state establishments continued to rise steadily from 2·1 millions in 1925–1926 to 2·5
millions in 1928–1929, though the ratio of state employees to the
total labour force declined from 21·1 per cent in 1925–1926 to
20·6 per cent in 1928–1929.[3]

The " régime of economy " campaign of 1926 seems to have
made its first impact on the staffs of economic establishments,
which were subject to a sharp decline in 1926–1927 ; the much
smaller reduction in the category of " administrative and judicial "
employees did not set in till 1927–1928.[4] At first, the rapid
expansion of staffs in the period 1924–1926 was slowed down
rather than reversed ; Orjonikidze at the seventh trade union
congress in December 1926 produced a table purporting to show
that dismissals from Soviet institutions had been more than
balanced by staff increases in the current budgetary year.[5] But
dismissals occurred on a considerable scale ; and what was probably a not unfair picture of them was drawn by another delegate
at the congress :

[1] *Pyatiletnii Plan Narodno-Khozyaistvennogo Stroitel'stva SSSR*(1929), i, 77.
[2] See pp. 542-544 below.
[3] See Table No. 21, p. 955 below ; for slightly different figures see *Ekono-micheskoe Obozrenie*, No. 4, 1929, pp. 159-160.
[4] See Table No. 22, p. 956 below.
[5] *Sed'moi S"ezd Professional'nykh Soyuzov SSSR* (1927), p. 447.

They turn out the least qualified people, i.e. the mass of workers and peasants who were forcibly thrust into the apparatus. The bureaucrat resisted ; we forced them in ; and now, when cutting down begins, these are cut out first of all. . . . The bureaucrat remains, and the new worker in virtue of his lack of qualification, his lack of experience, is turned out.[1]

On October 1, 1928, 250,000 employees were registered as unemployed (the largest single category next to the general one of " unskilled workers ") — a result of the " curtailment and rationalization of our administrative and service apparatus " ; and one-quarter of unemployed women were non-manual workers. The number of unemployed workers in Soviet trading institutions had more than doubled in the past two years.[2] But the incidence of the cuts was uneven. The number of social, scientific and cultural workers, including doctors and teachers, continued to rise, and by 1928–1929 accounted for about one-half of the total of state employees. On the other hand, the number of employees in administrative and judicial establishments continued to decline slightly, and in 1928–1929 amounted to rather more than one-quarter, or, together with employees in state economic institutions, about one-third, of all state employees. These were the only categories which an expanding economy found it possible to keep stable or slightly reduce.[3] The number of all state employees in towns increased from 1,260,200 on May 1, 1925 to 1,462,310 on January 1, 1928 (a rise of 16 per cent), the number in the countryside during the same period from 705,499 to 907,968 (a rise of 28·7 per cent).[4]

[1] *Ibid.* p. 463.
[2] *Vos'moi S"ezd Professional'nykh Soyuzov SSSR* (1929), p. 323.
[3] See Table No. 22, p. 956 below ; for some percentage calculations see *Ekonomicheskoe Obozrenie*, No. 4, 1929, pp. 161, 169.
[4] *Ibid.* p. 171.

CHAPTER 18

THE DRIVE FOR PRODUCTIVITY

WHEN the fourteenth party congress in December 1925 proclaimed industrialization, and first and foremost the development of heavy industry, as the fundamental aim of Soviet economic policy, it ushered in a period of increasing pressure on the industrial worker. The disproportion between a deficiency of capital and a super-abundance of labour was characteristic of every part of the Soviet economy, urban as well as rural. Much of the equipment of Soviet industry was still in a calamitous condition of neglect and obsolescence ; and capital for its renewal was unobtainable. Of the resources required for industrial expansion, human labour power was the only one in abundant supply ; and it was only by the lavish use of this resource that the policy could be brought to fruition. The reserve of labour power provided by the peasant, moving in increasing numbers from country to town, was, however, from the industrial standpoint, unskilled labour of the lowest grade. To impose on the raw peasant the discipline of factory work was a task of enormous difficulty, which invited, and perhaps necessitated, stern measures of compulsion. The beginnings of industrialization have rarely been painless. Industrialization in the Soviet Union, launched in a backward economy and without the support of foreign capital, placed an exceptionally harsh burden on the worker.

The campaign to raise the productivity of labour (proizvoditel'-nost' truda) had been actively pursued since 1924.[1] An ambiguity was latent in the term. The physical reality represented in calculations of the " productivity of labour " was " output per man ", measured on a yearly, monthly, or sometimes daily or hourly basis. But output per man did not depend solely on the effort of the individual worker. The amount of capital in the form of equip-

[1] See *Socialism in One Country, 1924–1926*, Vol. 1, pp. 382-389.

ment, mechanical power, etc. available per worker was a major factor in determining his productivity ; and in the Soviet Union this fell far behind what was available in the great industrial countries.[1] Factory organization and the trained skill of the worker were hardly less important ; the argument that in the Soviet Union in the nineteen-twenties productivity was held back largely by " the need for improved techniques " and " the insufficient skill of our workers " [2] had much to commend it. The term " productivity of labour " came, however, in the course of the discussions, increasingly to carry the connotation that its rise or fall depended, primarily or exclusively, on the intensity of individual effort. The capital element in productivity, severely limited by scarce resources, was treated as constant ; the variable was the intensity of labour. To increase the effort of the individual worker had always been an important element in the campaign for higher productivity ; and, as the pressure of industrialization increased and the shortage of capital became more acute, the demands on the worker were intensified, both relatively and absolutely. The party central committee at its session in April 1926, which endorsed the wages standstill, proposed to raise productivity " by means of the rationalization of production " : this included both improvements in plant and organization and " the intensification of the working day, the strengthening of labour discipline and the struggle with absenteeism etc." [3] The party

---

[1] A table in the Gosplan control figures for 1927–1928 showed the percentages of energy (calculated in horse-power hours) derived from different sources in the three principal countries :

	Human Power	Animal Power	Mechanical Power
USA	1·1	9·1	89·8
Great Britain	2·3	3·2	94·5
USSR	9·3	58·0	32·7

(*Kontrol'nye Tsifry Narodnogo Khozyaistva SSSR na 1927–1928 god* (1928), pp. 444-445). In the Soviet Union " productivity " was highest in the oil, rubber, leather and chemical industries, which worked with modern machinery, and lowest in coal-mining and in the glass and match industries (*Kontrol'nye Tsifry Narodnogo Khozyaistva na 1926–1927 god* (1926), pp. 324-325). In the autumn of 1928, Kviring noted that in Norway, owing to the high degree of mechanization, only a few hundred workers were required to build a hydro-electric station ; at that time 12,000 workers were employed at Dnieprostroi (*Dneprostroi*, No. 2-3, 1928, p. 4 ; *Torgovo-Promyshlennaya Gazeta*, October 6, 1928).

[2] *Na Agrarnom Fronte*, No. 7-8, 1926, p. 37.

[3] See *Socialism in One Country, 1924–1926*, Vol. 1, pp. 402-403.

appeal of April 25, 1926, on the " régime of economy " included an emphatic demand to increase labour productivity, and was followed by a decree of May 18, 1926, calling for a 10 per cent increase in productivity before the end of the economic year.[1] The decree of June 11, 1926, on the same theme included provisions for the rational utilization of labour and for the punishment of infractions of labour discipline, and called for the cooperation of the trade unions and other public organizations.[2]

The campaign for the " régime of economy " thus became linked, through the ambiguous conception of the " productivity of labour ", with a campaign for an intensification of effort on the part of the worker. Dzerzhinsky in a speech at the Yugostal works in May 1926 launched a campaign against absenteeism, which he treated as a product of anti-proletarian tendencies and proposed to counter by tough measures :

> Where there is absenteeism without due cause, I shall recommend the administration automatically to reduce the establishment, irrespective of the state of the production programme.[3]

The Vesenkha newspaper gave publicity to reports of workers absent after holidays through drunkenness, or returning to their villages without permission to do agricultural work, or simulating sickness or accident.[4] Semashko, the People's Commissar for Health, accused workers of " drunkenness, malingering and exaggeration of illnesses ".[5] These malpractices were attributed primarily to unskilled workers newly recruited from the countryside and subject to the anti-proletarian tendencies of a peasant background.[6] But skilled workers were also said to be well aware that they were indispensable, and to resist discipline ; the common complaint was made of failure by the trade unions to support the managers in applying disciplinary measures.[7] Art. 47 of the labour code provided that a worker absent without cause on three successive days, or six times in a month, could be dismissed.

[1] For the appeal and the decree see pp. 334-335 above.
[2] For this decree see p. 335 above.
[3] The speech was belatedly reported in Torgovo-Promyshlennaya Gazeta, October 1, 1926 ; absenteeism was said to have been two or three times as great as before the war (Torgovo-Promyshlennaya Gazeta, August 10, 1927).
[4] Ibid. June 8, 1926.   [5] Izvestiya, July 2, 1926.
[6] Bol'shevik, No. 13, July 15, 1926, p. 50.
[7] Torgovo-Promyshlennaya Gazeta, July 2, 3, 1926.

Managers now began to clamour for sterner measures. The organ of Vesenkha reported, under the heading " How to Combat Absenteeism ", that a Leningrad factory had made the rule that any worker late more than five times in three months would be " unconditionally dismissed ", and proposed that no sickness benefit should be paid for absences of less than three days, and that a factory doctor should be required to certify all cases of sick leave.[1] Kraval, whose post and personality as head of the labour economics department of Vesenkha[2] became increasingly influential at this time, proposed to the first congress of labour economics departments of the trusts, which met from June 29 to July 8, 1926, that, in order to discourage absenteeism, wages for sickness up to two weeks should no longer be paid in full but at a rate of two-thirds ; this proposal was endorsed in a resolution of the congress.[3] The congress also discussed ways and means of strengthening the hands of factory managers ;[4] and Kalinin wrote an article on the régime of economy which " one of the workers' newspapers " hesitated to publish on the ground that it was " too much in favour of the managers ", though, reflected the sentimental Kalinin, " nobody so much values a good manager as the workers ".[5]

From the time of the sixth trade union congress of November 1924 onwards, it had been clearly laid down that increased productivity was a condition precedent of higher wages.[6] The programme of rapid industrialization approved by the fourteenth party congress in December 1925 was based on the unspoken

---

[1] Ibid. July 1, 1926.   [2] See p. 286 above.

[3] Predpriyatie, No. 7, 1926, pp. 79-80.

[4] Torgovo-Promyshlennaya Gazeta, July 3, 14, 1926. The campaign continued throughout the year. In September 1926 the labour economics department of Vesenkha in conjunction with representatives of the Moscow trusts drew up new regulations for factory labour ; meetings, the reading of newspapers, distribution of library books and collection of trade union dues were to be prohibited in working hours ; absentees for more than four days were to be dismissed. Simulation of sickness was to be punished, on a first offence, by a reduction in grade, on a second, by dismissal (Torgovo-Promyshlennaya Gazeta, September 26, 1926 ; it is not clear whether these rules were in fact approved or applied). For an order of July 19, 1927, containing a long list of offences against discipline punishable on a first occasion by reprimand and on a subsequent occasion by dismissal see S. Zagorsky, Wages and Regulation of Conditions of Labour in the USSR (Geneva, 1930), pp. 15-16.

[5] Derevenskii Kommunist, No. 13, July 15, 1926, p. 7.

[6] See Socialism in One Country, 1924-1926, Vol. 1, pp. 389-392.

premiss that, if capital was to be accumulated for the expansion,
first and foremost, of heavy industry, the worker, like the peasant,
must for the present forego a full " equivalent return " for his
labour. He must produce more than he consumed ; productivity
must increase faster than wages. At the session of the party
central committee in July 1926 the opposition invoked the converse argument, and claimed that, since productivity had risen
rapidly during the past 12 months, an increase in wages was over-
due. When Shmidt, as People's Commissar for Labour, delivered
a report which concentrated entirely on productivity, Trotsky
reproached him with evading the crucial issue of wages and with
failing to condemn the administrative pressures exercised on the
workers by " a considerable proportion of managers ", and called
for the appointment of a commission to consider the operation of
the régime of economy, and to prevent it from being used to
depress the vital interests of the workers.[1] The views of the opposition were as a matter of course rejected, and no resolution was
passed on the labour question. But the demand for some improvement in the position of the workers proved irresistible ; and in
August 1926 the decision was taken to accord to the industrial
worker an all-round increase in wages.[2]

The wages increase of the autumn of 1926 challenged the all-
important principle, implicit in the whole productivity campaign,
that productivity should rise faster than wages. The Vesenkha
estimates for the coming economic year issued in July 1926 had
proposed a rise of productivity in industry of 12·3 per cent and a
rise in industrial wages of 7·2 per cent.[3] The Gosplan control

[1] Shmidt's report has not been available ; Trotsky's comments are in the
Trotsky archives, T 887. A pamphlet entitled *The Labour Question*, illicitly
circulated about this time, apparently not by the united opposition, but by
the Democratic Centralists, alleged that the régime of economy had been converted into a " means of pressure " on the worker, and that " a complete
autocracy of the administration " reigned in the factories (quoted in *XV
Konferentsiya Vsesoyuznoi Kommunisticheskoi Partii (B)* (1927), pp. 631-632);
Bukharin called it " an utterly and exceptionally disgusting leaflet " (*ibid.*
p. 579).

[2] See pp. 522-523 below ; for the joint party and government declaration of
August 16, 1926, condemning " distortions " of the " régime of economy "
at the expense of the workers see pp. 335-336 above.

[3] *Torgovo-Promyshlennaya Gazeta*, July 21, 1926 ; the final results for the
current year 1925-1926 showed a rise in productivity of 12 per cent (see Table
No. 24, p. 957 below).

figures for 1926–1927, prepared independently and issued in the
following month, provided for a rise in productivity in census
industry of 8·4 per cent and a rise in wages in Vesenkha-planned
industry of 7·7 per cent ; but a caveat was added that, if wages
throughout the whole of census industry were taken into account,
the rise would be 8·3 or 8·4 per cent.[1] These calculations were
angrily contested in the industrial newspaper, which demanded a
far larger margin between productivity and wages.[2] Shmidt, in
an interview in *Pravda* prompted by the wage increases, announced
that norms of production were also to be raised ; [3] and the official
economic newspaper wrote that the fundamental task of the collective agreements was now to guarantee a rise in the productivity of
labour and a lowering of costs of production.[4] Kraval made
explicit in particularly harsh and uncompromising terms the
demand of Vesenkha that a rise in productivity must outstrip any
increase in wages.[5] But this intense pressure provoked a corresponding reaction from critics within the party. In the course of a
discussion at the Communist Academy Sokolnikov described the
process of socialist construction as " painful ", and declared that
" the masses feel on their backs " the weight of industrialization.[6]
Radek, in the same discussion, reproached Kraval with treating a
rise in the productivity of labour as " a bureaucratic reform " to be
achieved " simply by circulars without the participation of the
masses " : the physical strength of the working class was not " a
barrel from which one can go on drawing *ad infinitum* ".[7] The
compromise arrived at between Vesenkha and Gosplan foreshadowed a rise of 12·6 per cent in productivity in 1926–1927 and
of 9·9 per cent in real wages.[8] The upward movement in wages
was irresistible, but was to be compensated by an all-out drive to
increase output and reduce costs of production.

[1] *Kontrol'nye Tsifry Narodnogo Khozyaistva na 1926–1927 god* (1926), pp. 86-
88 ; Gosplan assumed that prices would remain stable throughout the year and
that it was unnecessary to differentiate between nominal and real wages.
[2] *Torgovo-Promyshlennaya Gazeta*, September 2, 14, 1926.
[3] *Pravda*, September 24, 1926.
[4] *Ekonomicheskaya Zhizn'*, October 6, 1926.
[5] *Torgovo-Promyshlennaya Gazeta*, October 10, 1926.
[6] *Vestnik Kommunisticheskoi Akademii*, xvii (1926), 203.
[7] *Ibid.* xvii, 248.
[8] *Torgovo-Promyshlennaya Gazeta*, October 22, 1926 ; for the discussion
about cost reduction see pp. 338-340 above.

R 2

When the fifteenth party conference met on October 26, 1926, relations between Vesenkha and the trade unions, and between industrial managers and industrial workers, were tense, and tempers frayed. Tomsky's report on the trade unions, introducing theses which had, as usual, been approved in advance by the party central committee, provoked a bitter rejoinder from Teplov, a factory director who had attained the status of party membership. Teplov complained that, though the agreed theses contained a substantial passage on labour discipline, Tomsky had not so much as mentioned the subject. Absenteeism in factories commonly amounted to 15 per cent, and sometimes reached 30 per cent. Foremen had no means of enforcing discipline in the shops ; on the other hand, managers were subject to controls from all kinds of authorities.[1] The speech made a bad impression. Melnichansky called Teplov's figures " impossible " ; deliberate absenteeism was about 1·5 to 2 per cent. Ryazanov described Teplov as " the sort of director who, even when he is right, provokes a conflict by his mere appearance, his mere manner of speaking to the workers ".[2] But the problem of discipline remained. The section of the theses on the régime of economy admitted that some economic organs had been guilty of applying the prescribed policy " not by rationalization of the processes of production and curtailment of overheads, but by violation of the essential needs and interests of the workers ". But it enjoined on the trade unions " planned and constant effort to strengthen trade union and labour discipline, a decisive struggle against the anarchistic methods employed by some groups of workers (' walk-outs ', strikes unauthorized by the union etc.) ", and instructed them to counter

[1] XV Konferentsiya Vsesoyuznoi Kommunisticheskoi Partii (B) (1927), pp. 314-318.
[2] Ibid. pp. 321, 354 ; Tomsky also referred to Teplov's " unsuccessful " début at a party conference (ibid. p. 406). Teplov was, however, supported by another manager (ibid. pp. 344-347). The category of " deliberate " or " malicious " (zlostnyi) absenteeism was obviously difficult to define ; Tomsky threw some light on it when he explained that many excusable absences were due to the needs of children or to housing problems (ibid. pp. 403-404). Teplov, in a brief reply, admitted that widespread absenteeism occurred only among unskilled workers (ibid. p. 417). According to later statistics the number of days lost in industry through absences without due cause rose from 7·43 per worker in 1925 to 7·86 in 1926 ; the Donbass coal-miners had the worst record of absenteeism (Sotsialisticheskoe Stroitel'stvo SSSR (1934), p. 339 ; for later figures see p. 510 below).

" absenteeism, slackness, and an unconscientious attitude to obligations " among the workers.[1] Nobody wished to stress the incompatibility of rapid industrialization with the short-term interests of the workers, who had to sustain the burdens and tensions of the pace now being set.

Meanwhile Vesenkha did not allow the grass to grow under its feet. On November 5, 1926, immediately after the end of the conference, it issued a circular stressing the need to correct the existing " disproportion " between wages, productivity and the investment of capital, and arguing that " the scissors between wages and the productivity of labour must be brought into a normal relation ".[2] This provoked a retort in *Trud* from Frumkin, who particularly objected to the introduction of capital accumulation into the equation between wages and productivity.[3] The theme was cautiously handled at the seventh trade union congress in December 1926. Rykov, in his introductory speech, contrasted " the rationalization of production in capitalist countries ", which took place " independently of the will and against the interests of the working masses ", with the processes of socialist construction, which could be carried out " only with the most active participation of the working masses themselves and in their interests ".[4] Tomsky rejected the claim advanced by Trotsky for priority of wages over productivity, and eloquently reinforced Rykov's argument by contrasting the rôle of the communist in bourgeois countries, where he is " wholly and fully and always obliged to support all demands of workers for an improvement in their economic position " with his rôle under a dictatorship of the proletariat where " the interests of today must be subordinated to the general class interests of tomorrow and of the ensuing period of time ".[5] A critical delegate from the floor of the congress alleged that the managers " wanted first of all to use the régime of economy to squeeze the workers " ; another quoted a rhymed couplet in

---

[1] *KPSS v Rezolyutsiyakh* (1954), ii, 315-316, 320.
[2] *Torgovo-Promyshlennaya Gazeta*, November 7, 1926.
[3] *Trud*, November 9, 1926.
[4] *Sed'moi S"ezd Professional'nykh Soyuzov SSSR* (1927), pp. 15-16.
[5] *Ibid.* pp. 49-50 ; a few days earlier Tomsky had used the same argument in almost the same words (this was evidently a considered set-piece) at the third Ukrainian trade union congress in Kharkov (*Stenograficheskii Otchet 3^{go} Vseukrainskogo S"ezda Profsoyuzov* (1927), pp. 17-18).

which the régime was equated with pressure (nazhim) on the worker, who " feels this pressure on his shoulders ". Yet another said bluntly that it was " no secret " that measures like the rise in productivity and the régime of economy " amounted to pressure on the muscle-power of the workers ", and that less attention has been paid to the rationalization and equipment of production.[1] After Kuibyshev had alleged that " wages expressed in chervontsy have risen more than the productivity of labour ", and cautiously added that this " could not, of course, have a favourable reaction on cost movements ",[2] Krol, the president of the food workers' union, training his guns on Kraval rather than on Kuibyshev, denounced the labour economics department of Vesenkha : " a dozen people, who claim to know ' everything ', have the audacity to assert a whole lot of things tending to lead to a worsening of the workers' situation ".[3] The resolutions of the congress rejected " distortions of the régime of economy " resulting in " a deterioration of the material position of the workers ", but left no doubt of the support required from the unions for the policy of industrialization : " the most important task of the trade unions is further persistent work to raise the productivity of labour through the rationalization of production ".[4]

" Rationalization " had now supplanted " the régime of economy " as the current economic slogan.[5] The resolution of the party central committee of March 24, 1927, on rationalization again broached the question of the organization of labour and labour discipline : absences without due cause of more than three days in a month were not to be condoned.[6] The fifth Komsomol conference of March 1927 raised its voice in support of improved labour discipline, advocating " a struggle against absenteeism " and " the inculcation in the young worker of a responsible attitude to the work-bench, to his materials and to his tools " ; the member of the Komsomol should serve as an example to his fellow-workers in these respects.[7] In the following month at the fourth Union Congress of Soviets a recalcitrant trade union delegate protested that in existing conditions " we shall scarcely succeed in pushing

[1] *Sed'moi S"ezd Professional'nykh Soyuzov SSSR* (1927), pp. 467, 486, 522-523.   [2] *Ibid.* p. 507.   [3] *Ibid.* p. 531.
[4] *Ibid.* pp. 745, 796.   [5] See pp. 340-344 above. [6] See pp. 341-342 above.
[7] *VLKSM v Rezolyutsiyakh* (1929), p. 292.

production higher ", and that what was required to raise productivity was " the re-equipment, mechanization and also rationalization of production ".[1] The resolution on the development of industry sponsored by Kuibyshev uncompromisingly declared it " essential to raise further the productivity of labour, while at the same time the ratio of wages to costs must be systematically reduced." It endorsed the demand of the party resolution for stricter penalties for absenteeism ; the number of unauthorized absences entailing automatic dismissal was reduced from six to three a month.[2] A few months later the trade union central council exhorted all trade union organizations to intensify the campaign for " socialist rationalization ".[3] In the event, the logic of the economic situation prevailed. Rationalization both of technical processes and of the organization of labour was pursued. But, while the scarcity of capital resources limited the rate at which technical equipment could be improved, the drive for economy continuously encouraged the more intensive and " rational " utilization of the labour force.

The issue once more came to a head with the preparation of the control figures for the forthcoming economic year 1927–1928 — an example of the impact of planning on every fundamental question of policy. The final results for 1926–1927 showed a rise in productivity of only 9 per cent as compared with a target figure of 12·6 per cent ; and wages had risen by 12 per cent as compared with a target of 9·9 per cent.[4] The attempt to keep the rise in productivity ahead of wages increases had proved unsuccessful. This was a lapse to be retrieved ; and Vesenkha boldly budgeted for a rise in productivity of 13·8 per cent and in wages of 6 per cent in the forthcoming economic year.[5] These estimates were substantially accepted by Gosplan, which, noting defensively that, " in the period of reconstruction, an increase in the productivity of labour is conditioned by technical-organizational improvements, and not by increased intensity of labour ", foreshadowed in its control figures a rise in productivity of 12·6 per cent in capital

[1] SSSR : 4 S"ezd Sovetov (1927), pp. 70-71.
[2] S"ezdy Sovetov v Dokumentakh, iii (1960), 124.
[3] Trud, August 21, 1927.
[4] See Tables 24, 25, pp. 957, 958 below ; for the target figures see p. 489 above.
[5] Torgovo-Promyshlennaya Gazeta, September 6, 1927.

goods industries and 13·7 per cent in consumer goods industries, and a rise of 6 per cent in wages ; this, on the assumption of the projected fall in prices, was reckoned to be equivalent to a rise of 12-13 per cent in real wages.[1] The renewal of the collective agreements at the beginning of the economic year in the autumn of 1927 led to the usual haggling between Vesenkha and the trade union central council. An article in *Torgovo-Promyshlennaya Gazeta* of October 18, 1927, accused the trade unions of taking an " unduly optimistic " view of productivity and of its relations to wages, and was sharply answered in *Trud* on the following day. But, lest anyone should speculate on friction between Vesenkha and the trade unions, a directive was issued to trade unions and economic organs, in the joint names of Kuibyshev and Tomsky, explaining that, " in the relation between the productivity of labour and wages, it is indispensable to achieve a decisive turn in the direction of raising the rate of growth of productivity above the rate of growth of wages " : the respective rates now prescribed were 13·8 and 6·8 per cent.[2]

These policies proved highly vulnerable to the criticisms of the opposition. The opposition assault was indeed not free from demagogy. The opposition was even more heavily committed than the official leaders to intensive industrialization ; and every practicable method of attaining this goal involved increased pressure either on the worker, or on the peasant, or on both. Trotsky, when he occupied the seats of power, had been known as a disciplinarian in his attitude to labour.[3] But the paradox of a self-styled workers' state which brought harsh pressure to bear on the worker to increase production, while at the same time paring

---

[1] *Kontrol'nye Tsifry Narodnogo Khozyaistva SSSR na 1927–1928 god* (1928), p. 220 ; see also *Pravda*, September 10, 1927.

[2] The directive was published both in *Torgovo-Promyshlennaya Gazeta* and in *Trud*, October 30, 1927, and in *Pravda*, November 1, 1927 ; for the results achieved in 1927–1928 see p. 507 below.

[3] See *The Bolshevik Revolution, 1917–1923*, Vol. 2, p. 215. Trotsky was no doubt alive to the charge of inconsistency, and attempted to meet it ; on September 21, 1926, he wrote to an unnamed correspondent that " measures of war communism and intensified pressure " could be effective only for a limited period, and that " in the conditions of the long-term building of socialism workers' discipline must rest more and more on the self-activization of the workers and on their interest in the results of their work " (Trotsky archives, T 895).

his wages, was too easy a target to be spared. The opposition platform of September 1927 complained that higher productivity meant only increased " pressure on the muscles and nerves of the workers ". It protested against the intensification of discipline in the factories :

> The administrative organs are striving more and more to establish their unlimited authority. The hiring and discharge of workers is actually in the sole hands of the administration. Pre-revolutionary relations between master and workmen are not rarely to be found.

It demanded a rise in wages at least proportional to the rise in the productivity of labour, and a radical cessation of " every inclination to lengthen the eight-hour day ".[1]

The party leaders, always especially sensitive to the charge of exploiting the workers, reacted more sharply to this than to any other part of the opposition campaign. They decided to outbid the opposition on this point by a bold and unexpected stroke. The eight-hour day had been hailed as one of the great achievements of the revolution, and had led to a gradual, but progressive, reduction in the length of the working day.[2] On October 12, 1927, at the end of a long speech to the Moscow provincial trade union congress, Bukharin raised the question, evidently with the authority of the Politburo, of " a slow but sure transition *to a shorter working day* ", and spoke of a seven-hour day as setting " new tasks before the trade unions and the working class ". At the same time he demanded higher productivity of labour, and denounced " the slave-labour tempo " of work in the building industry. But this part of the speech was not published for nearly a week, and seems

---

[1] L. Trotsky, *The Real Situation in Russia* (n.d. [1928]), pp. 36, 49, 52. The theme that rationalization of production meant primarily increased pressure on the worker was a staple theme of opposition criticism at this time ; Bukharin attempted to meet it in his optimistic speech of October 26, 1927, in which he lyrically described rationalization as implying " a higher type of worker, a higher tempo of labour, a higher intensity of labour, and at the same time a higher capacity in the labour force to develop a greater intensity of labour " (for this speech see pp. 35-36 above).

[2] According to statistics quoted in S. Strumilin, *Problemy Ekonomiki Truda* (1957), p. 481, the average number of hours per day worked in industry fell from 8·9 in 1917 to 7·6 in 1925, and 7·5 for each of the years 1926 and 1927 ; it fell further to 7·4 in 1928.

to have attracted no particular attention.[1] The first publicity
came in another form. One of the tasks of the session of the TsIK
of the USSR in October 1927 was to issue a manifesto for the
tenth anniversary of the October revolution. A draft of the manifesto was submitted on October 15, 1927, on the eve of the session,
to the party fraction of the delegation. It announced a programme of which the following was the first and most sensational
item :

> To assure to workers in production in factories and work-
> shops a transition in the next few years to a seven-hour day with-
> out reduction in earnings ; and for this purpose to instruct the
> presidium of TsIK and the Sovnarkom of the USSR to initiate,
> at the latest within a year, the gradual execution of this resolu-
> tion in several industries, in accordance with the progress made
> in re-equipping and rationalizing factories and workshops and
> with the rise in productivity of labour.[2]

It was clear that the same wages were to be paid for the reduced
time worked, but on condition that output was also maintained —
or even increased. One practical advantage of the seven-hour day,
though not much publicized either by the supporters of the scheme
or by its opposition critics, had been from the first in the minds of
those who propounded the scheme : it would facilitate a transition
to three-shift working. A month earlier, Mezhlauk at a meeting
of the Vesenkha commission to re-examine the five-year plan, had
urged consideration of the question : " *Can we go over to a
reduced working day, and introduce three-shift working in those
industries where it is necessary and appropriate ?* " ; and Kraval
commented that in some industries a reduced working day was
possible to combat unemployment and to force the utilization of

---

[1] *Pravda*, October 16, 18, 1927 ; the passage came in the second instalment
(in section 8 of the speech). Neither the brief record of the debate on Bukharin's
speech (*ibid*, October 14, 1927) nor the record of the simultaneous session of the
trade union central council (*ibid*. October 13, 14, 1927) mentioned the seven-
hour day. This was the speech in which Bukharin had announced the " reinforced offensive against the *kulak* " (see pp. 32-33 above). Piquancy was added
to the choice of Bukharin to launch the slogan by the fact that, at the fifteenth
party conference of October 1926, he had referred contemptuously to the seven-
hour day as the sort of demagogic proposal which Menshevik or social-democrat
heretics might have been expected to make (*XV Konferentsiya Vsesoyuznoi
Kommunisticheskoi Partii (B)* (1927), pp. 592-593).

[2] For this manifesto see p. 33 above.

" morally depreciated " [i.e. obsolescent] equipment.[1] Strumilin, at the presidium of Gosplan on October 14, 1927, spoke of the prospective increase in the number of shifts as a way of reducing the number of unemployed.[2] *Pravda*, in a leading article of October 18, 1927, explained that the seven-hour day would be " linked in a number of branches [of industry] with an increase in the number of working shifts, and with a diminution of unemployment ". Sabsovich claimed that the three-shift system, made practicable by the seven-hour day, would enable the textile industry to increase its output by 40 per cent.[3]

Whatever other calculations may have lain behind it, it seems clear that one motive for this sudden move was to disconcert and outwit the opposition. This purpose was fulfilled. When the proposal was discussed in the party fraction, Zinoviev complained that most of those present had heard of the proposal for the first time " yesterday or the day before on their arrival in Moscow or Leningrad " ; [4] none of the current draft plans had so much as mentioned the idea. He denied that the length of the working day

---

[1] *Torgovo-Promyshlennaya Gazeta*, September 18, 1927 ; for this commission see pp. 866-867 below.

[2] *Informatsionnyi Byulleten' Gosplana SSSR*, No. 11-12, 1927, p. 21. For a previous use by Strumilin of the same argument see note 4 below ; Rykov repeated it at the fifteenth party congress in December 1927 (*Pyatnadtsatyi S"ezd VKP(B)*, ii (1962), 874).

[3] *Pravda*, October 19, 1927 ; for Sabsovich see p. 309 above.

[4] Trotsky knew of the proposal by October 10, 1927, on which date he wrote a memorandum criticizing it (*ibid*. T 3097). It was afterwards claimed that the proposal had in fact been prepared and discussed in advance ; but evidence quoted for this assertion was scanty. At the seventh trade union congress in December 1926, the two-shift system had been spoken of as normal in the textile industry, and the three-shift system as a remote possibility (*Sed'moi S"ezd Professional'nykh Soyuzov SSSR* (1927), p. 861). Reference was made in *Pravda*, October 18, 1927, to an article in *Planovoe Khozyaistvo*, No. 5, 1927, pp. 59-72, and to a Gosplan draft of the five-year plan, and in *Pravda*, October 25, 1927, to an alleged proposal of Dzerzhinsky 18 months earlier. But the *Planovoe Khozyaistvo* article was a utopian excursion into the prospect of achieving the six-hour day by 1940; and the only trace of the Gosplan proposal seems to be a reference by Strumilin at the second Gosplan congress of March 1927 to a " shortening of the working day and an increase in the number of shifts " as a means of dealing with unemployment, which he appeared to regard as desirable, but impracticable (S. Strumilin, *Ocherki Sovetskoi Ekonomiki* (1928), p. 481). Larin, a notorious eccentric, had proposed at the fourth Union Congress of Soviets in April 1927 to introduce four six-hour shifts in skilled trades, including printing (*SSSR : 4 S"ezd Sovetov* (1927), p. 369).

was now the main grievance of the workers. The questions of wages, unemployment and housing were all more important ; and Zinoviev reiterated the terms of the opposition platform.[1] Trotsky followed in a similar, though more acid, vein. He spoke cuttingly of " a policy of surprises and unexpectedness " and " a political expedient for one acute emergency, designed for its political effect — and no more ". The proposal was entirely out of accord with the general line : " all the wheels of the machine are turning from Left to Right — and for the holiday from Right to Left ".[2] These objections did not prevent the submission of the draft manifesto to TsIK, where it was carried by acclamation and without discussion ; Rykov called it " the second stage of the process of the rationalization and reconstruction of industry ", and explained that, whereas under capitalism rationalization meant " intensified exploitation of the working class and increased profits for the capitalist ", under socialism it meant " a simultaneous improvement in conditions of labour and in the material position of the working class ".[3]

During the next few days the adoption of the seven-hour working day was widely acclaimed in the press. When the party central committee met on October 21, 1927, Evdokimov repeated amid constant interruptions the strictures of the opposition on the manner in which the seven-hour day slogan had been launched, and complained once more that " we tie up the question of a rise of wages in industry exclusively with an increase in the intensity of the worker's labour ". Trotsky, whose speech was shouted down, called the project, with reference to the tenth anniversary celebrations, a " jubilee zigzag ", and alleged that Tomsky had been against it from fear that " the workers will demand a reckoning from the trade unions ".[4] As a retort to these attacks, a special resolution approving the manifesto of October 15, 1927, was

[1] Trotsky archives, T 1029.

[2] Trotsky archives, T 3098 ; both Zinoviev's and Trotsky's speeches were published in German in Die Fahne des Kommunismus, No. 35, November 11, 1927.

[3] 2 Sessiya Tsentral'nogo Ispolnitel'nogo Komiteta Soyuza SSR 4 Sozyva (n.d. [1927]), p. 34 ; the resolution of the ninth IKKI of Comintern in February 1928 also hailed the seven-hour day as evidence that the Soviet Union was in advance of the capitalist countries in its treatment of the workers (Kommunisticheskii Internatsional v Dokumentakh (1933), p. 746).

[4] For Evdokimov's and Trotsky's speeches see p. 35 above.

adopted by the committee, the opposition voting against it.[1] The introduction of the three-shift system soon emerged as the essential item of the reform. The textile workers' trade union agreed to the experimental introduction of the system in five factories.[2] By a decree of November 11, 1927, a governmental commission was set up, consisting of representatives of Narkomtrud, of the trade union central council and of Vesenkha, to arrange for the carrying out of the project ; [3] and on November 17, 1927, the presidium of the trade union central council set up a commission to consider its trade union aspects, including the vexed question of night work for women and juveniles.[4]

The fifteenth party congress, which met early in December 1927, paid strikingly little attention to labour problems. Chaplin, the Komsomol spokesman, suggested that, if the seven-hour day was introduced, the standard working-day for juveniles ought to be reduced from six hours to five. Evdokimov again attacked the whole proposal in a speech which was shouted down.[5] While the congress was in session, 15 members of the former Democratic Centralism group, headed by Sapronov and V. M. Smirnov, handed in a declaration which described " rationalization " (in inverted commas) as " a substitute for technical progress ", alleging that the workers had been " deprived in practice of the possibility of profiting from the workers' democracy achieved in the October revolution ".[6] Tomsky declared that the workers, and especially the non-party workers, were indifferent to the agitation in the party and would be glad to see the opposition silenced.[7]

[1] *VKP(B) v Rezolyutsiyakh* (1941), ii, 195 ; the vote was hailed with satisfaction in a leading article in *Pravda*, October 26, 1927, which noted that the opposition " was obliged to answer clearly : yes or no ", and " voted not only against the seven-hour working day, but against the whole manifesto of TsIK " (the comments in S. Schwarz, *Labor in the Soviet Union* (N.Y., 1952), p. 260, note 4, are based on a mis-reading of this article).
[2] *Torgovo-Promyshlennaya Gazeta*, November 4, 1927.
[3] *Sobranie Zakonov, 1927*, No. 65, art. 662.
[4] *Professional'nye Soyuzy SSSR 1926-1928: Otchet k VIII S"ezdu* (1928), p. 416.
[5] *Pyatnadtsatyi S"ezd VKP(B)*, i (1961), 259-262.
[6] The declaration was not published, and is known only from quotations in an article in *Partiya i Oppozitsiya Nakanune XV S"ezda*, ii (1928), 16c-179, and in *Pyatnadtsatyi S"ezd VKP(B)*, i (1961), 380 ; according to Tomsky's speech at the congress (*ibid.* i, 331), it had been received " yesterday ", i.e. December 5, 1927.   [7] *Ibid.* i, 335.

Otherwise he scarcely touched on the grievances of the workers ; and other trade union leaders were equally reticent. Only Uglanov, reverting to the three-shift system, spoke emphatically of " the concrete task of how to realise this most important measure ", and wanted to make the question a " corner-stone " of policy.[1] The resolution of the congress on the report of the central committee praised the policy of " rationalization of production and administration ", and noted, without special emphasis, that the party had " announced a gradual transition to the seven-hour working day ".[2] The overthrow of the opposition, and the exile of its principal members, enabled the party leaders to pursue their course untrammelled by public criticism or by fears of an appeal behind their backs to recalcitrant workers. The grain collections crisis of the winter of 1927–1928 put the whole programme of industrialization in jeopardy, and confronted the régime with its most acute internal crisis since 1921. The year 1928 was one of desperate pressure on all sides to maintain and increase production, whose full weight fell on the industrial workers. Its most direct and conspicuous instruments were the introduction of the three-shift system and the revision of working norms.

The first practical application of the seven-hour day came in the form of the introduction in January 1928 of three seven-hour shifts in the textile industry to replace the former two eight-hour shifts. This measure was obviously dictated by the urgent need to increase the supply of textile goods to the peasantry and thus stimulate the supply of grain to the market.[3] Circumstances made the transition to three-shift working in this context a highly practical proposition. In the textile industry machinery was often old ; managers argued that, since the machinery was obsolete and due

---

[1] *Pyatnadtsatyi S"ezd VKP(B)*, i (1961), 141.

[2] *KPSS v Rezolyutsiyakh* (1954), ii, 439.

[3] A party writer later explained that the seven-hour day was " inseparably bound up with the introduction of an additional shift and with the necessity for a significant concentration of work ", and that " the demands of the market " made the change urgent (*Bol'shevik*, No. 8, April 30, 1928, pp. 41-42) ; the announcement of an immediate transfer of 14 textile factories to the three-shift system cited the need to improve supply of textiles to the countryside (*Togorvo-Promyshlennaya Gazeta*, January 8, 1928).

for replacement, it paid meanwhile to wear it out to the maximum extent.[1] The change was confined in the first months of 1928 to the Moscow, Leningrad and Central Industrial regions,[2] and almost exclusively to the textile industry. In May 1928, 7·2 per cent of workers in cotton and linen mills, and 35·2 per cent of those in woollen mills, were on a three-shift basis.[3] By October 1, 1928, 28 factories employing 126,500 workers had completed the transition to the seven-hour day ; of these, 20 employing 113,000 workers were textile factories, and this accounted for 22·4 per cent of all textile workers.[4] In 20 textile factories the number of workers rose from 91,200 on January 1, 1928, to 113,900 six months later ; in some factories the increase was as high as 46 per cent.[5] By the end of 1928 the change-over had been approved for 255 factories employing 369,000 workers ; and it was optimistically estimated that by October 1, 1929, one-fifth of all industrial workers would be on a seven-hour day basis.[6]

The costs of the change-over to the three-shift system had also to be counted. A discussion of the project in the directors' club dwelt on many practical difficulties, including the strain on machines and equipment and shortage of raw materials. The consensus of opinion was that the reform would involve a temporary fall in productivity per hour, and could be introduced only " very slowly and with great exertions ".[7] An article in the party journal admitted that the introduction of the third shift had led to increased absenteeism and unpunctuality, resulting in a temporary fall in productivity of from 5 to 15 per cent : this was attributed to the low quality of the new labour recruited.[8] According to a report on the first five months of the operation of the scheme, continuous working resulted in an increased number of stoppages from mechanical breakdowns, and the increase in hours worked

[1] Predpriyatie, No. 11, 1927, p. 6.
[2] Gosudarstvennoe Regulirovanie Truda i Profsoyuzy (1929), p. 62.
[3] Ekonomicheskoe Obozrenie, No. 8, 1928, p. 43.
[4] Obzor Deyatel'nosti NKT SSSR za 1927–1928 gg. (1928), pp. 15-16.
[5] Planovoe Khozyaistvo, No. 10, 1928, p. 304.
[6] Obzor Deyatel'nosti NKT SSSR za 1927–1928 gg. (1928), p. 18 ; mines in the Stalino department were reported to have gone over to the six-hour day, and a plan was announced to introduce it in the Shakhty region (Pravda, September 29, October 18, 1928).
[7] Predpriyatie, No. 1, 1928, pp. 86-88.
[8] Bol'shevik, No. 8, April 30, 1928, pp. 43-44.

was offset by lower productivity. But these were treated as teeth-ing troubles ; and figures were quoted to show that productivity, though lower than before the change, was now rising again.[1] A resolution of the party central committee of May 20, 1928, on the preliminary results of the scheme attributed its shortcomings to lack of preparation, including shortage of raw materials, and the poor quality of the labour recruited (" well-to-do peasants etc.").[2] In particular, the three-hour interval during which work ceased was said to be inadequate for the proper cleaning and ventilation of the factories and maintenance of the machines.[3] Uglanov, at a meeting of the Moscow party committee on June 30, 1928, criti-cized excessive haste to apply the system in factories not suited to it.[4]

The most frequent charge, however, against the three-shift system was that a reform originally announced as a plan to ease the worker's lot by reducing his working time had been transformed into a device to place fresh burdens on him. The one point in the scheme to meet with open objections from the textile workers' union was the proposal that workers should work not in continuous seven-hour shifts, but in two half-shifts of three-and-a-half hours each every 24 hours. This was resisted by the union as tending to disrupt the lives of the workers ; and Narkomtrud decided against it.[5] It seems, however, to have been widely used.[6] The three-shift system implied a complete abandonment of the prohibition in the labour code of the RSFSR on night-work for women (a majority of the textile operatives were women) ; but this had long been a dead letter.[7] It was replaced in January 1928 by a decree prohibiting night-work for women after five months of pregnancy and for nursing mothers for seven months after the birth of a

[1] Ekonomicheskoe Obozrenie, No. 8, 1928, pp. 51-54.
[2] Izvestiya Tsentral'nogo Komiteta VKP(B), No. 16-17 (237-238), May 25, 1928, pp. 9-10.
[3] Ekonomicheskoe Obozrenie, No. 8, 1928, p. 43. Productivity on the night-shift was 4·1 per cent below that on the day-shifts ; this was partly due to the fact that the night shift was the third continuous shift, and the atmosphere was hot and damp (ibid. No. 6, 1929, p. 110).   [4] Pravda, July 5, 1928.
[5] Trud, January 12, 1928 ; it was also opposed by some managers (Pred-priyatie, No. 1, 1928, p. 86).
[6] Trud, October 1, 1928, where the split shift was said to be in force " almost everywhere ".
[7] See Socialism in One Country, 1924–1926, Vol. 1, pp. 361-369.

child.[1] Even this prohibition was reported to have encountered resistance from the women themselves, who objected to transfer to unfamiliar shifts with possible diminution of wages ; and it was not generally applied.[2] Shmidt in a report to the trade union central council of October 19, 1928, declared that, while the aim of the seven-hour day was to increase production, " our task is to keep the resulting burden from falling exclusively on the shoulders of the workers ". He admitted an increased sickness and accident rate among workers employed on these shifts.[3] Later still, a party report deplored " direct opposition " to the scheme from " backward groups of workers ", especially in the textile industry.[4]

The party central committee at its session of November 1928 devoted a special resolution to the seven-hour day, making it clear that this was the thorniest labour problem of the moment. It recapitulated the defects of the system and the measures necessary to remedy them. While accepting by implication the legality of night work for women, it called for the strict application of legislative provisions " on the exemption of pregnant and nursing women from work in the night shift in enterprises transferred, or in course of being transferred, to the seven-hour day ". But the resolution also dealt with the projected extension of the system. Its application to industry and transport was to be increased by " about 20 per cent " in 1928–1929, and by " not less than 20 per cent " in the following year. A list of enterprises ripe for transition to the seven-hour day, drawn up by the commission in charge of the question, was approved in principle ; but attention was drawn to the need to extend the system to the most important productive enterprises, notably in heavy industry.[5] A certain

---

[1] Trud, January 7, 1928 ; the seven-month limit was reduced a year later to six months (Sobranie Zakonov, 1929, No. 4, art. 30 ; No. 16, art. 133). A woman delegate at the eighth trade union congress in December 1928 complained that the trade unions did nothing to enforce the prohibition on night work for pregnant and nursing women (Vos'moi S"ezd Professional'nykh Soyuzov SSSR (1929), pp. 158).

[2] Obzor Deyatel'nosti NKT za 1927–1928 gg. (1928), pp. 161-162.

[3] Trud, October 31, 1928 ; for the accident rate see p. 612 below.

[4] Izvestiya Tsentral'nogo Komiteta VKP(B), No. 8-9 (267-268), March 31, 1929, p. 2 ; see M. Fainsod, Smolensk under Soviet Rule (1958), p. 51, for a report of resistance by workers in a local textile factory.

[5] VKP(B) v Rezolyutsiyakh (1941), ii, 303–305 ; this resolution was omitted from later editions. The commission referred to was the one originally set up on November 11, 1927 (see p. 499 above), which was instructed in January 1928

ambivalence marked the attitude of the eighth trade union congress in the following month. Tomsky in his formal introductory speech hailed the seven-hour day as a harbinger of " further successes in the rationalization of labour ",[1] but avoided the subject in his main report. Tolstopyatov, the deputy commissar who took Shmidt's place as spokesman of Narkomtrud, admitted that, in textile factories which had gone over to the seven-hour day and three shifts, while the number of workers employed had increased by 24·9 per cent, production had increased only by 24·5 per cent, and the average daily wage had fallen to 92·1 per cent of its former level ; meanwhile accidents had increased by 35·7 per cent. These grim results were attributed to the fact that the transition was inadequately prepared, and took place " without participation of the working masses " : Narkomtrud would work to remedy defects.[2] The congress did not fail to greet the seven-hour day as " an immense achievement of the working class ", and to approve the decision to convert all industry and transport to it within five years, but called for further attention to the material needs of the workers.[3] A decree of the TsIK of the USSR of January 2, 1929, provided for the transition of all productive enterprises to the seven-hour day within the period of the five-year plan.[4]

The other conspicuous instrument of pressure on the workers at this time was to raise " norms " of output (or to cut " the rate for the job ") ; norms were a key factor in fixing piece-rates, and therefore in determining the relation of productivity to earnings. The resolution of the party central committee of August 19, 1924, which for the first time cautiously pronounced that " the rise in

---

to examine the extension of the system to other industries (*Sobranie Zakonov, 1928*, No. 8, art. 72) ; for a somewhat confused account of its work, and of controversy between Vesenkha and the trade union central council, see *Professional'nye Soyuzy SSSR : Otchet k VIII S"ezdu* (1928), pp. 419-421.

[1] *Vos'moi S"ezd Professional'nykh Soyuzov SSSR* (1929), p. 3.

[2] *Ibid.* pp. 332-333.   [3] *Ibid.* pp. 524-525, 557.

[4] *Sobranie Zakonov, 1929*, No. 4, art. 30 ; the plan as approved in April 1929 contained detailed figures for the proposed transition in Group A and B industries (*Pyatiletnii Plan Narodno-Khozyaistvennogo Stroitel'stva SSSR* (1929), ii, ii, 182). The Ford factories in Detroit, which worked round the clock six days a week, though the individual worker worked only for five days, were quoted at this time as an instructive example of the intensive use of fixed capital (*Planovoe Khozyaistvo*, No. 2, 1929, p. 187).

the productivity of labour must overtake the rise in wages ", and removed the limitation on piece-work,[1] had also demanded " the periodical revision of norms of output ". But little — or not enough — appears to have been achieved in this direction. In April 1926 at a conference on state industry, Kraval alleged that norms had in many cases not been re-examined for 18 months, and that actual output was now often double the norm ; and he reverted to the theme on the occasion of the negotiation of new collective contracts in August 1926.[2] After the wages increase of August–September 1926 Vesenkha reiterated once more that " the new wages policy obliges the trusts to raise the question of re-examining output norms " in order to bring the " wages-productivity scissors " into a normal relation ;[3] and the fifteenth party conference of October 1926 spoke of a necessary revision of norms of production.[4] These demands met, however, with unusually obstinate resistance from the workers and the trade unions ; and the authorities exhibited noteworthy caution. The decree of the party central committee on rationalization of March 24, 1927, called for " special attention " to the fixing of norms in new enterprises ; in other enterprises where " organizational and technical improvements in production have been, or are being, carried out ", norms should be revised to correspond to these improvements, but in such a way as " not to reduce the daily wage of the worker ".[5] Kuibyshev told the plenum of Vesenkha in August 1927 that, in order to increase productivity in relation to wages, norms must be increased and surplus workers discharged.[6] It was not till the autumn of 1927 that, in face of opposition attack, the party insisted on a closing of the ranks. Kraval once more put the case for Vesenkha with his usual pertinacity ;[7] and the trade union central council, evidently under pressure, agreed to a general

[1] See *Socialism in One Country, 1924–1926*, Vol. 1, p. 387.
[2] *Torgovo-Promyshlennaya Gazeta*, August 23, 26, 1926 ; according to the journal of the Red directors, norms in the Putilov works had not been changed between March 1924 and April 1926 (*Predpriyatie*, No. 4, 1926, pp. 85-86). *Trud*, August 22, 1926, described a struggle by the trusts to increase norms in Leningrad factories in the new collective contracts.
[3] *Torgovo-Promyshlennaya Gazeta*, November 7, 1926.
[4] For this resolution see pp. 490-491 above.
[5] For this decree see pp. 341-342 above.
[6] *Torgovo-Promyshlennaya Gazeta*, August 17, 1927.
[7] *Ibid.* October 15, 1927.

re-examination of norms.[1] A final attempt to compose the quarrel
was made in the joint Kuibyshev–Tomsky directive of October
1927.[2] This firmly laid down that norms were to be revised
where no revision had taken place for a long time, or where they
had become " erroneous and out-of-date ", or where " rationalization and improvements in organization and technique have raised
the productivity of labour ". But norms remained a sore and
vulnerable point. A month later, at the fifteenth party congress,
Kuibyshev related with indignation that " one of our provincial
committees recently at a conference with managers and trade
unionists gave a directive on no account to revise the norms of
payment for work, in view of the situation created by the struggle
with the opposition ".[3] The control of norms was more and more
clearly seen as an essential instrument of the planned control of
wages.

Here, as elsewhere, the elimination of the opposition paved the
way for more vigorous policies and lessened the danger of unwelcome publicity. Resistance in trade union quarters continued.
In December 1927 the trade union central council issued a circular
censuring the refusal of some local trade union organs to re-
examine out-of-date norms.[4] But the trade union newspaper
complained that " in a vast majority of cases the economic organs
demand a wholesale revision of norms in all enterprises, leading to
a reduction of wages " ; [5] and Lepse, at the congress of the metal
workers' union in February 1928, protested that norms should be
revised only where processes of production had been technically
improved, and not as a means of forcing down wages.[6] At a
conference of labour economics departments in June 1928, Kuibyshev admitted that, during the economic year 1927–1928, norms
had improved (from the point of view of the industrialists) in
the metal industry, and were generally satisfactory in the textile
industry. The conference passed a resolution demanding a revision of norms in light industry, and proposing that in future

[1] *Torgovo-Promyshlennaya Gazeta*, October 22, 1927.
[2] For this see p. 494 above.
[3] *Pyatnadtsatyi S'ezd VKP(B)*, ii (1962), 961.
[4] *Torgovo-Promyshlennaya Gazeta*, June 30, 1928, which also cited recent
instances of trade union resistance to revision of norms ; the circular has not
been traced.   [5] *Trud*, January 6, 1928.
[6] *Torgovo-Promyshlennaya Gazeta*, February 17, 1928.

norms should be subject to revision, not only once a year on the occasion of the renewal of the collective agreements, but at any time during the year.[1]

The argument about the relation of productivity to wages was reopened in the autumn of 1928 by the preparation of the Gosplan control figures for 1928–1929 and of the first five-year plan. The results for the year 1927–1928 had been encouraging. For the first time since 1924–1925 the rise in productivity had clearly outstripped the rise in wages. Productivity in census industry had risen by 12 per cent, the increase being greater in Group A than in Group B industries ; [2] and nominal wages had increased only by 10 per cent.[3] The compilers of the control figures for 1928–1929 claimed that, except in coal-mining, productivity had everywhere risen faster than real wages in 1927–1928. In the metal industries productivity had risen by 14 per cent and real wages by 7 per cent ; in the more efficient electrical industries productivity had risen by 25 per cent and real wages by 7 per cent ; in the cotton textile industry productivity had risen by 12 per cent and real wages by 5 per cent ; in the food industry productivity had risen by 22 per cent and real wages had remained stationary.[4] Vesenkha, in the first draft of its control figures for 1928–1929, proposed that productivity in Group A industries should rise by 14·7 per cent and in Group B industries by 11·6 per cent ; wages were to rise by 6 per cent in the former category and by 4·8 per cent in the latter.[5] Gosplan, more generous in the matter of wages, performed an act of faith in its estimate of productivity. Recording a rise of 13 per cent in productivity in 1927–1928, and repeating that the primary condition of an increase of productivity was " the organizational-technical improvement of

---

[1] *Ibid.* June 17, 27, 1928.

[2] See Table No. 24, p. 957 below.

[3] See Table No. 25, p. 958 below ; the report of the trade union central council to the trade union congress of December 1928 claimed an increase of 14 per cent in productivity in 1927–1928, while real wages had been stationary or had fallen (*Professional'nye Soyuzy SSSR, 1926–1928: Otchet k VIII S"ezdu* (1928), pp. 316–317).

[4] *Kontrol'nye Tsifry Narodnogo Khozyaistva SSSR na 1928–1929 god* (1929), p. 153.

[5] *Torgovo-Promyshlennaya Gazeta*, June 10, 1928.

production, not a growth in the intensity of labour ", it projected
an increase of productivity in census industry for the forthcoming
year of 17·5 per cent.[1] The trade union central council pleaded in
vain to reduce the figure to 16 per cent.[2]

In the summer of 1928 the unremitting drive for productivity
led to increased tension in labour relations, though it is difficult to
say how far this was due to a deterioration in the discipline of the
workers and how far to attempts by managers, in the pursuit of
ever more production, to impose sterner measures of control. In
May 1928 a " weakening of labour discipline " was reported in the
coal-mining industry, and gradually spread to other branches of
production.[3] The main trouble was in heavy industry. Acute
anxiety about the situation in coal-mining was expressed in the
official economic newspaper :

> The productivity of labour has recently decreased somewhat,
> the output of coal is falling. Costs are rising. Equipment is
> shockingly bad. In the pits there is slackness, excess of labour
> power, and extensive absenteeism.[4]

Articles in the industrial newspaper drew attention to the decline
in output in Yugostal between February and July 1928, which it
attributed to the decline in labour discipline. The number of
stoppages in April–June 1928 exceeded that for the same quarter
in the previous year, and the seasonal drop in production in the
summer months had been greater.[5] An article in an official journal
enumerated current forms of indiscipline : (1) drunkenness at

---

[1] *Kontrol'nye Tsifry Narodnogo Khozyaistva SSSR na 1928–1929 god* (1929),
pp. 151-155 ; for a table showing rates of increase industry by industry see *ibid.*
p. 468.

[2] *Torgovo-Promyshlennaya Gazeta*, October 16, 1928.

[3] *Ekonomicheskoe Obozrenie*, No. 3, 1929, p. 10 ; an earlier article had
referred to " the new wave of a weakening of labour discipline " in the summer
of 1928 (*ibid.* No. 11, 1928, pp. 14-15 ; this journal reflected Vesenkha views).
A report of the trade union central council of December 1928 admitted that
" in the summer of 1928 we had in some places a weakening of labour discipline,
which to a certain extent slowed down the growth of the productivity of labour "
(*Professional'nye Soyuzy SSSR, 1926–1928: Otchet k VIII S"ezdu* (1928), pp.
316-317).

[4] *Ekonomicheskaya Zhizn'*, August 12, 1928 ; for a vivid description of the
hard conditions of work in the Donbass mines see H. R. Knickerbocker, *The
Soviet Five-Year Plan* (1931), pp. 168-172.

[5] *Torgovo-Promyshlennaya Gazeta*, September 7, 12, 1928.

work, (2) absenteeism, (3) hooliganism, (4) unpunctuality, (5) sleeping at work, (6) abuse or beating up of specialists and administrators, (7) refusal to work on religious holidays, (8) deliberate reduction of productivity, (9) theft. Among the reasons assigned for the decline in discipline were " the cultural and technical backwardness " and " low cultural level " of the workers, especially of former peasants recruited into industry (" the general cultural growth of the working class does not keep up with the growth of large-scale industry ") ; " the resistance of capitalist elements and the sharpening of the class struggle in the country " ; and bad relations between workers and technical personnel bred by the Shakhty affair.[1] A later report referred to " the high percentage of absenteeism without due cause, lateness in beginning work, leaving work before time, refusal of workers to obey legiti mate orders of the administrative and technical staff " as " almost a mass phenomenon ".[2] The campaign against non-party specialists following the Shakhty trial had helped to undermine the authority of managers. The journal of the Red directors complained that " Soviet principles of leadership of enterprises and of production are being replaced by principles of election and, in practice, of responsibility to voters ".[3] The resolution of the party central committee of April 1928 on the Shakhty affair instructed Vesenkha to apply the statute on trusts of June 29, 1927, in such a way as " to ensure to the managements of enterprises real leadership and administrative powers over the enterprise ".[4]

The state of factory discipline was extensively ventilated at the fourth Vesenkha plenum of November 1928. The theses presented by Kuibyshev declared that cost reduction and labour productivity

---

[1] *Ekonomicheskoe Obozrenie*, No. 3, 1929, pp. 5-6 ; for the Shakhty affair see pp. 584-587 below.

[2] *Ekonomicheskoe Obozrenie*, No. 10, 1929, p. vi.

[3] *Predpriyatie*, No. 12, 1928, p. 12 ; for the controversy over " one-man management " see *The Bolshevik Revolution, 1917–1923*, Vol. 2, pp. 187-191.

[4] *KPSS v Rezolyutsiyakh* (1954), ii, 507 ; for this resolution see p. 586 below. For the statute on trusts see p. 372 above. The question continued to give trouble ; on September 5, 1929, the party central committee issued a decree " On Measures to Regulate the Management of Production and to Establish One-Man Command ", which required party and trade union organs to support " measures introduced by the director of an enterprise to strengthen discipline in production " (*Direktivy KPSS i Sovetskogo Pravitel'stva po Khozyaistvennym Voprosam*, ii (1957), 102-106).

plans would be fulfilled " only if the party and trade union organizations take all necessary measures to ensure that the decline in
labour discipline and growth of absenteeism observed last year do
not recur in 1928–1929 ".[1] Speaker after speaker complained of
the indiscipline of the workers and of the complacent attitude of
the trade unions. Birman, the president of Yugostal, put the
blame on managers and engineers as well as on workers. The one
openly dissentient voice was that of L. I. Ginzburg, the representative of the trade union central council, who gave the trade unions
credit for a rise in productivity more rapid than the rise in wages,
and attributed shortcomings to worn-out equipment and shortages
of raw material. He claimed that breaches of discipline were local
occurrences and that, taking industry as a whole, absenteeism had
fallen. This apologia was not well received. Kuibyshev devoted
his reply to the debate to a refutation of Ginzburg's case and a
criticism of the trade union attitude.[2] While relations between
workers and managers indubitably deteriorated during 1928, all
the evidence points to a steady rise in productivity in this period ; [3]
and Ginzburg's claim that absenteeism actually declined seems to
have been substantiated. According to official figures, days lost
in industry through absenteeism without due cause fell from 7·86
per worker in 1926 to 6·94 in 1927, 5·72 in 1928, and 4·09 in 1929.[4]
Other statistics recorded the average number of days worked in
industry — 261·36 in 1926, 260·85 in 1927, 263·02 in 1928, and
264·19 in 1929, with sharp falls in the succeeding years.[5] Whatever the explanation of the growing tension in labour relations, it
was clear that, if the drive for rapid industrialization was to suc-

[1] Torgovo-Promyshlennaya Gazeta, November 27, 1928.
[2] The debate was reported ibid. November 28, 29, 30, 1928 ; for L. Ginzburg see p. 525 below.
[3] See p. 507 above, and Table No. 24, p. 957 below.
[4] Sotsialisticheskoe Stroitel'stvo SSSR (1934), p. 339 ; at the eighth trade
union congress in December 1928, Ginzburg claimed that the average number
of days per year worked by the worker had increased by two in 1927–1928, and
that absenteeism had diminished (Vos'moi S"ezd Professional'nykh Soyuzov
SSSR (1929), p. 411). Statistics quoted in Statisticheskoe Obozrenie, No. 12,
1929, p. 30, showed that the figure of absenteeism for 1928–1929 was only 74·4
per cent of the figure for 1927–1928.
[5] Trud v SSSR (1936), p. 96 ; according to Ekonomicheskoe Obozrenie, No.
3, 1929, p. 115, the average number of days worked in Group A industries fell
from 261·6 in 1926–1927 to 255·2 in 1927–1928, and in Group B industries
rose from 261·3 to 263·5.

ceed, no means could be neglected of increasing the productivity of the worker.

Ever since 1925 the destiny of the worker had rested on an uneasy compromise between Vesenkha and the managers, eager to increase the efficiency of industry and to cut down costs, and the trade unions, solicitous for the immediate material interests and welfare of the workers ; between these organs there had always been the " certain amount of pulling and hauling " to which Dzerzhinsky had once complacently referred.[1] But, as the drive for industrialization became more intense, the trade unions fought a losing battle ; the needs of industry were the paramount consideration. In this battle Tomsky had been content to conduct an orderly retreat, saving what he could by the way. He had never been one of the irreconcilables, and had vigorously repelled the criticisms of the opposition. When, however, the eighth trade union congress met on December 10, 1928, the split had just occurred in the Politburo which ranged Bukharin, Rykov and Tomsky together as leaders of a Right opposition anxious to slow down the pace of industrialization ; and, if Bukharin and Rykov were chiefly concerned to protest against the excessive pressure imposed on the peasant, Tomsky in the same context was the natural champion and protector of the industrial worker. Nothing in his report to the congress openly challenged official policy. It contained nevertheless some significant remarks. Tomsky criticized the arrogance of the planners. " Planning is often understood to mean : speak according to the plan, and outside the plan not a word." He declared firmly that " we have never thought it a disgrace, but on the contrary a sacred duty, to strive for a greater and greater rise in the productivity of labour and for greater labour discipline ", but went on to remark that " we have moved away from the period of war communism when — it may as well be confessed — some unions came near to setting up houses of detention ".[2] Kozelev, president of the metal workers' union, described " methods of compulsion in regard to the working masses " as the policy of " Trotsky and the Trotskyites " ; a delegate from

[1] See *Socialism in One Country, 1924-1926*, Vol. 1, p. 417.
[2] *Vos'moi S"ezd Professional'nykh Soyuzov SSSR* (1929), pp. 42-44.

Leningrad protested against the attempts of managers to rationalize production " by pressure on the workers ", and declared " nothing further can be squeezed out of the workers ".[1] These isolated voices, however, did not affect the conclusions of the congress. The resolution on wages was prefaced by a strong call for " maximum discipline and restraint " and for " ever new heroic exertions ". The principle that the rise in productivity must outstrip the rise in wages was once more unequivocally proclaimed :

> The turning-point is the year 1927–1928, when the rise in productivity for the first time overtakes the rise in wages — a fact which ensured a reduction of costs and corresponding capital accumulations for industry. Nevertheless, even in this past year the planned tasks were not fulfilled. The rate of increase in productivity must be continued and expanded in the future.[2]

Kuibyshev put before the congress a lengthy analysis of the five-year plan, based on the theme of progressively rising productivity and wages, and concluded :

> The working class, if it wishes to industrialize the country, if it wishes to catch up with and overtake the capitalist world, will carry out the tasks which history has set before it.[3]

The resolution on Kuibyshev's report urged all trade unions " to give all manner of support to the economic organs in measures directed to raise the productivity of labour ", while proclaiming that this could be attained only on the condition of an improvement in the material situation of the worker.[4] Whatever ambiguities lurked in these formal pronouncements, the congress marked an unqualified acceptance of the paramount demands of industrialization. To these every minor desideratum must be sacrificed. It was within the limits imposed by this overriding aim that the trade unions henceforth pursued their traditional policies. The congress ended with the silent elimination of Tomsky from his long-standing rôle as leader of the Soviet trade union movement.[5]

The next few months were marked by mounting pressure on the labour front. The continuous improvement in productivity over the past two years [6] served only as a spur to fresh efforts. The first five-year plan, which was receiving its finishing touches at this

---

[1] *Vos'moi S"ezd Professional'nykh Soyuzov SSSR* (1929), pp. 96, 419.
[2] *Ibid.* pp. 519, 522.   [3] *Ibid.* p. 401.   [4] *Ibid.* p. 554.
[5] See pp. 558–560 below.   [6] See Table No. 24, p. 957 below.

time, envisaged a rise in the productivity of labour in industry during the five-year period of 85 per cent (" basic variant ") or 110 per cent (" optimum variant "). The framers of the plan professed themselves unable to measure the relative importance of the two major contributory factors in this improvement : the increased application of mechanical power, and " the increased intensity of effort of the worker himself ".[1] But no doubt was left of the importance of the second factor. Moral appeals to the worker to improve discipline and raise productivity had been familiar for the past two years. The resolution of the party central committee of March 24, 1927, on rationalization [2] called for " a conscious attitude on the part of the workers to rationalization and their active participation in carrying it out ". This note was constantly sounded throughout 1927. Kuibyshev at the fourth Union Congress of Soviets in April 1927 explained that the Soviet worker felt himself " the master of his industry ", and did not react to it as " something alien to himself which was necessary to him only from the point of view of receiving his wages ".[3] From the summer of 1927 onwards the element of competition was introduced into the campaign. Since September 1926 factory competitions for " the best young worker " had been popular and had been encouraged by the Komsomol.[4] On September 1, 1927, the Vesenkha newspaper announced a competition for the best enterprise in the country with a jury presided over by Kuibyshev ; the criteria of excellence were to be success in reducing costs of production, improvement in quality of products, and improvement in the conditions and safety of labour.[5] This led to numerous local competitions, and the results of the Union competition were finally announced in April 1928.[6] Kuibyshev struck a new note when he pleaded for " a certain element of emulation between directors of enterprises, separate trusts, etc." [7] The tenth anniversary of the revolution in the autumn of 1927 saw a revival,

---

[1] *Pyatiletnii Plan Narodno-Khozyaistvennogo Stroitel'stva SSSR* (1929), i, 94.
[2] See pp. 341-342 above.
[3] *SSSR : 4 S"ezd Sovetov* (1927), pp. 263-264.
[4] For particulars of these competitions and references to the Komsomol press see L. Rogachevskaya, *Iz Istorii Rabochego Klassa SSSR* (1959), pp. 152-155.   [5] *Torgovo-Promyshlennaya Gazeta*, September 1, 1927.
[6] L. Rogachevskaya, *Iz Istorii Rabochego Klassa SSSR* (1959), pp. 148-150 ; *Torgovo-Promyshlennaya Gazeta*, April 28, 29, 1928.
[7] *Torgovo-Promyshlennaya Gazeta*, September 27, 1927.

under Komsomol inspiration, of the "communist Saturdays" instituted with the blessing of Lenin during the civil war, when workers worked for a certain number of extra hours without pay ; "Saturdays" were worked in Moscow, in Leningrad, in Kiev and in the Donbass mines.[1] "Shock brigades" of workers committed to the performance of exceptional tasks, and "challenges" by one factory or group of workers to another to increase production, were popular innovations at this time.[2] The artificial element in these campaigns, and the pressure put on recalcitrant or indifferent workers to participate in them, were plain enough. But without some ground-work of genuine enthusiasm they could hardly have been launched at all.

The problem of labour discipline, and growing friction between workers and managers, in the summer of 1928 [3] called not only for measures of repression, but for further attention to incentives. These preoccupations evidently inspired a decree of STO of June 14, 1928, providing that, when a reduction of estimated costs had been achieved in a state industrial enterprise, from 25 to 50 per cent of the saving should be credited to a fund to be used by the director for further rationalization of production and for improvement in the living and working conditions of the workers.[4] Intangible incentives were not neglected. A year earlier, a decree of July 27, 1927, had instituted the title of "Hero of Labour" to be conferred on persons who had shown particular merit in any form of public service ; gainful employment for 35 years was named as one of the qualifications for eligibility. Heroes of labour enjoyed pensions, certain tax exemptions and priority in housing.[5] In

[1] L. Rogachevskaya, *Iz Istorii Rabochego Klassa SSSR* (1959), pp. 165-168, and the sources there quoted ; the party central committee passed a resolution supporting the call of the Komsomol for a "communist Saturday" in commemoration of the tenth anniversary of the revolution (*Izvestiya Tsentral'nogo Komiteta VKP(B)*, No. 37-38 (210-211), October 8, 1927, p. 9). The Moscow textile factories worked "communist Saturdays" (probably two or three hours' unpaid overtime) on January 14, 21 and 28, 1928 (G. Konyukhov, *KPSS v Bor'be s Khlebnymi Zatrudneniyami* (1960), pp. 94-96). For the communist Saturdays of 1919 see *The Bolshevik Revolution, 1917–1923*, Vol. 2, p. 208.

[2] A later commentator using archival material traced shock brigades back to 1926, and connected competition between factories with the factory production conferences (*Voprosy Istorii*, No. 6, 1953, p. 38) ; for the production conferences see pp. 568-573 below.   [3] See pp. 508–509 above.

[4] *Sobranie Zakonov, 1928*, No. 42, art. 384 ; No. 43, art. 387. For this fund see also pp. 609-610 below.   [5] *Sobranie Zakonov, 1927*, No. 45, art. 456.

September 1928 the Order of the Red Banner of Labour was created. It followed closely the institution of Heroes of Labour of the previous year, except that it could be awarded not only to individuals but to enterprises, institutions and collectives of workers.[1]

Early in 1929 these diverse incentives to production were organized round the slogan of " socialist emulation ", which appears to have been first used in the campaign for the re-elections to the Soviets.[2] On January 20, 1929, *Pravda* printed an article written by Lenin early in January 1918, but laid aside under the impact of the Brest–Litovsk crisis, and hitherto unpublished, entitled *How to Organize Emulation.* It contrasted " emulation " (sorevnovanie) with capitalist " competition ", the effect of which was to exploit the workers in the interests of their employers, and hailed emulation as the correct way of appealing to the workers for increased production in the building of socialism.[3] This publication touched off an extensive campaign. Lenin's article was printed as a pamphlet which was said to have sold 3,500,000 copies in six weeks.[4] The Komsomol newspaper described " the shock brigades, the challenges to production, the competitions sponsored by the Komsomol " as " the beginning of broad socialist emulation ", and appealed to Komsomol members to apply it on a Union-wide scale.[5] A resolution of the party central committee in March 1929 deplored the low productivity of labour in textile factories and called for the introduction of " emulation " there.[6] Factories and mines took up the slogan and organized competitions.[7] In

[1] *Sobranie Zakonov, 1928*, No. 59, arts. 523, 524.
[2] This campaign will be discussed in a subsequent volume.
[3] Lenin, *Sochineniya*, xxii, 158-167.
[4] *Economic Review of the Soviet Union* (Washington), iv, No. 18, September 15, 1929, p. 313.
[5] *Komsomol'skaya Pravda*, January 26, 1929 ; for resolutions of the Ukrainian party on the subject from March to May 1929 see *Istoricheskie Zapiski*, xliii (1953), 203-204. A number of collections of documents relating to emulation and shock brigades in Moscow, Leningrad, the Ukraine and elsewhere are listed in *Voprosy Istorii*, No. 2, 1965, p. 126.
[6] *Izvestiya Tsentral'nogo Komiteta VKP(B)*, No. 10 (269), April 12, 1929, pp. 13-15.
[7] Reports on these activities to the Komsomol central committee and to the trade union central council are printed from the archives in *Politicheskii i Trudovoi Pod"em Rabochego Klassa SSSR* (1956), pp. 214-217, 236-239 ; the same volume contains many detailed reports from factories. For examples of emulation within or between factories see *Ekonomicheskoe Obozrenie*, No. 5, 1929, pp. 3-4 ; increases of 20 per cent or more in productivity were claimed.

April 1929 *Pravda* reported that, thanks to " socialist emulation ", absenteeism had entirely ceased in a factory formerly notorious for drunkenness among the workers ; and *Trud* declared that the month of March had been a turning-point in the campaign for better labour discipline.[1] A contemporary foreign observer commented aptly on the psychology that lay behind these manifestations :

> The lack of discipline which is so noticeable in Russian industry is not due . . . to any lack of rules and regulations, or to their non-enforcement ; it is an inner self-discipline that is wanting. The average Russian worker's background is agricultural. His habits of work, his attitude of mind have been shaped on the farm and inherited from generations of peasants. Thus he is accustomed to working hard in the summer when the crops must be cared for and to hibernating in the winter. He has no predisposition for regularity of effort, for the sustained cooperative labour which is a part of an industrial system. Transplanted to a factory community, he must be stimulated by mass-meetings, by bands and speeches, and by every device of propaganda. . . . Following such a mass-meeting plant production usually shows a great increase. But then inevitably comes the reaction.[2]

The popularity of these campaigns did not, of course, imply any relaxation in the conventional pressures of factory discipline. A resolution of the party central committee of January 17, 1929, painted a gloomy picture of conditions in the Donbass mines, alleging " a decline of labour discipline both among the workers

[1] *Pravda*, April 17, 1929 ; *Trud*, April 24, 1929 ; both were quoted at the sixteenth party conference (*Shestnadtsataya Konferentsiya VKP(B)* (1962), p. 146). On the other hand a party report from the Western region of the RSFSR recorded strong resistance to " socialist emulation ", which was attacked as " bondage for the workers " and a device to increase norms (M. Fainsod, *Smolensk under Soviet Rule* (1958), pp. 312-313). Stalin, in his famous article of November 1, 1929, boasted that " in the past year . . . we were able to achieve *a decisive break-through* in the sphere of the productivity of labour " (Stalin, *Sochineniya*, xii, 119).

[2] Quoted from *Harper's Monthly Magazine*, December 1931, in J. Freeman, *The Soviet Worker* (1932), p. 95 ; a similar diagnosis was made by another foreign observer : " The Russian easily gets bored and hankers after novelty ; he is capable of a burst of intense enthusiasm and energy, usually succeeded by a period of reaction and apathy, for which the climate, with its short urgent summer and long torpid winter, no doubt is partly responsible." (L. Hubbard, *The Economics of Soviet Agriculture* (1939), p. 7.)

and among the technical and lower supervisory personnel " and
" an insufficient growth in the productivity of labour ".[1]   The
trade union newspaper, now thoroughly brought into line, wrote
in favour of the revision of norms.[2]   An editorial in *Pravda* of
January 31, 1929, called for campaigns led by older workers for
improved discipline in the factories. On February 21, 1929, an
appeal for measures to strengthen labour discipline went out from
the party central committee to all party organizations.[3]   This was
followed up by an appeal from the presidium of the trade union
central council " to all men and women workers ".[4]   Kraval protested in an indignant article against inadequate sanctions for
breaches of discipline :

> The manager sacks a man, the RKK reinstates him ; if the
> RKK also sacks him, the labour inspector or the court reinstates
> him ; if all the authorities accept the sacking as correct, the
> labour exchange sends back the trouble-maker to the same job,
> to the same enterprise.[5]

A stern decree of Sovnarkom of March 6, 1929, purported to
detect a relaxation of labour discipline and an increase in absenteeism and unpunctuality in factories — phenomena attributed to the
influx of new workers and to slackness on the part both of trade
unions and of administrations. Administrations were instructed
to inflict on defaulters the full penalties laid down in the regulations, and labour exchanges to give priority to workers who had
not been dismissed for breaches of discipline.[6]

The sixteenth party conference of April 1929, the main business of which was to register party approval of the five-year plan,
gave full endorsement both to the demand for stricter labour discipline and to the socialist emulation campaign. Kuibyshev, who,

[1] *Direktivy KPSS i Sovetskogo Pravitel'stva po Khozyaistvennym Voprosam*,
ii (1957), 7.   [2] *Trud*, January 22, 1929.
[3] *Direktivy KPSS i Sovetskogo Pravitel'stva po Khozyaistvennym Voprosam*,
ii (1957), 12-17 ;   the copy in the Smolensk party archives was apparently
marked " Not for publication " (M. Fainsod, *Smolensk under Soviet Rule*
(1958), p. 309).
[4] *Trud*, March 3, 1929.
[5] *Ekonomicheskaya Zhizn'*, March 3, 1929 ; for the RKKs see p. 564 below.
[6] *Sobranie Zakonov, 1929*, No. 19, art. 167 ; Rykov at the sixteenth party
conference in April 1929 referred to " the recent law of the government on the
strengthening of labour discipline " (*Shestnadtsataya Konferentsiya VKP(B)*
(1962), p. 12).

of the three *rapporteurs* on the plan,[1] most distinctly represented the party line, made a firm pronouncement on labour discipline. In order to meet the needs of an expanding industry it was necessary, and would be still more necessary in the future, to draw on " a relatively large number of workers from the countryside ". But it was precisely " these elements, these strata of the working class " who were as a rule " the least disciplined, the least amenable to labour discipline ". Kuibyshev quoted the famous article of 1918, *Current Tasks of the Soviet Power*, in which Lenin had called for an increase in the intensity of labour, and spoken of the need to match revolutionary enthusiasm " with *iron* discipline in work time ", and of " the *unquestioning obedience* of the masses to the single will of the director of the working process ".[2] He also quoted — it was now an obligatory embellishment of major party speeches — the article of 1918 on socialist emulation, and, at the conclusion of the debates, proposed, without further discussion, to issue an appeal " To All Workers and Toiling Peasants of the Soviet Union ".[3] It proclaimed in militant language the determination to proceed with " the rapid industrialization of the country and the socialist reconstruction of agriculture ". It invoked further quotations from Lenin, together with a resolution of the ninth party congress in 1920, which had described emulation as " the mightiest force to raise the productivity of labour ". The last paragraphs of the appeal were built round the theme of " emulation ". The trade unions and economic organs were to introduce " a system of *encouraging* those who engaged in emulation " ; " *emulation* and the *five-year plan* " were described as " inseparably bound up with one another ".[4] The resolution of the conference on the five-year plan endorsed the demand for an increase of 110 per cent in productivity during the period of the plan.[5]

A few days after the end of the conference the party central committee adopted a resolution instructing party workers to

[1] For this debate see pp. 892-894 below.
[2] *Shestnadtsataya Konferentsiya VKP(B)* (1962), pp. 72-73 ; for another quotation from the same article, referring to piece-rates, Taylorism, and the relation of wages to output, see *The Bolshevik Revolution, 1917–1923*, Vol. 2, p. 111. [3] *Shestnadtsataya Konferentsiya VKP(B)* (1962), pp. 615-617.
[4] *KPSS v Rezolyutsiyakh* (1954), ii, 615-619 ; it appeared in *Pravda*, May 4, 1929. The resolution of the ninth party congress had been drafted by Trotsky (see *The Bolshevik Revolution, 1917–1923*, Vol. 2, pp. 213-214).
[5] *KPSS v Rezolyutsiyakh* (1954), ii, 574 ; for this figure see p. 513 above.

encourage "socialist emulation" on a mass scale between factories and workshops, and to extend the principle of collective emulation to Sovkhozy, kolkhozy and cooperatives.[1] The same theme was pursued a month later at the fifth Union Congress of Soviets. Kuibyshev demanded a further increase in the productivity of labour, which had, he said, risen in the past year by no more than 10 per cent, and concluded his report with a peroration on "socialist emulation"; the spokesman of Narkomtrud argued that the task posed by the first five-year plan of reducing costs of production by 35 per cent was "stiff, but fully realizable"; and the resolution of the congress on the work of the government sang the praises of socialist emulation and of the seven-hour day.[2] The session of the trade union central council at the end of May 1929 issued an appeal, dated June 1, 1929, on the tasks of leadership in socialist emulation.[3] By this time two million workers were said to be engaged in various forms of socialist emulation.[4] The results of the year 1928–1929 demonstrated the striking successes achieved by the drive for productivity. Productivity increased by 15 per cent (14·4 in Group A, 16·6 in Group B, industries).[5] Most of the increase occurred in the half-year April–September 1929, when production, stimulated by the emulation campaign, exceeded that of the previous year by 20 per cent.[6] In the years from 1925–1926 to 1928–1929, productivity increased by no less than 42 per cent.[7] While part of this increase could be attributed to a restoration of pre-war standards, its dimensions were none the less impressive; and these achievements helped to foster the spirit of self-induced faith, a blend of spontaneous enthusiasm and deliberate calculation, in which the first five-year plan was launched.

[1] *Direktivy KPSS i Sovetskogo Pravitel'stva po Khozyaistvennym Voprosam'* ii (1957), 59-61; *Pravda*, May 9, 1929. For the extension of this campaign to agriculture see p. 262 above.
[2] *SSSR: 5 S"ezd Sovetov* (1929), No. 9, pp. 23, 27; *S"ezdy Sovetov v Dokumentakh*, iii (1960), 152-153.
[3] *Profsoyuzy SSSR* (1963), ii, 491-493; the debate was reported in *Trud*, June 2, 8, 1929. For this session see p. 562 below.
[4] *Politicheskii i Trudovoi Pod"em Rabochego Klassa SSSR* (1956), p. 236.
[5] See Table No. 24, p. 957 below; the figures for 1928–1929 are "preliminary"; nominal wages increased by only 11 per cent (see Table No. 25, p. 958 below). For the target figure of 17 per cent for productivity see p. 508 above.
[6] *Statisticheskoe Obozrenie*, No. 12, 1929, p. 32, which gives, however, slightly different (and perhaps later) figures from those in Table No. 24 (see following note).   [7] See Table No. 24, p. 957 below.

CHAPTER 19

WAGES

WAGES under NEP were in principle determined by individual or collective contracts between employer and worker without state intervention. The campaign to link wages to productivity, actively pursued since the autumn of 1924,[1] did not necessarily contravene this principle. The new factor which gradually made itself felt in labour policy from 1926 onwards, and soon came to dominate it, was the principle of planning. That planning involved some measure of direction of labour was not immediately apparent in a period of mass unemployment. But the relation between wages and planning, even in the absence of any formal pronouncement, quickly made itself felt. The national wages bill was far too important an item in the economy to be exempt from the calculations and control of the planners. Both the total amount of the wages bill and its distribution between different branches of industry were vital elements in any comprehensive plan. And this in turn required a degree of centralized control incompatible with the free negotiation of wage-rates between employers and workers or between economic organs and trade unions — a conclusion which, however cogent, aroused strong resistance in trade union circles and was the subject of prolonged controversy. As Tomsky once remarked, wages were " a profoundly political question " which concerned " millions of people who shout and get excited and want to drink and eat ", and " not to understand the political difference between the regulation of wages affecting millions of workers and questions of fuel, raw materials etc. means to approach the question too schematically ".[2] But the current trend was foreshadowed by the gradual introduction and extension of the principle of state fixing of wages for

[1] See *Socialism in One Country, 1924–1926*, Vol. 1, pp. 389-392.
[2] *Sed'moi S''ezd Professional'nykh Soyuzov SSSR* (1927), p. 240.

employees in state and public institutions,[1] and, more significantly, by the events of the summer of 1926, when a general revision of wages was effected by governmental action on a decision taken in the Politburo.

After a halt in the winter of 1924–1925, wages had moved upward again in the summer of 1925 only to come to a standstill in the autumn of that year ; and during the following winter, though wages remained stable in monetary terms, real wages declined.[2] The " régime of economy " announced in the spring of 1926 was interpreted by Dzerzhinsky as precluding any rise in wages.[3] Shtern, Pyatakov's adjutant in Vesenkha, hoped to postpone any wages increase till the second quarter of 1926–1927 (i.e. January–March 1927).[4] The decree of June 11, 1926, on the régime of economy demanded among other means of reducing costs " a prohibition on any kind of concealed increase of wages, a contraction of overtime work, a contraction of the number and duration of journeys on business, particularly abroad, and payment of wages in strict accordance with the set norms ".[5] But this hard policy proved difficult to maintain. The wages question was one of the main planks in the programme of the newly formed united opposition at the session of the party central committee in July 1926. The " declaration of the 13 " complained of " the rejection at the April plenum of the most legitimate and indispensable proposal for a guarantee of real wages ", which had been denounced as demagogy. The opposition demanded " some rise in wages in the autumn ", beginning with the lowest categories.[6] Trotsky, in his speech, criticized Shmidt's report for ignoring the question of wages : he pointed out that the average monthly wage of employees had risen in the quarter January–March 1926 from 98·39 to 101·42 rubles, and that of industrial workers had fallen from 52·14 to 51·44 rubles. His immediate proposals were to end the unpunctual payment of wages, which " continues in spite of all decrees on the

---

[1] See pp. 542-544 below.
[2] See *Socialism in One Country, 1924–1926*, Vol. 1, pp. 398-399, 402 ; Smilga in a speech at the Communist Academy in September 1926 claimed that real wages had first topped the pre-war level in September 1925, but had fallen back to 88 per cent of that level in March 1926, and had since recovered only to 91 per cent (*Vestnik Kommunisticheskoi Akademii*, xvii (1926), 254).
[3] *Torgovo-Promyshlennaya Gazeta*, May 9, 1926.
[4] *Ibid.* June 4, 1926.   [5] For this decree see p. 335 above.
[6] For the declaration see p. 5 above.

subject ", to restore real wages to the level at which they stood at the end of 1925, and to increase wages " within the measure of existing economic possibilities ", especially in the backward branches of industry (mining and metallurgy) and in transport.[1] The proposals of the opposition were rejected or ignored. But the pressure for wage concessions was irresistible. Industry was advancing rapidly ; the financial situation seemed less desperate than it had been in the spring ; harvest prospects were excellent. After the session of the party central committee the Politburo, on which Trotsky was now the sole remaining opposition representative, gave way.[2] The party and government declaration of August 16, 1926, going back on the attitude to wages adopted two months earlier, denounced " the masked reduction of wages " as a distortion of the " régime of economy ".[3] On August 17, 1926, Sovnarkom, acting on the motion of the trade unions, and " in view of the successes achieved in the economic position of the country ", set up a commission under Narkomtrud, composed of representatives of the trade unions and of the departments concerned, to report within two weeks on possible wage increases.[4] No attempt was made to treat the decision as a triumph for the worker or for the trade unions. On the following day Tomsky, reporting to the trade union central council, recommended " *profound caution* " in the approach to wage increases ; a resolution was passed welcoming the decision and reserving details for further examination.[5] A month later the presidium of Vesenkha issued an order explaining that it had " recognized it as necessary to carry out some increase in wages ", and giving directives how this was to be met.[6] But the presidium of Gosplan, in a report on industrial costs of September 20, 1926, sounded a note of extreme caution :

[1] Trotsky archives, T 887 ; for Shmidt's report and Trotsky's speech see p. 488 above. For unpunctual payment of wages see pp. 537-538 below.

[2] Tomsky and Bukharin subsequently gave similar accounts of what happened (*XV Konferentsiya Vsesoyuznoi Kommunisticheskoi Partii (B)* (1927), pp. 286, 599) ; for another account by Tomsky, connecting the decision with the good harvest, see *Sed'moi S"ezd Professional'nykh Soyuzov SSSR* (1927), p. 240.

[3] See pp. 335-336 above.

[4] *Sobranie Zakonov, 1926*, No. 57, art. 418.

[5] *Trud*, August 19, 1926 ; a speech of a similar tenor by Rykov was reported in *Izvestiya*, August 20, 1926.

[6] *Torgovo-Promyshlennaya Gazeta*, September 23, 1926.

The increase of wages in industries where they have lagged behind, which is now being worked out by a special commission of Sovnarkom under the presidency of comrade Shmidt, must not be made universal, but must be put into effect only in conformity with rises in labour productivity. Moreover, a system of wage payments must be adopted which will provide an incentive for workers to increase their skill.[1]

No detailed public announcement of wage increases was made ; the increases became generally effective in September 1926.[2]

This first example of wage regulation (fortunately, in this case, a wage increase) by the central authority on a planned basis was followed by a prolonged controversy about the relation of wages to productivity.[3] This in turn involved the status of the collective agreements by which wages were regulated, and which were of two kinds, central, comprising all workers in the given branch of production, and local, confined to particular trusts or regions.[4] Wage-fixing was now subject to two separate processes. The first was a decision of principle, generally reached in the Politburo after prolonged wrangling between Vesenkha and the trade unions, on the coefficients of proposed increases in productivity and in wages, and on the relation between them. This decision was registered in the control figures for the coming year, and was in principle taken in the early autumn.[5] The second process was the conclusion of collective agreements between the industrial trusts and the relevant trade unions, which had hitherto been concerned only with wages, not with productivity and norms of output. At a session of the presidium of Vesenkha on October 7, 1926, Kviring demanded that norms of productivity as well as of wages should be written into the collective contracts, and that responsibility should rest on the glavki to ensure that this was done.[6] Kraval, at this time the most austere advocate of productivity at all costs and of

---

[1] *Informatsionnyi Byulleten' Gosplana SSSR*, No. 9, 1926.
[2] See Table No. 25, p. 598 below.   [3] See pp. 488-489 above.
[4] By way of reaction against undue centralization in the middle nineteen-twenties, a slight trend away from central to local agreements occurred in 1927 and 1928 ; but in 1928 nearly 40 per cent of workers were still covered by central agreements (*Professional'nye Soyuzy SSSR, 1926–1928: Otchet k VIII S"ezdu* (1928), pp. 340-341). Pressure for increased centralization came from Vesenkha and was resisted by the trade unions (*Trud*, November 16, 1928).
[5] For examples of this procedure see pp. 488-489, 493-494, 507-508 above.
[6] *Torgovo-Promyshlennaya Gazeta*, October 8, 1926.

unlimited pressure on the worker, scarcely concealed his disapproval of recent wage increases, and his determination that they
should not become a precedent :

> Such a rate of increase in wages as we have had in the
> current year we cannot have in the coming year — and still less
> in future years : that is completely indubitable in view of the
> slowing down in the rate of increase in productivity.[1]

The trade union newspaper reacted with some acrimony to this
assault, repeating the familiar argument that the rise in wages now
lagged behind the rise in productivity.[2] The keenest resentment
was aroused by the attack on the status of the collective agreements concluded by the trade unions with enterprises employing
labour. The danger had long been apparent that these " agreements " would degenerate into instruments for imposing wages
and conditions of labour on the workers ; [3] the provision of art. 21
of the labour code of 1923 that such agreements became valid only
on registration by Narkomtrud, though originally designed to protect the worker, gave an added impression of state control.[4] For
the trade unions the collective agreements were a symbol of their
authority. On October 12, 1926, *Trud* printed under the heading
" Against Capricious Interpretations " an angry reply to Kraval's
intervention, protesting against " attempts under various pretexts
to ' revise ' the decision of Sovnarkom on the raising of wages ",
and to introduce extraneous demands into the collective agreements. This article was attacked in turn by Kraval, who insisted
that the wage figures in the plan must take precedence of the collective agreements. The plan was drafted in advance of the agreements, and in any case piece-rates depended on productivity. It
was the business of the *glavki* to see that wage increases were compatible with the plan, and that norms of productivity were laid
down in the collective agreements.[5] Meanwhile, the declaration
of the opposition leaders to the Politburo of October 3, 1926, had
put first among the targets of their criticism the fall in real wages

---

[1] *Torgovo-Promyshlennaya Gazeta*, October 10, 1926.
[2] *Trud*, October 10, 1926.
[3] See *Socialism in One Country, 1924–1926*, Vol. 1, pp. 414-415.
[4] The fact that registration was necessary sometimes led to consultation
with Narkomtrud during negotiations (*Obzor Deyatel'nosti NKT SSSR za
1927–1928 gg* (1928), pp. 47-48).
[5] *Torgovo-Promyshlennaya Gazeta*, October 21, 1926.

and the rise of unemployment.[1] The illicit pamphlet *The Labour Question* alleged that since 1924, when the campaign for higher productivity began, real wages had not risen, and had even declined. As regards the wages increase of August 1926, " the ' course for higher wages' turned out to be pure demagogy, and was dropped as soon as the opposition was defeated ".[2] The famous Maizlin article had proposed to use part of the proceeds of an increase in wholesale industrial prices to raise wages ;[3] Zinoviev, in his speech of October 1, 1926, at the Aviapribor factory, also proposed to devote some of the savings which he hoped to realize to an increase in wages.[4] These reinforcements cannot have helped the defensive action on which the trade unions were engaged.

When the fifteenth party conference met towards the end of October 1926, the issue of wage regulation simmered not far beneath the surface. L. I. Ginzburg, the member of the trade union central council in charge of wage negotiations, touched delicately on the dilemma, remarking that " the system of regulating wages by collective agreements is beginning to encounter rather serious difficulties ". But he claimed that there were " no internal contradictions between a planned economy . . . and the system of collective agreements ", so long as planning did not lead to " excessive, unnecessary centralization ". Tomsky refused to take up the challenge, and reserved the issue for the forthcoming trade union congress.[5] The conference showed more interest in questions of productivity and discipline than of wages.[6] The recent wage increase had taken some of the sting out of the wages issue ; and not even Trotsky, who again raised the issue of the relation of wages to productivity,[7] demanded a further increase. Stalin did not speak in the economic debate ; but, in winding up the political debate on the errors of the opposition, he observed brusquely that the party would not allow the opposition to " come out on the streets with demagogic proclamations of an immediate 30 or 40

[1] This declaration will be discussed in a subsequent volume ; the passage is quoted in *XV Konferentsiya Vsesoyuznoi Kommunisticheskoi Partii (B)* (1927), p. 497.
[2] Quoted *ibid.* p. 631 ; for this pamphlet see p. 488, note 1 above.
[3] For this article see p. 10 above.
[4] For this speech see pp. 286-287 above.
[5] *XV Konferentsiya Vsesoyuznoi Kommunisticheskoi Partii (B)* (1927), pp. 338, 402-403.   [6] See pp. 490-491 above.
[7] *XV Konferentsiya Vsesoyuznoi Kommunisticheskoi Partii (B)* (1927), p. 507.

per cent rise in wages ", the purpose of which was " to cultivate discontent among the backward sectors of the workers, and to organize dissent against the party ".[1]

The fundamental issue of the regulation of wages came into the open at the seventh trade union congress in December 1926. The report prepared by the central council for the congress noted " an inclination on the part of the economic organs to replace real contractual relations by one-sided fixing of wages and conditions of labour ", and admitted that this had received the support of the authorities in some of the national republics.[2] A few days before the congress met, Tomsky, speaking at the third Ukrainian trade union congress, had put the rhetorical question : " Is it possible to plan . . . without knowing the basic elements of the plan, without regulating a basic element of the planned economy — wages ? " He had concluded that the relation between wages in different industries could not be allowed to depend on profits, and that some " centralization " was essential. The president of the Ukrainian trade unions, Radchenko, defended collective agreements as a half-way house between the extremes of state-fixed wages and " anarchy ".[3] At the seventh congress Tomsky embarked on the question in his opening report. He was helped by the wages increase of the autumn which was fresh in everyone's mind : a single decision at the centre had done something which could not have been achieved by months of collective bargaining. Planning was " a fundamental pre-supposition of a socialist economy ". Hence arose " the indispensability of planning in the matter of raising wages " — Tomsky bravely brushed aside the idea that a reduction of wages could be in question. Once the general decision had been taken to raise wages in a given industry, it was the function of the collective agreement to allocate the increase between different categories of workers.[4] Ginzburg ironically confessed to being one of those trade unionists whose " brains are confused about this question ". When " regulation " meant a decision by a government commission not merely on a wage

[1] Stalin, Sochineniya, viii, 352.
[2] Professional'nye Soyuzy SSSR, 1924–1926: Otchet k VII S"ezdu (1926), p. 191.
[3] Stenograficheskii Otchet 3go Vseukrainskogo S"ezda Profsoyuzov (1927), pp. 19, 46.
[4] Sed'moi S"ezd Professional'nykh Soyuzov SSSR (1927), pp. 51-54.

increase for heavy industry, but on specific increases for regions and enterprises, was not this " a beginning of state-fixing ", which " clashes with our policy of collective agreements " ? He protested against the idea of a plan for wages " under the presidency of comrade Shmidt ".[1] But opposition was limited to isolated protests. After Tomsky had described the dissentients as " people who struggle against something which in fact already exists ",[2] a resolution was adopted which explained that " the strengthening of the planning principle in the economy, and the centralized planned regulation of the growth of wages, inevitably entail a somewhat greater centralization than hitherto in the work of the unions on collective agreements ".[3] The resolution went on to define the working of the system :

> The distribution between different branches of industry and different economic organs and trusts of the fund allocated for the raising of wages must be carried out by agreement between the central organs of the trade unions and the central controlling economic organ (Vesenkha). Collective agreements between trade unions and corresponding economic organs must be concluded on the basis of these agreements.[4]

A decree of STO issued while the congress was in session prescribed that collective agreements should be concluded by industrial enterprises, according to the size and importance of the enterprise, either with the central committee of the trade union concerned or with the local branch of the union : disputes arising over the conclusion or implementation of the agreements were to be settled by Narkomtrud.[5] The struggle between Vesenkha and the trade unions was finally composed by the issue in October 1927 in the name of Vesenkha and of the central council of trade unions of a joint directive on the collective agreements, which stoutly denied any incompatibility between the principle of the agreements and the principle of the plan.[6]

This compromise lasted without substantial change for two years. The difficulty of making the process of negotiation effective, and of making it appear effective to the workers, was evident

[1] *Sed'moi S"ezd Professional'nykh Soyuzov SSSR* (1927), pp. 132-133.
[2] *Ibid.* p. 700.   [3] *Ibid.* pp. 782-783.   [4] *Ibid.* pp. 783-784.
[5] *Sobranie Zakonov, 1926*, No. 77, art. 637.
[6] For this directive see p. 494 above.

from the outset. The agreements were discussed at general meetings of the workers, as well as at special meetings of active members of the unions.[1] The resolution of the seventh congress instructed the unions " to take measures to improve their leadership of the workers' meetings at which draft agreements are discussed " and to keep the workers informed of the progress of negotiations ; [2] and the implied criticism was echoed in the platform of the opposition of September 1927 which demanded that " collective agreements shall be made after real and not fictitious discussions at workers' meetings ".[3] After the defeat of the opposition at the end of 1927, the necessity of integrating wages into the planned economy was not again challenged. The statute of Narkomtrud of September 1928 [4] included among its functions " the general regulation of wages " and the registration and supervision of collective agreements. The compilers of the Gosplan control figures for 1928–1929 listed wages among the big questions " which in former years had been decided independently of the control figures ", but had now been brought into closer relation with them.[5] As a result of complaints that the existing system did not " guarantee a sufficiently planned character in the growth of wages ",[6] a new procedure was tried in the autumn of 1928. Before the negotiation of the collective agreements began, Vesenkha and the trade union central council reached an agreement of principle on the vital questions of wages, productivity and norms of production, and issued a joint declaration, which also included a pronouncement that " the conclusion of collective agreements is the surest method of arousing the interest of the working masses in production and its needs ", and called for " general meetings "

[1] Professional'nye Soyuzy SSSR, 1924–1926: Otchet k VII S"ezdu (1926), p. 192.
[2] Sed'moi S"ezd Professional'nykh Soyuzov SSSR (1927), p. 784.
[3] L. Trotsky, The Real Situation in Russia (n.d. [1928]), p. 54. According to a statement at the eighth trade union congress in December 1928, the attendance at such meetings had increased ; in Moscow 60-65 per cent of workers attended, and even higher percentages were quoted elsewhere (Vos'moi S"ezd Professional'nykh Soyuzov SSSR (1929), p. 65).
[4] See p. 465 above.
[5] Kontrol'nye Tsifry Narodnogo Khozyaistva SSSR na 1928–1929 god (1929), p. 21 ; the importance of the question was indicated by the calculation that wages accounted for 40 per cent of the costs of production in Group A industries, and 19-20 per cent in Group B (ibid. p. 281).
[6] Obzor Deyatel'nosti NKT SSSR za 1927–1928 gg. (1928), p. 71.

of workers to discuss these problems. The two separate processes
— the initial agreement of principle between Vesenkha and the
trade union central council and the collective agreement between
a trade union or its local branch and the management of the
industry or enterprise concerned — were thus brought into a
formal relation, in which the former took precedence over the
latter.[1] The new procedure also gave effect to the demand put
forward by Vesenkha in 1926 that the relation between productivity and wages should find expression in the collective agreements. The wages structure of particular industries was thus
subordinated to basic central decisions of economic policy ; the
economic plan became in the last resort the decisive factor in
regulating wages.

   The direct intervention of the highest party and Soviet authorities in the fixing of wages was bound to reopen the vexed question
of discrimination between different grades of worker, between
skilled and unskilled. Since the early days of the régime, and more
specifically since the introduction of NEP, a running battle had
been fought between the desire of the policy-makers for increased
differentials in the interests of efficiency and the egalitarian principles inscribed in the party programme and upheld — falteringly
and intermittently — by the trade unions.[2] The growing spread
between the highest and lowest wage levels, aggravated by the
extension of piece-rates, still from time to time provoked sharp
protests. One such protest was voiced by a Komsomol leader at
the seventh Komsomol congress in March 1926 :

   Among the young . . . the tendency towards equalization is
   highly developed : to make all workers, skilled and unskilled,
   equal. The mood is such that young workers come to us and
   say that we do not have state enterprises, enterprises of a consistently socialist type as defined by Lenin, but that what we
   have is exploitation.[3]

   [1] *Trud*, November 3, 1928 ; *Professional'nye Soyuzy SSSR, 1926–1928:
Otchet k VIII S"ezdu* (1928), pp. 341-342.
   [2] See *Socialism in One Country, 1924–1926*, Vol. 1, pp. 376-377.
   [3] *VII S"ezd Vsesoyuznogo Leninskogo Kommunisticheskogo Soyuza Molodezhi* (1926), p. 49 ; a resolution of the fifth Komsomol conference in March
1927 named " egalitarian moods " as an " unhealthy " symptom discernible

On the eve of the decision to raise wages in August 1926, Trotsky complained of " an unhelpful, even disagreeable, attitude to unskilled and semi-skilled workers, as to a ' grey mass ' which has not yet attained the ' high ' level of the bureaucrats, and therefore dreams of equality ", and denounced this attitude as a symptom of divorce from the masses.[1] Tomsky, in his report on the decision to the trade union central council, demanded that the wages of unskilled workers should be brought more nearly into line with those of skilled workers ; and a resolution was passed in this sense.[2] At the seventh trade union congress in December 1926 Tomsky reiterated the traditional view in a noteworthy passage :

> When foreigners visit us, they are especially astonished by the circumstance that, in the world of the proletarian dictatorship, in our revolutionary trade unions and with all our influence, the difference between the pay of the skilled and the unskilled worker here is of colossal dimensions such as are not found in western Europe. Of course this is explained by many causes ; briefly, one of the causes is that our technical equipment is still too backward, personal skill, the craft tradition etc. still play too large a rôle, automatic machines which simplify the labour of the worker, and introduce automatic methods, are too little used. But an explanation is one thing, and elementary class justice another. We must in future move in the direction of modifying the gap between the wages of the skilled and of the ordinary worker.

Dogadov quoted examples to show that skilled workers earning three times as much as unskilled workers in the same trade were common, and thought that " the gap in earnings between skilled and unskilled labour demands the most serious attention ".[3] The " pulling up " (podtyagivanie) of the wages of the lowest paid

---

among " backward sections of young workers " (*VLKSM v Rezolyutsiyakh* (1929), p. 283).
    [1] Memorandum of July 11, 1926 (Trotsky archives, T 2993) ; it is not clear whether this memorandum was circulated to the committee or was merely a brief for Trotsky's remarks at the session of July 1926.
    [2] *Trud*, August 19, 1926 ; for this report see p. 522 above. Similar comments by Rykov were reported in *Izvestiya*, August 20, 1926 ; this suggests that the principle had been approved by the Politburo.
    [3] *Sed'moi S"ezd Professional'nykh Soyuzov SSSR* (1927), pp. 51, 87.

categories of workers was named as an objective both in the general
resolution of the congress on the report of the central council and
in the resolution on wage-scales.[1] Even the resolution on Kuibyshev's report to the fourth Union Congress of Soviets in April 1927,
which was principally concerned to promote productivity and
rationalization, cautiously advocated " pulling up the level of remuneration of the lowest paid groups of workers ".[2]

Determination to " pull up " the wages of the lowest paid
workers concealed, however, an ambiguity already latent in an
earlier period.[3] Was this a continuation of the long-standing party
demand to equalize wages, to reduce the gap between higher and
lower grades of labour, between skilled and unskilled workers ?
Or was it a new demand to " pull up " wage levels in those industries which had been least favoured in NEP conditions, but were
now seen to be vital to an expansion of the national economy ? In
the first years of NEP, the level of wages in consumer goods
industries owed much both to the wide demand for their products,
which were relatively free from price controls, and to the low
relative proportion of the wages component in costs of production ;
wages in industries producing means of production, notably coal-
mining and the metal industries, had suffered from the opposite
conditions.[4] The consumer goods industries had recovered more
easily under the régime of profitability introduced by NEP. Most
of these industries, with the notable exception of textiles, paid
relatively high wages. This situation, under the growing pressure
of industrialization, it was now urgent to reverse.[5]

The new emphasis quickly made itself felt. The decision of

---

[1] *Ibid.* pp. 735, 783.

[2] *S"ezdy Sovetov v Dokumentakh*, iii (1960), 124.

[3] See *Socialism in One Country, 1924–1926*, Vol. 1, p. 377, note 1.

[4] The compilers of the Gosplan control figures for 1928–1929 noted that
the ratio of wages to costs of production was twice as high in Group A as in
Group B industries (see p. 528, note 5 above).

[5] The depressed wages of capital goods industries were a reversal of the
pre-1914 situation when metal workers and miners were the most highly paid
workers ; in 1925–1926 metal workers received only 75·3 per cent, and miners
only 65·2 per cent of their pre-1914 wages, at a time when most industries had
achieved higher wages than before 1914 (*Ekonomicheskoe Obozrenie*, No. 10,
1929, pp. 145-146). The textile industry, with its predominance of female
workers, had always been badly paid : before 1914 its wages were only 68 per
cent of average wages, and less than half those of metal workers (*ibid.* p. 147).

August 1926 to raise wages was described by *Pravda* as designed
" in the first instance " to help " backward groups of time-
workers ".[1] The fifteenth party conference in October 1926 recorded its approval of the decision " to raise the level of wages . . .
in backward branches of production and of especially low paid
groups of workers " [2] (apparently the first time the policy had been
defined in this dual form) ; and the same two aims in the same
order were proclaimed in the wages resolution of the seventh trade
union congress in December 1926 :

> The starting point must be the importance of a given branch
> [of industry] in the general economic system and the necessity
> of guaranteeing a flow of labour power to it ; the regulation of
> wages should also be directed to pull up the wages of the lowest
> groups of workers and employees.[3]

These formulas appeared at first sight to reconcile current insistence on the relation of wages to productivity, and the pragmatic
view of differential wages as an incentive to output, with the
egalitarian tradition.   But, when planners and industrializers subscribed to the demand to " pull up " the wages of low-paid workers, they thought in terms not of the relation of unskilled to skilled
workers, but of low-paid industries vital to the economy.   These
were especially the metal and mining industries and transport,
and (from the point of view of supplies to the peasant market) the
textile industry.   To raise wages in these industries as an incentive
to higher production was a demand which satisfied both schools of
thought ; and this became the first achievement of a planned and
centralized wages policy.   For the year 1926–1927 a total of 94
million rubles was allocated for an increase in wages.   Of this, 42
millions were to go to the transport workers, and the other major
beneficiaries were the metal workers, textile workers and miners ;
all these, except the metal workers (who were in the middle range),
were conspicuously low-paid industries.   Nothing was given to the
consumer goods industries (other than textiles), whose workers
already enjoyed relatively high wages.   For the year 1927–1928 the
total increase was reduced to 32 million rubles ; nothing more was

---

[1] *Pravda*, September 24, 1926.
[2] *KPSS v Rezolyutsiyakh* (1954), ii, 309.
[3] *Sed'moi S"ezd Professional'nykh Soyuzov SSSR* (1927), p. 783.

given to the transport workers, but miners and metal and textile
workers were again the main beneficiaries.[1] At the eighth trade
union congress in December 1928, low wages in the textile industry
and in mining were still a grievance.[2] While, however, something
was done to " pull up " wages in the lower-paid industries, it is
not clear whether the wage-levelling policies of the later nineteen-
twenties affected in any way the relations between the wages of
skilled and unskilled workers in the same industry.[3] In the summer of 1928 some party members in Moscow were said to be
shocked by the growing rift between skilled workers, who were
distinguished by " their way of life, costume, diet and housing ",
and the unskilled workers chronically at the mercy of penury and
unemployment.[4] A Komsomol member remarked to Bukharin
that " one lot of our workers strut like peacocks (pizhonyat'sya),
and another lot have to go about almost like beggars ".[5] But
this was not the primary preoccupation of wages policy at this
time.[6]

[1] Professional'nye Soyuzy SSSR, 1926–1928: Otchet k VIII S"ezdu (1928),
p. 320.
[2] Vos'moi S"ezd Professional'nykh Soyuzov SSSR (1929), pp. 73, 90,
121.
[3] A. Bergson, The Structure of Soviet Wages (Harvard, 1944), p. 188, claims
that, in the metal, woollen textile, and shoe and leather industries, differentiation between skilled and unskilled workers was reduced from 1926 to 1928.
But figures quoted in S. Zagorsky, Wages and Regulation of Conditions of Labour
in the USSR (Geneva, 1930), pp. 116-117, from Statistika Truda appear to
show conclusively that differentiation between skilled and unskilled metal
workers increased in these years ; the proportion of metal workers earning less
than 70 per cent, or more than 120 per cent, of the average wage of the factory in
which they worked increased in 1927-1928 (Ekonomicheskoe Obozrenie, No. 9,
1929, p. 142). Later, when Tomsky's record came under fire, it was alleged
that the eighth trade union congress of December 1928 had given the signal for
" an extensive development of petty bourgeois egalitarianism " (Voprosy Truda,
November–December 1932, p. 29).
[4] Trotsky archives, T 2021 ; for this report see p. 83, note 3 above.
[5] VIII Vsesoyuznyi S"ezd VLKSM (1928), p. 37.
[6] Another discrepancy which attracted less attention, and was justified in
part by differences in cost of living, was between wages paid in different regions.
In 1929 the average daily wage of a Leningrad metal worker was 5·06 rubles,
ranging from 8·13 as the highest wage to 3·79 as the lowest ; of a corresponding
worker in the Urals 2·67 rubles, ranging from 4·38 to 1·90. The average daily
wage of a Leningrad cotton textile worker was 3·02 rubles, ranging from 5·22
to 2·18 ; of an Ivanovo-Voznesensk cotton textile worker 2·45 rubles, ranging
from 3·86 to 1·79 (Sostav Fabrichno-Zavodskogo Proletariata SSSR (1930), pp.
60, 62).

The system was in fact less rigid and less water-tight than it appeared. Earnings were, to a varying but always considerable extent, determined not by basic wage-rates, but by a number of alternative or supplementary forms of remuneration which could not be calculated in advance. Of these the most important were piece-rates. After the general approval of piece-rates in 1925,[1] it was found necessary to introduce bonus or incentive payments to workers on time-rates,[2] so that, for virtually all workers, wage-rates no longer determined actual earnings. In March 1926 16 per cent of all workers in the RSFSR, 30 per cent of all workers in the Ukraine, and 70 per cent of workers in the metallurgical industry were said to be in receipt of overtime pay.[3] At the same date wages paid to piece-workers in large-scale industry exceeded basic rates on an average by 68·1 per cent, and in December 1927 by 69 per cent, the excess being greatest for metal workers (103·6 and 122·9 per cent for the two dates respectively) and lowest for textile workers (41·8 and 43 per cent). Excess payments for time-workers were smaller, but still substantial, averaging 27·8 per cent of wage-rates in March 1926, and 34·1 per cent in December 1927.[4] Total earnings in industry rose by 12·1 per cent in 1926–1927, and by a further 11 per cent in 1927–1928, making a two-year rise of 23·3 per cent ; though metal workers scored the largest rise over this period (28·1 per cent), the relative position of other industries showed little change.[5]

This loophole in the planned control of wages had to be closed.

[1] See *Socialism in One Country, 1924–1926*, Vol. 1, pp. 390-392. A table in *Ekonomicheskoe Obozrenie*, No. 10, 1929, p. 148, covering 24 large factories employing 30,000 workers, showed that the proportion of workers on piece-rates increased heavily between 1924 and 1928 (figures for intermediate years were not given) ; from 60 to 90 per cent of the workers were on piece-rates in 1928.

[2] *Professional'nye Soyuzy SSSR, 1924–1926: Otchet k VII S"ezdu* (1926), pp. 215-216.   [3] *Bol'shevik*, No. 13, June 15, 1926, p. 52.

[4] *Professional'nye Soyuzy SSSR, 1924–1926: Otchet k VII S"ezdu* (1926), p. 220 ; *Professional'nye Soyuzy SSSR, 1926–1928: Otchet k VIII S"ezdu* (1928), p. 331. Piece-work in 1928 accounted for rather more than 60 per cent of hours worked in large-scale industry (*ibid.* p. 323) ; *Ekonomicheskoe Obozrenie*, No. 3, 1929, p. 117, gives figures of 57·5 per cent for Group A industries and 64·5 per cent for Group B industries ; *Trud v SSSR* (1936), p. 97, gives the figure of 57·5 per cent, probably in error, for all large-scale industry in 1928. In one factory 90 per cent of the workers were said to be on piece-work in 1927 (*Torgovo-Promyshlennaya Gazeta*, July 13, 1927).

[5] See Table No. 25, p. 958 below ; *Professional'nye Soyuzy SSSR, 1926–1928: Otchet k VIII S"ezdu* (1928), p. 314.

Reasons for a change were cogent. Piece-rates were disliked not only by the planners, who saw their control over the wages bill placed in jeopardy,[1] but by the trade unions, which saw in them both a traditional instrument of pressure on the workers, and a device through which wages eluded their control.[2] At the fifteenth party conference in October 1926, Lepse had argued that the existing system, which combined the 17-grade wage-scale with bonuses and piece-rates, had become impossibly complicated, and demanded " a simplification of the existing wage system, i.e. to include a part of piece-rate earnings, a part of the bonuses, in the wages scale, and make the workers' wage-scale more real ".[3] The task was immensely complex, and inevitably involved the vexed issue of the wide spread between the wages of skilled and unskilled workers. The seventh trade union congress in December 1926 showed no desire to plunge into this awkward question. But in a resolution on wages, it strongly condemned the complexities of the existing system, assumed that any reform must move in the direction of levelling out inequalities between different categories of workers, and instructed the trade unions, with the aim of " the successful regulation of wages in enterprises and of the relation between different trades and groups of workers ", to draw up a new series of wage-scales for manual workers in industry, with separate scales for engineers and technicians, for trainees and for employees.[4] The trade union central council in March 1927 decided on a scale of 8 grades for manual workers, 6 grades for trainees, 16 for engineers and technicians, and 16 for employees, and instructed the trade unions to draw up scales on this basis for their respective industries. Of the grades for manual workers the standard basic rate of the top grade (i.e. the eighth) was 2·8 times

[1] As the Gosplan control figures for 1926–1927 coyly observed, " a sufficient percentage of persons engaged on piece-work guarantees an automatic increase in wages proportional to an increase in the productivity of labour " (*Kontrol'nye Tsifry Narodnogo Khozyaistva na 1926–1927 god* (1926), p. 88).

[2] At a congress of representatives of labour departments in June 1926, a trade union delegate spoke of piece-rates as a " slave survival of the past, reflected in the psychological assumption that the worker works better when he receives a low basic wage and has the opportunity to earn a bonus of several hundred per cent " (*Torgovo-Promyshlennaya Gazeta*, July 2, 1926).

[3] *XV Konferentsiya Vsesoyuznoi Kommunisticheskoi Partii (B)* (1927), pp. 390-391.

[4] *Sed'moi S"ezd Professional'nykh Soyuzov SSSR* (1927), pp. 786-787 ; for existing scales see *Socialism in One Country, 1924–1926*, Vol. 1, pp. 376-377

that of the lowest, though rates varied in different industries, and not all unions adopted the eight-grade scale. Most of the new scales were not ready till the end of the year, and came into force at the beginning of January 1928: some were still outstanding at that time.[1] The major result — and, it is fair to assume, purpose — of the new scales for manual workers was to increase the proportion of fixed wage-rates in total earnings and reduce the proportion of supplementary payments and piece-rates. Fixed wage-rates were stepped up ; this was achieved in part by suppressing the lowest two or three grades in the old scales, which had come to be reserved mainly for juveniles (now transferred to separate scales), so that the lowest grade in the new scales corresponded to the third or fourth in the old ones. This was, however, the moment of a general increase of norms sufficiently drastic to ensure that productivity rose more rapidly than wages in the year 1927–1928, so that the rise in fixed wage-rates was counter-balanced by a corresponding reduction in bonus and piece-rate payments. Such payments, which at the end of 1927 represented 56·1 per cent of total earnings in large-scale industry, were reduced by March 1928 to 31 per cent ; extra payments to metal workers fell from 105·4 to 47·7 per cent of their basic wage-rates.[2] Conversely, it was calculated that, whereas at the end of 1927 only 65 per cent of industrial earnings came from fixed wage-rates, the proportion had risen in May 1928 to 75·4 per cent.[3] This reform was clearly favoured by the planners, since it made a higher proportion of the wages fund amenable to planning. The attitude of the managers was " passive ", no doubt from fear that it tended to diminish incentives. The change seems also to have been unpopular with the workers — partly, perhaps, from suspicion that the readjustment was designed to conceal a reduction of earnings, or to forestall an increase, partly because it was accompanied by a simultaneous raising of norms for piece-rates,[4] and was resented as a trick to put fresh pressure on the worker. Unrest in the summer of 1928 was probably attributable in large part to this source.[5] At the eighth

---

[1] *Professional'nye Soyuzy SSSR, 1926–1928: Otchet k VIII S"ezdu* (1928), pp. 324-326 ; by March 1928 83·5 per cent of workers were on the new scales (*ibid.* p. 327).   [2] *Ibid.* pp. 325-327, 331.   [3] *Ibid.* p. 336.
[4] See pp. 504-507 above.
[5] For a report from a worker in the Kremenchug wagon works, received in May 1928, of stiff opposition to the reform see Trotsky archives, T 1390, 1586.

trade union congress, meeting in December 1928 in an atmosphere of political tension, it was left to Krupskaya to claim that " the trade unions had rightly set their course to pull up the more backward strata, not only in the matter of wages and conditions of labour, but in the cultural sense " ; and she added that this process went on " half spontaneously ".[1] The congress in its resolution noted with satisfaction that the reform, though " far from completed ", had strengthened " the regulating rôle of the collective agreement in fixing the amount of wages ". It claimed that one result of the reform had been " to achieve, in full agreement with the policy of the unions, some reduction of the gap between the earnings of skilled and untrained workers ". Its only novelty was the proposal that, " with the increasing mechanization of the processes of production " (the conveyor-belt was the innovation principally in mind), " piece-rates should be replaced by a system of collective bonuses ".[2] This suggestion was to bear fruit in the ensuing period.

The long-standing scandal of the unpunctual payment of wages, which had been partially overcome by 1926,[3] still gave rise to complaint.[4] In the winter of 1927–1928 Vesenkha issued no less than three instructions to its subordinate organs on the need to pay wages punctually ; [5] and the report of the trade union central council to the eighth trade union congress in December 1928 mentioned strikes due to unpunctual payment of wages.[6] Special attention continued to be given to unpunctual wage payments in private industry. Decrees of September 9, 1927, and June 22, 1928, were designed to penalize such offences on the part of private concerns engaged on public work or of concession enterprises ; [7] and in 1929 an amendment to the labour code of the

---

[1] *Vos'moi S"ezd Professional'nykh Soyuzov SSSR* (1929), p. 134.
[2] *Ibid.* pp. 521-522.
[3] See *Socialism in One Country, 1924–1926*, Vol. 1, p. 373.
[4] *Trud*, August 17, 1926 ; see also Trotsky's comment pp. 521-522 above.
[5] S. Zagorsky, *Wages and Regulation of Conditions of Labour in the USSR* (Geneva, 1930), pp. 90-92 ; an order of January 27, 1928, stated that, in spite of a previous order of November 23, 1927, delays still occurred, and instructed heads of *glavki* to investigate these cases personally (*Torgovo-Promyshlennaya Gazeta*, February 2, 1928).
[6] *Professional'nye Soyuzy SSSR, 1926–1928: Otchet k VIII S"ezdu* (1928), p. 360.
[7] *Obzor Deyatel'nosti NKT SSSR za 1927–1928 gg.* (1928), pp. 87-88.

RSFSR imposed on all private employers an obligation to pay wages punctually.[1] Non-payment of wages during stoppages due to the fault of the management was cited as an abuse in a party resolution of April 1928.[2] During these years, wages of industrial workers in terms of rubles moved continuously upward.[3] The establishment of the stable currency in 1924 had led to an abandonment of the payment of " real " wages in terms of current prices ; and, when inflation crept in again in the autumn of 1925, this was not resumed. Tomsky at the fifteenth party conference in October 1926 confessed that the trade unions had " hesitated for a long time before making the transition from the goods index to the chervonets reckoning ", but that the stable currency had conferred immense benefits on the worker, and to abandon it now would be " an absurd and politically irresponsible proposition ".[4] At the seventh trade union congress two months later he spoke more specifically of "the slogan of the maintenance of real wages ", and explained why the trade union central council had refused to support it :

This means — count up the rise in the index, the increase in the goods ruble, and say : Now pay wages in goods rubles. And this means an official recognition, not only that the chervonets has fallen, but that it is falling, sliding down, travelling on an inclined plane, and that it is doomed to devaluation.[5]

Refusal publicly to admit inflation or the decline in value of the chervonets currency was a steady feature of Soviet financial policy in this period.[6] The Gosplan control figures for 1926–1927 calculated the total wages fund in pre-war, goods and chervonets rubles, but average individual wages, industry by industry, only in chervonets rubles ; [7] the control figures for wages in subsequent years used only chervonets rubles. Percentage rises in productivity were still expressed by Gosplan in terms of pre-war prices,

---

[1] *Sobranie Uzakonenii, 1929*, No. 11, art. 120.
[2] *KPSS v Rezolyutsiyakh* (1954), ii, 508.
[3] See Table No. 25, p. 958 below.
[4] *XV Konferentsiya Vsesoyuznoi Kommunisticheskoi Partii (B)* (1927), pp. 285-286.
[5] *Sed'moi S"ezd Professional'nykh Soyuzov SSSR* (1927), p. 50.
[6] See pp. 777-778 below.
[7] *Kontrol'nye Tsifry Narodnogo Khozyaistva na 1926–1927 god* (1926), pp. 302-303, 376-378.

and compared with a percentage rise in real wages ; [1] and from 1926 onwards a cost-of-living index based on a hypothetical worker's budget was regularly published. Statements about " real wages " were frequently made. On the eve of the fifteenth party congress in December 1927, a member of the opposition was allowed to publish an article in the party journal in which he claimed that, while conflicting estimates of the relation of real wages to productivity were in circulation, productivity in 1925–1926 had in fact reached 110·6 per cent of the pre-war level, and real wages only 91·3 per cent. This was answered by an official spokesman who argued that productivity in 1925–1926 had reached only 91·6 per cent of the pre-war level and real wages 93·7 per cent, and that these ratios had risen to 104·2 per cent and 105·1 per cent respectively in 1926–1927.[2] It was claimed at the eighth trade union congress in December 1928 that real wages had risen by 12·5 per cent in 1926–1927 and by 10·8 per cent in 1927–1928.[3] But such calculations were based on the official price level ; [4] and, since the extent to which consumer needs could be met in state or cooperative shops at official prices varied widely, and was far from complete, they were largely nugatory. All wage calculations were rendered to some extent illusory by a variety of conditions affecting purchasing power of the wages — availability of works canteens or cooperative stores, housing, and social services of varying efficacy.[5]

While statistics remain an inadequate guide, all the evidence

[1] *Kontrol'nye Tsifry Narodnogo Khozyaistva SSSR na 1927–1928 god* (1928), pp. 211, 218 ; productivity was, however, sometimes measured in 1926–1927 prices and wages in current prices.

[2] *Bol'shevik*, No. 22, November 30, 1927, pp. 115-130.

[3] *Vos'moi S"ezd Professional'nykh Soyuzov SSSR* (1929), p. 63.

[4] According to Gosplan statistics real wages rose by 13·9 per cent in 1927–1928, but more than half the increase was due to falling prices (*Planovoe Khozyaistvo*, No. 4, 1934, p. 154) ; private market prices rose sharply during this year (see Table No. 31, pp. 964-965 below).

[5] For the various forms of social insurance see pp. 605-608 below ; for the concept of " the socialized part of wages " see *Socialism in One Country, 1924–1926*, Vol. 1, p. 374, note 5. Social and cultural additions to wages were said to amount to 32 per cent in 1925–1926 against 9 per cent before the revolution (*SSSR: Ot S"ezda k S"ezdu (Mai 1925 g.–April 1927 g.)* (1927), pp. 30-31). According to calculations from other Soviet sources, social insurance benefits, including unemployment insurance, in 1928 amounted to an average 7 per cent of wages ; all social service benefits (including education) amounted to 18 per cent of wages (J. Chapman, *Real Wages in Soviet Russia* (1963), pp. 126-138).

points to a sharp fall in real wages in the summer and autumn of 1928. Hitherto the rise in the cost of living consequent on the falling value of the ruble had been more or less effectively balanced by wage increases ; and during 1927 some success was achieved in reducing retail prices.[1] But, with the grain crisis of the spring and summer of 1928, prices soared rapidly.[2] Molotov, in an article in *Pravda*, admitted that rising agricultural prices were " bound up with certain sacrifices on the part of the working class ".[3] The now illicit opposition harped in its underground propaganda on the fall in the standard of living of the industrial worker, which took place " against a background of increased incomes for other sectors of the population ".[4] Some party circles were openly unsympathetic to the worker's claims. Remarks alleged to have been made by Bubnov in a Moscow factory on September 12, 1928, were quoted in an opposition bulletin :

> The worker has grown fat and developed pretensions ; however much you give him, he is not satisfied. Before the revolution workers slept on rags in barracks : now they sleep in bed. They did not eat meat ; now they eat meat with macaroni.[5]

Kuibyshev at the fourth plenum of Vesenkha in November 1928 protested against the annual " mechanical increase " in wages which frustrated the campaign for reducing costs.[6] L. I. Ginzburg told the eighth trade union congress at the end of the year that since July " the workers have begun to lose considerably through the rise in prices " : the general price level had risen by 4 per cent, the index of agricultural prices by 6 per cent.[7] The Gosplan control figures for 1928-1929 provided for an increase of 8·1 per cent (against an actual increase of 9·6 per cent in 1927–1928) in wages in census industry, and an increase of 7·4 (against 7·9 per cent in 1927–1928)

[1] See pp. 688-689 below.   [2] See pp. 691-695 below.
[3] *Pravda*, August 5, 1928; for this article see pp 84-85 above.
[4] See opposition report of September 1928 in Trotsky archives, T 2574.
[5] Trotsky archives, T 2560 ; the report added that only 50 out of 3000 workers waited to hear Bubnov's concluding speech.
[6] *Torgovo-Promyshlennaya Gazeta*, November 28, 1928 ; for Kuibyshev's report see pp. 328, 509-510 above.
[7] *Vos'moi S"ezd Professional'nykh Soyuzov SSSR* (1929), p. 412 ; this is confirmed by a calculation in S. Zagorsky, *Wages and Regulation of Conditions of Labour in the USSR* (Geneva, 1930), p. 201, which shows real wages rising to a peak in the first quarter of 1928 and declining fairly sharply during the rest of the year.

in all wages, reckoned as equivalent to an increase of 4·9 per cent
in real wages. The formula of " pulling up the wages of backward sectors of labour and groups of workers " was again invoked ;
and it was observed that, since the wages reform of 1928 had
reduced " the need for a mechanical increase of wages ", it might
be hoped that planned rates of increase would not be exceeded in
1928–1929.[1]

The anxieties of the present were, however, tempered by optimism for the future. An early version of the first five-year plan as
reported by Kuibyshev to the fifteenth party congress in December
1927, contemplated a rise of 24·6 per cent in nominal wages and of
46 per cent in real wages during the period of the plan.[2] At the
eighth trade union congress in December 1928 Ginzburg pointed
out that the provision in the draft plan presented by Kuibyshev to
the congress for a rise of more than 50 per cent in real wages rested
on the assumption of a substantial fall in prices, and that previous
prognostications of wage movements by the planners had proved
" unreal ". He concluded that " we cannot accept the control
figures as an obligatory document for the fixing of wages ".[3] But
this scepticism found no echo in other speeches or in the resolutions of the congress. The final version of the five-year plan provided for an increase of wages in industry in the five-year period of
38 per cent (basic variant), not including the " social component "
which would raise the figure to 42 per cent, or 48 per cent (optimum variant) ; and this would be reinforced by a fall of 10 per
cent (basic variant) or 14 per cent (optimum variant) in the cost of
living, so that the increase in real wages would amount to 53 per
cent (basic variant) or 66 per cent (optimum variant).[4] The sixteenth party conference in April 1929 in its resolution endorsing
the plan forecast a rise of no less than 71 per cent in the real
wages of the industrial worker.[5] It was to be an ironic comment
on these hopes and expectations that real wages of workers and

[1] *Kontrol'nye Tsifry Narodnogo Khozyaistva SSSR na 1928–1929 god* (1929),
pp. 150–151 ; for tables see *ibid*. pp. 452–455.
[2] *Pyatnadtsatyi S"ezd VKP(B)*, ii (1962), 955.
[3] *Vos'moi S"ezd Professional'nykh Soyuzov SSSR* (1929), p. 412 ; for this
draft see pp. 881–884 below.
[4] *Pyatiletnii Plan Narodno-Khozyaistvennogo Stroitel'stva SSSR* (1929), i,
95–96.
[5] *KPSS v Rezolyutsiyakh* (1954), ii, 572.

employees in 1932 were no more than 88·6 per cent of those of 1928.[1] Increased nominal wages paid to the industrial worker inexorably created a demand for agricultural products higher than peasant production for the market could satisfy, and a demand for consumer goods competing with the minimum demand of the peasant market. Where there was not enough to go round, every belt had to be tightened.

The uniform state regulation of wages of employees in all state organs and institutions, including those working on *khozraschet*, which had been inaugurated in 1925,[2] was progressively extended during the three following years. Though the essence of the change was to " establish fixed official salaries in place of the determination of wages by collective agreements ",[3] willingness to keep the trade unions formally in the picture was manifested by a provision in the decree of September 21, 1926, that wages fixed by the state should nevertheless be embodied in collective agreements covering the different categories of workers affected.[4] At the seventh trade union congress in December 1926, Dogadov, a leading member of the trade union central council, deplored the effective exclusion of the trade unions from work among " the immense mass of employees ", but had nothing to propose. Tomsky defended the system as a necessary protection against the bureaucratic inflation of wages in state establishments. A resolution of the congress approved the extension of state regulation " to enterprises on *khozraschet* and to staffs of state trading institutions in which the system of regulation of wages by collective agreements still exists " (thus apparently sweeping away the convenient fiction that the two systems were mutually compatible), but stipulated that this should be done " with full agreement between the unions

---

[1] A. Malafeev, *Istoriya Tsenoobrazovaniya v SSSR* (1964), p. 174.

[2] See *Socialism in One Country, 1924–1926*, Vol. 1, pp. 381-382.

[3] *Professional'nye Soyuzy SSSR, 1924–1926: Otchet k VII S"ezdu* (1926), p. 222 ; the trade union central council, in announcing its acceptance of the change, had admitted that a system of fixed salaries " renders impracticable the conclusion of collective agreements " (*Trud*, July 18, 1925).

[4] *Sobranie Zakonov, 1926*, No. 67, art. 514 ; Narkomtrud reported " a significant expansion " of this practice in 1927–1928 (*Obzor Deyatel'nosti NKT SSSR za 1927–1928 gg.* (1928), p. 85).

and the state establishments concerned " ; [1] and a decree of April
15, 1927, provided that wages in institutions subject to state regulation of wages should be fixed by Narkomtrud in consultation with
other commissariats and with the trade union concerned.[2] In
effect, where state regulation of wages applied, it excluded even
the form of the collective bargain on wages ; this was recognized
in a resolution of the trade union central council of September 9,
1927, which instructed trade unions to " concentrate on the
application of the labour code and on the correct application of
state regulation itself ". Collective agreements were to be concluded on such matters as engagement and dismissal of workers,
promotion, or the protection of labour.[3] A decree of September
30, 1927, prescribed the extension of state regulation to employees
of credit institutions, of central and local offices of social insurance,
of workers' savings banks and of the administrations of industrial
syndicates, and proposed to the Sovnarkoms of the republics to
ensure that state regulation of wages was applied to all institutions
carried on republican or local budgets by April 1, 1928.[4]

By the end of 1928, state regulation of the wages of employees
had been introduced in virtually all public institutions of the
USSR and of the Russian, Ukrainian and White Russian republics;
in the other republics progress was slower and more patchy.[5] At
the eighth trade union congress in December 1928, Tomsky took
under his protection the despised category of employees, declaring
that it was time to recognize that the employee was " no longer
what he was ", and to drop ironical references to " Soviet employees " and " Soviet young ladies ". The spokesman of Narkomtrud claimed that 94·9 per cent of employees on state budgets
throughout the USSR, and 73·8 per cent of those on budgets of
local authorities, were now covered by the system of state regulation ; it was essential to extend it in 1928–1929 to all personnel
" of establishments on *khozraschet* and of syndicates and banking

---

[1] *Sed'moi S"ezd Professional'nykh Soyuzov SSSR* (1927), pp. 154, 242, 787-788.
[2] *Sobranie Zakonov, 1927*, No. 20, art. 230.
[3] *Gosudarstvennoe Normirovanie Zarabotnoi Platy* (1928), p. 58.
[4] *Sobranie Zakonov, 1927*, No. 59, art. 589.
[5] For detailed reports see *Obzor Deyatel'nosti NKT SSSR za 1927–1928 gg.* (1928), pp. 76-85 ; *Gosudarstvennoe Normirovanie Zarabotnoi Platy* (1928), pp. 65-78.

institutions ", where resistance to it was still encountered.¹ The element of compromise remained. No attempt was made to extend the system to industrial workers ; and within its limited scope it was accepted by the trade unions. But, where industry was nationalized, the theoretical line of demarcation between the two methods of wage-fixing was not altogether clear. The system was freely described as " a transition to the planned regulation of wages ".² Dislike continued to be felt in trade union circles of a principle which might one day be susceptible of wider application ; and the use of collective agreements to register terms of employment regulated in this way seemed to vitiate the whole principle of the collective agreement.

---

¹ *Vos'moi S"ezd Professional'nykh Soyuzov SSSR* (1929), pp. 30, 332.
² *Obzor Deyatel'nosti NKT SSSR za 1927–1928 gg.* (1928), p. 84.

CHAPTER 20

TRADE UNIONS

(a) Organization and Policy

THE processes which determined the evolution of the trade unions in the middle nineteen-twenties [1] operated with gathering force throughout the rest of the decade. Industrial expansion and improved organization ensured a rising membership. By the middle of 1926 the trade unions had 9,278,000 members, two years later more than 11 millions.[2] A break-down of trade union membership on April 1, 1927, classified the members by occupation as follows (in thousands) :

Agriculture	1,122·3
Industry	3,456·1
Building	624·8
Transport and Communications	1,556·9
Employees	2,556·7
Communal Services	244·4
Food Industries	267·4
Total	9,828·6 [3]

Owing to the structure of Soviet trade unions, which included all workers of every grade in the same branch of production, technical and clerical staffs belonged to the same unions as manual workers ; thus 12·6 per cent of members of industrial unions, 25·3 per cent of transport workers and 33·4 per cent of all trade unionists were

[1] See *Socialism in One Country, 1924–1926*, Vol. 1, pp. 409-416.
[2] *Sed'moi S"ezd Professional'nykh Soyuzov SSSR* (1927), p. 76 ; *Vos'moi S"ezd Professional'nykh Soyuzov SSSR* (1929), p. 57 ; for a detailed breakdown of these totals by union and by region see *Professional'nye Soyuzy SSSR, 1924–1926: Otchet k VII S"ezdu* (1926), pp. 19-25 ; *Professional'nye Soyuzy SSSR, 1926–1928: Otchet k VIII S"ezdu* (1928), pp. 25-34. For earlier figures see *Socialism in One Country, 1924–1926*, Vol. 1, p. 410.
[3] *Spravochnik Partiinogo Rabotnika*, vi (1928), ii, 575-576 (the total has been corrected).

non-manual workers.[1] But Tomsky at the fifteenth party conference in October 1926 rebutted a suggestion that the increase in
trade union membership consisted largely of employees.[2]
The rapid growth of the unions diluted the hard core of
experienced industrial workers round which the unions had originally been built, and emphasized the rôle of the unions as representatives of a potential, rather than of an existing, proletariat.
The persistence of unemployment bred a sense of helplessness
among the workers. " The passive attitude of some groups of
workers to entry into the trade unions " was deplored in the party
journal. It was necessary to exclude from the union " obstinate
non-payers ", who were three months in arrears with their dues ;
in a Kharkov locomotive factory 20,000 workers were reported to
have been expelled from the union for non-payment of dues.[3] A
hostile critic from Leningrad attributed the weakness of the
unions to the large peasant element in the labour force :

> In the fearful years of devastation and hunger a large part of
> the mass of workers was dissolved in the peasant cauldron
> (kotel), and renewed its link with the land. New cadres are
> being formed in the corrupting environment of terror, and
> simply do not know what an organized proletarian struggle is.[4]

The emphasis already laid in 1925 on the educational and cultural
work of the trade unions and on the indoctrination of the new
working class [5] became increasingly apposite in the ensuing period.
A new philosophy of trade union leadership emerged, and was
expounded by Kuibyshev in unqualified terms at the fourth
plenum of Vesenkha in November 1928 :

> It is wrong to think that the trade unions are some arith-
> metical aggregate of all the workers in a given enterprise, and
> that the will of the trade unions, their line, is expressed by a
> majority of persons belonging to a given organization raising
> their hands and taking a particular decision. This would not

[1] Sed'moi S"ezd Professional'nykh Soyuzov SSSR (1927), p. 77.
[2] XV Konferentsiya Vsesoyuznoi Kommunisticheskoi Partii (B) (1927), pp.
267-268.
[3] Bol'shevik, No. 23-24, December 31, 1928, pp. 37-38, 42.
[4] Sotsialisticheskii Vestnik (Berlin), No. 10 (176), May 18, 1928, p. 13 ; for
the influx of peasants into urban employment see pp. 453-454 above.
[5] See Socialism in One Country, 1924-1926, Vol. 1, p. 411.

be a Bolshevik approach, it would be tail-endism. . . . It is necessary to lead the masses, to direct them along a definite line, to set oneself definite aims and to bring about the achievement of these aims by exercising leadership of the corresponding section of the working class.[1]

These anomalous conditions helped to explain not only a lack of solidarity among the rank and file of the unions, but what was often noted and deplored in party circles — the " bureaucratization " of the unions and the loss of contact between leaders and mass membership. It was remarked that only a small proportion of those elected to the executive organs of the unions or even of delegates to trade union congresses and conferences were now workers from the bench.[2] A new class of trade union officials had grown up and had taken charge. The " triangle " or " triple alliance " of party, management and trade unions in control of industry had been cautiously discussed at the fourteenth party congress in December 1925, and had led to fears of a " managerial deviation " in the unions ; [3] and it was the subject of some sharp criticism in an article in the party journal in July 1926, which detected " a sort of ' growing together ' of trade union organs with economic organizations ".[4] Tomsky took up the challenge at the fifteenth party conference in October 1926. He claimed that the " economic deviation " of constant support of the managers by the trade unions had been " to a significant extent overcome ", but admitted that the " triangle " sometimes led to passivity in the unions, and that in disputes between managers and workers the trade union representatives were inclined to stand aside ; an interrupter later in the proceedings exclaimed that there was " no

---

[1] *Torgovo-Promyshlennaya Gazeta*, November 30, 1928 ; for " tail-endism " see *The Bolshevik Revolution, 1917–1923*, Vol. 1, p. 18.

[2] *Pravda*, July 23, 1927 ; this was quoted in the 1927 platform of the opposition (L. Trotsky, *The Real Situation in Russia* (n.d. [1928]), p. 51). The party central committee at this time passed a resolution requiring that, in elections to trade union (and cooperative) congresses, steps should be taken to ensure " adequate representation of non-party people, of women and workers at lower levels, and also of rank-and-file members " (*Izvestiya Tsentral'nogo Komiteta VKP(B)*, No. 22-23 (195-196), July 17, 1927, p. 5).

[3] See *Socialism in One Country, 1924–1926*, Vol. 1, pp. 399-401, 417 ; in the individual factory the " triangle " consisted of secretary of the party cell, director of the factory and president of the trade union factory committee (see L. Trotsky, *The Real Situation in Russia* (n.d. [1928]), p. 51).

[4] *Bol'shevik*, No. 13, July 15, 1926, pp. 49-50.

triangle, but a one-angle ", i.e. a managerial monopoly.[1] At the seventh trade union congress in the following month, Andreev read a lesson to the trade unions themselves. The managers, he admitted, were sometimes indifferent to the wages and to the material needs of the workers, and attempted to exclude the trade unions from participation in economic questions. On the other hand, the trade unions often fell into " a narrow workshop deviation ", which made them concentrate exclusively on " the defence of the material interests of their members " and forget that their rôle in the proletarian state also included " direct participation in the work of socialist construction ".[2] The congress warned the trade unions against two opposite deviations : a " narrow workshop attitude " which ignored the rôle of the unions in socialist construction, and neglect of the economic interests of the workers reflected in unconditional support of managers and economic organs.[3]

The factor which first seriously undermined the independence of the trade unions was the drive for increased productivity of labour. When the trade unions were called on to throw their full weight behind the campaign for the régime of economy, Tomsky's sophisticated argument that, under the dictatorship of the proletariat, " the interests of today must be subordinated to the general class interests of tomorrow and of the ensuing period of time "[4] was more likely to appeal to the party conference to which it was addressed than to workers engaged in a harsh struggle for bare means of subsistence. The dilemma of an organization whose professed function was to defend the interests of the workers, but which could not perform that function without incurring the charge of setting the organization in opposition to the party and to the workers' state, could not really be turned by the assurance that separate interests of the workers did not in practice exist. It would, however, be premature to assume that the unions at this time had no independent policy or outlook of their own, or that they did not defend the interests of their members. According to a delegate at the seventh trade union congress in December 1926, an old trade union placard with a rhymed couplet to the effect that " the worker alone is weak, the trade union defends him from the

[1] XV Konferentsiya Vsesoyuznoi Kommunisticheskoi Partii (B) (1927), pp. 274, 321.   [2] Sed'moi S"ezd Professional'nykh Soyuzov SSSR (1927), p. 717. [3] Ibid. p. 796.   [4] See p. 491 above.

employers' clutches " could still be seen even in state enterprises and institutions.[1] During the second half of 1926 and the greater part of 1927 the issue of the relation of wages to productivity was the subject of constant and often bitter debate between the trade unions and Vesenkha, which was carried on at conferences and congresses and in the columns of their respective newspapers.[2] The attempt to secure priority for trade union members in applications for employment was a conspicuous example of the defence of a sectional interest. A rare attempt by a trade union organ to enforce restrictive practices was recorded in 1926, but was quickly overruled. Women workers in a Yaroslavl textile factory volunteered to work four looms instead of two. The proposal was vetoed by the provincial section of the textile workers' union ; but on appeal to the trade union central council the decision was reversed.[3]

With the advent of planning the situation was more clearly defined. The thesis that planning under socialism involved the participation of the workers through their trade unions took little account of the position of the rank-and-file membership and seemed in existing circumstances utopian. One delegate at the seventh trade union congress in December 1926 declared that workers were " automatically regarded as military conscripts ", whom it was not necessary to consult, and that, when meetings of workers were summoned, only a small proportion thought it worth while to attend. Krol, the strong-minded president of the food workers' union, complained that " the trade unions cannot take an appropriate part in the framing of the plan, since everything is done in a hurry, figures are not checked, and are sometimes simply invented ".[4] The trade unions were in a cleft stick. They could not resist the principle of planning, which in any case meant the expansion of industry and of the industrial proletariat. Yet planning meant the submission of the unions to the planning authority. The unions were integrated slowly but surely into the structure of government.[5]

[1] *Sed'moi S"ezd Professional'nykh Soyuzov SSSR* (1927), p. 175.
[2] See pp. 491-495 above.
[3] *Pervye Shagi Industrializatsii SSSR 1926–1927 gg.* (1959), p. 274.
[4] *Sed'moi S"ezd Professional'nykh Soyuzov SSSR* (1927), pp. 96, 532.
[5] For the anomalous position of members of trade unions in private industry see Note E, pp. 938-939 below.

Closer links between trade union and planning authorities led to an increasing centralization which was reflected in friction between the trade union central council and individual unions. Radchenko complained at the fifteenth party conference in October 1926 of " syndicalist tendencies " among some Ukrainian trade unionists, who believed that all would be well if the unions were left alone and not interfered with from the centre.[1] A month later, in advance of the seventh trade union congress, Krol published an article criticizing the central council for abuse of its power, and arguing that " only in exceptional cases, in extremely important questions ", should the council put decisions into effect without consulting the central committees of the unions.[2] Tomsky at the congress denounced this attitude as " complete decentralization " leading to " federalism " — the weakness which had brought about the defeat of the British general strike. He went on :

> We will not play at hide-and-seek, we will say straight out that we have centralization of the trade union movement. We will not conceal from anyone that the trade union movement has been led, is led, and will be led, by the VKP, by the party of the working class.

The leadership of the party could be realized only " in a centralized way ".[3] Krol retorted angrily that the central council had made its pronouncement on the wage increases in the previous August without consulting the central committees of the unions, and had fixed the age of admission to the unions at 16 in defiance of the statutes of unions which admitted youths at 14.[4] But such protests represented a struggle of lesser against greater bureaucrats rather than of rank-and-file members against bureaucracy.

[1] *XV Konferentsiya Vsesoyuznoi Kommunisticheskoi Partii (B)* (1927), p. 375.
[2] *Trud*, November 19, 1926.
[3] *Sed'moi S"ezd Professional'nykh Soyuzov SSSR* (1927), pp. 47-48 ; according to the report of Tomsky's speech in *Trud*, December 8, 1926, he prefaced the passage on party leadership with a remark which was omitted from the official record : " Our trade union organizations are still not sufficiently well educated not to need a stern hand ". One of the weapons of centralized control was financial : Tomsky claimed that the central council had carried out a " purification " of the finances of a number of trade union organizations. For previous denunciations of " federalism " in the trade union movement see *Socialism in One Country, 1924–1926*, Vol. 1, pp. 413-414.
[4] *Sed'moi S"ezd Professional'nykh Soyuzov SSSR* (1927), p. 102.

The struggle took one particularly acute form. For several years a rivalry had existed between the central committees of individual trade unions and regional inter-union organizations which purported to deal locally with matters of common concern to all unions, and were supported by the trade union central council. The draft resolution on organization submitted by the council to the seventh trade union congress in December 1926 contained a section delimiting the respective functions of the central committees of unions and the regional inter-union organizations, and providing that decisions of the trade union central council of a " general character " should be communicated to lower trade union organs, not by the central committees of the unions, but by the regional inter-union organizations. This proposal excited violent opposition at the congress, being denounced by one delegate as the revival of a long-standing ambition of the central council to fuse all trade unions into a " single union ". When the representative of the central council at last offered to withdraw the unpopular proposal, he was not permitted to do so, and it was voted down by a large majority.[1] It may be doubted whether this gesture of independence — the last occasion on which a trade union congress defied the wishes of the central council — did much to curb the growing monopoly of power in the hands of the official leaders. So long as the central council was the repository of party authority and party policy in the trade unions, its position was both theoretically and practically impregnable. As Kaganovich, more flat-footed than Tomsky and less alive to trade union tradition, had told the third Ukrainian trade union congress a few days earlier, it was necessary " *to educate the workers in the spirit of the unity of interests of the working class and of the Soviet state, of the unity of interests of the trade unions and of the Bolshevik party* " : in fact, " the party and the trade unions are something inseparable ".[2]

The year 1927 was probably the high-water mark in the attempt to gear the trade unions into the machinery of production

---

[1] For the text of the proposal and the vote see *Sed'moi S"ezd Professional'-nykh Soyuzov SSSR* (1927), pp. 870-871, 873 ; for the attack on it *ibid.* p. 188.

[2] *Stenograficheskii Otchet 3-go Vseukrainskogo S"ezda Profsoyuzov* (1927), pp. 310-311 ; for earlier pronouncements see *Socialism in One Country, 1924-1926*, Vol. 1, pp. 412-413.

and planning without wholly undermining their independent rôle
as the mouthpiece of the workers.   A joint *communiqué* of Vesenkha
and the trade union central council of March 10, 1927, announced
that a trade union representative would henceforth be present at
all meetings of the presidium of Vesenkha with a consultative
voice.[1]   This gave the trade unions a tenuous footing in the
supreme organ responsible for the management of industry ; and,
while it did nothing to promote cooperation between managers
and workers at factory level,[2] it may have helped to ease relations
between the principal officials concerned in the framing of industrial and trade union policy.   While the vexed question of productivity and wages continued to give trouble, caution and conciliation prevailed on both sides.   Throughout 1927 it was above all
necessary to present a united front to the opposition ; and Tomsky
was a key figure in the Politburo.   Tomsky's speech at the fifteenth party congress in December 1927 was devoted to trouncing
the opposition, and raised no trade union issues at all ; and Dogadov, another leading member of the trade union central council,
confined himself to a modest complaint that the makers of the five-
year plan paid insufficient attention to labour questions.[3]   But, once
the policy of planning had been endorsed by the congress, the
opposition crushed and expelled, and a programme of industrialization adopted which necessitated a still more intensive drive for
increased productivity with curbs on consumption, the crisis could
not be long delayed.   It is difficult to judge how far Tomsky's
association with the Right opposition in 1928 was due to realization that large-scale planned industrialization would bring to an
end the traditional rôle and status of the trade unions, or how far
his association with the Right placed the trade unions in a position
of sharper opposition than might otherwise have developed to the
official policy.

A cloud on the horizon, which at first attracted little notice,
presaged the coming storm.   For more than two years acute
friction had occurred between the trade unions and the Komsomol over problems of juvenile labour ;[4] and the Komsomol

[1] *Spravochnik Partiinogo Rabotnika*, vi (1928), ii, 527.
[2] For the production conferences which were intended to serve this purpose
see pp. 568-573 below.
[3] *Pyatnadtsatyi S"ezd VKP(B)*, ii (1962), 919.   [4] See pp. 474-480 above.

newspaper, *Komsomol'skaya Pravda*, had thrown itself into the fray with its usual controversial vigour.[1] In May 1928, about the time when the Right opposition was beginning to take shape, Stalin spoke at the closing session of the eighth Komsomol congress. He took as his theme the evils of " bureaucratism ", mentioning the trade unions among the organs in which this disease was prevalent ; and he urged the Komsomol and its newspaper *Komsomol'skaya Pravda* to be active in the struggle against it. A week later, on the occasion of its third anniversary, *Komsomol'-skaya Pravda* printed a congratulatory message from Stalin hailing it as " a warning bell, which awakes sleepers, encourages the weary, drives on laggards, and scourges the bureaucratism of our institutions ".[2] Whether or not such words reflected a deliberate policy, the knowledge that the Komsomol enjoyed Stalin's patronage must have encouraged the campaign against the trade unions and the trade union newspaper *Trud*, which was conducted in the columns of *Komsomol'skaya Pravda* with increasing asperity during the summer and autumn of 1928. Early in June 1928, the party central committee publicly referred to " violations of democracy " in the trade unions, and urged the party fractions in them to combat the growth of " bureaucratism ".[3] A meeting of the party fraction in the presidium of the trade union central council on November 9, 1928, discussed the position of Yaglom, the editor of *Trud*, who had evidently been under attack in party circles for his controversy with *Komsomol'skaya Pravda*. Melnichansky ironically referred to those who made a profession of seeking out Right deviations ; and Yaglom complained that a situation had been created round the trade unions in which it was impossible to work — " a state of total collapse ".[4] According to reports reaching Trotsky in Alma-Ata, Lozovsky, Tomsky's rival and Stalin's principal henchman in the trade union central council, denounced the way in which delegates were being chosen for the forthcoming trade union

---

[1] The party central committee, in a long congratulatory message to *Komsomol'skaya Pravda* on its second anniversary on July 13, 1927, had warned its editors to exercise " a stricter check on denunciatory material " (*Spravochnik Partiinogo Rabotnika*, vi (1928), ii, 171-173) ; this evidently referred to its quarrel with the trade unions.

[2] Stalin, *Sochineniya*, xi, 72-74, 78.

[3] *Pravda*, June 3, 1928.

[4] *XVI S"ezd Vsesoyuznoi Kommunisticheskoi Partii (B)* (1930), p. 680.

T 2

congress, but was voted down by the majority.¹

Relations between the industrialists and the trade unions also deteriorated at this time, perhaps not without some prompting from Stalin.² Throughout the summer and autumn of 1928 the industrial managers kept up an active campaign against the unions for their alleged unwillingness to check breaches of labour discipline in the interests of increased productivity. A protest from Birman, the director of Yugostal, to the Ukrainian committee of the mineworkers' union was ignored ; and at a meeting of the Ukrainian party central committee the representative of the mineworkers was said to have been the only member to dissent from measures proposed to improve discipline and raise productivity.³ *Trud* was accused of persistently playing down the evils of indiscipline, absenteeism and other abuses.⁴ The trade unions were suspected of giving surreptitious encouragement to the growing animosity of the workers against managers and specialists.⁵ It was on the eve of the session of the party central committee in November 1928 that the first open dissensions occurred in the Politburo on the rate of industrialization; Bukharin, Rykov and Tomsky for the first time directly challenged the policy of the majority.⁶ The trade union question is not known to have played any specific part in this quarrel. But the resolution adopted at the session on the recruitment of members to the party contained a significant passage which, though couched in general terms, referred primarily and directly to the trade unions :

Our mass organizations (trade unions etc.) often do not show the necessary sensitivity to the needs and demands of men and women workers, in many cases lag behind the growing activity of the masses, and therefore altogether inadequately utilize their immense potentialities for mobilization of the resources of the working class to solve the fundamental tasks confronting it,

¹ Trotsky archives, T 2850.
² Stalin, in a letter to Kuibyshev of August 31, 1928, wrote : " I hear that Tomsky intends to slate you. He is a malicious man, and not always honest. I think he is wrong. I read your report on rationalization. A sound report. What more does Tomsky want of you ? " (Stalin, *Sochineniya*, xi, 220 ; for a further quotation from this letter see p. 909 below.)
³ *Torgovo-Promyshlennaya Gazeta*, September 12, 1928.
⁴ *Ibid.* September 7, 1928.
⁵ See pp. 588-589 below.   ⁶ See pp. 92-93 above.

and to overcome the difficulties involved in the building of socialism.

The trade unions were also warned to be more active among new workers recently recruited to industry and among agricultural workers, and to conduct " a relentless struggle against a bureaucratic divorce from the workers ".[1] Tomsky's ingenious formula of reconciliation of the short-term and long-term interests of the worker[2] no longer sufficed. Kuibyshev, in his reply to the debate at the fourth plenum of Vesenkha in November 1928, demanded a less equivocal recognition of priorities : trade union organizations could serve as a channel for workers' interests " in so far as that is necessary in our conditions ".[3] *Pravda* called for a strengthening of party leadership in the trade unions, and published a further article accusing them of " a conspiracy of silence " about the important issues confronting them.[4] A leading article in the industrial newspaper described bad discipline in the factories as " an almost universal phenomenon ", and repeated the charge that managers received insufficient support from the trade unions.[5]

The session of the party central committee had one unexpected sequel. Shmidt was deposed from the post of People's Commissar for Labour, which he had occupied for ten years, and was replaced by Uglanov.[6] Since Shmidt had always been an exponent of an independent trade union policy, it was reasonable to connect his loss of office with the desire of a majority of the Politburo to establish firmer control over the unions.[7] The motive of Uglanov's appointment was probably desire to remove him from the key

---

[1] *KPSS v Rezolyutsiyakh* (1954), ii, 542 ; a charge of insufficient attention to " the defence of the daily needs of the workers " had already been levelled at the trade unions by the party central committee in April 1928 (*ibid.* ii, 509).

[2] See p. 491 above.

[3] *Torgovo-Promyshlennaya Gazeta*, November 30, 1928 ; for this speech see p. 510 above.   [4] *Pravda*, November 21, 24, 1928.

[5] *Torgovo-Promyshlennaya Gazeta*, November 29, 1928.

[6] *Pravda*, November 30, 1928 ; *Trud*, November 30, 1928. The announcement in *Trud* revealed that Uglanov's name had been formally proposed by the presidium of the trade union central council three days earlier ; Tomsky's statement to the council proposing confirmation of the appointment was reported *ibid.* December 8, 1928.

[7] For a striking instance of favour shown by Shmidt to the trade unions see *The Interregnum, 1923–1924*, p. 66.

position of secretary of the Moscow party organization.[1] He did not play any significant rôle in Narkomtrud, and held the post of People's Commissar only for a few months. The clash with the Right opposition on industrialization had revealed a danger that Tomsky might encourage trade union opposition to the demands of the planners ; and it was clear that the impending eighth trade union congress would be a crucial occasion.

When Tomsky opened the congress on December 10, 1928, when Rykov made a ceremonial speech of greeting on behalf of the party central committee and the Soviet Government, and when on the next day Tomsky delivered the usual report of the central council to the congress, and received the usual ovation on its conclusion,[2] the proceedings seemed normal and harmonious. The first danger signal was an article in *Pravda* on December 12, 1928, which warned the trade unions against taking an " a-political " line, and paying insufficient attention to " the new tasks of the reconstruction period ". This was a revival of the old charge against the unions of encouraging a narrow " workshop " attitude, and neglecting the higher needs of production. The article concluded with a reference to " the bureaucratic ossification of a part of the trade union apparatus ". Such criticism from *Pravda*, launched at the outset of an important congress, was a political move. It was at once denounced at the congress by Kozelev, one of the leaders of the metal workers and a member of the trade union central council, who bluntly called it " a slander on the trade union movement ", and compared it with the attacks on the unions in recent weeks in *Komsomol'skaya Pravda*. He detected in it " a contemptuous attitude to the consumer interest of the working masses " and " a recrudescence of Trotskyism " — reminiscent of Trotsky's policy in the famous trade union controversy of 1921. The road to industrialization could be paved only by " an increase of attention to the ' personal ' day-to-day interests and needs of the working masses ".[3] The *Pravda* article opened the way for the violent speech delivered at the congress by Zhdanov, a leading member of the central committee of the Komsomol. This, for the first time in public, included a veiled attack on Tomsky. In

[1] For Uglanov's misdemeanour see pp. 88-89, 91-92 above.
[2] *Vos'moi S"ezd Professional'nykh Soyuzov SSSR* (1929), pp. 3-6, 10-14, 24-55.   [3] *Ibid.* pp. 95-97.

what was no doubt a carefully pondered phrase, Zhdanov observed that " he who cannot perceive the full depth of our disagreements of principle . . . will not be able, as is necessary, to strengthen in his daily work the link between these two organizations in the task of serving the young worker ". Tomsky in his reply to the debate tore aside the veil : commenting on " the disagreeable tone, the disagreeable character " of Zhdanov's speech, he added that " it seems as though Zhdanov is demanding the replacement of Tomsky ".[1] The link between the future of the trade unions and Tomsky's own political fate had been brought into the open.

Tomsky's speech in reply to the debate on the report was followed by another painful incident. The debates on organization which had occupied the seventh congress were resumed at the eighth congress two years later ; and charges of " centralization " and counter-charges of " federalism " were exchanged.[2] Tomsky, in his reply to the debate, spoke of a " healthy centralism " which consisted in the control exercised by the central council, and declared emphatically that, " *if we are to maintain in the country a single trade union movement based on the principle of democratic centralism, such centralism on our part there will be* ".[3] Krol, who had drawn fire on this issue at the previous congress, did not speak in the debate : he was no longer president of the food workers' union, though he retained his seat on the central council pending fresh elections at the congress. But, when at the end of Tomsky's reply, the usual resolution was submitted formally approving the report and activity of the central council, Krol rose to submit an alternative resolution. The text of his proposal did not appear in the records. As soon as he attempted to read it, he was met with shouts of " Shakhty affair " and " Down with the Mensheviks ". The president, having curtly dismissed Krol's counter-resolution as " Menshevik ", put the original motion to the vote. It was approved unanimously. A delegate then rose to denounce Krol's

[1] *Vos'moi S"ezd Professional'nykh Soyuzov SSSR* (1929), pp. 110-111, 193. In quoting Zhdanov's phrase, Tomsky made the reference to himself more pointed by substituting " the leader who " for " he who " ; it is impossible to be sure which was the authentic text, but the difference was slight. For further details of Zhdanov's speech see p. 480 above ; the brief press report in *Trud*, December 15, 1928, omitted the controversial passages.
[2] *Vos'moi S"ezd Professional'nykh Soyuzov SSSR* (1929), pp. 74-75, 90.
[3] *Ibid.* pp. 199-200.

" sally ", which he ranged with " the Shakhty affair " and " the Trotsky affair " as attempts " to divert the proletariat from the true Leninist path ". He proposed to deprive Krol of his mandate (as a member of the central council he was a " consultative ", though not a voting, delegate), and to expel him from the union. Tomsky followed. He thought it deplorable that " undisciplined members of our party " should behave in a way which made them " undistinguishable from Mensheviks " ; this showed " how far Trotskyism has gone ". The party of Lenin needed " not only iron, but steel, discipline ". It was open to the congress to deprive Krol of his mandate, though, since Krol would presumably not be re-elected to the central council, this was an empty gesture. He begged the congress not to expel Krol from the union : this was a penalty which should be reserved for " a very heinous crime against the working class ". The proposal to expel Krol was silently dropped. When the vote was taken to deprive him of his mandate only four dissentient votes were recorded, with two abstentions.[1] Ironically, this halting and embarrassed utterance was Tomsky's last appearance on a trade union platform. At a later session Shmidt delivered a valedictory speech, in which he described himself, without further explanation, as " a former worker in Narkomtrud ".[2] Uglanov did not appear at the congress, and the spokesman for Narkomtrud was Tolstopyatov, the deputy commissar.

The party was now clearly bent on intervention. The Politburo proposed that a representative of the party central committee should be appointed to the presidium of the trade union central council ; Kaganovich, who for the past three years had been secretary of the Ukrainian party, was designated for the post.[3] Since the evident purpose was to supervise and curb Tomsky's activities, it is not surprising that he resisted it on the ground that such an arrangement would create a " dual centre " ; and, in the wrangle which followed in the party fraction of the trade union delegation, he obtained the support of other trade union leaders.[4]

---

[1] *Vos'moi S"ezd Professional'nykh Soyuzov SSSR* (1929), pp. 206-207.
[2] *Ibid.* p. 317.
[3] According to *Sotsialisticheskii Vestnik* (Berlin), No. 7-8, April 12, 1929, p. 20, Kaganovich, a former trade union worker, was well regarded in the trade union movement, where he had supported Tomsky against Lozovsky in the affairs of the Anglo-Russian committee and of relations with IFTU.
[4] Information on this episode is derived from the resolution of the party

Exactly what transpired is not clear. But the will of the party prevailed. Tomsky's long report and reply to the debate were, as usual, printed in *Trud* in several instalments, which were completed only on December 21, 1928. Thereafter Tomsky's name disappeared for many months from the columns of *Trud*, and was never again mentioned except in terms of opprobrium. On December 24, 1928, the party fraction, having heard a report by Dogadov, endorsed " wholly and completely " the November resolution of the party central committee, which had rejected " moods appearing in the ranks of the party directed to a weakening of the tempo of industrialization ". The fraction declared that the Soviet trade union movement had " never taken its stand on a workshop, so-called ' purely workers' ', point of view ", and called for " mobilization of the working masses and of the toilers in the countryside for the active performance of the tasks of socialism ". The resolution ended by stressing the need for an " intensified struggle against the Right danger and against any compromise with it ".[1] No allusion was made to the question of the leadership. On the same evening the congress held its final meeting to approve the outstanding resolutions and to elect the central council. Tomsky, Kaganovich and Uglanov all appeared among the 234 members elected, Tomsky's name still standing first on the list. Dogadov then made the formal speech bringing the congress to a close. The trade unions, he declared, would " *march boldly and unflinchingly along the path marked out by a Leninist party and a Leninist central committee* " — the path of " *a strengthening of the tempo of industrialization* ".[2] Nobody referred to Tomsky's

---

central committee of February 9, 1929 (see p. 561 below), and from an account in *Voprosy Istorii KPSS*, No. 4, 1960, p. 71, which is based on unpublished archives, but quotes no documents textually. The trade unions under Tomsky were said to have favoured " a weakening of the activity of the trade unions in socialist construction ", to have " cultivated political neutralism, a closed workshop attitude ", and to have " opposed the organization of emulation and shock work ". On the other hand, Tomsky and his friends found a Trotskyite flavour in the proposed " shake-up " of the trade unions (see *The Bolshevik Revolution, 1917–1923*, Vol. 2, p. 221) ; Trotsky had also been the first champion of " shock work " (*ibid.* Vol. 2, p. 217).

[1] *Vos'moi S"ezd Professional'nykh Soyuzov SSSR* (1929), pp. 504-505 ; the resolution, which was first published in *Pravda*, December 29, 1928, was printed with the records of the congress.

[2] *Vos'moi S"ezd Professional'nykh Soyuzov SSSR* (1929), pp. 573-574, 579-580.

absence. At some point during these proceedings he tendered his resignation as president of the central council,[1] and silently disappeared from the scene where he had so long and so recently been the principal actor.

The congress devoted considerable attention to the cultural and educational work of the trade unions.[2] The seventh congress in December 1926 had adopted a lengthy resolution dealing with such familiar topics as workers' clubs, adult education, the liquidation of illiteracy, the need for popular libraries and literary and technical publications, sport and physical culture.[3] At the eighth congress two years later a new emphasis was apparent. The *rapporteur* on the question claimed that " the tasks of cultural and educational work " were " linked in the closest and most direct way with the fundamental economic and political tasks of the working class "; this was because " the reconstruction of the economy presupposes a corresponding cultural growth in the masses ".[4] The resolution of the congress on organization spoke of " new workers arriving from the countryside ", who were " without experience of the class struggle and least dependable in the class sense ", and were liable to " the influence of petty bourgeois elements " and to " purely consumer attitudes ". The trade unions must " take all steps to raise their cultural level, to defend their economic interests, and to explain to them the necessity of increasing by all means the productivity of labour, of reducing absenteeism, etc.". This was the function of the " agitational and cultural work " of the unions.[5] The resolution on cultural and educational work opened with the statement that " *its fundamental purpose* " was to prepare the broad masses of the proletariat " *for conscious and active participation in socialist construction* ", and referred once more to workers newly arrived from the countryside who were " inclined to stand aside from the basic mass of proletarians, from its interests and its social life ". In

[1] At the seventeenth party congress in December 1934 Tomsky expressed remorse for his " completely impermissible, self-willed departure from the post of president of the trade union central council ", and added that this had compelled the party central committee to " remove the whole leadership of the trade unions " (*XVII S"ezd Vsesoyuznoi Kommunisticheskoi Partii (B)* (1934), p. 144).   [2] See p. 546 above.
[3] *Sed'moi S"ezd Professional'nykh Soyuzov SSSR* (1927), pp. 766-781.
[4] *Vos'moi S"ezd Professional'nykh Soyuzov SSSR* (1929), p. 699.
[5] *Ibid.* p. 514.

addition to a reiteration of the well-known forms of activity, the resolution contained a novel section on " questions of daily life ".

This exhorted the trade unions " to intensify their struggle against such phenomena as drunkenness, gambling, uncultural habits of behaviour, a brutal attitude to women, and other survivals of the old way of life ". Among these survivals were cited the preaching of religion, " the kindling of national dissension and hatred " and, in particular, anti-Semitism : the trade unions were to " *intensify the struggle against anti-Semitism, revealing its counter-revolutionary essence and unmasking all the evil of an indifferent and passive attitude to it* ". The concluding paragraph of the resolution looked forward to " *the consummation of the cultural revolution* as the indispensable and most important prerequisite of the socialist transformation of society ".[1] The conception of the new man, regenerated intellectually and morally by the revolution, blended with the conception of the new industrial worker, schooled by proletarian discipline for the factory where the building of socialism would proceed. The task of forming and educating the new man and the new worker had become a major responsibility of the trade unions.

For three months Tomsky and Kaganovich were both members of the presidium of the trade union central council, though there is no evidence to show what part either of them took in the proceedings. On February 9, 1929, a joint session of the Politburo and of the presidium of the party central control commission recited Tomsky's offences side by side with those of Bukharin, accused him of carving out for himself a " feudal principality in the trade unions ", and summoned him " loyally to carry out all decisions of IKKI, of the party and of its central committee ".[2] Finally, on April 23, 1929, the party central committee, in passing sentence on the Right opposition, detailed its errors in trade union affairs :

> In the question of the trade unions, Bukharin, Rykov and Tomsky stand for a dangerous opposition of the trade unions to the party, carry on in practice a course designed to weaken party leadership of the trade union movement, play down defects in trade union work, conceal " trade-unionist " tendencies and

[1] *Ibid.* pp. 531-532, 542, 546 ; Dogadov in his report to the congress had mentioned a revival of anti-Semitism and clericalism, especially in White Russia (*ibid.* p. 66).   [2] *KPSS v Rezolyutsiyakh* (1954), ii, 556-567.

562 THE ECONOMIC ORDER PT. I

phenomena of bureaucratic rigidity in part of the trade union apparatus, and depict the struggle of the party with these defects as a Trotskyite " shake-up " of the trade unions.

The resolution ended by relieving Tomsky of his post in the trade union central council.[1] With the trade union leadership in total disarray, no spokesman of the unions addressed the sixteenth party conference in April 1929. Shatskin, the Komsomol delegate, recalled the controversy between *Komsomol'skaya Pravda* and *Trud* in the previous autumn, classed Tomsky with those who had been blind to the " serious maladies " of the trade unions, and demanded a " radical reformation " of their methods.[2] But this attack stirred no echo ; and otherwise the trade unions were scarcely mentioned throughout the proceedings.[3] When the trade union central council met at the end of May 1929 for the first time since the fateful congress of December 1928, it complied with the party ruling by removing Tomsky from his post as member and president of the presidium, and by appointing a secretariat of five which included Dogadov and Shvernik.[4] During the session, on May 29, 1929, the party fraction in the council held a meeting at which it accused the Right of resisting the policies of rapid industrialization, the five-year plan, and pressure on the *kulak*, and of standing for " a most dangerous opposition of the trade unions to the party ", and expressed its entire approval of the desire of the party central committee to strengthen party leadership in the trade unions.[5]

Five years later, speakers at the seventeenth party congress of December 1934 attempted to provide an explanation and justification of these events. Kaganovich depicted Tomsky as wedded to

---

[1] *KPSS v Rezolyutsiyakh* (1954), ii, 554-556 ; for these sessions see p. 247-248, 250-252 above. The term " trade-unionist " in the resolution represents a Russian transliteration of the English word — the customary method of condemning a non-political, non-party attitude in the unions (see *The Bolshevik Revolution, 1917-1923*, Vol. 2, p. 101).

[2] *Shestnadtsataya Konferentsiya VKP(B)* (1962), pp. 115-116.

[3] For the appeal to the workers, which included an instruction to " trade unions and economic organs " to " apply on a broad scale a system of *encouragement* of those who participate in emulation ", see p. 513 above.

[4] *Trud*, June 2, 1929.

[5] The long resolution adopted at this meeting was published " with abbreviations " in *Pravda*, June 9, 1929, together with an article summarizing it and stressing its importance ; the *Pravda* text, further abbreviated by the omission of a fierce attack on the Right opposition and on the Trotskyites, is in *Profsoyuzy SSSR* (1963), ii, 487-491.

the view that the defence of the interests of the workers was incompatible with participation in the management of industry, and declared that throughout 1928 the trade union central council had never discussed problems of production. Tomsky, who appeared at the congress in the rôle of a penitent, confessed that he had " diverted the trade unions from tasks demanding the most rapid solution ".[1] Shvernik accused the Right opposition of " setting the trade unions against the party " ; and another delegate alleged that the former leaders had " persistently warned the unions against working to raise the productivity of labour, and opposed the defensive work of the unions to the tasks of participation in socialist construction ".[2] A grain of truth could be found in these extravagant charges. The onset of planning and industrialization had insensibly changed the rôle of the unions. The downfall of Tomsky and the adoption of the plan ended the period during which the trade unions had, with increasing difficulty, enjoyed a certain independence within the Soviet economy. Henceforth they would become an integral part of a vast machine geared to the implementation of an over-all economic plan. Increased pressure on the worker was dictated by the increasingly intense demands of industrialization ; and the shackling of the trade unions made it beyond question easier to apply.

(b) Industrial Disputes

The machinery for the settlement of industrial disputes, which had been a subject of complaint at the fourteenth party congress in December 1925,[3] began to work more effectively : 2426 disputes involving 3,212,300 workers were settled in 1925–1926, 3155 involving 2,463,000 workers in 1926–1927, and 2661 involving 1,874,300 workers in 1927–1928. Of disputes occurring in 1926–1927 12·9 per cent, and in 1927–1928 9·4 per cent, were with private employers ; but, in view of the small size of private enterprises, the number of workers involved in these disputes was insignificant.[4] The issues on which disputes occurred were classified as follows : rate of basic wage ; communal services supplied ;

[1] XVII S"ezd Vsesoyuznoi Kommunisticheskoi Partii (B) (1934), pp. 63, 144.   [2] Ibid. pp. 648, 680.
[3] See Socialism in One Country, 1924–1926, Vol. 1, p. 416.
[4] Obzor Deyatel'nosti NKT SSSR za 1927–1928 gg. (1928), pp. 90-91.

THE ECONOMIC ORDER PT. I

addition to wages ; compensation for dismissal or for non-utilized holidays ; procedure of engagement and dismissal ; and protection of labour.[1] The conclusion of the collective agreements was a prolific occasion for disputes. In 1927 43·2 per cent, and in 1928 22·9 per cent, of all workers covered by collective agreements were involved in disputes arising out of the negotiation of the agreements ; in the major industrial unions the proportion was higher still, rising in these years to 68·1 and 55·1 per cent for the metal workers and 55·4 and 33·8 for the textile workers.[2]

Concern continued to be expressed about the method of settling these disputes. The normal procedure was through a Conflict and Assessment Commission (RKK).[3] The seventh trade union congress in December 1926 pressed for a strengthening of the RKK, considered that " the organization and experience of the work of shop RKKs as auxiliary organs of the general factory RKK have given positive results ", and proposed that transport and such branches of industry as had not yet adopted this measure of decentralization should hasten to do so.[4] By 1928 84·9 per cent of all disputes were said to be settled by the RKKs.[5] Less satisfactory was what happened when the disagreement was not settled by the RKK, and became a " dispute " in the proper sense of the word. The labour code provided in that event for recourse to a conciliation court and, in the event of failure there, to an arbitral tribunal. It was perhaps indicative of the character of relations between workers and managers that the conciliation courts remained unpopular and ineffective. A joint appeal of the Narkomtrud of the RSFSR and the trade union central council to make more use of the conciliation courts [6] proved unavailing. A

---

[1] Obzor Deyatel'nosti NKT SSSR za 1927–1928 gg. (1928), pp. 94-95. Tomsky told the third Ukrainian trade union congress in November 1926 that the largest number of disputes occurred over the fixing of norms and assessments for piece-work (Stenograficheskii Otchet 3⁰⁰ Vseukrainskogo S"ezda Profsoyuzov (1927), p. 20). In 1927 with the rationalization campaign disputes about dismissals became common ; 10·9 per cent of all disputes (17·1 per cent in the textile industry, and 45·7 per cent among Soviet trade employees) were attributed to this cause (Professional'nye Soyuzy SSSR, 1926–1928: Otchet k VIII S"ezdu (1928), pp. 365-366).   [2] Ibid. p. 346.

[3] See Socialism in One Country, 1924–1926, Vol. 1, pp. 393, 416.

[4] Sed'moi S"ezd Professional'nykh Soyuzov SSSR (1927), pp. 788-789.

[5] Professional'nye Soyuzy SSSR, 1926–1928: Otchet k VIII S"ezdu (1928), p. 367 ; disputes about the negotiation of collective agreements were apparently not referred to the RKKs.   [6] Trud, June 4, 1926.

trade union delegate at the fifteenth party conference in October 1926 complained that " the managers, and in part also the trade unionists, are afraid to take responsibility for the conclusion of a collective agreement, and transfer the whole responsibility to a third party or a third force — the super-arbiter ".[1] At the seventh trade union congress a few weeks later Tomsky protested against the habit of referring " every trivial question . . . *direct to the arbitral tribunal*, avoiding the conciliation court " ; it was stated that 69 per cent of all disputes went direct to arbitration without being submitted to the conciliation courts at all. A delegate from the Ukraine declared that there " the work of the conciliation courts comes to nothing " and " their authority has collapsed completely ", and blamed the managers who refused to make any serious attempt at conciliation. The congress passed a resolution to " extend the practice of dealing with questions in conciliation courts " and to " relieve the arbitral tribunals of petty conflicts ".[2] Yet in the next two years not more than 20 per cent of outstanding disputes were settled there, the remainder being reserved for arbitration.[3]

Even the decision of the arbitral tribunal was not always final. The right of appeal to the labour sections of the People's Courts was supposed to be restricted to legal issues ; but this covered any alleged infringement of the labour code or of a collective agreement. Moreover, the dissatisfied party, if influential enough, could always appeal to the Narkomtrud of the republic or even to the Narkomtrud of the USSR to override the decision. Shmidt at the seventh trade union congress complained that, in this way, " the dismissal of a single worker sometimes costs the state several thousand rubles ".[4] A massive decree of August 29, 1928, attempted to clarify the situation by defining precisely the scope and competence of the organs concerned in the settlement of disputes, beginning with the RKKs, but introduced nothing new.[5] The spokesman of Narkomtrud at the eighth trade union congress in December 1928 again complained that the recommendations of the seventh congress had not been carried out, and that " the great mass of disputes

[1] *XV Konferentsiya Vsesoyuznoi Kommunisticheskoi Partii (B)* (1927), p. 382.
[2] *Sed'moi S"ezd Professional'nykh Soyuzov SSSR* (1927), pp. 56, 344, 394, 751.　　　[3] *Obzor Deyatel'nosti NKT SSSR za 1927–1928 gg.* (1928), p. 92.
[4] *Sed'moi S"ezd Professional'nykh Soyuzov SSSR* (1927), pp. 345-346.
[5] *Sobranie Zakonov, 1928*, No. 56, art. 495.

are settled by the vote of a super-arbiter, i.e. the manager and the unions try to unburden themselves of the responsibility and place it on the arbiter ".[1] But the resolution of the congress did no more than repeat the same exhortations that had been heard in the past.[2]

During this period strikes were almost completely, though never formally, eliminated from the armoury of the Soviet trade unions and of the Soviet worker. No large-scale wave of strikes, such as that which had marked the spring of 1925,[3] recurred. A distinction was sometimes drawn between strikes in nationalized and in private enterprises; but a strike in a private factory in Minsk in May 1926 was perhaps the last industrial strike in the Soviet Union to be reported sympathetically in the Soviet press.[4] At the seventh trade union congress in December 1926 Dogadov reported a satisfactory decline in the number of strikers in the first half of 1926 : 58 strikes had involved only 11,000 workers.[5] The official attitude was well summarized in a confidential directive from the central committee of the wood-workers' union to its branches in January 1927 :

A strike in a state enterprise, in whose successful work we are directly concerned, is an extreme measure, and can only be the result of a clearly bureaucratic approach on the part of the economic organ or of an unconscious attitude on the part of some groups of workers and trade unionists who have not fully realized that we must not do damage to the state economic organizations. Therefore the most important task of the trade union organs is to take prompt preparatory measures in order to forestall a strike movement in state enterprises.

In case of demands to call a strike in a state enterprise, regardless of the size of the enterprise and the number of workers in it, the strike must be sanctioned beforehand by the central committee of the trade union, without which the calling of a strike is categorically forbidden.[6]

Strikes received little or no publicity in the next two years. But the official trade union report to the eighth congress in December

[1] *Vos'moi S"ezd Professional'nykh Soyuzov SSSR* (1929), p. 333.
[2] *Ibid.* pp. 526, 559.
[3] See *Socialism in One Country, 1924–1926*, Vol. 1, pp. 393-394.
[4] *Pravda*, May 21, 1926 ; for relations between the trade unions and private industry see Note E, pp. 938-939 below.
[5] *Sed'moi S"ezd Professional'nykh Soyuzov SSSR* (1927), p. 90.
[6] M. Fainsod, *Smolensk under Soviet Rule* (1958), p. 318.

1928 gave fuller statistics than before. In 1926 43,200 workers had been involved in strikes (32,900 in state enterprises), in 1927 25,400 (20,100 in state enterprises), in the first half of 1928 9700 (8900 in state enterprises) ; the number of working days lost had fallen from 140,056 in 1926 (64,530 in state enterprises) to 48,597 in 1927 (27,417 in state enterprises). Rather more than one-third of disputes leading to strikes had been settled wholly in favour of the workers, less than one-third in favour of managements, the rest had given divided results : these proportions remained constant throughout the period. In 1926 2·1 per cent of strikes, and in 1927 1·9 per cent, took place with the approval of the union : these were presumably in private enterprises. But the great majority of strikes " arise spontaneously and not by the will of the union ". The reassuring conclusion was that " strikes with us remain an incidental, transitory phenomenon, affect enterprises only partially, and are quickly liquidated ".[1] Tomsky at the congress mentioned " strikes which arise from time to time ' *without the knowledge of the trade unions* ' ", and treated them, as he treated them in 1925, as proof of inattention on the part of the unions to the grievances of the workers ; and Dogadov rehearsed the statistics from the official report.[2] But the congress did not attempt to discuss the question, which had ceased to be a serious menace. The trade unions were pledged up to the hilt to increase productivity ; and any action which interfered with output was bound to encounter resistance.[3]

[1] *Professional'nye Soyuzy SSSR, 1926–1928: Otchet k VIII S"ezdu* (1928), pp. 358-360.
[2] *Vos'moi S"ezd Professional'nykh Soyuzov SSSR* (1928), pp. 26, 65. *Sotsialisticheskii Vestnik* (Berlin), No. 14 (156), July 18, 1927, p. 16, reported strikes in many parts of the country which were not supported by the trade unions or mentioned in the press, but admitted that they were less numerous than in the previous year ; a year later strikes were reported in the Putilov works and in a textile factory in Leningrad and in the Serp i Molot metal works in Moscow (*ibid.* No. 8-9 (174-175), May 3, 1928, p. 30). For an apparently successful strike or walk-out over norms as late as 1929 see M. Fainsod, *Smolensk under Soviet Rule* (1958), p. 312. In the autumn of 1929 a strike for higher pay occurred among workers on the Dnieprostroi site when the stone-crushing equipment broke down and work had to be done manually (Arzhanov and Mikhalevich, *Dneprostroi k XVI S"ezdu VKP (B)* (1930), pp. 38-44).
[3] A. Ciliga, *Au Pays du Grand Mensonge* (1938), p. 31, quotes the case of a woman worker excluded from work by her trade union as a punishment for having organized a strike ; the writer constantly comments on the passivity of the workers.

An apparently unique and little reported episode in the history of Soviet strikes was a wave of strikes among agricultural workers or *batraks* employed on vegetable- or fruit-growing farms in the southern and south-eastern regions in the summer of 1929. It began in the neighbourhood of Odessa, spread rapidly eastwards as far as Orenburg, and culminated in " a massive strike of *batraks* in the vineyards of German colonists " in Georgia ; not more than 5000 *batraks*, however, are said to have been involved in these strikes. The embarrassed reaction of the trade unions was significant. The central committee and the sixth congress of Vserabotzemles in December 1928 had taken a decision that " in the struggle against the *kulaks* the trade unions should not stop short of a strike ". The local organization of Vserabotzemles was weak, and these instructions " were forgotten on the spot ". When the strike broke out at Rostov, a regional representative of the union appeared on the scene for a quarter of an hour, and left without giving any lead to the strike committee ; elsewhere it was alleged that the president of a *batraks'* committee, appointed by the regional committee of the union, " drinks with the *kulaks* and follows their line ". Still more noteworthy was the attitude of other unions. The regional inter-union organizations took no interest in a strike of *batraks* ; and in Orenburg the printers' union refused to print leaflets and proclamations for them. Notwithstanding these discouragements, it was claimed that the strikes ended with a victory for the *batraks*, that they " raised the political and class consciousness of the *batraks* ", and — not very plausibly — that they " brought the *batraks* nearer to the party, to the trade unions and to the industrial workers in the towns ".[1] The episode was evidently of no great intrinsic importance. But it illustrated the diversity of conditions in the Soviet Union, as well as the complexity of relations between town and country and between different elements in the trade union movement.

(c) Production Conferences

The guarded approval of production conferences in factories voiced by Tomsky at the fourteenth party congress in December

---

[1] *Na Agrarnom Fronte*, No. 10, 1929, pp. 81-92 ; strikes of *batraks* also occurred at this time in the Ukraine (*Istoriya Sovetskogo Krest'yanstva i Kol khoznogo Stroitel'stva v SSSR* (1963), p. 198).

1925 [1] did not conceal the difficulties attending this form of organized relations between workers and management ; and such initial popularity as they enjoyed appears to have suffered a decline.[2] The trade union central council in June 1926 noted the weakness of trade union work in the production conferences.[3] Dzerzhinsky, in a note of June 22, 1926, to Kraval, attributed their lack of success to " our managers who have not hitherto shown active good will in this matter ", adding that " the trade unions are unable by themselves to put life into these conferences ". He instructed Kraval to discuss the question with the heads of trusts and with the trade unions, and to prepare material for a meeting at which he himself would address the managers.[4] The result of this initiative was a joint directive issued by Vesenkha and the trade union central council in July 1926, a few days before Dzerzhinsky's death, which sought to revive flagging interest in the conferences ; [5] and the trade union central council passed a resolution calling for the creation in all factories of production commissions to make proposals and prepare the agenda of the production conferences.[6]

When the fifteenth party conference met in October 1926, Tomsky explained that production conferences might be of two kinds : they might deal with day-to-day practical grievances of the workers in the factory, or they might discuss issues of economic policy. Hitherto he had favoured the former alternative : now, however, it was time to carry the workers a step further — " to raise them from the interests of the bench to the interests of the whole shop, to the interests of the whole factory, to the interests of the whole trust ". The conferences should from time to time appoint " control commissions " to go into particular points, though the directors and managers were, he admitted, apt to resent this as an intrusion on their functions and a revival of

[1] See Socialism in One Country, 1924–1926, Vol. I, p. 400.
[2] L. Rogachevskaya, Iz Istorii Rabochego Klassa SSSR (1959), p. 85 ; for an unpublished report of the party central committee of April or May 1926 see Pervye Shagi Industrializatsii SSSR 1926–1927 gg. (1959), pp. 274-278.
[3] Bol'shevik, No. 13, July 15, 1926, p. 47.
[4] Istoricheskii Arkhiv, No. 2 (1960), pp. 89-90.
[5] Trud, July 18, 1926.
[6] Ibid. August 15, 1926 ; such commissions apparently already existed in some factories (Bol'shevik, No. 13, July 15, 1926, p. 47).

" workers' control ".[1] This proposal had a poor reception from other delegates. Uglanov was pessimistic about the production conferences, and thought that Tomsky had " over-simplified the question ". Two managerial delegates protested against the control commissions as an aggravation of an already excessive burden of controls. Ryazanov attacked the production conferences as useless, and liable to undermine the authority of the trade unions. Tomsky again defended his project.[2] The resolution of the conference, mindful of the need to discredit the opposition, declared that, " contrary to the panic cries of the opposition ", the production conferences had developed and that the first stage of their work was " almost complete ". It was now time to " deepen " their activities by leading them " to work out bigger general questions " of production and organization. For this purpose it would be useful to create " temporary control commissions of the workers of a given enterprise ", whose precise functions would be defined by Vesenkha and by the trade union central council.[3] At the seventh trade union congress in December 1926 Tomsky touched lightly on the problem of the production conferences and the control commissions ; [4] and the main resolution of the congress contained the significant *caveat* that the organization of the commissions should " in no case be interpreted as an attempt at direct interference in the functions of administrative or economic management of the enterprise ".[5] The temporary control commissions, which were elected by the production conferences and generally consisted of from five to seven skilled workers and members of the technical staff, dealt with such questions as sources of wastage, conditions of rationalization, causes of high costs, and deficiencies in the utilization of the labour force.[6]

The organization of temporary control commissions was approved in a joint decision of Vesenkha and the trade union central

[1] *XV Konferentsiya Vsesoyuznoi Kommunisticheskoi Partii (B)* (1927), pp. 276-283.
[2] *Ibid.* pp. 298-299, 317, 346-347, 356, 408-410.
[3] *KPSS v Rezolyutsiyakh* (1954), ii, 316-319.
[4] *Sed'moi S"ezd Professional'nykh Soyuzov SSSR* (1927), pp. 58-59.
[5] *Ibid.* pp. 793-794.
[6] *Shestnadtsataya Konferentsiya VKP(B)* (1962), p. 814, note 279 ; the information appears to be drawn from unpublished archives.

council on February 2, 1927. By that time nine trade unions had been responsible for the creation of 26 commissions ; [1] by the end of the year 241 commissions had been set up by 16 unions. [2] But the commissions, which were the chosen instrument of the trade unions, enjoyed only intermittent support in party and governmental circles, which sought to discredit them as unnecessary rivals of the production conferences. [3] The fourth Union Congress of Soviets in April 1927 commended production conferences as a means of encouraging the initiative of the workers and interesting them in rationalization, but said nothing about the commissions. [4] At the fifteenth party congress in December 1927, S. V. Kosior hailed the growth of production conferences, but professed that the results of the work of the control commissions had " not yet been collated " ; and the supporters of the commissions found themselves on the defensive. Uglanov deplored the fact that, in spite of a number of promising experiments, this work had never " got into its stride ", and Dogadov complained of the negative attitude of managers and factory directors. [5] At the session of the party central committee in April 1928 the trade unions were blamed for the poor organization of the production conferences, for the rarity of their meetings, and for failure to explain their importance to the workers ; but work on the temporary commissions was also dismissed as inadequate. [6]

After this reproof, a joint directive of Vesenkha and the trade union central council led to an increase in the number of control

[1] *Spravochnik Partiinogo Rabotnika*, vi (1928), ii, 534-536. For a list of the 26 commissions and some account of the work done by them see *Pervye Shagi Industrializatsii SSSR 1926-1927 gg.* (1959), pp. 388-400 ; further details can be found in L. Rogachevskaya, *Iz Istorii Rabochego Klassa SSSR* (1959), pp. 122-126.

[2] *Professional'nye Soyuzy SSSR, 1926-1928: Otchet k VIII S"ezdu* (1928), p. 445.

[3] According to a later account, " the practice of replacing production conferences by commissions was cultivated mainly by Right-opportunist elements in the leading trade union organs ", which, by weakening the production conferences, " kept the masses of the workers away from participation " in the discussion of questions of production (L. Rogachevskaya, *Iz Istorii Rabochego Klassa SSSR* (1959), p. 116). The suggested motive is far-fetched ; but the association of the commissions with Tomsky and the Right trade union leaders probably sharpened the opposition to them.

[4] *S"ezdy Sovetov v Dokumentakh*, iii (1960), 121.

[5] *Pyatnadtsatyi S"ezd VKP(B)*, i (1961), 95-96, 143 ; ii (1962), 923.

[6] *KPSS v Rezolyutsiyakh* (1954), ii, 503.

commissions to nearly 2000, including commissions not only in industry, but in transport, in state institutions, and in trading and cooperative organizations.[1] But this did nothing to allay the criticism that the commissions " turned themselves into a sort of independent self-sufficient organ, carried on their work outside the production conferences and rendered no account to them " ; and they received only " weak cooperation " from administrative and technical personnel.[2] At the eighth trade union congress in December 1928 Tomsky continued to assert that the production conferences had made no progress, that statistics of them were " ' adapted ' to the needs of the moment ", and that most of them met only three times a year.   In effect, they had been replaced by the control commissions.   Of the reputed 2000 control commissions, however, only 1000 had apparently yet come into existence.[3] The congress resolution, adopted after Tomsky's downfall, commended the production conferences as the most effective means of discharging " the fundamental task of the trade unions — the preparation of broad masses of the workers for the administration of the whole apparatus of the proletarian state, and the initiation of these masses into the work of actively and consciously building socialism " ; but it also urged the trade unions " to extend the *net of temporary control commissions and gradually to include in it all large and medium-sized enterprises* ".[4] This extension did not, however, enjoy unqualified approval elsewhere.   A semi-official article on the congress in an economic journal spoke of the production conferences in conventional terms, and did not mention the control commissions at all.[5] After this, the commissions seem to have faded gradually out of the picture.   During 1929 numerous reports were drawn up of a " review " of the production conferences pointing to their increased activity.[6] But, as a stimulus to

[1] *Professional'nye Soyuzy SSSR, 1926–1928: Otchet k VIII S"ezdu* (1928), p. 446.
[2] *Ibid.* pp. 447-448.
[3] *Vos'moi S"ezd Professional'nykh Soyuzov SSSR* (1929), pp. 41-43.
[4] *Ibid.* pp. 527-528.
[5] *Ekonomicheskoe Obozrenie*, No. 12, 1928, pp. 6-7.
[6] For the inauguration of the review see *Pravda*, October 28, 1928.   For a number of reports on it from the archives see *Politicheskii i Trudovoi Pod"em Rabochego Klassa SSSR* (1956), pp. 129-155 ; the final results of the review were announced in *Pravda*, August 8, 1929.

productivity, such dramatic and occasional expedients as shock brigades, competitions between factories or bonuses for workers' inventions seem to have proved more effective than the regular production conferences.

CHAPTER 21

THE SPECIALISTS

THE privileged position of the " specialists ", which had been a source of friction and embarrassment since the early days of the régime,[1] continued to present an intractable problem : as the status of the group came to be more secure and clearly defined, the attitude of party and government towards it grew increasingly ambivalent. It is difficult to arrive at any precise estimate of the number of specialists or of the qualifications entitling to this description. In the census of December 1926 37,988 persons were returned as " managing personnel ", and 81,241 as " engineering-technical personnel ", in factory industry ; the latter category included 13,094 engineers and designers, 15,552 technicians and 13,536 " foremen ".[2] A survey made by Vesenkha in 1928 found 50,798 " engineers and technicians " working in large-scale industry. Of these only 15,415 were trained engineers with professional qualifications ; 15,399 were trained technicians ; 19,984 were " foremen " without special training, who had learned

---

[1] See *The Bolshevik Revolution, 1917–1923*, Vol. 2, pp. 182-187 ; *Socialism in One Country, 1924–1926*, Vol. 1, pp. 115-122, 379-381.

[2] *Vsesoyuznaya Perepis' Naseleniya 1926 goda*, xxxiv (1930), 122, 144. The " foreman " (the traditional translation of the Russian " master ") represented an anomalous category. He was as a rule a promoted worker without technical training ; his duties included the supervision and enforcement of labour discipline and the supply of materials. He was, however, often paid less than the highly skilled worker, so that workers did not readily seek promotion to foremen ; the authority of the foreman was not adequately supported by the trade unions (*Predpriyatie*, No. 12, 1926, pp. 13-14, 22). On the other hand, many foremen clearly did acquire technical skills : schools or courses for foremen were reported in the electrical and metal industries (*ibid.* No. 4, 1926, pp. 94-95 ; No. 12, 1926, p. 16). Complaints that foremen were not admitted to meetings of engineers (*ibid.* No. 12, 1926, p. 22), and were not all admitted to the engineers' and technicians' sections of the trade unions (*ibid.* No. 2, 1927, pp. 74-75, No. 4, 1927, p. 82, No. 6, 1927, p. 74 ; for these sections see p. 576 below) are evidence of their indeterminate status. Statistically, they appear normally to be classified with engineers and technicians.

their skills on the job.[1] The framers of the first five-year plan counted 20,200 engineers working for state industry in 1927–1928, of whom 13,100 were directly engaged in production ; it was proposed to increase the total to 41,500 by 1932–1933.[2] In 1929 an investigation of the specialists employed in 25 of the largest industrial establishments yielded the following classification :

Directors and Assistant Directors, Managers and Assistant Managers	125
Heads of Shops, Departments, and Workshops and their Assistants	1771
Engineers	1658
Foremen (Mastera)	1761
Technicians	987
Designers (Konstruktora)	568
Scientific Workers	789
Other Administrative and Technical Staff	1336
Total	8995 [3]

It is uncertain how many of the directors and managers or the higher administrative personnel who ranked as specialists had engineering qualifications ; the original criterion of the specialist was apparently that his rate of remuneration was independent of the regular wage-scales. But " engineers and technicians " formed the hard core of the specialists, and provided such organization as they possessed ; and not all of these enjoyed the privilege of personal salaries.[4] The status of the " technicians ", poised between engineers and workers, was often indeterminate ; in Tomsky's words " the former (the engineers) have left them

---

[1] *Torgovo-Promyshlennaya Gazeta*, June 28, 1928 ; the total of 50,798 was said to compare with a total of 46,500 in 1913 (*Voprosy Istorii KPSS*, No. 2, 1966, p. 30).

[2] *Pyatiletnii Plan Narodno-Khozyaistvennogo Stroitel'stva SSSR* (1929), i, 74 ; later Gosplan figures gave 17,900 engineers with professional qualifications and 19,900 technicians employed in industry and transport in 1928 (*Itogi Vypolneniya Pervogo Pyatiletnego Plana* (1933), pp. 215-219).

[3] *Ekonomicheskoe Obozrenie*, No. 12, 1929, p. 103 ; of the engineers, 714 worked in factories, 223 in trusts, and 415 in research institutes ; of the scientific workers, 765 worked in research institutes.

[4] For the salaries of specialists see pp. 601-604 below.

behind, but they have not yet joined the latter (the workers) ".[1]

A professional organization of engineers under the name of the All-Russian Association of Engineers (VAI), the heir of a similar body dating from the Tsarist period, continued to exist throughout the nineteen-twenties. Its president was a non-party engineer working in Vesenkha, Dolgov ; and it had branches in the principal centres. It discussed technical and professional problems and from time to time made representations to the authorities on the status of engineers.[2] But it was soon rivalled by another organization which, being of Soviet origin, wielded greater influence. From 1925 onwards every industrial trade union comprised an " engineers' and technicians' section " (ITS) ; and in the same year an All-Union Inter-Sectional Bureau of Engineers and Technicians (VMBIT) was set up to coordinate the work of these sections.[3] During 1925 and 1926 the number of sections rose from 350 to 3340, and of members from 23,000 to 91,600.[4] A spokesman of VMBIT addressed the seventh trade union congress in December 1926 ; and the resolution of the congress on questions of organization laid down that " the engineers' and technicians' sections, being integral parts of the unions, cannot rest on a foundation of voluntary membership, and must embrace all members of the union in a given group ".[5] The third congress of VMBIT, which met in April 1927 and was the first to be heavily publicized,[6]

[1] Vos'moi S"ezd Professional'nykh Soyuzov SSSR (1929), p. 30.

[2] Torgovo-Promyshlennaya Gazeta, April 20, May 22, 1928. VAI was later reproached with its political neutralism and called " an academy of inertia " (ibid. December 14, 1928) ; it was dissolved in 1929 (S. Fedyukin, Sovetskaya Vlast' i Burzhuaznye Spetsialisty (1965), p. 225).

[3] At the " industrial party " trial in 1930 Ramzin in his confession mentioned the creation at the end of 1925 or early in 1926 of an " engineers' centre " out of which the conspiratorial " industrial party " developed (Le Procès des Industriels de Moscou (1931), p. 57) ; this may be a perverted reflexion of the setting up of VMBIT.

[4] Sed'moi S"ezd Professional'nykh Soyuzov SSSR (1927), p. 122 ; for more detailed but less up-to-date figures see Professional'nye Soyuzy SSSR, 1924–1926: Otchet k VII S"ezdu (1926), p. 409.

[5] Sed'moi S"ezd Professional'nykh Soyuzov SSSR (1927), pp. 122-125, 807 ; a similar Ukrainian organ (VUMBIT) reported in the previous month to the third Ukrainian trade union congress (Stenograficheskii Otchet 3⁰⁰ Vseukrainskogo Soyuza Profsoyuzov (1927), pp. 51-60 ; see also the resolution ibid. pp. 324-325).

[6] The previous congresses have not been traced ; one of them may have been the congress of engineers in 1924 (see pp. 581-582 below), though this preceded the formal constitution of VMBIT.

was attended by 574 delegates and observers from 4108 local organizations representing 105,000 members — a total which must have been achieved by opening the net fairly wide — and was addressed by Rykov and Tomsky. Tomsky was evidently concerned about the status of VMBIT in the trade union movement and anxious to forestall any claims to independence :

> No union of engineers [he said] could secure an improvement in the economic position of the engineers against the will of the working class and against its wishes. Your section has sufficient rights. It is a working-class organization designed to serve a special category of working people.[1]

With the pressure for industrialization and the advance of planning the shortage of engineers was acutely felt. Kuibyshev told a conference in September 1927 that the shortage had seriously delayed the preparation of specifications for machinery to be imported on German credits, and had prevented the development of artificial silk production and the study of the latest American methods for the production of copper.[2] One result of the shortage was that trained technicians and even untrained mechanics were doing engineers' jobs.[3] It was calculated that the 50,798 " engineers and technicians " (including " foremen ") recorded by the Vesenkha survey of 1928 represented only 2·3 per cent of all workers engaged on production ; this was, according to Kuibyshev, only one-third of the proportion found in western European and American industry.[4] The long-standing difficulty of inducing specialists to work outside the great cities [5] was still in evidence ; several decrees of 1927 offered additional inducements to those accepting employment in remoter parts of the Soviet Union.[6] Rykov at the fifteenth party congress in December 1927 commented sharply on unemployment among non-manual

---

[1] *Pravda*, April 7, 1927 ; for further reports of the congress see *ibid*. April 8, 12, 13, 15, 1927.

[2] *Torgovo-Promyshlennaya Gazeta*, September 28, 1927.

[3] *Ibid*. October 28, 1927.

[4] *Ibid*. March 8, 1928, June 17, 1928 ; for the Vesenkha survey see p. 574 above.   [5] See *Socialism in One Country, 1924–1926*, Vol. 1, p. 378.

[6] *Sobranie Zakonov, 1927*, No. 25, arts. 269, 270 ; No. 38, art. 380 ; No. 43, art. 436 ; specialists were said to prefer work in the central administrative organs to jobs in production which brought them into direct contact with " dirty workers " (Trotsky archives, T 2021).

U

workers " at a time when there is an immense hunger for non-
manual workers in the provinces and in the countryside ", and
thought that those who " prefer unemployment in the city to work
in the countryside " should not be allowed to count as unemployed. He admitted, however, that the "régime of economy " had
sometimes led to the dismissal of " qualified specialists, laboratory
workers and technicians, working for the improvement of production ".[1] Another complaint heard at this time was that a decree of
December 2, 1925, promising living accommodation to medical
personnel willing to work in the villages had been ignored by the
local authorities, who did nothing to make the necessary provision.[2]
The problems of the direction of professional workers presented
even greater complications than those relating to the industrial
worker.

The most serious charge against the specialists was that of
hostility to the workers and to the workers' state. Bad relations
between workers and specialists at the factory level were chronic,
and were aggravated by the ideological cleavage. The fact that
engineers and technicians, through membership of the ITS, were
members of the trade union did nothing to bridge the gap.
Managements were said to look askance at engineers or technicians who appeared at production conferences as trade union
delegates, and wished them to be treated as representatives of the
administration.[3] The workers — or at any rate the trade unions —
resented the high salaries paid to specialists whose origin and outlook alike made them alien to the proletariat.[4] Among the abuses
of the régime of economy named in the declaration of August
16, 1926, were " intolerable patronage accorded to ' big bosses ',
who should not be confused with honest specialists devoted to
their job ", the granting to " big bosses " of such privileges as
automobiles and bonuses, and disguised forms of wage increases
for " high officials ".[5] Paradoxically the specialists came to be

    [1] *Pyatnadtsatyi S"ezd VKP(B)*, ii (1962), 874-875. In 1928 15,000 spe-
cialists were said to be unemployed, including 2000 in Moscow and 2500 in
Leningrad ; of this total, 43 per cent had been qualified for less than a year, and
63 per cent for less than two years (*Torgovo-Promyshlennaya Gazeta*, June 15
1928).
    [2] *Vos'moi S"ezd Professional'nykh Soyuzov SSSR* (1929), p. 285.
    [3] *Sed'moi S"ezd Professional'nykh Soyuzov SSSR* (1927), p. 123.
    [4] See *Socialism in One Country, 1924-1926*, Vol. 1, pp. 378-379.
    [5] For this declaration see pp. 335-336 above.

regarded in the eyes of the workers both as the principal agents
and as the beneficiaries of the régime of economy and of rationalization, with all the pressures which these imposed on the workers.[1]
Constant complaints were made of their harsh and brutal attitude
to the workers, generally regarded as a legacy of pre-revolutionary
habits. Syrtsov at the fifteenth party conference in October 1926
convicted the specialists of " an exaggerated opinion of themselves " and of " rudeness, self-importance and sometimes bully-
ing of workers ".[2] Kuibyshev at the fourth Union Congress of
Soviets in April 1927 warned the engineers that " the social environment of our country imperatively requires the engineering
profession to adapt itself to our special features " ; the old
methods of command would no longer work.[3] A more sympa-
thetic observer attributed the trouble to " excessive nervousness "
among the specialists, many of whom worked twelve hours a day.[4]

Wherever the blame lay, the depth of the antipathy between
specialists and workers in the middle and later nineteen-twenties
could not be denied. Specialists resented the protection accorded
by the trade unions and the party to the workers, which prevented
them from enforcing order and discipline in the traditional
manner.[5] The report of VUMBIT to the third Ukrainian trade
union congress in November 1926 professed to find an improvement in labour relations : " cases of hostile action against engineering and technical staff are now isolated exceptions, and in
any case are incidental, not mass, phenomena ". But it was admitted that " we still have a more dangerous form of concealed

---

[1] *Pravda*, April 13, 1927 ; party and trade union representatives in the
factories may sometimes have preferred to leave responsibility for enforcing
disagreeable decisions to the non-party managers.

[2] *XV Konferentsiya Vsesoyuznoi Kommunisticheskoi Partii (B)* (1927), p. 176.

[3] *SSSR: 4 S"ezd Sovetov* (1927), p. 398 ; managers who adopted a high
and mighty attitude to the workers were known as " hats " (shlyapy) (*Torgovo-
Promyshlennaya Gazeta*, December 1, 1928).

[4] *Stenograficheskii Otchet 3ᵍᵒ Vseukrainskogo S"ezda Profsoyuzov* (1927),
p. 54.

[5] See p. 490 above for Teplov's remarks at the fifteenth party conference
and the comments provoked by them ; at the " industrial party " trial in 1930,
Fedotov, one of the accused, complained that the engineer " has no possibility
of influencing the discipline of the factory, and is at the same time obliged to
exercise this discipline ", adding that " this dilemma is very acute and many
engineers suffer from it ", and that " the situation has reached a point where the
worker can at any moment insult the engineers with impunity " (*Le Procès des
Industriels de Moscou* (1931), p. 310).

'spets-baiting'", particularly when the specialist was concerned in the enforcement of "strict economic accounting ".[1] The seventh trade union congress in Moscow in the following month recognized the "melancholy phenomenon" of "excesses" against engineers and technicians by ordinary workers, which sometimes took on " the colour of hooliganism " ; [2] and in the summer of 1927 it was reported from the Ukrainian mines that orders of managers were met by " curses, threats and calls to violence ", and that several attempts had been made on the lives of specialists.[3] It was sometimes suspected that such attitudes were encouraged or tolerated from above.   Early in 1928, on the very eve of the Shakhty affair, Shein, the president of VMBIT, again protested against attacks on the Soviet engineering profession by prominent leaders of industry and of the trade unions.[4]

Tense as were the relations between workers and specialists, relations between the specialists and the party and governmental authorities were still more ambiguous.   In discussions of the attitude of the specialists to the régime, they were commonly divided into three groups.   Active opponents were not thought to be very numerous : before the Shakhty trial of March 1928, suspicions of positive disloyalty among specialists were not widely entertained. Active supporters of the régime were also not numerous.   Of 3000 members of the ITS of the metal workers' union only 110-115 were party members, and this proportion was well above the average among specialists ; according to another estimate, only 0·81 per cent of all trained engineers and technicians belonged to the party.[5]   The third, or middle, group, which was by common consent much the largest, was described as basically apathetic, addicted to mild anti-Semitic and anti-party gossip : instead of

[1] *Stenografcheskii Otchet 3ᵍº Vseukrainskogo S"ezda Profsoyuzov* (1927), p. 54 ; see also *ibid.* p. 325.   For VUMBIT see p. 576, note 5 above.
[2] *Sed'moi S"ezd Professional'nykh Soyuzov SSSR* (1927), p. 124.
[3] *Torgovo-Promyshlennaya Gazeta*, June 18, 1927.
[4] *Ibid.* March 7, 1928.
[5] *Ibid.* April 13, July 4, 1928 ; Kraval, speaking of engineers alone, put the number of party members in the autumn of 1928 at 139 in the whole of Union industry, of whom only 12 were in the mining, and 7 in the textile, industry (*Puti Industrializatsii*, No. 11, 1928, p. 8).   The situation was quite different among directors and managers of trusts, syndicates and state enterprises : the highest posts were commonly reserved for party members, often without technical qualifications.

pursuing their studies in their spare time, " engineers prefer to visit one another in the evenings, to drink and to play preference ".[1] This group had no strong political convictions, and professed to be politically neutral, being concerned only to do a practical job.[2] But this neutralism masked the unconscious assumptions of a past epoch. At the " industrial party " trial in 1930, Ramzin, the principal defendant, described the corps of engineers as " an isolated structure, a caste having class interests and a class ideology ", animated by " a pronounced dissatisfaction with the Soviet régime ". As a whole, they had " a firm belief in the salutary effects of private enterprise " ; on the other hand they accepted NEP as " a gradual movement towards state capitalism ".[3] Larichev, another defendant, said that " the majority of them were encrusted in bourgeois and democratic ideas, most of them springing from the bourgeoisie or from various petty bourgeois environments ". Yet another, Kalinnikov, described himself as " reared in the bourgeois class in capitalist conditions, like any other engineer ".[4] These statements were not seriously exaggerated.

The attitude of party and government to the specialists had been ambivalent ever since Trotsky first employed former Tsarist officers in the Red Army. Only for a short time, in the hectic days of workers' control, was the illusion entertained that industry could work without managers and engineers inherited from the old régime ; and by the time of the ninth party congress in March 1920 " comradely cooperation between workers and the specialist-technicians " was being actively preached.[5] As industry revived, the rôle of the specialists became more important. It was something of a landmark when Rykov, as president of Sovnarkom, attended a congress of engineers in December 1924, and offered a charter of rights to " the specialist, the engineer, the man of science

[1] *Torgovo-Promyshlennaya Gazeta*, May 26, 1928.
[2] *Sotsialisticheskii Vestnik* (Berlin), No. 18 (160), September 22, 1927, p. 13, claimed that the specialists at this time were either Menshevik (though without formal affiliation) or non-party ; well-defined Menshevik or ex-Menshevik groups existed in the higher economic bureaucracy, but not apparently among the engineers or technicians.
[3] *Le Procès des Industriels de Moscou* (1931), pp. 58, 204.
[4] *Ibid.* pp. 108, 141.
[5] See *The Bolshevik Revolution, 1917–1923*, Vol. 2, pp. 182-186 ; for workers' control see *ibid.* Vol. 2, pp. 66-73.

582 THE ECONOMIC ORDER PT. I

and technology ".[1] Dzerzhinsky told the fourteenth party conference in April 1925 that it was wrong to look on the technicians as " traitors and hirelings ", and went on : " We can conquer them as colleagues, as comrades with whom we work jointly ".[2] As president of Vesenkha, Dzerzhinsky seems to have done much to restore the status and morale of the specialists ; after his death, one of them gratefully said of him : " He made us into people again ".[3] Stalin, at the party central committee in April 1926, denounced those who sought to " slate " the managers, and demanded support for them " in the task of building industry ".[4] A resolution of the fifth Komsomol conference of March 1927 reproached " backward sections of young workers " with " an incorrect attitude to specialists and foremen ".[5]

These official pronouncements did not, however, remove the mistrust of the specialists felt in party circles or the corresponding fears and animosities on the side of the specialists. As party policy turned towards the Left, and doubt was cast on the durability of the compromises introduced by NEP, relations not only between specialists and workers, but between specialists and party, tended to deteriorate. In February 1927 Bukharin significantly felt called on to deny rumours, " current especially in Leningrad ", of a reversion by the party to the attitudes of 1918 in regard to the specialists.[6] Kuibyshev at the fourth Union Congress of Soviets told the story of an engineer who said that he did not care whether what was produced was right or not : he simply carried out orders. This was censured as " a formal, bureaucratic attitude " in conditions where " economic vision " was required.[7] Lomov, an old Bolshevik who was now president of Donugol, was concerned with the same problem of apathy among specialists. Engineers in the Donbass feared to introduce new plant because of the investigations which would take place if anything went wrong. In one district all the mine managers and chief engineers were under

[1] See *Socialism in One Country, 1924–1926*, Vol. 1, p. 121.
[2] *Chetyrnadtsataya Konferentsiya Vserossiiskoi Kommunisticheskoi Partii (Bol'shevikov)* (1925), p. 173.
[3] *Sotsialisticheskii Vestnik* (Berlin), No. 19 (137), October 2, 1926, p. 16.
[4] See *Socialism in One Country, 1924–1926*, Vol. 1, p. 381.
[5] *VLKSM v Rezolyutsiyakh* (1929), p. 283.
[6] *Pravda*, February 2, 1927.
[7] *SSSR : 4 S"ezd Sovetov* (1927), pp. 396–397.

investigation by a court ; some of them had as many as five cases to answer. These conditions made engineers unwilling to take part in management ; Lomov thought that " the element of scope and discretion should not be taken away from the technician and engineer ".[1] A constant minor complaint was the volume of paper-work, and of meetings and conferences, which took up a substantial part of the engineer's working day.[2]

In the autumn of 1927, when on every major issue new lines of policy were being formulated, an attempt was made to secure the active support of the " technical intelligentsia ", which may be looked on either as a last attempt to enlist their voluntary enthusiasm or a first attempt to coerce them into active conformity. A declaration was published by a group of prominent scientists and engineers, including Aleksandrov, president of the Dnieprostroi technical council, Dolgov, president of VAI, and Shein, president of VMBIT, initiating an Organization of Scientific and Technical Workers to Assist Socialist Construction (Ornito). It was a political manifesto, speaking of the country's recovery " under the leadership of the communist party ", and of the need for members of the organization to be " socialist-minded ". " In a class society scientific and technical workers cannot remain politically neutral " ; there were two classes and two world outlooks, and the aim was to unite scientific and technical forces " on a definite ideological foundation ".[3] During the next few days lists of names of supporters were published. They included a few prominent non-Bolsheviks such as Groman ; [4] but the support forthcoming was evidently small. Ipatiev in his memoirs relates that Zbarsky, the principal party spokesman, asked him and other prominent chemists to join, promising that members would be immune from OGPU control or criticism. Ipatiev replied that he " never participated in political affairs ", and comments that the organization was " still-born ".[5] In February 1928 Sovnarkom approved a statute of the new organization under the name Varnitso

[1] *Pravda*, May 8, 1927.
[2] For typical complaints see *Torgovo-Promyshlennaya Gazeta*, April 20, 1926, April 5, 1928.
[3] *Izvestiya*, October 15, 1927 ; the initiative had been taken by a group of intellectuals meeting in April 1927 (*Istoriya SSSR*, No. 6, 1959, p. 96).
[4] *Torgovo-Promyshlennaya Gazeta*, October 21, 1927.
[5] N. Ipatieff, *The Life of a Chemist* (Stanford, 1946), p. 451.

(All-Union Association of Scientific and Technical Workers to Assist Socialist Construction of the USSR). On April 23–26, 1928, Varnitso held its first conference, which was attended by 170 delegates of whom 98 were described as professors and 32 as engineers : 113 of the delegates were non-party. Bakh, a leading chemist who had been one of the prime movers, was elected president of the association.[1] But Zbarsky struck a jarring note at the conference by bitterly criticizing the " top stratum of the intelligentsia ", which was said to be hostile to the declaration initiating the society on the ground that it would split the intelligentsia, and declared that this stratum " has learned nothing and forgotten nothing in ten years ".[2] A resolution of the conference expressed the view that " the intelligentsia should not be neutral, but should participate actively in the work of planning and of the capital construction of the whole industry of the country ".[3]

At this juncture the sensational Shakhty affair threw the limelight on the prevailing mistrust of the specialists, and exacerbated all their relations with the authorities for the next two years. Early in March 1928 it was announced that a counter-revolutionary organization carrying out sabotage in the mines of the Shakhty district of the Donbass had been unmasked, and 55 persons, mainly technical personnel and including three German engineers, arrested ; of these some 30 had confessed their guilt, wholly or in part.[4] The directing centre of the conspiracy had been an organization of former mine-owners and shareholders in Paris : contacts had also been maintained with " German industrial firms " and with the Polish counter-espionage department. " Organized sabotage " was said to have begun as early as 1922, but evidence was mainly of a later date. Since 1925 sabotage was alleged to have been directed from the headquarters of Donugol, the coal-mining trust, in Kharkov ; since 1926 a sabotage centre

[1] *Istoriya SSSR*, No. 6, 1959, pp. 97-98 ; for Bakh see p. 421 above.
[2] *Torgovo-Promyshlennaya Gazeta*, April 24, 1928 ; the opening of the conference was briefly reported in *Pravda* of the same date.
[3] Quoted from the archives in S. Fedyukin, *Sovetskaya Vlast' i Burzhuaznye Spetsialisty* (1965), p. 223 ; for a resolution of the conference on the Shakhty affair see *Ekonomicheskaya Zhizn'*, May 17, 1928.
[4] *Pravda*, March 10, 1928. The indictment was published *ibid.* May 8–12, 1928 ; even this lengthy text was apparently an abbreviated version.

had existed in Moscow. Among those arrested were Rabinovich, president of the technical council of Donugol and alleged founder of the Moscow centre, and Skorutto, deputy director of a department of Vesenkha. Apart from specific acts of destruction in the mines, the charges of sabotage included such items as unpunctuality in the payment of wages and neglect of safety measures for workers, the deliberate purchase of unsuitable or unnecessary machinery, capricious changes in organization, and the falsification of accounts. The trial opened on May 19, 1928, and lasted for six weeks. It received maximum publicity, and was extensively reported in the press.[1] By way of contrast with the tenuous nature of the evidence of particular acts, the " social-political significance " of the trial as an element in the class struggle against the implacable hostility of the bourgeoisie at home and abroad was thrown strongly into relief. Grinko, a deputy president of Gosplan, Shein, the president of VMBIT, and two other speakers dilated on this theme before the final speech of Krylenko, the prosecutor, who demanded the death penalty for more than 20 of the accused. The court acquitted four of the accused, sentenced 11 to death, and the remainder to terms of imprisonment. Rabinovich, who had protested his innocence throughout, was sentenced to three years' imprisonment, Skorutto, who gave evidence in closed session of large sums of money received from France, to ten. Of the three German engineers two were acquitted, and the third sentenced to one year's imprisonment on a minor charge. Of those sentenced to death, five were executed.[2]

Even in the early stages of the Shakhty affair some of the party leaders showed alarm at the consequences of the passions that had been aroused. Orjonikidze and Rykov, speaking immediately after the first disclosures, both gave emphatic warnings against indiscriminate " spets-baiting ".[3] Rykov is said to have spoken in the

[1] *Pravda* carried full reports daily from May 22 to July 4, 1928; the sentences and the full text of the judgment appeared on July 6 and 7, 1928. For a melodramatic account by an eye-witness see E. Lyons, *Assignment in Utopia* (1938), pp. 114-133.

[2] The opinion was widespread in party circles that the sentences had been too light; this was expressed in all three reports of party meetings in July-August 1928 preserved in the Trotsky archives (T 2021, 2066, 2167).

[3] *Torgovo-Promyshlennaya Gazeta*, March 11, 1928.

Politburo in opposition to the campaign against the specialists, and to have quoted " a whole portfolio " of passages from Lenin in their defence.[1] The central committee of the mine-workers' union issued an appeal to its members, calling, among other things, for " *a stubborn struggle against saboteurs, but a comradely attitude to honest specialists, a struggle against spets-baiting, but at the same time control and checking of the work of the specialists* ".[2] Later in March 1928 Kuibyshev spoke in defensive terms to a meeting of Moscow engineers and technicians. He rejected the allegations in the foreign press that the Shakhty affair had been staged by the authorities in order to cover up the failures of Soviet industry, or to " incite the workers against the specialists ". He blamed both " the slovenliness and technical ignorance of our economic organs " and " the formalism, inertia and caste-like seclusion of the engineers' and technicians' environment ", and concluded with an assurance that the Soviet Government did not intend to change its attitude to the specialists : the saboteurs were " an insignificant handful ".[3] I. Kosior reiterated that " *creative work in industry is impossible without some risk* " ; engineers should not be penalized for honest mistakes.[4] The resolution of the party central committee of April 1928, adopted on a report by Rykov, displayed a cautious ambivalence. It recognized that " a large part of the technical intelligentsia came over to sincere collaboration with the Soviet power ". But it referred to " the group of hitherto exceptionally privileged specialists " in the Donbass, and criticized Red directors for their " blind confidence " in their technical colleagues. Its conclusions were suitably balanced :

> While mercilessly punishing evil saboteurs and wreckers, it is essential at the same time to improve the conditions of work of the mass of honest worker-specialists devoted to their job.

The struggle against " spets-baiting " must be carried on " with all consistency and firmness ".[5]

These expressions of good intent were, however, overtaken and

---

[1] This account was given by Orjonikidze to the sixteenth party congress in July 1930, when Rykov was already in disgrace (*XVI S"ezd Vsesoyuznoi Kommunisticheskoi Partii (B)* (1931), p. 319). [2] *Pravda*, March 14, 1928. [3] *Torgovo-Promyshlennaya Gazeta*, March 29, 1928. [4] *Ibid.* April 8, 1928. [5] *KPSS v Rezolyutsiyakh* (1954), ii, 500-505.

nullified — as happened on many occasions later — by the campaign of denunciation which accompanied them. On the day after the announcement of the arrests, the Vesenkha newspaper wrote of " very probable centres of treason " in other industries, and of the need to be " on guard " (na cheku) — a play on the name Cheka, still in common use as a synonym for the OGPU.[1] The frightened engineers held meetings at which they condemned the Shakhty plot, and defended the conduct of the engineers as a whole : one speaker complained of " the mass passion for finding some fault in the work of an engineer ".[2] But this did not stem the tide. Shein, who testified for the prosecution at the Shakhty trial, sought to cover himself further by a sweeping criticism of the ITS. The political neutralism of the older engineers in the Donbass, and their loyalty to bourgeois ideology and even to their old masters, had isolated the ITS from the trade union movement and kept their leadership in counter-revolutionary hands. This state of affairs must be remedied :

> While practising the broadest democracy, it is essential that the trade unions and VMBIT should accomplish the task of putting at the head of the ITS workers really devoted to the cause of socialist construction.[3]

The conduct of the trial, which riveted attention on the bourgeois affiliations and sympathies of the accused rather than on their specific acts, and articles in the press inspired by the sentences, inflamed opinion against the specialists. It was alleged, though nobody seems to have noticed it at the time, that engineers and technicians had been " principal figures " in a majority of cases of bribery and corruption which had come before the courts between 1925 and 1928.[4]

---

[1] *Torgovo-Promyshlennaya Gazeta*, March 11, 1928.
[2] *Ibid.* April 20, 1928.
[3] *Ibid.* June 12, 1928 ; for Shein's rôle at the trial see p. 585 above.
[4] A. Fabrichny, *Chastnyi Kapital na Poroge Pyatiletki* (1930), p. 46. Other specialists were certainly arrested at this time in addition to those publicly tried. In May 1929 an announcement was made of the execution for counter-revolutionary activities of three specialists who held high posts in economic administration (*Pravda*, May 23, 1929 ; for particulars of those concerned see M. J. Larsons, *An Expert in the Service of the Soviet* (1929), pp. 199-207). One of the three, Palchinsky, was later named by Ramzin at the " industrial party " trial in 1930 as having been arrested " in the first half of 1928 " (*Le Procès des Industriels de Moscou* (1931), p. 65).

The issue of the specialists was ventilated once more at the eighth trade union congress in December 1928. The impression made on them by the Shakhty affair and its sequel was described in the report of the trade union central council to the congress :

> For the mass of engineers and technicians the possibility of such a crime was completely unexpected. The discovery of a widespread counter-revolutionary organization among the technical personnel staggered the members of the ITS. Moods of panic appeared among the specialists, and were aggravated when the slogan of a healthy proletarian mistrust was proclaimed. The first reactions of nervous and apprehensive expectations were somewhat mitigated by declarations of the government and of leading organs that not the whole technical personnel, but only a criminal stratum which had nothing in common with it, was being brought to judgment.[1]

At the congress itself, Rykov again deplored the prevalence of " spets-baiting ", and pleaded that, " without decisively overcoming this sickness, we shall not be able to press forward the technical revolution at a rapid tempo ". Tomsky more cautiously spoke of the task confronting the workers " of preparing from their own ranks their own cadres of new specialists ", and pointed the moral of the Shakhty affair : " Work with the specialists *hand in hand, a maximum of confidence, a maximum of comradely support, learn from them,* but do not forget that *you should keep watch,* since *there are specialists and specialists,* and this is a rather *peculiar* stratum ". Nevertheless an end must be put to " certain anti-specialist moods " and to " cases of persecution of specialists ". The conclusion was pointed by a quotation from Lenin.[2] The resolution of the congress on organization reproached the trade unions with exercising an " insufficiently strong ideological influence " on engineers and technicians, and pronounced that " the work of the trade unions and of the engineers' and technicians'

[1] *Professional'nye Soyuzy SSSR, 1926–1928: Otchet k VIII S"ezdu* (1928), p. 519.
[2] *Vos'moi S"ezd Professional'nykh Soyuzov SSSR* (1929), pp. 11, 29 ; the appeal of the party central committee of February 21, 1929, for improved labour discipline (see p. 517 above) also included a warning against spets-baiting. Cases were frequently quoted in which engineers were afraid to enforce discipline for fear of denunciation or dismissal ; see, for example, an article by Tolstopyatov in *Ekonomicheskaya Zhizn'*, March 3, 1929.

sections should be so ordered as to preclude any possibility of a repetition of recent events (the Shakhty affair) " ; [1] and a further resolution treated the Shakhty affair as a result both of the failure of the trade unions to maintain contact with the masses and of their insufficient attention to " important economic organs in which wrecking elements had made their nest ".[2]

In this atmosphere, relations between workers and specialists went from bad to worse. From the Mariupol iron-works came reports of " undisciplined action by workers " seeking to " settle personal accounts with the technical personnel ".[3] At the Skorokhod factory a worker named Bykov, dismissed for drunkenness, absenteeism and spoiling material, attempted to shoot the foreman with a revolver.[4] Three hooligans beat up a mining engineer and wrecked his apartment. Two of them were Komsomol members ; but neither the Komsomol nor the party took any action.[5] Many complaints of this character were voiced at the Vesenkha plenum at the end of November 1928. " The formula ' Public opinion is against him ' ", observed Kuibyshev, " has already become typical " ; in such cases, the leader of the trust or the enterprise " has to take his departure, to flee from the place ".[6] Technical personnel were " exposed to attacks and curses for any justified requirement of labour discipline ", and were " literally hounded ". At one large factory water was poured over an engineer, and a technical manager pelted with melon rind.[7]

Apart from the not unfounded suspicion that a majority of the specialists were unsympathetic to the Soviet régime, and were consciously or unconsciously wedded to " bourgeois " ways of life and thought, a less plausible attempt was sometimes made to associate them with successive oppositions within the party. In 1927 the specialists were likely to feel alarmed by a policy which

---

[1] Vos'moi S"ezd Professional'nykh Soyuzov SSSR (1929), p. 512 ; the membership of these sections had risen at the beginning of 1928 to 129,000 (Professional'nye Soyuzy SSSR, 1926–1928: Otchet k VIII S"ezdu (1928), p. 520) ; for earlier figures see pp. 576-577 above.
[2] Vos'moi S"ezd Professional'nykh Soyuzov SSSR (1929), p. 569.
[3] Torgovo-Promyshlennaya Gazeta, August 24, 1928.
[4] This episode received extensive publicity in the industrial newspaper, being referred to as the " Bykovshchina " ; Bykov was sentenced to ten years' deprivation of liberty (ibid. November 15, 24, December 21, 1928).
[5] Ibid. November 15, 1928.   [6] Ibid. November 30, 1928.
[7] Ibid. November 29, December 1, 1928.

led to a break with the west — if only because this closed the door on hopes of much-needed foreign capital for industry — and which seemed about to jettison the compromises of NEP and point the way back to the hated practices of war communism. But these were not the points on which Trotsky and Zinoviev challenged Stalin, and it is difficult to believe that they found much support among the predominantly non-party specialists. After the Shakhty affair had envenomed the atmosphere, and the opposition within the party came no longer from the Left but from the Right, the situation changed. Bukharin's lukewarm and sceptical attitude to intensive planning and industrialization was an approach to views long held by most specialists ; Rykov, of all Soviet leaders since the death of Dzerzhinsky, had shown most understanding of their grievances and their difficulties. No specific evidence linked the specialists with the Right opposition of the winter of 1928–1929. But knowledge where their sympathies were likely to lie in that quarrel inflamed the growing mistrust of them entertained in official circles. The formation in April 1929 of a group of specialists professing a desire to cooperate with Rabkrin in the campaign to raise industrial efficiency [1] was doubtless a move to counteract these suspicions, but apparently remained without a sequel.

Reliance on specialists inherited from the former régime and steeped in bourgeois ideology was tempered by the assumption that they would be replaced in course of time by Soviet-trained specialists. It was, however, gradually realized that this process would be slow, and that, in a highly critical period for the Soviet economy, reliance on these alien elements in key positions would still be inevitable. Meanwhile, no clear conception had yet emerged of the new type of Soviet specialist or of the methods required to train him. Before 1927 no special attention seems to have been given to the training of engineers and technicians for industry ; and the principal aim was to secure the admission to training establishments of a proper quota of workers and peasants. A decree of the party central committee of June 8, 1926, prescribed that, among those possessing the necessary intellectual qualifications for admission to institutions of higher

[1] *Istoriya SSSR*, No. 1, 1966, p. 87.

education (VUZy), priority should be given to workers, *batraks*, poor and middle peasants, party members and trade unionists, and that 75 per cent of places in technical schools should be reserved for young workers and peasants.[1]   These intentions were not fully realized.   A resolution of the committee of April 13, 1927, noted that the proportion of workers admitted to VUZy had fallen off in 1926, though the quota of those entering technical schools had been maintained.   Nine months later, a further resolution of the party central committee recorded improved percentages of admission to the VUZy :

	1926	1927
Workers (and children)	28·7	31·7
Peasants ,,	22·2	24·3
Employees ,,	49·1	41·0

The resolution welcomed these results, but at the same time deplored the low educational standards of those admitted.[2]

Another problem now loomed on the horizon.   The VUZy and the technical schools, like other forms of education, were under the control of Narkompros.   But the traditional educators of Narkompros gave professional training no high priority ; and only a small proportion of VUZy were institutions specializing in engineering and technology (these were generally referred to as VTUZy). Between 1926 and 1928 the training establishments of the RSFSR turned out from 5500 to 6000 qualified engineers — not a very impressive figure.[3]   The position in the technical schools where lower-grade technicians were trained was even less favourable.   In the RSFSR in 1928, when the number of students in the VTUZy had risen to 36,000, the technical schools had only 16,000 — a ratio of technicians to qualified engineers which was considered far too low.[4]   Any deficiency appears to have been due to the lack of facilities rather than of candidates ; a report of the autumn of 1927 described the pressure of students to enter higher educational

---

[1] *Spravochnik Partiinogo Rabotnika*, vi (1928), i, 694-696, 696-697 ; see also p. 476 above.
[2] *Izvestiya Tsentral'nogo Komiteta VKP(B)*, No. 5 (226), February 22 1928, pp. 3-4.   [3] *Torgovo-Promyshlennaya Gazeta*, April 21, 1928.
[4] *Ibid.* June 28, 1928.

institutions, and especially the Moscow Polytechnic, since engineers were " well paid ".[1] Following the tradition of higher education in the universities, the VTUZy provided broad and theoretically based professional courses in engineering lasting from six to eight years. The more impatient industrialists, mistrustful of the tradition of Narkompros, demanded shorter courses and highly specialized practical training.[2] A good deal of training at a lower level was probably undertaken on an *ad hoc* basis without much attention to recognized procedures. When the Turksib railway was under construction, a building school was established in Semipalatinsk, and it was proposed to set up schools for young Kazakh technicians and apprentices.[3]

A Union conference on industrial and technical education held in September 1927 seems to have been the first concerted attack from the side of industry on this easy-going tradition. Kuibyshev, who dominated the conference, condemned past neglect of the training of engineers. The slogan of industrialization had been proclaimed ; but the capital invested would have been more productive if more skilled labour had been available to use it. As it was, " *technology comes to us essentially through foreigners and through old specialists, not through the schools* ". In spite of the clamour about investment and output, no industry had raised the question of the training of skilled workers. Kuibyshev quoted with approval a remark of Lunacharsky, the People's Commissar for Education, that Narkompros should " really work to the orders of the managers ", but remarked cuttingly that, " in order to commend yourself as a supplier, you must do something " : Narkompros was turning out far more electrical engineers and technicians than were required and far fewer metallurgists and textile engineers. He pursued the comparison of skilled labour with a commodity :

> The client is not indifferent to the way in which the output, for which an advance has sometimes been paid, is organized. . . . The client (i.e. Vesenkha) is bound to adopt a critical attitude to

[1] *Sotsialisticheskii Vestnik* (Berlin), No. 21-22 (163-164), November 10, 1927, p. 22.
[2] These alternatives were canvassed in an editorial in *Torgovo-Promyshlennaya Gazeta*, August 18, 1927, which sagely concluded that both types were needed.
[3] *Turkestano-Sibirskaya Magistral'* (1930), pp. 262-263 ; for the training of industrial labour generally see pp. 475-481 above.

the supplies that are delivered. He must set definite conditions, and perhaps in some cases refuse to accept the output, and indicate to the supplier, i.e. to the organs of Narkompros, that a correction must be made in fulfilling the next order.

In a confused defence of Narkompros, Lunacharsky complained of a lack of precision in the demands of industry : Narkompros had to guess future requirements. Referring to the clash between broad and specialized systems of training, he rather feebly remarked that out of this clash would come the end-product of people who were both efficient experts and pillars of the proletarian power. Kuibyshev replied in a conciliatory vein. He deprecated " the tendency which is quite strong in many of our business circles " to exclude Narkompros from control of technical education : this was " psychologically understandable ", but mistaken. He disclaimed any plan to " subordinate education to the interests of industry ".[1]

The Shakhty affair disturbed this uneasy balance. The moral, as Rykov pointed out at the session of the TsIK of the USSR in April 1928, was that the technical expert could twist the responsible director round his finger if the latter was not technically qualified : the only remedy was to have " a large cadre of better specialists, standing nearer to the working class and the peasantry, and to the task of building a new society ".[2] The party central committee, at its session in April 1928, in its resolution on the Shakhty affair exhorted Vesenkha in general terms to concern itself with the training of " new cadres of Red specialists ",[3] and invited the Politburo " to put on the agenda of an early session [of the central committee] the general question of the training of cadres of specialists ".[4] Stalin after the session spoke at length of the need for Red specialists and managers.[5] Both Kuibyshev and

[1] The conference was fully reported in *Torgovo-Promyshlennaya Gazeta*, September 28, 29, 30, 1927.

[2] *3 Sessiya Tsentral'nogo Ispolnitel'nogo Komiteta Soyuza SSR 4 Sozyva* (1928), p. 343.

[3] *KPSS v Rezolyutsiyakh* (1954), ii, 506; for this resolution see p. 586 above.

[4] Quoted from the archives in *Voprosy Istorii KPSS*, No. 2, 1966, p. 31 ; according to the same source (*ibid.* p. 33) Rykov on this occasion proposed to treat this " as a business question " and to resolve it " in one way or another without touching the class issue ".

[5] Stalin, *Sochineniya*, xi, 58-60 ; later Stalin specifically connected the drive to train Red specialists with the Shakhty affair (*ibid.* xii, 11).

Kraval pleaded, the urgency being what it was, for short courses : [1] this naturally ruled out a " broad " education, and made for practical specialized courses — for the production of what had come to be known as " the Ukrainian type of engineer ".[2] Stalin, without overtly taking sides in this controversy, spoke at the eighth Komsomol congress in May 1928 of the need " to create in rapid tempo new cadres of specialists from people of the working class, from communists, from members of the Komsomol ".[3]

During the summer of 1928 an active campaign was waged to remove the control of technical education from the hands of Narkompros. The first attempts appear to have encountered objections not only from Narkompros, but from some students.[4] But the well-known Mendeleev Institute of Chemical Technology in Moscow requested that it should be transferred to Vesenkha, alleging that it was starved of funds.[5] At a conference convened by the editorial board of Pravda on June 22, 1928, on the training of " Red specialists ", the VTUZy were once more criticized as too theoretical ; this was said to result from their subordination to Narkompros.[6] Meanwhile the initiative recorded at the session of the party central committee in April 1928 had resulted in the appointment by the Politburo of a representative commission which reported to the July session of the committee.[7] Discussion at this session was evidently keen ; according to one account, a proposal supported by Stalin to transfer control of the VTUZy to Vesenkha was defeated by a two-thirds majority headed by Rykov.[8] The resolution as finally adopted left this delicate issue open ; steps were to be taken in the year 1928–1929 " to proceed . . . to the unification of systems of technical education in the USSR ". But on specific points the resolution was more emphatic. Industry was declared to suffer from employing too low a per-

[1] Torgovo-Promyshlennaya Gazeta, March 29, April 21, 1928.
[2] For this phrase see ibid. September 29, 1927.
[3] Stalin, Sochineniya, xi, 75.
[4] See the discussion at the central bureau of proletarian students reported in Torgovo-Promyshlennaya Gazeta, April 21, 1928 ; opposition in party circles in Moscow was recorded in a report in the Trotsky archives, T 2021.
[5] Torgovo-Promyshlennaya Gazeta, May 13, 1928.
[6] Pravda, June 26, 29, 1928 ; for further articles on this controversy by Lunacharsky and others see ibid. June 27, July 5, 1928.
[7] Voprosy Istorii KPSS, No. 2, 1966, p. 31.
[8] Trotsky archives, T 1588 ; the authenticity of this source is uncertain.

centage of engineers, and a still lower percentage of technicians ;
the flow of " new cadres of young specialists " was inadequate.
Far-reaching proposals were made to reform and reinvigorate
technical education at all levels throughout the Soviet Union.
" VTUZy of a new type " were to be set up with courses not
exceeding 3 or 4 years. The network of technical schools was to
be extended. Six VTUZy and five technical schools were to be
placed under the management of ʹVesenkha, and two VTUZy
under that of Narkomput'. It was proposed that 1000 party
members should be admitted to the VTUZy in the current year,
and that 65 per cent of all those admitted to the schools should be
children of workers or peasants.[1]

These proposals inspired in August 1928 the first comprehensive decree of the USSR on the training of " new specialists ". A
100 per cent increase in the number of qualified engineers in heavy
industry was contemplated over the period of the plan with a ratio
of technicians to engineers of 3 : 2. Technical training establishments were to be attached to the principal industrial institutions.
But training was not to be exclusively technical : political economy
and at least one foreign language were to figure in the courses.
Foreign specialists and foreign text-books were to be employed,
and student specialists were to be encouraged to travel abroad.
Not less than 65 per cent of the places in these establishments were
to be reserved for the children of workers.[2] The party central
committee, in a further resolution of November 9, 1928, complained that the decision of the previous July on the VTUZy and
technical colleges was being applied very slowly ;[3] and Kraval
continued to attack the VTUZy, protesting that the training of
engineers was not sufficiently specialized, and was " below the

---

[1] KPSS v Rezolyutsiyakh (1954), ii, 518-524 ; for the decree carrying out
this decision see Sobranie Zakonov, 1928, No. 46, art. 409. In the discussions
following the session (see reports in the Trotsky archives, T 2021, 2167) it was
pointed out that 60 per cent of the professors in the VTUZy were " not ours ",
and that the admission of workers and peasants was incompatible with the
maintenance of a competitive entrance examination, which was " a Chinese wall
to workers wanting to enter the VTUZy ".

[2] Sobranie Zakonov, 1928, No. 58, art. 513.

[3] Izvestiya Tsentral'nogo Komiteta VKP(B), No. 33 (255), November 22,
1928, pp. 1-12 ; for a confused account of obstruction from Glavprofobr,
surprisingly supported by some circles in Vesenkha, see Voprosy Istorii KPSS,
No. 2, 1966, pp. 33-34.

level of western European and American technical achievements
and also behind the technical innovations which have already been
applied in our industry".[1] The first five-year plan, drafted at the
moment of this intensive drive, provided for an increase of the
number of Soviet engineers from 20,200 in 1927–1928 to 35,200
five years later, and an increase in the number of trained technicians from 20,000 to 60,000.[2] But all these measures took time
to fructify. The new Soviet-trained engineer still failed to make
his mark.[3] Down to the end of the nineteen-twenties, or even
later, the characteristic partnership at the head of industrial trusts
and factories was of a technically and culturally untutored party
president or director and a technically qualified manager or
engineer, whose affiliations linked him naturally with the beliefs
and practices of the old régime, and whose loyalty to the ruling
party and government was hesitant or suspect. Such was the
background of the first years of the industrialization drive, and
of the series of trials of alleged traitors and wreckers among
industrialists and economists which began with the Shakhty trial
in 1928.

A further source of jealousy which sometimes affected the
efficiency of the corps of engineers as a whole arose between older
and younger engineers. Of the specialists covered by the investigation of 1929, 23·3 per cent were aged 45 or over, 30·2 per cent
from 35 to 44, and 46·5 per cent less than 35 ; 30·7 per cent had
worked in this capacity before 1917, 32 per cent had begun work
between 1918 and 1925, and 37·3 per cent since 1926.[4] Friction
between generations was a familiar phenomenon, and the blame
could not be fastened exclusively on one side. The spokesman of
VUMBIT at the third Ukrainian trade union congress in Novem-

[1] *Puti Industrializatsii*, No. 11, 1928, pp. 12-14.
[2] *Pyatiletnii Plan Narodno-Khozyaistvennogo Stroitel'stva SSSR* (1929), i, 74-75.
[3] A decree of Sovnarkom of July 3, 1929, instructed Vesenkha and Narkom-put' to take measures to improve the training of engineers (*Sobranie Zakonov, 1929*, No. 43, art. 382) ; and a leading article in the party journal criticized the VTUZy for their lack of contact with industry and for continuing to employ reactionary professors, and the party and the trade unions for failing to pay sufficient attention to the matter, concluding that " the five-year plan cannot be fulfilled unless it is guaranteed by *cadres of new proletarian specialists* " (*Bol'shevik*, No. 20, October 31, 1929, pp. 3-8).
[4] *Ekonomicheskoe Obozrenie*, No. 12, 1929, pp. 104, 106; for detailed tables see *ibid.* pp. 120-121.

ber 1926 had a simple explanation of the friction between old and young specialists : the young lacked experience, but did not want to learn from the old.[1] The old engineers were severely criticized early in 1928 for their failure both to make use of foreign engineers and to train the young,[2] though a defender of the older generation put the blame on the young engineers, who " treat the just demands of the old engineer on the young as oppressive ".[3] The party central committee at its session in April 1928 noted curtly that " the newly arrived young Red specialists frequently meet with an openly hostile attitude on the part of the old specialists ".[4] The issue was inconclusively debated at the trade union central council in December 1928. One speaker said that the young engineer did not frequent the engineers' clubs because the environment was alien to him ; another suspected the older engineers of exercising a reactionary influence on the young.[5] But jealousy between generations seems to have been a less disturbing factor than the traditional background and ideology common to all but a few of the specialists. Even of those who had received their training and entered the profession since the revolution, a large majority belonged by their social origins and affiliations to the pre-revolutionary order. Of 14,800 scientific workers in the RSFSR enrolled in the educational workers' trade union (Rabpros) on October 1, 1928, over half had begun to work before the revolution ; only 7·8 per cent were of worker, and 5·8 per cent of peasant, origin, and only 4·6 per cent were party members.[6] The higher the qualification, the greater was the proportion of those whose roots were in the past. Of engineers with higher professional education in 1929 only 6·2 per cent were workers by origin.[7]

The training of " Red " directors and managers was a less extensive, but equally troublesome, problem. It had originally been raised as early as 1925.[8] But two years later a survey

[1] *Stenograficheskii Otchet 3ᵍᵒ Vseukrainskogo S"ezda Profsoyuzov* (1927) p. 149.   [2] *Pravda*, March 4, 1928.
[3] *Torgovo-Promyshlennaya Gazeta*, June 3, 1928.
[4] *KPSS v Rezolyutsiyakh* (1954), ii, 502.
[5] *Torgovo-Promyshlennaya Gazeta*, December 13, 1928.
[6] *Istoriya SSSR*, No. 6, 1959, p. 95.
[7] *Eko nomicheskoe Obozrenie*, No. 12, 1929, p. 107.
[8] See *Socialism in One Cou ntry, 1924–1926*, Vol. 1, pp. 379–381.

disclosed that 46 out of 66 presidents of Union trusts, and 601 out of 823 factory directors, included in the enquiry had received only "domestic" education, often dating back some 20 years.[1] In January 1928, nine-tenths of all directors were party members, but only 2·8 per cent had received higher education, whereas 58 per cent of the few non-party directors had had higher education.[2] Anecdotes of ignorant directors and managers issuing impracticable orders to qualified specialists were widely current,[3] and certainly did not lack foundation. The only course for managers set up in 1925 was a short part-time course of 10 hours a week : 141 men were enrolled and 79 finished the course.[4] In the following year arrangements were made for six-week or three-month full-time courses and part-time evening courses in various centres.[5] In 1927, on the proposal of Vesenkha, an academy for administrative and managerial staff, which came to be known as the Industrial Academy, was established in Moscow. It offered three-year courses, and candidates with insufficient formal education were put through a ten weeks' preliminary course in Russian, mathematics, drawing, physics and chemistry. The first enrolment in August 1927 was of 80 students ; the number was raised to 100 in 1928.[6] In addition, 280 directors and managers were sent abroad by Vesenkha in 1926–1927 to study the methods of foreign firms ; [7] this practice continued for several years. The decree on factory management of September 5, 1929, attempted to improve the status of Red directors by giving them greater security of tenure, and by proposing to grant them from one-and-a-half to two months' supplementary leave (presumably annual) " for the purpose of raising their theoretical qualifications ".[8]

During this period the prestige of foreign, and especially American, technical achievements still stood high ; and consider-

[1] *Torgovo-Promyshlennaya Gazeta*, August 6, 1927.
[2] *Bol'shevik*, No. 15, August 15, 1928, p. 27.
[3] N. Borodin, *One Man in his Time* (1955), pp. 73-74, 81-83 ; *Pravda*, April 13, 1927.   [4] *Torgovo-Promyshlennaya Gazeta*, July 4, 1926.
[5] *Ibid.* August 6, 1927.
[6] *SSSR : 4 S"ezd Sovetov* (1927), p. 394 ; *Torgovo-Promyshlennaya Gazeta*, August 6, 1927, April 1, 1928.   [7] *Ibid.* August 6, 1927.
[8] *Direktivy KPSS i Sovetskogo Pravitel'stva po Khozyaistvennym Voprosam*, ii (1957), 125.

able effort was made to attract foreign engineers, technicians and skilled workers into the service of Soviet industry. In 1924 only 23 foreign engineers had worked in the Soviet Union; the number had risen to 80 in 1925 and to 127 in November 1927, not counting a larger number of foremen and skilled workers : they were mainly, though not exclusively, employed in capital goods industries.[1]   This influx, however trivial in numbers, was little to the taste of Soviet engineers, who were reproached with their jealousy of foreign specialists and their reluctance to learn from western techniques. Tomsky, who shared some of the workers' mistrust of engineers, spoke candidly of this "jealousy" at the fifteenth party conference in October 1926 :

> If you have ever happened to have a heart-to-heart talk with our technicians and engineers, and to touch on such questions as that, say, in western Europe the situation is fine as regards technology, you have probably noticed how sensitively they react to this. "What are you saying about western Europe ? We know this business as well as they do. If we had had the resources, we should know how to fix this up just as they do".[2]

The first open pronouncement from the side of the specialists seems to have come from a spokesman of VUMBIT who told the third Ukrainian trade union congress in November 1926 that " we of course adopt a negative attitude " to the employment of foreign engineers in Soviet industrial concerns, but that they would be accepted " in very limited numbers and on condition of the strictest selection and corresponding agreement on the question with the engineers' and technicians' sections ".[3]   By this time the

---

[1] *Torgovo-Promyshlennaya Gazeta*, November 13, 1926, November 24, 1927.
[2] *XV Konferentsiya Vsesoyuznoi Kommunisticheskoi Partii VKP(B)* (1927), p. 279.
[3] *Stenograficheskii Otchet 3⁰⁰ Vseukrainskogo S"ezda Profsoyuzov*, p. 144 ; friction often occurred with American engineers. A secretary of a party cell said : " We made the revolution ourselves, and we will be able to organize production ourselves ". Americans disliked party members without technical qualifications being placed at the head of important projects ; Soviet engineers lacked practical experience, and refused to go into the plant and work side by side with the workers (E. Friedman, *Russia in Transition* (1932), pp. 252-253, 257-258). When friction occurred between Russian and American engineers working on the Stalingrad tractor factory, where Calder, who had built the Ford

industrial leaders were convinced that the design and execution of projects using modern technology required the employment of foreign engineers and consultants. In May 1927 Mezhlauk, the president of Glavmetall, emphasized the need to use foreign experts, " transferring whole projects and their sections abroad ", and sending Soviet engineers and technicians abroad.[1] Later in the year at the fifteenth party congress Mikoyan once more light-heartedly rebutted the prejudice against the foreign specialist :

> If the art of the barber has already been discovered, it is pointless to learn it all over again on our own cheeks. We do not need harmful amateurism. We need the achievements of the latest European and American techniques. We should not recapitulate all the stages of development of technical thinking.

He added that three million rubles had been spent on foreign drawings and patents in 1926–1927, and twice this amount would be spent in the current year.[2]   At the third plenum of Vesenkha early in March 1928 many reservations were expressed about the employment of foreign engineers.   Shein, the president of VMBIT, declared deprecatingly that the engineers and technicians were not opposed to the employment of foreign engineers, but wished them to be used for training rather than directly in production.   Lomov, the president of Donugol, said that excellent results had been achieved in the Donbass by employing foreign engineers in project-making, but not in production ;   and Sukhomlin, speaking for the Ukrainian Vesenkha, put the main emphasis on the training of Soviet engineers.   Kuibyshev and Rukhimovich stood out stoutly for the employment of foreign engineers, stressing the gap which still existed between Russian and western technology.[3]   The revelations of the Shakhty affair did not alter the official attitude.

---

factories in the United States, was the chief construction engineer, a contemporary Soviet source blamed the Russians for conservatism, chauvinism, sabotage and remoteness from the workers ; while American engineers were active on the site, looking very little different from workers, Russian engineers sat in their offices (I. Taskaev, *Pervyi Traktornyi* (Saratov, 1930), pp. 7-8).

[1] *Pravda*, May 11, 15, 1927.
[2] *Pyatnadtsatyi S"ezd VKP(B)*, ii (1962), 1100.
[3] *Torgovo-Promyshlennaya Gazeta*, March 7, 8, 1928 ; for Lomov see p. 582 above.

A few weeks later Kuibyshev again insisted on the importance of foreign technical aid and derided those Soviet specialists who treated invitations to foreign engineers as " almost an insult " ; [1] and the party central committee in April 1928, in its resolution on the Shakhty affair, still proposed " to organize the systematic recruitment of foreign specialists to work in our enterprises "[2]. Shein, in his speech at the Shakhty trial, referred to the " self-delusion " of some engineers and technicians, and to their " un-willingness to utilize foreign aid in full measure "[3]   In August 1928 an agreement was reached with the Freyn Engineering Company of Chicago, which designed the Kuznetsk iron and steel works, that twelve of its engineers would work permanently in the USSR.[4] The Soviet leaders came to rely increasingly on foreign assistance to introduce the latest technology into industry in general and in particular to prepare major projects, and often supported American engineers against the " conservatism " of the Russian engineers.[5] By 1929 the number of foreign " engineers and technicians " employed in Soviet industry had risen to 550, and the complaint was made that this number was " utterly insufficient to obtain serious results ".[6] It seems clear that at this time the Soviet leaders were less mistrustful of foreign — and in particular American — engineers than of the former bourgeois specialists who still dominated the field at home.

The question of the remuneration of specialists continued to give trouble. The plan mooted in 1925 for the introduction of a separate salary-scale for specialists [7] was continually discussed, but made no progress. The seventh trade union congress in December 1926 assumed that, with the introduction of a salary scale for specialists, the need for " supplements, bonuses and, as a rule, special rates " would disappear, though " in indispensable cases " rewards in the forms of bonuses might be awarded " for really

[1] *Torgovo-Promyshlennaya Gazeta*, March 29, 1928.
[2] *KPSS v Rezolyutsiyakh* (1954), ii, 506.
[3] For this speech see p. 585 above.
[4] *Torgovo-Promyshlennaya Gazeta*, June 29, July 15, August 8, 1928.
[5] See pp. 909-910 below.
[6] *Promyshlennyi Import*, ed. S. Aralov and A. Shatkhan (1930), p. 159.
[7] See *Socialism in One Country, 1924-1926*, Vol. 1, p. 380.

practical achievements in production ".[1] But the way was now open for a somewhat confused compromise. The idea of a salary-scale for specialists was tacitly dropped. But by a decree of March 7, 1927, " leading administrative and technical personnel " (i.e. those above the levels covered by existing wage-scales for non-manual workers) were entitled to receive " incentive payments " on the basis of individual achievements in promoting rationalization and increased profitability. The total allocation to the enterprise was made by the Sovnarkom, TsIK or other organ of the republic concerned ; the allocation to individuals was made by the management of the enterprise.[2] In June 1927 incentive payments were extended to state and cooperative trading enterprises.[3] The substitution of incentive payments for bonuses seems to have been a distinction without a difference, but served to emphasize the gearing of rewards not so much to profits as to higher productivity. Meanwhile the commission which had been in control of personal salaries since 1924 was disbanded, and its functions assigned to Narkomtrud ; [4] and some lower specialists were transferred to the category of employees whose salary-scales were fixed by the state.[5] Thanks to these measures, the total of personal salaries, which had stood at 5 million rubles a month in 1926–1927, was reduced to 3·8 millions in 1927–1928.[6]

Information regarding the income of specialists in these years is scarce, and wide variations occurred. Engineers and technicians fell into two categories : those on the ordinary salary-scale of " employees ", and those in receipt of personal salaries (the latter including most fully qualified engineers). Under the salary-scales the pay of " engineering and technical personnel and employees " was throughout these years less than twice that of manual

[1] *Sed'moi S"ezd Professional'nykh Soyuzov SSSR* (1927), p. 788.
[2] *Sobranie Zakonov*, *1927*, No. 16, art. 167.
[3] *Ibid.* No. 34, art. 357.
[4] *Ibid.* No. 33, art. 346 ; the new statute of Narkomtrud of September 1928 (see p. 465 above) required it to keep a register of all specialists.
[5] Early in 1927 the trade union central council decided that employees of trusts and trading organizations should be placed on regular state-fixed salaries, and the employees of factory administrations on ordinary wage-scales ; but this proved too complicated, and was evidently carried out only to a limited extent (*Professional'nye Soyuzy SSSR*, *1926–1928: Otchet k VIII S"ezdu* (1928), pp. 325, 328).
[6] *Obzor Deyatel'nosti NKT SSSR za 1927–1928 gg.* (1928), p. 86.

workers, and the differentiation tended to diminish. The following table shows monthly pay in rubles :

	Workers	Engineers, Technicians and Employees
1925	45	88
1926	57	106
1927	63	115
1928	69	123
1929	75	134 [1]

But these rates had no relation to those paid to higher specialists. In March 1926, when the average monthly wage of the worker was 58·64 rubles, the average monthly salary of a manager was 187·90 if he was a party member, 309·50 if he was non-party.[2] In June 1926, to ease the position of the party specialist, a new ruling on the party maximum was issued by the party central committee :

> In cases where the earnings of party members working in production, but not paid according to the tariff for responsible workers, exceed the party maximum, the excess over the party maximum is not liable to confiscation.[3]

When personal salaries were transferred to the control of Narkomtrud in May 1927, it was laid down that salaries of more than 360

[1] *Trud v SSSR* (1936), p. 96.
[2] S. Zagorsky, *Wages and Regulation of Conditions of Labour in the USSR* (Geneva, 1930), pp. 176, 178.
[3] *Izvestiya Tsentral'nogo Komiteta VKP(B)*, No. 26 (147), June 30, 1926, p. 8 ; a subsequent instruction was issued (it is not clear on what occasion) explaining that this rule applied to technical personnel (*ibid*. No. 1 (222), January 10, 1928, p. 6). On the other hand party members could not accept bonuses (tantièmes) : these must be paid into party funds (*ibid*. No. 11 (232), April 4, 1928, p. 7). Figures of the "party maximum" (i.e. the maximum remuneration which a party member was allowed to receive) were no longer published at this time. The Politburo on September 20, 1928, decided to raise it by 20 per cent to 270 rubles a month in Moscow and Leningrad (lower rates were in force elsewhere), but to confine the increase to responsible workers "working without regular limitation of the working day" ; Narkomtrud was to define the category of "responsible workers" more strictly and confine it to those properly qualified (Trotsky archives, T 2606). The decision was apparently taken on the recommendation of a Politburo "commission on the party maximum" presided over by Tomsky, which on August 27, 1928, pronounced in favour of raising the salaries of responsible workers (*ibid*. T 2394).

rubles a month must be registered at Narkomtrud : [1] salaries up to that amount were evidently regarded as normal. Salaries of specialists on the staff of Gosplan in 1926–1927 ranged from 250 to 500 rubles a month.[2] A plan for the newly created Machine-Tractor Stations put forward in 1928 proposed monthly salaries of 300 rubles for the director and 250 for the chief engineer.[3] By a decree of April 1928 salaries of from 360 to 500 rubles a month required the approval of the Narkomtrud of one of the republics, and above 500 rubles of the Narkomtrud of the USSR ; a later decree referred to the possibility of the same individual holding two jobs separately assessed, the limit requiring the approval of the Union Narkomtrud being fixed at 540 rubles a month.[4] At the "industrial party" trial in 1930, Ramzin, the principal defendant, reckoned his monthly earnings at 1500 rubles, and the Gosplan engineer Kalinnikov put his at 1000 : both these figures included literary earnings.[5] These were probably among the highest incomes received by specialists.

[1] For this decree see p. 602, note 4 above.
[2] See p. 803, note 2 below.
[3] A. Markevich, *Mezhselennye Mashino-Traktornye Stantsii* (2nd ed. 1929), p. 101.
[4] *Sobranie Zakonov, 1928*, No. 26, art. 236 ; No. 59, art. 531.
[5] *Le Procès des Industriels de Moscou* (1931), pp. 210, 242.

CHAPTER 22

SOCIAL POLICIES

(a) Social Insurance

SOCIAL insurance for the industrial worker was now firmly established, though with many shortcomings, in the Soviet administrative system.[1] The number of those insured rose steadily from 6,500,000 in 1924 to 8,491,000 on October 1, 1926, and 9,245,000 on October 1, 1927 ;[2] a year later it had reached 9,658,000.[3] The principal benefits were permanent disability pensions, maternity and funeral benefits, benefits in case of temporary sickness or incapacity, and unemployment benefits.[4] It had been intended to pay full wages in cases of temporary incapacity to workers earning less than 180 rubles a month — a high limit. But in the summer of 1926, under the stress of the " régime of economy ", payments were curtailed on the ground that they encouraged malingering.[5] Medical care for workers was provided free, and absorbed a larger proportion of the insurance fund than any other item except disability pensions.[6] This, together with the provision of sanatoria and rest houses for workers, was the only service which did not take the form of monetary payments. Information about the health of workers is scarce. But of 3170 chemical workers in Moscow on January 1, 1926, 1051 were reported

[1] See Socialism in One Country, 1924–1926, Vol. 1, pp. 403-404.
[2] Pervye Shagi Industrializatsii SSSR 1926–1927 gg. (1959), p. 231 ; Sed'moi S"ezd Professional'nykh Soyuzov SSSR (1927), p. 355.
[3] Vos'moi S"ezd Professional'nykh Soyuzov SSSR (1929), pp. 322, 368 ; this total was said to include 200,000 batraks for whom contributions were levied from employers, but who, for practical reasons, had no access to benefits.
[4] For the amounts payable to beneficiaries see Pervye Shagi Industrializatsii SSSR 1926–1927 gg. (1959), p. 232 ; maternity benefit was said in 1926 to have averaged a lump payment of 23 rubles plus 5·75 rubles a month for nine months (Sed'moi S"ezd Professional'nykh Soyuzov SSSR (1927), pp. 354-355).
[5] Ibid. p. 360.
[6] For the total amounts paid out in these years see Table No. 26, p. 959 below.

to be cases, or suspected cases, of tuberculosis, and 779 had afflictions of the heart or the blood vessels. Of a total of 144,750 workers in Moscow, 86,000 had received medical treatment ; of these 31,000 were cases of tuberculosis.[1] At the fifteenth party congress in December 1927 Stalin spoke of the sanatoria and rest houses, the subventions to the unemployed, and the pensions to disabled workers and veterans of the civil war, as evidence of the improved material situation of the working class.[2]

Relief for the unemployed was still the weakest link in the chain. It was severely restricted, partly, no doubt, by financial considerations, but partly also by the difficulty of defining *bona fide* unemployment and the danger of opening the gates too wide, by trade union jealousy of aid for any who were not members of unions, and by fear of weakening the incentive to seek work. But the rising tide of unemployment gradually sapped these inhibitions. In 1926 about 350,000 unemployed were in receipt of relief which averaged 10 rubles a month for unskilled workers and 15 rubles for skilled workers, supplemented by additional allowances for children ; highly skilled workers in Moscow (rates varied in different piarts of the country) might receive as much as 22·50 rubles, wh ch approximated to the lowest wage of an unskilled worker.[3] Two years later, 765,000 unemployed were in receipt of relief, and rates of relief had risen by 16 per cent — or, for the highest category of workers, by 26 per cent.[4] But such high rates were exceptional. The average rate of unemployed relief rose from 12·55 rubles a month in October 1926 to 13·51 rubles in July 1928.[5]

The initial social insurance scheme made no provision for old-age pensions (other than disability pensions). But the manifesto of October 15, 1927, on the tenth anniversary of the revolution, promised the gradual introduction of " insurance at state expense

---

[1] *Predpriyatie*, No. 8, 1926, pp. 3-4.

[2] Stalin, *Sochineniya*, x, 314 ; the veterans' pensions, though rarely mentioned, were at a higher rate than the workers' disability pensions (*Pervye Shagi Industrializatsii SSSR 1926-1927 gg.* (1959), p. 232).

[3] *Vos'moi S''ezd Professional'nykh Soyuzov SSSR* (1929), pp. 355-356.

[4] *Ibid.* p. 324.

[5] *Pervye Shagi Industrializatsii SSSR 1926-1927 gg.* (1959), p. 232 ; the average rate of disability pension rose during the same period from 17·95 to 22·35 rubles a month. The period was one of stable retail prices (see Table No. 31, pp. 964-965 below), but of increasing shortages.

of persons of advanced age ", to include even " the poorer strata of the peasantry " — an addition which led Trotsky to dismiss the scheme as " plain nonsense ".[1] Twelve months later, the eighth trade union congress of December 1928 announced the introduction of retirement pensions for industrial workers. Hitherto only the textile workers' union had made any attempt to provide for the old age of its members. It was now proposed to pay retirement pensions, amounting to four-ninths of wages, to railwaymen, metal workers and miners : this was expected to cover 40,000 workers in the year 1928–1929.[2] A delegate at the congress made the perhaps unrealistic assumption that " the expenses incurred by transferring aged workers to a pension will be covered by a reduction of the costs of furnishing material aid to the unemployed ".[3] The resolution of the congress enthusiastically welcomed the innovation and called for its extension to other industries, where its absence prejudiced " not only the interests of particular groups of the proletariat, but also the needs of the corresponding sectors of the national economy, the rationalization of which is impeded by the retention of elderly workers, involving a diminution of the productivity of labour ".[4] The project was realized in a decree of May 18, 1929, providing for old-age pensions for workers in the mining, metal, electrical and textile industries and in transport.

---

[1] Memorandum in Trotsky archives, T 3097 ; for the anniversary manifesto see p. 33 above. Some scruples were evidently felt at this time about the virtual restriction of insurance to the industrial worker ; the insurance journal in its anniversary article declared that " social insurance, far from being an institution created for urban workers, must be converted into an institution covering also the peasantry " (*Voprosy Strakhovaniya*, No. 44, 1927, p. 3).

[2] *Vos'moi S"ezd Professional'nykh Soyuzov* (1929), p. 322. The scheme had been worked out in the control figures for 1928–1929 submitted by Narkomtrud to Gosplan in November 1928 ; it was to be limited to workers of 60 or over (55 or over for women) who had worked in the industry for not less than 25 years. It was described as being calculated " to assist the rejuvenation of the labour force and the mitigation of unemployment " (*Kontrol'nye Tsifry po Trudu na 1928–29 god* (1929), pp. 52-53).

[3] *Vos'moi S"ezd Professional'nykh Soyuzov SSSR* (1929), p. 344.

[4] *Ibid.* p. 563 ; an article in the journal of Narkomtrud stated that " the specific purpose of the law is to eliminate old people from production ", and added that " the new law has great importance for our unemployed youth, who will have the opportunity to take jobs vacated by the old " (*Voprosy Truda*, March–April 1929, pp. 118, 120). Strumilin had advocated the measure as early as March 1927 as a means of relieving unemployment (S. Strumilin. *Ocherki Sovetskoi Ekonomiki* (1928), p. 481).

Men of 60 who had worked for 25 years and women of 55 who had worked for 20 years were eligible for pensions, which were to be paid at the rate of half the wage paid before retirement.[1] The control figures of 1928–1929 reckoned on the payment of 70,000 old-age pensions at an annual cost of 17 million rubles.[2]

By the year 1928–1929, therefore, a comprehensive social insurance scheme, restricted almost exclusively to the employed urban population, was in operation in the Soviet Union, its most striking features being the large and growing cost of disability pensions, and the rising, but still comparatively modest, allocation to unemployment relief. The grading of benefits to wages, which had been adopted from the outset as the basis of the Soviet system, as well as the consistently cautious attitude to unemployment relief, were beyond doubt prompted by the strong desire to maintain and strengthen incentives to production. Nevertheless, down to 1929, the eleemosynary character of the system appeared to predominate. The compilers of the first five-year plan drafted in the autumn of 1928, looked forward confidently to a doubling of the insurance fund over the five-year period, with old-age pensions firmly established, and substantially higher payments to the disabled and the unemployed, and to the medical services.[3] The financial implications of the scheme were at first, perhaps, not taken very seriously. The trade union central council at its session of June 1926 had been obliged to recognise that " the financial position of the insurance fund is very strained ".[4] At the seventh trade union congress in December 1926, the *rapporteur* on social insurance issued a warning against reductions, conceded on various pretexts, in the percentage of wages payable by employers to the insurance fund, and declared that a continuation of this process " threatens the very foundations of insured assistance to the workers ".[5] At the eighth congress two years later the same

---

[1] *Sobranie Zakonov, 1929*, No. 32, art. 289.

[2] *Kontrol'nye Tsifry Narodnogo Khozyaistva SSSR na 1928–1929 god* (1929), p. 48. This is the estimate for a full year; the figure for 1928–1929 in Table No. 26, p. 959 below, is 8 million rubles.

[3] *Pyatiletnii Plan Narodno-Khozyaistvennogo Stroitel'stva SSSR* (1929), i, 97-98.　　　　[4] *Trud*, June 6, 1926.

[5] *Sed'moi S"ezd Professional'nykh Soyuzov SSSR* (1927), p. 361. Employers' payments were graded according to the degree of danger to life or health inherent in the occupation concerned ; but exemptions or favourable rates were also granted in special conditions.

rapporteur drew a gloomy picture of the state of the fund. Since 1924–1925, when it achieved a surplus of 37 million rubles, it had been faced by a constant struggle to make both ends meet. The two succeeding years had produced deficits of 19 and 3 million rubles respectively. In 1927–1928 reserves were completely exhausted, and some offices had been obliged to suspend payment for a time. It was only thanks to this partial default that the fund had balanced at the end of the year. During the past two years the average percentage of wages payable by the employer to the fund had been reduced from 13·4 to 12·7 (of which 0·5 per cent went to the housing fund) ; this meant that receipts had risen more slowly than the demands on the fund. The collection of arrears of contributions had helped, but this resource was now virtually exhausted. A diversion of 35 million rubles during the past two years from the medical fund to the pensions fund could not be repeated. A provision to advance the date of payment of employers' contributions (which meant that payments for 13 months would in fact be made during the current year), as well as to retard certain disbursements, enabled the fund not merely to present a balanced budget for 1928–1929, but to estimate for a surplus of 50 million rubles by way of a reserve.[1] These expedients, and the embarrassments which they were intended to relieve, were symptomatic of strain placed by the process of industrialization on every sector of the economy.

In addition to social insurance benefits, the workers had since 1925 derived some rather precarious advantages from a welfare fund created by setting aside 10 per cent of the profits of state trusts and trading organizations.[2] Complaints were made that the fund, the major part of which went to subsidize housing, but which also provided crèches, dining-rooms, bath-houses, clubs, etc. for the workers, was administered centrally, and did not cater specifically for the workers in the enterprise from whose profits it was drawn.[3] But the statute on trusts also allocated a share of savings in cost to a " director's fund " ; and, where an enterprise achieved a reduction in costs of production substantially in excess

[1] *Vos'moi S"ezd Professional'nykh Soyuzov SSSR* (1929), pp. 336-338.
[2] See *Socialism in One Country, 1924–1926*, Vol. 1, p. 407.
[3] *Professional'nye Soyuzy SSSR, 1926–1928: Otchet k VIII S"ezdu* (1928), 414-416.

X

of the planned reduction, the decree of June 14, 1928, allowed this fund to be used at the discretion of the director for betterment of living and working conditions of the workers.[1] The director's fund later assumed increasing importance both as an incentive to production and as a welfare agency.

(b) Protection of Labour

The accident rate in large-scale industry, which had begun to cause serious concern in 1924–1925,[2] increased by more than 50 per cent in the next two years, rising from an average for the principal industries of 26 accidents per 1000 workers in the last quarter of 1925 to 44·3 in the last quarter of 1927 ; the highest rate was in mining, the lowest in the textile industry.[3] The claim that the increase was due in part to better reporting of accidents probably had some justification ; and the number of accidents was certainly swelled by the employment of untrained workers fresh from the countryside, and by the high turnover of labour. Increased consumption of alcohol was also named as a cause.[4] But the general consensus of opinion associated the increase with the campaign for higher productivity. From 1925 onwards a system was instituted of annual agreements between the trade unions and economic establishments controlled by Vesenkha under which the latter undertook to set aside a given sum to be spent on measures to improve the health and safety of the workers. In 1925–1926 20 million rubles were allocated for this purpose.[5] Concern, however, continued to be widely expressed. A speaker at the third Ukrainian trade union congress in November 1926 quoted American statistics to show that the accident rate in American industry was the highest in the world, but admitted the alarming increase

---

[1] For this decree see p. 514 above ; for the statute on trusts see p. 372 above.

[2] See *Socialism in One Country, 1924–1926*, Vol. 1, pp. 392-393.

[3] *Obzor Deyatel'nosti NKT SSSR za 1927–1928 gg.* (1928), p. 119 ; the opposition platform of September 1927 quoted a Narkomtrud figure of 97·6 accidents per 1000 workers in 1925–1926 (L. Trotsky, *The Real Situation in Russia* (n.d. [1928]), p. 49).

[4] *Ekonomicheskii Byulleten' Kon"yunkturnogo Instituta*, No. 11-12, 1927, p. 89.

[5] The system was described by Shmidt at the seventh trade union congress in December 1926 (*Sed'moi S"ezd Professional'nykh Soyuzov SSSR* (1927), p. 340).

of accidents in Soviet industry from 1925 to 1926.[1] At the seventh
trade union congress a few days later Shmidt spoke of the continuous growth of the accident rate which he considered inevitable
" in view of the intensity of labour, of the loading of our factories,
in conjunction with the worn-out character of our plant " ; the
greatest difficulties were encountered in the Ural region, where
" industry is technically most backward " and equipment dated
from " before the flood ".[2] This conclusion was endorsed in the
resolution of the congress, which also suggested that economic
organs should be held responsible for the safety of workers under
" a tariff of incentives and penalties ".[3] But progress was slow.
Under agreements concluded between the trade unions and
Vesenkha for 1926–1927 the sum allocated for the improvement of
factory conditions was raised to 37 million rubles. But the agreements were not finally settled till the spring of 1927 ; only 20
millions were spent in the current financial year, and most of this
went to improvements in sanitation and ventilation, which were
especially important in the textile industry, rather than to the pre-
vention of accidents.[4] The Gosplan control figures for 1927–1928
for the first time contained a section on the protection of labour,
and proposed an allocation of 43 millions for this purpose during
the year.[5] At the fifteenth party congress of December 1927
Dogadov accused Vesenkha of " a purely bookkeeping accountancy
approach " when it " mechanically " closed unspent credits at the
end of the financial year.[6] It appears that they were eventually
released, and the money spent.[7]

From this time onwards, growing sensitiveness to the ele-
mentary needs of the worker seems to have been stimulated by
recognition that this was an essential condition of the expansion
of industrial production. More systematic attention was paid to
problems of health and safety.[8] Though the conclusion of the

---

[1] *Stenograficheskii Otchet 3go Vseukrainskogo S"ezda Profsoyuzov* (1927),
p. 248.   [2] *Sed'moi S"ezd Professional'nykh Soyuzov SSSR* (1927), pp. 339-341.
[3] *Ibid.* p. 750.
[4] *Obzor Deyatel'nosti NKT SSSR za 1927–1928 gg.* (1928), pp. 105-106.
[5] *Kontrol'nye Tsifry Narodnogo Khozyaistva SSSR na 1927–1928 god*
(1928), pp. 230-232.   [6] *Pyatnadtsatyi S"ezd VKP(B)*, ii (1962), 920.
[7] *Obzor Deyatel'nosti NKT SSSR za 1927–1928 gg.* (1928), p. 106.
[8] The longest chapter in the report of Narkomtrud for the years 1927 and
1928 to the eighth trade union congress was devoted to " the protection of
labour " (*ibid.* pp. 105-154).

agreements for the year 1927–1928 was again delayed till the spring of 1928, the sums allocated were fully expended by the end of the calendar year 1928.[1] In a report to the trade union central council of October 19, 1928, on the seven-hour day Shmidt once more referred to the increased accident rate [2] ; and, on the eve of the eighth trade union congress in December 1928, the protests were renewed at a conference in Moscow on the protection of labour.[3] At the congress itself the spokesman of Narkomtrud spoke at length of the continued rise in the accident rate (though statistics later than the end of 1927 do not appear to have been available), and blamed both the inexperience of the workers and delay and obstruction on the part of managers. The resolution of the congress had no remedies to propose other than increased funds and a strengthening of the labour inspectorate.[4] A rather more encouraging picture emerged from the control figures prepared by Narkomtrud for 1928–1929. The report introducing these quoted several instances of industries and factories which had substantially reduced their accident rates. Of the increased allocations for 1928–1929 the lion's share was to go to the metal and electrical industries.[5] The Gosplan control figures for 1928–1929, which provided for an increase from the 45 million rubles expended under this head in the previous year to 49·7 millions, cautiously observed that " the insignificant size of these allocations calls for a particularly careful and rational expenditure and for the exclusion from this head of everything but direct expenditure on the protection of labour ".[6]

(c) Housing

The drive for more and better housing was a legacy of the year 1925,[7] and was intensified by the needs of industrialization, which

[1] Obzor Deyatel'nosti NKT SSSR za 1927–1928 gg. (1928), pp. 106-107; the figures given ibid. pp. 108-109 appear to include sums available from all sources, not merely from the trade union agreements.
[2] For this report see p. 503 above ; for a detailed discussion of the subject see Trud, November 7, 1928.   [3] Ibid. December 12, 1928.
[4] Vos'moi S"ezd Professional'nykh Soyuzov SSSR (1929), pp. 328-330, 555-557.
[5] Kontrol'nye Tsifry po Trudu na 1928–29 god (1929), pp. 42-44 ; for detailed figures see ibid. p. 74.
[6] Kontrol'nye Tsifry Narodnogo Khozyaistva SSSR na 1928–1929 god (1929), p. 48.   [7] See Socialism in One Country, 1924–1926, Vol. 1, pp. 407-409.

brought a fresh influx of workers into towns and factories. The importance of the question, and of the provision of necessary finance, was stressed in a special resolution adopted by the party central committee at its session in July 1926, which observed that the housing shortage " delays the further development of industry ", and demanded the establishment of a permanent fund drawn from various sources to build dwellings for the workers.[1] The question was not raised at the fifteenth party conference in October 1926, but received some attention at the seventh trade union congress a few weeks later. The congress resolution stressed the significance of the issue from the angle of production :

> The most important question of the material life of the workers at the present time is the housing question. It is not only acute from the point of view of the real material demands of the workers, but is profoundly important also from the point of view of the future development of the national economy. Hard living conditions are one of the fundamental hindrances in the way of drawing skilled workers into production, establishing normal conditions of work, and raising the productivity of labour.[2]

Rykov at the fourth Union Congress of Soviets in April 1927 mentioned the " many notes " sent to him by delegates about housing, but said little to encourage optimism : in face of difficulties every effort must be made " not only to put an end to the reduction of living-space per person, but to begin an upward movement ".[3] The shortage of housing for workers became a favourite target of the opposition, and party and government were forced into a defensive position ; the opposition platform of September 1927 alleged that industrial workers with an average living space of 5·6 sq. metres per person were less favourably treated than employees (6·9 sq. metres), members of the professions (10·9 sq. metres) and even the " non-working element " (7·1 sq. metres), and that the gap was widening.[4] But the magnitude of the problem continued to defy every attempt to find a quick and comprehensive solution.

---

[1] *KPSS v Rezolyutsiyakh* (1954), ii, 286-289.
[2] *Sed'moi S"ezd Professional'nykh Soyuzov SSSR* (1927), p. 796.
[3] *SSSR : 4 S"ezd Sovetov* (1927), pp. 210-211.
[4] L. Trotsky, *The Real Situation in Russia* (n.d. [1928]), p. 47.

Detailed evidence was hardly required to illustrate the appalling housing conditions under which the mass of the population suffered. " We live in huts, in cowsheds, in barns ", exclaimed Dogadov at the seventh trade union congress in December 1926, " . . . in the summer we live simply under the trees." In the Urals, the worker's living space reached " coffin standard ". Those employed on building houses had themselves nowhere to live.[1] The decline in living-space per head of town and factory population had not yet been checked. The control figures of Gosplan for 1926–1927 frankly admitted that " living conditions for workers will deteriorate still further ", and that " the problem of the construction of housing has not yet been solved by the measures hitherto taken " ; [2] and the control figures for the following year recorded that the decline in living-space per head of population had not yet been arrested.[3] In 1927–1928 the position was said to have been stabilized at the following low average levels per head :

Total Urban Population	5·9	sq. metres
Workers	4·9	,, ,,
Factory Workers	4·75	,, ,,
Textile Workers	4·15	,, ,,
Miners	3·7	,, ,,
Employees	7·05	,, ,,
In Organizations	7·65	,, ,,
In Factories	6·6	,, ,,

The situation was, however, not uniform. The figures for Moscow (owing to the abnormally large influx of population) and for the Central Industrial region (which contained a large number of

[1] *Sed'moi S"ezd Professional'nykh Soyuzov SSSR* (1927), pp. 148-149, 200, 372 ; at the third Ukrainian trade union congress a few days earlier a delegate complained that the offices of industrial trusts in Kharkov had taken over a building formerly occupied by workers' dwellings, and that a new house of industry was being built while workers were homeless (*Stenograficheskii Otchet 3go Vseukrainskogo S"ezda Profsoyuzov* (1927), pp. 215-216).

[2] *Kontrol'nye Tsifry Narodnogo Khozyaistva na 1926–1927 god* (1926), p. 219 ; detailed statistics of housing conditions and building programmes in 1926–1927 were published in *Statisticheskii Spravochnik SSSR za 1928 g.* (1929), pp. 820-847. It was claimed that in 1926–1927 new investment in housing for the first time caught up with depreciation (*Kontrol'nye Tsifry Narodnogo Khozyaistva SSSR na 1928–1929 god* (1929), p. 184).

[3] *Kontrol'nye Tsifry Narodnogo Khozyaistva SSSR na 1927–1928 god* (1928), p. 201.

textile factories) were below the national average, for Leningrad substantially above it ; 62·5 per cent of the urban population and 73·1 of workers had less than 6 square metres of living-space, 20·9 per cent of the urban population and 27·4 per cent of workers less than 3 square metres.[1]   In some factories in the Ural region the average living-space per head was as low as 2 sq. metres ; in some textile factories in Vladimir province it fell to 1·8 sq. metres.[2] Workers in the electrical industry were the best (or least badly) housed of industrial workers, having since 1926–1927 more than 6 sq. metres per head : then followed oil, chemical and metal workers, with coal-mining, forestry and textile workers at the bottom of the scale.[3]

The scarcity of resources to cope with so vast and intractable a problem presented itself primarily as a question of public finance. As late as 1927–1928 52 per cent of urban dwelling-space, measured in square metres, was privately owned, the proportion not having significantly changed since 1924–1925.[4] At the end of 1926, 46 per cent of all workers and employees lived in private housing.[5] Dwellings built privately in 1925–1926 and 1926–1927 actually exceeded in extent those built out of public funds, and fell only slightly below them in 1927–1928.[6] Much private building, however, being undertaken by individuals and their families, was of low quality and value in comparison with public building. " The individual builder ", it was explained in the commentary to the first five-year plan, " takes no account of any sanitary or technical standards, and builds his house of the cheapest,

---

[1] *Pyatiletnii Plan Narodno-Khozyaistvennogo Stroitel'stva SSSR* (1929), ii, ii, 273-274.

[2] *Obzor Deyatel'nosti NKT SSSR za 1927-1928 gg.* (1928), p. 165 ; *Vos'-moi S"ezd Professional'nykh Soyuzov SSSR* (1929), p. 341. For housing conditions in the Western region of the RSFSR see M. Fainsod, *Smolensk under Soviet Rule* (1958), pp. 315-316.

[3] *Kontrol'nye Tsifry Narodnogo Khozyaistva SSSR na 1928-1929 god* (1929), p. 164 ; the difference in standard corresponded to a difference in wage levels (see Table No. 25, p. 958 below).

[4] *Kontrol'nye Tsifry Narodnogo Khozyaistva SSSR na 1927-1928 god* (1928), p. 533.

[5] *Pyatiletnii Plan Narodno-Khozyaistvennogo Stroitel'stva SSSR* (1929), ii, ii, 271 ; the percentage of employees in private housing was only 35·5 — an interesting indication that they enjoyed some priority in the new public housing.

[6] *Obzor Deyatel'nosti NKT SSSR za 1927-1928 gg.* (1928), pp. 167-168.

frequently scrap, material." The result was "low-grade, but very cheap, houses, scattered for the most part on the boundaries of towns, generally without any plan ".[1] Almost all private building was in wood, only 3·3 per cent of it from 1923 to 1926 being in brick.[2]

With industrialization on the way, the need to provide accommodation for a rapidly expanding urban and factory population called for the construction of large-scale apartment houses by public enterprise and with public finance.[3] In December 1926, an attempt was made to put the housing fund on a firmer financial basis. Employers were required to make a contribution for workers' housing supplementary to their basic contribution to the social insurance fund ; and out of the basic contribution a further one-half per cent was to be set aside for housing.[4] Fresh impetus was given to the question by the introduction at the end of 1927 of the three-shift system. On January 4, 1928, a decree was issued by the TsIK and Sovnarkom of the USSR which dealt in detail with every aspect of the housing problem, including the building of new, and the maintenance and management of old, housing, and the provision of finance from public, cooperative and even private sources. Building costs were to be reduced by methods of rationalization by not less than 15 per cent in the following year. The rule was laid down that the construction of workers' housing should be undertaken by industrial and transport enterprises and

---

[1] *Pyatiletnii Plan Narodno-Khozyaistvennogo Stroitel'stva SSSR* (1929), ii, ii, 275. Privately built houses usually consisted of one room and a kitchen which also served as a living room ; their average cost per square metre of floor space was 40-50 rubles, whereas that of publicly built housing was 130-160 rubles (*Kontrol'nye Tsifry Narodnogo Khozyaistva SSSR na 1927–1928 god* (1928), p. 201).

[2] *Ekonomicheskoe Obozrenie*, No. 9, 1928, p. 144. In the middle nineteen-twenties, more than half of urban dwellings throughout the USSR (except in the Transcaucasian federal republic, which had 64·2 per cent of brick dwellings) were in wood ; the highest proportion of wooden dwellings (93·5 per cent) was found in White Russia (*ibid.* p. 139). Of new building between 1923 and 1926 18·4 per cent was in brick (*ibid.* p. 147).

[3] Two decrees of the RSFSR of October 1926 and November 1927 laid the foundations of a conception of town planning (*Sobranie Uzakonenii, 1926*, No. 65, art. 512 ; *Sobranie Uzakonenii, 1927*, No. 117, art. 799).

[4] *Sobranie Zakonov, 1927*, No. 2, art. 19 ; the decree was dated December 31, 1926. Two further decrees of June 15, 1927, were designed to put the fund on a permanent basis (*ibid.* No. 36, arts. 368, 369). For previous contributions to the housing fund see *Socialism in One Country, 1924–1926*, Vol. 1, p. 407.

by building cooperatives, and that private building should be restricted to regions " where living and economic conditions have not yet permitted the development to a sufficient extent of large-scale state and cooperative house-building ". Since housing legislation fell within the competence of the republics, not of the USSR, the decree took the form of proposals to the republican governments.[1] The restriction on private building was reversed in a decree of April 17, 1928, the aim of which was to encourage house-building by individuals or share companies " without participation of state or cooperative capital ".[2] Results were, however, negligible ; a Rabkrin report of 1929 showed that only one share company had been set up in Moscow, and two in the Ukraine.[3]

Some attention was given to building cooperatives, which built housing to the value of 24 million rubles in 1925, of 47 millions in 1926, of 86 millions in 1927 and 91 millions in 1928 ; these figures represented from 15 to 21 per cent of all house-building in these years.[4] The following statistics of housing cooperatives were quoted in the Gosplan control figures for 1927–1928 :

	No. of Organizations	No. of Members
October 1, 1926	19,651	712,000
October 1, 1927	21,100	1,050,000
October 1, 1928 (Plan)	13,900	1,250,000 [5]

Two-thirds of members of housing cooperatives in the RSFSR and the Ukrainian SSR were workers.[6] Contributions from

[1] *Sobranie Zakonov, 1928*, No. 6, art. 49.
[2] *Ibid.* No. 26, art. 231.   [3] *Voprosy Istorii*, No. 12, 1964, p. 16.
[4] *Kontrol'nye Tsifry Narodnogo Khozyaistva SSSR na 1928–1929 god* (1929), p. 111 ; their share in the construction of workers' dwellings rose from less than one-sixth in 1926–1927 to rather less than one-quarter in 1927–1928 (*Obzor Deyatel'nosti NKT SSSR za 1927–1928 god* (1928), p. 164). Most cooperative building was done in Moscow, where in 1928 2·4 per cent of the population were housed in " cooperative and communal " dwellings ; percentages elsewhere were negligible (*Pyatiletnii Plan Narodno-Khozyaistvennogo Stroitel'stva SSSR* (1929), ii, 272, where the building cooperatives are referred to as " a new category of house-owners ").
[5] *Kontrol'nye Tsifry Narodnogo Khozyaistva SSSR na 1927–1928 god* (1928), p. 379. The figures for 1928 are estimates ; no explanation was suggested for the reduction in the number of organizations.
[6] *Kontrol'nye Tsifry Narodnogo Khozyaistva SSSR na 1928–1929 god* (1929), p. 118.

X 2

members averaged only 6 rubles a month ; and a major, though diminishing, part of the cost of building was met by subventions and credits.[1] The housing cooperatives, like other cooperatives, were eyed by the trade unions with a certain jealousy. At the fifteenth party congress in December 1927, Dogadov deprecated the tendency to rely for housing development on the building cooperatives ; it was more practical for housing to be provided by the factories, which should regard it as " an essential instrument of production ".[2] Like private building, nearly all cooperative building (89 per cent in 1926) was in wood.[3]

As the housing shortage grew more acute, and threatened the very basis of industrialization, investment in building increased, though far less rapidly than investment in industry and in the other main sectors of the economy (except private agriculture).[4] The proportion of investment in housing that went during these years to the socialized sector (public and cooperative building) also increased at the expense of private building :

	1925–1926	1926–1927	1927–1928 (Preliminary)	1928–1929 (Plan)
	(in thousand rubles)			
Socialized Sector	235·7	313·3	402·2	458·0
Private Building	87·0	110·0	120·0	130·0
Total	322·7	423·3	522·2	588·0

This meant that the major part of new building was financed by state industry, including transport, or by Soviet organs of government — mainly by regional or city executive committees ; but, in addition to these subventions, substantial credits were made available through Tsekombank.[5] The construction of new housing for 1,030,000 persons (580,000 by public, and 450,000 by private,

---

[1] *Kontrol'nye Tsifry Narodnogo Khozyaistva SSSR na 1928–1929 god* (1929), pp. 115-116.   [2] *Pyatnadtsatyi S"ezd VKP(B)*, ii (1962), 922.
[3] Yu. Larin, *Chastnyi Kapital v SSSR* (1927), pp. 97-98.
[4] See Table No. 47, p. 979 below.
[5] *Kontrol'nye Tsifry Narodnogo Khozyaistva SSSR na 1928–1929 god* (1929), p. 487. The totals are somewhat lower for all years than those shown in Table No. 47, p. 979 below ; the corrected figures for 1928–1929 given in the control figures for the following year (*Kontrol'nye Tsifry Narodnogo Khozyaistva SSSR na 1929/30 god* (1930), p. 519) were somewhat higher. For Tsekombank see *Socialism in One Country, 1924–1926*, Vol. 1, pp. 417, 474-475.

enterprise) was planned for the year 1928–1929; but urban population was expected to increase by 1·1 millions.[1] At the end of 1928 Kviring admitted that " the reduction in the standard of living-space per head of population in the towns " had not yet been arrested. He hoped that 1929 would at length be a " breakthrough year " on this front. But he dismissed the possibility of actually raising the living-space per head of urban population as " beyond our powers in the short run ".[2]

Apart from difficulties of finance, the main obstacles to the acceleration of the housing programme were handicaps affecting the building industry as a whole : scarcity of labour and shortage of raw materials. Climatic conditions made building operations peculiarly difficult. June, July and August were the only months well suited to building operations in the northern and central regions : it was also the period when the urban worker tended to return to his home in the country to bring in the harvest.[3] In spite of a large influx of casual labour from the countryside,[4] the report of Narkomtrud for 1927–1928 spoke of " competition among employers for the hire of seasonal workers " and consequent " excessive wage demands ".[5] Competition between different organizations for scarce building materials was deplored by a speaker at the seventh trade union congress as a cause of the rise in building costs.[6] At the fifteenth party congress a year later Krzhizhanovsky spoke of the backwardness of the building industry and of the high cost of building, building materials costing from 250 to 290 per cent of pre-war prices.[7] In the autumn of 1928, Kviring predicted " an acute shortage of building materials in this

[1] *Kontrol'nye Tsifry Narodnogo Khozyaistva SSSR na 1928–1929 god* (1929), pp. 184-186. Investment in urban housing was planned to increase by 14 per cent ; but this increase, which included investment in industrial housing paid for out of the capital investment allocation to industry, was still far smaller than the percentage increase in capital investment as a whole (*ibid.* pp. 428-429).

[2] G. Krzhizhanovsky and others, *Osnovnye Problemy Kontrol'nykh Tsifr Narodnogo Khozyaistva na 1928/29 god* (1929), pp. 100, 145.

[3] *Obzor Deyatel'nosti NKT SSSR za 1927–1928 gg.* (1928), pp. 47-48 ; the building year was more generously estimated in *Kontrol'nye Tsifry Narodnogo Khozyaistva SSSR na 1927–1928 god* (1928), p. 209, at 150-160 days.

[4] See pp. 453-455 above.

[5] *Obzor Deyatel'nosti NKT SSSR za 1927–1928 gg.* (1928), p. 49.

[6] *Sed'moi S"ezd Professional'nykh Soyuzov SSSR* (1927), pp. 715-716.

[7] *Pyatnadtsatyi S"ezd VKP(B)*, ii (1962), 906.

and next year " ; and one government institution was said to have issued an order " not to begin to build where there are no building materials ".[1]

The last major discussion of the housing question in this period took place at the eighth trade union congress in December 1928. Tomsky, in his report to the congress, rather grudgingly referred to housing as an " important requirement " which nevertheless had to take second place to the imperative need to catch up the capitalist countries in industrial development, but thought that something could be achieved by improved techniques of building.[2] A woman delegate described the shocking conditions in which textile workers lived under the three-shift system : three families, all on different shifts, occupied one room, so that there was constant going and coming throughout the 24 hours.[3] Other delegates spoke of the wretched housing conditions of railway workers, who lived in cellars or broken-down wagons or caves, and of dock workers in Odessa who lived in " damp buildings without roofs " ; a silk factory in Uzbekistan had been unable to recruit workers for lack of anywhere to house them.[4] Many complaints were made of the distance at which workers were compelled to live from their work.[5] The representative of Narkomtrud could do little but rehearse the sums voted for past and projected increases in housing ; and the resolution of the congress reiterated the need " to raise the average level of living space for the working population during the five-year period to minimum standards of health ".[6] But official prognostications did not encourage any extravagant optimism. The framers of the five-year plan noted that in order to attain an average " minimum health standard " of 6 square metres per head for all groups of the urban population, it would be necessary to increase the existing living-space by 50 per cent ; the average living-space per worker was to increase from 4·8 to 6·6 square metres during the currency of the plan, and per head of urban

---

[1] G. Krzhizhanovsky and others, *Osnovnye Problemy Kontrol'nykh Tsifr Narodnogo Khozyaistva na 1928/29 god* (1929), pp. 100, 113.
[2] *Vos'moi S"ezd Professional'nykh Soyuzov SSSR* (1929), pp. 26-27.
[3] *Ibid.* p. 78 ; similar conditions were reported from a porcelain factory working in three shifts (*ibid.* p. 120).
[4] *Ibid.* pp. 143, 161, 168.
[5] *Ibid.* pp. 79, 106.
[6] *Ibid.* p. 560.

population from 5·7 to 6·8 square metres.[1] A further decree was issued in January 1929 on " measures to assist the building of workers' dwellings " ;[2] and Krzhizhanovsky, at the sixteenth party conference in April 1929, expressed the hope that the provision of more housing would make it possible to deal with the problem of labour turnover.[3]

House-rents continued to present a thorny problem. Though the provision of housing for workers was always treated as a social service, and not as an enterprise conducted on the principles of *khozraschet*, it had been accepted policy since 1925 to raise rents to a level which would cover upkeep ; and provisions for this purpose had been included, though without avail, in the first Gosplan control figures for 1925-1926.[4] Strumilin, in his report to the first Gosplan congress in March 1926 reverted to the proposal in the language of strict financial orthodoxy :

> Gosplan has insisted for several years that rents should be re-examined and increased, so that dwellings should pay for themselves and make some profit, even though it is small. But unfortunately this idea has not yet been put into practice. A very modest increase in rents has taken place, tied to the wage increases of manual and office workers. But this supplement is quite inadequate for the building of dwellings to become profitable. Without profitability every incentive to this construction will cease, particularly if it is a matter of attracting private capital.[5]

A decree of June 4, 1926, laid down the principle that rent must be sufficient to cover costs of maintenance and normal depreciation, and fixed a new scale for house-rents.[6] The resolution of the party central committee of July 1926 repeated that " rent should

---

[1] *Pyatiletnii Plan Narodno-Khozyaistvennogo Stroitel'stva SSSR* (1929), ii, ii, 276-277 ; for the figures said to have been reached in 1927-1928 see p. 614 above.

[2] *Sobranie Zakonov, 1929*, No. 9, art. 83.

[3] *Shestnadtsataya Konferentsiya VKP(B)* (1962), p. 52.

[4] See *Socialism in One Country, 1924-1926*, Vol. 1, pp. 405, 409.

[5] *Problemy Planirovaniya (Itogi i Perspektivy)* (1926), pp. 47, 50.

[6] *Sobranie Zakonov, 1926*, No. 44, art. 312. How far the official scales were effective cannot be guessed ; they were probably not much observed outside the large cities. The example was quoted of a miner in the Donbass who paid 20 per cent of his wage for one small room, and let a share of this to another worker, thus becoming an exploiter in his turn (*Sed'moi S"ezd Professional'nykh Soyuzov SSSR* (1927), pp. 167-168).

guarantee current repair of houses and their renewal ", but at the same time, anxious to forestall opposition criticism, stipulated that any increase in rent should be " in direct relation to the rate of general increase in the real wages of workers and employees ".[1] But the two aims were difficult to reconcile. A concrete proposal to add a percentage to rents concurrently with the rise in wages was shelved and referred to the trade unions ; [2] and at a meeting of Gosplan Strumilin returned to the proposal to raise rents and to devote the proceeds to the fund for workers' housing.[3] The control figures for 1927–1928, which estimated the monthly cost of maintenance and amortization of dwellings at 70 kopeks per square metre in the large cities and 55 kopeks in the smaller towns, compared with an average monthly rent of 32 kopeks per square metre, called categorically for an increase in rents of from 20-25 per cent to cover costs of maintenance and renovation.[4] None of these recommendations appears to have been followed.

The decree on housing policy of January 4, 1928, once more attempted to reconcile the two principles at stake. It provided for a general increase in rents by 10 kopeks per square metre per month, but exempted from the increase unemployed workers and those earning less than 20 rubles a month (a very low category), and added the stipulation that rent must in no case exceed 10 per cent of the family budget of the worker or employee. The governments of the republics were left with the task of applying this injunction.[5] None of the republics appears to have done so except the RSFSR, which established an elaborate system of rents graded not only to the income of the tenant, but to the number of members of his family.[6] A table published in the first five-year plan showed that in 1927–1928 the graduated rents paid by workers earning less than 80 rubles a month (about two-thirds of all workers) did not cover building costs, those paid by workers earning from 80 to 140 rubles just covered costs, and those paid

---

[1] For this resolution see p. 613 above.

[2] *Torgovo-Promyshlennaya Gazeta*, August 1, 1926.

[3] *Ibid.* August 4, 1926 ; for the previous proposal see *Socialism in One Country, 1924–1926*, Vol. 1, pp. 408-409.

[4] *Kontrol'nye Tsifry Narodnogo Khozyaistva SSSR na 1927–1928 god* (1928), pp. 202-203.

[5] For this decree see pp. 616-617 above.

[6] See table in *Obzor Deyatel'nosti NKT SSSR za 1927–1928 gg.* (1928), p. 173.

by the insignificant number earning more than 140 rubles more than covered costs.[1] Rents were raised everywhere under the new scheme in the autumn of 1928, and the increase was defended at the eighth trade union congress in December of that year as "economically indispensable".[2] In the Soviet Union, as elsewhere, housing policy was involved in a tissue of inconsistencies. But the conception that it was a social obligation, however imperfectly fulfilled in practice, to provide decent housing for the workers continued to predominate.

---

[1] *Pyatiletnii Plan Narodno-Khozyaistvennogo Stroitel'stva SSSR* (1929), ii, ii, 282 ; cf. the statement *ibid.* ii, ii, 290 that 90 per cent of workers paid rents which did not cover costs.

[2] *Vos'moi S"ezd Professional'nykh Soyuzov SSSR* (1929), pp. 364-365 ; in practice the long-term effect of these measures was largely nullified by a currency inflation which allowed wages to rise faster than rents, so that in Moscow the 9·2 per cent of the worker's budget spent on rent in 1927 fell to 6·2 per cent in 1933 and 3·7 per cent in 1938 (D. Broner, *Ocherki Ekonomicheskogo Khozyaistva Moskvy* (1946), p. 104).

D : *Trade and Distribution*

*

CHAPTER 23

THE MARKET AND THE PLAN

THE growth of internal trade under NEP was a logical process : NEP was essentially a market policy designed to meet the needs of the consumer through the mechanism of the market. It encouraged, first and foremost, the recovery of consumer industries.[1] But, when recovery spread to heavy industry, hitherto mainly occupied with the fulfilment of state orders, this too had its contribution to make to the market economy. At the fourteenth party conference in April 1925 Dzerzhinsky saw direct sales on the consumer market as the key to the future development of the metal industry :

> The arguments of two years ago about whether the metal industry should be directed to the consumer market or be exclusively based on state customers are now past history. Now the fundamental base of our metal industry as a whole (not the special locomotive works, but our main metal industry) is the consumer market. It is here that the whole strength and future of our metal industry is to be found.[2]

Later at the same conference Dzerzhinsky made this assumption quite explicit :

> Our plan is a process of uncovering the chain connections of our state industry and its separate branches with each other, and of each of these separate branches with our market, with those for whom we work, i.e. the peasantry. The interconnection of each branch and of all industries taken together, and the uncovering of these inter-relationships and interconnections, is a process which takes place in our agriculture, on which in the last resort we are dependent financially, economically, and in every other respect.[3]

[1] See *Socialism in One Country, 1924–1926*, Vol. 1, pp. 329-332.
[2] *Chetyrnadtsataya Konferentsiya Rossiiskoi Kommunisticheskoi Partii (Bol'shevikov)* (1925), pp. 160-161.
[3] *Ibid.* p. 212.

Nor, though this development coincided naturally with the policy of " Face to the Countryside " and the favour shown to the well-to-do peasant, who provided the lion's share of the consumer market, should it be assumed that Dzerzhinsky was thinking merely in terms of an expedient concession to peasant interests. It was the expansion of the consumer market which had provided the main impetus to the recovery of industry in the first years of NEP. If industry under the Tsars had been geared mainly to serve the interests of the government and the capitalists, socialist industry would work for the masses : this was the firm basis of the " link " between worker and peasant. It would be an exaggeration to say that the peasant called the tune, for his economic position relative to the urban worker was less favourable than before the revolution. But the imperative need not to antagonize the peasant was the main constraint on economic policy, and a satisfactory relation between government and peasantry through the market was the *sine qua non* of every other economic relation. Market relations were described in a report prepared for the fifteenth party congress of December 1927 as " the predominant form of the economic link between town and country ".[1]

From the outset a group within the party — not confined to the opposition — took a positive view of planning, and, without openly challenging the market basis of NEP, stressed the struggle against market forces rather than the need to adapt policies to them. As early as 1924 Krzhizhanovsky wrote of the need for the workers' state to control commodity exchange and currency circulation, the " Holy of Holies " of capitalism's Old Believers and fetish-worshippers :

> The existence of a dictatorship of workers and peasants furnishes the key to the resolution of the contradiction between the market and the plan, reducing all this contradiction, to use Lenin's terminology, to changed forms of " approach " in carrying out the state economic plan.[2]

[1] *K Voprosu o Sotsialisticheskom Pereustroistve Sel'skogo Khozyaistva* (1928), p. 397 ; Lenin had called trade " the only possible economic link between the tens of millions of small cultivators of the soil and large-scale industry " (Lenin, *Sochineniya*, xxvii, 83).
[2] *Ekonomicheskaya Zhizn'*, January 13, 1924.

But at this period it was confidently assumed that the struggle would be waged within the NEP framework. Lenin had made this clear when NEP was first introduced :

> Neither political nor any other ways round this problem are possible, since this is a test of competition with private capital. Either we win this test . . . or complete failure will ensue.[1]

It was Trotsky who at the twelfth party congress in April 1923 had preached a policy of overcoming NEP " on its own foundation and to a large extent by using its own methods ".[2] If the Soviet economy under NEP was conceived as a market economy in which the " commanding heights " of industry were held by the state, these heights were none the less governed, in their relations with the rest of the economy, by the laws of the market.   NEP and the link with the peasantry carried with them the assumption that the peasantry should be handled not by force or by administrative orders, but through the " commodity-money relations " of the market.   Strumilin in 1924 reiterated what was then a universally accepted truth :

> We have no intention of " abolishing " NEP, for we believe that we are strong enough to overcome its negative sides *by economic means* with its own weapons, by the method of " driving in a wedge ".

He specified that the means would be those used by " any financial concern, trust or cartel in a capitalist country to drive out its competitors ".[3]   Similarly Vesenkha declared in 1925 that " the capacity of the market (emkost' rynka) will in the main direct our course in resolving the very difficult national economic task of establishing new industry ".[4]   When Preobrazhensky opposed the " law of value " of the market to the " law of primitive socialist accumulation " by which the state sector attempted to expand, it was not implied that the state sector should triumph by other than economic means ; [5] and he justified his support for increased

[1] Lenin, *Sochineniya*, xxvii, 235.
[2] See *The Interregnum, 1923–1924*, p. 23.
[3] *Ekonomicheskaya Zhizn'*, November 7, 1924.
[4] *Perspektivy Promyshlennosti na 1925–26 Operatsionnyi god* (1925), p. 87.
[5] See *Socialism in One Country, 1924–1926*, Vol. 1, pp. 205-206.

industrialization by referring to the goods shortage on the market and the high prices of home-produced industrial goods in relation to world market prices.[1] The advent of planning slowly sapped the foundations of this assumption. Strumilin, during the discussion of the first 1925–1926 control figures, condemned Sokolnikov for wishing to replace Gosplan by " the peasants' plan " (krestplan) : Sokolnikov wanted to adapt the plan to the market environment, whereas " the only reliable way of developing our socialist economy painlessly and without crisis is not to *adapt oneself* to [the market environment] but to *adapt* the market environment consciously to our planning efforts ".[2] Strumilin's attitude found ready support in Vesenkha, which cautiously argued that " one of the most important and most positive methods of rational industrial construction is to manœuvre between the objective conditions of the developing state of the market and the possibilities of conscious correction of market demand in the direction of industrial policy ".[3] The summer of 1926, which saw the rise of the united opposition, the death of Dzerzhinsky and the appointment of Kuibyshev to Vesenkha, strengthened this reaction. As the starting-point of NEP had been a policy for internal trade, so it was in this field that the fundamental dilemma of NEP first became apparent.[4] The private trader had been allowed and encouraged to play his part in the revival of the economy. But this encouragement, like the favour shown for the same reasons to the well-to-do peasant, was bound to enrich and strengthen a class whose basic outlook was inimical to the régime, and might threaten the foundations of the proletarian dictatorship. A new spirit began to assert itself.

[1] *Vestnik Kommunisticheskoi Akademii*, xvii (1926), 227-228 ; *Bol'shevik*, No. 6, March 15, 1927, p. 61.
[2] S. Strumilin, *Na Planovom Fronte* (1958), p. 225.
[3] *Perspektivy Promyshlennosti na 1925–26 Operatsionnyi god* (1925), p. 89.
[4] At the Menshevik trial in 1931, Zalkind, an ex-Menshevik official of Narkomtorg, explained that in the first years of NEP, it had been easy to reconcile Menshevism with the " free-trade elements " in official policy ; but " we outlived our Menshevik illusions more quickly than other Mensheviks ". This was because the reaction against the retreat, and the beginning of the offensive, came earlier in Narkomtorg than elsewhere, i.e. in 1925–1926 (*Protsess Kontrrevolyutsionnoi Organizatsii Men'shevikov* (1931), p. 89). This view must be accepted with some caution ; but it is correct that the scissors crisis of 1923 made the first serious breach in the system of NEP (see *The Interregnum, 1923–1924*, pp. 110-113).

The gradual overtaking of the private sector of internal trade by the socialized sector, i.e. by state and cooperative trading, which had begun in the period 1924–1926,[1] gathered momentum in the following years. Strumilin, summing up the situation in 1926, admitted that in form " our Soviet trade " did not differ radically from pre-revolutionary trade.

But [he went on] it is being gradually penetrated by elements, alien to this [i.e. the capitalist] world, of planned regulation of prices and distribution of goods in bulk in accordance with the needs of different regions and groups of population.[2]

The fifteenth party conference of October 1926 spoke of " the strengthening of the dominant position of the cooperatives and of state trade in the field of the exchange of goods ", and insisted that this line must be " prolonged still further ".[3]   A leading official in Vesenkha pointed the same moral :

The weaknesses and shortcomings of the state and cooperative system are one of the chief causes of the development of private capital.   Therefore the exclusion of private capital depends first and foremost on the internal strengthening and improvement of the work of the state and cooperative system.[4]

The dilemma was illustrated by a theoretical controversy about the " two regulators " of the Soviet economy, variously described as " the principle of spontaneity " and " the planning principle ", or " the law of value " and " the law of socialist accumulation ". Preobrazhensky argued that conflict between the two laws or regulators was the essence of the NEP economy and could be resolved only through the victory of planned accumulation ; a long debate on this theme took place at the Communist Academy in January 1926.[5]   Trotsky remained uneasy about the extent to which Preobrazhensky's approach might be used, on the one hand to accuse the opposition of wishing to break the link with the peasantry, and on the other hand to justify the thesis of " socialism in one

---

[1] See Socialism in One Country, 1924–1926, Vol. 1, pp. 423-428.
[2] Planovoe Khozyaistvo, No. 9, 1926, p. 7.
[3] KPSS v Rezolyutsiyakh (1954), ii, 307.
[4] A. Ginzburg, Chastnyi Kapital v Narodnom Khozyaistve SSSR (1927), p. 18.
[5] See the report of the discussion in Vestnik Kommunisticheskoi Akademii, xiv (1926), 3-254.

country ".[1] But for planners of whatever shade of opinion the restrictions imposed by the market economy always seemed trivial compared with the magnitude of the larger goal. They saw the compromise with the peasantry as an interlude; they conceded that the interlude must be ended by persuasion and not by force, but their eyes were on the road to full state planning which lay ahead. The drive for rapid industrialization, which became paramount in 1927, shifted the emphasis away from the production of consumer goods for the market to the production of capital goods for the equipment of industry, and aggravated the chronic " goods famine " of these years. The market was gradually relegated to a secondary place in economic calculations ; planning was in a sense the antithesis of the market. In the struggle for a planned economy the gradual exclusion of private capital from retail trade was an important factor.

The decisive rôle of the cooperatives and of state trade on the market [declared the party central committee in February 1927], won by them in recent years, is an achievement which, by comparison with the initial stage of NEP, raises us to a higher stage of development.[2]

The issue was more emphatically defined in the resolution of the fifteenth party congress of December 1927 :

The socialist sector of trade, expanding by way of the extrusion of private capital, introducing the planning principle into the sphere of the exchange of goods through rationalization of the trading network, through the maximum curtailment of unproductive costs in the sphere of exchange, will strengthen all the immense economic advantages of the new socialist system of distribution, and in future, with the successes of socialist construction, will be transformed into the apparatus of the socialist distribution of goods.

[1] In a memorandum dated May 2, 1926, directed against the " neophytes of socialist accumulation " in the party majority, Trotsky argued that the analysis of the economy from the point of view of the relation between the law of value and the law of socialist accumulation was legitimate as a method, but could not be transformed into a philosophy of " the development of socialism in one country " ; he also stressed the need to achieve " the overthrow of the legend of the treatment of the countryside as ' a colony ' " (Trotsky archives, T 2984).

[2] KPSS v Rezolyutsiyakh (1954), ii, 353 ; for this resolution, which was mainly concerned with price policy, see pp. 568-686 below.

The overriding aim of policy " in the sphere of the organization of exchange " was now " *to overcome the anarchy of the market* ".[1] Nobody as yet, however, openly rejected the assumption that the socialized sector competed with the private sector in the conditions of a market economy, and that the struggle between them was essentially an economic struggle. As Mikoyan put it in October 1927, the market was " *the point of contact of all the fundamental class contradictions and the battle-field of all contradictory economic forms* ".[2] When Vainshtein, in the bulletin of the *Konjunktur* institute, referred to the reappearance of " certain characteristics of the economy of war communism ",[3] this was vigorously denied by a party spokesman, who claimed that " the forward movement of the socialist sector takes place within the framework of the New Economic Policy ".[4]

The conception of a market economy established by NEP, and based on a free exchange of goods between socialized and private sectors, had already been undermined in the winter of 1926–1927. Goods shortages on the market had been seen up to this time as a manifestation of disequilibrium which the central authorities should seek to eliminate. In an article in the party journal in December 1926, Mikoyan frankly argued that investment in industry might result in an increased shortage of goods over a period of two or three years ; the shortage was a sign of economic growth and helped to drive industry forward.[5] In the following month at a discussion in STO, Rykov, while fearing that a serious goods shortage might create the danger of " antagonism between countryside and town ", also suggested that " a certain excess of demand over supply is a stimulus for industrialization ".[6] The acute goods shortage of the summer and autumn of 1927, resulting from the rise in purchasing power due to the increased expenditure on capital construction, and aggravated by the price reductions

[1] *KPSS v Rezolyutsiyakh* (1954), ii, 462.
[2] *Voprosy Torgovli*, No. 1, October 1927, p. 6 ; a commentator a year earlier had called prices " the chief arena of the struggle of the principle of price regulation with the private capitalist market " (Ts. Kron, *Chastnaya Torgovlya v SSSR* (1926), p. 85).
[3] *Ekonomicheskii Byulleten' Kon'yunkturnogo Instituta*, No. 11-12, 1927, p. 15.
[4] *Ekonomicheskoe Obozrenie*, No. 3, 1928, p. 79.
[5] *Bol'shevik*, No. 23-24, December 31, 1926, pp. 25-26.
[6] *Ekonomicheskaya Zhizn'*, January 7, 1927.

THE ECONOMIC ORDER PT. I

of the previous few months, confirmed the view of the more enthusiastic supporters of planning and industrialization in the party that planned regulation of the market should be maintained and strengthened even at the cost of increasing shortages. Speaking at the plenum of Vesenkha in August 1927, Kuibyshev roundly asserted that the achievement of price reductions at a time when the war danger had led to stock-piling, when demand had increased, and when speculation in certain goods was taking place, was " a very great achievement of the planning principle " :

> If we succeed in this manœuvre, the future historian will evaluate it as one of our most brilliant victories. To reduce prices when there is a goods shortage is indeed a direct contradiction of the normal laws of development of capitalist society.[1]

At the fifteenth party congress in December 1927, even Sokolnikov, now returned to the ranks of the majority, was prepared to concede that " the goods shortage is a concomitant of the first stages of industrialization ".[2] The failure of the grain collections in the winter of 1927-1928 strengthened the argument that the laws of the market could be overcome by administrative measures. In January 1928, at a meeting of the party cell in Vesenkha, Kuibyshev uttered a strong warning against what he called the " Konjunktur approach ", i.e. the taking of decisions in the light of market trends. " Konjunktur ", he declared, " may be one current in the stream, but a communist and a Bolshevik has always been able and is now able to swim against the stream " ; and he called for a militant struggle against " the iron laws of Konjunktur ".[3] Shortly afterwards, he attributed the increase in grain deliveries to " administrative pressure ", and enthusiastically declared that " the will of the state opposed itself to the Konjunktur, and, thanks to all the levers at the disposal of the proletarian state, this Konjunktur was broken ".[4] The processes of trade were henceforth to be governed, not by the laws of the market or by the need to bring about a balance between supply and demand, between industry and agriculture, but, like the processes of industry, by deliberate decisions of policy.

---

[1] Torgovo-Promyshlennaya Gazeta, August 14, 1927.
[2] Pyatnadtsatyi S"ezd VKP(B), ii (1962), 1133.
[3] Istoricheskii Arkhiv, No. 3, 1958, pp. 65-67 ; see also pp. 59, 308-309 above.   [4] Torgovo-Promyshlennaya Gazeta, February 4, 1928.

632

The dangers inherent in such a course were plain enough ; and consciousness of them was revealed by constant protestations that no departure was intended from the principles of NEP.[1] The compilers of the Gosplan control figures for 1928–1929 had occasion to criticize " tendencies to excessive centralization of the exchange of goods, to a too primitive, schematic approach to questions of regulation ".[2] The issue of trade played a subsidiary, though substantial, rôle in the dispute with the Right opposition. The charge against Bukharin in the Politburo resolution of February 9, 1929, of supporting those who demanded " the unleashing of capitalist elements in town and country "[3] evidently referred to a demand for the relaxation of restraints on private trade. At the session of the party central committee which preceded the sixteenth party conference in April 1929, Rykov and Bukharin proposed to " normalize " the market, to " create healthy conditions " for the exchange of goods, and to remove " pressure in the sphere of trade " ;[4] and Stalin, in his reply to the debate, cautiously re-defined NEP as meaning " freedom of private trade within *certain* limits, within a *certain* framework, *under guarantee of the regulating function of the state in the market* ", and denied that any departure from NEP was contemplated. On the contrary, " the new mass forms of exchange of goods between town and country by the method of *kontraktatsiya* " had arisen precisely " on the basis of NEP ".[5] The argument was sophistical ; in fact, commodity exchange on the market was gradually being transformed into planned supply and distribution. The resolution adopted by the party conference accused the opposition of " an interpretation of NEP in a liberal sense, leading in practice to a rejection of the control of market relations by the proletarian state ".[6] But not much attention was devoted at the conference to the problems of trade. Though changes so great as

---

[1] See p. 631 above.
[2] *Kontrol'nye Tsifry Narodnogo Khozyaistva SSSR na 1928–1929 god* (1929), p. 298.
[3] For this resolution see p. 248 above.
[4] For these unpublished speeches see pp. 250, 329 above ; the above phrases are quoted without further detail in *Shestnadtsataya Konferentsiya VKP(B)* (1962), p. 793, note 133 ; at the conference a delegate accused Rykov of wanting " to unleash free exchange on the market " (*ibid.* p. 399).
[5] Stalin, *Sochineniya*, xii, 43, 49.
[6] *KPSS v Rezolyutsiyakh* (1954). ii, 552.

THE ECONOMIC ORDER

to amount to something like a reversal of policy had taken place, they had taken place within a well established framework. At the time of the creation of Narkomtorg in May 1924, the thirteenth party congress had enunciated the two purposes which the new commissariat was to serve : the conquest of the market by the strengthening of state and cooperative trade and by the eclipse of the private trader, and the regulation of prices by government action.[1] These purposes continued to sum up Soviet trade policy in the ensuing years.

[1] See *Socialism in One Country, 1924–1926*, Vol. 1, p. 423 ; the framers of the Gosplan control figures for 1928–1929 added a third aim of policy : " an extension of the planned *kontraktatsiya* of mass products and their planned distribution " (*Kontrol'nye Tsifry Narodnogo Khozyaistva SSSR na 1928–1929 god* (1929), p. 296). For *kontraktatsiya* see pp. 219-226 above.

CHAPTER 24

THE SOCIALIZED SECTOR

AN analysis of the figures of internal trade for the years 1925–1926 to 1927–1928 reveals a rapid growth of all forms of trade, accompanied by a steady expansion of the " socialized sector " (i.e. state and cooperative trade) at the expense of the private sector. The value of internal trade increased from 23 milliard rubles in 1925–1926 to nearly 43 milliards in 1928–1929 ; in the former year the socialized sector accounted for about 70 per cent of all trade, in the latter year for 94 per cent.[1] In wholesale trade, the share of the private trader was by 1926 negligible,[2] or was diverted into illicit channels which escaped control and record. In retail trade, the share of the private trader declined rapidly, especially after 1927.[3] It was characteristic of this period that trade in rural areas increased faster, though from a much lower level, than in the towns ; this may have been in part a statistical increase, since rural trade was now better organized and more amenable to record and control. In the years from 1923–1924 to 1928–1929 the volume of retail trade per head of population doubled in the towns and increased five-fold in the countryside. As a result of this, the share of the countryside in the retail trade of the USSR rose from 18·3 per cent in 1923–1924 to 29·9 per cent in 1926–1927 and 31·5 per cent in 1927–1928. A corresponding increase occurred in the number of trading institutions serving the countryside.[4]

Within the socialized sector, state trade increased absolutely, but declined relatively. The cooperatives advanced at the expense

---

[1] *Kontrol'nye Tsifry Narodnogo Khozyaistva SSSR na 1928–1929 god* (1929), p. 492 ; see also Table No. 27, p. 960 below.
[2] See Table No. 28, p. 961 below.   [3] See Table No. 29, p. 962 below.
[4] G. Neiman, *Vnutrennyaya Torgovlya SSSR* (1935), pp. 12-122 ; for statistics of employees in trading institutions — state, cooperative and private — from 1925 to 1929 see *Ekonomicheskoe Obozrenie*, No. 9, 1929, p. 123.

of private trade and, in a lesser degree, of state trade.[1] Conditions varied considerably from region to region : state trading organs held their own best in the remoter regions.[2] Of the organs of state trade the syndicates were by far the most powerful ; and, since some at any rate of the share companies or other enterprises trading in industrial goods on *khozraschet*, though with state capital, seem to have been created or controlled by them, the preponderance of the syndicates in state trade was perhaps even greater than the bare figures suggest. The torgi,[3] and some of the share companies and *khozraschet* concerns, also formed part of the machinery for the state collection of agricultural products ; but in this field they were gradually overtaken and eclipsed by the cooperatives.[4] In trade in industrial goods the torgi occupied a peripheral position, which they maintained with difficulty under constant pressure from the syndicates on the one hand and the consumer cooperatives on the other.

(a) Syndicates

The selling syndicates set up by the industrial trusts from 1922 onwards were powerful instruments in bringing wholesale and retail trade in industrial goods under public control. But conditions, and the rate at which this process took place, varied widely from industry to industry. In the first years of NEP, when the consumer market was still more important than the market for capital goods, the All-Union Textile Syndicate (VTS) was the most influential and best organized of the syndicates, beginning from an early date to monopolize selling arrangements at the expense of factories and trusts.[5] By 1926 immense changes had occurred in its sales machinery. In the early years of NEP, the factory sent sample-cards to representatives of the wholesale and retail trading organizations, which selected what they wanted ; by the autumn of 1926, each factory delivered its output to a named division of the syndicate.[6] Before the revolution, each factory had

[1] See Table No. 27, p. 960 below.   [2] See p. 650 below.
[3] See pp. 650-653 below.   [4] See pp. 15-16 above.
[5] For the encroachment of the syndicates on the trusts see pp. 373-375 above ; for their origin see *The Bolshevik Revolution*, Vol. 2, pp. 314-315.
[6] *Torgovo-Promyshlennaya Gazeta*, September 22, 1926.

its own commercial traveller ; [1] now trading activities had passed to VTS, destroying the direct links of the factories with the market.[2] The importance of the market in textiles as the counterpart of the grain collections gave VTS a key position in the economy and enhanced its authority. During 1926 and 1927 it took over first the trading departments and then the warehouses and major stores of the textile trusts.[3]

In the metal industry, responsibilities were at first divided between a number of syndicates ; and the metal syndicates were much weaker than VTS. Some centralized sales were controlled not by the syndicates but by Vesenkha direct, and much of the output of the industry was sold by the trusts themselves. Gradually the metal syndicates were unified and their importance increased. In 1924 the syndicates combined in a " convention " ; and in June 1926 an All-Union Metal Syndicate (VMS) was established to replace the convention. The long-standing rivalry and conflict of interests between Ukrainian and Ural industries led to the breakdown of negotiations to incorporate the Urals into the system ; and, in spite of its name, VMS, like the pre-revolutionary syndicate Prodamet, at first handled only the output of the Ukrainian industry.[4] In the next year, it made several attempts to take over the sales of the Ural trusts ; and these efforts succeeded in September 1927, when a single metal trust was formed in the Urals, and ceded its selling functions to VMS.[5] A similar process of rationalization was applied to sales of machinery. In 1923–1926 the syndicate responsible for these sales had been mainly concerned with warehouse sales of metal. A separate specialized " Mashinosindikat ", later known as VMTS, was formed at the same time as VMS.[6] At first it sold only a small proportion of the production of its constituent trusts, and tended to get from the trusts only products which they found difficult to sell direct. As late as the middle of 1928, only one-third of the output of its members was being sold through VMTS. But, with the growth

[1] *Ekonomicheskaya Zhizn'*, January 4, 1927.
[2] *Pravda*, March 23, 1927.
[3] *Torgovo-Promyshlennaya Gazeta*, August 25, 1926, October 18, 1927.
[4] *Protokol Zasedaniya Prezidiuma VSNKh SSSR, 1925–1926*, No. 11, art. 367.
[5] *Torgovo-Promyshlennaya Gazeta*, June 20, 1926, September 3, 1927.
[6] See p. 375 above.

of central planning, VMTS set itself the aim of taking over the sale of all batch and mass production, leaving only custom-built machinery as a direct responsibility of the trusts.[1] The target set for VMTS for the year 1928–1929 was to control 75 per cent of that part of engineering production designated by a special commission of Glavmetall as appropriate for syndicate control.[2] A notable example of the emergence of a new syndicate, though it was only partly effective, was in the building materials industry. Shortages consequent upon the expansion of construction led to the formation of Stromsindikat in July 1927. The syndicate was at first intended to cover only cement and fire-resistant materials, but the crisis of the summer of 1928 led to an endeavour to bring the output of the vast number of kilns and quarries, most of which were under local or republican control, under the authority of this single organization.[3]

The timber industry for a long time successfully resisted syndicalization. Timber sales were more subject to market conditions and pressures than sales of metals or textiles. The industry had a dispersed character ; its products were difficult to standardize and, doubtless for these reasons, timber prices escaped any large degree of central regulation. In 1926, serious attempts were made to control sales both of standing and of sawn timber. Measures were introduced to keep prices at auctions within a ceiling of 216 per cent of the pre-war level ;[4] Narkomput' and the Vesenkhas of the USSR and RSFSR cooperated to divide up the purchases of standing timber and avoid competitive bidding.[5]

---

[1] *Torgovo-Promyshlennaya Gazeta*, July 16, December 4, 5, 1926, September 16, October 22, 1927, June 12, 1928.

[2] *Metall*, No. 4, 1929, pp. 100-110. These developments were of course resisted by the trusts ; a case was quoted in which, after Yuzhmashtrest had been prohibited from making a direct offer of locomotives required by Dnieprostroi, VMTS failed to deliver them on time, so that they had to be ordered from abroad (*Dnieprostroi*, No. 4, 1928, pp. 111-113).

[3] " The interests of the separate republican trusts ", Vesenkha declared, "must be subordinated to national economic interests. Overlapping in the work of syndicate and trusts disorganizes the market for building materials, and creates an artificial shortage of some materials and a great surplus of others " (*Torgovo-Promyshlennaya Gazeta*, August 17, 1928 ; see also *Promyshlennost' SSSR v 1926/27 godu* (1928), p. 287).

[4] *Byulleten' Finansovogo i Khozyaistvennogo Zakonodatel'stva*, *1926*, No. 32, pp. 1299-1301 ; No. 37, pp. 1452-1455 ; No. 39, p. 1535.

[5] *Ibid.* No. 35, p. 1391.

Stricter controls were introduced to limit or reduce prices of sawn timber.[1] In June 1926, a timber syndicate (Lesosindikat) was established under the Vesenkha of the RSFSR ;[2] the Vesenkha of the USSR ordered its trusts to make all their arrangements for the purchase of sawn timber by contracts with the producing trusts or the syndicate.[3] Both conditions of shortage and conditions of surplus were used as arguments for closer central control of the timber market. Supporters of central control claimed that organized distribution was necessary if expanding consumer demand was to be satisfied,[4] but also argued that " unhealthy competition " between timber trusts must be avoided at a time of overproduction.[5] A Rabkrin survey in August 1927 complained of " the weak syndicalization of the timber industry, the absence of a single operative regulating centre for timber materials, and the disorganization of the timber market thanks to the multitude of sellers ",[6] and recommended that Lesosindikat should take over the whole output of the trusts.[7] The process of transfer was, however, slow. In 1927–1928 Lesosindikat covered only 21·1 per cent of timber sales, and in 1928–1929 26·3 per cent.[8] In April 1928, all consumers of timber were required by Vesenkha to submit annual claims for 1928–1929 to Lesosindikat ;[9] and in that year the first national balance or budget of timber production and consumption was prepared. In 1929 STO transferred to the syndicate the control of all timber sales.[10]

Thus, in the middle and later nineteen-twenties, syndicates representing all the principal industries [11] played a more and more

---

[1] *Ibid.* No. 34, p. 1358 ; *Torgovo-Promyshlennaya Gazeta*, November 10, December 4, 1926.   [2] *Ibid.* June 3, 24, 1926.

[3] *Ibid.* November 10, 1926.   [4] *Ekonomicheskaya Zhizn'*, July 21, 1925.

[5] *Ibid.* January 4, 1927 ; *Torgovo-Promyshlennaya Gazeta*, August 20, 1927.

[6] *Planovoe Khozyaistvo*, No. 2, 1929, p. 267.

[7] *Torgovo-Promyshlennaya Gazeta*, August 20, 1927.

[8] *Voprosy Torgovli*, No. 6, March 1929, p. 7 ; the much higher figures quoted in the table on p. 641 below are dubious.

[9] *Torgovo-Promyshlennaya Gazeta*, April 18, 1928.

[10] A. Khavin, *Kratkii Ocherk Istorii Industrializatsii SSSR* (1962), pp. 74-75 ; *Lesnaya Promyshlennost' SSSR, 1917–1957* (1957), ii, 137, 144-145.

[11] A party resolution of June 1927 named Metallosindikat, Tekstilsindikat, Prodasilikat, Kozhsindikat, Rybsindikat and Sol'sindikat as the six leading syndicates (*Izvestiya Tsentral'nogo Komiteta VKP(B)*, No. 24-25 (197-198), June 30, 1927, pp. 10-11). For a list of " the 12 largest syndicates " in 1925–1926 see A. Malafeev, *Istoriya Tsenoobrazovaniya v SSSR* (1964), p. 78.

dominant rôle in the marketing of industrial products. The syndicate gradually came to usurp the selling functions of the trust, and to act as the national negotiating body between industry and consumer. Already in the autumn of 1925 the 12 largest syndicates had 121 sections and 35 agencies in the provinces which accounted for 75 per cent of all sales of the goods handled by them.[1] On May 6, 1926, the presidium of Vesenkha endorsed a resolution of an industrial conference which had " recognized the syndicates as the main transmitter to the market of the state principle " ;[2] and Dzerzhinsky gave blunt expression to the current policy :

> The supreme economic organs of the Union consider it appropriate to take trading work away from the trust machinery. Trading work will be transferred to the syndicates.[3]

Moreover, the syndicates were quickly successful in asserting the principle of central control against the organs of the republics. In December 1926, the presidium of the council of syndicates, the coordinating organ of the syndicates, agreed that each syndicate should control the whole Union market of the product handled by it.[4] The principle that a syndicate responsible for sales throughout the whole Union should be placed under Union control came to be generally accepted.[5] The one important exception was the timber syndicate which remained under RSFSR control.[6] In consumer industries such as leather, and pottery and glass, where most of the output was produced by local and republican trusts, or even by artisans, the Vesenkha of the RSFSR argued that, if it was to plan production, it should also control the syndicate : " control of the sphere of circulation must not be separated from control of the sphere of production ".[7] This battle was, however, soon lost. Attempts even by local trusts to sell their products independently and without the approval of the Union syndicate

---

[1] Ts. Kron, *Chastnaya Torgovlya v SSSR* (1926), p. 114.
[2] *Protokol Zasedaniya Prezidiuma VSNKh SSSR, 1925–1926*, No. 8.
[3] *Torgovo-Promyshlennaya Gazeta*, May 9, 1926.
[4] *Ibid.* December 24, 1926.
[5] See the discussion on the preserved food syndicate *ibid.* December 24, 1926.
[6] See p. 639 above.
[7] *Torgovo-Promyshlennaya Gazeta*, November 23, 1926 ; *SSSR : 4 S"ezd Sovetov* (1927), p. 376.

were generally defeated,[1] though as late as April 1929 a writer in
the Narkomtorg journal still argued that it was more advantageous
for the cooperatives to deal direct with the trusts than with the
syndicates.[2]

The process once set in motion was progressive. The following table illustrates the rapid increase in some typical industries in
the percentage of total output controlled by the syndicates :

	1923–1924	1924–1925	1925–1926	1926–1927	1927–1928	1928–1929
Textiles	34·6	39·5	64·6	79·6	90·7	88·6
Oil	98·2	98·9	98·0	98·0	98·0	98·0
Leather	49·8	49·3	54·4	67·5	90·5	93·8
Makhorka	13·2	31·8	37·0	42·8	73·0	100
Timber	—	—	—	35·0	68·0	93·0 [3]

In 1928 the syndicates were said to handle from 80 to 95 per cent
of the output of all Vesenkha-planned industry.[4] In heavy
industry, the metal and chemical syndicates handled 100 per cent
of the output of their respective trusts, the oil syndicate 98·3 per
cent, the machinery syndicate 80·2 per cent ; the laggards in this
field were the building materials syndicate (57·8 per cent) and the
timber syndicate (26·3 per cent). Of the output of planned
industry for the consumer market, the syndicates handled about
86 per cent.[5]

The rise of the syndicates formed part of the general process
of the erosion of market relations. From 1924 onwards, direct
administrative controls by the trading agencies played an increasing part in the wholesale and retail market for industrial consumer

[1] Such an attempt by a perfume and cosmetics trust of the Moscow Sov-
narkhoz was reported in *Torgovo-Promyshlennaya Gazeta*, May 26, June 22,
1928.   [2] *Voprosy Torgovli*, No. 7, April 1929, p. 72.

[3] Yu. Moshinsky, *Ekonomika i Organizatsiya Obrashcheniya Sredstv
Proizvodstva v SSSR* (1936), p. 115. The figures quoted, except for timber,
correspond closely with those in *Voprosy Torgovli*, No. 6, March 1929, p. 6,
which, however, gives only planned totals for 1928–1929 ; for the unexplained
discrepancy in the timber figures see p. 639, note 8 above.

[4] *Voprosy Torgovli*, No. 12, September 1928, p. 20.

[5] *Kontrol'nye Tsifry Narodnogo Khozyaistva SSSR na 1928–1929 god* (1929),
pp. 317-318.

Y

goods. In existing market conditions some goods were always in short supply ; in the autumn of 1925, and again in the autumn of 1927, the " goods famine " became general. Every shortage provided an urgent reason for extending direct control of the distribution of scarce output ; as shortages grew worse, controls became tighter over the major materials such as metal and fuel, which had been subject to some administrative controls even in the early years of NEP. But the rise of the syndicates cannot be explained simply as an attempt to organize conditions of scarcity. In the late autumn of 1926, when there was a glut of some goods, it was sometimes successfully argued that the appropriate syndicate should be stronger so as to help the trusts to handle the glut — a reversion to the original rôle which the syndicates had been created to fill.[1] Economic expediency was the main inspirer of the tendency to centralize. But the principle that each syndicate should monopolize the whole output of its industry also possessed a momentum of its own, and gathered strength as planning was gradually extended to every sector of the economy.

The next crucial problem in which the syndicates became involved was the sharing of the distribution of consumer goods to the urban and rural population between state, cooperative and private agencies, the eventual exclusion of the private trader from the field being proclaimed as the goal. By a decree of August 18, 1926, STO recognized general contracts between the syndicates and Tsentrosoyuz as the best method of organizing retail trade and reducing costs of distribution. " The rôle of chief distributor of industrial goods to consumers ", declared the decree, " belongs to the system of consumer cooperatives " ; and it sought to restrict the functions of the torgi to the supply of raw materials to local and artisan industries and to the sale of their products. On the other hand, it did not formally prohibit direct relations between the syndicates and lower cooperative organs, though its aim was evidently to discourage them.[2] Whatever the embarrassments and

---

[1] For an example of the use of both arguments in the timber industry see p. 639 above.

[2] *Sobranie Zakonov*, *1926*, No. 59, art. 445. On the following day, a resolution of the party central committee on the agricultural cooperatives instructed STO to examine " the practice of general contracts concluded by state industry with agricultural cooperatives " and " the causes of the unprofitability of some of these contracts ", and suggested that the principal

imperfections of the system of general contracts, it marked a move in the direction of planned and centralized control of distribution ; and a pronouncement of the party central committee at its session of February 1927, ostensibly related to the campaign to reduce prices, proposed to take the system a step further :

> Industry will be in a position to react sensitively to changes in demand only when the cooperatives and state trading organs, and especially the cooperatives, which possess a widespread network of distribution, . . . observe in good time the changes which occur and make themselves felt on the market, and promptly signal them to state industry. As the cooperatives master this new, important and difficult task, they must go over to a system of orders in advance.[1]

During the discussion which preceded this reform, Mikoyan spoke of it as a transition to " a higher stage of planning, when plans will be compiled on basis of orders in hand ".[2]

The system of orders in advance was first introduced in the textile industry. A decree of STO dated August 26, 1927, ruled that, as part of the annual negotiations for general contracts between VTS and the cooperatives and torgi, the latter were to place specific and detailed orders for the products which they required ; the scheme was to cover 50 per cent of the total amount agreed in the contract for the period from January 1 to July 1, 1928, and 100 per cent thereafter.[3] The aim of the textile syndicate was to secure an arrangement whereby it could place firm precise orders with the factories well in advance, and simultaneously to mould the market to the pattern of output which the producing trusts could most easily achieve. A leading administrator in the textile industry put it frankly. The idea in " some circles, mainly in the cooperatives ", he declared, was that " the task of industry amounts only to a continuous adaptation to consumer demand ". While it was necessary to study the consumers and

---

function of the agricultural cooperatives was to supply raw materials to state industry ; for this resolution see p. 146 above. This was evidently a move in the rivalry between consumer and agricultural cooperatives (see pp. 15-16, 47 above).

[1] *KPSS v Rezolyutsiyakh* (1954), ii, 351.   [2] *Pravda*, March 2, 1927.
[3] *Ibid.* September 2, 1927 ; *Torgovo-Promyshlennaya Gazeta*, September 2, 1927.

adapt oneself to their needs, " the main thing is to have an organizing influence on them ". He went on :

> There can be no serious talk about the rationalization of production in the textile industry if industry has to reorient itself (perezapravlyat'sya) in accordance with the initial requirements of the market, as disclosed by the trading organizations and presented by them to industry. . . . The basis for the rationalization of production, the specialization of factories and the reduction of costs must be the organizing influence of industry on consumer demand, so that it may develop in accordance with the objective possibilities of industry.[1]

A little later, it was explained that the system of orders in advance had a dual function. It was concerned not only to communicate popular demand to industry, but " to assist in broadening the influence of cooperative centres and of state industry in forming consumer demand ".[2] If the syndicates seemed to have forfeited some of their independence to Tsentrosoyuz, their authority vis-à-vis the trusts, and the authority of syndicates and Tsentrosoyuz together over the market, had been greatly strengthened. The syndicates and Tsentrosoyuz together now occupied key positions in the new planning complex which determined both what was to be produced and what was to be consumed. But the result of the new system, in conditions in which most consumer goods were in short supply on the market, was to preclude any serious attention to consumer demand. This applied even to ready-made clothing, where the articles supplied too often consisted of " uncomfortable ' bourgeois jackets ' " for men, and " complicated women's dresses on which much unnecessary material is expended without real benefit to the customer ".[3]

The introduction of planned trade and distribution and the exclusion of the private trader were seriously hampered both by deficiencies in the state and cooperative agencies of distribution and by the continuing rivalry between them. Friction between Vesenkha and the cooperatives had been endemic throughout the

---

[1] *Torgovo-Promyshlennaya Gazeta*, May 18, 1928.
[2] *XLI Sobranie Upolnomochennykh Tsentrosoyuza* (1928), p. 339 ; for an account of the working of the system of " orders in advance " see *ibid.* pp. 186-188.   [3] *Voprosy Torgovli*, No. 7, April 1929, p. 57.

preceding period.[1] The situation was further complicated by the
rise of the syndicates, whose attempts to make use of existing torgi
as selling agencies,[2] or themselves to set up agencies for retail trade,
were a direct challenge to the cooperatives. The problem had not
been solved by the decree of August 18, 1926.[3] The syndicates
refused to believe that the cooperatives were well enough organized
or financed to sell their products, and feared " a dissipation of their
resources on the cooperative periphery, without a hope that the
latter would discharge the financial obligations incurred by it ".[4]
Even when they professed to dismantle their retail network, they
evaded this concession to the cooperatives by various " roundabout
devices " such as share companies for the marketing of their products, formed sometimes on an industrial, sometimes on a local,
basis. The most successful examples of the former appear to have
been Tekstil'torg and Metallosklad, of the latter (which were formed
in partnership with local authorities) Sibtorg, Uzbektorg, Turkmen-
torg and Kirtorg.[5] The syndicates sometimes concluded general
contracts for the supply of goods to private traders, though this
practice was afterwards condemned as a potential cover for
" speculation ".[6] Constant friction arose from the reluctance of
the syndicates to sell through the cooperatives scarce goods which
they could dispose of to better advantage elsewhere, and from the
reluctance of the cooperatives to take goods in abundant supply
which the syndicates were eager to let them have.[7] Larin at the

---

[1] See Socialism in One Country, 1924–1926, Vol. 1, pp. 434-435.

[2] It seems to have been true that in the outlying regions the torgi were more
effective than the cooperatives, and often received support from the syndicates
(see pp. 651-652 below).   [3] See p. 642 above.

[4] Voprosy Torgovli, No. 2-3, November–December 1927, p. 63.

[5] XLI Sobranie Upolnomochennykh Tsentrosoyuza (1928), p. 38 ; Voprosy
Torgovli, No. 6, March 1929, p. 58. The aim of Tekstil'torg was said to be
" to demonstrate the superiority of state trade to the consumer cooperatives "
(ibid. No. 2-3, November–December 1927, p. 68). Regional torgi pre-dated
the syndicates (see p. 650 below).

[6] Voprosy Istorii, No. 12, 1964, p. 15 ; a charge of re-selling goods to private
traders was brought against the consumer cooperatives (XV^{ya} Sessiya Soveta
Tsentrosoyuza (1926), p. 69).

[7] Voprosy Torgovli, No. 2-3, November–December 1927, p. 62. Goods
in abundant supply at this time were salt, matches, kerosene, tobacco, sugar
(formerly " scarce "), earthenware and galoshes ; leather goods and footwear,
heavy metals, and wool and cotton textiles were scarce (Planovoe Khozyaistvo,
No. 5, 1928, pp. 79-88 ; for a more detailed list see Kontrol'nye Tsifry Narodnogo
Khozyaistva SSSR na 1927–1928 god (1928), p. 238). It was claimed that the

fifteenth party conference in October 1926 accused the trusts and syndicates of deliberately reducing the proportion of their goods sold through the cooperatives, and denounced this as an example of the " opposition " policy of Pyatakov, though some separate selling organizations set up by the syndicates had admittedly been disbanded.[1]

While therefore the syndicates were increasingly successful in asserting their exclusive right to bring to the market the output of the trusts, far less success attended the efforts of Tsentrosoyuz to establish a monopoly position in the retailing of these products. The consumer cooperatives claimed, not without reason, that they alone possessed a widely spread network of shops and stalls equipped for retail trade ; they complained that the trusts or syndicates supplied only inferior goods to workers' cooperatives and reserved the best for state shops, and that this hampered the struggle against the private trader.[2] Specific causes of trouble were unpunctual deliveries by the syndicates and demands for payment in advance of up to 30 per cent of the price.[3] A further difficulty arose from the desire of lower cooperative organs, some-times encouraged by the syndicates, to deal directly with the syndicates and not subordinate themselves to the centralized organization of Tsentrosoyuz. Direct transactions between the syndicates and local cooperatives continued, especially in the out-lying regions ; the Siberian cooperatives complained that the failure of Tsentrosoyuz to keep up an adequate supply of goods compelled them to make separate agreements with the suppliers.[4] In spite, however, of these frictions and handicaps, the system of general contracts between syndicates and Tsentrosoyuz made pro-gress. Between 1925-1926 and 1926-1927 the proportion of the output of the chemical industry covered by general contracts rose from 44 to 55·8 per cent, of sugar from 29 to 43·9 per cent and of

---

general contracts covered mainly scarce goods ; of the items covered by the original contracts of 1925-1926, 70 per cent were scarce, 62·7 per cent being textiles (*Voprosy Torgovli*, No. 7, April 1929, p. 55).

[1] *XV Konferentsiya Vsesoyuznoi Kommunisticheskoi Partii (B)* (1927), pp. 166, 225-226.
[2] *XV^va Sessiya Soveta Tsentrosoyuza* (1926), p. 37 ; *XLI Sobranie Upolno-mochennykh Tsentrosoyuza* (1928), pp. 80, 88.
[3] *XV^va Sessiya Soveta Tsentrosoyuza* (1926), pp. 25, 35.
[4] *XLI Sobranie Upolnomochennykh Tsentrosoyuza* (1928), p. 143.

textiles from 25·4 to 37·6 per cent : these were the highest proportions.[1] In 1927–1928 Tsentrosoyuz claimed to have covered 80
per cent of the output of cotton textiles and 60 per cent of textiles as a whole, 65 per cent of rubber goods, and 62 per cent of
sugar and tobacco.[2] These claims, put forward at a conference of
enthusiastic delegates of the consumer cooperatives, probably did
not suffer from understatement. Elsewhere it was stated that 48·2
per cent of all industrial goods handled by the consumer cooperatives in 1927–1928 were covered by general contracts, and 54·9
per cent in 1928–1929.[3] An unwanted consequence of these
arrangements appears to have been an increased tendency, of
which Sokolnikov complained at the beginning of the grain collections crisis of 1928, to give preference to the urban over the rural
market in the supply of consumer goods.[4] The party central committee decided in April 1928 to recommend an increased supply of
industrial goods to the grain-producing regions " even at the cost
of a temporary denuding of the towns ".[5] But the increasing goods
shortage in the towns obviously made this policy difficult to enforce ;
and Mikoyan later commented that " we lacked the revolutionary
harshness to denude the town for the sake of the countryside ".[6]

In the spring and summer of 1928 the syndicates, with the
support of Vesenkha, made a concerted assault on the ambition of
Tsentrosoyuz to establish a monopoly in retail trade in industrial
goods. The presidium of Vesenkha, in a communication to Gosplan, complained of " clumsiness ", " complexity " and " lack of
flexibility " in the existing arrangements, declared that some " decentralization " of orders and requisitions was indispensable, and
called for a revision of the whole system of general contracts.
About the same time " a plan of work of the syndicates for 1928–
1929 " was drawn up in Vesenkha. This called for decentralization of orders, and for direct contact between regional sections of the
textile syndicate and local cooperative organizations. It proposed

---

[1] *Voprosy Torgovli*, No. 2-3, November–December 1927, pp. 62, 68.
[2] *XLI Sobranie Upolnomochennykh Tsentrosoyuza* (1928), pp. 33-34.
[3] *International Cooperation, 1927–1929* (International Cooperative Alliance,
1930), p. 219.
[4] *Torgovo-Promyshlennaya Gazeta*, January 8, 14, 1928.
[5] *KPSS v Rezolyutsiyakh* (1954), ii, 494 ; for Mikoyan's advocacy of this
course see p. 38 above.
[6] *XLI Sobranie Upolnomochennykh Tsentrosoyuza* (1928), p. 288.

among other items that the leather syndicate should organize
" a special network of regional footwear stores " where cooperatives
and state organs had failed to do so ; that the metal syndicate
should extend its trading network ; and that the salt syndicate
should curtail its credits to consumer cooperatives.[1] At a
Tsentrosoyuz conference in July 1928,[2] loud protests were voiced
at the attempts of Vesenkha and the syndicates to restrict the rôle
of the cooperatives in the marketing of industrial goods. Particular
indignation was expressed at the setting up of shops in rural areas
by the textile syndicate ; these were described by one delegate,
amid applause, as " the best and most perfect disorganizers of the
market ".[3] Mikoyan, who addressed the conference as People's
Commissar for Trade, tried to pour oil on the waters. The textile
syndicate had 100 shops, the cooperatives 60,000 ; were " demands for the liquidation of these 100 shops " really necessary ?
The important point was for the syndicates and the cooperatives
to form " a single front in the struggle against private capital ".
In the past disputes between them had " threatened our common
development ". But now the issue was settled : 80 per cent of all
textiles were covered by general contracts. Mikoyan, while refusing to support the claim of Tsentrosoyuz for a monopoly in the
marketing of industrial goods, upheld the authority of Tsentrosoyuz as the central organ of the consumer cooperatives, and was
against the conclusion of independent agreements by the syndicates with lower cooperative organs ; Vesenkha, he claimed, had
now come round to this view.[4] These exhortations and assurances
failed in the long run to improve relations. " Disputes and
clashes " between the syndicates and Tsentrosoyuz continued to
occur over the general contracts, and were attributed by a spokesman of the cooperatives to " the top-level apparatus of industry
struggling for its bureaucratic existence ".[5] But, in an environment of increasing shortage of consumer goods and ever greater

---

[1] These documents are quoted in XLI Sobranie Upolnomochennykh Tsentrosoyuza (1928), pp. 36, 100. See also Torgovo-Promyshlennaya Gazeta, May 8,
12, 15, 1928 ; many industrialists called for the replacement of " general
contracts " by more flexible " general agreements ".
[2] For this conference see pp. 656, 662 below.
[3] XLI Sobranie Upolnomochennykh Tsentrosoyuza (1928), p. 90.
[4] Ibid. pp. 302, 304-305, 314.
[5] Voprosy Torgovli, No. 5, February 1929, p. 26.

concentration on heavy industry, the scales were weighted in favour of Vesenkha and the syndicates.[1]

The increasing strength of the syndicates was illustrated by their success from 1927 onwards in dictating to the cooperatives the retail prices at which their merchandise should be re-sold. It was an old reproach that the cooperatives were more interested in earning profits than in reducing prices.[2] The practice grew up of specifying retail prices in the contracts between the syndicates and Tsentrosoyuz " for the purpose of coordinated release on the market ", such prices being sometimes fixed, or " confirmed ", by Narkomtorg.[3] Where no contracts were in existence, the syndicates supplied important consumer goods on the basis of " a system of indicated prices ".[4] Moreover, as the producer goods industries expanded, direct transactions between industrial concerns, which were often handled by the syndicates but did not enter the cooperative network at all, became increasingly important ; the compilers of the Gosplan control figures for 1928–1929 regarded " the rationalization of turnover in the organized sector of the economy, primarily of transactions between industries ", as the central problem confronting the syndicates.[5] In spite of the growth in the value of goods covered by general contracts between the syndicates and Tsentrosoyuz, in 1927–1928 it still represented less than 40 per cent of the turnover of the syndicates.[6] The syndicates had moved a long way from their original function as voluntary organizations which helped the trusts to dispose of part of their products, and were concerned mainly with sales handled directly through their own warehouses. By 1928 they were part of the national organization of industry responsible

---

[1] A decree of July 3, 1929, attempted to regulate relations between the syndicates and Tsentrosoyuz by providing for the submission of disputed questions to Narkomtorg for decision (*Sobranie Zakonov, 1929*, No. 45, art. 394).

[2] *Voprosy Torgovli*, No. 2-3, November–December 1927, p. 67.

[3] *Ibid.* No. 7, April 1928, pp. 95-96.

[4] *Ibid.* No. 6, March 1929, p. 10.

[5] *Kontrol'nye Tsifry Narodnogo Khozyaistva SSSR na 1928–1929 god* (1929), pp. 51, 318.

[6] G. Neiman, *Vnutrennyaya Torgovlya SSSR* (1935), p. 113, quotes figures of 528 million rubles for 1925–1926, 1049 millions for 1926–1927, and 2032 millions for 1927–1928 ; a cooperative source quoted in *Postroenie Fundamenta Sotsialisticheskoi Ekonomik iv SSSR* (1960), p. 440, gives a figure of 3396 million rubles for 1928–1929, or 70 per cent in advance of the previous year.

Y 2

for the allocation of scarce supplies among industrial and private consumers, and mainly concerned with planning and issuing instructions for direct (tranzit) sales from producer to consumer. In 1924–1925, 82 per cent of the sales of the principal syndicates passed through their warehouses ; in the plan for 1927–1928, this figure had fallen to 27 per cent.[1] The major function of the syndicates was now to organize and supervise the processes of planned trade and distribution.

(b) Torgi

State trading establishments (gostorgi or torgi) had existed since the early days of NEP.[2] Many of them were set up by provincial Sovnarkhozy. But their development is described as " to a large extent spontaneous ", and " the organizers of these trading enterprises were not themselves clearly aware what rôle in the national exchange of commodities they were intended to play ". In the European provinces of the RSFSR and in the Ukraine, they were active mainly in wholesale trade, some of them trading in factory products from the large industrial centres, others in products of local and artisan industry ; many of them participated from the first in the state collections of grain and other agricultural products. State retail shops were set up in towns ; but, in the European regions of the RSFSR, only the State Universal Store (GUM) with headquarters in Moscow and branches in other large cities achieved outstanding success. In the non-European parts of the USSR, where the cooperatives had made little or no impact, and trade organization was still primitive or non-existent, the torgi played an important part in retail trade, though they appear to have operated mainly in towns. By 1926–1927 a network of 71 provincial or regional torgi had been established, with numerous county and local torgi working under their direction. The total turnover, wholesale and retail, of the torgi rose from 470 million rubles in 1923–1924 to 1272 millions in 1925–1926.[3]

---

[1] Yu. Moshinsky, *Ekonomika i Organizatsiya Obrashcheniya Sredstv Proizvodstva v SSSR* (1936), p. 119.
[2] See *The Bolshevik Revolution, 1917–1923*, Vol. 2, pp. 340-341.
[3] *Voprosy Torgovli*, No. 6, 1929, p. 17 ; G. Neiman, *Vnutrennyaya Torgovlya SSSR* (1935), p. 111. For GUM see *The Bolshevik Revolution, 1917–1923*, Vol. 2, p. 336.

While, however, the work of the torgi continued to increase with the growing expansion of trade, they were from the outset subject to heavy pressure of competition from several sides. The powerful industrial syndicates, which had at first been inclined to use the torgi as channels for the disposal of their products in outlying centres, began to set up their own local selling agencies.[1] The rôle of the torgi in the agricultural collections was gradually eroded by the agricultural and consumer cooperatives.[2] Most important of all, the consumer cooperatives put up a stubborn resistance to the encroachment of the torgi on the retail market ; and, in places where the cooperatives were already established, the plea that they enjoyed a prestige, and possessed a knowledge of consumer needs, which the torgi could not emulate, was well justified. When the thirteenth party congress in May 1924 set out to organize a People's Commissariat of Internal Trade and to improve trading procedures, it favoured the maximum development of the consumer cooperatives in retail trade, and pronounced that state trade " should be confined more and more within the limits of wholesale and wholesale-retail trade ".[3] This injunction, which was less than mandatory in tone, had little immediate effect, thanks no doubt to the weakness of the cooperatives. But it was reinforced by the decree of August 18, 1926, which was designed as a charter for the consumer cooperatives, and which sought to limit the functions of the torgi to the supply of raw materials to local and artisan industries and to the marketing of their products, especially in outlying regions.[4] Meanwhile the Exchanges, set up at the time of the scissors crisis as an instrument for controlling prices,[5] were reduced in number and lost their obligatory character, becoming little more than " organs of Narkomtorg for the registration and supervision of wholesale commercial transactions ".[6] In the following year a commission on the rationalization of trade, set up by STO under the presidency of Tsyurupa, in a resolution of May 30, 1927, defined in greater detail the functions of the torgi.

[1] See p. 645 above.   [2] See pp. 15-16 above.
[3] KPSS v Rezolyutsiyakh (1954), ii, 43 ; for this resolution see Socialism in One Country, 1924–1926, Vol. 1, p. 430.
[4] For this decree see p. 642 above.
[5] See The Interregnum, 1923–1924, p. 109.
[6] Sobranie Zakonov, 1926, No. 71, art. 545 ; Sobranie Zakonov, 1927, No. 6, art. 56 ; G. Neiman, Vnutrennyaya Torgovlya SSSR (1935), p. 120.

Their participation in retail trade in consumer goods was to be
confined to the sale of products of local industry, and primarily to
" remote and peripheral regions having a poorly developed network of cooperative trade ". Three tasks were entrusted to them :
to serve as wholesalers to private retail trade, thus ousting the
private wholesaler ; to supply artisans with raw material and to
market their products ; and to act as selling agents for trusts and
syndicates where empowered to do so by special agreements.[1]
This was immediately followed by an instruction to the torgi
from Narkomtorg to reduce their network of local branches.[2] On
August 17, 1927, Sovnarkom promulgated a statute for the torgi
in which they were defined as " independent trading organizations
set up by a state institution and acting on the principles of khozraschet " ; the statute related, however, only to torgi of Union or
republican status having a capital of not less than 100,000 rubles.[3]
On April 27, 1928, STO, harking back to the resolution of the
Tsyurupa commission of May 1927, issued an elaborate regulation
for the torgi, which were authorized to engage in small and medium
wholesale trade and also in retail trade. " In regions with sufficiently developed cooperatives ", the torgi would " gradually contract their enterprises ". The functions specifically assigned to
them were to supply artisans with raw materials and market their
products, and to act as wholesalers for " commercial undertakings
which have no sales apparatus of their own ", supplying provincial
and regional cooperative organizations.[4] The implication was
strong that the torgi were being relegated to the performance of
secondary functions not otherwise provided for. From this time
the most important work of the torgi appears to have been the
marketing of the output of local and artisan industries : they were
sometimes referred to as " the syndicates of local industry ".[5] In
outlying regions, where consumer cooperatives were weak or non-
existent, the torgi still held their own.[6] Protests were, however,

[1] Torgovo-Promyshlennaya Gazeta, July 8, 1927 ; G. Neiman, Vnutrennyaya
Torgovlya SSSR (1935), p. 112.
[2] Voprosy Torgovli, No. 6, March 1929, p. 57.
[3] Sobranie Zakonov, 1927, No. 49, arts. 501, 502.
[4] Sobranie Zakonov, 1928, No. 29, art. 265.
[5] Voprosy Torgovli, No. 6, March 1929, p. 56.
[6] Ibid. No. 2-3, November–December 1927, p. 61. In 1926 the Siberian
regional torg (Sibtorg) was so much better supplied with goods than the regional

made as late as July 1928 that state retail stores in other areas served as a brake on recruitment of members by the consumer cooperatives and on the collection of dues, and that such stores were still being opened, not only in towns but in the countryside, and were selling consumer goods in direct competition with the cooperatives.[1]

Competition from the syndicates on one side and the cooperatives on the other finally clipped the wings of the torgi. The period of spectacular increase in turnover ended with the year 1925–1926 ; in 1926–1927 turnover increased only by 8·6 per cent and in 1927–1928 by a further 2·8 per cent — a relative decline in a period of expanding trade.[2] Nevertheless their position had been to some extent stabilized, and nobody seriously thought it possible to dispense with them. A survey of the torgi in the journal of Narkomtorg in March 1929 deprecated " the conclusion that the work of the torgi has no future ".[3] An official report of the same period pilloried " a contraction of state retail trade carried out by order of local organs " as " incorrect ", and looked forward to " some expansion " of it in the current year.[4] But it was evident the torgi were no match for two such powerful, well integrated and aggressive organizations as the syndicates and the consumer cooperatives, and would continue to operate mainly in the sphere of small-scale local industry, which the syndicates did not find it worth while to penetrate, and in outlying and thinly populated regions, where the cooperatives had not gained a foothold.

(c) Consumer Cooperatives

After the revival of the consumer cooperatives in 1925,[5] and their gradual integration into the system of marketing industrial goods through the syndicates, their membership and trade turnover progressively expanded. Party mistrust of them did not

cooperative union (Sibkraisoyuz) that local cooperatives were obliged to buy from it ; or alternatively Sibkraisoyuz itself bought from Sibtorg (XV^{va} Sessiya Soyuza Tsentrosoyuza (1926), pp. 68, 90).

[1] XLI Sobranie Upolnomochennykh Tsentrosoyuza (1928), pp. 95, 143.
[2] Voprosy Torgovli, No. 6, March 1929, p. 18.
[3] Ibid. No. 6, March 1929, pp. 17-19.
[4] SSSR : Ot S"ezd k S"ezdu (Aprel' 1927 g.–Mai 1929 g.) (1929), p. 76.
[5] See Socialism in One Country, 1924–1926, Vol. 1, pp. 433-435.

entirely evaporate. But they were too convenient an instrument
to be discarded. The consumer cooperatives had an important
place in the central theme of economic policy. Their function
was " to establish the link between working class and peasantry,
between consumer and producer ".[1] As in the grain collections,
so in the marketing of industrial goods, the cooperatives proved
more effective than the state trading organs as competitors of the
private trader. Dzerzhinsky looked to the consumer cooperatives
as " the future grave-digger of private capital ", and went on :

> The whole strength of private capital derives from the weak-
> ness of the cooperatives. . . . Without good and cheap coopera-
> tives the private trader will beat us ; and we shall not get out of
> our economic difficulties.[2]

The party central committee at its session of February 1927 referred to " the enormously rapid growth " of the cooperatives, and
recommended them to broaden their activities, both by driving
out private trade and by replacing state trade, in so far as this
could be done without raising prices to the consumer and without
opening the way for a return of private trade.[3]

Thus officially encouraged, membership of the consumer cooperatives grew rapidly. The number of societies throughout the
Soviet Union remained constant at about 28,500 (this suggests an
unwillingness or inability to branch out into the remoter regions).
The following statistics (in millions) show a progressive rise in
membership :

	Rural	Urban	Transport
October 1, 1926	7.2	4.4	0.72
October 1, 1927	9.8	5.3	0.85
October 1, 1928	13.8	7.7	0.98
1928–1929	19.9	12.8	— 4

[1] XV^{va} Sessiya Soveta Tsentrosoyuza (1926), p. 68.
[2] Letter of March 1926 quoted by Larin in Na Agrarnom Fronte, No. 7-8,
1926, p. 23.   [3] KPSS v Rezolyutsiyakh (1954), ii, 352-353.
[4] Kontrol'nye Tsifry Narodnogo Khozyaistva SSSR na 1928–1929 god (1929),
p. 102 ; Kontrol'nye Tsifry Narodnogo Khozyaistva SSSR na 1929/30 god
(1930), p. 571. In 1927 the proportion of peasant households belonging to the
consumer cooperatives was 39 per cent ; in the two following years it rose to
54 and 58 per cent (Istoriya Sovetskogo Krest'yanstva i Kolkhoznogo Stroitel'stva
SSSR (1963), p. 67).

In the RSFSR alone, according to Tsentrosoyuz statistics, the number of consumer cooperative shops and stalls in town and country increased from 42,424 in 1925–1926 to 63,890 in 1928–1929.[1] Of the urban members in the summer of 1926, 60–65 per cent were trade-unionists, the proportion of members of the co-operatives being highest among railway workers (75 per cent) and in large-scale factory industry, and lowest among building and food workers (25 and 21 per cent).[2] The rise in membership was accompanied by a rise in turnover.[3] But the consumer cooperatives, thanks to the system of general contracts with the syndicates, played a larger rôle in the distribution of industrial goods than of agricultural products. In 1928 68 per cent of all goods purchased by workers from the consumer cooperatives were industrial goods, though more than half the workers' total expenditure was on foodstuffs.[4] In the period of the first five-year plan it was estimated that the proportion of retail trade handled by the cooperatives would rise to 88 per cent of industrial goods and 56 per cent of agricultural products.[5]

Though these advances were welcomed, the social composition of the consumer cooperatives, especially of the rural branches, was subject to the same suspicions as that of other cooperatives. When a delegate at the council of Tsentrosoyuz in February 1926 quoted an article in the Tsentrosoyuz journal complaining that " the richest families are drawn into the consumer cooperatives ", and that " the consumer cooperatives consist of a cluster (sgustok) of the wealthiest households in the countryside ", Khinchuk could only reply that statistics of social composition were misleading and contradictory.[6] " As in other forms of cooperatives ", observed the compilers of the Gosplan control figures for 1928–1929, " the participation of the higher groups in the consumer network

---

[1] *Voprosy Torgovli*, No. 4, January 1929, p. 70.
[2] *Bol'shevik*, No. 3, February 1, 1927, pp. 49–50 ; many of these were no doubt members of workers' cooperatives (see pp. 660–661 below).
[3] See Table No. 27, p. 960 below.
[4] *XLI Sobranie Upolnomochennykh Tsentrosoyuza* (1928), p. 40. In *Voprosy Torgovli*, No. 4, January 1929, p. 68, the figure of 68 per cent is quoted for the RSFSR alone ; owing to the dual status of Tsentrosoyuz (see p. 662 below), cooperative statistics are often subject to this ambiguity.
[5] *Shestnadtsataya Konferentsiya VKP(B)* (1962), p. 188.
[6] *XVᵛᵃ Sessiya Soveta Tsentrosoyuza* (1926), p. 19.

is high ".[1] These suspicions led to growing insistence on stricter party control. In June 1927 the party central committee gave its attention to the leading personnel of the consumer cooperatives. Party workers in responsible positions were said to be changed too rapidly ; the number of party members and party workers engaged in cooperative work was insufficient ; and a review of existing personnel was demanded.[2] The council of Tsentrosoyuz at its session in the same month, in a long resolution on organization, coupled reminders of " the enlargement of the rôle of the consumer cooperatives in the national economy as a whole, and their enhanced responsibility for the condition of the market " with recommendations for closer links with the party.[3] Increasing intervention of the party in their affairs brought with it more direct subordination of the cooperatives to the organs of government. At the fifteenth party congress in December 1927, when Lyubimov, the president of Tsentrosoyuz, complained of excessive interference from the centre, especially from Narkomtorg, and of the small number of cooperative delegates elected to party and Soviet congresses, he was listened to with unconcealed impatience.[4] The Tsentrosoyuz conference in July 1928, at which jealousy of the authority of Narkomtorg was freely expressed, passed a resolution demanding that " mutual relations with Narkomtorg should be based on a recognition of the consumer cooperatives, not as an object of regulation, but as a fundamental factor in the organization and regulation of the market ".[5] At the sixteenth party conference in April 1929 Lyubimov again protested bitterly that Tsentrosoyuz had to contend " with two Sovnarkoms [of the USSR and the RSFSR], two Gosplans, two Narkomtorgs and two Vesenkhas ". But he won little sympathy from his audience. He was refused an extension of time for his main speech ; and his second speech was frequently interrupted.[6] Between January and

---

[1] *Kontrol'nye Tsifry Narodnogo Khozyaistva SSSR na 1928–1929 god* (1929), p. 118 ; a complaint of inadequate statistics on this subject made in the control figures for the previous year was emphatically repeated *ibid*. pp. 116-117. For the agricultural cooperatives see pp. 149-152 above.

[2] *Izvestiya Tsentral'nogo Komiteta VKP(B)*, No. 24-25 (197-198), June 30, 1927, p. 10 ; a leading article *ibid*. pp. 1-2, called for better training of personnel.

[3] *Spravochnik Partiinogo Rabotnika*, vi (1928), ii, 560-564.

[4] *Pyatnadtsatyi S"ezd VKP(B)* (1962), ii, 1037-1039.

[5] *XLI Sobranie Upolnomochennykh Tsentrosoyuza* (1928), pp. 229-230, 345.

[6] *Shestnadtsataya Konferentsiya VKP(B)* (1962), pp. 187, 538, 541.

April 1929 *Pravda* had conducted a " review " of the party cell in Tsentrosoyuz, which brought to light a number of bureaucratic shortcomings, and now resulted in " an improvement and purge of the apparatus ".[1] The consumer cooperatives had become an indispensable part of the Soviet machinery of administration. In spite of past traditions of independence, serious deviations on their part could no longer be tolerated.

The finances of the consumer cooperatives (as of other cooperatives) were dependent on bank credits and state subsidies in various forms.[2] In response to constant pressure to reduce prices, the trading margins of the consumer cooperatives were cut from year to year ; [3] and they had to manage with a lower rate of profit. At the Tsentrosoyuz conference in July 1928, Lyubimov reported that profits, now pared to a minimum, had reached 147 million rubles in 1926 and only 85·5 millions in 1927 ; [4] working capital was provided mainly by loans, amounting to more than a milliard rubles. Rykov observed that, though the government had helped and would help the consumer cooperatives, it was time that they should finance themselves mainly from their own funds.[5] While

---

[1] *Shestnadtsataya Konferentsiya VKP(B)* (1962), p. 818, note 309 ; for particulars of a drastic purge in the following year see *40 Let Sovetskoi Torgovli* (1957), pp. 179-180.

[2] Competition for state finance was an important element in the rivalry between consumer and agricultural cooperatives (see pp. 15-16, 47 above). In the 1925–1926 budget allocation of 35 million rubles for the cooperatives, 8 millions were initially assigned to the consumer, and 18 millions to the agricultural, cooperatives ; protests from the consumer cooperatives brought about a revision of these figures to 12·5 and 14·5 millions respectively (*XV*ᵛᵃ *Sessiya Soveta Tsentrosoyuza* (1926), pp. 7-8).

[3] Costs remained substantially higher than those of the syndicates and torgi, no doubt because they operated in smaller units ; the following comparative table of costs as percentages of turnover appeared in the control figures for 1927-1928 :

	1925–1926	1926–1927	1927–1928 (plan)
Syndicates	2·55	1·43	1·21
Torgi	3·25	2·17	1·86
Consumer cooperatives :			
Wholesale	2·9	2·0	1·7
Retail	7·5	6·4	5·5

Labour costs in all cases accounted for from 50 to 60 per cent of the total (*Kontrol'nye Tsifry Narodnogo Khozyaistva SSSR na 1927–1928 god* (1928), p. 250).   [4] *XLI Sobranie Upolnomochennykh Tsentrosoyuza* (1928), p. 44.

[5] *Ibid.* p. 280 ; Rykov had always been a stern critic of cooperative finances (see *Socialism in One Country, 1924–1926*, Vol. 1, p. 431).

the consumer cooperatives were certainly in a sounder financial position than the other cooperatives, neither Rykov's exhortation, nor Kalinin's suggestion a few months later that their profits should be used to finance producer cooperatives,[1] could be called realistic.

The question of membership dues remained a sore point. In 1926 the average annual dues paid by members of consumer cooperatives were 4·32 rubles in the towns and 2·86 rubles in the country ;[2] and insistence on full and punctual payment was incompatible with the desired increase in the recruitment of poor peasants. The council of Tsentrosoyuz, at its session in February 1926, noted that a strengthening of the lower social groups in the countryside in the membership of the cooperatives " depends to a significant extent on the prompt receipt from the state of the necessary means, in the form of long-term credit, to make available to the poor peasant population the maximum exemptions from the payment of membership dues ".[3] A party resolution of September 1, 1927, advocated the raising of annual dues to 10 rubles for urban, and 7 rubles for rural, cooperatives, with exemption for poor peasants.[4] At the Tsentrosoyuz conference in July 1928, Lyubimov claimed that 50 million rubles had been collected in members' dues in the first half of the financial year 1927–1928 (nearly twice as much as for the previous year), and that an attempt was being made to enforce a standard rate of 10 rubles a year for rural, and 15 rubles for urban, members. But " backwardness in the payment of contributions " was a standing difficulty.[5] Differential rates of contribution continued to prevail, and were recommended in the Gosplan control figures for 1928–1929 as a way to " extract money from middle and well-to-do groups ".[6] In 1929 the standard rate was raised to 19·5 rubles for urban, and 15 rubles

[1] SSSR : 5 S"ezd Sovetov (1929), No. 15, p. 38.
[2] XV Konferentsiya Vsesoyuznoi Kommunisticheskoi Partii (B) (1927), p. 227.
[3] XV^va Sessiya Soveta Tsentrosoyuza (1926), p. 109.
[4] Spravochnik Partiinogo Rabotnika, vi (1928), i, 658.
[5] XLI Sobranie Upolnomochennykh Tsentrosoyuza (1928), p. 46 ; exemptions or reduced rates were accorded to, among others, Red Army men, " the poorest strata of the population " and second members of the same family (ibid. pp. 62, 207).
[6] Kontrol'nye Tsifry Narodnogo Khozyaistva SSSR na 1928–1929 god (1929), p. 293.

for rural, members.[1] As time went on, these devices were evidently inadequate to meet financial needs ; and the dependence of the consumer cooperatives on credits and subventions played an important rôle in their evolution into organs of public policy geared to a governmental machinery of distribution.

A running fight went on throughout this period between Narkomtorg, which desired to use the consumer cooperatives as the main channel of distribution of consumer goods to the whole population, and Tsentrosoyuz, which desired to reserve cooperative shops and stalls for members only ; if these were open to all, membership of the cooperatives lost its attraction. In theory two kinds of preferential treatment for members were possible : to allow them a discount on purchases, or to distribute an annual dividend out of profits.[2] But both these methods seem to have been too complicated or too expensive for general adoption. Practice evidently varied in different parts of the country. In Smolensk, in the winter of 1926–1927, scarce goods were reserved for members, and membership doubled in consequence. In Tula, 47 per cent of those questioned in a party enquiry said that they could not afford to join the cooperative ; but 75 per cent of their income was spent in cooperative shops.[3] The acute food shortages and the introduction of rationing in 1927–1928 evidently helped the cooperatives, which alone supplied scarce commodities at official prices.[4] Mikoyan, who openly desired to use rationing as a means of discrimination against nepmen and non-workers,[5] appears to have assumed that all workers belonged to the cooperatives. A cooperative membership card was, he declared, equivalent to a ration book ; there was even a black market in such cards.[6] On the other hand credit cooperatives were criticized for their refusal, in spite of government instructions, to finance the

---

[1] *Shestnadtsataya Konferentsiya VKP(B)* (1962), p. 189.
[2] *XV^{va} Sessiya Soveta Tsentrosoyuza* (1926), p. 78.
[3] *Bol'shevik*, No. 3, February 1, 1927, pp. 52–53.
[4] A cooperative writer admitted that, " but for the goods famine and other connected circumstances, the cooperatives would often have been in grave danger in their struggle both with private capital and with state trade, thanks to the low level of their commercial equipment " ; inadequacy of shops, warehouses, bakeries and refrigerated space was quoted as an instance of their inefficiency (*Voprosy Torgovli*, No. 5, February 1929, p. 27).
[5] See pp. 700–701 below.
[6] *XLI Sobranie Upolnomochennykh Tsentrosoyuza* (1928), p. 311.

supply of agricultural machines to non-members;[1] and in the crisis of the grain collections of 1928–1929, consumer cooperatives were instructed to deliver goods to "those who deliver grain", whether they were members of the cooperatives or not.[2] This conflict was still unresolved in the spring of 1929, by which time the consumer cooperatives were the principal agents in the distribution of industrial goods, and had a substantial rôle in the distribution of foodstuffs. Two alternative courses were open. The cooperatives might confine their services to due-paying members, in which case everyone not branded as a *kulak* or nepman (and therefore excluded from privileges) would be obliged to join the cooperatives; this was what the cooperative leaders themselves desired. Or the cooperatives might cease to discriminate between members and non-members, in which case the cooperatives would lose their distinctive character and their membership, and become simply state selling agencies; this was on the whole the eventual aim of Narkomtorg.[3] In this contest neither side was strong enough to win an outright victory. The situation remained confused, with wide varieties of practice in different localities. But nothing seriously qualified the ultimate dependence of the cooperatives on state finance and on the will of the party.

The workers' cooperatives, which in the preceding period had served as a spearhead in the Soviet campaign to establish effective control over the consumer cooperatives,[4] continued to function as recognized, though semi-autonomous, units in the network of consumer cooperatives. But the relation of the "central workers' section", which acted as their central organ, to Tsentrosoyuz was uneasy and undefined. When the Tsentrosoyuz council met in February 1926, a proposal to put the question on the agenda was resisted on the ground that the administration of Tsentrosoyuz had not yet reached agreement on the subject.[5] At a later stage in the proceedings, Dogadov explained the point of view of the trade

---

[1] *Voprosy Torgovli*, No. 12, September 1928, p. 55; for credits for agricultural machines see pp. 201-203 above.
[2] *Voprosy Torgovli*, No. 4, January 1929, p. 16.
[3] *Ibid.* No. 5, February 1929, p. 26.
[4] See *The Bolshevik Revolution, 1917–1923*, Vol. 2, pp. 236-238.
[5] *XV*va *Sessiya Soveta Tsentrosoyuza* (1926), p. 5.

unions. To liquidate the central workers' section altogether (as
had apparently been done in the Ukraine) would be wrong ; on
the other hand, it would be equally wrong to make it completely
independent of Tsentrosoyuz. The difference between workers
and peasants must, however, be respected, and the central workers'
section must be integrated in the system of consumer cooperatives
in a manner which would be acceptable to the trade unions. Two
representatives of workers' cooperatives, though not members of
the council, were allowed to address the meeting, and complained
of the neglect of the workers' cooperatives shown by Tsentrosoyuz.[1] Khinchuk, the president of Tsentrosoyuz, then announced
the view of a majority of the council. The virtual independence
claimed by some members of the central workers' section could not
be conceded. The principle of unified leadership must be established ; and Tsentrosoyuz must accept responsibility for maintaining supplies to the workers' cooperatives.[2] But no resolution
was passed, and it seems clear that no substantive agreement had
been reached. The central workers' section, comprising 165
workers' cooperative societies, continued to enjoy a large measure
of autonomy, holding separate conferences and controlling its own
funds. In 1928 it claimed 2,845,000 due-paying members, or 42
per cent of all due-paying members of the consumer cooperatives ;
and 47 per cent of the turnover of the consumer cooperatives in
the towns was in the hands of the workers' cooperatives. Moreover, the effective independence of the workers' section was increasing. In 1925-1926 it received 59·7 per cent of its supplies
direct from state industry (meaning the trusts and syndicates) and
30·4 per cent from Tsentrosoyuz, in 1926-1927, 74·4 per cent
from state industry and 19·8 per cent from Tsentrosoyuz. This
anomalous situation led, as the spokesman of the workers' cooperatives admitted at the conference of Tsentrosoyuz in July
1928, to " a series of misunderstandings between the cooperatives
and the workers' sections ". Tsentrosoyuz could neither dispense
with this powerful autonomous unit in its structure, enjoying
party and trade union support, nor completely master it.[3]

[1] *Ibid.* pp. 29, 30-32, 33-34.   [2] *Ibid.* pp. 52-53.
[3] The above particulars are taken from the report of the delegate of the
workers' section to the conference (*XLI Sobranie Upolnomochennykh Tsentrosoyuza* (1928), pp. 61-67) ; divergent figures quoted can be reconciled only on
the assumption that some workers' cooperatives affiliated to Tsentrosoyuz did

662 THE ECONOMIC ORDER PT. I

A formal constitutional change was effected in Tsentrosoyuz in this period. From the time of the formation of the USSR down to 1928 the Tsentrosoyuz of the RSFSR had " simultaneously fulfilled the functions of a central organ for all the cooperatives of the USSR ".¹ This created particular difficulties in the Ukraine, where a central cooperative council, Vukospilka, functioned on parallel lines to the Tsentrosoyuz of the RSFSR ; ² and similar councils existed in the White Russian, Georgian, Armenian and Azerbaijan republics.³ At the Tsentrosoyuz conference of July 1928, it was decided to divide the existing functions of Tsentrosoyuz between two separate organs — a Tsentrosoyuz of the RSFSR and a Tsentrosoyuz of the USSR — as from October 1, 1928.⁴ After the conference each of the two new bodies held a formal session to elect a council and a board of administration.⁵ The administrative structure of the consumer cooperatives followed that of the Soviets. The village and urban consumer cooperatives (Sel'po and Gorpo) were grouped under district unions, district unions under provincial or regional unions, and provincial or regional unions under republican unions subject to the ultimate authority of the Tsentrosoyuz of the USSR. The presidents and principal officers of the higher unions, though in theory elected from below, seem for the most part to have been party nominees.

not belong to the workers' section. The uneasiness of relations is confirmed by the paucity of references to the workers' section by other speakers or in the resolutions of the conference. For the independent financial status of the workers' section see *ibid.* pp. 383-384, 385 ; references to the workers' co-operatives at the eighth trade union congress in December 1928 (*Vos'moi S"ezd Professional'nykh Soyuzov* (1929), pp. 173, 467-475) suggested some reservations about them, even in trade union circles.

¹ See *Socialism in One Country, 1924–1926*, Vol. 1, p. 429, note 3.
² Its rôle in the grain collections was recognized in the resolution of the party central committee of April 1928 (*KPSS v Rezolyutsiyakh* (1954), ii, 499).
³ *International Cooperation, 1927–1929* (International Cooperative Alliance, 1930), pp. 240-254.
⁴ *XLI Sobranie Upolnomochennykh Tsentrosoyuza* (1928), p. 257.
⁵ *I⁰ Sobranie Upolnomochennykh Tsentrosoyuza RSFSR* (1928) ; *I⁰ Sobranie Upolnomochennykh Tsentrosoyuza SSSR* (1928).

CHAPTER 25

THE PRIVATE SECTOR

WHILE the share of the private merchant in wholesale trade was now insignificant, having fallen to 9 per cent in 1925–1926, 40 per cent of retail trade still passed through his hands.[1] Since toleration of private trade was inherent in NEP, it is not surprising that, according to Narkomfin statistics for 1925–1926, the largest volume of private capital (agriculture excepted) was invested in trade — an estimated 800 million rubles, compared with only 200 millions in industry.[2] Internal trade was described in 1926 as " the outstanding branch of the national economy of the USSR in which private capital can find significant utilization ".[3] Pyatakov in July 1926 estimated the turnover of private trade during the year 1925–1926 at a milliard rubles and its net profits at 500-600 millions ; Rykov at the fifteenth party conference three months later quoted an expert estimate of a profit of 100-200 millions.[4] Gosplan figures for 1927–

[1] See Table No. 29, p. 962 below ; for slightly different figures see *Socialism in One Country, 1924–1926*, Vol. 1, p. 424. In absolute figures this was the peak year for private retail trade (*Chastnaya Torgovlya SSSR*, ed. A. Zalkind (1927), p. 4 ; *40 Let Sovetskoi Torgovli* (1957), p. 6).

[2] *Voprosy Istorii*, No. 12, 1964, p. 11. The most varied estimates of private capital in trade, based on different calculations, were current at this time. Narkomtorg estimated the capital of licensed private trading enterprises in October 1925 at 450 million rubles. According to Narkomfin returns, the category of tax-payers classified as engaged in private trade and industry, or property owners, or money-lenders, numbered 752,000 in the first half of 1925–1926 ; the highest category of these, numbering 320,000, had an average income of over 175 rubles a month (*Chastnyi Kapital v Narodnom Khozyaistve SSSR*, ed. A. Ginzburg (1927), pp. 5-6).

[3] Ts. Kron, *Chastnaya Torgovlya v SSSR* (1926), p. 3.

[4] *Bol'shevik*, No. 21-22, November 30, 1926, p. 17 ; *XV Konferentsiya Vsesoyuznoi Kommunisticheskoi Partii (B)* (1927), p. 129 (Rykov also quoted Preobrazhensky's estimate of 600 million rubles for 1923). The higher figures were apparently obtained by treating as profit the total income of the private trader derived from his business ; Dzerzhinsky in his speech of July 20, 1926 (see p. 281 above) rejected Kamenev's estimate of 400 million rubles on this

1928 indicated that 15·2 per cent of income derived from trade went to the private sector.[1] Private trade had two main characteristics. In the first place, it worked mostly in small units. In the middle nineteen-twenties only one quarter of private traders in the countryside had permanent shops (against two-thirds before 1914), the remainder selling from temporary booths or working as itinerant pedlars.[2]

> Engaged primarily in petty trade [reported a Narkomtorg publication], in selling through hawkers and pedlars, or at most from booths, kiosks etc., private capital is by this very fact distinguished from state and even cooperative organizations.[3]

Of the six categories into which trade was now officially classified for the purpose of issuing licences,[4] the private trader had almost disappeared from the two highest categories, which were concerned mainly with wholesale trade. On the other hand, the first category — pedlars and hawkers — was almost entirely monopolized by private traders, who held 158,000 of the 160,000 licences issued in this category in April–September 1926[5]. In 1926–1927 there were 21·59 private trading units to every 10,000 inhabitants of rural areas, compared with 7·64 cooperative and 1·35 state trading establishments.[6] Figures for rural trade alone showed that the private capital invested in first category trade had more than doubled between October 1, 1926 and October 1, 1927. But

---

score, and dismissed the total net accumulation of the private trader as " completely insignificant " (*Pravda*, August 1, 1926).

[1] *Kontrol'nye Tsifry Narodnogo Khozyaistva SSSR na 1929–1930 god* (1930), p. 466.

[2] *Chastnyi Kapital v Narodnom Khozyaistve SSSR*, ed. A. Ginzburg (1927), p. 125.

[3] *Chastnaya Torgovlya SSSR*, ed. A. Zalkind (1927), p. 31.

[4] See *The Bolshevik Revolution, 1917–1923*, Vol. 2, p. 337, note 2. On September 24, 1926 a decree was issued re-defining the categories of licence : these were (1) trade in bazaars, markets and other open places conducted by single salesmen with portable equipment ; (2) trade in bazaars conducted by single salesmen or members of their families from small stalls or booths, with a turnover of up to 300 rubles a month ; (3) trade in small shops with a turnover of up to 800 rubles a month ; (4) retail or semi-wholesale trade in agricultural products, timber, building materials, coal, iron, etc., with a turnover of up to 2000 rubles a month ; (5) similar trade with a turnover up to 5000 rubles a month ; (6) trade in larger establishments (*Sobranie Zakonov, 1926*, No. 63, art. 474).

[5] *Planovoe Khozyaistvo*, No. 9, 1926, p. 9.

[6] *Materialy po Istorii SSSR*, vii (1959), 121.

even so it represented only 6·1 per cent of private trading capital.[1] The number of private establishments still predominated in the second and third categories, and remained substantial in the fourth category. But the number of units was falling, and their size increasing ; and this increased the share of the cooperatives and the state, to which the larger units belonged. Figures of private trade in the RSFSR showed that the number of cooperative and state units in these three categories fell from 93,814 in 1926–1927 to 88,443 in 1927–1928, of private units from 226,760 to 159,254. In the same period the average retail turnover per cooperative and state unit rose from 66,500 to 84,400 rubles, and per private unit fell from 12,000 to 11,900 rubles.[2]

Secondly, as might have been expected, private trade survived. longer in rural areas than in the more important urban centres, where it first came under pressure from the authorities. The turnover of private trade in towns declined from 4421 million rubles in 1925–1926 to 3992 millions in 1926–1927 ; in the countryside in the same period it rose from 1164 to 1274 millions.[3] The increase in the countryside was spread over all categories of trade except the third (small shops), where the competition of the cooperatives was most strongly felt ; turnover actually doubled in the lowest and least important category.[4] In 1926–1927, private trade accounted for about 23 per cent of the total turnover of rural trade. Its incidence was unequally spread, being highest in Central Asia and Transcaucasia, and lowest in the northern region and in western Siberia.[5] The ratio of private trade appears to have varied inversely to the strength of the cooperatives in the region in question. Of rural private trade, two thirds was said to be devoted to " groceries and miscellaneous trade ",

[1] Ibid. vii, 132-133.
[2] Voprosy Torgovli, No. 4, January 1929, pp. 64-65 ; some allowance must be made for illicit private trade which escaped registration and taxation.
[3] Materialy po Istorii SSSR, vii (1959), 90, 153. A table in Planovoe Khozyaistvo, No. 9, 1926, p. 14, showed private trade progressively declining in the towns and increasing in the countryside from 1922–1923 to 1924–1925 ; 1925–1926 yielded an increase of about one third in the towns and of 90 per cent in the countryside.
[4] Materialy po Istorii SSSR, vii (1959), 157 ; in 1926–1927 more than 80 per cent of the profits of rural private trade came from second and third category enterprises (ibid. p. 164).
[5] Ibid. p. 154 ; figures for 1927–1928 for the RSFSR alone are quoted in Voprosy Torgovli, No. 4, January 1929, pp. 67-68.

one-sixth to " live animals, poultry and meat ", and only one-
tenth to " manufactured goods, haberdashery etc." ¹ From 1925
onwards private traders began to interest themselves in the
products of rural artisan industry.²

Since competition occurred mainly between the private trader
and the cooperatives, much discussion took place on their relative
efficiency. It was commonly accepted that private capital, though
insignificant in amount compared with state and cooperative
capital, enjoyed the advantages of " more rapid turnover, extreme
mobility and higher profitability ".³ The salt syndicate reported
that the private trader turned over his capital far more rapidly
than the cooperatives, and " is therefore in a position to accept the
rather severe terms (credits two or three times as small and prices
two or three times as high) proposed by the salt syndicate ". The
private trader had better facilities for selling salt in " localities
remote from railway or water transport ", and coped more efficiently with the technical problems of marketing a bulk product
on which profit margins were small. In these circumstances,
recourse to private traders was " a plus, not a minus " — especially for goods in plentiful supply ; and the salt syndicate would
have liked to see 30 per cent of its turnover passing through this
channel. Similar views were expressed by the sugar trust, which
counted on disposing of from 26 to 28 per cent of its turnover to
private traders, and the yeast industry, which found the private
trader more attentive to quality and to the delivery of the product
in fresh condition. Trusts and factories were said often to purchase their requirements from private traders rather than from
state or cooperative organs, though this was described as a " distortion " of the procedures of wholesale trade.⁴ In general, the
cooperatives demanded nearly three times as much credit as the
private trader and for longer periods.⁵ Strumilin admitted that
the private trader " enjoys all the advantages of private initiative,
is very resourceful, calculating, hard-working etc.", while the
cooperatives " have not yet outlived a deadening bureaucratism,

¹ *Materialy po Istorii SSSR*, vii (1959), 146.
² Ts. Kron, *Chastnaya Torgovlya v SSSR* (1926), p. 137.
³ *Chastnyi Kapital v Narodnom Khozyaistve SSSR*, ed. A. Ginzburg (1927),
p. 7.   ⁴ *Ekonomicheskaya Zhizn'*, June 9, 1927.
⁵ *Chastnyi Kapital v Narodnom Khozyaistve SSSR*, ed. A. Ginzburg (1927),
pp. 18-20.

show a striking lack of culture in their lower personnel, and suffer
deeply from extensive waste and embezzlement " : yet the cooperatives worked with smaller margins, and their profits accrued
to the whole country.[1] Larin argued that the private trader owed
his advantage to the possession of more working capital :

> This is a question of resources, not of any innate unalterable
> advantages of private trade.[2]

In fact, the advantage of the private trader turned on the issue of
price. The private trader, largely untrammelled by official price
regulation, was able to charge higher prices to the consumer and
earn higher profits. But, whatever the merits of the argument,
private trade was bound in the end to succumb to official pressure
and official support of the consumer cooperatives.

The campaign against private trade may be said to have dated
back to the creation of Narkomtorg in May 1924 with a mandate to
ensure " the conquest of the market " by state and cooperative
trade.[3] But, apart from occasional sallies against nepmen, pressure
on the private trader remained intermittent and half-hearted till
the autumn of 1926. The framers of the 1926–1927 Gosplan
control figures pointed out that the socialized and private sectors
dealt largely with different categories of goods, and that " notwithstanding an illusory quantitative ' independence ', any market
rift between the sectors will adversely affect the whole economy ".[4]
By this time, however, the continued attempt to conciliate the
peasantry without any relaxation of the intensive drive for industrialization was leading to a strong demand to reduce retail
prices.[5] On October 14, 1926, STO instructed Narkomfin to
carry out a selective enquiry into private trade in towns ; about
2700 enterprises, all in categories (2) to (6), were covered by the
enquiry.[6] The fifteenth party conference of October 1926 noted
that " the rôle of private capital, especially in the sphere of trade,
still remains important ", and called for " special attention . . . to
questions of the struggle against private capital ".[7] Hitherto it

---

[1] *Planovoe Khozyaistvo*, No. 9, 1926, pp. 22-23.
[2] Yu. Larin, *Chastnyi Kapital v SSSR* (1927), p. 201.   [3] See p. 634 above.
[4] *Kontrol'nye Tsifry Narodnogo Khozyaistva na 1926–1927 god* (1926), p.
191.   [5] See pp. 679-684 below.
[6] *Materialy po Istorii SSSR*, vii (1959), 79 ; detailed results of the enquiry,
which was carried out in 1928, follow *ibid.* vii, 80-120.
[7] *KPSS v Rezolyutsiyakh* (1954), ii, 307-308.

had been assumed that " the conquest of the market " would be achieved by competition in market conditions rather than by administrative measures. When the party central committee in February 1927 passed its resolution on prices, it significantly observed that, " side by side with the task of progressively overcoming private capital in trade and industry by *economic* measures, the task of subjecting private capital to the controlling influence of the proletarian state emerges into first place ".[1] But caution still prevailed in some quarters. The thirteenth Congress of Soviets of the RSFSR in April 1927 pronounced it "incorrect to set as an immediate task the complete exclusion of the private trader from the market ", and recorded the view that " in many branches of trade private capital will occupy an important place for a number of years ".[2] According to Mikoyan, the most effective weapon in the campaign to exclude the private trader from the grain collections was the priority accorded to state and cooperative collecting organs on the railways ; in view of the shortage of wagons, this amounted to a virtual denial of railway transport to the private trader in grain.[3] Supplements of from 50 to 100 per cent are said to have been levied in 1926 on private consignments of grain ; on some occasions later the supplement reached 400 per cent.[4] The private trader was also subject to financial pressures in the form of restriction of credit, increased rents for premises and sites in bazaars, and, above all, increased taxation.[5] But these

---

[1] *KPSS v Rezolyutsiyakh* (1954), ii, 354 ; for this resolution see pp. 685-686 below.

[2] *S"ezdy Sovetov v Dokumentakh*, iv, i (1962), 95.

[3] *Bol'shevik*, No. 19-20, October 31, 1926, pp. 82-84 ; Mikoyan surprisingly looked forward to a withdrawal of the restrictions. Strumilin justified discrimination on the ground that the railways were subsidized out of public funds (*Planovoe Khozyaistvo*, No. 9, 1926, p. 32).

[4] A. Malafeev, *Istoriya Tsenoobrazovaniya v SSSR* (1964), p. 133. Discrimination at first took the form of insisting that private consignments should be carried by express trains charging higher rates ; later the consignments were sent by slow train at express rates (*SSSR : Svodnye Materialy o Deyatel'nosti Soveta Narodnykh Komissarov i Soveta Truda i Oborony za I Kvartal (Oktyabr'-Dekabr') 1927–28 g.* (1928), pp. 69-70).

[5] *Materialy po Istorii SSSR*, vii (1959), 164-166 ; the report relates to rural trade, but conditions of urban trade were in this respect comparable. A report from Novgorod showed that 171 former private traders who replied to a questionnaire on their reasons for going out of business stated their reasons as follows : 21 per cent, taxation ; 22 per cent, sanitary or other regulations of Narkomtorg ; 16 per cent, shortage of goods ; 11 per cent, shortage of capital

measures would scarcely have affected first category (pedlars and hawkers) trade ; and the contraction of private trade in 1927 was due to indirect as well as direct administrative measures. The most important factor of all was probably the growing shortage of goods ; in January 1927 it was reported that private traders in many places had closed down for lack of supplies.[1] Limited supplies of industrial goods were channelled through the syndicates to the cooperatives, and the surpluses available to the private trader disappeared.[2]

By the end of 1927, when industrialization and planning were everywhere under discussion, the campaign against private trade had made sufficient progress to warrant both congratulation and doubts about some of its consequences. It was reported that in Moscow, between January 1 and July 1, 1927, 20 per cent of private retailers and 32 per cent of private wholesale and semi-wholesale traders had gone out of business, and that in the whole calendar year the number of private trading units had sunk from 9223 to 6812.[3] The general resolution of the fifteenth party congress of December 1927 on the report of the party central committee noted that " the private capitalist elements of the economy " had grown in absolute terms, though less rapidly than the socialist sector, and that " a policy of still more decisive economic exclusion should and can be applied " to them.[4] But two embarrassing consequences attended this campaign.

In the first place, the pressures hitherto applied had not only tended to drive the private trader into the illegal or semi-legal underworld of the Soviet economy, but had brought him into

---

or credit ; 7 per cent, competition from the cooperatives ; 4 per cent, fines for breaches of regulations ; the remainder were presumably indeterminate (*Ekonomicheskaya Zhizn'*, October 15, 1927). For the sharp reduction of bank credits to private trade and industry in 1927 see *Materialy po Istorii SSSR*, vii (1959), 27–30. A spokesman of private traders and manufacturers in Irkutsk listed among their demands the removal of restrictions on the admission of their children to higher educational institutions (A. Fabrichny, *Chastnyi Kapital v SSSR na Poroge Pyatiletki* (1930), p. 51).

[1] *Torgovo-Promyshlennaya Gazeta*, January 22, 1927.

[2] This may explain why the proportion of textile goods in rural private trade, which amounted to 13·46 per cent in 1925–1926, fell to 7·38 per cent in 1926–1927 (*Materialy po Istorii SSSR*, vii (1959), 148).

[3] *Ekonomicheskaya Zhizn'*, March 20, 1928.

[4] *KPSS v Rezolyutsiyakh* (1954), ii, 438.

association with those peripheral groups which were least amenable to central control and most mistrusted by official policymakers. A report prepared for the fifteenth party congress in December 1927 noted that the private trader, excluded from the market in major industrial products, had acquired " decisive positions in the market for artisan products ", and that local trade in agricultural products was in the hands of private traders and *kulaks*. " The still powerful influence of the private trader in the market for agricultural products and the recent strengthening of his operations among artisans "[1] brought nearer the moment when he would be regarded unconditionally as an enemy of the régime. The congress resolution took up and expanded this point :

> Private capitalist strata in town and country, combining with certain bureaucratic elements in the Soviet and economic apparatus, strive to intensify their opposition to the offensive of the working class, and try to exercise an influence hostile to the proletarian dictatorship on definite strata of officials and of the intelligentsia, on backward strata of artisans and craftsmen, of peasants and workers.[2]

It was also alleged that, whereas the proportion of merchandise passing through the hands of the private trader was still falling, " *within private trade* a strengthening of the rôle of large-scale capital has taken place ". The increased influence of the private wholesaler and of private loan capital were cited as sinister symptoms.[3] During the year after the fifteenth congress, the growth of state and cooperative retail trade seems to have satisfied party opinion, though " a tendency of private capital to contract its activity in the sphere of *legal* trade " and " a direct transition to *illegal* work " were also noted.[4] Illegality frequently consisted in

[1] Ya. Yakovlev, *K Voprosu o Sotsialisticheskom Pereustroistve Sel'skogo Khozyaistva* (1928), pp. 447, 450 ; according to a report in *Ekonomicheskaya Zhizn'*, March 20, 1928, the private trader who was put out of business turned to artisan production, or to bogus cooperatives, or to valuta transactions.   [2] *KPSS v Rezolyutsiyakh* (1954), ii, 439.
[3] Yu. Larin, *Chastnyi Kapital v SSSR* (1927), p. 291.
[4] Several local party reports are summarized in A. Fabrichny, *Chastnyi Kapital na Poroge Pyatiletki* (1930), pp. 12-15 ; this pamphlet contains much miscellaneous material about the misdeeds of private capitalists, often operating on the borderline between legality and illegality, in 1927 and 1928.

collusion between private traders and state or cooperative officials.
Well-organized local meat rings were said to have monopolized
the meat market during the critical winter 1928–1929 ; [1] and a
private share company in Ryazan dealing in leather goods acquired
such importance in 1929 that its warehouses were visited by
merchants from Moscow, Leningrad and other cities.[2] In 1928–
1929 some private traders on the famous Sukharevsky market in
Moscow went over from retail to wholesale trade : from 60 to 70
per cent of the goods offered by them came from the syndicates.[3]
It was noted that " private capital, driven out of urban trade, transferred its activity to the grain market, playing on price differences
and earning a super-profit from this kind of speculation ".[4] The
revival of " bagging ", under the impetus of the grain shortage and
the failure of the official collections, dated from the autumn of
1928.[5] The picture of private trade during these years which
emerges from the disjointed evidence is of an offensive against the
nepman parallel to the offensive against the kulak and leading to
similar results. Frumkin at the TsIK of the USSR in April 1928
reported that Narkomfin had been given a specific directive " to
fix the tax so that private mills will close ", and added that " in
some places we have almost completely abolished private trade by
our tax policy ".[6] The private trader, expelled by slow degrees
from his customary and hitherto legally tolerated sources of profit,
and actuated by a new animosity against the régime which perse-
cuted him, resorted more and more to illegal activities, which in
turn provoked still severer reprisals. The year 1928–1929 was
said to have been marked in general by his failure to pay taxes and
by his " migration from the legal to the illegal sphere ".[7]

Secondly, the offensive against private trade produced other
consequences which were no more convenient or gratifying to the
authorities. The resolution of the thirteenth party congress in
May 1924 on the regulation of trade had added a rider on the
necessity to avoid taking, " in the sphere of private trade, any

[1] Ibid. pp. 27-28.
[2] Izvestiya, September 7, 1929 ; this affair is also referred to in A.
Fabrichny, Chastnyi Kapital na Poroge Pyatiletki (1930), p. 33.
[3] Ibid. p. 31.   [4] Ekonomicheskoe Obozrenie, No. 11, 1929, p. 138.
[5] See p. 86 above.
[6] 3 Sessiya Tsentral'nogo Ispolnitel'nogo Komiteta Soyuza SSR 4 Sozyva
(1928), pp. 243-244.   [7] Planovoe Khozyaistvo, No. 8, 1929, p. 9.

measures which would lead to a curtailment of, or interference
with, the general process of exchange of goods ".[1] This caution
was in the nature of things not fully observed. The term " empty
spaces " (pustyni) was said to have been currently applied in the
nineteen-twenties to regions from which private trade had been
ousted, but which were not yet served by state or cooperative
organizations ; at the end of 1925, according to Tsentrosoyuz
figures, only 10 per cent of all villages had cooperative shops.[2] It
was even a matter of reproach that, between 1926 and 1929,
" nepmen again and again liquidated their undertakings, taking
no account of the state, hoping to preserve what was left of their
resources for operations on the black market ".[3] The resolution
of the fifteenth party congress in December 1927 noted hopefully
that the socialized sector of trade was " expanding at the cost of
the exclusion of the private trader ", but repeated the same word
of caution as its predecessor three years earlier :

> The further exclusion of the private trader from the market
> by the cooperatives and by state trade must proceed in line with
> their organizational and material capacities, so that this exclu-
> sion does not entail a breach in the trading network and inter-
> ruptions in supplies to the market.[4]

Rykov at the TsIK of the USSR in April 1928 protested mildly
against exaggerated applications of the policy :

> The Moscow Soviet . . . and comrade Uglanov are discussing
> what state machinery can replace the old woman with a tray
> who goes along the street and sells rolls or matches. This kind
> of replacement of " private traders " is not necessary at all.[5]

Mikoyan at the Tsentrosoyuz conference of July 1928 spoke of

---

[1] For this resolution see *Socialism in One Country, 1924–1926*, Vol. 1, p. 425.
[2] *Na Agrarnom Fronte*, No. 7-8, 1926, p. 29 ; according to the counter-
theses of the opposition on the five-year plan issued on the eve of the fifteenth
party congress of December 1927 (see p. 36, note 2 above), the mass consumer
purchased more than 50 per cent of what he needed from the private trader.
[3] *Voprosy Istorii*, No. 12, 1964, p. 17.
[4] *KPSS v Rezolyutsiyakh* (1954), ii, 462 ; about the same time the *Konjunktur* institute of Narkomfin noted that the replacement of the private trader
led to a contraction of rural trade (*Ekonomicheskii Byulleten' Kon"yunkturnogo
Instituta*, No. 11-12, 1927, pp. 7-8, 11).
[5] *3 Sessiya Tsentral'nogo Ispolnitel'nogo Komiteta Soyuza SSR 4 Sozyva*
(1928), p. 348.

" the class struggle over shops " between the cooperatives and the private trader in the previous year, which had led to the closing of 100,000 shops or stalls and the throwing of a million stall-holders with their dependants (perhaps an exaggerated number) on to the labour market.[1] In the cities the increase of population rendered existing warehouse and shop accommodation inadequate, and the closing down of those in private hands made the shortage more acute.[2] In the countryside, the old-established private village or small-town booth or stall was often more efficient and enterprising than its hastily installed cooperative replacement. A delegate at the Tsentrosoyuz conference lamented that the cooperatives could not keep " the microscopic shops left behind by the departing private trader ", and had no funds to open new ones ; and a failure in supplies of meat to Moscow in April 1927 was attributed by Mikoyan to the campaign against the private trader, who was being driven from the market more rapidly than the cooperatives could replace him.[3] An article in the journal of Narkomtorg admitted that hold-ups had occurred in supplies due to " the closing of a significant number of private trading establishments which could not be replaced at short notice by state or cooperative trade ". Cases were quoted of potatoes brought to Kiev from a distance of 100 versts, because the private traders who handled local supplies had gone out of business, and of fishermen in Leningrad province ceasing to fish because nobody was available any longer to buy their catch.[4]

In the grain collections crisis of 1928 not much attention was given in public pronouncements to other forms of trade. But Stalin at the party central committee in July 1928 gave an uncompromising definition of current policy :

> We often say that we are developing socialist forms of economy in the sphere of trade. What does this mean ? It means that in this very way we are driving out of trade thousands and thousands of small and medium traders.[5]

[1] *XLI Sobranie Upolnomochennykh Tsentrosoyuza* (1928), p. 287.
[2] *Voprosy Torgovli*, No. 4, January 1929, pp. 26-27.
[3] *XLI Sobranie Upolnomochennykh Tsentrosoyuza* (1928), pp. 118, 300-301.
[4] *Voprosy Torgovli*, No. 9-10, June–July 1928, p. 12 ; No. 4, January 1929, pp. 21-22.
[5] Stalin, *Sochineniya*, xi, 170.

The issue of trade played only a secondary rôle in the struggle with the Right opposition in the winter of 1928–1929. But the defeat of the Right wing may be said to have heralded, among other things, the final defeat of the private trader as a recognized element in the Soviet economy. In the year 1929 private retail trade amounted to only 13·5 per cent of total retail trade as against 42·3 per cent in 1925–1926.[1]

[1] See Table No. 29, p. 962 below.

CHAPTER 26

CONTROL OF PRICES

THE first steps towards industrialization in the summer and autumn of 1925 had led to inflationary pressures resulting in rising industrial prices. Alarm was caused by the " wholesale-retail scissors ", the margin between wholesale and retail prices of industrial goods, as well as by the more familiar " scissors " between the prices of industrial and agricultural products.[1] Since effective control was exercised by the state over industrial prices only at the wholesale stage, the margin between wholesale and retail prices continued to increase ; retail prices were said to have exceeded wholesale prices by 60 per cent in the spring of 1926 as against 20 per cent before 1914.[2] Meanwhile, agricultural prices, under the impetus of a good harvest and successful grain collections, began to fall sharply after April 1926, thus opening further the scissors between agricultural and industrial prices.[3] The makers of official policy hoped to solve both the problem of the " wholesale-retail scissors " and the problem of the " agricultural-industrial scissors " by forcing down the retail prices of industrial goods. The cooperatives had proclaimed in February 1926 the aim of closing the " wholesale-retail price scissors ".[4] The party central committee at its session of April

[1] For the wholesale-retail scissors see *Socialism in One Country, 1924–1926*, Vol. 1, pp. 438, 440 ; for the agricultural-industrial scissors, which were the ratio of the retail prices at which the peasants purchased the products of industry to the wholesale prices received by them for their products, and which had led to the original scissors crisis of 1923, see *The Interregnum, 1923–1924*, Part I, *passim*.

[2] *Ekonomicheskoe Obozrenie*, No. 5, 1926, p. 52 ; figures from Vesenkha, which was always eager to put the blame for high prices on the retailer, showed retail prices exceeding wholesale prices by 51 per cent on October 1, 1925, and by 68 per cent on October 1, 1926 (*Voprosy Torgovli*, No. 2-3, November–December 1927, p. 66).

[3] See Tables Nos. 34, 35, pp. 967, 968 below.

[4] *XV^{ya} Sessiya Soveta Tsentrosoyuza* (1926), p. 17.

1926 resolved that it was essential to bring about a reduction in retail prices and to narrow the gap between wholesale and retail prices.[1]

This policy incurred criticism from two different quarters. To the expert advisers of Narkomfin, it seemed impracticable ; only if the over-strained programme of investment in industry were slowed down, and the earnings of factory workers restricted, could the prices of industrial goods be reduced and the scissors between industrial and agricultural prices be further closed. Some of the experts argued that, in the situation existing in the early months of 1926, official prices, both wholesale and retail, for industrial goods, had been fixed too low, and should be allowed to rise to what the market would bear. The underlying conception of NEP as a market economy implied the maintenance of a market on which prices adjusted themselves to supply and demand. Though the reign of unregulated market prices had been ended by the scissors crisis of 1923, nobody, even in the party, yet openly attacked the theoretical presuppositions of NEP.[2] It was the market, declared a writer in the journal of Narkomfin, which, " by controlling prices, orders *what shall be produced, how much, and in what way* " ; a " non-commercial price policy " would represent a step backwards from a money economy to an economy in kind. What the market required was an increase in industrial prices to limit the demand for scarce goods.[3] " To restrain price increases which owe their origin to currency emission ", wrote another Narkomfin adviser, "essentially means not to cut your coat according to your cloth ".[4]

The other challenge to the demand for lower industrial prices

---

[1] See *Socialism in One Country, 1924–1926*, Vol. 1, pp. 437-441.

[2] Bukharin, in a refutation of Preobrazhensky, ingeniously attempted to reconcile them with the modest price-fixing policies hitherto adopted : " The process of Soviet price-formation is a previous anticipation of what, under spontaneous regulation, would be established *post festum* " (*Pravda*, July 1, 1926).

[3] *Vestnik Finansov*, No. 2, 1926, pp. 90-96 (V. Novozhilov) ; the same doctrine, expressed in slightly more ambiguous terms, appeared simultaneously in an article in the journal of Gosplan : " The market retail price, emerging on the basis of an equilibrium of supply and demand, must be the departure point in our work of controlling prices. . . . The ' spontaneously ' formed retail prices at any given moment must be accepted as objectively given " (*Planovoe Khozyaistvo*, No. 2, 1926, p. 118).

[4] *Vestnik Finansov*, No. 4, 1926, p. 16.

came from the party opposition, which reached the same conclusion from totally different premises.[1] Unlike the Narkomfin
experts, who attributed the goods famine and inflated prices to
excessive investment in heavy industry, the opposition found the
cause of the trouble in the backwardness of industrial development, and sought the remedy in more, not less, industrialization.
This view, which possessed undoubted long-term validity, was
less convincing on the shorter prospect, and was received " nega-
tively, and sometimes even ironically ", by the experts of Narkomfin.[2] It was, however, deeply rooted in the philosophy of the
opposition. Trotsky, though he hedged on the question of prices,
had spoken in 1923 of the " dictatorship " belonging " not to
finance, but to industry ".[3] Pyatakov in the same year had issued
the notorious instruction from Vesenkha to the trusts on the duty
of earning maximum profits.[4] Preobrazhensky's paper of 1924 on
The Law of Primitive Socialist Accumulation commended " a price
policy consciously directed to the exploitation of the private
economy in all its forms ".[5] When, after a brief respite, the price
question again became acute in the winter of 1925–1926, the
opposition reacted sharply against the proposal to reduce industrial prices. Preobrazhensky, in an article in the party journal,
pointed out that the shortage of mass consumption goods enabled
private traders to widen the " wholesale-retail scissors " and snatch
profits which were denied to the state industrial trusts, and called
for " an increase in the wholesale prices of trusts for those mass
consumption goods in relation to which the goods shortage is
greatest and out of which private capital makes most profit ",
adding optimistically that this increase should not lead to a further
increase in retail prices.[6] V. Smirnov, another opposition spokesman, argued that the increasing gap between wholesale and retail
prices should be closed not by lowering the latter, but by raising
the former ; only in this way could the flow of resources from

[1] The coincidence of views between the two opposite groups was remarked
in an article in *Planovoe Khozyaistvo*, No. 5, 1926, p. 29.
[2] *Vestnik Finansov*, No. 4, 1926, p. 14.
[3] See *The Interregnum, 1923–1924*, p. 125.
[4] See *ibid.* p. 9.
[5] See *Socialism in One Country, 1924–1926*, Vol. 1, p. 204.
[6] *Bol'shevik*, No. 6, March 31, 1926, pp. 61-64 ; an article in *Pravda*, April
10, 1926, proposed that the cooperatives and state trading organs should raise
their prices to the level of those of private traders.

industry into trading capital be replaced by a flow of resources into industry in a sufficient quantity for it to undertake investment.[1] Trotsky, at the session of the party central committee in April 1926, also favoured an increase in wholesale, but not in retail, prices.[2]

Arguments in favour of raising industrial prices, from whatever source they came, made little impression on party leaders who remembered the scissors crisis of 1923, and were still apprehensive of rousing the antagonism of the peasantry. The Osvok plan and the first Gosplan draft of a five-year plan, both drawn up in 1926, assumed the prospect of a substantial fall in the price of industrial goods on the peasant market.[3] But, while the orthodox party view was that the increase in retail prices should be curbed, and if possible reversed, ways and means of attaining this desirable end eluded the policy-makers. The familiar distinction between " economic " and " administrative " measures of control was no less applicable to price policy ; the view was firmly held that " measures of an economic character must be regarded as the best form of price regulation ", and that " methods of administrative regulation should be reduced to a minimum ".[4] But this theoretical preference was ineffective in practice. From 1924 onwards fixed prices (sometimes called " ticket prices ") had been set for standard items of mass consumption subject to excise such as tea, matches, tobacco and cigarettes. Where this method was inapplicable, an attempt was made to fix retail prices by a percentage addition to cost of production : this proved inconvenient and was quickly replaced by a surcharge on wholesale prices.[5] In a period of chronic goods famine, when rising demand constantly outstripped production, these initial attempts at retail price fixing were largely abortive. Sometimes they clashed with prices fixed by syndicates and other selling organizations which were also approved by Narkomtorg. Though the fixed prices were supposed to apply to private traders, and increasingly severe penalties were announced

[1] *Krasnaya Nov'*, No. 5, 1926, pp. 171-174.
[2] See *Socialism in One Country, 1924–1926*, Vol. 1, p. 326.
[3] See pp. 847-848, 853 below ; a party spokesman at this time argued that " *the policy of cutting prices* " was a weapon against " the hostile force " of private capital (Ts. Kron, *Chastnaya Torgovlya v SSSR* (1926), p. 85).
[4] *XVva Sessiya Soveta Tsentrosoyuza* (1926), p. 112.
[5] G. Neiman, *Vnutrennyaya Torgovlya SSSR* (1935), p. 139.

for their infringement, it proved quite impossible to enforce them.
An official wrote cautiously in 1926 that private traders sold goods
identical with those produced by state industry at free prices, and
that " ticket prices have only recently been extended to private
concerns ".[1] The complaint was heard that price-fixing orders
by Narkomtorg were merely communicated to traders and not made
public, so that nobody knew what prices had been fixed.[2] One
difficulty was that prices for industrial goods were not uniform,
being considerably higher in the countryside than in towns : a
fixed price which meant a reduction for the former might spell an
increase in the latter.[3]

Consciousness of the dilemma brought mounting pressure to
bring down industrial prices. In March or April 1926 a tentative
proposal by Vesenkha to reduce retail prices by 10 per cent was
rejected by Gosplan ; [4] in the latter month, Kamenev as People's
Commissar for Trade, Dzerzhinsky as president of Vesenkha, and
Lyubimov as president of the consumer cooperatives, sent a joint
appeal to all trading organizations to cut retail prices.[5] In June
1926 a fresh start was made. Vesenkha proposed to STO that
prices of industrial goods produced by state enterprises should be
reduced by an average of 10 per cent by administrative decree.[6]
STO rejected this crude method, but approved the aim. On June
28, 1926, a joint session of Sovnarkom and STO resolved that the
reduction of retail prices was " a shock (udarnyi) economic task ".[7]
On July 2, 1926, a resolution of STO " on the reduction of retail
prices of products of state industry in short supply " required that
the price of such goods should be reduced by August 1 to levels
10 per cent below those of May 1, but left the reduction to be

---

[1] *Chastnyi Kapital v Narodnom Khozyaistve SSSR*, ed. A. Ginzburg (1927),
p. 17 ; for the growing divergence between official and private prices see p. 691
below.

[2] For an article condemning this practice see *Revolyutsionnaya Zakonnost'*,
No. 5-6, 1926, pp. 3-4 ; another commentator pointed out that this prevented
" pressure of organized public opinion in the form of party, Soviet, trade union
and other organizations, and in the press " (*Voprosy Torgovli*, No. 2-3,
November–December 1927, p. 67).

[3] *Ibid.* No. 2-3, November–December 1927, p. 60.

[4] *Torgovo-Promyshlennaya Gazeta*, October 1, 1926.

[5] *Ibid.* April 24, 1926.

[6] *Protokol Zasedaniya Prezidiuma VSNKh SSSR, 1925–1926*, No. 9, art.
285 (June 3) ; *Na Agrarnom Fronte*, No. 3, 1927, pp. 10-11.

[7] *Sobranie Zakonov, 1926*, No. 54, art. 396.

effected by Narkomtorg through the ordinary commercial channels : in practice only a small reduction was achieved.[1] The price question was not on the agenda of the session of the party central committee in July 1926, and the united opposition was evidently not eager to attack the official policy of price reduction — possibly owing to divided counsels in its own ranks.[2] Only Pyatakov addressed himself to the theme :

A fundamental task is to channel this margin between wholesale and retail prices to some extent into state industry, and not into private capital, and in this way to expand the work of industry and provide the foundation for a reduction of retail and wholesale prices. If it is necessary and possible, why not make a manœuvre, why not raise the prices of those goods of which we have a shortage and which we issue to the private trader, keep this up for some time and later, on the basis of expanded production, make a parallel reduction of both retail and wholesale prices ?[3]

The enigmatic language did not save Pyatakov from the anger of Dzerzhinsky, who called the proposal to increase wholesale prices " senseless, anti-Soviet and anti-proletarian ".[4] Shortages of goods had long been endemic in the Soviet economy ; and nobody wanted to face the hard fact that to reduce or hold down prices aggravated shortages by increasing effective demand. Rykov at this time observed realistically, if complacently, that shortages " will be chronic for many years to come ", especially in textiles and metal goods.[5]

While the party majority recognized that a policy of higher industrial prices would endanger the link with the peasantry, practical ways and means of achieving a reduction remained elusive. The acuteness of the problem was illustrated by an obsti-

[1] *Na Agrarnom Fronte*, No. 3, 1927, pp. 10-11 ; for the resolution see *Sobranie Zakonov, 1926*, No. 51, art. 374. The initiative in this decision was taken by Dzerzhinsky as president of Vesenkha (*Voprosy Torgovli*, No. 2-3, November–December 1927, p. 66) ; according to A. Malafeev, *Istoriya Tsenoobrazovaniya v SSSR* (1964), p. 103, state trading organs received it " without enthusiasm ", being interested in the maintenance of profits.

[2] See p. 683 below.

[3] Cited by Rykov in *Pravda*, August 17, 1927, and (in part) by G. Krumin in *Bol'shevik*, No. 7-8, April 15, 1927, p. 48.

[4] *Pravda*, August 1, 1926 ; for this speech see pp. 281-282 above.

[5] *Torgovo-Promyshlennaya Gazeta*, August 13, 1926.

nate difference of opinion which occurred in Gosplan in the course
of preparing the control figures for 1926–1927. A minority calculated that grain prices would decline in the forthcoming year by
8 per cent, and agricultural prices as a whole by 4·2 per cent ; if
the industrial-agricultural price scissors were not to be widened
further, this required a reduction of at least 4 per cent in retail
industrial prices. The majority was sceptical of the possibility of
such a reduction in industrial prices ; and, since it agreed with the
necessity of keeping the price scissors stable, it also declared
against a reduction in agricultural prices (except, perhaps, for
particular products or in particular regions).[1] What was clear was
that " any noticeable reduction in grain prices " was possible only
on the condition of " a corresponding reduction in the actual
retail prices for industrial goods ". The general conclusion was
that the price level in 1926–1927 would remain substantially unchanged.[2] It was significant that any widening of the scissors was
rejected by both groups, and that neither advocated an increase in
industrial prices. The STO decree of August 18, 1926, on relations
between state industry and the cooperatives [3] proposed measures
for improving the machinery of distribution, which it declared to
be essential if retail prices of industrial products and the gap
between wholesale and retail prices were to be reduced ; it made
no further attempt to enforce the ineffective resolution of July 2,
1926. Meanwhile voices continued to be raised in favour of
increased prices. The illicit pamphlet on *The Labour Question*
circulated after the session of the party central committee continued to attack " the policy of low prices carried out mainly to
the advantage of the speculator " ; [4] Maizlin's article of September 1926 argued that wholesale and retail prices were three times
as high as before 1914 ; that the policy of reducing retail prices
had failed ; and that the surplus profit was being swallowed up by
speculators and by inflated state and cooperative staffs. To close
the gap, he advocated gradually raising wholesale industrial prices
by 30 per cent ; this would yield an additional profit of 1200
million rubles, out of which 180 millions could be devoted to an

---

[1] *Kontrol'nye Tsifry Narodnogo Khozyaistva na 1926–1927 god* (1926), pp.
109-116.
[2] *Ibid.* pp. 81, 88, 220.
[3] See p. 642 above.   [4] For this pamphlet see p. 488, note 1 above.

increase in the wages of workers by way of compensation for the inevitable further increase in retail prices.[1]

By this time the whole economic policy of the opposition was falling into disarray, and the proposal to raise industrial prices had few friends left. At a discussion in the Communist Academy in September 1926, opposition speakers avoided the price issue, and Pyatakov, when directly challenged, hedged uncomfortably :

> The price question is a most complicated one, and you cannot make do with a Yes or a No ; we have to be able to manœuvre with prices on the market. The general party policy of reducing prices is absolutely right, but it must cover both retail and wholesale prices. If we reduce wholesale prices of goods in short supply for which retail prices are rising, we shall make a crude mistake ; in accordance with the specific conditions of the market, we can also raise certain wholesale prices, in order to reduce them later on the basis of the extension of production. Who does not understand this, understands absolutely nothing. If you put the simple question, Are you for raising or for lowering ?, I cannot answer you ; only an idiot can put questions like that.[2]

At the fifteenth party conference in October 1926, Rykov came out emphatically against the Maizlin proposal to raise wholesale prices, which was also attacked by Chubar and Larin, and found no defenders.[3] Syrtsov complained that some organizations had raised retail prices in order afterwards to make show of reducing them. Trotsky hedged on the price question, declaring that more rapid industrialization would " yield a larger quantity of commodities, and this will reduce retail prices ", but did not refer to previous opposition proposals to increase prices.[4] Bukharin drew attention to the silence of the opposition on this " cardinal element in their policy ", and reported that on the price issue " we hear whispers that Kamenev does not agree with Pya-

---

[1] *Bol'shevik*, No. 18, September 30, 1926, pp. 116-117 ; for this article see p. 10 above.

[2] *Vestnik Kommunisticheskoi Akademii*, xvii (1926), p. 215.

[3] *XV Konferentsiya Vsesoyuznoi Kommunisticheskoi Partii (B)* (1927), pp. 134, 149, 538-541 ; see also Maretsky's reply to Maizlin in *Bol'shevik*, No. 18, September 30, 1926, pp. 118-128, and a further article *ibid.* No. 21-22, November 30, 1926, pp. 8-24.

[4] *XV Konferentsiya Vsesoyuznoi Kommunisticheskoi Partii (B)* (1927), pp. 173, 514.

takov, Pyatakov with Kamenev and Trotsky, that Trotsky does not agree with Zinoviev, and so on ".[1] The conference in its economic resolution described as " profoundly erroneous ", and " decisively " rejected, the proposals of " a number of comrades from the opposition to raise wholesale prices of industrial goods as a source of additional resources to hasten the industrialization of the country ". It noted that the retail price-index for industrial goods, which had stood at 271 on May 1, 1926 (as against 225 a year earlier), had been reduced by October 1, 1926 to 264, but refused to recognize this reduction as sufficient ; a further closing of the gap between wholesale and retail prices must be brought about through improved organization.[2] These arguments and declarations of principle did nothing to improve the position on the market. Between April and July 1926, the agricultural-industrial scissors widened from a ratio of 150 to 164 (1913 = 100), and still stood at 160 in December 1926.[3] The wholesale-retail price scissors also showed no signs of closing. Everyone recognized the vital importance of this question for relations with the peasantry.

> With the question of prices [wrote the peasant newspaper] is bound up *the basic question of the link.* Either we shall cheapen prices and demonstrate *in action* the superiority of a socialist economy, or prices will remain high — and then there can be no question of any kind of link.[4]

Other increases had occurred which affected the cost of living, even though they did not affect the price index. In June 1926 urban rents had been increased ; [5] and during the summer and autumn of 1926 passenger fares on the railways were substantially raised.[6] Attention increasingly turned to the use of direct administrative measures to force down the retail prices of industrial

---

[1] *Ibid.* p. 580.   [2] *KPSS v Rezolyutsiyakh* (1954), ii, 306-307.
[3] See Table No. 35, p. 968 below.
[4] *Bednota*, October 30, 1926 ; " the relation of industrial and agricultural prices ", wrote Trotsky at this time, ". . . must be the decisive factor in the question of the relation of the peasantry to capitalism and socialism " (Trotsky archives, T 3015).
[5] See p. 621 above.
[6] Increases in railway tariffs during 1926 are listed in *Perspektivy Razvertivaniya Narodnogo Khozyaistva SSSR na 1926/27–1930/31 gg.* (1927), pp. 266-268.

goods. The new criminal code of the RSFSR made " a malicious raising of prices of merchandise by way of buying up, concealing or withholding from the market " an offence punishable with one year's (or, in case of conspiracy, three years') imprisonment with confiscation of property.[1] Mikoyan, in a characteristic utterance of this period, declared that cooperatives should be compelled " almost with the big stick " to lower prices, and that people should be prosecuted " for refusal to lower prices and for failure to carry out government orders in this question ".[2] At the same time, towards the end of the calendar year 1926 some signs appeared that the goods shortages were lessening for the first time since the spring of 1925 ; fears were even expressed at this time in industrial circles of a glut of certain goods.[3] By the end of 1926 prices of industrial consumer goods had begun to fall, and demand was becoming " selective " even for items hitherto in short supply, e.g. roofing iron.[4]

In this atmosphere of determination to assert the control of the state over the market and of hope that the economic situation was favourable to such action, the Politburo decided in December 1926 to initiate a fresh campaign to reduce both wholesale and retail industrial prices.[5] Vesenkha had earlier been opposed to any suggestion of a reduction of wholesale prices in the absence of any reduction in retail prices ; [6] that it still regarded this prospect without enthusiasm was indicated by a speech of Kuibyshev at the seventh trade union congress in the same month. Kuibyshev, while accepting a curb in wholesale industrial prices as a stimulus to rationalization and to a lowering of costs, rejected the idea of an all-embracing price reduction such as had been undertaken in the autumn of 1923, and stressed that " a reconsideration of wholesale prices must be made dependent on real progress in the reduction of retail prices ".[7] A leading article in *Pravda*, on January 9, 1927,

---

[1] For this code see p. 50, note 7 above.
[2] *Na Agrarnom Fronte*, No. 9, 1926, p. 10.
[3] *Torgovo-Promyshlennaya Gazeta*, December 10, 17, 1926.
[4] *Informatsionnyi Byulleten' Gosplana SSSR*, No. 2-3, 1927, pp. 1-7.
[5] *Bol'shevik*, No. 4, February 15, 1927, pp. 20-21.
[6] In a report to the presidium of Vesenkha in November 1926, Sokolovsky declared that no general reduction of prices in industries producing scarce goods could take place (*Torgovo-Promyshlennaya Gazeta*, November 28, 1926).
[7] *Sed'moi S"ezd Professional'nykh Soyuzov SSSR* (1927), pp. 507-508.

described price reductions as a first condition of the building of socialism ; and the price question was the main issue at the session of the party central committee which opened on February 7, 1927. The line was laid down in a decision of the Politburo of February 3, 1927 ; [1] and the policy was expounded at length by Mikoyan in an article in the party journal, entitled *The Pivot of Current Economic Policy*. Since the early days of NEP, he argued, " we have climbed some rungs higher on the ladder of the construction of the economic basis of socialism ". It was no longer the market, but the " organized sector " of the economy, which played the decisive rôle in fixing prices. But " a change in the price relation " in favour of agriculture was essential if the link with the peasant was to be maintained. [2] Reports were made to the central committee by Mikoyan and Kuibyshev, representing Narkomtorg and Vesenkha respectively. The opposition was caught without an alternative policy to propose, and showed up badly. It appears to have promised cooperation in the policy of price reduction ; but Trotsky explained that the opposition was doubtful whether so large a reduction as was proposed by the Politburo could be passed on *in toto* to the consumer. [3] Nikolaeva, a defecting member of the opposition, described the speeches of the opposition leaders as " unclear " and " ambiguous ", and explained that she — and, she claimed, some other members of the opposition — had never shared Preobrazhensky's desire to raise wholesale prices. [4] The resolution " On the Reduction of Wholesale and Retail Prices ", which was carried unanimously, noted that, while success had been recorded in every other field of economic policy, the aim of reducing retail prices of industrial goods was still unfulfilled ; the decisions of the party central committee of April 1926 and of STO of July 2, 1926, to lower retail prices by 10 per cent had been " carried out in a far from sufficient degree ". An attack was made on the " wholesale-retail price

---

[1] The text of the decision has not been published, but was referred to in the resolution of the party central committee (see below).

[2] *Bol'shevik*, No. 4, February 15, 1927, pp. 18-27 ; an article in the following number drew attention to the recent widening of the scissors (*ibid.* No. 5, March 1, 1927, pp. 21-22).

[3] See memorandum by V. Smirnov in the Trotsky archives, T 922.

[4] *Pravda*, February 15, 1927, which reported Nikolaeva's speech and commented on it at length in a leading article.

' scissors ' ", and state and cooperative trading organs were instructed to cut their costs by 15 per cent. The desired result could not, however, be achieved simply at the expense of distribution. A reduction of wholesale prices was now also recognized as " a timely and altogether indispensable measure ". The view that " the interests of accumulation and of the rate of industrialization dictate a policy of high industrial prices " was dismissed as " absolutely erroneous and unfounded ". The resolution described price policy as " the nodal point of the whole economic policy of the Soviet state ", determining the rate of development of industry, of agricultural production, and of " socialist accumulation ", as well as the limits of private accumulation, the stability of the currency, and the level of wages. The immediate objective was a reduction " at all costs " of 10 per cent by June 1, 1927, in the retail prices prevailing on January 1.[1]

The party decision was at once translated into legislative action. On February 16, 1927, a far-reaching decree of STO required Narkomtorg within two months to lower retail prices of industrial goods in all departments of state and cooperative trade ; again within two months, to fix a maximum percentage of profit on such goods ; to extend the system of fixing and publishing " ticket " prices for all principal commodities ; to instruct state factories to sell goods to private traders only if they complied with these conditions ; and to prohibit the sale of scarce commodities to private traders.[2] A few days later Mikoyan told the TsIK of the USSR that " questions of the market and of price policy " now occupied " a central place in our economic policy ", and that industrial prices must be reduced if agriculture was to expand.[3] A decree was duly issued noting with satisfaction that the prices of kerosene and agricultural machines were at pre-war level, and demanding that attention should be given to reducing the prices of articles of peasant mass consumption, such as leather and metal goods and salt.[4]

---

[1] *KPSS v Rezolyutsiyakh* (1954), ii, 344-355.
[2] *Sobranie Zakonov, 1927*, No. 11, art. 117 ; " the small retailer must know ", wrote Strumilin at this time, " that he will receive goods from state organs only if he binds himself to sell them at firmly fixed ticket and list prices " (S. Strumilin, *Ocherki Sovetskoi Ekonomiki* (1928), p. 298).
[3] *SSR : Tsentral'nyi Ispolnitel'nyi Komitet 3 Sozyva : 3 Sessiya* (1927), pp. 834, 845-846.   [4] *Sobranie Zakonov, 1927*, No. 12, art. 125.

Wrangling with the opposition on the price issue still continued. After the close of the session of the party central committee, an article in *Pravda* taunted the opposition leaders with having voted for a policy contrary to that which they had hitherto preached, and called this attitude " a political speculation unworthy of Bolsheviks " ; [1] this provoked on the following day a letter of protest from the opposition to the Politburo and the central control commission. Trotsky in an unpublished memorandum a few days later admitted that a reduction of industrial prices had become " tactically urgent " to appease the dissatisfaction both of the wage-earner and of the peasant ; but this would be achieved only through increased industrial development and larger investment in industry.[2] Articles in the press by opposition leaders abandoned altogether the demand for higher wholesale prices, and criticized the authorities only for their unjustified optimism and for their failure to overcome the " goods famine " and to bring down retail prices.[3] In May 1927 the " declaration of the 83 " complained that, although the opposition had voted for price reduction at the February session of the central committee, official propaganda still persistently asserted that the opposition was against it, and also pointed out that the price reduction was taking effect " only on an extremely small scale ".[4]

Meanwhile a leading article in the journal of the party central committee in March 1927 called for a mass campaign by housewives and others to bring down retail prices of articles of mass consumption ; and the party central committee passed a resolution in the same sense.[5] The fourth Union Congress of Soviets in April 1927 remarked on " the immense importance of systematic work on the reduction of prices of industrial goods ", to be

[1] *Pravda*, February 15, 1927 ; a leading article in *Bol'shevik*, No. 4, February 15, 1927, pp. 3-7, declared that " only a madman would propose to raise wholesale prices ".
[2] Trotsky archives, T 3026, 3027, 3028.
[3] *Pravda*, March 25, 1927 (Trotsky) ; *Bol'shevik*, No. 6, March 15, 1927, pp. 57-65 (Preobrazhensky), pp. 66-77 (Smilga). The two last articles were followed by an editorial note stating that they had been published " by way of exception " as representing the views of the opposition ; a long article by Krumin rebutting them appeared in this and the succeeding issue (*ibid.* pp. 78-95 ; No. 7-8, April 15, 1927, pp. 27-54).
[4] For this declaration see pp. 24-25 above.
[5] *Izvestiya Tsentral'nogo Komiteta VKP(B)*, No. 10-11 (183-184), March 21, 1927, pp. 1-2 ; No. 13 (186), April 8, 1927, pp. 3-4.

achieved both by rationalization of distribution and by cutting the costs of production in the factory.[1] The trade union central council issued an appeal for price reductions ;[2] and the party central committee ordered propaganda in favour of rationalization and lower prices to be conducted through party schools and the agitprop sections of local party committees.[3] In May and June 1927, Narkomtorg organized " a mass investigation of retail trade ", in which " tens of thousands " of people participated, and which turned into a public campaign for lower prices. In the first stages of the campaign, some state and cooperative organizations resisted price reductions. This provoked judicial and administrative measures against those responsible : such " repressive measures " are said to have been particularly frequent in the Ukraine.[4] High prices and shortages were still attributed to speculations by private traders who bought up scarce goods for re-sale ; a writer in the Vesenkha newspaper recorded that the OGPU had taken effective action against speculators in GUM, and concluded that " *the work of large-scale buyers can be limited to a considerable extent by measures of repression* ".[5]

Between January 1 and October 1, 1927, thanks to these exertions, retail prices of industrial goods fell by over 7 per cent in state and cooperative trade, and free market prices by over 6 per cent.[6] The party central committee at its session in July 1927 was not primarily concerned with price questions. While welcoming " successes achieved in the sphere of reducing prices of industrial goods ", it drew attention to " the general level of prices for industrial goods, which still remains high, and the large gap between wholesale and retail prices ".[7] STO, having heard a report by Mikoyan, summed up with cautious satisfaction the

---

[1] *S"ezdy Sovetov v Dokumentakh*, iii (1960), 115-116. A similar resolution in even stronger terms was passed by the thirteenth congress of Soviets of the RSFSR in the same month (*ibid.* iv, i (1962), 91-96).

[2] *Spravochnik Partiinogo Rabotnika*, vi (1928), i, 544-545.

[3] *Izvestiya Tsentral'nogo Komiteta VKP(B)*, No. 29 (202), July 30, 1927, p. 8 ; for this campaign see pp. 340-341 above.

[4] *Voprosy Torgovli*, No. 2-3, November–December 1927, pp. 70-71.

[5] *Torgovo-Promyshlennaya Gazeta*, September 15, 1927.

[6] See Table No. 31, pp. 964-965 below ; the peasant newspaper complained, however, that such reductions as took place in the towns were not effective in the countryside (*Bednota*, May 20, 1927). For the shortages of foodstuffs, and consequent rise in free market prices, at this time see pp. 699-700 below.

[7] *KPSS v Rezolyutsiyakh* (1954), ii, 374, 378.

summer campaign for the reduction of retail prices.[1] On the other hand Frumkin, in an article in *Pravda* on September 8, 1927, drew attention to the wide disparity between grain collection prices and retail prices for industrial goods ; and Kuibyshev at the session of the TsIK of the ·USSR in October 1927 called confidently for " the maximum contraction of the scissors ".[2] The compilers of the Gosplan control figures for 1927–1928 wrote of " the sharp break-through in the direction of a lowering of industrial, especially retail, prices " as " the greatest success of the past year " ; and, though this hyperbolic language was not reflected in their positive recommendations, they planned a further reduction in wholesale agricultural prices by 5·2 per cent, and in wholesale industrial prices by 4·5 per cent. So far as retail prices were concerned, they considered that the first half of the forthcoming year should be devoted to " consolidation of the achievements in reducing prices of mass consumption goods " ; a further reduction of these prices would be undertaken in approximately the third quarter of the economic year, but " only as the situation on the market is clarified ".[3] As a result of the reduction in retail industrial prices, the official index of the agricultural-industrial scissors presented in the latter part of 1927 a reassuring picture. The ratio fell from 160 in December 1926 to 145 in April 1927 and 135 by January 1928.[4]

This paper improvement was, however, almost wholly illusory. The success of the price reduction campaign did not improve the real ability of the peasant or of the industrial worker to purchase industrial consumer goods, since it was accompanied by now chronic shortages of these goods in both town and country. The opposition platform of September 1927 continued to stress the price scissors between industrial and agricultural products as the main grievance of the peasantry ;[5] and Yakovlev, in a report prepared for the fifteenth party congress, described " the relation of prices of industrial and agricultural goods " as " the factor which

---

[1] *Pravda*, August 18, 1927.

[2] *2 Sessiya Tsentral'nogo Ispolnitel'nogo Komiteta Soyuza SSR 4 Sozyva* (n.d. [1927]), p. 251.

[3] *Kontrol'nye Tsifry Narodnogo Khozyaistva SSSR na 1927/1928 god* (1928), pp. 233, 300-301.

[4] See Table No. 35, p. 968 below.

[5] L. Trotsky, *The Real Situation in Russia* (n.d. [1928]), p. 29.

in large measure determines the tempo and direction of the development of agriculture ".[1]   But this diagnosis missed the now cardinal factor of the failure of goods to reach the consumer in adequate quantity at the listed prices.   The fifteenth party congress of December 1927 was primarily an occasion for celebrating the achievements of the régime and refuting the slanders of the opposition, and had little to say about price policy as such.   Stalin in his report regretted " the slow progress made in reducing costs of production in industry and in lowering retail prices ".[2]   Mikoyan warned his hearers that the goods famine would increase rather than diminish in the current year, and foresaw serious market difficulties.[3]   The resolution of the congress on the five-year plan admitted the existence of " a disproportion *between industry and the peasant economy* ", but rejected both " *a rise in industrial prices* " (which the opposition had advocated " down to the most recent time ") and " *a reduction of agricultural prices* ".   The only correct method was " *a reduction in the cost of industrial production* " ;   and the price question thus became merged in the broader campaign for the rationalization of industry, through which the congress hoped to achieve " a rise in the purchasing power of the chervonets ".[4]   When in November 1927, as a measure of economy, central, republican and local commissions for the reduction of retail prices were disbanded, and their functions transferred to the Union and republican Narkomtorgs and their agencies,[5] this may be said to have marked the end of a campaign which had been abandoned as a lost cause.   As an attempt to combine the drive for industrialization with a closing of the scissors between industrial and agricultural prices and with improved standards of living in both town and country, the price reduction campaign had failed ;   the next three or four years were to be a period of rising prices due to the pressures of industrialization.   The significance of the campaign of 1927 lay rather in the considerable increase in administrative planning of prices and

[1] Ya. Yakovlev, *K Voprosu o Sotsialisticheskom Pereustroistve Sel'skogo Khozyaistva* (1928), p. 397.
[2] Stalin, *Sochineniya*, x, 312.
[3] *Pyatnadtsatyi S"ezd VKP(B)*, ii (1962), 1103.
[4] *KPSS v Rezolyutsiyakh* (1954), ii, 455-456, 458, 463 ;   for currency policy see pp. 719-720, 773-777 below.
[5] *Sobranie Zakonov, 1927*, No. 65, art. 669.

control of the market which it entailed.

The mood of complacency of the autumn of 1927, encouraged by the tactical exigencies of the struggle against the opposition, was of short duration. After the end of 1927, the questions of price policy which had so long preoccupied and baffled party and government authorities took different forms, or were merged in more pressing and more specific problems — the grain collections crisis, the tempo of industrialization, and the mounting currency inflation. As the advent of planning insensibly undermined the foundations of NEP, price levels — one of the main pillars on which NEP rested — could no longer be envisaged as an independent or autonomous entity determining the shape of the economy. It was not prices, as the orthodox economists of Narkomfin had tried to maintain, which dictated the decisions of the planners. It was the function of the planners in the last resort to dictate prices.[1] But this conception was embarrassing not only to economists grounded in the pre-revolutionary tradition, but to all who had whole-heartedly embraced NEP ; and it was assimilated with difficulty. The dilemma was expounded in an article in the journal of Gosplan in the spring of 1928 :

> Price is the focus of economic relations, in which we find a reflexion of changes taking place in the productivity of labour and of the achievements of man in his obstinate struggle to master matter and the phenomenon of energy.

At the same time, all planning calculations had to be made in fixed prices : otherwise the plan would be falsified.[2] The function of price in a planned economy long remained a notorious crux in Soviet economic thought.

The winter of 1927–1928, the winter of the grain collections crisis, brought to a head the problem of the relation between prices fixed by the state and those of the private market. From the moment when price-fixing became accepted policy, the official prices had applied rigidly only to state and cooperative shops, and goods were sold by private traders at slightly higher prices. In 1923–1924 private market prices were estimated to exceed official prices by 3 per cent, in 1924–1925 by 7·2 per cent, in 1925–1926

---

[1] *Planovoe Khozyaistvo*, No. 5, 1928, p. 46.
[2] *Ibid.* No. 4, 1928, pp. 19-20.

by 10·4 per cent.[1] Between October 1925 and January 1927, prices of industrial goods on the private market rose by 9 per cent, so that the gap between prices of industrial goods in the private and socialized sector rose to 21 per cent.[2] In 1927, with growing scarcities both of foodstuffs and of industrial consumer goods, and with official pressure increasing to hold down retail prices in face of an incipient (though still officially ignored) currency inflation, a determined effort was made to subject prices on the private market to effective control. At the session of the party central committee in February 1927 Mikoyan drew attention to the excessive profit margins of the private trader ; in provincial towns, cotton goods were sold by the cooperatives at 15 per cent, by private traders at 73 per cent, above wholesale prices.[3] The resolution adopted by the committee demanded that private traders, as a condition of receiving supplies from socialized industry, should bind themselves to sell at official retail prices ; [4] and between January and October 1927 prices of industrial goods in the private sector were reported to have fallen to approximately the same extent as prices in the socialized sector.[5] But they still remained considerably higher than in the socialized sector ; and the campaign to reduce costs of distribution drew attention to the much higher margins of profit in private trade.[6] At the end of the year cooperative prices were said to be still from 20 to 22 per cent below those of the private trader.[7] The reduction of official prices meant that such scarce commodities as soap and tea almost disappeared from state and cooperative shops, and were available only on the private market, where prices remained unchanged, or moved upwards with increased demand.[8] It is nevertheless clear

---

[1] A. Malafeev, *Istoriya Tsenoobrazovaniya v SSSR* (1964), p. 85 ; for comparative monthly figures from October 1924 onwards see *ibid.* pp. 382-385.
[2] See Table No. 31, pp. 964-965 below.
[3] Quoted in Yu. Larin, *Chastnyi Kapital v SSSR* (1927), p. 196.
[4] See p. 688 above.
[5] See Table No. 31, pp. 964-965 below ; another table prepared by the *Konjunktur* institute of Narkomfin showed private market prices of a number of commodities exceeding cooperative prices on June 1, 1927, by percentages varying from nil to 60, and margins widening in almost all cases since January 1 (*Voprosy Torgovli*, No. 2-3, November–December 1927, p. 71).
[6] *Ibid.* No. 2-3, November–December 1927, p. 33.
[7] *Pyatnadtsatyi S"ezd VKP(B)*, ii (1962), 1033 ; for the rôle of the syndicates in holding down cooperative retail prices see p. 649 above.
[8] *Na Agrarnom Fronte*, No. 11-12, 1927, pp. 121-122.

that the state succeeded in establishing a considerable degree of control over the rapidly declining private trade in industrial goods. By October 1928 the index of retail prices of industrial goods in the private sector stood only at 247 against 235 in October 1927 ; and even by January 1929 it had risen only to 254.[1] The problem was much more serious in the case of agricultural goods. Here what emerged in practice after 1927 was a dual price system in which official prices fixed by the state in response to exigencies of policy or to calculations of the planners were confronted by widely divergent " free " or " private " prices dictated by the market. The conflict between the planners and the private market reflected the " clash " of interests between industry and agriculture.[2] The private market paid higher prices than the official collecting agencies for agricultural products, and this enabled the peasant to resist the demands of the industrializers. Between October 1927 and July 1928 the index of retail agricultural prices in the private sector rose from 215 to 293.[3] The private trader was more and more openly pilloried as the partner or ally of the kulak. Throughout 1928 official price policies remained fluctuating and chaotic. A main cause of the grain collections crisis, which dominated all economic thinking in the first months of the year, appeared to be the disproportion between the supply of industrial goods to the countryside and the demand of the peasantry for these goods. A confused and embarrassed article in the journal of Narkomtorg explained that equilibrium might in theory be established either by reducing agricultural prices or by raising industrial prices. But both these ways of curtailing the purchasing power of the peasant were rejected as impracticable ; and the conclusion was that the supply of industrial goods to the countryside must be increased either by curbing industrial wages (and thus limiting urban demand) or by " a further forcing of the development of light industry ".[4] These proposals were, however,

---

[1] See Table No. 31, pp. 964-965 below.

[2] Rykov at the Tsentrosoyuz conference of July 1928 referred to " the clash (styk) between town and country " in the sphere of trade (*XLI Sobranie Upolnomochennykh Tsentrosoyuza* (1928), p. 280.

[3] See Table No. 31, p. 964-965 below.

[4] *Voprosy Torgovli*, No. 6, March 1928, pp. 5-9 ; this was an unsigned editorial article. For the development of the consumer goods industries in this period see pp. 49, 307-310 above.

equally unacceptable, and nobody had anything else to suggest. A campaign conducted in general terms to reduce prices [1] led nowhere.

The next landmark was the acute controversy about prices which arose at the session of the party central committee of July 1928, when the out-and-out industrializers, now cautiously supported by Stalin, faced a head-on collision with the group headed by Bukharin and Rykov, who still thought it necessary to conciliate the peasant. The Sovnarkom decree of July 19, 1928, which embodied the compromise reached in the committee, provided for a substantial increase in the official prices for grain.[2] On August 7, 1928, Sovnarkom and STO, on the proposal of Mikoyan, authorized Narkomtorg to bring the new prices into force on August 15, 1928.[3] It was explained that one purpose of the increase was to reduce the gap between official and free market prices, and thus assist the struggle with the " speculative, inflated prices " of the market.[4] This was in effect a forced move, dictated by the impossibility of extracting grain in significant quantities from the peasant at current official prices. But it failed to defeat the persistent activities of the free market. The rise in free prices for grain was resumed in September and continued thereafter without remission, varying in intensity with the shortage of supplies in the region concerned. In December 1928 free prices of rye and wheat in the Ukraine exceeded the official prices by 27 and 44 per cent respectively, in the middle Volga region by 48 and 22 per cent, in the Ural region by 42 and 30 per cent.[5] In Smolensk province inflation in the prices of agricultural products enabled the private trader to monopolize the market ; rye flour on the free market in 1928–1929 rose to almost three times the price of the previous year, and the price of wheat flour almost doubled. As the party report which supplied these particulars sententiously observed :

> The high percentage of influence of the private market in the supply of the agricultural group of goods, and the scissors between the prices of the cooperatives and prices on the free market, which have been especially apparent of late, testify to

---

[1] See, for example, an interview with Mikoyan in *Bednota*, March 23, 1928, and articles in *Pravda*, March 22, 26, 31, 1928.   [2] See pp. 83-84 above.
[3] *Pravda*, August 12, 1928.   [4] *Ekonomicheskoe Obozrenie*, No. 7, 1928, p. 142.
[5] *Ibid.* No. 11, 1929, p. 137 ; see *ibid.* pp. 136, 141, for tables showing that free market prices of rye and wheat rose in every month of the agricultural year July 1928–June 1929 except August 1928 and May 1929.

the fact that the workers' cooperatives were unable to fulfil their tasks in preserving the real level of wages.[1]

In 1928–1929 average prices for grain paid by the official collecting agencies were said to have risen by 19·6 per cent ; prices for wheat rose by 19·5 per cent, for rye by 21·5 per cent. But 23 per cent of the grain marketed was taken by private traders at prices from two or three times as high as the official prices.[2] The retail price index for agricultural products in the private sector rose steadily from 293 in July 1928 to 381 in April and 450 in July 1929 ; the margin between prices in the socialized and in the private sectors widened rapidly throughout this time.[3] The rise in agricultural prices resulted in a continuation of the partial closing of the agricultural-industrial price scissors, which had begun in 1927 ; the ratio fell to 127 in October 1928.[4] But the relatively more favourable prices at which the peasant could in theory obtain industrial products were still nullified by the continuing shortages. Mikoyan showed a realistic appreciation of the situation when he remarked at the session of the central committee in July 1928 that " the scissors will long remain, it is impossible to close them ".[5]

Price policies in the winter of 1928–1929 had thus led to a paradoxical situation. Effective control of wholesale and retail prices of industrial products had been established. Strumilin could in this respect convincingly claim that the economy was no longer bound by the laws of the market : " We now already in practice regulate both market prices and the norms of accumulation which are inseparably linked with them ".[6] Within the state sector, prices could be kept stable in order to simplify planning calculations, or altered to promote the transfer of financial resources from one part of the state sector to another. But no such success could be claimed for agricultural prices. Control of prices in the state sector had been accompanied by a dramatic rise in prices of agricultural products on the private market, and by increasing shortages of foodstuffs in the towns and of industrial products in both town and country. Market relations between

[1] M. Fainsod, Smolensk under Soviet Rule (1958), p. 314.
[2] A. Malafeev, Istoriya Tsenoobrazovaniya v SSSR (1964), p. 119.
[3] See Table No. 31, pp. 964-965 below.   [4] See Table No. 35, p. 968 below.
[5] The remark was quoted by Sokolnikov in his conversation with Kamenev on July 11, 1928, for which see p. 82, note 1 above.
[6] Planovoe Khozyaistvo, No. 5, 1928, p. 46.

town and country had broken down. The state was driven to introduce rationing on the urban market, and to adopt administrative measures of increasing severity in an effort to maintain even limited food supplies to the towns. In face of chronic and severe goods shortages and rising inflation, the assumption, which lay behind the price reduction campaign of 1927, that price reductions would both strengthen the link with the peasantry and improve the standard of living in the towns belonged to a bygone age. While successive drafts of the five-year plan in 1928 and 1929 retained the optimistic view that retail prices could be drastically reduced,[1] current economic policy was more realistic. The proposals of the summer of 1927 for a reduction in wholesale industrial prices were silently abandoned.[2] The compilers of the Gosplan control figures for 1928–1929 in the autumn of 1928 were obliged to recognize that " a policy of price reduction cannot be realized ". Their modest objectives for the forthcoming year were an average reduction in wholesale prices of 1·1 per cent (nil for consumer goods and 3 per cent for producer goods), together with " stability of retail prices for industrial and agricultural products ".[3] The mood was now one of resignation, and the desire was general to shelve the embarrassing issue of price policy while insisting that the state must not abandon its measures of control over the market. When Bukharin at a party central committee in April 1929 described the policy of the majority as an attempt to " leap over " NEP, Stalin retorted that " NEP does not at all mean . . . *free* play of prices on the market ", and accused Bukharin of wanting " licence for the free play of prices on the market and higher grain prices".[4] When the sixteenth party conference met in the same month, the general rise in agricultural prices and the shortage of industrial and agricultural goods were accepted facts, and little could be gained by discussing the question of responsibility. Only the spokesman of Tsentrosoyuz complained that " everything was blamed on to the trading organizations and, in particular, the consumer cooperatives ", and pointed out that increased official prices left the cooperatives with no option but to raise theirs.[5]

[1] See p. 689 above.   [2] See p. 690 above.
[3] *Kontrol'nye Tsifry Narodnogo Khozyaistva SSSR na 1928–1929 god* (1929), pp. 275-276.
[4] Stalin, *Sochineniya*, xii, 43, 60 ; for this debate see pp. 250-251, 633 above.
[5] *Shestnadtsataya Konferentsiya VKP(B)* (1962), p. 190.

CHAPTER 27

CONSUMPTION AND RATIONING

THE period 1923–1926 had been one of rising standards of living throughout the Soviet Union. The peasants, though still at a bare subsistence level which placed them at the mercy of any natural calamity, had escaped from the immediate menace of hunger ; and supplies sufficient to maintain the necessities of life flowed into the towns. Official statistics of the average consumption of foodstuffs per head of population published during these years cannot claim to be more than crude estimates, but give what is probably a fair general picture. The consumption of grain products per head of population reached a peak in the middle nineteen-twenties, and then began to decline. The countryman consumed substantially larger quantities of bread and dairy products than the town-dweller ; the town-dweller, on the other hand, consumed more sugar and meat. In the towns workers' families consumed larger quantities of bread than the families of employees ; employees consumed more sugar, meat and dairy products. But all categories of the population down to 1927 steadily and substantially increased their consumption of meat, dairy products and sugar.[1] It seems probable that by 1926 both urban workers (and a fortiori employees) and peasants were eating better than before the revolution, though some of the claims made were plainly exaggerated. A survey of 130,000 Moscow workers conducted between 1924 and 1927 showed that average height, chest measurement and weight, especially of the younger workers, were substantially greater than before the revolution.[2] Statistics were published

---

[1] See Table No. 36, pp. 969-970 below. According to statistics submitted to the fifteenth party congress in December 1927, consumption of bread per head of population fell by 8 per cent between 1923 and 1926 ; in the same period consumption of butter rose by 52 per cent, of meat and milk by 74 per cent, of sugar by 133 per cent and of eggs by 157 per cent (*Pyatnadtsatyi S"ezd VKP(B)*, ii (1962), 1102).

[2] *Statisticheskoe Obozrenie*, No. 8, 1927, pp. 88-93.

698 THE ECONOMIC ORDER PT. I

showing that in October 1926 peasants in the consuming zone
consumed 98 per cent, and in the producing zone 96 per cent, of the
quantities of grain consumed before the revolution ; [1] but they
too had to some extent replaced bread by more valuable foodstuffs.
Strumilin in the summer of 1927 criticized the view that owing to the
scissors the peasant was worse off than before the war :

> The level of well-being of the mass of the people in town and
> country is already higher than before the war ; and, if in rela-
> tion to the countryside this is still disputed, in a year or two all
> dispute about it will already be impossible.[2]

Bread, in spite of its partial replacement by other foodstuffs,
remained the staple diet of worker and peasant alike ; Moscow,
with a population little more than two-fifths of that of Berlin,
consumed more bread.[3] With a slow, but steady, growth in the
individual consumption of bread, the rapidly rising population
meant a significant increase in total consumption of grain, especially in the great cities. It was calculated that the consumption of
grain in towns had risen from 4,713,300 tons in 1924–1925 to
5,367,800 tons in 1925–1926 and 5,944,400 tons in 1926–1927.[4] A
striking feature of the nineteen-twenties was a gradual substitution
of wheat-bread for rye-bread as the staple item of consumption,
especially in the towns, and a corresponding fall in the consumption of rye flour.[5] Oganovsky noted at the beginning of 1928 that
the demand for wheat was growing " at a gigantic rate ", and that
even the peasant wanted " not sour rye-bread, but sweet wheaten
bread ".[6] In the late nineteen-twenties rye-bread, the food of the
poorest section of the population, was sold at a loss, which was
covered by a profit on wheaten bread.[7]

From 1927 onwards detailed statistics of consumption do not
seem to have been published, and the situation deteriorated. The

---

[1] *Itogi Desyatiletiya Sovetskoi Vlasti v Tsifrakh 1917–1927* (n.d. [1927]),
p. 357.

[2] *Planovoe Khozyaistvo*, No. 8, 1927, p. 18.   [3] *Pravda*, March 15, 1929.

[4] *Ekonomicheskoe Obozrenie*, No. 9, 1928, p. 44.

[5] See Table No. 36, pp. 969-970 below ; between 1923 and 1926 consumption of rye flour per head was said to have declined by 51 per cent, while that of
wheat flour increased by 52·5 per cent (*Pyatnadtsatyi S"ezd VKP(B)*, ii (1962),
1102).   For the shift from rye to wheat see p. 70 above.

[6] *Ekonomicheskaya Zhizn'*, January 13, 1928.

[7] *Kontrol'nye Tsifry Narodnogo Khozyaistva SSSR na 1929/30 god* (1930),
p. 230.

falling off in the grain collections, and the concentration of industrial effort and investment on producer goods industries, limited supplies available for consumption. The rapid growth of urban population and the rise in purchasing power, both in the towns and in the countryside, tended to increase demand, so that the shortages, which NEP had never entirely overcome, recurred in an acute form. At the fifteenth party conference in October 1926 " a butter crisis " was reported in Moscow.[1] But the fact that a temporary shortage of a single foodstuff was worth mentioning showed that it was still exceptional. This relatively satisfactory state of affairs was, however, soon to come to an end. The turning-point seems to have been the alarm inspired by the diplomatic break with Great Britain and the disasters in China in the spring of 1927.[2] In May–June 1927 serious signs of strain began to appear. In the Volga and North Caucasian regions, and in Kazakhstan, free market prices for grain moved sharply ahead of the official prices.[3] About the same time symptoms of a general scarcity made themselves felt, after a long interval, in the food-shops of Moscow and other large cities.[4] By the autumn of 1927 shortages in the cities had become widespread and chronic. A writer in the Vesenkha newspaper, referring primarily to textiles and other manufactured goods, described how groups gathered in shops discussing the shortages and recalling the famine years, and went from shop to shop in search of scarce goods, aggravating the impression of a crisis.[5] In Moscow, butter, cheese and milk were no longer to be had — or not at prices which most people could afford ; and supplies of bread were irregular.[6] A Moscow newspaper referred to the shortage of flour, meat and butter, blaming " various trusts and trading organs " for failure to distribute

---

[1] *XV Konferentsiya Vsesoyuznoi Kommunisticheskoi Partii (B)* (1927), p. 176.

[2] Rykov at the fifteenth party congress in December 1927 mentioned " complications of an international character ", leading to hoarding, as one cause of the shortages (*Pyatnadtsatyi S"ezd VKP(B)*, ii (1962), 858.

[3] *Ekonomicheskoe Obozrenie*, No. 7, 1928, p. 138.

[4] *Na Agrarnom Fronte*, No. 8-9, 1927, p. 77.

[5] *Torgovo-Promyshlennaya Gazeta*, September 15, 1927.

[6] A. Ciliga, *Au Pays du Grand Mensonge* (1938), p. 28 — the account of a critical eye-witness, who adds : " The public queued patiently for whole hours. No indignation, no protest meetings. The newspapers passed over the facts in silence."

supplies.[1]   But at the climax of the struggle with the opposition any publicity for these unwelcome facts was sedulously avoided. Rykov at the fifteenth party congress in December 1927 admitted a scarcity of flour " in some isolated cases ".[2] The failure of the grain collections in the winter of 1927-1928 deepened the crisis and brought the threat of worse privations to come. In February 1928 Moscow was reported as lacking butter, tea, soap, and white flour ; only " grey " bread was to be had.[3] In March 1928 a grain shortage occurred in the cotton-growing area of Central Asia, which depended on European supplies of grain.[4] On May 5, 1928, Trotsky wrote from Alma Ata that the price of a pud of wheat flour, which since his arrival in January had stood at 8-10 rubles, had suddenly risen to 25 rubles ; one of his correspondents reported a few weeks later from Barnaul that there bread queues had " become a habit ", that 10 kilograms of bread a month were issued on bread-cards, and that no butter had been available for two months.[5]   Between April and June 1928 the co-operatives began to restrict supplies of bread to customers.[6] The retail prices of agricultural products on the free market, which had been slowly rising during the winter, moved up very sharply in April and May, and by July 1, 1928, were 60 per cent in excess of official prices.[7] Bukharin speaking at the party central committee in July 1928 referred to " grievous symptoms of under-consumption in a whole number of regions " ; [8] and the resolution of the committee admitted " the appearance of queues and the partial introduction of bread-cards in a number of places ".[9] Mikoyan

[1] *Rabochaya Gazeta*, November 22, 1927.
[2] *Pyatnadtsatyi S"ezd VKP(B)*, ii (1962), 856.
[3] *Sotsialisticheskii Vestnik* (Berlin), No. 4 (170), February 21, 1928, p. 14 ; no white bread had been seen for half a year (*ibid.* No. 14 (180), July 23, 1928, p. 13).   An article in *Voprosy Torgovli*, No. 5, February 1928, p. 46, recommended the mixing of rye and maize in wheat flour in order to release wheat for export, and claimed that this was practised in western Europe and the United States.
[4] G. Konyukhov, *KPSS v Bor'be s Khlebnymi Zatrudneniyami* (1960), p. 66.
[5] Trotsky archives, T 1429, 1531.
[6] *Ekonomicheskoe Obozrenie*, No. 11, 1929, p. 134.
[7] See Table No. 31, pp. 964-965 below.
[8] For this unpublished speech of Bukharin see p. 79 above.
[9] *KPSS v Rezolyutsiyakh* (1954), ii, 515 ; for queues and bread-cards in the Ural region see G. Konyukhov, *KPSS v Bor'be s Khlebnymi Zatrudneniyami* (1960), pp. 159-160.   The introduction of bread-cards was also mentioned in Astrov's article in *Pravda*, July 1, 1928 (see p. 75 above), which added that

justified rationing as a way of discriminating between workers and nepmen :

> Why must we supply the full 100 per cent of the population ? Why must we supply nepmen ? The easiest way is to establish a norm, a ration-card.[1]

Tomsky, on the other hand, declared at the trade union central council that the chief cause of the falling off in labour discipline in the summer of 1928 was the bread crisis :

> In many enterprises, in connexion with the shortage of bread, the need to stand in queues and also the prevalence of " bagging ", absenteeism, lateness at work and departure from work before time have increased. . . . The bread situation has undoubtedly affected the fulfilment of the programme, and also mutual relations between the workers and the economic, trade union and party organizations.[2]

These accumulating shortages were a foretaste of what was to come. The Gosplan control figures for 1928–1929, drawn up in the late autumn of 1928, called for " a firm plan for bread supplies, based on the principles of a certain limitation and rationalization of consumption " : this included " a strict limitation of fine grinding throughout the whole year, the mixing in of maize and barley, a standardization of the consumption of bread in public eating places, and a whole series of other measures of the same kind ".[3] In Leningrad in October 1928 " black-grey " bread containing

---

grain was changing hands at five or six times the official price ; it does not seem to have been directly reported in the press.

[1] *XLI Sobranie Upolnomochennykh Tsentrosoyuza* (1928), p. 311 ; a later commentator defined the purpose of rationing as twofold : " the security in the first place of the working class at the cost of limiting the consumption of non-worker, capitalist elements in town and country, and the distribution of market supplies according to occupations, enterprises, districts and regions, taking into account their importance to the national economy " (A. Malafeev, *Istoriya Tsenoobrazovaniya v SSSR* (1964), p. 137).

[2] The document is in the Trotsky archives, T 1829, and appears to be a report or resolution presented by Tomsky to the trade union central council ; it has not been traced elsewhere. For the weakening of labour discipline at this time see pp. 508-511 above.

[3] *Kontrol'nye Tsifry Narodnogo Khozyaistva SSSR na 1928–1929 god* (1929), p. 50.

40 per cent rye was being sold as white.[1] In the Nizhny-Novgorod region in the spring of 1929 peasants were eating bread with an admixture of dried grass.[2] Potatoes were handled by the agricultural collecting agencies, but, according to Mikoyan, " in a haphazard way, each acting on its own account in competition with the others " (i.e. no fixed prices were enforced); from 1½ to 2 rubles was paid for a pud of potatoes as compared with one ruble for a pud of rye. Even at this price the supply was not sufficient, in the winter of 1928–1929, to satisfy the demands of Moscow, Leningrad and the Donbass.[3]

The first decree on the introduction of ration-books in Leningrad was issued by the Leningrad Soviet in November 1928. The corresponding decree for Moscow was staved off for another three months. At a session of the Moscow city Soviet in December 1928, the deputy president attempted to excuse temporary " interruptions " in bread supplies, and Molotov promised that, whereas in the past year the population of Moscow had received only 600 grammes of bread daily per head, the figure for the coming year would be 700 grammes.[4] A decree of the Moscow Soviet on rationing in Moscow was finally issued on February 21, 1929. It divided those entitled to ration-books into four categories in order of priority : (1) workers (i.e. industrial workers) who were paying members of consumer cooperatives ; (2) workers not belonging to consumer cooperatives ; (3) other members of the working population (trudyashchiesya) who were members of consumer cooperatives ; and (4) members of the working population not belonging to cooperatives. Members of cooperatives had pink ration-books, other members of the working population blue ; books of workers

[1] Sotsialisticheskii Vestnik (Berlin), No. 20 (186), October 28, 1928, p. 13 ; Mikoyan later claimed that in the year 1928–1929 258,000 tons of grain were saved by mixing barley and maize for milling with rye and wheat, and 260-280,000 tons by coarser grinding (Bol'shevik, No. 15, August 15, 1929, pp. 16-17).
[2] SSSR : 5 S"ezd Sovetov (1929), No. 16, p. 4 ; Bukharin at the session of the party central committee in July 1928 had noted the topsy-turvy situation in which horses ate bread and people grass (myakina) (for this speech see p. 79 above). For the feeding of bread to animals see p. 105 above.
[3] Pravda, June 27, 1929. Potatoes were not a popular item of consumption, especially in the countryside ; in the late nineteen-twenties, when the area under grain in the USSR was about 100 million hectares, the area under potatoes barely reached 6 million hectares (Sotsialisticheskoe Stroitel'stvo SSSR (1934), pp. 222-223).
[4] Pravda, December 18, 1928.

were specially marked. Persons deprived of electoral rights got no ration-books. At the same time the impending introduction of bread-rationing in " a number of industrial centres and regions of the consuming zone " was announced.[1] An attempt was made to mitigate the hardship, and secure preferential treatment, for those whose services were most essential by establishing " closed co-operatives " and " closed stores " available only to those working in specified factories or institutions.[2] A leading article in *Pravda* attempted to place the unwelcome necessity in its proper perspective. Though the January grain collections had fallen off owing to " inertia ", it would be a mistake to attribute the decision exclusively to this failure. Three years ago Moscow had consumed only 220,000 tons of rye flour, two years ago 239,000 tons, and in 1928 268,000 tons ; in the current year the demand might well exceed 300,000 tons. The rise was due both to an increase in population and to an increase in well-being which raised individual consumption. Bread-cards were necessary in the interests of the working population. No cards would be issued to non-workers, who would be obliged to buy bread in the open market at inflated prices.[3]

The sale of bread on ration-books began in Moscow on March 17, 1929 ; a coupon was available for each day, but the amount obtainable on it varied with the state of supplies.[4] But the system did not at first extend beyond a few large cities and industrial centres ; the rest of the country had to make do with local supplies. In the consuming zone an attempt was apparently made to supply bread on ration to poor peasants.[5] But it is doubtful whether much came of this. In April 1929 Rykov replied to a number of questioners at the Moscow provincial congress of Soviets :

> We shall not be able this year to guarantee the grain require-ments of the whole population of our Union from the state and

---

[1] *Pravda*, February 21, 1929 ; G. Neiman, *Vnutrennyaya Torgovlya SSSR* (1935), pp. 173-174 ; the other centres named were Odessa, Kiev and Kharkov. Rationing in the consuming zone had been necessitated by " mass speculation in bread and a flow of bread from the large towns to the small towns and into the countryside " (*Planovoe Khozyaistvo*, No. 10, 1929, p. 93).
[2] *Ekonomicheskaya Zhizn' SSSR : Khronika Sobytii i Faktov* (1961), p. 201, dates this system from the end of 1928.
[3] *Pravda*, February 22, 1929.   [4] *Pravda*, March 16, 1929.
[5] *Planovoe Khozyaistvo*, No. 5, 1929, p. 61.

cooperative collections. .... In some regions grain requirements for the current year will not be fully satisfied.[1]

In the Western region the industrial worker was limited to 600 grammes of bread a day with an additional 300 for each member of his family, and to from 200 grammes to one litre of vegetable oil a month — " and that not every month ". Tea, cotton cloth, thread and leather goods were all in short supply.[2] It was cautiously claimed that total urban consumption of food had increased in 1928–1929, though, owing to the rise in population, consumption per head, especially of bread, vegetables and butter, had declined. The situation had deteriorated in the quarter April to June 1929, but improved somewhat in the following quarter.[3] Molotov congratulated himself that, owing to the timely introduction of bread-cards, it had not been necessary to repeat last year's importation of grain.[4] But the failure of the grain collections meant that people went hungry and tightened their belts. The financing of the five-year plan, observed the Gosplan journal, involved " putting a steel hoop round consumption ".[5] In the spring of 1929 rationing was extended to sugar and tea ; and meat, dairy products and potatoes were added later.[6] By the summer of 1929, acute shortages of foodstuffs had become chronic and general.[7]

[1] *Pravda*, April 14, 1929.

[2] M. Fainsod, *Smolensk under Soviet Rule* (1958), p. 315.

[3] *Planovoe Khozyaistvo*, No. 8, 1929, p. 18.

[4] *Pravda*, July 20, 1929 ; for the grain imported in July 1928 see p. 66 above.

[5] *Planovoe Khozyaistvo*, No. 3, 1929, p. 283.

[6] G. Neiman, *Vnutrennyaya Torgovlya SSSR* (1935), p. 174.

[7] Orjonikidze, speaking at a Moscow regional party conference, painted a gloomy picture : " Whatever we may say here, however much we may praise our achievements, the growth of our industry and of the whole economy, we cannot conceal the queues from ourselves, or conceal them from the working class. In this respect we have great difficulties. We can on no account shut our eyes to that. As we approach the twelfth anniversary of the Soviet power, we have shortages of almost all agricultural products " (*Pravda*, September 29, 1929). In 1930 about 26 million people had bread-cards (A. Malafeev, *Istoriya Tsenoobrazovaniya v SSSR* (1964), p. 138).

CHAPTER 28

FOREIGN TRADE

THE aims pursued in Soviet foreign trade were those of the economic system as a whole. During the first four years of NEP, the restoration of foreign trade, like that of industry, was not inspired by any conscious desire to strike out in new directions. To re-knit foreign trade relations proved, however, a particularly arduous task. The control vested in the monopoly of foreign trade was more complete than that exercised over industry by Vesenkha. But in 1926, when Soviet industrial production reached its pre-war level and agricultural production approached it, foreign trade still lagged far behind. World trade in that year was back to its pre-war dimensions, and European trade had achieved 87 per cent of its former level. Soviet foreign trade reached only 32 per cent or, taking account of the territories lost since 1917, 40 per cent; this meant that, while Tsarist Russia had accounted before 1914 for 3·7 per cent of world trade, the corresponding figure for the Soviet Union in 1926 was 1·2 per cent.[1] In 1913 the foreign trade turnover of Tsarist Russia represented 13·2 per cent of the national production; the corresponding figures for the Soviet Union in 1925–1926 and 1926–1927 were 4·9 and 4·7 per cent.[2]

Various explanations were offered for the decline, including "the hostility of capitalist countries, especially of Russia's former creditors", and the low price of timber, now one of Russia's major exports, on the world market.[3] But the major factor was the

[1] *Kontrol'nye Tsifry Narodnogo Khozyaistva SSSR na 1927–1928 god* (1928), pp. 451-452.
[2] *Voprosy Torgovli*, No. 1, October 1927, p. 25. After the industrial expansion of the five-year plan the proportion exported declined further; *Vneshnyaya Torgovlya SSSR*, ed. D. Mishustin (1938), p. 93, gives a figure of 3·2 per cent in 1929 and less than 1 per cent by the middle nineteen-thirties.
[3] *Kontrol'nye Tsifry Narodnogo Khozyaistva na 1926–1927 god* (1926), pp. 155, 157.

2 A   705

collapse of grain exports, by far the largest item in Russia's pre-war exports. In the four years before 1914, Russia had provided 25·1 and 33·4 per cent respectively of world exports of wheat and rye : the Soviet Union in 1925–1926 provided 3·9 and 16·7 per cent.[1] The decline in other agricultural exports, though considerable, was less steep ; but these were also less important. The reasons for the decline in agricultural exports were not far to seek. Owing to the break-up of the larger units of production, smaller surpluses had been available for the market ; and of the lower proportion of the crop to be marketed home consumption had taken a larger share. In 1926–1927 industrial exports topped the average of the years 1907–1913 by 6·7 per cent ; but agricultural exports still reached only 25·5 per cent of the pre-war average. Before 1914 agricultural exports constituted 80·8 per cent of total exports, in 1926–1927 only 52 per cent.[2] The pattern of imports was also significantly changing. The proportion of producer goods (including raw materials) in total imports, which had stood at an average of 65 per cent for the five years before 1914, climbed to nearly 90 per cent in 1926–1927.[3]

Partly, no doubt, because of its traditionally minor rôle in the economy of Tsarist Russia, and still smaller rôle in the Soviet economy, foreign trade enjoyed no prestige among Soviet theorists, and was regarded by politicians (Krasin was almost the sole exception) as a necessary, and sometimes lucrative, nuisance. The Soviet approach to foreign trade was pragmatic. The Soviet Union accepted the " co-existence " of antagonistic socialist and capitalist systems, and, owing to its economic backwardness, had to resort to " a ' borrowing ' . . . of the rich experience of the industrial countries ".[4] But this did not in the long run imply readiness to accept the traditional position of Russia as exporter of grain and timber and importer of industrial equipment, which would, in Soviet eyes, have meant the subordination of Soviet

---

[1] Voprosy Torgovli, No. 1, October 1927, p. 35.
[2] Voprosy Torgovli, No. 5, February 1928, p. 41. These calculations were made in pre-war prices ; according to other calculations, industrial exports did not exceed the pre-war level before 1928–1929.
[3] See Table No. 37, p. 971 below.
[4] Kontrol'nye Tsifry Narodnogo Khozyaistva na 1926–1927 god (1926), p. 146 ; for Trotsky's views a year earlier see Socialism in One Country, 1924–1926, Vol. 1, pp. 453–454.

interests to those of economically more powerful countries. The point was succinctly made in a report to the fifteenth party congress in December 1927 :

> We do not in the least intend to strengthen the existing international division of labour, we do not intend to be an agrarian appendage of the capitalist economic system.

Foreign trade was necessary, but in the interests of Soviet industrialization, including the industrialization of agriculture.[1] In a planned economy foreign trade appeared as a recalcitrant element. However strictly the Soviet authorities might control imports and plan exports, their foreign trade operations took place on a world market. As Mikoyan pointed out, sharp fluctuations of the prices of important commodities like cotton and rubber on the world market created unforeseen difficulties and " set limits on our planning and our prediction ".[2] The framers of the five-year plan listed the uncertain prospects of foreign trade and foreign credits as one of the factors which might decide the issue between the basic and optimum variants of the plan.[3]

The inescapable fact of the influence exercised by world market prices on Soviet foreign trade seems to have encouraged the illusion, rooted in the tradition of free markets and free international exchanges, that the level of Soviet domestic prices was a determining factor in foreign trade. For the brief period from the spring of 1924 to the spring of 1925, when the ruble was effectively exchangeable for foreign currency, such calculations retained a certain validity ; but they were automatically continued long after these conditions had ceased to exist. Dzerzhinsky, in his last speech at the party central committee in July 1926, declared that " we in the USSR . . . have to be on a level with foreign price co-efficients, qualities etc., or they will destroy us ".[4] A few weeks later Preobrazhensky, in an address to the Communist Academy, believed that " the dangers of the situation increase every year as our connexions with the world economy grow ". World prices

---

[1] Ya. Yakovlev, *K Voprosu o Sotsialisticheskom Pereustroistve Sel'skogo Khozyaistva* (1927), p. 339.
[2] *XLI Sobranie Upolnomochennykh Tsentrosoyuza* (1928), pp. 285-286.
[3] *Pyatiletnii Plan Narodno-Khozyaistvennogo Stroitel'stva SSSR* (1929), i, 99 ; for the other factors see p. 895 below.
[4] For this speech see p. 281 above.

pressed on the USSR ; world capitalism was knocking at the
artificial wall which surrounded it. " The wall may break ; this is
the danger for our existence." [1] The compilers of the control
figures for 1926–1927 held rising domestic prices and falling world
prices responsible for " the unprofitability of a number of the
largest items of our export " ; [2] of actual exports in 1926–1927,
448 million rubles represented, according to Narkomtorg calculations, transactions at profit, and 346 millions transactions at a loss
(including 235 millions at a serious loss).[3] To use world costs and
prices as a touchstone to challenge the efficiency of Soviet trade
and industry was fair enough. But Soviet domestic prices were
increasingly determined by government action ; and from 1926
onwards the official exchange rate for the ruble was no longer
influenced by changes in Soviet or world prices. In these circumstances, calculations of the profitability of exports and imports in
terms of the official exchange rate were misleading, and were in
fact no longer applied, in deciding what to export and to import.
V. Smirnov had already argued that the gap between world prices
and Soviet internal prices provided no argument for refusing to
raise Soviet prices ; the gap could be handled as a technical
problem.[4] The price level played less and less part in a context in
which the demands of self-sufficiency were pitted against such
practical considerations as the need for prompt delivery of industrial equipment ; [5] and the availability of goods for export had
less and less to do with their price on the home market.

The monopoly of foreign trade, having survived earlier attacks,[6]
was subject to no challenge of principle in this period. Mikoyan
at the fifteenth party congress in December 1927 called it " the
impregnable condition of the building of socialism in a capitalist
environment ", not only a bulwark against capitalist intervention
from without, but " a bulwark of the planning principle of socialist
construction against the element of the capitalist market ". The
qualifications required of its representatives were, however, formi-

---

[1] *Vestnik Kommunisticheskoi Akademii*, xvii (1926), 227-228 ; see also
Preobrazhensky's article in *Bol'shevik*, No. 15-16, August 31, 1926, pp. 74-76.
    [2] *Kontrol'nye Tsifry Narodnogo Khozyaistva na 1926–1927 god* (1926), pp.
78-79.   [3] Yu. Larin, *Chastnyi Kapital v SSSR* (1927), p. 202.
    [4] *Krasnaya Nov'*, No. 5, 1926, p. 165.
    [5] For such choices between Soviet and imported machines see pp. 408-412
above.   [6] See *Socialism in One Country, 1924–1926*, Vol. 1, pp. 445-451.

dable — knowledge of languages, knowledge of markets and of technology, and " the greatest devotion to the cause ", since they had to work " in the corrupting conditions of the capitalist world " and were exposed to these influences.[1] Behind the impressive façade of torgpreds which represented the monopoly of foreign trade in the eyes of the foreign trader, the business of import and export was conducted in the USSR by a mass of corporations, usually in the form of share companies with state capital set up under the decree of October 1925 [2] — Mashinoimport, Stankoimport, Tekhnopromimport, Eksportkhleb, Eksportlen' among others. The agricultural cooperatives, in view of their past record in Russian export trade, had a favoured position. The specialized cooperative organizations, such as Khlebotsentr and L'notsentr, were constituents of the export companies, Eksportkhleb and Eksportlen' ; and the agricultural cooperatives had offices in the principal foreign capitals, registered under the name of Sel'skosoyuz and working under the general supervision of the torgpreds.[3] The annual plans of imports and exports were prepared by Gosplan on the advice of Narkomtorg, and handed down through Narkomtorg to the import and export companies. But in this period, in contrast with what happened later, control of trading operations and accounts in each country rested with the torgpred and its agencies.[4] This provided a reasonable compromise between centralized control and the specialized knowledge of particular commodities required for trade negotiations. Less complaints were heard in this period than before of the corruption of the organizations conducting foreign trade.

From 1926 onwards, industrialization and planning gave a more positive direction to foreign trade policy. By an elaborate decree of March 30, 1926, STO set up a " licensing commission (soveshchanie) " under the Narkomtorg of the USSR, with similar commissions under the direction of the foreign trade plenipotentiary of Narkomtorg in each Union republic. The Union commission, which comprised representatives of Vesenkha, Narkomfin,

[1] *Pyatnadtsatyi S"ezd VKP(B)*, ii (1962), 1104-1105 ; for insinuations against the torgpreds see *Socialism in One Country, 1924–1926*, Vol. 1, pp. 447-448.
[2] See *ibid.* pp. 450-451.
[3] G. Ratner, *Agricultural Cooperation in the Soviet Union* (1929), pp. 63-65.
[4] *Vneshnyaya Torgovlya SSSR*, ed. D. Mishustin (1938), p. 314.

the Narkomzems of the republics and the cooperatives, was responsible for preparing an import plan, to be submitted to STO, and for allocating quotas to the Union and to the republics ; the import quota for the Union was divided between categories of imports. Licences were then issued by the Union or republican commissions within the limits laid down in the import plan.[1] At a session of Sovnarkom and STO in August 1926 the representative of Narkomtorg called for " a total revolution in the structure of the import plan for 1926–1927 ", reducing imports of finished goods and consumer goods and increasing those of raw materials and semi-manufactured goods for industry.[2] The over-riding motive was now to acquire such imports from abroad as would help to develop Soviet industrial production. The resolution of the fifteenth party conference in October 1926 was categorical on this point :

> The realization of industrialization at the present stage results in the necessity for a maximum import of machinery, the possibility of expanding which depends on the development of export and on the exclusion from imports of those goods which can be produced within the USSR.[3]

The dual need to speed up industrialization by importing the maximum amount of raw materials and equipment, and at the same time make the country independent of such imports in the future, was generally accepted by party opinion.[4] The total of imports rose steadily ; within the total the main increase fell on producer goods, imports of consumer goods progressively de-

---

[1] *Sobranie Zakonov, 1926*, No. 29, art. 183 ; *Vestnik Finansov*, No. 12, 1926, p. 10.

[2] *Torgovo-Promyshlennaya Gazeta*, August 20, 1926.

[3] *KPSS v Rezolyutsiyakh* (1954), ii, 308.

[4] A curious exchange of views between Trotsky and Bukharin occurred at the seventh enlarged IKKI in December 1926. Industrialization, said Trotsky, " means, for an immediate, and fairly prolonged, period, not a diminution, but a growth, of our relations with the outside world, and our increasing dependence (mutual, of course) on the world market " ; Bukharin, sensing an attack on " socialism in one country ", retorted that this was " only *half* the truth and therefore untrue ", since " we become *all* the time more independent " (*Puti Mirovoi Revolyutsii* (1927), ii, 101, 107). Bukharin in his *Notes of an Economist* of September 30, 1928 (see pp. 89–90 above) wrote : " We should *develop our own heavy industry* and gradually free ourselves from our dependent position ". For an earlier observation by Trotsky on Soviet dependence on trade with capitalist countries see *Socialism in One Country, 1924–1926*, Vol. 1, p. 453.

clining in this and succeeding years ; and within the total of producer goods, " Raw Materials " and " Equipment " were the
items which rose most rapidly ; the sub-heading " Electrical
Equipment " increased three-fold between 1925–1926 and 1927–
1928.[1] By 1927 the Soviet Union was the largest importer of
machinery in the world next to Great Britain,[2] though it was
pointed out at the fifteenth party congress in December 1927 that
one-third of Soviet imports consisted of raw material for industry
— cotton, wool and leather — which could be produced within
the Soviet Union.[3]

Another factor in the work of industrialization which made
further demands on foreign currency was the resort to foreign
technical aid, oddly but correctly described as " an industrial
import of a particular kind ". Industrial missions to the number
of 418 were sent abroad in 1926–1927, and more than 500 in each
of the two following years, two-thirds of them to study foreign
industrial techniques. The cost of these missions was more than
a million rubles a year.[4] A joint session of the presidiums of the
Vesenkhas of the USSR and the RSFSR in the autumn of 1928
urged that trusts and syndicates should order more foreign technical literature, and that more experts in management should be
sent abroad.[5] Apart from the foreign specialists employed in the
Soviet Union, agreements were concluded between 1923 and 1929
with 72 foreign firms providing for the communication of technical
information and advice ; in 1929, 64 of these were still in operation. Of these 29 were with German, and 21 with American, firms,
the remainder being shared between France (7), Sweden (3), Great
Britain (2), Switzerland and Italy. On the Soviet side the agreements were almost all concluded by the large industrial trusts,
some of which had several such agreements ; most of them were
in the metal, mining, chemical and electrical industries.[6] While

[1] See Table No. 39, pp. 972-973 below.
[2] *Kontrol'nye Tsifry Narodnogo Khozyaistva SSSR na 1928–1929 god*
(1929), p. 394.
[3] *Pyatnadtsatyi S"ezd VKP(B)*, ii (1962), 931.
[4] *Promyshlennyi Import*, ed. S. Aralov and A. Shatkhan (1930), p. 158 ;
Puti Industrializatsii, No. 10, 1928, p. 75.
[5] *Protokol Ob"edinennogo Zasedaniya Prezidiumov VSNKh SSSR i VSNKh
RSFSR, 1928–1929*, No. 3, Prilozhenie.
[6] *Promyshlennyi Import*, ed. S. Aralov and A. Shatkhan (1930), pp. 160-165 ;
for foreign specialists in the Soviet Union see pp. 598-601 above.

relations between the Soviet authorities and foreign experts sometimes bred mutual mistrust, the debt of Soviet industry to foreign technical advice and training was widely acknowledged, and the only serious complaint was that there was too little of it. The resolution of the fifth Union Congress of Soviets of May 1929 on the five-year plan recognized " the full utilization of the recent achievements of world science and technology " as one of the " indispensable conditions of the successful realization of the five-year plan ".[1]

Rising imports meant pressure on scarce reserves of foreign currency and raised in an acute form the problem of the financing of Soviet foreign trade. Substantial credits had been forthcoming from Germany in 1925 and 1926.[2] Rykov informed a German workers' delegation in August 1926 that the German credit of 300 million German marks (equal to 140 million rubles) would be used to import equipment for industry ; [3] and two months later he told the fifteenth party conference that " we must now energetically and without being afraid, as some people are, set out to get more long-term credits abroad ".[4] According to a report to Vesenkha a year later, foreign credits amounting to 600-700 million rubles were received in 1926–1927.[5] Apart from this windfall, which was not repeated in the following year, financial facilities were limited to the discounting by foreign banks of bills of exchange accepted by Soviet importers ; and this involved high rates of interest which were reflected in the price of the goods. In 1926–1927, thanks to high prices on the world market for wheat, flax and feathers, important Soviet exports, and low prices for cotton, a major import, as well as to the success in obtaining credits from Germany for machinery and equipment, a favourable trade balance was achieved. A repetition of this " exceptionally favourable *Konjunktur* " could not be expected in 1927–1928.[6]

---

[1] *S"ezdy Sovetov v Dokumentakh*, iii (1960), 159.

[2] See *Socialism in One Country, 1924–1926*, Vol. 3, pp. 279, 431, 438.

[3] *Torgovo-Promyshlennaya Gazeta*, August 13, 1926.

[4] *XV Konferentsiya Vsesoyuznoi Kommunisticheskoi Partii (B)* (1927), p. 198.

[5] *Torgovo-Promyshlennaya Gazeta*, August 12, 1927.

[6] *Kontrol'nye Tsifry Narodnogo Khozyaistva SSSR na 1927–1928 god* (1928), pp. 254-255, cf. *ibi¹*. p. 234 ; the year 1926–1927 was quoted as the first for which the foreign trade plan had been fulfilled (*Voprosy Torgovli*, No. 2-3, November–December 1927, p. 203).

The break with Great Britain in 1927 had increased the sense of isolation and encouraged fears of an economic boycott. At the fifteenth party congress in December 1927 Mikoyan predicted a difficult year for foreign trade owing to the complete collapse of grain exports, and called exports the " bottleneck " of the economy.[1] The resolution of the congress contributed little to the issue. It deprecated " the maximum expansion of grain export at the expense of industrial investment ", but proclaimed the necessity for " an active trade balance ", and for the formation of reserves " in kind, in goods and in currency ".[2] The underlying mood, at the moment of the grain collections crisis, was one of anxiety. Kuibyshev in a speech in Vesenkha on January 18, 1928, which was not published at the time, explained that exports in November 1927 had fallen 20 per cent below those of November 1926 and that planned imports had had to be cut in order to avoid a deficit in the trade balance.[3] A widespread campaign was undertaken to stimulate exports. A resolution of STO in May 1928 recorded successful meetings organized by local Soviets, but listed areas in which insufficient efforts had been made by local organizations and especially by the cooperatives ; in republican and local budgets investment in export industries was to be treated as " shock " expenditure.[4] Everything now seemed to turn on the prospect of increasing exports. The compilers of the Gosplan control figures for 1928–1929 drew attention to " the limiting rôle of export and the direct dependence of imports on exports ".[5] Complaints were frequently made of the inefficiency of Soviet exporting organizations. Products were not standardized, so that " one and the same commodity is exported from different regions with different packing, different marking etc.". No sufficient attempt was made to study market demands ; and " commercial flexibility and manœuvre " were lacking.[6]

---

[1] *Pyatnadtsatyi S"ezd VKP(B)*, ii (1962), 1104, 1108; the compilers of the Gosplan control figures for 1926–1927 had described exports as one of two " bottlenecks ", the other being transport (*Kontrol'nye Tsifry Narodnogo Khozyaistva na 1926–1927 god* (1926), p. 217).

[2] *KPSS v Rezolyutsiyakh* (1954), ii, 455–457.

[3] *Istoricheskii Arkhiv*, No. 3, 1958, p. 56.

[4] *Torgovo-Promyshlennaya Gazeta*, May 26, 1928.

[5] *Kontrol'nye Tsifry Narodnogo Khozyaistva SSSR na 1928–1929 god* (1929), p. 392.

[6] *Ekonomicheskoe Obozrenie*, No. 3, 1929, p. 107.

Throughout these years the illusion was entertained that the interruption, total or partial, in grain exports, was a temporary phenomenon. In May 1927 the Soviet delegates at the world economic conference in Geneva held out confident hopes of a renewal of grain exports : " in 1927 the pre-war surplus would be equalled " and " Russia was practically back in her old position ".[1] An early draft of the five-year plan budgeted for an export of 1250 million puds of grain during the currency of the plan, or nearly 4 million tons a year — an estimate which even Rykov found unduly optimistic.[2] Stalin at the party central committee in July 1928 put great emphasis on the accumulation of " grain reserves for export " :

> What does the disappearance of grain from our exports mean ? It means the loss of the source with the help of which we imported, and must import, equipment for industry, tractors and machines for agriculture.[3]

And two months later Bukharin, in his *Notes of an Economist*, remarked that " it would be fantastic if we were to renounce for ever all export of grain merely because we have had to stop exporting it now as a result of the grain crisis ".[4] The framers of the five-year plan estimated that by the end of the five-year period annual exports would have reached anything from 5 to 8 million tons.[5] The fact remained, however, that in the crucial years 1927–1928 and 1928–1929 the export of grain was negligible, and, though it was temporarily resumed in 1930 and 1931 (reaching 5 million tons in the latter year), never again resumed its former importance as an asset in foreign trade. In 1925–1926 agricultural products still accounted for 63·3 per cent of Soviet exports (grain 29·3 per cent) ; in 1927–1928 the proportion had declined to 48

---

[1] *Report and Proceedings of the World Economic Conference* (Geneva, 1927), i, 121 ; ii, 187.   [2] *Pyatnadtsatyi S"ezd VKP(B)*, ii (1962), 873.

[3] Stalin, *Sochineniya*, xi, 178 ; for imports of grain in 1928 see pp. 65-66 above.

[4] For this article see pp. 89-90 above ; the same hope was expressed in the Gosplan control figures for 1928–1929, where it was based on the claim that " our grain is fully competitive " in terms of world prices (*Kontrol'nye Tsifry Narodnogo Khozyaistva SSSR na 1928–1929 god* (1929), p. 393).

[5] *Pyatiletnii Plan Narodno-Khozyaistvennogo Stroitel'stva SSSR* (1929), i, 99 ; the control figures for 1929–1930 predicted a resumption of grain exports in the third year of the five-year plan, i.e. 1930–1931 (*Kontrol'nye Tsifry Narodnogo Khozyaistva SSSR na 1929/30 god* (1930), p. 328).

per cent (grain 7·5 per cent).[1]   Falling agricultural prices on the
world market were a constant preoccupation.   In the winter of
1928–1929, prices of butter and eggs on the London market were
said to be not high enough to cover the official collection prices in
the Soviet Union plus transport and export costs.[2]

A serious effort was initiated to relieve the situation by expanding the production of gold for export which, except for the mainly
abortive episode of the Lena Goldfields concession,[3] had been
neglected since the revolution.   In September 1927, a Union share
company was formed to unify all gold-fields in the USSR ; [4] and
the fifteenth party congress of December 1927 demanded, in the
context of the need for a favourable foreign trade balance, " an
increase in the mining of gold in the country ".[5] Serebrovsky, a
deputy president of Vesenkha, was placed in charge of the
industry, which was shortly afterwards significantly transferred to
Narkomfin.[6]   At the sixteenth party conference in April 1929
Serebrovsky called for the transformation of gold-mining into a
modern mechanized industry.[7]   But no effective results were
achieved during this period.   The major exports from the Soviet
Union now fell under the classification of " raw materials and semi-
manufactured products ", the largest being oil and furs, exports of
which handsomely exceeded their pre-war value, and timber and
timber products, which approached it.[8]   The following figures of
exports in 1927–1928, expressed as percentages of the corresponding exports of 1913, were quoted in the Gosplan control figures for
1928–1929 : oil, 228 ; timber, 45 ; flax and flax waste, 19 ;
manganese, 38 ; asbestos, 80 ; sugar, 87.   The replacement of

[1] *Kontrol'nye Tsifry Narodnogo Khozyaistva SSSR na 1928–1929 god* (1929),
p. 418 ; for the export figures for these years see Table No. 37, p. 971 below.
[2] *Statisticheskoe Obozrenie*, No. 3, 1929, pp. 76-77.
[3] See *Socialism in One Country, 1924–1926*, Vol. 3, p. 415.
[4] *Torgovo-Promyshlennaya Gazeta*, September 21, 1927.
[5] *KPSS v Rezolyutsiyakh* (1954), ii, 456 ; for this passage in the resolution
see p. 713 above.
[6] *Torgovo-Promyshlennaya Gazeta*, October 26, 1927, August 1, 1928 ;
Promyshlennost' SSSR v 1927/28 godu (1930), p. 171.   See also J. Littlepage and
D. Bess, *In Search of Soviet Gold* (1938), pp. 20-26.
[7] *Shestnadtsataya Konferentsiya VKP(B)* (1926), p. 79 ; the journal of the
party central committee followed this up with an article on the importance of
party work in the gold-producing districts (*Izvestiya Tsentral'nogo Komiteta
VKP(B)*, No. 16 (275), June 14, 1929, pp. 4-5).
[8] See A. Baykov, *Soviet Foreign Trade* (Princeton, 1946), Table V.

grain by oil as the major item in Soviet exports, quaintly referred
to as " the mineralization of export ", was attributed not only to
increased demand for oil in world markets but to the skill of Soviet
exporters in adapting themselves to market needs.[1]
The most noteworthy features of the geographical distribution
of Soviet foreign trade during this period were the large trading
surplus with Great Britain, the marked deficit with the United
States and the more equally balanced trade with Germany ; these
three countries remained the most important trading partners.[2]
Early in 1929 the tension between the Soviet Union and the
western world had begun to lift, and the obstacles to the development of trade were disappearing.[3] It was in this mood that the
framers of the five-year plan estimated that Soviet exports would
increase twofold (basic variant) or two-and-a-half times (optimum
variant) during the period of the plan ; though in 1928–1929 they
reached only 40 per cent of the pre-war level, it was hoped that in
five years' time they might exceed it.[4] But Soviet foreign trade
in the ensuing period did not reach even the modest dimensions of
foreign trade under the Tsarist régime, and never came to occupy
a position of major importance in the Soviet economy.

The records of this period confirm the failure already noted in
1925 of the high hopes once placed in concessions as a way to

---

[1] *Kontrol'nye Tsifry Narodnogo Khozyaistva SSSR na 1928–1929 god*
(1929), pp. 392-393. Down to 1925 Soviet oil was distributed abroad by foreign
oil companies ; as the result of a boycott by Standard Oil and Shell, the USSR
was obliged to organize direct sales abroad (*Ekonomicheskaya Zhizn'*, May 7,
1926). The success of ROP, the company created for the purpose in Great
Britain, was recorded in an order of Vesenkha of December 1926 (*Torgovo-
Promyshlennaya Gazeta*, December 30, 1926). In 1927–1928 a fall in world
prices for oil hit Soviet exports (*SSSR : Ot S"ezda k S"ezdu, Aprel' 1927–Mai
1929* (1929), p. 87).
[2] See Table No. 40, p. 973 below.
[3] *Kontrol'nye Tsifry Narodnogo Khozyaistva SSSR na 1928–1929 god* (1929),
p. 391. This passage must have been written after February 1929, since it
refers to an agreement with Deterding concluded in that month ; if a mention
of " two years " dating from the breach in Anglo-Soviet relations is to be taken
strictly, it cannot have been written before May 1929. The foreign relations
aspect of these questions will be discussed in a subsequent volume.
[4] *Pyatiletnii Plan Narodno-Khozyaistvennogo Stroitel'stva SSSR* (1929), i,
99 ; ii, ii, 410 ; for the optimistic prediction about grain exports see p. 714
above.

attract foreign capital. Investment by foreign companies was always looked on in principle as a potential auxiliary source of capital ; in 1925 important concessions had been granted to the Lena Goldfields Company and to the Harriman interests in Georgia.[1] But increasing emphasis on the need to industrialize the Soviet Union on its own resources restricted the scope for concessions. In 1926 and early in 1927 the Politburo decided, in a more or less piecemeal fashion, that major construction projects, while bolstered by foreign technical advice, should be built with Soviet internal resources.[2] The international crisis of the summer of 1927 further dimmed the prospect of attracting foreign capital. On October 1, 1926, 19 " mixed " companies with joint Soviet and foreign capital were active in foreign trade, in timber and in transport. A year later the number had fallen to one-half ; it was evidently the smaller companies which disappeared, since the total capital was only slightly reduced. But, in these enterprises, Soviet capital increasingly preponderated over foreign capital :

	Soviet Capital (in thousand rubles)		Foreign Capital (in thousand rubles)	
	1926	1927	1926	1927
Companies for :				
Trade with the West	515	1272	1259	1014
Trade with the East	3773	3772	1207	1207
Timber	3240	1902	3222	1882
Transport	479	1171	179	407
Total	8007	8118	5867	4510

Both timber and transport companies were said to have made losses in 1926–1927, and only companies trading with the east earned large profits.[3] Besides the mixed companies, 62 foreign concessions were operating in 1926 and 53 in 1927, with 38 million rubles of foreign, and 28 millions of Soviet state, capital. Of these the largest were engaged in mining, and Soviet investment in mining concessions was substantial. Agricultural and timber

[1] For the previous history of concessions policy, see *Socialism in One Country, 1924–1926*, Vol. 1, pp. 454-455 ; Vol. 3, pp. 415-416, 483-485.

[2] For the decision not to offer Dnieprostroi and its associated plants to foreign firms as concessions see p. 909, note 4 below.

[3] The above account is taken from *Materialy po Istorii SSSR*, vii (1959), 48-55.

concessions worked at a loss. Concessions as a whole yielded in 1926–1927 a favourable balance in foreign exchange of 12·5 million rubles ; [1] this was perhaps their principal importance. A discouraging verdict seemed unavoidable. Mikoyan reported to the fifteenth party congress in December 1927 that " the concessions policy has not yielded the results which it might have had " ; [2] and the journal of Gosplan summed up in the same sense :

> Experience of the work of foreign enterprises in the USSR has not been particularly large, and it is also true that it has not been particularly successful. [3]

In view of these verdicts, it is surprising that the year 1928, which saw the cancellation of the Harriman manganese concession, [4] was also marked by a belated attempt to revive the concessions policy. In September 1928 it was announced that Sovnarkom, on July 24, 1928, on a report from the chief concessions committee, had drawn up a list of enterprises available for development by foreign capital, adding that this list was not exclusive. [5] A subsequent statement emphasized that the growth of Soviet industry was now such as to permit, without danger to its independence, the utilization of " foreign finance and technical assistance in more considerable amounts than before ". A more positive policy of attracting foreign capital was promised. [6] But this initiative appears to have had no sequel ; and during the next two or three years most of the outstanding concessions were gradually wound up. [7]

---

[1] *Materialy po Istorii SSSR*, vii (1959), 55-61 ; a figure of 60 million rubles for foreign capital invested in concessions in 1927, given to the fifteenth party congress (*Pyatnadtsatyi S"ezd VKP(B)*, ii (1962), 1689-1690), seems to have been exaggerated.
[2] ii, 1099.
[3] *Planovoe Khozyaistvo*, No. 1, 1928, p. 80.
[4] This will be discussed in a subsequent volume.
[5] *Torgovo-Promyshlennaya Gazeta*, September 15, 1928.
[6] *Ekonomicheskaya Zhizn'*, October 11, 1928.
[7] *Postroenie Fundamenta Sotsialisticheskoi Ekonomiki v SSSR* (1960), p. 209.

E : *Finance*

*

CHAPTER 29

FINANCE AND PLANNING

THE major instruments of financial policy during the period of NEP were the state budget and the credit plan. The quarterly state budget and the quarterly credit plan were regularly considered by Narkomfin, Gosplan and STO; the annual budget, the cornerstone of the whole edifice, was also examined by Sovnarkom and given final approval by TsIK.[1] The budget and the credit plan together controlled the level of financial activity in the economy; the budget surplus or deficit and the net volume of credit were crucial factors in determining the amount of currency in circulation and the stability of the ruble. While the budget and the credit plan were approved as separate acts of policy, their mutual impact was a major preoccupation of the authorities; these arrangements already constituted a kind of rudimentary financial planning of the economy as a whole.

The problem of the later nineteen-twenties was not, therefore, so much to design an efficient system of financial planning as to bring the existing system into line with the policy of rapid industrialization. The supporters of planning and industrialization sought to use the financial powers of the state to allocate resources to economic and cultural development, and in particular to investment in industry. Narkomfin, on the other hand, was both parsimonious in its attitude to the claims of economic development and extremely sceptical about the validity of such financial planning as already existed, believing that unforeseen changes in *Konjunktur* would make it necessary to revise decisions taken even on a quarterly basis.[2] The supporters of the claims of industry tended to assume that the conflict arose solely from the inherent conservatism of Narkomfin officials, and failed to recognize that it also reflected

---

[1] See *Socialism in One Country, 1924–1926*, Vol. 1, p. 460.
[2] See p. 727 below.

an underlying incompatibility between industrialization and financial stability. In 1926, all economists and politicians shared the
assumption that the purchasing power of the ruble should be
maintained and if possible increased ; the need for a stable currency was not challenged even by the "super-industrialists" of the
united opposition.[1] But in practice the victory of the industrializers over Narkomfin gave the industrialization drive precedence
over the stability of the currency ; the subordination of state
budget and credit plan to the requirements of the national economic plan made it possible to remove the financial restraints on
industrialization.

As late as March 7, 1925, the budget was described in a resolution of TsIK as the " basis of the economic plan of the USSR " ; [2]
and at that time few would have contested this principle. A few
months later the first control figures of the national economy, prepared by Gosplan during the summer of 1925, presented a challenge
to the supremacy of the budget ; the challenge was for the time
being successfully rebuffed by Narkomfin.[3] But within three
years the subordination of the budget to the plan had gone farther
than even the most optimistic Gosplan official would have anticipated. The head of the budget and financial section of Gosplan
could already claim at the time of the compilation of the budget
for 1925–1926 that his section was able to exercise a considerable
influence on the budget through the presidium of Gosplan.[4] In
the summer and autumn of 1926, as in the previous year, the discussion in Sovnarkom and STO of the control figures prepared by
Gosplan preceded the discussion of the budget ; and Sovnarkom
in the course of this discussion adopted decisions which treated
both the control figures and the budget as essential elements in the
formation and application of economic policy.[5] In December 1926
discussion of the budget in Sovnarkom took place in the context

[1] In its declaration to the Politburo on October 3, 1926, for example, the
opposition included the fall in the purchasing power of the ruble in its list of
the failures of official economic policy (quoted in *XV Konferentsiya Vsesoyuznoi
Kommunisticheskoi Partii (Bol'shevikov)* (1927), p. 497) ; for an example of
financial caution displayed by Preobrazhensky see p. 741 below.
[2] *Sobranie Zakonov, 1925*, No. 17, art. 126.
[3] For these events see *Socialism in One Country, 1924–1926*, Vol. 1, pp.
499-508.
[4] Cited in G. Krzhizhanovsky, *Sochineniya*, ii (1934), 272-273.
[5] For these decisions see pp. 741-742 below.

and under the influence of the preceding discussions about the
control figures.[1] The same procedures were followed in preparing
the budget for 1927–1928. The law on the budgetary powers of
the USSR and the Union republics adopted on May 25, 1927,
provided that Sovnarkom should fix the total capital investment
of state industry, and the amount to be invested in agriculture, in
the light both of a report from Narkomfin on the prospects for
state revenue and expenditure and of the report from Gosplan on
the control figures.[2] The position of Gosplan in the process of
compiling the budget was thus formally recognized. Larin had
already suggested at TsIK in February 1927 that the association
between the budget and economic planning should be taken
further than this, and that the budget should be considered as part
of the economic plan.[3] At the session of TsIK in April 1928 which
discussed the 1927–1928 budget, Rykov suggested that, as the
budget was an important part of the national economic plan, the
report on the budget " *should be made to the session of TsIK
together with and as part of the general economic plan of the Union* ".[4]
Rykov envisaged that this proposal would not take effect for a year
or two. On April 30, 1928, as an interim measure, a joint decree of
TsIK and Sovnarkom on the procedures for framing the 1928–
1929 budget declared firmly that all economic and operational
plans should be compiled on the basis of the control figures as
adopted by Sovnarkom and merely " adjusted " when the budget
was approved ; the time-table of the process was to be worked out
by Gosplan. The same decree ruled that the 1928–1929 budgetary
estimates of expenditure on the national economy should be
allocated as undivided sums for each major sector of the economy,
such as industry and transport ; all further subdivision was the
responsibility of the spending authority concerned.[5] The effect of

---

[1] *Torgovo-Promyshlennaya Gazeta*, December 28, 1926 ; *Ekonomicheskaya
Zhizn'*, January 7, 1927. Reports on the budget were made by representatives
of Gosplan and Rabkrin as well as of Narkomfin.
[2] *Sobranie Zakonov, 1927*, No. 27, art. 286.
[3] *SSSR : Tsentral'nyi Ispolnitel'nyi Komitet 3 Sozyva : 3 Sessiya* (1927), p.
771.
[4] *3 Sessiya Tsentral'nogo Ispolnitel'nogo Komiteta Soyuza SSR 4 Sozyva*
(1928), pp. 344-345.
[5] *Sobranie Zakonov, 1928*, No. 25, art. 218 ; the decree included several
other provisions for accelerating the adoption of the budget. The delay had
been a matter of concern for some years. The budgets for 1923–1926 were

these measures was drastically to simplify and accelerate budgetary procedure, while simultaneously curbing the authority of Narkomfin. Henceforth the budget was subordinate to the plan both in law and in fact.[1] The process of subordination was completed in November 1928 with the recognition of the control figures as the annual national economic plan ;[2] as a result of the simplifications of procedure the 1928–1929 budget was adopted by TsIK only one month after the approval of the control figures, on December 15, 1928.[3]

From 1927 onwards official policy required that the annual control figures or economic plans should be firmly based on the five-year perspective plan ; a corollary of this was that the annual budget, and the other financial plans, should also conform to the five-year plan. The first estimates of the 1927–1928 budget prepared in Narkomfin were based on the current Gosplan draft of the five-year plan ; they were later said to have been too low precisely because the Gosplan draft had under-estimated the possibilities of growth.[4] During 1928 so many drafts of the five-year plan followed one another in swift succession that it was impossible to use them as a satisfactory basis for planning the 1928–1929 budget. Narkomfin made more than one attempt to compile its own perspective financial plan.[5] But the initiative remained in

---

all considerably delayed (see *Socialism in One Country, 1924–1926*, Vol. 1, pp. 457-469). The budget of the USSR for 1926–1927 was adopted in February 1927, earlier in the year than any of the earlier budgets ; even so TsIK resolved that the five months' delay " to a considerable extent deprives of value the planning rôle of the state budget in national economic construction " (*Sobranie Zakonov, 1927*, No. 12, art. 120, dated February 25, 1927). The budget for 1927–1928 was not approved by TsIK until April 1928. At the session of TsIK, Rykov attributed the delay to delays in compiling the national economic plan (*3 Sessiya Tsentral'nogo Ispolnitel'nogo Komiteta Soyuza SSR 4 Sozyva* (1928), pp. 344-345) ; another speaker pointed out that, " since at least three or four months are needed for compiling and elaborating the budget, it is inevitable, if the control figures are adopted in September, that the state budget will not be adopted until January of the following year at the earliest " (*ibid.* p. 209).

[1] Haensel, a former leading tax official of Narkomfin, who did not return to the USSR after a visit abroad in 1928, saw this decree as a turning-point in the history of Soviet finance (P. Haensel, *The Economic Policy of Soviet Russia* (1930), p. 114).
[2] See pp. 820-821 below.   [3] *Sobranie Zakonov, 1928*, No. 69, art. 638.
[4] *Ekonomicheskoe Obozrenie*, No. 4, 1928, p. 14.
[5] See pp. 740-741 and 881, note 1 below.

the hands of Vesenkha and Gosplan, whose successive drafts of the five-year plan included estimates of the growth of budgetary revenue and expenditures. When Yurovsky, a prominent Narkomfin official, complained that proposals made by Gosplan were unrealistic, an official of its budgetary and financial section replied :

In constructing the budget, the budgetary and financial section has assumed that the budget plays a subordinate rôle in relation to the economy, and that the budget has always served and always must serve the aim of developing the productive forces of the country. If national economic plans are worked out more or less correctly, the budget must correspond to them, and fully coincide with the national economic plan.[1]

The amount actually received by a spending authority did not depend entirely on the annual budget as approved by TsIK. For a large part of the year, arrangements had to be made in anticipation of an annual budget which was not yet authorized. Quarterly budgets supplemented the annual budget and did not keep strictly to its estimates ; the precise sum to be allocated to each spending authority was often settled from month to month. Delays in the receipt of revenue meant that appropriations could not be issued in full, so that some spending authorities had to be temporarily kept short. Unexpected needs which arose in the course of the year impelled the spending authorities to reallocate the approved appropriations between their subordinate institutions and to demand *ad hoc* supplementary appropriations.[2] All these matters were settled whenever possible by direct negotiation between Narkomfin and the spending authorities. But major spending authorities such as Vesenkha or Narkomput' frequently exercised their right to appeal to STO ; and, as might be expected, STO was often prepared to over-rule Narkomfin where appropriations to Vesenkha were concerned.[3] The decree of April 30, 1928, gave Vesenkha and the other economic authorities much more control over their annual appropriations.[4] The report of the fifth Union

[1] *Informatsionnyi Byulleten' Gosplana SSSR*, No. 8-9, 1928, pp. 30-36.
[2] See *Torgovo-Promyshlennaya Gazeta*, August 31, September 29, 1927 (allocations before approval of annual budget) ; July 24, 1927 (monthly allocations within quarterly budget) ; May 25, 1926 (request for reallocation of original appropriation between subordinate units of a spending authority) ; May 6, 30, 1926 (distribution of supplementary allocation).
[3] See for example *ibid.* September 3, 1927.   [4] See p. 721 above.

Congress of Soviets about the activities of the government between April 1927 and May 1929 frankly declared :

> If there is any breakdown of the budgetary plan, the government exerts all its efforts to carry out in any event the budgetary provisions for expenditure relating to production, on which all our economic plans depend. This again underlines the fact that our budget is in the first place a plan of economic expenditure.[1]

The budgetary powers of Narkomfin were further weakened by changes in the system of auditing and control. In November 1923, all powers of financial control had been removed from Rabkrin and placed in the hands of Narkomfin.[2] The system of auditing then adopted was extremely elaborate : it required inspection by the control organs of Narkomfin of all documents relating to the budgetary expenditure of spending authorities. On November 16, 1926, Sovnarkom accepted a report from Rabkrin which proposed a drastic simplification of the system. Auditing was now limited to selective periodic checks ; in addition institutions financed by the budget were required to submit regular accounts.[3] This change was seen at the time as an encouragement to Narkomfin to concentrate its attention on the efficiency with which money was spent rather than on the formal accuracy of the accounts.[4] Its practical consequences were more drastic. The agencies of State Financial Control, as the Narkomfin department was now called, appear to have henceforth been excluded from auditing the budgetary expenditure of institutions on *khozraschet*, a category which included nearly all industrial enterprises.[5] In the event, the reform of November 1926 proved to have been a step on the road to the abolition of effective auditing by Narkomfin.[6]

---

[1] *SSSR : Ot S"ezda k S"ezdu (Aprel' 1927 g.–Mai 1929 g.)* (1929), p. 59.

[2] See *Socialism in One Country, 1924–1926*, Vol. 1, p. 461.

[3] *Sobranie Zakonov, 1926*, No. 76, art. 608 ; *Vestnik Finansov*, No. 8, 1927, p. 67.

[4] A further decree issued by TsIK on April 21, 1928, encouraged the control organs of Narkomfin to move in this direction (*Sobranie Zakonov, 1928*, No. 34, art. 210).

[5] *Vestnik Finansov*, No. 8, 1927, p. 68.

[6] State Financial Control was abolished in 1930, and Narkomfin agencies for auditing the budget were not re-established until 1933 (see R. W. Davies, *The Development of the Soviet Budgetary System* (1958), p. 242).

The extent to which credit would be planned by the central authorities was quite unclear when Gosbank and the special banks were first established in 1922 and 1923.[1] Some kind of commercial market for credit was expected to emerge : each of the special banks would autonomously attract free resources on a commercial basis both from the private market and from state and cooperative enterprises ; to some extent Gosbank would also operate on ordinary commercial principles. As late as 1926 and even 1927, Narkomfin and Gosbank officials still hankered after a credit market in which the state, cooperative and private sectors would all participate.[2] Such expectations altogether failed to materialize. No effective commercial rate of interest existed in Soviet conditions, particularly where the state sector was concerned. As a Narkomfin commentator pointed out :

> Even if the bank rate were high, and borrowing at this rate involved losses for a client trust, the trust would continue to apply for credit, since the principle of commercial profitability has so far been less significant in the industry of the USSR than the principle of planned production.[3]

The interest of 8-10 per cent per annum which the special banks paid on deposits did not attract substantial deposits from state or cooperative organizations, and completely failed to attract personal savings or the savings of the private market. The resources of the banks in fact consisted primarily of the deposits of state and local budgets.[4] Decisions of the banks to grant credit were also taken on administrative grounds rather than on grounds of profitability. Loans at a rate as low as 3-3½ per cent were made by the Central Municipal Bank, and even loans made by the agricultural credit societies, which often charged 7-10 per cent, were not based on market rates.[5] The volume of credit was in practice planned by

[1] For the special banks see *Socialism in One Country, 1924–1926*, Vol. 1, pp. 473-474.
[2] For examples of these views see *Vestnik Finansov*, No. 4, 1926, pp. 21, 24 ; *Problemy Dolgosrochnogo Kreditovaniya Promyshlennosti*, ed. A. Sokolov (1928), p. 44.
[3] *Vestnik Finansov*, No. 5-6, 1926, p. 7 ; for the rôle of profit see also pp. 370-372 above.
[4] The relevant figures are set out in A. Z. Arnold, *Banks, Credit and Money in Soviet Russia* (N.Y., 1937), pp. 252-253, 289, 298, 306, 311, 314.
[5] *Problemy Dolgosrochnogo Kreditovaniya Promyshlennosti*, ed. A. Sokolov (1928), pp. 111-131 ; A. Z. Arnold, *Banks, Credit and Money in Soviet Russia*

the state. As Strumilin put it, " credit resources are directed to
each sector of the economy not by the spontaneous operation of
supply and demand, but by conscious action to carry out the
general plan of the national economy ".[1]

The planned volume of credit, and the related proposal for the
net amount of currency to be issued, were included in the annual
control figures of the national economy prepared by Gosplan, and
were debated at length in STO and Sovnarkom each year. But
these annual plans for currency and credit were ineffective : as
late as the autumn of 1928, Gosplan commented in its control
figures for 1928–1929 that " in this matter the accuracy of planning
forecasts is of course extremely limited ".[2] In practice, control by
the state over currency and credit was exercised through a quarterly
credit plan. The credit plan showed on its debit side the planned
net volume of credit to be made available during the quarter by
both Gosbank and the special banks ; the crucial figure for the net
quarterly issue of currency appeared on the credit side of the plan,
and was determined by the level of net credits and deposits. The
credit plan could thus influence the volume of currency independently of the state budget ; even when the budget was in surplus,
new currency could be issued by increasing the volume of credit.[3]
Although Gosbank was responsible both for compiling the
credit plan and for managing credit and currency issues, its powers
were limited by the provision that its quarterly credit plans, like
other operational economic plans, were discussed and approved by
STO : the credit plan approved by STO, including the figure for
currency issue, was in theory binding on the bank. At the same
time Gosbank was hampered by the ability of the special banks to
issue credits in excess of the plan.[4] In practice, the quarterly
credit plan was a very imperfect instrument, with the result that

(N.Y., 1937), pp. 254, 274-275. The principal exception, or partial exception, to
this picture of non-commercial activity was the Moscow city bank, which used
sums voluntarily deposited by institutions attached to the Moscow Soviet to make
loans for periods between eighteen months and three years at the high interest rate
of 9-10 per cent. Its outstanding loans to municipal services, building repair and
local industry amounted to 67 million rubles on October 1, 1926 (*Problemy Dolgosrochnogo Kreditovaniya Promyshlennosti*, ed. A. Sokolov (1928), pp. 114-117).
   [1] S. Strumilin, *Ocherki Sovetskoi Ekonomiki* (1928), p. 300.
   [2] *Kontrol'nye Tsifry Narodnogo Khozyaistva SSSR na 1928–1929 god*
(1929), p. 32.
   [3] See p. 772 below.   [4] See p. 779 below.

the quarterly currency issue frequently diverged considerably from the plan.[1]

In this uncertain situation, a stubborn struggle was waged for the control of credit and credit planning. During 1926 and the first half of 1927, Gosbank pressed strongly for the abolition of the quarterly credit plan, using the pragmatic argument that the plans were in practice ineffective, and that three months was in any case too long a period over which to plan so sensitive a regulator as credit. As a writer in the journal of Narkomfin put it :

> Plans hypnotize : the fulfilment of the plan figure, which is unconditionally treated as obligatory, blunts sensitivity to the economic situation and to changes in *Konjunktur*.[2]

The weakening of control by the central authorities over credit which would have resulted from the abolition of the quarterly credit plan would undoubtedly have carried with it an immense accession of authority to the bank. The proposal was hotly contested. This was partly a matter of normal inter-departmental rivalry. But the issues ran deeper. Gosbank was even more notoriously committed than Narkomfin to currency stability and financial restraint, and was evidently anxious to assume fuller control of credit policy and to prevent any repetition of the inflationary crisis of the summer of 1925. For their part, Gosplan and Vesenkha rightly feared that an increase in the powers of the bank would hinder economic development. Shtern, head of the finance department of Vesenkha, reproved Gosbank for attributing too much importance to credit and to its own rôle in relation to credit, and reminded it that capital investment and production targets were also important levers of control over industrial enterprises.[3]

---

[1] This is shown in the following table, which compares the net currency issues (+) or withdrawals (-) planned in the quarterly credit plan with the amount actually issued (in million rubles at current prices) :

	October–December		January–March		April–June		July–September	
	Plan	Actual	Plan	Actual	Plan	Actual	Plan	Actual
1926–1927	+ 101	+ 63	- 75	- 70	(No plan)	+ 136	+ 75	+ 209
1927–1928	+ 170	+ 40	- 150	- 150	+ 125	+ 179	+ 250	+ 270

(A. Z. Arnold, *Banks, Credit and Money in Soviet Russia* (N.Y., 1937), p. 279.)

[2] *Vestnik Finansov*, No. 5, 1927, p. 46.

[3] *Torgovo-Promyshlennaya Gazeta*, December 7, 1926 ; he still believed, however, that in principle " the method of influence ' by the ruble ' is far more

728 THE ECONOMIC ORDER PT. I

In spite of strong opposition, the pretensions of Gosbank were at first successful. It was permitted to make monthly changes in the quarterly credit plan, and in the January–March quarter of 1926 STO merely " noted " the plan.[1] In January 1927, the practice of examining credit plans in STO was dropped altogether.[2] No credit plan was prepared by Gosbank or by the other banks for April–June 1927. But the triumph of the bank was short-lived. In its first and last " unplanned " credit quarter it unexpectedly conducted itself in a manner quite at variance with its tradition of financial caution, and permitted substantial over-issues of bank credit.[3] The bank had used the difficulties of planning as a pretext to take over control of credit into its own hands ; its enemies now used its lack of restraint as a pretext for restoring the previous arrangements. The presidium of Gosplan triumphantly complained that the bank had given way to pressure from economic bodies ; the president of Prombank added that the loans made by Gosbank had included unnecessary credits to local industry ; both Gosplan and Prombank attributed these failures to the absence of a properly approved credit plan.[4] On July 25, 1927, STO agreed to the immediate reintroduction of overall quarterly credit plans.[5]

This decision proved to be more far-reaching than a return to the old system.[6] The committee on banks, established in 1924 with the object of coordinating credit policy and the banking system, had been supposed to scrutinize the quarterly credit plans before they were submitted to STO.[7] But in practice it had been

---

effective and viable than the method of ' instructions ' from the People's Commissariats " ; for Shtern see p. 279 above.
[1] *Vestnik Finansov*, No. 5-6, 1926, p. 8.
[2] *Ibid.* No. 2, 1927, p. 56, No. 5, 1927, p. 31 ; *Informatsionnyi Byulleten' Gosplana SSSR*, No. 8-9, 1927, pp. 4-7.
[3] The reasons for these over-issues are discussed on pp. 773-774 below.
[4] *Torgovo-Promyshlennaya Gazeta*, July 15, 1927 ; *Informatsionnyi Byulleten' Gosplana SSSR*, No. 8-9, 1927, pp. 4-7.
[5] *Informatsionnyi Byulleten' Gosplana SSSR*, No. 8-9, 1927, pp. 4-7.
[6] Gosbank unsuccessfully attempted to reduce the effect of the first of the resumed credit plans for the quarter July–September 1927 by proposing to retain 45 per cent of the planned credit as a reserve to use at its own discretion ; the budget and financial section of Gosplan commented that this was " only the ghost of a plan " (*Informatsionnyi Byulleten' Gosplana SSSR*, No. 8-9, 1927, pp. 4-7).
[7] See *Socialism in One Country, 1924–1926*, Vol. 1, pp. 473-474.

ineffective. The president of Gosbank was by statute president of the committee; and both Gosplan and Vesenkha complained that it acted in practice not as an independent organizer of the banking system, but as a mere auxiliary of Gosbank; by 1926, it had even ceased to meet regularly.[1] In July 1927, the committee was reconstituted as the " committee for bank affairs ". The new committee reassumed the power to scrutinize the quarterly credit plans, but in conditions which made it far more independent of Gosbank than the old committee; its president was henceforth not the president of Gosbank but the People's Commissar for Finance.[2] But the main pressure for an expansionist credit policy came from the other government departments represented in STO; as the industrialization drive accelerated, the credit plans approved by STO became, as Gosbank had feared, an instrument for the rapid expansion of credit, and a major means of overcoming the conservative policies of Narkomfin and Gosbank.[3] Henceforth the volume of credit was determined not by the standards of financial orthodoxy upheld by Narkomfin and Gosbank, but by the demands of the policy of industrialization voiced by Vesenkha and Gosplan.

The state budget and the credit plan did not include all the financial transactions of state institutions and enterprises. The social insurance budget, though financed by methods analogous to taxation, was administratively quite separate from the state budget.[4] Local budgets came only in part within its scope.[5] State and co-

---

[1] *Informatsionnyi Byulleten' Gosplana SSSR*, No. 7, 1926, p. 11; *Torgovo-Promyshlennaya Gazeta*, July 1, 17, 1926; A. Z. Arnold, *Banks, Credit and Money in Soviet Russia* (N.Y., 1937), pp. 266-267.

[2] *Torgovo-Promyshlennaya Gazeta*, July 17, 1927; the statute of the committee was approved by Sovnarkom on October 31, 1927 (*Sobranie Zakonov, 1927*, No. 64, art. 648).

[3] In September 1928 the procedure for approving the credit plans was greatly accelerated (M. Atlas, *Razvitie Gosudarstvennogo Banka SSSR* (1958), pp. 74-75).

[4] For the social insurance budget see pp. 605-609 above.

[5] The " unified budget " (edinyi byudzhet) approved by Sovnarkom and TsIK included only the Union and republican budgets; what was known as the " comprehensive budget " (svodnyi byudzhet) included the local budgets as well as the unified budget, but was treated merely as background material by Sovnarkom and TsIK and did not receive formal approval.

operative organizations on *khozraschet* paid taxes into the budget
and received grants from it, and their loans and deposits appeared
in the credit plan, but their current incomes and expenditures
were not included either in the budget or in the credit plan. The
promfinplans of state industry, in which financial transactions were
prominent, were examined and approved by the central authorities
as a separate act of policy.[1]

In party circles it was widely recognized that successful planning of the national economy required a more comprehensive
system of financial planning; how far this would involve the re-
modelling or fusion of existing instruments of financial policy was
not yet clear. In successive annual discussions of the budget,
some members of the budget commission of TsIK proposed to
enlarge the coverage of the state budget. In April 1926, Vetosh-
kin, one of the most prominent members of the commission, proposed that all the income and expenditure of state industry should
be included in the budget.[2] In February 1927, during the discussions at the commission on the 1926–1927 budget, Ryazanov
supported this view, and added that social insurance and trade
should also form part of the budget.[3] Another speaker cited the
example of transport, where the pre-revolutionary practice of including its total income and expenditure in the budget continued,
and commented:

> The growth of planned economy in our country must in-
> evitably involve a greater and greater extension of the bounds of
> our budget, not only as a result of the natural growth of its
> revenue, but also as a result of including new spheres of state
> property in the budget.[4]

But belief in *khozraschet* and memories of the unhappy experiments of war communism stood in the way of proposals to incorporate all state income and expenditure in the budget. At the
session of TsIK in April 1926, Bryukhanov, People's Commissar
for Finance, had commented that " this is not a practical idea,

---

[1] For the *promfinplans* see pp. 823-827 below.
[2] *SSSR: Tsentral'nyi Ispolnitel'nyi Komitet 3 Sozyva: 2 Sessiya* (1926),
pp. 169-170.
[3] *Plenum Byudzhetnoi Komissii TsIK Soyuza SSR* (1927), p. 117.
[4] *Ibid* pp. 123-124.

at least for the immediate future ", and added that such an
arrangement would be " somewhat oppressive for industry ".[1]

A more immediate and practical problem was to achieve better
coordination of the existing instruments of financial policy. Progress was slow. The control figures of the economy for 1926–1927
prepared by Gosplan in the summer of 1926 included a section on
the budget, but made no serious attempt to link the discussion of
the budget either with the other aspects of the financial system or
with the rest of the economic plan.[2] In February 1927, Larin proposed at the budget commission of TsIK that the budget, the
credit plan and the *promfinplan* should all be discussed together by
TsIK as part of the state economic plan.[3] In the following month,
TsIK resolved, presumably as a concession to the critics, that the
promfinplan should be presented to it simultaneously with the
state budget in 1927–1928.[4] But the control figures of the national
economy for 1927–1928 prepared by Gosplan in the summer of
1927 again failed to draw together the various financial plans.[5] In
1927–1928 Sovnarkom discussed the *promfinplan* and the budget
separately, and the *promfinplan* was not submitted to TsIK.[6] The
credit plan was still approved only on a quarterly basis, and only
by STO. At the session of TsIK in April 1928, the *rapporteur* for
the budget commission complained that its work had been weakened by its inability to consider, together with the budget, " questions of the planning of our whole credit system ", and stressed
that " the amount received by the national economy through the
budget is insignificant in comparison with what it receives through
credit ".[7]

In November 1928, the central committee of the party accepted
the main proposals in a revised version of the control figures of

[1] *SSSR: Tsentral'nyi Ispolnitel'nyi Komitet 3 Sozyva: 2 Sessiya* (1926),
pp. 374-375.
[2] *Kontrol'nye Tsifry Narodnogo Khozyaistva na 1926–1927 god* (1926), pp.
93-100.
[3] *Plenum Byudzhetnoi Komissii TsIK Soyuza SSR* (1927), pp. 141-142.
[4] *Sobranie Zakonov, 1927,* No. 12, art. 120.
[5] *Kontrol'nye Tsifry Narodnogo Khozyaistva SSSR na 1927–1928 god* (1928),
pp. 302-321.
[6] The *promfinplan* was approved by Sovnarkom on March 20, 1928
(*Sobranie Zakonov, 1928,* No. 20, art. 180), the budget by TsIK on April 21
(*ibid.* No. 24, art. 207).
[7] *3 Sessiya Tsentral'nogo Ispolnitel'nogo Komiteta Soyuza SSR 4 Sozyva*
(1928), pp. 48-49.

Gosplan as " the economic plan for 1928–1929 ".[1] The volume of
control figures for 1928–1929 prepared by Gosplan at that time
included a section entitléd " The System of Finance ", which
attempted a general survey of the financial system of the country and
tried to coordinate the various financial plans ; [2] and in December
1928, in the annual budget debate at TsIK, the spokesman of the
budget commission again complained of having to examine the
budget for 1928–1929 in isolation from the credit plan and the other
financial plans, and insisted on the need to compile " a unified financial plan, which would be a general survey, a general summary of all
measures in the economy ".[3] By this time the planning department
of Narkomfin had already begun work on the preparation of a
" unified financial plan " for the following year 1929–1930. Events
now moved rapidly. On February 20, 1929, TsIK and Sovnarkom
resolved that a " unified budget of social insurance " should be
compiled annually and approved by Sovnarkom ; it was to incorporate social insurance financed through the republican budgets,
the insurance budget for transport workers, and the estimates of
the Central Administration of Social Insurance and Narkomtrud.[4]
On April 24, 1929, TsIK and Sovnarkom resolved that, when
Narkomfin presented the 1929–1930 budget, it must also present
a " comprehensive (svodnyi) financial plan of the economy ", prepared jointly with the control figures, and including all sources of
income.[5] For the moment, however, the annual state budget and
the quarterly credit plans continued to be the practical instruments of financial planning.

The subordination of the financial system to the emerging
system of national economic planning carried with it the decay of
Narkomfin as an institution in its traditional form. The limita-

[1] See p. 820 below.
[2] *Kontrol'nye Tsifry Narodnogo Khozyaistva SSSR na 1928–1929 god* (1929),
pp. 53-55, 325-341.
[3] *4 Sessiya Tsentral'nogo Ispolnitel'nogo Komiteta Soyuza SSR 4 Sozyva*
(1928), No. 3, pp. 2, 9.   [4] *Sobranie Zakonov, 1929*, No. 16, art. 132.
[5] *Ibid.* No. 27, art. 245 ; what was described as a " first attempt " at a
unified financial plan was presented to an all-Russian financial conference in
November 1929, and later published as *Edinyi Finansovyi Plan na 1929–30
god* (1930). At this time no clear distinction was made between the " unified
financial plan " and the " comprehensive financial plan " ; for the distinction
which was made later see R. W. Davies, *The Development of the Soviet
Budgetary System* (1958), pp. 152, 178.

tions imposed between 1926 and 1929 on the powers of Narkomfin in relation to the budget and the credit plan were accompanied by vigorous attempts to bring the policies and personnel of Narkomfin into line with official economic policy. This was a difficult task. Narkomfin had long been notorious for its conservative financial policies. Sokolnikov, People's Commissar for Finance from 1921 until January 1926, showed himself to be strongly influenced by those members of the Narkomfin staff who most actively resisted the policy of industrialization. The staff of Narkomfin included professional economists such as Kondratiev, director of its *Konjunktur* institute, A. L. Vainshtein, Kondratiev's deputy, Yurovsky, head of its currency section, and Litoshenko ; these men were thoroughly versed in contemporary western economics and published articles in professional journals in western Europe and the United States.[1] Three common features may be distinguished in the attitude to the Soviet economy of the members of this school. First, they predicted that, as a result of the backwardness of the economy, the lack of private accumulation and the absence of foreign investment, the level of investment and the rate of growth of the national income in the USSR would in future necessarily be lower than in the Tsarist period or in western capitalist countries.[2] Secondly, they shared with the " neo-*narodniks* " a firm belief in the importance of developing agriculture rather than industry ;[3]

[1] Kondratiev's famous article on long waves appeared in *Archiv für Sozialwissenschaft und Sozialpolitik*, Vol. 56, No. 3 (1926), and he wrote on " The Static and Dynamic View of Economics " in *Quarterly Journal of Economics*, xxxix (1925), 575-583. Litoshenko, a specialist on Soviet national income, published an article on the subject *ibid* xlii (1928), 70-93. Accounts by Kondratiev of the work and organization of the *Konjunktur* institute appeared *ibid.* xxxix (1925), 320-324, and in *International Labour Review*, xvii (1928), 231-240 ; reports by the institute on Soviet economic conditions appeared regularly in *London and Cambridge Economic Service* until January 1928. For Kondratiev and his school see also pp. 20-22 above.

[2] *Planovoe Khozyaistvo*, No. 4, 1927, pp. 14-15 ; *Vestnik Finansov*, No. 7, 1927, pp. 48-49.

[3] Kondratiev and his associates were often lumped together in polemical discussion with former SRs in Narkomzem and the Central Statistical Administration (see pp. 20-22 above). At a discussion in January 1928 Lyashchenko, an ex-Menshevik economist, pointed out to Strumilin, who frequently described Kondratiev as a neo-*narodnik*, that " Professor Kondratiev not only does not belong to the neo-*narodniks*, but on the contrary is a sufficiently definite figure of another complexion " (*O Pyatiletnem Plane Razvitiya Narodnogo Khozyaistva SSSR : Diskussiya v Kommunisticheskoi Akademii* (1928), p. 45).

while they did not after 1926 openly decry industrialization as such, they consistently argued that the planned rate of industrialization was too high, and pressed the claims of other sectors of the economy. Thirdly, they were disposed to favour the spontaneous decisions of the market in preference to conscious economic control, the private sector of the economy in preference to the state sector, and voluntary investment by individuals in preference to compulsory investment by the state.[1] These attitudes coloured every aspect of their proposals for budgetary and credit policy. At the lower levels of Narkomfin, the staff had at first included many former officials of the Tsarist Ministry of Finance ; only a handful of the staff were party members.[2] Between 1922 and 1925, a systematic effort had been made to increase the number of party members.[3] On January 1, 1926, 17 per cent of a total staff of Narkomfin amounting to 61,000 persons, and 27 per cent of its 19,500 " responsible and trained officials " belonged to the party or the Komsomol.[4] The complaint continued to be frequently heard, however, that Narkomfin was dominated by ex-Tsarist officials.[5] On June 27, 1927, a decree of the party central committee reported that a survey of Gosbank and the special banks had shown that the majority of their middle-level staff were qualified non-party specialists who had many years of experience of banking, but were " insufficiently subject to the influence of the party ".[6]

The appointment of Bryukhanov to succeed Sokolnikov as People's Commissar for Finance in January 1926 [7] marked a change in the fortunes of the commissariat. Bryukhanov, an old

---

[1] For examples of these views see *Vestnik Finansov*, No. 4, 1926, p. 24 ; *Problemy Dolgosrochnogo Kreditovaniya Promyshlennosti*, ed. A. Sokolov (1928), pp. 43-44, 98, 140.

[2] See R. W. Davies, *The Development of the Soviet Budgetary System* (1958), pp. 66-67.

[3] For the first stages in the process see *Socialism in One Country, 1924–1926*, Vol. 1, p. 116, note 2.

[4] *Vestnik Finansov*, No. 7, 1926, p. 128. By this time only 11 per cent of the " outside " staff of Narkomfin had been working as financial officials before the revolution, and over 40 per cent of its tax officials were party members (*ibid*. No. 3, 1926, pp. 90, 95).

[5] A. Fabrichny, *Chastnyi Kapital na Poroge Pyatiletki* (1930), p. 52 ; in 1929, 37 per cent of the personnel of Narkomfin were reported to be former Tsarist officials (*Socialism in One Country, 1924–1926*, Vol. 1, p. 117).

[6] *Spravochnik Partiinogo Rabotnika*, vi (1928), i, 561-564 ; middle-level staff included heads and deputy heads of bank departments.

[7] See *Socialism in One Country, 1924–1926*, Vol. 1, p. 468.

Bolshevik who had previously been Sokolnikov's deputy, appears to have accepted without reserve the increasing emphasis on industrialization, remaining in office until 1930. In January 1927, he stated at a Moscow provincial party conference that " the whole of financial policy " was directed towards acquiring supplementary resources for industrialization ; [1] at a session of TsIK in the following month he insisted that " it is not our fate to prepare an easy budget " :

> Our obligation, our duty, is to obtain for the use of the state all those resources which it is possible to obtain, and to throw the maximum quantity of these resources into the needs of the economy, for its development and rapid growth.[2]

Kuznetsov, one of his deputies, was also insistent on the importance of increasing capital investment in industry.[3] On the other hand Frumkin, the other deputy People's Commissar, seems to have remained faithful to the old tradition of Narkomfin, and in the following year came out as an outspoken adherent of the party Right.[4]

The appointment of Bryukhanov did not remove the mistrust of Narkomfin among party members, and among non-party supporters of the industrialization policy in Gosplan and Vesenkha, as a centre of financial conservatism. By 1926, the long-standing antipathy between Gosplan and Narkomfin had reached the point at which protests were made in Gosplan against the unqualified publication of the views of Narkomfin officials.[5] In the summer of 1927, hostility between the party members in Gosplan who supported rapid industrialization and the Narkomfin experts greatly increased.[6] At the same time, the united opposition denounced the Kondratiev group as agents of counter-revolution. In a bitter attack on them in *Bol'shevik*, Zinoviev described what he called

---

[1] *Ekonomicheskaya Zhizn'*, January 11, 1927.
[2] *SSSR: Tsentral'nyi Ispolnitel'nyi Komitet 3 Sozyva: 3 Sessiya* (1927), p. 530.
[3] *Torgovo-Promyshlennaya Gazeta*, July 13, 1927.
[4] See pp. 74-75, 320, 323 above.
[5] A critic in *Planovoe Khozyaistvo*, No. 6, 1926, p. 226, argued that a pamphlet by Yurovsky published by Narkomfin would hinder the ordinary reader from understanding the causes of the difficulties of 1925, and should not have been published without a critical preface.
[6] See pp. 856-861 below.

" Kondratievshchina " as " a complete ideology of the new bour-geoisie ".[1] In an extensive review of the results of the economic year 1926–1927, published at the beginning of 1928 as a number of the bulletin of the *Konjunktur* institute, prominent members of the institute, including Vainshtein, launched a full-scale attack on the pace of industrialization, and on the policy of curbing the private sector of the economy.[2] During March 1928, after the publication of this number of the bulletin, a vigorous campaign was carried on against the Kondratiev group in the economic and daily press. They were castigated as " bourgeois economists ", who were attempting " a bourgeois revision of the main lines of Leninism on economic construction ", and as " apologists of capitalism ", whose nonsensical talk about the use of the methods of war communism reflected "the ideology of the men of the private sector ".[3] Kraval complained that the printing of their views as " leading articles in the official organs of government departments without appropriate remarks by the editors leads us to sad reflexions on how deeply tendencies hostile to the proletariat have seeped in." [4] Soon after these attacks Kondratiev, Vainshtein and others were removed from their posts in Narkomfin, and the editorial board of the bulletin was replaced.[5]

The discussion of the budget for 1927–1928 by TsIK in April 1928 revealed the extent to which these events had undermined the position of Narkomfin. Larin, who for some years had taken on the function of a public scourge of capitalistic influences in Narkomfin, strongly criticized Bryukhanov's report on three grounds. First, Bryukhanov had relied on data provided by the

[1] *Bol'shevik*, No. 13, July 15, 1927, pp. 33-47 ; for this article and the editorial note on it see p. 31 above.

[2] *Ekonomicheskii Byulletin' Kon"yunkturnogo Instituta*, No. 11-12, 1927 ; for references to this number of the bulletin see pp. 389, 631 above. For an expression of similar views by another senior Narkomfin official see L. Yurovsky, *Denezhnaya Politika Sovetskoi Vlasti (1917–1927)* (1928), p. 371, cited in part on pp. 775-776 below.

[3] *Ekonomicheskaya Zhizn'*, March 15, 1928 ; *Ekonomicheskoe Obozrenie*, No. 3, 1928, pp. 78-79.

[4] *Puti Industrializatsii*, No. 1, 1928, pp. 26-35.

[5] On April 12, 1928, Larin stated that Kondratiev had been " removed only recently " (*3 Sessiya Tsentral'nogo Ispolnitel'nogo Komiteta Soyuza SSR 4 Sozyva* (1928), p. 76) ; on April 13, 1928, Bukharin referred to the control of the bulletin by " Kondratiev, Vainshtein, etc. " in the past tense (*Pravda*, April 19, 1928).

Konjunktur institute, which was "under the leadership of the ideologists of capitalism". Secondly, Narkomfin had consistently underestimated revenue possibilities. Thirdly, it had treated profits of private industry and trade as "super-normal" for taxation purposes only when they exceeded a figure which was sometimes as high as 30 per cent, and this indicated "a loss of revolutionary feeling and communist sensitivity in relation to our class enemies ".[1] As on other occasions, Larin had moved into a troubled area. Each of his three accusations dealt with a major aspect of the conflict between Narkomfin and the party. His first charge struck at the influence on Narkomfin of the Kondratiev group, the first centre of resistance to the industrialization policy against which official action had been taken. His second charge was aimed at the part played by Narkomfin in its long battle for conservative finance and against inflation. His third charge drew attention to the resistance of Narkomfin to the policy of squeezing out the private sector. In the speeches which followed Larin's attack, its political implications were angrily rebutted. Kuznetsov claimed that Larin had been "irresponsible ", remarking scathingly that, " if it had not been Larin who said this, one could have been more insulted ". He accused Larin of raising party matters in a state organization, hinted at Larin's Menshevik past, and praised the firmness of Frumkin, who was in charge of tax matters in Narkomfin.[2] Later in the session Rykov joined in the defence of Narkomfin :

> I do not think that accusations of an ideological influence of the bourgeoisie on comrades Bryukhanov, Frumkin and Kuznetsov, or on Narkomfin as a whole, are in any way correct. . . .
> *It is impermissible to utter, without any proof, accusations that*

---

[1] *3 Sessiya Tsentral'nogo Ispolnitel'nogo Komiteta Soyuza SSR 4 Sozyva* (1928), pp. 74-84. In January 1928, Larin attacked the Narkomfin of the RSFSR and the tax commission of the Narkomfin of the USSR for their leniency in taxing the incomes of the bourgeoisie ; the editors of *Pravda* supported Larin in substance while disassociating themselves from the tone of his article (Larin's article, a reply by Frumkin, president of the commission, and counter-replies by Larin and Frumkin, appeared in *Pravda*, January 11, February 1, 25, April 5, 1928 ; for editorial comments see *ibid.* February 25, April 5, 1928).

[2] *3 Sessiya Tsentral'nogo Ispolnitel'nogo Komiteta Soyuza SSR 4 Sozyva* (1928), pp. 139-143.

2 B

bourgeois influence is felt in this most sensitive and responsible place, in our financial policy.[1]

And at the end of the debate Bryukhanov tried to brush off the attack :

> We all know comrade Larin's habits well, we know that nobody else has put him up to all the unpleasant things he says and all his mistaken assertions. They belong to nobody except himself. Let them remain with him.[2]

Larin's attack heralded what was soon to become a commonplace attitude to Narkomfin. The summer of 1928, which was marked by the trial of the Shakhty engineers,[3] saw an active campaign throughout the Soviet administration against those who resisted policies of industrialization ; and Narkomfin was particularly vulnerable. Frumkin continued throughout the summer and autumn his attacks on the rate of industrialization, using many of the traditional Narkomfin arguments. But his independence was exceptional, and was due to his standing in the party and to the reluctance of the leaders to take action against him.[4] Though no publicity appears to have been given to the removal of any officials or experts of Narkomfin other than the members of the *Konjunktur* institute, in the course of the year 1928 the Narkomfin experts rapidly lost any remaining influence.[5] In the summer of 1928 Narkomfin put forward five-year budget estimates which it would have regarded as completely unacceptable twelve months before.[6] In October 1928, the change in Narkomfin was symbolized by the appointment of Pyatakov, former " super-industrialist " and member of the united opposition, who had now been received back into the party, as deputy president of Gosbank and a member of the collegium of Narkomfin.[7] A few months later, Pyatakov took over the office of president of Gosbank from Sheinman, who had in that

---

[1] *Ibid.* pp. 348-349.   [2] *Ibid.* p. 361.
[3] See pp. 584-585 above.   [4] See pp. 74-75, 320, 323 above.
[5] Bryukhanov later summed up the position in measured terms by saying that " the cadres of old financial specialists " had been used " not unsuccessfully " in the restoration period, but were " for the most part unsuitable for the new objectives of financial construction " (*Edinyi Finansovyi Plan na 1929-30 god* (1930), pp. 11-13).
[6] See p. 881, note 1 below.
[7] *Sobranie Zakonov, 1928*, ii, No. 58, art. 229 ; he was also authorized to represent Gosbank in STO (*ibid.* ii, No. 67, art. 274).

office firmly supported the principles of financial orthodoxy for a number of years.[1] At the session of the party central committee in November 1928, Stalin, while strongly criticizing Frumkin's behaviour as a member of the central committee, conceded that Narkomfin was " bound to be stingy ".[2] But this hint of magnanimity towards Narkomfin was scarcely typical. In 1928 and 1929 it lost all influence on the making of policy and was reduced to the status of a technical administrative organ.

[1] *Sobranie Zakonov, 1929*, ii, No. 17, art. 96 ; Sheinman also relinquished his post as a deputy People's Commissar for Finance and his membership of STO (*ibid.* ii, No. 17, arts. 93, 95). For Sheinman see *The Bolshevik Revolution, 1917–1923*, Vol. 2, p. 351.

[2] Stalin, *Sochineniya*, xi, 276 ; for other aspects of this speech see pp. 93, 326-328 above.

CHAPTER 30

THE STATE BUDGET

(a) Expenditure

THE expenditure of the state budget more than doubled between 1925–1926 and 1928–1929.[1] Over half the total increase was absorbed by expenditure on " financing the national economy ". Under this head, allocations to industry increased most, but there was also a substantial rise in expenditure on agriculture.[2] Expenditure on " social and cultural measures ", primarily the health and education services, also grew rapidly, though less than budgetary expenditure as a whole. Defence expenditure, in spite of the alarms of 1927, rose more slowly, and recorded expenditure on the defence industries, which was classified as part of expenditure on the national economy, was not large.[3] Expenditure on administration, perhaps as the result of a series of campaigns to keep it down,[4] also increased at a much slower rate than budgetary expenditure as a whole.

An increase in budgetary expenditure of this magnitude was not at first regarded as a necessary or automatic prerequisite of the policy of industrialization. It was widely held in the late nineteen-twenties that planning would involve no increase in the rates of direct or indirect taxation, and that the budget would not expand more rapidly than the national income as a whole. A three-year financial plan compiled by a Narkomfin expert, Nikitsky, at the end of 1925 even assumed that the ratio between the budget and the gross national product would be somewhat lower in 1927–

[1] See Table No. 41, p. 974 below.
[2] For detailed figures, see R. W. Davies, *The Development of the Soviet Budgetary System* (1958), p. 83.
[3] Budgetary expenditure on the defence industries was 36 million rubles in 1926–1927 (*ibid.* p. 132, note 4) and was planned to be 50 million rubles in 1927–1928 (*Vestnik Finansov*, No. 7, 1927, p. 7).
[4] For these campaigns see R. W. Davies, *The Development of the Soviet Budgetary System* (1958), pp. 132–133.

1928 than it had been in 1913.[1] Eighteen months later, its author declared that in future the budget should expand less rapidly than the national income as a whole.[2] While Narkomfin by this time officially conceded that the budget should increase more rapidly than the national income, Kuznetsov also stressed " the need for caution in calculating the revenue side of the financial plan ".[3] Caution about the possible rate of growth of the budget was not confined to Narkomfin. Groman, in assessing the prospects for 1927–1928, declared that " the sources of revenue are exhausted to the point of refusal to pay ", and looked forward to no more than " a parallel growth of the budget and the mass of goods in circulation ".[4] The compilers of the second Gosplan draft of the five-year plan, more enthusiastic in their support of industrialization, advocated a more rapid expansion of the budget than of the national income, but stressed that the rate of both direct and indirect taxation should not be increased.[5] Even Preobrazhensky found himself caught between his support for industrialization and his acceptance of the prevailing financial caution. In a speech in the budget debate at TsIK in February 1927, he unexpectedly argued that the rate of increase in the budget for 1926–1927, which exceeded the rate of increase in the national income, would lead to great disproportion and overstrain, objected to the proposals of the budget commission to increase expenditure, and insisted that the growth of the budget must be halted.[6]

In practice, Narkomfin yielded year by year to the pressure of the spending departments. In July 1926, its initial proposals for the 1926–1927 budget contemplated an increase of 16·5 or 17 per cent; this figure, which already exceeded the expected growth of the

---

[1] *Planovoe Khozyaistvo*, No. 11, 1925, pp. 152-153 ; No. 1, 1926, p. 130.

[2] *Vestnik Finansov*, No. 7, 1927, p. 45 ; he suggested that the growth of the budget was dependent on the growth of agriculture, arguing that " the rate of growth of the total budget as a whole in every country has always been and will always be close to the rate of growth of the social segment or group of the national income which is largest in proportion to the total, if the financial system itself is not changed " (*ibid.* p. 51). There is an interesting ambiguity in the last clause.

[3] *Torgovo-Promyshlennaya Gazeta*, July 23, 1927.

[4] *Planovoe Khozyaistvo*, No. 7, 1927, p. 131.

[5] *Perspektivy Razvertivaniya Narodnogo Khozyaistva SSSR na 1926/27–1930/31 gg.* (1927), pp. 31, 420-436 ; for this draft see pp. 854-858 below.

[6] *SSSR: Tsentral'nyi Ispolnitel'nyi Komitet 3 Sozyva: 3 Sessiya* (1927), pp. 762-768 ; for other aspects of this speech see p. 747 below.

national income, was accepted by Gosplan.[1] But on August 3, 1926,
Sovnarkom issued a directive for a further increase in expenditure
on the national economy in the 1926–1927 budget, stipulating
that budgetary allocations to investment in industry should exceed
those of the previous year, that the working capital of industry and
allocations to transport should be increased, and that provision
should be made for starting the construction of a number of new
power stations and for the encouragement of exports.[2] This
directive was further reinforced on September 8, 1926, when
Sovnarkom and STO again insisted that the proposed budgetary
allocations to industry should be expanded ; the budget surplus
and the budget reserve were also to be increased.[3] In the next few
months the budget estimates were further increased. In December 1926, Bryukhanov proposed to a joint meeting of Sovnarkom
and STO that the budget for 1926–1927 should exceed that of the
previous year by about 24 per cent.[4] In fact, budgetary expenditure increased by as much as 41 per cent in 1926–1927, while
national income increased by only 6·3 per cent.[5]

The estimates for the year 1927–1928 followed a similar course.
In the summer of 1927, Narkomfin recommended that the budget
should be increased by 9 or 10 per cent in 1927–1928, as compared
with a rise in national income of 6·5 to 7 per cent. The initial
proposals of Gosplan, reached independently of Narkomfin, were
almost identical.[6] But the upward trend in the estimates was soon
resumed. Early in 1928, Kuznetsov reported that an increase in
the budgetary estimates was permissible because the original proposals had underestimated the rate of growth of trade turnover,
and particularly of the sales of sugar and vodka, on which a high
revenue would be received.[7] The proposals approved by the
session of TsIK in April 1928 involved a much more rapid

[1] *Torgovo-Promyshlennaya Gazeta*, August 3, 1926.
[2] *Torgovo-Promyshlennaya Gazeta*, August 12, 1926 ; *SSSR : Svodnye
Materialy o Deyatel'nosti Soveta Narodnykh Komissarov i Soveta Truda i Oborony
za IV Kvartal (Iyul'-Sentyabr') 1925–26 g.* (1926), p. 78.
[3] *Pravda*, September 21, 1926 ; see also pp. 284-285 above and 813-814
below. Both the August and the September resolutions emphasized the
importance of reducing administrative expenditures.
[4] *Torgovo-Promyshlennaya Gazeta*, December 28, 1926.
[5] See Tables No. 41 and 45, pp. 974, 977 below.
[6] *Vestnik Finansov*, No. 7, 1927, p. 4.
[7] *Ekonomicheskoe Obozrenie*, No. 4, 1928, pp. 13-24.

increase in budgetary expenditure than the expected growth in the
national income : they provided for budgetary expenditure 17 per
cent in excess of the actual expenditure in 1926–1927. Narkomfin,
attacked by Larin at the session for persistently underestimating
budgetary revenue,[1] still tried to exercise some restraint. Of the
two deputy People's Commissars for Finance, Kuznetsov offered
a mild defence of a policy of caution :

> A Narkomfin and a government which propose a budget the
> fulfilment of which, with some small surplus, is guaranteed, are
> better than a Narkomfin and a government which propose a
> budget the 100 per cent fulfilment of which cannot be guaran-
> teed.[2]

Frumkin went further, expressly defending the efforts of Narkomfin to oppose the " inflated programmes for capital construction
presented by many organizations ", which could not be carried
out.[3] Nevertheless, supplementary estimates to finance the economy, to the value of nearly 300 million rubles, were added to the
1927–1928 budget between April and September 1928.[4] At the
session of the party central committee in July 1928, Osinsky
strongly criticized the rapid growth in budgetary expenditure,
claiming that " our budget is the budget of a country which is
living beyond its means ".[5] In 1928–1929, after another round of
argument, TsIK resolved on an increase in the budget of 14·3 per
cent, as against an increase in the national income of 10·7 per cent.[6]
Before the end of the economic year, supplementary estimates
amounting to a further 370 million rubles were approved.[7] In each
year, the budget approved by TsIK was substantially larger than the
initial estimates of Narkomfin, and actual expenditure showed a

---

[1] See p. 737 above.
[2] *3 Sessiya Tsentral'nogo Ispolnitel'nogo Komiteta Soyuza SSR 4 Sozyva*
(1928), p. 139.
[3] *Ibid.* p. 238.
[4] *Sobranie Zakonov, 1928*, No. 24, art. 207 ; *Sobranie Zakonov, 1929*, No.
75, art. 721.
[5] Trotsky archives, T 1834 ; for an account of this session see pp. 76–81
above.
[6] *SSSR : Deyatel'nost' SNK i STO : Svodnye Materialy : I Kvartal (Oktyabr'-Dekabr') 1928–29 g.* (1929), p. 43.
[7] *SSSR : Deyatel'nost' SNK i STO : Svodnye Materialy : IV Kvartal
(Iyul'-Sentyabr') 1928–29 g.* (1929), p. 78.

further substantial increase.[1] The increases were partly due
to an initial underestimation of the rate of growth of budgetary
revenue; but in the main they resulted from pressure of the claims
of the economy on budgetary resources.[2] Between 1925–1926 and
1928–1929, state budgetary expenditure increased by 105 per cent
as against an increase in the national income of at most 40 per cent.[3]
The budget thus became increasingly an instrument for financing
industrialization. The following table prepared by Narkomfin shows
the various sources from which capital investment and increases
in working capital in industry were financed (in million rubles):

	1925–1926	1926–1927	1927–1928	1928–1929
Budgetary Allocations	171	487	642	900
Profits and Depreciation				
Allowances	934	1060	1252	1580
Bank Credits	295	423	469	463
Other Sources	170	91	86	100
Total	1570	2061	2449	3043

[1] This is illustrated by the following figures (in million rubles), which,
unlike those in Table No. 41, p. 974 below, include the *gross* expenditure on
transport, posts and state loans (initial estimates of expenditure have not been
traced):

	Initial Estimates of Revenue by Narkomfin	Budget Expenditure Approved by TsIK	Actual Expenditure
1926–1927	4600 [a]	4902 [b]	5179 [c]
1927–1928	5413 [d]	6038 [e]	6353 [f]
1928–1929	?	7682 [c]	8105 [g]

[a] *Torgovo-Promyshlennaya Gazeta*, August 3, 1926.
[b] *Sobranie Zakonov, 1927*, No. 12, art. 119 (February 23, 1927).
[c] *Sobranie Zakonov, 1928*, No. 69, art. 640 (December 15, 1928).
[d] *Torgovo-Promyshlennaya Gazeta*, July 14, 1927.
[e] *Sobranie Zakonov, 1928*, No. 24, art. 207 (April 21, 1928).
[f] *Sobranie Zakonov, 1929*, No. 75, art. 721 (December 8, 1929).
[g] *Sobranie Zakonov, 1931*, No. 5, art. 62 (January 10, 1931).

[2] For the similar tendency to expand the budget in 1923–1924, 1924–1925
and 1925–1926 see *Socialism in One Country, 1924–1926*, Vol. 1, pp. 456–469.

[3] See Table No. 41, p. 974 below; according to the official statistics, the
national income increased in this period by 25 per cent when measured in 1913
prices (see Table No. 45, p. 977 below) and by 41 per cent when measured in
current prices (G. Krzhizhanovsky and others, *Osnovnye Problemy Kontrol'nykh
Tsifr Narodnogo Khozyaistva SSSR na 1929/30 god* (1930), appendix table 1).
The state budget, excluding the self-balancing items transport and posts,
increased between 1925–1926 and 1928–1929 from 12 to 18 per cent of the

The importance of the state budget in financing industry steadily increased, while the relative importance of the internal resources of industry and of bank credits declined. According to the Narkomfin figures, industry made a net payment to the budget in 1925–1926 of 45 million rubles, but in 1928–1929 received a net payment from the budget of 401 million rubles.[1]

This development was reflected in the changing emphasis of official pronouncements on the financing of industry. In April 1926, Stalin included the budget as one item in a list of potential sources of capital accumulation, speaking of " state power which controls the state budget and collects a certain amount of money for the further development of the economy in general and our industry in particular ".[2] The fifteenth party conference of October 1926, while still treating accumulation within industry as of prime importance, nevertheless declared that this " cannot be enough to serve the necessary speed of industrial development, at any rate in the near future ", and added :

> One of the main instruments for the redistribution of the national income is the state budget. In the state budget of the USSR the interests of the industrialization of the country should find full expression.[3]

This view was repeated even more strongly by the fourth Union Congress of Soviets in April 1927.[4] In April 1928, one of the speakers at TsIK declared that the aim should be to achieve " every possible increase in the rôle and proportion of the budget in the national economy of the country " ; [5] and even an official of Narkomfin argued that, in the absence of loans, the budget must be " *the main method of financing industrial capital construction* ".[6]

In spite, however, of this realistic assessment, the compilers

---

national income measured in current prices, while local budgets and social insurance budgets increased from 8 to 10 per cent of the national income.
[1] *Planovoe Khozyaistvo*, No. 3, 1932, p. 150 ; which taxes were assumed to be paid by industry for the purposes of this calculation is not made clear.
[2] Stalin, *Sochineniya*, viii, 125.
[3] *KPSS v Rezolyutsiyakh* (1954), ii, 296.
[4] *S"ezdy Sovetov v Dokumentakh*, iii (1960), 119.
[5] *3 Sessiya Tsentral'nogo Ispolnitel'nogo Komiteta Soyuza SSR 4 Sozyva* (1928), p. 148.
[6] F. D. Lifshits in *Problemy Dolgosrochnogo Kreditovaniya Promyshlennosti*, ed. A. Sokolov (1928), p. 82 ; other Narkomfin officials still strongly contested this view.

of successive drafts of the five-year plan, both in Gosplan and in
Vesenkha, had visions of an industrialization programme financed
primarily from the increased profits of industry itself. Early in
1928, Sabsovich declared that the net allocation of the budget to
industry should be reduced as nearly as possible to zero in the
course of the five years.[1] Later in the year the president of the
budget and financial section of Gosplan declared that by the end
of the first five-year plan the weight of the budgetary system in the
financial system as a whole would decline in view of the growth of
the resources of economic organizations.[2] The first five-year plan, as
adopted in the spring of 1929 by the sixteenth party conference and
the fifth Union Congress of Soviets, still assumed that the profits of
economic enterprises would provide the major source for financing
the economy, and that the rôle of the budget would decline.[3] These
calculations were to prove quite unrealistic; industry became increasingly dependent on the budget throughout the period of the
first five-year plan.

(b) Revenue

It was taken for granted in discussions about the size of the
budget that any increase in budgetary expenditure must be
matched by a corresponding increase in revenue. In the Soviet
Union, as in the rest of the world at that time, a budgetary deficit
was assumed to indicate grave mismanagement of the finances of
the country.[4] In each of the years from 1925–1926 to 1928–1929 a
budgetary surplus was achieved :

State Budget Surplus
(in million rubles)

1925–1926	13
1926–1927	66
1927–1928	204
1928–1929	187 [5]

[1] *Puti Industrializatsii*, No. 2, 1928, p. 56; for Sabsovich see p. 309 above.
[2] M. Bogolepov, *Finansovyi Plan Pyatiletiya* (1929), p. 12.
[3] For the financial aspects of the draft five-year plans see pp. 848-849,
852-853, 856, 863-864, 888, 891 below, and R. W. Davies, *The Development of
the Soviet Budgetary System* (1958), pp. 194-197.
[4] In a discussion at the Communist Academy in September 1926, the
official spokesman indignantly repudiated Sokolnikov's charge that there had been
a budget deficit of 200 million rubles in 1925–1926 instead of the planned surplus
of 117 million rubles (*Vestnik Kommunisticheskoi Akademii*, xvii (1926), 201, 271).
[5] See Tables No. 41 and 42, pp. 974, 975 below. These are revised figures;

To achieve this result in face of the rapid rise in expenditure required a doubling of budgetary revenue between 1925–1926 and 1928–1929. The effort to obtain these large increases finally settled the fate of the traditional socialist policy, to which the party in principle still adhered, of reliance on direct taxation as the main source of budgetary revenue.[1] In February 1924, the second Union Congress of Soviets had stressed the importance of progressive direct taxation,[2] and as recently as April 1925, Sokolnikov, then People's Commissar for Finance, had defended the system of direct taxation as one " which guarantees the possibility of a class approach ".[3] In December 1926, Gosplan suggested that the proportion of direct taxation should be increased in future budgets.[4] For several years Larin continued to campaign for higher taxation of the nepman and the kulah ;[5] and this was a standard theme in the campaigns of the united opposition. Preobrazhensky, in his speech in the budget debate at TsIK in February 1927, argued that the income of the " new bourgeoisie " was rising and was not sufficient.y taxed.[6] The opposition counter-theses on the five-year plan for the fifteenth party congress called for increased taxation of the nepman.[7] But, even though the opposition claims were repudiated, a hankering for direct taxation as a major means of raising revenue was still sometimes expressed. In April 1928, Rykov at the session of TsIK called it a weakness that " elements of direct progressive taxation have so far occupied a small part of the budget " ; the

the official reports on the fulfilment of the budget approved by TsIK at the time showed a substantially higher surplus of 277 million rubles for 1925–1926 and 447 million rubles in 1926–1927 ; in each year these official reports showed a budgetary surplus which was considerably larger than had been planned in the estimates (*Sobranie Zakonov, 1926*, No. 45, art. 323 ; *Sobranie Zakonov, 1927*, No. 12, art. 119 ; *Sobranie Zakonov, 1928*, No. 24, arts. 207, 209 ; No. 69, arts. 638, 640 ; *Sobranie Zakonov, 1929*, No. 75, art. 721 ; *Sobranie Zakonov, 1931*, No. 5, art. 62).

[1] For the earlier stages in this conflict see *The Bolshevik Revolution, 1917–1923*, Vol. 2, p. 141 ; *Socialism in One Country, 1924–1926*, Vol. 1, pp. 458–459, 465-466.

[2] *Vtoroi S"ezd Sovetov SSSR : Postanovleniya* (1924), pp. 12-16.

[3] See *Socialism in One Country, 1924–1926*, Vol. 1, p. 465.

[4] *Torgovo-Promyshlennaya Gazeta*, December 28, 1926.

[5] See p. 737 above.

[6] *SSSR : Tsentral'nyi Ispolnitel'nyi Komitet 3 Sozyva : 3 Sessiya* (1927), p. 767 ; for other aspects of this speech see p. 741 above.

[7] For the counter-theses see p. 36 above.

progressiveness of direct taxation should in future be increased.[1] The compilers of the first five-year plan were on the defensive about " the large rôle of indirect taxation ", but claimed that the direct taxes which were proposed provided " sufficient levers to guarantee the proper class character of the revenue side of the budget ".[2] The weakness of any proposal to increase direct taxation was the absence of wealthy capitalist or landowning classes in the USSR from which substantial revenues could be extracted. In the towns, the main direct taxes introduced or restored in the first years of NEP were the personal income tax, imposed on employers of labour, self-employed persons, and wage-earners, and the industrial tax, imposed on both private and socialized sectors of industry.[3] But direct taxes on the socialized sector were hardly taxes in the sense of an impost by the state on personal incomes.[4] Direct personal taxation could have yielded the large increase in revenue required by the state only if the income tax paid by the mass of wage-earning workers and employees had been substantially increased. This possibility was never seriously discussed ; and in the period from the spring of 1926 to the summer of 1929 the rates of income tax on wage-earners were not increased.[5] Direct taxation was, however, extensively used as a means of squeezing out the nepman. Increased taxation of the nepman was discussed in detail in Narkomfin during the first few months of 1926.[6] On June 18, 1926, a " temporary state tax on excess profits " was introduced. It was to be paid from the second half of the year 1925–1926 onwards by those individuals whose income was four times the exempted minimum, and could rise to a maxi-

[1] 3 Sessiya Tsentral'nogo Ispolnitel'nogo Komiteta Soyuza SSR 4 Sozyva (1928), p. 347.

[2] Pyatiletnii Plan Narodno-Khozyaistvennogo Stroitel'stva SSSR (1929), i, 110.

[3] For the income tax see Socialism in One Country, 1924–1926, Vol. 1, p. 459 ; an income tax was also imposed on the socialized sector of the economy (see R. W. Davies, The Development of the Soviet Budgetary System (1958), pp. 119-120). For the industrial tax see The Bolshevik Revolution, 1917–1923, Vol. 2, p. 347. The main direct taxes in the towns are listed as items 1-5 in Table No. 42, p. 975 below.

[4] The industrial and income taxes on the socialized sector are discussed in relation to other revenues from that sector on pp. 763-764 below.

[5] For state loans from individuals, which became a form of compulsory savings or concealed tax during this period, see pp. 766-770 below.

[6] Vestnik Finansov, No. 1, 1926, pp. 72-77 ; No. 7, 1926, pp. 35-41.

mum of 50 per cent of the income tax for which the individual was liable.[1] In September 1926, a resolution of Sovnarkom and STO again called for a " maximum increase in the taxation of private capital " in the course of 1926–1927.[2] A new statute on personal income tax, approved on September 24, 1926, increased the maximum marginal rate of tax on employers of labour from 30 to 45 per cent, while at the same time reducing the incidence of the tax on self-employed persons with low incomes, and, in certain areas, on employed persons.[3] In addition to the income tax paid to the state budget, local authorities were entitled to impose a surcharge amounting to a maximum of 25 per cent of income tax ; [4] the richer employers of labour continued to be liable to pay excess profits tax amounting to a maximum of 50 per cent of income tax. At the fifteenth party conference in October 1926, Rykov pointed out that the maximum rate of tax on the nepman could now in certain cases amount to as much as 90 per cent of income.[5] The

---

[1] *Sobranie Zakonov, 1926*, No. 42, art. 307.

[2] *SSSR : Svodnye Materialy o Deyatel'nosti Soveta Narodnykh Komissarov i Soveta Truda i Oborony za IV Kvartal (Iyul'-Sentyabr') 1925–26 g.* (1926), p. 70.

[3] *Sobranie Zakonov, 1926*, No. 64, art. 484. The following table shows the amount of income tax collected from the main tax categories in the year preceding and the year following the reform :

	1925–1926		1926–1927	
	Number of Persons Taxed (thousands)	Amount Paid (million rubles)	Number of Persons Taxed (thousands)	Amount Paid (million rubles)
Manual and Office-workers	805	2·5	775	13·5
Self-employed	1,050	12·0	418	18·0
Employers in Trade and Industry	477	68·0	380	105·0
Total	2,332	82·5	1,573	136·5

(*Finansy SSSR za XXX Let 1917–1947*, ed. N. Rovinsky (1947), pp. 253-254 ; *SSSR : Ot S"ezda k S"ezdu (Aprel' 1927 g.–Mai 1929 g.)* (1929), p. 66 ; G. Sokolnikov and others, *Soviet Policy in Public Finance, 1917–1928* (Stanford, 1931), p. 174) ; these figures differ slightly from those in Table No. 42, p. 975 below. The larger amount paid by manual and office workers in 1926–1927 is presumably due to rises in money incomes which resulted in an increase in the proportion of the income of the more highly-paid worker liable to taxation.

[4] *Sobranie Zakonov, 1926*, No. 31, art. 198 (dated April 25).

[5] *XV Konferentsiya Vsesoyuznoi Kommunisticheskoi Partii (B)* (1927), p. 130 ; the figure of 90 per cent was based on the assumption, which Rykov

highest rate of tax was, however, paid by only a small minority of private capitalists, and then only on a part of their income : the average rate of tax paid by private employers, excluding the local addition of up to 25 per cent, amounted in 1926–1927 to about 11 per cent of assessed income.[1] In November 1927 the opposition in its counter-theses on the five-year plan proposed that the taxes on the excess profits of private *entrepreneurs* should be increased by 150-200 million rubles a year ; Mezhlauk retorted that the capitalist elements from which the opposition wanted to extract this sum were being steadily driven out of the economy, and quoted Narkomfin statistics purporting to show that the total accumulation of private *entrepreneurs* did not now exceed 200-250 million rubles a year.[2] A month later, on December 14, 1927, a further statute on the income tax increased the maximum rate of tax on personal income payable by employers of more than two persons from 45 to 54 per cent.[3]

Apart from personal income tax, the other main form of tax on the private businessman was the industrial tax, imposed on the value of the turnover of trade and industry : in 1925–1926, 109 million out of the 349 million rubles collected in industrial tax came from the private sector. Though some minor changes were made in the industrial tax in September 1926,[4] the tax was still

---

did not explain, that the local authorities could impose a surcharge as high as 50 per cent on income tax.
    [1] In 1926–1927 the tax paid by different income groups of employers was as follows :

Annual Income (rubles)	Number of Tax-payers (thousands)	Income Taxed (million rubles)	Tax Paid (million rubles)
1000 or less	124	93	3
1000-5000	219	480	29
5000-10,000	28	190	27
10,000-20,000	8	97	22
20,000 and over	2	70	24
Total	380	930	105

(G. Sokolnikov and others, *Soviet Policy in Public Finance, 1917–1928* (Stanford, 1931), p. 174).
    [2] The counter-theses and Mezhlauk's article both appeared in *Pravda*, November 17, 1927, *Diskussionyi Listok*, No. 5 ; for the counter-theses see p. 36 above.   [3] *Sobranie Zakonov, 1928*, No. 1, art. 2.
    [4] *Sobranie Zakonov, 1926*, No. 63, art. 474 (dated September 24).

strongly criticized as being insufficiently discriminatory against the private sector. At the session of TsIK in February 1927, Bryukhanov admitted that the effect of the changes had in fact been to reduce the relative rate of tax on the private sector ; whereas the private trader had paid tax at two-and-a-half times the rate payable by the state trading organizations, he now paid only twice the rate.[1] A year later, the budget commission of TsIK recommended that the rate of tax on the private sector should be raised.[2] When the tax was reformed on August 10, 1928, the rate of tax imposed on both private and socialized trade and industry was substantially increased.[3]

Legislation imposing higher rates of tax on the nepman could be effective only if it was accompanied by measures to enforce the collection of the tax. Resolutions of the fifteenth party conference of October 1926 and of the session of TsIK in February 1927 criticized the under-assessment of tax in the private sector and called for a strengthening of the tax collecting machinery.[4] A drive to collect tax from private businessmen more efficiently or more ruthlessly formed part of the general offensive against private capital which began in the summer of 1927.[5] After a relaxation of pressure in the winter of 1927–1928 the tax drive was again intensified in the autumn of 1928. One study listed the devices by which private traders had evaded tax pressure, and complained of the " mass " corruption of Narkomfin officials.[6] But the drive against the nepman, of which discriminatory taxation formed a part, automatically eliminated the sources of income on which the taxes were imposed. In 1927–1928, as a result of the increased rates of tax, revenue from direct taxation was greater than in the previous

---

[1] *SSSR : Tsentral'nyi Ispolnitel'nyi Komitet 3 Sozyva : 3 Sessiya* (1927), pp. 534-535.

[2] *3 Sessiya Tsentral'nogo Ispolnitel'nogo Komiteta Soyuza SSR 4 Sozyva* (1928), p. 54.

[3] *Sobranie Zakonov, 1928*, No. 50, arts. 442, 443 ; *4 Sessiya Tsentral'nogo Ispolnitel'nogo Komiteta Soyuza SSR 4 Sozyva* (1928), No. 1, pp. 17-18. For other forms of tax discrimination against the private businessman introduced between 1927 and 1929 see R. W. Davies, *The Development of the Soviet Budgetary System* (1958), pp. 111-112.

[4] For these developments see *ibid.* pp. 112-113.

[5] *3 Sessiya Tsentral'nogo Ispolnitel'nogo Komiteta Soyuza SSR 4 Sozyva* (1928), pp. 243-244.

[6] A. Fabrichny, *Chastnyi Kapital na Poroge Pyatiletki* (1930), pp. 41-45 ; the devices included taking out licences in another person's name, changing the name of the firm, and dividing capital among relatives.

year ; but it fell short of the estimate owing to the decline in the number and activity of private firms.[1] In the first quarter of 1928–1929, only 30 million rubles were collected from the private sector instead of the 60 million rubles estimated ; the total taxable private turnover, which was expected to decline by 25 per cent in the first six months of 1928–1929, in fact fell by 40-45 per cent.[2] The total amount collected from personal income tax and from industrial tax on the private sector did not exceed 7 per cent of budgetary revenue throughout this period.[3]

Apart from the wage-earner and the nepman in the towns, the other main potential source of direct taxation was the peasant. In the period from 1924–1925 to 1926–1927 the money incomes of the peasantry increased rapidly, both absolutely and as a proportion of total personal income, though peasant income per head remained far below urban incomes.[4] In the spring of 1925, when the policy of conciliating the peasant was at its height, the fourteenth party conference decided to reduce the absolute amount of the agricultural tax, the only major direct tax on the peasant, for the year 1925–1926 ; and the provisions of the tax law for that year were strongly criticized as tending to favour the better-off peasant.[5] In the event, the actual amount collected in 1925–1926, 252 million rubles, was less even than the 280 million rubles planned, and represented a substantial easing of the burden of

[1] SSSR : Ot S"ezda k S"ezdu (Aprel' 1927 g.–Mai 1929 g.) (1929), p. 61.

[2] SSSR : Deyatel'nost' SNK i STO : Svodnye Materialy : I Kvartal (Oktyabr'-Dekabr') 1928–29 g. (1929), p. 55 ; II Kvartal (Yanvar'-Mart) 1928–29 g. (1929), p. 47.

[3] The following table shows the approximate amounts collected each year from the private sector (in million rubles). The 1928–1929 figure of industrial tax is not comparable with that for the previous years ; in 1928–1929, local additions were for the first time incorporated in the industrial tax included in the revenue of the state budget :

	1925–1926	1926–1927	1927–1928	1928–1929
Personal Income Tax	86	114	153	166
Tax on Excess Profits	—	11	22	19
Industrial Tax on Private Sector	94	109	86	170

(For sources see Table No. 42, p. 975 below ; SSSR : Deyatel'nost' SNK i STO : Svodnye Materialy : IV Kvartal 1928–29 g. (1929), p. 74.)

[4] See table in Kontrol'nye Tsifry Narodnogo Khozyaistva SSSR na 1927–1928 g. (1928), p. 548.

[5] See Socialism in One Country, 1924–1926, Vol. I, pp. 265, 269-270 ; agricultural tax is listed as item 6 in Table No. 42, p. 975 below.

direct taxation on the peasant.[1] In the winter of 1925–1926, the
future of the tax was thoroughly discussed. The discussion turned
on the question whether the tax could be so constructed as to
discriminate against the *kulak* and assist the poor peasant, while
at the same time encouraging the development of the peasant
economy. The difficulty of the problem was greatly increased by
the complexity of assessing and collecting the tax from 25 million
peasant households, which received their income from a variety of
sources, and in which the head of the household was often illiterate.
Narkomfin had established by 1926 an elaborate network for tax
assessment and collection. The principal tax agencies were the
village Soviet and the executive committee (ispolkom) of the rural
district (volost') Soviet. Under the guidance of the rural district
ispolkom, the village Soviet compiled " a household register "
which showed the liability of each household for taxation ; on the
basis of this register tax assessments prepared by the rural district
ispolkom were distributed to each household. A " tax commission " of every rural district ispolkom granted exemptions and
considered complaints from the peasant : it included representatives of the higher county agricultural and financial agencies, and
two representatives of the peasantry.[2] But statistical and tax
machinery was not equal to the task of assessing the income of each
household individually ; and in 1925–1926, as in previous years,
the unit of taxation was a desyatin of land, into which cattle and
horses were converted at conventional rates.

The main outlines of a reform in the tax were approved in a
decision of Sovnarkom in March 1926 on the method of assessment to be used in the collection of the tax in 1926–1927. The
tax was to be imposed on assessed income and not, as hitherto, on
units of land ; earnings from subsidiary occupations were to be

[1] See table in R. W. Davies, *The Development of the Soviet Budgetary
System* (1958), p. 82. The amount collected in 1924–1925 was 326 million
rubles, and represented a substantially higher proportion of the money income
of the peasantry (see p. 758, note 5 below).
[2] *Sobranie Zakonov, 1925*, No. 31, art. 209 (dated May 7) ; one of the
peasants was to be chosen by the rural district committee of peasant aid ; the
other place was filled in turn by a representative of each village Soviet as the
taxation for the village was considered. Special commissions were also formed
at the province and county levels ; according to *Derevenskii Kommunist*, No.
17 (113), September 14, 1929, p. 27, the village Soviet also in theory had such a
commission, but the work was in practice done by the secretary of the Soviet.

included in taxable income ; the tax was to be made more progressive.[1] At the session of the party central committee in April
1926, Trotsky was joined by Kamenev in advocating a more progressive agricultural tax ; the committee, while formally rejecting
Trotsky's amendments, also approved the decision of Sovnarkom
to reform the tax.[2] In the same month, Bryukhanov presented to
a session of TsIK detailed proposals which would " amount to a
change in the whole existing system of the agricultural tax " ; [3]
they were subsequently endorsed by the session.[4] The change in
the method of assessment to an " income " basis was a change in
form rather than in content : the tax continued to be assessed on
a conventional " norm " of income, and not on the actual income
of each household. A " norm " of income for each desyatin of
land worked, and each horse and cow held, by an average peasant
household was fixed for each republic by the TsIK of the USSR on
the basis of information about the average income of the peasantry
over several years, and then used by the local Soviets to calculate
a hypothetical income for each household. The income thus calculated was divided by the number of members of the household,
as the land units had previously been, to obtain the income per
head.[5] A great deal was still left to the discretion of the local
authorities. The Union republics were permitted to apply different
income-norms to different provinces, provided that the overall
assessed income for the republic as a whole remained unchanged ;
and a similar right of adjustment was given to the provincial
authorities. The province decided whether to make liable for
tax non-agricultural earnings and such previously untaxed agricultural activities as pig-farming and bee-keeping, and fixed the
norms of income for these purposes. Practice must have varied
greatly in different areas. But the regulations themselves con-

[1] See *Socialism in One Country, 1924–1926*, Vol. 1, p. 320.

[2] See *ibid.* Vol. 1, pp. 326-327 ; according to Kraval, a " prominent opposi-
tionist " proposed at the Aviapribor meeting on October 1, 1926, to raise
taxes on the peasantry from 300 to 600 million rubles (*Torgovo-Promyshlennaya
Gazeta*, October 10, 1928 ; for this meeting see pp. 286-287 above).

[3] *SSSR : Tsentral'nyi Ispolnitel'nyi Komitet 3 Sozyva : 2 Sessiya* (1926),
p. 640.

[4] *Sobranie Zakonov, 1926*, No. 30, art. 192 (dated April 25, 1926).

[5] In the Ukraine, the income of the whole household was taken as the basis
for the tax, and a fixed sum out of this income was exempted from tax for each
member of the household (see p. 758, note 5 below).

tained an inherent arbitrary element in the assessment of income. Within each rural district, all peasants were assumed to obtain the same income from one horse, one cow or one desyatin of land : this favoured the more efficient, whose land was more productive and whose cattle were of higher quality.[1] The rate of progression of the tax was, however, sharply increased in April 1926 : the maximum marginal rate was 25 per cent, and the rates of tax on the lower income groups were reduced.[2] The increased progression of the tax was primarily responsible for the increase in the total amount of tax in 1926–1927. The tax was expected to yield 300 million rubles against 250 million rubles collected in 1925–1926. In the outcome this proved to have been an underestimate ; 358 million rubles were in fact collected.[3]

The agricultural tax law for 1927–1928, adopted on April 2, 1927, made no significant change either in the total amount of tax or in its progression.[4] Failure to make the tax more progressive was once more strongly criticized by the united opposition, which argued in the " declaration of the 83 " in May 1927 that the proposal of the opposition to relieve 50 per cent of peasant households of agricultural tax, thus doubling the 25 per cent so far exempt, was proving more and more justified.[5] The opposition platform of September 1927 claimed that " the agricultural tax in the village is imposed, as a general rule, in an inverse progression : heavy upon the weak, lighter upon the strong and upon the *kulak* ".[6] In

---

[1] *Na Agrarnom Fronte*, No. 11-12, 1926, pp. 159-160 ; later examples are given in *ibid*. No. 2, 1928, pp. 3-10.

[2] See tables illustrating the change in incidence of taxation in different areas in *Vestnik Finansov*, No. 4, 1927, pp. 8-10.

[3] See R. W. Davies, *The Development of the Soviet Budgetary System* (1958), p. 82.

[4] *Sobranie Zakonov, 1927*, No. 17, art. 189. Local authorities were encouraged, however, to increase the assessment of non-agricultural earnings of better-off households liable to tax. Some partial data appear to show that in 1927–1928 a large part of the difference between the assessed incomes of middle and upper peasant income groups was due to the much higher value at which non-agricultural earnings were assessed in the upper income groups (*Vestnik Finansov*, No. 6, 1929, pp. 104-105).

[5] For this declaration see pp. 24-25 above.

[6] L. Trotsky, *The Real Situation in Russia* (n.d. [1928]), p. 28 ; according to the platform, poor peasants, constituting 34 per cent of all peasants, received 18 per cent of all net income and paid 20 per cent of the total tax, while the highest group, containing 7·5 per cent of the peasants, also received 18 per cent of all net income and paid 20 per cent of the total tax.

the opposition counter-theses of October 1927, a proposal was made to supplement the agricultural tax with an obligatory grain loan, levied on the " well-to-do or *kulak* households ", and amounting to 150 or 200 million puds.[1] The October manifesto of TsIK went part of the way to meet the criticism that poor peasants were taxed too heavily ; it announced a decision to increase the number of households exempt from agricultural tax by a further 10 per cent, making 35 per cent in all ; [2] but throughout the year 1927 no official attempt was made to increase the incidence of the tax on the upper groups of the peasantry.

From the beginning of 1928, the atmosphere changed. The " extraordinary measures " were accompanied by an attempt to speed up the collection of agricultural tax ; and the view that the incidence of the tax on the well-to-do must be sharply increased now became a commonplace. Stalin, in his instruction of February 13, 1928, condemned the " insufficiency " of the agricultural tax, and called for further pressure to collect tax debts from the well-to-do peasants.[3] Articles now began to appear which purported to show that *kulaks* had not been sufficiently taxed.[4] The new approach was confirmed by the party central committee in April 1928 ; [5] and on April 21, 1928, TsIK approved a tax law for 1928–1929 which took several important steps to increase the rate of tax on the upper groups of the peasantry. First, the maximum rate of tax was raised from 25 to 30 per cent. Secondly, each republic was to estimate the total income received in each province by peasant households whose incomes were above a stated sum, and then to impose a surcharge (nadbavka) on the province varying between 5 and 25 per cent of the tax due from this group ; the surcharge was to be allocated among the top 10 or 12 per cent of households by the provincial authorities concerned. The rural

---

[1] For the counter-theses see p. 34 above.
[2] For this manifesto see p. 33 above.
[3] Stalin, *Sochineniya*, xi, 14, 18 ; for this instruction see pp. 51-52 above. Mikoyan declared a few months later that " we made a colossal mistake in leaving the tax unchanged for the upper strata of the village " ; dissatisfaction had been produced by unnecessary taxation of the poor and middle peasant (*XLI Sobranie Upolnomochennykh Tsentrosoyuza* (1928), p. 288).
[4] An article in *Na Agrarnom Fronte*, No. 2, 1928, pp. 3-10, listed methods which favoured well-to-do peasants, and pointed out that, as long as assessment was collective not individual, it was difficult to penalize them.
[5] *KPSS v Rezolyutsiyakh* (1954), ii, 494, 498.

district might also withdraw from well-to-do households exemptions hitherto accorded in virtue of the number of members of the household. Thirdly, the incomes of the top 2 or 3 per cent of households were to be individually assessed by the local tax commissions.[1] A tax official later summarized all these measures as follows :

> In constructing the tax law, we started from the point that, in addition to the 35 per cent of households freed from tax, about a further 20 per cent of peasant households would pay a somewhat reduced tax in comparison with the previous year. The increase in tax for the remaining households was to begin with minimum amounts and rise for the highest groups to an increase of 80-90 per cent.[2]

As a result of these changes, the total amount of tax to be collected in 1928–1929 was estimated at 400 million rubles, an increase of one-third on the estimates for 1927–1928. In the autumn of 1928, when the tax campaign began, fears were expressed that tax pressure was being applied too rigorously to the upper strata of the peasantry. In a speech to the Moscow Soviet on September 18, 1928, Kalinin complained that "many local organs have understood the new law as implying dekulakization ", and declared that the Soviet government did not want the tax campaign to lead to the destruction of *kulak* farms.[3] At the party central committee in November 1928, Stalin complained that, in spite of the Politburo decision that only 2-3 per cent of households should be individually assessed, in many areas 10, 12 or more per cent of households had been assessed individually, thus damaging relations with the middle peasants ; he condemned this as a " crime ".[4] During the course of the winter of 1928–1929, in a number of areas the initial taxes on the upper groups and the

---

[1] *Sobranie Zakonov, 1928*, No. 24, art. 212 ; *Finansy i Kredit SSSR*, ed. V. Dyachenko and G. Kozlov (1938), p. 140 ; *SSSR : Ot S"ezda k S"ezdu (Aprel' 1927 g.–Mai 1929 g.)* (1929), pp. 67-68.

[2] *Vestnik Finansov*, No. 2, 1929, p. 24.

[3] *Pravda*, September 23, 1928 ; see also editorial *ibid.* September 25, 1928. According to *Vestnik Finansov*, No. 2, 1929, p. 39, as a result of " mistakes and distortions " which were reported " from the end of July and particularly in August " 1928, directives were issued at the beginning of September 1928 forbidding the individual assessment of middle-peasant households and of any household which did not have income of an exploiting character, and restricting the total tax in every province to 50 per cent above the 1927–1928 level.

[4] Stalin, *Sochineniya*, xi, 264-265.

number of households individually assessed were reduced.[1] It
was reported that on average only 1·7 per cent of households had
in fact been individually assessed, but that a survey had shown that
the tax on this group had been increased by a total of 178 per cent.[2]
At the sixteenth party conference in April 1929, Kalinin complained of " excesses " in individual assessment which had to some
extent recalled a " landlord's approach " (barskii podkhod) :

> A man pays 100 rubles in tax and is assessed for another 100
> rubles by individual assessment. The man naturally crawls to
> the wall.[3]

The excesses were attributed to the failure of local Soviets to apply
the law correctly, and to the failure of Narkomfin and of provincial
presidents of Soviets and party secretaries to put things right.[4]
The total tax collected in 1928–1929 was eventually reported at
449 million rubles against the estimate of 400 millions ; even so,
the agricultural tax was believed to constitute a smaller proportion
of the total money income of the peasantry in 1928–1929 than in
1924–1925.[5] In December 1928, a proposal to increase the agricultural tax and reduce the tax on vodka was rejected ; [6] and on

[1] *Vestnik Finansov*, No. 2, 1929, pp. 39-40.
[2] According to incomplete and preliminary data, the 1·7 per cent of households which were individually assessed paid 15·8 per cent of the total tax while
a further 10·5 per cent were subject to the surcharge and paid 39·1 per cent of
the total tax (*Vestnik Finansov*, No. 2, 1929, pp. 24-26).
[3] *Shestnadtsataya Konferentsiya VKP(B)* (1962), p. 286.
[4] *Ibid.* p. 287 ; N. Bryukhanov, *Khozyaistvennyi Pod"em Sovetskogo
Soyuza i ego Finansovaya Baza* (1929), pp. 25-28.
[5] In April 1928, Kalinin estimated that the agricultural tax would amount
to 7·4 per cent of the total money income of the peasantry in 1928–1929 against
10·6 per cent in 1924–1925, 5·8 per cent in 1925–1926, 7·1 per cent in 1926–1927
and 6·0 per cent in 1927–1928 (*3 Sessiya Tsentral'nogo Ispolnitel'nogo Komiteta
Soyuza SSR 4 Sozyva* (1928), p. 408). Analysis of the effects of the tax changes
in 1928–1929 is particularly difficult because of the simultaneous decision to
adopt throughout most of the USSR the practice introduced in the Ukraine
in 1926–1927 of taxing households not on a " per head " basis but on a " per
household " basis (see p. 754, note 5 above). The effect of the new system in
practice was to increase the rate of taxation on larger households, and thus
encourage the division of households (in cases cited in *Na Agrarnom Fronte*,
No. 11, 1928, pp. 20-21, the amount of tax could be reduced by 60-100 per cent
by splitting the household) ; in November 1928 the party central committee
issued a warning that changes in the tax " should not encourage the fragmenta-
tion of households ", but without practical result (*KPSS v Rezolyutsiyakh*
(1954), ii, 534).
[6] N. Bryukhanov, *Khozyaistvennyi Pod"em Sovetskogo Soyuza i ego Finansovaya Baza* (1929), pp. 25-28.

February 8, 1929 a decree provided for a reduction of the agricultural tax for 1929–1930 to 375 million rubles.[1] In the whole
period from 1926 to 1929, the increasingly vigorous efforts of the
Soviet authorities to tax the upper groups of the peasantry were
accompanied by great reluctance to raise the level of direct taxation on the peasantry as a whole.[2]

The other major form of taxation — indirect taxes or excise
duties — was throughout these years the subject of bitter controversy.[3] The retention or even the increase of excise duties had
long been advocated by many economists and officials.[4] But
excise duties were open to strong social and political objections.
They were unambiguously a tax on the consumer, and could most
easily be imposed on mass consumer goods for which demand was
not very elastic — tobacco, sugar, and above all vodka. A large
part of budgetary revenue had come from these sources before the
revolution, and the Bolsheviks had played their part with other
opponents of the Tsarist régime in condemning this practice. The
case for reducing excise rates was strongly argued at successive
sessions of TsIK. In February 1927, Ryazanov demanded that
the excise duties on tea and sugar should be abolished, pointing
out that the excise on tea had not been introduced until October
1916.[5] Such proposals were usually rejected on the grounds that
the commodity concerned was in short supply, so that the abolition
of the tax would merely increase the profits of the private trader.[6]
But excise policy continued to be a sensitive topic. The authorities
indignantly repudiated documents said to have been circulated in

[1] *Sobranie Zakonov, 1929*, No. 10, art. 95 ; R. W. Davies, *The Development
of the Soviet Budgetary System* (1958), p. 116, mistakenly assumed that the
proposed reduction related to the financial year 1928–1929.
[2] For state loans from the peasantry, which in part became compulsory
during this period, see pp. 767–770 below.
[3] The revenue from excise duties is set out by major products in Table No.
43, p. 976 below ; excise and customs duties, the two main forms of indirect
taxation, are listed as items 7 and 8 in Table 42, p. 975 below.
[4] See *Socialism in One Country, 1924–1926*, Vol. 1, p. 466 ; *Planovoe
Khozyaistvo*, No. 1, 1926, p. 104 ; *Plenum Byudzhetnoi Komissii TsIK Soyuza
SSR* (1927), pp. 307-308.
[5] *SSSR ; Tsentral'nyi Ispolnitel'nyi Komitet 3 Sozyva : 3 Sessiya* (1927),
pp. 701-703.
[6] *Ibid.* pp. 536-537 ; *Plenum Byudzhetnoi Komissii TsIK Soyuza SSR*
(1927), pp. 159, 310.

Narkomfin in the autumn of 1928, proposing that financial stability should be maintained in 1928–1929 by increasing excise duties and railway charges by four or five hundred million rubles.[1]

The excise on vodka was by far the most important means of indirect taxation, and met with most public criticism. At a session of TsIK in April 1926, Bryukhanov reported that the question had been discussed " by all organs, from the smallest village Soviet to the central executive committee ", and that the government " became convinced in practice that the struggle against alcoholism cannot be carried on by a simple system of suppression " ; the only result would be to enrich " *kulaks*, middle-men and village leeches ".[2] The opposition platform of September 1927 rejected the state sale of vodka as " completely unsuccessful ", arguing that the losses to industry from " idle days, careless workmanship, defective products, broken machines, increased industrial accidents, fires, fights, injuries, etc." were as great as the revenue accruing to the budget;[3] and the opposition counter-theses of October 1927 proposed " the ending of the state sale of vodka in the shortest possible time (2-3 years) ".[4] In the same month, Stalin told a French workers' delegation that the vodka monopoly was essential as an alternative to foreign loans, adding :

> Vodka now gives us more than 500 million rubles in revenue. To give up vodka at present would mean to give up this revenue ; but there are no grounds for believing that alcoholism would be less, because the peasant would begin to produce his own vodka, poisoning himself with *samogon* (home-distilled spirit).

He conceded, however, that as other sources of revenue grew the production of vodka should gradually be reduced and then cease altogether.[5] At the session of TsIK in April 1928, the budget commission recommended that the state sale of vodka should not

[1] G. Krzhizhanovsky and others, *Osnovnye Problemy Kontrol'nykh Tsifr Narodnogo Khozyaistva na 1928/29 god* (1929), pp. 111-112.
[2] *SSSR : Tsentral'nyi Ispolnitel'nyi Komitet 3 Sozyva : 2 Sessiya* (1926), p. 24 ; three years later, he repeated the same argument (N. Bryukhanov, *Khozyaistvennyi Pod"em Sovetskogo Soyuza i ego Finansovaya Baza* (1929), p. 31).   [3] L. Trotsky, *The Real Situation in Russia* (n.d. [1928]), p. 91.
[4] For the counter-theses see p. 34 above.
[5] Stalin, *Sochineniya*, x, 232-233 ; a month later, at the fifteenth party congress, he suggested that the vodka duty should be replaced by such sources of revenue as the radio and the cinema (*ibid.* x, 312).

be increased in 1928–1929, and should then be reduced ; [1] the
party central committee at its session in July 1928 called for " a
persistent struggle against *samogon* ".[2]

The extent and notoriety of the effects of vodka were responsible
for many troubled consciences in the party. A woman factory
worker from Ivanovo-Voznesensk spoke at the session of TsIK in
April 1928 of " drunkenness and the most frightful hooliganism ",
of " bestial murders " in her small town, and complained that
" drunken hooligans stop us walking down the street " ; [3] another
delegate to TsIK reported that in one village on a holiday nearly
all the peasants had been drunk all day long.[4] At the fifth Union
Congress of Soviets in May 1929, the number of arrests for
drunkenness in Moscow was reported to have increased from
36,000 in 1926 to 122,000 in 1928.[5] The argument that any
reduction in the amount of state-distilled spirit would merely
lead to an increase in the distilling of *samogon* was constantly
invoked. On March 2, 1929, the presidium of Gosplan pointed
out that production by the state had failed to drive out *samogon* :
according to surveys by Narkomfin experts between 320 and 480
million litres of *samogon* had been consumed in the Soviet countryside in 1924–1925, while in 1927–1928 an investigation by the
Central Statistical Administration revealed that 600 million litres
of *samogon* had been consumed in the RSFSR alone.[6] In 1928

  [1] *3 Sessiya Tsentral'nogo Ispolnitel'nogo Komiteta Soyuza SSR 4 Sozyva*
(1928), pp. 54-55, 86-87.   [2] *KPSS v Rezolyutsiyakh* (1954), ii, 516.
  [3] *3 Sessiya Tsentral'nogo Ispolnitel'nogo Komiteta Soyuza SSR 4 Sozyva*
(1928), pp. 58-59.   [4] *Ibid.* p. 207.
  [5] *SSSR : 5 S"ezd Sovetov* (1929), No. 13, p. 23. Nearly 90 per cent of
those arrested for drunkenness in Moscow and Leningrad were workers ;
nearly 10 per cent were party members ; the number of drunks " unable to
reach home " in Leningrad was said to have been twice as great in 1927–1928
as in pre-revolutionary Russia. In other large towns, however, only half the
pre-war quantity of vodka was sold by the state in that year (G. Sokolnikov and
others, *Soviet Policy in Public Finance, 1917–1928* (Stanford, 1931), p. 197).
  [6] *SSSR : 5 S"ezd Sovetov* (1929), No. 13, pp. 23-24. For contradictory
evidence see G. Sokolnikov and others, *Soviet Policy in Public Finance, 1917–
1928* (Stanford, 1931), p. 197 ; an article by the president of Tsentrospirt
claimed that, while *samogon* used up 50 per cent more grain than factory-
distilled vodka, consumption had been reduced to between 1 and 3 litres per
head a year according to the region, as compared with 6 litres before the war
(*Bednota*, February 3, 1928). Such figures seem to have been the product of
guess-work or wishful thinking. In a note to the Politburo in June 1928 Stalin
remarked that " the struggle against *samogon* started in January of this year "
(Stalin, *Sochineniya*, xi, 125).

and 1929 the rate of excise on vodka and beer was substantially increased, even though the excise on vodka was already a much higher proportion of cost than in 1913.[1] Statements of an intention to reduce state sales of vodka continued to be made.[2] The first five-year plan provided for a reduction in the consumption of vodka in the five-year period by 17·9 per cent (basic variant) by 35·7 per cent (optimum variant). The brunt of the reduction was to fall on the towns ; consumption in the countryside was actually to rise by 5 per cent in the basic variant, and decline by no more than 10 per cent in the optimum variant.[3] But, whatever the value of these prognostications or promises, the fact remained that the revenue from vodka had increased steadily throughout the period from 1926 to 1929, as a result both of an increase in excise rates and of an increase in sales more rapid than that of any other major commodity. In 1928–1929, the revenue from spirits, wines and beer was over two-and-a-half times as large as in 1925–1926.

Excise revenue from other commodities rose more slowly ; the increase between 1925–1926 and 1928–1929 averaged only 71 per cent. This increase was due to rising sales rather than to increased rates of taxation. Between 1925 and 1929 the rates charged on sugar and kerosene did not increase ; and on April 2, 1927, the excise duty on salt, which had incurred particularly strong criticism, was abolished.[4] The rates of excise on tobacco and cigarettes were increased on April 20, 1926, but further proposals for increases in the autumn of that year were not adopted.[5] In the

---

[1] *Finansovaya Entsiklopediya*, ed. G. Sokolnikov and others (1927), cols. 1009-1010 ; *Sobranie Zakonov, 1928*, No. 16, art. 131 ; No. 54, art. 483 ; *Sobranie Zakonov, 1929*, No. 10, art. 94 ; G. Sokolnikov and others, *Soviet Policy in Public Finance, 1917–1928* (Stanford, 1931), pp. 198-199. The excise on vodka rose from 14·96 rubles per *vedro* in 1925–1926 to 23 rubles per *vedro* in February 1929. In 1913 the excise had been 52 per cent of the retail price of 8·53 rubles ; in 1925–1926 it was 69 per cent of the retail price of 21·76 rubles.

[2] *Pravda*, May 6, 1929, announced that they were to be reduced by 20 per cent in the second half of 1928–1929.

[3] *Pyatiletnii Plan Narodno-Khozyaistvennogo Stroitel'stva SSSR* (1929), ii, ii, 337 ; an earlier draft of the plan had apparently contemplated an increase in production from 31·5 million *vedra* in 1926–1927 to 68 millions in 1930–1931 (*Pravda*, August 19, 31, October 4, 1928).

[4] See *Socialism in One Country, 1924–1926*, Vol. 1, p. 465, note 3 ; *Sobranie Zakonov, 1927*, No. 18, art. 195. The excise duty on coffee was also abolished, but a higher customs duty was introduced simultaneously.

[5] *Sobranie Zakonov, 1926*, No. 56, art. 408 ; *Torgovo-Promyshlennaya Gazeta*, November 5, 1926.

years from 1925–1926 to 1928–1929, revenue from excises increased in every year at a higher rate than budgetary revenue
as a whole, and at 1796 million rubles in 1928–1929 was more than
twice as large as in 1925–1926. This expansion, which was far
more rapid than even optimists had predicted,[1] was primarily due
to the increase in the revenue from spirits, wine and beer, which
rose from 43 per cent of the total revenue from excises in 1925–
1926 to 54 per cent in 1928–1929.

A further important source of budgetary revenue was provided by deductions from the profits of state enterprises. Although
these payments were in effect a tax on profits, they were classified
under the heading " non-tax revenue ".[2] Some Soviet economists
set great store by non-tax revenue as a means of solving the problem of increasing budgetary revenue. In November 1926, Strumilin declared at a session of Gosplan that budgetary policy must be
directed towards increasing non-tax revenue, because it was
received from the producer rather than the consumer ; [3] and a
month later at a session of Sovnarkom and STO Bryukhanov also
declared that the proportion of non-tax revenue should increase in
future budgets.[4] Others suggested that in circumstances in which
prices, incomes and taxes were planned by the state, no special
significance could be attached to deductions from profits and other
non-tax revenues. Deductions from profits, the industrial tax
which state enterprises paid on their turnover, the income tax on
state enterprises, and excises were all seen as performing similar
functions as instruments of the state. This view was maintained
by Rykov at the session of TsIK in April 1928 :

---

[1] The second Gosplan draft of the five-year plan completed in the spring of
1927 (see pp. 854-856 below) expected the excise revenue in the economic
year 1930–1931 would be only 1568 million rubles (*Vestnik Finansov*, No. 8,
1927, p. 64).
[2] Deductions from profits were paid by state industrial and trading enterprises, and by Gosbank and the special banks. Other " non-tax revenue "
included various payments for the use of natural resources owned by the state,
especially forests (stumpage and other fees) and ores ; these payments were
primarily made by state organizations. Non-tax revenue is listed as items 10
and 11 in Table No. 42, p. 975 below.
[3] *Torgovo-Promyshlennaya Gazeta*, November 23, 1926.
[4] *Ibid.* December 28, 1926.

In our conditions there is no great distinction of principle between non-tax and tax revenue. . . . Is there a great difference whether we receive ½ or ¼ kopek of profit per arshin of calico or the same ½ or ¼ kopek by indirect tax, by excise ? I think there is no difference here. In bourgeois countries this difference exists because there taxes go to the budget, and the incomes of industry to the capitalists. With us, from the point of view of the redistribution of the national income, there is no difference. We fix both prices and taxes ourselves. In just the same way, the system of prices is a means of redistributing the national income.[1]

Whatever the ultimate validity of these arguments, the different forms of revenue affected the financial situation in different ways. If increases in deductions from profit or industrial tax were passed on to the consumer in the form of price increases, they were certainly taxes on consumption scarcely distinguishable from excises.[2] But, if the state successfully maintained its controls over the prices paid to industry, then increases in revenue from these sources would represent merely a book-keeping transaction between the state enterprise and the budget ; the rôle of the budget would be at best to transfer resources from non-priority state enterprises to priority state enterprises, and at worst to take with one hand and pay back with the other. In the period from 1925–1926 to 1928–1929, a substantial and increasing proportion of the net income of state enterprises was in fact transferred to the budget ; [3] as a result, the ratio of these items to total budgetary revenue increased.[4]

[1] 3 Sessiya Tsentral'nogo Ispolnitel'nogo Komiteta Soyuza SSR 4 Sozyva (1928), p. 346 ; see also Puti Industrializatsii, No. 4, 1928, p. 51.

[2] A financial official claimed that in practice the industrial tax " as a general rule is transferred to the consumer . . . in essence, the industrial tax has the same character of a tax on consumption as excise duties " (Vestnik Finansov, No. 8, 1927, p. 54).

[3] According to Narkomfin data, the profits and depreciation allowances retained by state industry increased from 934 million rubles in 1925–1926 to 1580 millions in 1928–1929 ; the total deductions paid to the budget from state industry (excluding the industrial tax) increased from 216 to 499 million rubles in the same period (see pp. 744-745 above and Planovoe Khozyaistvo, No. 3, 1932, p. 150).

[4] For detailed figures, and for changes in the methods of assessing revenue from state enterprises from 1926 to 1929, see R. W. Davies, The Development of the Soviet Budgetary System (1958), pp. 82-83, 117-121.

Until the end of 1926, state loans were a very minor source of revenue : in the economic year 1925–1926, the net receipts of the budget from loans amounted to only 1 per cent of the total.[1] In the next two years, the increase was very rapid ; in 1928–1929 loans provided over 7 per cent of budgetary revenue.[2]

State loans were divided into three main groups, according to whether bonds were purchased by state enterprises, savings banks, or individual citizens. Loans were held by these three groups in the following amounts at the beginning of each economic year (in million rubles) :

	October 1, 1925	October 1, 1926	October 1, 1927	October 1, 1928	October 1, 1929
State Enterprises	65	104	212	315	489
Savings Banks	—	—	41	259	465
Individual Citizens	225	234	390	603	895
Total	290	338	643	1177	1849 [3]

The increase in loans from state enterprises had little significance. State enterprises were required to invest 60 per cent of their reserve capital in loans;[4] but, as the capital was originally advanced by the state, this provision, which formed part of the general drive to restrict the financial resources at the free disposal of state industry and trade, was not much more than a book-keeping device.[5]

Savings banks were an increasingly popular method of encouraging small savings by the individual. The number of savings offices increased from 7362 on October 1, 1925, to 20,364 on October 1, 1929 ; more than half of these were in the countryside.[6]

---

[1] For the earlier history of state loans see *Socialism in One Country, 1924–1926*, Vol. 1, pp. 469-470.

[2] Net receipts from loans are listed as item 13 in Table No. 42, p. 975 below.

[3] *Narodnoe Khozyaistvo SSSR* (1932), pp. 598-599; see also *3 Sessiya Tsentral'nogo Ispolnitel'nogo Komiteta Soyuza SSR 4 Sozyva* (1928), pp. 32-33, 45.

[4] See R. W. Davies, *The Development of the Soviet Budgetary System* (1958), p. 126, where the decrees authorizing these loans are listed.

[5] These loan holdings by state enterprises were quite separate from their subscriptions to the 300-million ruble " loan of economic restoration " issued in August 1925 by Gosbank (see *Socialism in One Country, 1924–1926*, Vol. 1, p. 346) and from the sums deposited by state enterprises in current accounts, which were used by the banks as a means of financing credit (see p. 779 below).

[6] *Finansy SSSR za XXX Let 1917–1947*, ed. N. Rovinsky (1947), p. 301. Most of these " offices " were in fact counters in post offices, financial departments and branches of Gosbank ; branches were also opened in factories,

To encourage the everyday use of these offices, new legislation entitled them to collect state and local taxes and payments for municipal services, and to pay out pensions.[1] The number of depositors increased from 1,300,000 on October 1, 1925, to 7,105,000 on October 1, 1929.[2] Deposits held by the savings banks increased rapidly, and special state loans were issued on June 1, 1927, and September 9, 1928, in which the banks invested the deposits received.[3] However, the average size of deposits remained small, and the savings banks did not succeed in attracting the free resources of the peasants, who had contributed a substantial part of the much larger total of deposits before the revolution.[4] As a result, administrative costs were heavy: the banks received 11 or 12 per cent interest on state loans, but were able to pay only 8 per cent interest to the individual depositor.

State loans subscribed by the individual citizen were an increasingly important source of budgetary revenue. They were thought to provide means of raising additional resources for industrialization by appealing to personal interest.[5] On September 3, 1926, a small test five-year loan was issued to the urban population, bearing lottery prizes: it was later reported that the 30 million rubles asked for were fully and voluntarily subscribed.[6] On February 4, 1927, encouraged by this success, the authorities

---

railway stations, chemists' shops, schools, reading rooms and army units (*Vestnik Finansov*, No. 7, 1927, p. 69); for their earlier history see *Socialism in One Country, 1924–1926*, Vol. 1, pp. 470-471.

[1] *Sobranie Zakonov, 1927*, No. 19, art. 220 (dated April 11); *Sobranie Zakonov, 1929*, No. 17, art. 140 (dated February 20). The journal of Narkomfin reported, however, that peasants preferred to deal with offices which did not have tax-collecting responsibilities (*Vestnik Finansov*, No. 7, 1927, p. 69).

[2] *3 Sessiya Tsentral'nogo Ispolnitel'nogo Komiteta Soyuza SSR 4 Sozyva* (1928), p. 36; *Narodnoe Khozyaistvo SSSR* (1932), pp. 600-601.

[3] *Sobranie Zakonov, 1927*, No. 31, art. 318; *Sobranie Zakonov, 1928*, No. 60, art. 540.

[4] On October 1, 1929, 36·3 per cent of total deposits came from institutions, 27·4 per cent from state employees, 12·1 per cent from workers, and only 5·5 per cent from peasants; total deposits on this date were 496 million rubles (*Narodnoe Khozyaistvo SSSR* (1932), pp. 600-601). On January 1, 1916, total deposits had been 2250 million rubles, 640 million rubles of which were from peasants (*SSSR : Tsentral'nyi Ispolnitel'nyi Komitet 3 Sozyva : 3 Sessiya* (1927), p. 562).

[5] *Pravda*, May 7, 1927.

[6] *Sobranie Zakonov, 1926*, No. 60, art. 449; *Torgovo-Promyshlennaya Gazeta*, October 1, 1927.

issued a further loan, bearing lottery prizes equivalent to an interest-rate of 10 per cent : this loan was for 100 million rubles and was to be repaid over a period of eight years.[1] The loan was again fully subscribed ; 61 million rubles came from small and medium savers, of which 26 million rubles were raised by mass subscriptions " on collective signature " at factories and offices : [2] under the new mass subscription system state workers and employees agreed that a proportion of their wages should be deducted over a period (in this case six months) and paid into loan subscriptions.[3] It proved far more difficult to place loans among the peasants than among the townsmen. An experimental " third peasant loan " was approved on March 11, 1927, bearing lottery prizes.[4] It yielded only 4 or 5 million rubles out of the 25 million rubles asked for ; but Narkomfin in its report to Sovnarkom hailed this, in comparison with previous efforts, as " a definite achievement ".[5]

On August 24, 1927, the first " state internal loan for the industrialization of the economy of the USSR " was issued for an amount of 200 million rubles, yielding lottery prizes and interest equivalent to an interest-rate of only 6 per cent ; the loan was to be repaid over ten years.[6] This loan was fully subscribed, partly through the use of mass subscription of a more or less compulsory kind. Kalinin, commenting that at a session of TsIK some months later " voluntary subscription " implied " tremendous social compulsion ", described the procedure :

A general meeting of workers was convened, a speaker demonstrated the advantages of the loan. After this, the meeting resolved that everyone receiving such-and-such a wage must

[1] *Sobranie Zakonov, 1927*, No. 7, art. 71.

[2] *Vestnik Finansov*, No. 7, 1927, pp. 84-86 ; *Torgovo-Promyshlennaya Gazeta*, October 1, 1927. A further 29 million rubles were subscribed by private capital.

[3] A Narkomfin circular of February 15, 1927, instructed that " special attention should be paid to the organization of mass subscription among workers and employees " (*Vestnik Finansov*, No. 1, 1929, p. 15).

[4] *Sobranie Zakonov, 1927*, No. 17, art. 182 ; for the first and second peasant loans see *Socialism in One Country, 1924–1926*, Vol. 1, pp. 469-470.

[5] *SSSR: Svodnye Materialy o Deyatel'nosti Soveta Narodnykh Komissarov i Soveta Truda i Oborony za I Kvartal (Oktyabr'-Dekabr') 1927–28 g.* (1928), p. 34.

[6] *Sobranie Zakonov, 1927*, No. 51, art. 508 ; the decree promised that 35 million rubles of the total would be provisionally earmarked for financing Dnieprostroi.

pay such-and-such a sum. This decision did not of course have juridical force, but at the factory perhaps only one in a thousand would decide not to subscribe after such a vote. He knows that every worker in sight may call out : " He's a White ! " [1]

The first industrialization loan was open to subscription in the countryside as well as in the towns and was more successful than the third peasant loan ; even so, only 10·5 million rubles out of the total of 200 millions were subscribed in the countryside.[2] At the end of 1927, the crisis in grain deliveries led to drastic measures aimed at reducing the purchasing power of the peasants in order to induce them to sell their grain. On December 30, 1927, a " state lottery loan to strengthen peasant economy " was announced for a total of 100 million rubles. This was a relatively short-term loan, repayable within three years ; and lottery prizes plus interest yielded a total return of 13 per cent.[3] Priority supplies of agricultural implements could be obtained in lieu of lottery prizes, and the bonds could be presented as payment for agricultural tax from April 1929 onwards. The official report of STO and Sovnarkom declared that the purpose was to remove surplus money from the market, and to take advantage of the *Konjunktur* to introduce state loan operations into the village on a stable basis. Teachers, agronomists, cooperatives and party organizations were all to endeavour to place the bonds ; but they were to be placed mainly through the rural district Soviet, which was to receive 10 per cent of the proceeds for local agricultural and cultural needs.[4] Eventually 140 million rubles were subscribed.[5] But, in spite of the favourable

---

[1] *3 Sessiya Tsentral'nogo Ispolnitel'nogo Komiteta Soyuza SSR 4 Sozyva* (1928), pp. 419-420. A general meeting of specialists working in the Vesenkha of the USSR resolved that it was desirable for specialists to contribute a month's pay, and that half a month's pay should be " an obligatory minimum subscription for every specialist " (*Torgovo-Promyshlennaya Gazeta*, October 23, 1927) ; payments were spread over a year. Out of 200 million rubles 113 millions were contributed on mass subscription (*Vestnik Finansov*, No. 1, 1929, p. 16).

[2] *SSSR : Svodnye Materialy o Deyatel'nosti Soveta Narodnykh Komissarov i Soveta Truda i Oborony za I Kvartal (Oktyabr'-Dekabr') 1927–28 g.* (1928), p. 34.   [3] *Sobranie Zakonov, 1928*, No. 3, art. 24.

[4] *SSSR : Svodnye Materialy o Deyatel'nosti Soveta Narodnykh Komissarov i Soveta Truda i Oborony za I Kvartal (Oktyabr'-Dekabr') 1927–28 g.* (1928), pp. 34-35.

[5] *SSSR : Deyatel'nost' SNK i STO : Svodnye Materialy : Kvartal (I Oktyabr'-Dekabr') 1928–29 g.* (1929), p. 64 ; a supplementary loan of 50 million rubles was floated on February 29, 1928 (*Sobranie Zakonov, 1928*, No. 14, art. 118).

terms of the loan, a considerable element of compulsion was involved.[1] The whole loan operation was criticized on this ground at the session of TsIK in April 1928. One speaker described the methods used in her locality :

> They gave the president of a village Soviet a target of placing so many rubles' obligations of the peasant loan. What could he do ? He went and simply asked : " Take the lot ! " The peasants said, " I have no money, I can't take it ", and the president said, " Sign then that you can't take it ". Well, naturally no one signed ; they were afraid and finally took it.

From the Urals it was reported that, " if they propose to a peasant to take 50-100 rubles and he is unable to, they arrest the peasant and hold him until he agrees to take it ".[2] In order to hinder the sale of bonds back to the state, " the liquidity of the loan was considerably restricted ".[3] At the end of March 1928, however, an instruction signed by Rykov as president of Sovnarkom prohibited the forced placing of the loan.[4]

On July 18, 1928, a " second industrialization loan " was issued on approximately the same terms as the first loan a year previously : the new loan was to amount to the large sum of 500 million rubles.[5] By January 1, 1929, subscriptions of 506 million rubles were reported, of which 465 millions were mass subscriptions with delayed payment.[6] The second industrialization loan was said to have enjoyed much greater popularity among the peasantry than the peasant loan of December 1927. After a two months' extension

---

[1] In his instruction to party organizations of February 13, 1928, Stalin required them to cease placing the loan by using administrative measures such as payment for grain in loan obligations and compulsory allocation of the loan to households, but urged them to continue the loan campaign (Stalin, *Sochineniya*, xi, 19).

[2] *3 Sessiya Tsentral'nogo Ispolnitel'nogo Komiteta Soyuza SSR 4 Sozyva* (1928), p. 192 ; see also *ibid.* pp. 117, 129, 456.

[3] *Vestnik Finansov*, No. 3, 1929, p. 74.   [4] See p. 62 above.

[5] *Sobranie Zakonov, 1928*, No. 40, art. 406 ; an additional sum of 50 million rubles was floated on December 19, 1928 (*Sobranie Zakonov, 1929*, No. 1, art. 5).

[6] *SSSR : Deyatel'nost' SNK i STO : Svodnye Materialy : I Kvartal (Oktyabr'-Dekabr') 1928–29 g.* (1929), p. 64. At this stage, although mass subscription was virtually compulsory at large factories and in government offices, the holder apparently retained the right to sell his obligations (*Vestnik Finansov*, No. 1, 1929, p. 21 ; No. 3, 1929, p. 23).

2 C

of the initial subscription period, the peasants agreed to subscribe over 100 million rubles of the 500-million ruble loan, and an
official report claimed that, " unlike the loan to strengthen the
peasant economy, the second industrialization loan was placed
everywhere in a completely voluntary fashion ".[1] But, in placing
loans with the peasants, as in applying the agricultural tax, official
policy was cautious during 1928–1929 : a financial official described 1928–1929 as " a year of breathing-space (peredyshka) in
relation to loan work in the countryside ".[2] Between 1925–1926
and 1928–1929, the amount of new subscriptions to state loans
increased every year. But by 1928–1929 the cost to the state of
servicing the loans was already high and increasing rapidly : in
that year interest, lottery prizes, and repayments on previous loans
rose to over 40 per cent of the gross receipts from new loans, and
the net receipts of the state budget from loans were slightly less
than in 1927–1928.[3]

Significant changes in the pattern of budgetary revenue
resulted from these developments.[4] In spite of the strenuous
efforts to increase direct taxation, the proportion of budgetary
revenue received from income tax on the population, industrial
tax on the private sector and the agricultural tax continued to
decline over the period. The main source of additional income was
indirect taxation : in spite of reluctance in principle to increase
excise duties, the revenue from this source increased as rapidly as
budgetary revenue as a whole, and contributed one-third of the
total increase in budgetary revenue between 1925–1926 and 1928–
1929. Revenue from the socialized sector, notably the industrial
tax and deductions from profits, also expanded very rapidly ; these
two items alone contributed a further quarter of the total increase
in revenue. The other major new source of revenue was state
loans from individuals, which increased much more rapidly than
any other item of the budget in 1926–1927 and 1927–1928, and
compensated for the relative decline in revenue from direct taxa-

---

[1] *SSSR: Deyatel'nost' SNK i STO: Svodnye Materialy: I Kvartal (Oktyabr'-Dekabr') 1928–29 g.* (1929), p. 65.   [2] *Vestnik Finansov*, No. 3, 1929, p. 25.
[3] See Table No. 42, p. 975 below, and table in R. W. Davies, *The Development of the Soviet Budgetary System* (1958), p. 126.
[4] For a summary of the changes see Table No. 42, p. 975 below.

tion of private income. The pattern underwent some changes
from year to year ; but, at the end of the period, the population as
a whole were paying a higher proportion of their incomes in taxation, direct and indirect, than at the beginning. Various attempts
were made to calculate the tax burden on different groups of the
population. Such calculations were necessarily difficult : they
involved, for example, distributing the different excise duties
among different groups of the population, and thus required a
detailed knowledge of household budgets. A substantial and
increasing part of total budgetary revenue, notably the industrial
tax and deductions from profits, could not meaningfully be divided
up between different social groups. Certain conclusions can, however, be drawn from the available information. First, within the
urban population, persons receiving incomes from private industry
and trade paid a much higher proportion of their income in taxes,
direct and indirect, than persons employed by the state, and this
proportion rose sharply with increases in income.[1] Secondly, the
peasantry paid a far lower amount per head in tax than the urban
population, probably less than a fifth as much ; only about 40 per
cent of total taxation, including indirect taxation, was paid by the
peasantry in 1926–1927.[2] While this difference was largely a
reflection of the much lower income per head in the countryside,
the peasant almost certainly paid a smaller proportion of his
income in tax than the town-dweller. This does not, however,
take account of the effect of prices on peasant incomes. The products of the countryside exchanged for the products of the town
at terms less favourable to the peasant than before the war. The
" scissors " were a major form of concealed taxation of the countryside by the state.[3]

[1] Some caution must be observed here ; indirect taxes imposed on commodities consumed primarily by lower-income groups are regressive in their
effects, and no studies are available of the consumption per head of commodities
bearing a high rate of excise (notably vodka and tobacco) in different urban
income-groups. The opposition platform of September 1927 claimed that
as a result of the increase in indirect taxation " the tax burden automatically
moves from the wealthier to the poorer levels " (L. Trotsky, *The Real Situation
in Russia* (n.d. [1928]), pp. 28-29).
[2] Calculated from data in *Vestnik Finansov*, No. 1, 1929, pp. 82-83.
[3] For data on the tax burden on different social groups, see *Vestnik Finansov*,
No. 10, 1925, p. 64 ; No. 8, 1926, p. 19 ; No. 1, 1929, pp. 82-83 ; and G. Sokolnikov and others, *Soviet Policy in Public Finance, 1917–1928* (Stanford, 1931),
p. 283.

CHAPTER 31

CREDIT, CURRENCY AND BANKING

BUDGETARY revenue thus sufficed to balance rapidly rising expenditure and to maintain a substantial surplus. But the achievement of a budget surplus did not necessarily ensure the stability of the ruble : inflation could result from the issuing of credits through the banks independently of the state budget.[1] In practice, net issues of credit by the banks far exceeded the state budget surplus in every year, and were reflected in a corresponding rise in currency circulation, shown in the following table :

Currency in Circulation
(net increase as compared with October 1 of preceding year)

	In million rubles	In percentages
October 1, 1926	217	20·3
October 1, 1927	337	26·1
October 1, 1928	343	21·0
October 1, 1929	671	34·0 [2]

Credit policy and currency issues were the inflationary instruments that promoted the industrialization drive.

Credit policy between the end of 1925 and the summer of 1929 may be divided into two main phases. In the first phase, which ran from the end of 1925 till approximately May 1927, caution predominated, in reaction against the inflationary credit issues of the summer of 1925. But the curbs imposed by Gosbank and Narkomfin were vigorously opposed by industry, particularly in the spring and summer of 1926, when they resulted in grave financial difficulties for some major trusts.[3] In April 1926, industrial circles claimed that there was no general inflation, and that

[1] See p. 726 above.
[2] For currency in circulation see Table No. 44, p. 976 below ; for the budget surplus see p. 746 above, and Tables No. 41, 42, pp. 974, 975 below.
[3] See p. 333 above.

further reduction of credits to industry would be harmful.[1] In June 1926, the presidium of Vesenkha criticized Gosbank for restricting essential credit ; [2] and at a Gosplan conference on the control figures for 1926–1927, Groman argued that recent credit restrictions were " not economically necessary " and would " merely slow down the essential capital *construction* which has begun in industry ".[3] The presidium of Gosplan castigated the restrictions as a " hunger ration " and as a " deviation in bank policy ".[4] Nevertheless, restraint prevailed. In the year 1925–1926, net currency issue was only 217 million rubles ; [5] and the same cautious rate of issue was maintained during the seven months October 1926 to April 1927.[6] During this period supply of goods kept pace with purchasing power, and there were even some fears of over-production of certain goods.[7]

A second and expansionist phase in credit policy began in May and June 1927. In these two months net currency issues, resulting from the expansion of credit, amounted to 119 million rubles ; in the corresponding months of 1926 the amount of currency in circulation had declined.[8] The change in direction was unplanned and apparently unintended, and was at first hardly noticed.[9] The rapid increase in credit in May and June 1927 was

---

[1] *Torgovo-Promyshlennaya Gazeta*, April 30, 1926.
[2] *Ibid.* June 30, 1926.   [3] *Ibid.* May 22, 1926.
[4] *Informatsionnyi Byulleten' Gosplana SSSR*, No. 8, 1926, pp. 7-9 ; the control figures approved by Gosplan in August 1926 referred, however, to " excessive saturation of processes of trade with money " (*Kontrol'nye Tsifry Narodnogo Khozyaistva na 1926–1927 god* (1926), p. 78).
[5] This represented an increase in total circulation of 20·3 per cent, against 85·7 per cent in 1924–1925.
[6] See Table No. 44, p. 976 below, for the currency issue in October–December 1926 and January–March 1927. Net currency issue in April 1927 was 16 million rubles as compared with 23 million rubles in April 1926 (*Pokazateli Kon"yunktury Narodnogo Khozyaistva SSSR za 1923/24–1928/29 gg.*, ed. A. Mendel'son (1930), p. 126).   [7] See p. 684 above.
[8] *Pokazateli Kon"yunktury Narodnogo Khozyaistva SSSR za 1923/24–1928/29 gg.*, ed. A. Mendel'son (1930), p. 126. An article in the financial journal later pointed out that before the war net currency issues had always been confined to the July–September quarter, and claimed, presumably on the basis of the experience of 1925–1926, that in the Soviet period net issues should occur in July to December, and net withdrawals in January–March ; the April–June quarter should be a period of stability. The seasonal fluctuation was due partly to the grain trade and partly to the industrial building season (*Vestnik Finansov*, No. 8, 1927, p. 16).
[9] The official report of Sovnarkom and STO for this quarter set out the

attributable to two major causes. First, the reduction of wholesale prices in the spring of 1927, which had not been foreseen at
the beginning of the economic year, reduced industrial profits,
resulting in a shortage of working capital in industry,[1] and, coin-
ciding with the reduction in retail prices, put a severe strain on
the working capital of trading organizations. In consequence,
industry and trade withdrew part of the deposits in their current
accounts with the banks ; this amounted in effect to a net credit
issue. The second and more important cause was the successful
pressure of industry for increased credit, arising principally from
the capital construction programme, which required additional
spending from the resources of industry itself as well as from the
budget.[2] The claims of industry, which had been rejected in the
corresponding period of 1926, were now satisfied by a large expansion of credit. Both the decline in deposits and the increase in
credit resulted in increased issues of currency. What happened in
May 1927 was a silent reversal of policy in favour of the demands
of industry. As a writer in the Narkomfin journal put it, " the
régime of strict correspondence between expenditure and available resources ", which characterized the summer and autumn of
1926, was " somewhat weaker " in the April–June quarter of 1927.[3]
Spunde, acting president of Gosbank, explained that, at a time
when more funds were needed for capital construction and an
increase in industrial production was needed in preparation for the
harvest, Gosbank had decided to meet the shortage of working
capital by increased credits : " the real needs of state industry
were satisfied in full ".[4] More than half the net increase in loans
and discounts went to industry, but this did not suffice to relieve
the strain on its financial position ; cash in hand and deposits fell
by 6 per cent.[5]

facts, and spoke of a " strained " cash position, but sounded no note of alarm
(*SSSR: Svodnye Materialy o Deyatel'nosti Soveta Narodnykh Komissarov i Soveta
Truda i Oborony za III Kvartal (Aprel'-Iyun')* 1926–27 g. (1927), pp. 37-40).
    [1] The textile industry was particularly affected (*Vestnik Finansov*, No. 10,
1927, p. 4).
    [2] *Ibid.* No. 8, 1927, p. 16 ; *SSSR: Svodnye Materialy o Deyatel'nosti
Soveta Narodnykh Komissarov i Soveta Truda i Oborony za III Kvartal (Aprel'-
Iyun')* 1926–27 g. (1927), pp. 38-39.   [3] *Vestnik Finansov*, No. 8, 1927, p. 16.
    [4] *Torgovo-Promyshlennaya Gazeta*, August 5, 1927.
    [5] *SSSR: Svodnye Materialy o Deyatel'nosti Soveta Narodnykh Komissarov i
Soveta Truda i Oborony za III Kvartal (Aprel'-Iyun')* 1926–27 g. (1927), pp. 39-40.

In reviewing the credit position in April–June 1927, Spunde emphasized the need for " maximum care " in July–September 1927, and announced that credits would be issued only to finance grain deliveries.[1] Vesenkha and Gosplan, however, argued vigorously against further restrictions ; and the industrial newspaper reported that a policy of " sharp credit and currency restrictions " had been rejected.[2] Under this pressure, the currency issue of 75 million rubles proposed in the credit plan for July–September 1927 [3] was greatly exceeded. Balances in current and deposit accounts, particularly those of industry, declined ; and, while short-term credits to industry did not increase, long-term credits to industry rose substantially. In the event, currency in circulation increased by 208 million rubles between July 1 and October 1, 1927, nearly three times as much as had been planned at the beginning of the quarter. An official report covering these three months explained " the strained situation in our monetary and credit sector " as due both to " the growth of expenditure on capital construction " and to " the increase in the standard of living of workers and peasants ".[4] In 1926–1927 as a whole, currency in circulation increased by 337 million rubles against the increase of 150 million rubles originally planned in the control figures for 1926–1927.[5] At the session of the central committee of the party in October 1927, Smilga, speaking on behalf of the opposition, referred to the " undoubted presence in our economy of currency inflation ", one of the results of which was " a consistent and undeviating fall in the exchange-rate of our chervonets ".[6] His analysis was later confirmed by Yurovsky, who offered the usual Narkomfin remedy :

The inflation of 1925–1926 was overcome by re-examining economic plans and programmes and by measures to reduce the

---

[1] *Torgovo-Promyshlennaya Gazeta*, August 5, 1927.
[2] *Informatsionnyi Byulleten' Gosplana SSSR*, No. 8-9, 1927, p. 7 ; *Torgovo-Promyshlennaya Gazeta*, July 27, August 19, 1927.
[3] See p. 727, note 1 above.
[4] *SSSR: Svodnye Materialy o Deyatel'nosti Soveta Narodnykh Komissarov i Soveta Truda i Oborony za IV Kvartal (Iyul'-Sentyabr') 1926–27 g.* (1927), p. 57.
[5] *Vestnik Finansov*, No. 8, 1927, p. 19 ; see Table No. 44, p. 976 below. The Narkomfin plan provided for an increase of only 120 million rubles in 1926–1927.
[6] For this speech see p. 35 above.

scale of the loans of banking institutions. Analogous measures are again becoming necessary on the eve of 1928.[1]

In the first six months of the economic year 1927–1928, credit and currency issues were again limited. This trend proved, however, to be no more than temporary. The quarter January–March 1928 was the last in this period in which the amount of currency in circulation substantially declined ; the industrialization drive gathered momentum with the opening of the building season in the spring of 1928, and credit and currency issues again expanded rapidly. In the economic year 1927–1928 currency in circulation increased by 343 million rubles.[2]

Those who directed economic policy were by now much less unwilling to throw off the financial restraints imposed by Narkomfin, and rejected as irrelevant the financial principles which were invoked to justify these restraints. At a meeting of Tsentrosoyuz in July 1928, Mikoyan spoke in terms of unalloyed optimism and unconcern :

> If we take other spheres, for example, currency circulation, which is a very important economic indicator, we shall see that last year at this time we had certain difficulties. At present we have the position that the total amount of money in the country is in full conformity with the requirements of the economy, of trade turnover, etc.[3]

Narkomfin continued to raise an ineffectual voice against the pressure for increased credit issues and the economic policy which lay behind it. When Gosplan, in preparing the control figures for 1928–1929, proposed an increase in currency circulation of 300 million rubles,[4] Narkomfin and Gosbank once more protested that this figure was too high. Frumkin in an article in a financial journal maintained that " we are carrying on a policy of providing finance which by its excess *disorganizes the economy* " ; and an

---

[1] L. Yurovsky, *Denezhnaya Politika Sovetskoi Vlasti (1917–1927)* (1928), p. 371.

[2] See Table No. 44, p. 976 below ; the planned increase was 200 million rubles (*Kontrol'nye Tsifry Narodnogo Khozyaistvo SSSR na 1927–1928 god* (1927), p. 565 ; *Bol'shevik*, No. 19-20, October 31, 1927, p. 36).

[3] *XLI Sobranie Upolnomochennykh Tsentrosoyuza* (1928), p. 284.

[4] *Ekonomicheskaya Zhizn'*, October 16, 1928.

editorial which accompanied the article lamented the blindness of the policy-makers :

It must be admitted that unfortunately an extensive use of currency issue has many supporters in our country. It is difficult to judge whether this is a concealed wish to make use of inflation . . . or simply heedlessness.[1]

Shanin, in the journal of Gosplan, argued that " *the inflationary provision of finance* for our economy inevitably *leads to a contraction of potential productive work in our country* ".[2] At a moment when industry was expanding at a spectacular rate, these strictures seemed merely carping, and were brushed aside rather than refuted. Discussion was obscured by the unwillingness of official publicists to admit the fact of inflation, and by the universal desire to keep currency issue within reasonable bounds. Kviring, on behalf of Gosplan, rejected the suggestion that currency issue might amount to 450-500 million rubles or more in 1928–1929 as quite unacceptable.[3] When Sovnarkom examined the control figures for 1928–1929 prepared by Gosplan, it left the planned rates of growth of the economy intact, but restricted the proposed currency issue to 200 million rubles, a figure which Gosplan opposed as " unrealistic ".[4] During 1928–1929, conflicts between expansionist policies, which required new credit issues, and the desire to restrict currency circulation were almost automatically resolved in favour of expansion. From February 1929 onwards the rate of net currency issue once more rose steeply, the total increase for the year 1928–1929 being 671 million rubles.[5] Yet Krumin, a party publicist, in an article in *Pravda*, emphatically rejected attempts to set up an opposition between a strengthening of the currency and the needs of socialist construction : party policy demanded " a stable currency ".[6]

The denial of inflation in the Soviet economy, continually

---

[1] *Finansy i Narodnoe Khozyaistvo*, No. 43, October 21, 1928.

[2] *Planovoe Khozyaistvo*, No. 10, 1928, p. 62.

[3] G. Krzhizhanovsky and others, *Osnovnye Problemy Kontrol'nykh Tsifr Narodnogo Khozyaistva na 1928/29 god* (1929), pp. 110-111.

[4] *Ibid.* p. 112 ; *Kontrol'nye Tsifry Narodnogo Khozyaistva SSSR na 1928–1929 god* (1929), pp. 336-337.

[5] See Table No. 44, p. 976 below ; for monthly figures see *Pokazateli Kon"yunktury Narodnogo Khozyaistva SSSR za 1923/24–1928/29 gg.*, ed. A. Mendel'son (1930), p. 126.

[6] *Pravda*, March 31, 1929.

2 C 2

repeated at this time by official spokesmen, appears to have had several motives. After the post-war currency crises in Europe, culminating in the fall of the German mark in 1923, inflation was regarded both in the capitalist countries and in the USSR as the most obvious sign of ill-health in an economy. Inflation was denounced by the new Right opposition as a pernicious symptom of the excessive pressure of the industrialization drive ; to admit its existence was to play into the hands of the Right. An official admission of the declining value of the currency might lead to panic buying in the towns, and add to the complication of the grain collections in the countryside. Most of all, perhaps, Soviet prestige in foreign as well as in domestic eyes had been connected, ever since the currency reform of 1924, with a stable Soviet ruble ; and, though the decision to jettison the gold basis of the currency had effectively been taken in March 1926,[1] nobody was prepared to recognize that the policy of the stable currency had been abandoned. It remained official policy to stabilize the ruble and to restore its value ; even in May 1929 the fifth Union Congress of Soviets, in accepting the financial programme of the five-year plan, specifically referred to the importance of " raising the purchasing power of the chervonets ".[2] But from the end of 1927 onwards little was heard about putting this policy into effect, and price reduction campaigns were quietly dropped. The divorce of the ruble from the world market was confirmed by a decree of March 21, 1928, which severely restricted the amount of foreign currency which could be purchased for travelling abroad or for sending abroad, and reiterated the absolute ban, which remained permanently in force, on the export of Soviet bank notes or coins.[3]

During the second half of the nineteen-twenties, radical changes were made in the organization and management of the credit system, which had developed in a somewhat haphazard fashion in the early years of NEP. Gosbank was the pivot of the banking system established in 1922–1924 ; it was responsible for the issue of banknotes, held the accounts of other banks and the

[1] See Socialism in One Country, 1924–1926, Vol. 1, pp. 483-489.
[2] S"ezdy Sovetov v Dokumentakh, iii (1960), 159.
[3] Sobranie Zakonov, 1928, No. 18, art. 152.

current accounts of many *khozraschet* enterprises, and made short-term and some long-term credit available to them ; it had branches in all important towns.[1] Its weakness was its lack of authority over the special banks. Unlike Gosbank, which was subordinate to Narkomfin, these banks were responsible to inter-departmental boards representing their shareholders, the People's Commissariats and other institutions, of which Narkomfin was only one ; the most important of the special banks, Prombank, was in practice completely under the control of Vesenkha. The delimitation of functions between the banks was by no means clear. While the special banks were primarily concerned with long-term and medium-term credit, and Gosbank with short-term credit, both Gosbank and the special banks handled current accounts and made both short-term and long-term loans. Different enterprises in the same industry might have accounts either in Prombank or in Gosbank, and the same customer might hold accounts in and receive advances from more than one bank. The special banks were able to use sums deposited with them in current accounts as a source of new credit in excess of the amount allowed in the credit plan, and as a result Gosbank was unable to control the total volume of credit.[2] Control over credit by Gosbank was also limited by the existence of " commercial credit " : state enter-

---

[1] According to M. Atlas, *Razvitie Gosudarstvennogo Banka SSSR* (1958), p. 72, outstanding short-term credit advances by the bank were made up as follows (in million rubles) :

	On October 1, 1925	On October 1, 1929
Discounted Bills of Exchange	741	1715
Loans for Grain Purchases	183	580
Loans on Commodities other than Grain	211	384
Loans for Production Purposes (including Loans for Seasonal Activities)	221	1345
Loans on Securities and Foreign Currency	53	107
Total	1409	4130

For the functions of Gosbank at this period see *ibid.* pp. 36-85 ; A. Z. Arnold, *Banks, Credit and Money in Soviet Russia* (N.Y., 1937), pp. 244-280 ; it had 486 branches, offices and agencies on October 1, 1926 (*ibid.* p. 265).

[2] *Vestnik Finansov*, No. 5-6, 1926, pp. 6-14 ; No. 5, 1927, p. 33. The special banks apparently also sometimes issued credits in excess of the deposits held by them and of the credit plan (see A. Z. Arnold, *Banks, Credit and Money in Soviet Russia* (N.Y., 1937), pp. 288-290, 297).

prises had the right to issue promissory notes to their suppliers ; although these notes were normally discounted in Gosbank, the arrangement nevertheless meant that a stream of credit emanated from industrial and trading organizations without preliminary control by the bank.

From the autumn of 1924 onwards, Gosbank gradually but systematically encroached on the functions of the special banks, using its position as issue bank for the state and as a supplier of resources to other banks.[1] A report from the presidium of Gosplan covering the quarter April–June 1926 complained that competition between Gosbank and the special banks was threatening the normal existence of the special banks and had reduced the banking system to a state of " extreme disorganization ".[2] Later in 1926, a proposal of Gosbank, with support from Narkomfin, to take over the administration of all short-term credit, was strongly resisted by both Vesenkha and Gosplan.[3] At the other extreme, several experts, including some Vesenkha officials, proposed that the powers of Gosbank should be drastically curtailed, and that it should be transformed into a " bankers' bank " along the lines of the pre-revolutionary State Bank : it would make loans to, and accept deposits from, other banks, but would not be permitted to make either short- or long-term loans direct to clients.[4] On June 15, 1927, a new statute " On the Principles of the Organization of the Credit System " was approved by Sovnarkom and TsIK.[5] The statute recognized Gosbank as being formally in control of the whole credit system, and as the sole custodian of all resources of the state budget, the savings banks, and state and social insurance ;[6]

---

[1] In the period from October 1, 1924 to April 1, 1926, the debt of state trade and industry to Gosbank rose from 302 to 908 million rubles, while the debt of state trade and industry to Prombank rose more slowly from 147 to 329 million rubles ; simultaneously the proportion of the current accounts of industry held by Gosbank also increased (*Planovoe Khozyaistvo*, No. 7, 1926, pp. 105-106, 109-110).

[2] *Informatsionnyi Byulleten' Gosplana SSSR*, No. 8, 1926, pp. 7-9.

[3] *Ibid.* No. 1, 1927, pp. 13-14 ; *Torgovo-Promyshlennaya Gazeta*, December 7, 1926.

[4] See *Vestnik Finansov*, No. 11, 1926, pp. 15-25 ; *Ekonomicheskaya Zhizn'*, November 21, December 1, 7, 1926 ; M. Atlas, *Razvitie Gosudarstvennogo Banka SSSR* (1958), pp. 95-96.

[5] *Sobranie Zakonov, 1927*, No. 35, art. 364.

[6] Between 1925 and 1929, the administration of revenues and expenditures of the state budget was transferred to Gosbank from the Narkomfin " exchequer

and it attempted to distribute clients systematically between Gosbank and the special banks. Gosbank was in future responsible
for short-term credits to grain collection agencies, transport, Union
state trading organizations and the largest industrial enterprises ;
the special banks were responsible for long-term credits and for
short-term credits to clients not served by Gosbank. The statute
also contained the important provision that clients should not
normally hold current accounts in, and draw short-term credits
from, more than one bank. After its publication Gosbank did not,
however, cease its drive to take over all short-term credit operations. A month later, Rukhimovich referred at a meeting of the
council of Prombank to the " struggle between the special banks
and Gosbank, which is trying to concentrate in its hands the vast
majority of short term credit operations " ; and the representative
of Narkomfin promised to deal with the " misdeeds " of Gosbank.[1]
In February 1928, Gosbank took over responsibility for short-
term credit to the amount of 290 million rubles from Prombank
and transferred to it responsibility for long-term credit to a total
of 364 million rubles.[2] During the year 1928–1929, further responsibilities for short-term credit were transferred to Gosbank.[3]
The course of events seemed to demonstrate the strong position
of Gosbank in relation to the special banks : there was now no
more talk of transforming it into a bankers' bank. But its administrative success was achieved at the moment when it lost effective
control over the volume of credit ; in 1928, Gosbank was brought

---

offices " (kassy), which had continued pre-revolutionary arrangements (see
A. Z. Arnold, *Banks, Credit and Money in Soviet Russia* (N.Y., 1937), p. 265,
and R. W. Davies, *The Development of the Soviet Budgetary System* (1958), pp.
203-205) ; the previous arrangements continued in military units and in the
countryside.
   [1] *Torgovo-Promyshlennaya Gazeta*, July 15, 1927 ; see also an article *ibid.*
July 17, 1927.   In the following month Rabkrin and Narkomfin reached a
further agreement on the delimitation of clients between banks ; it does not
seem to have gone further than the statute of June 15, 1927 (*ibid.* August 25,
1927).   For Rukhimovich see p. 300 above.
   [2] M. Atlas, *Razvitie Gosudarstvennogo Banka SSSR* (1958), p. 68.
   [3] *SSSR : Ot S"ezdu k S"ezdu (Aprel' 1927 g.–May 1929 g.)* (1929), p. 72 ;
in its quest for a centralized credit system over which it would have control,
Gosbank also attempted in 1928 and 1929 to bring commercial credit more
closely under its aegis (see A. Z. Arnold, *Banks, Credit and Money in Soviet
Russia* (N.Y., 1937), pp. 345-351 ; M. Atlas, *Razvitie Gosudarstvennogo Banka
SSSR* (1958), pp. 71-75).

under stronger central control and itself became an instrument of inflation.[1]

The special banks had always been primarily concerned with the supply of long-term credit ; as Gosbank took over control of short-term credit, long-term credit became their exclusive preoccupation. Their importance in economic development varied greatly according to the sector of the economy. In agriculture, which was almost entirely in private control, it was natural that investment funds supplied by the state should be issued, through the network of republican agricultural banks, credit societies and mutual assistance societies, in the form of long-term interest-bearing loans ; the chief exception was part of the investment in Sovkhozy, which was issued in the form of non-returnable grants.[2] Municipal construction, including housing, was also financed primarily through loans, as was some electric power construction.[3] But most expenditure on the construction of power plants, and almost all expenditure on capital construction in industry which was not financed by its own funds, was covered by allocations from the budget which were nominally loans, but were treated in practice as non-returnable grants. Here the special banks at first played no part : the grants were issued through the exchequer offices or the branches of Gosbank.[4] As industrialization got under way, the primary question was whether additional resources could be obtained to finance loans for capital investment. The schemes tried out by Vesenkha since 1924 had proved unsuccessful ; a new attempt was made with the formation on April 1, 1926, of a " department of long-term credit " (ODK) within Prombank, to be financed by budgetary and other funds.[5] The new department received little support from the budget in the first year of its existence : on April 1, 1927, its outstanding loans amounted only to 46 million rubles.[6] In 1927, a further attempt was made to

---

[1] See pp. 729, 738-739 above.
[2] See pp. 153-154 above; a statute stipulating which budgetary allocations to agriculture should be made as loans and which as grants was approved by TsIK and Sovnarkom on April 25, 1928 (*Sobranie Zakonov, 1928*, No. 27, art. 240).
[3] *Problemy Dolgosrochnogo Kreditovaniya Promyshlennosti*, ed. A. Sokolov (1928), pp. 127-131, 111-113, 119-121.   [4] *Ibid.* pp. 40-41.
[5] *Ibid.* pp. 39-40, 123-125 ; see also *Socialism in One Country, 1924–1926*, Vol. 1, pp. 340, 346-347, 487.
[6] *Problemy Dolgosrochnogo Kreditovaniya Promyshlennosti*, ed. A. Sokolov (1928), p. 17.

swell the resources of Prombank by a decision that 10 per cent of the profits of industrial trusts should be transferred to the bank and a further 12·5 per cent placed with it as a long-term deposit.[1]

During 1927 and the early part of 1928 the question of the control over Prombank and of appropriate methods for financing investment in industry generally became the subject of a sharp controversy.   Officials of Narkomfin insisted that long-term loans rather than outright grants were the best form in which to allocate budgetary resources to industry, and proposed that all long-term loans should be administered by an independent interdepartmental bank in the management of which Narkomfin would have some say.[2]   Vesenkha not unexpectedly insisted that any new long-term credit bank must remain under its control ; fear was expressed that without such control the bank would favour commercially profitable enterprises and restrain construction in heavy industry.[3]   More surprisingly, a strong current of opinion in Gosplan and Vesenkha as well as in Narkomfin supported the view that finance for capital investment in industry should be provided through loans rather than outright grants.   The presidium of Gosplan, after much debate, endorsed a proposal that capital investment should be financed by 25-year loans having a rate of interest varying between 3 and 6 per cent.[4]   In January 1928, the presidium of Vesenkha presented a compromise proposal to Sovnarkom which provided that, while defence projects and projects of an experimental nature should continue to be financed by grants, a substantial part of capital investment should be financed by loans repayable within 3-5 years of the completion of the project ; the maximum interest rate would be 6 per cent.[5]

[1] See R. W. Davies, *The Development of the Soviet Budgetary System* (1958), pp. 119-120.

[2] *Problemy Dolgosrochnogo Kreditovaniya Promyshlennosti*, ed. A. Sokolov (1928), pp. 20, 148 ; *Torgovo-Promyshlennaya Gazeta*, April 12, 1928, reported that Narkomfin wanted 51 per cent of the shares in the proposed new bank.

[3] *Puti Industrializatsii*, No. 6, 1928, pp. 13-14.

[4] *Informatsionnyi Byulleten' Gosplana SSSR*, No. 2, 1926, pp. 3-6 ; No. 5-6, 1927, pp. 23-28.

[5] *Torgovo-Promyshlennaya Gazeta*, January 14, February 9, 11, 1928.   At the presidium of Vesenkha on January 12, 1928, Shtern argued that the grants system was a " conservative factor " and led to investment being controlled by administrative decisions independently of economic criteria ; Mantsev, on the other hand, claimed that the use of loans for capital investment in industry would " mechanically transfer the methods of work of advanced capitalism into

On June 27, 1928, a decision of TsIK and Sovnarkom consolidated the financial control of Vesenkha over investment in industry by resolving that Prombank and Elektrobank should be fused into a new Long-Term Credit Bank for Industry and Electrification subordinate to Vesenkha and incorporating the former department of long-term credit (ODK) of Prombank. The new bank, which was still known as Prombank, was responsible for disbursing state budgetary allocations to industry and power construction, as well as for long-term loans to industry.[1] Under the new arrangements, Gosbank retained only the shadow of its former powers over long-term finance : but, as Prombank had very few local branches, it had to make use of the facilities of Gosbank.[2] When the new bank was established, it was assumed that the provision of the " long-term credit " referred to in its title would become its main function, and that budget grants would come to play a relatively minor part in the provision of finance for capital construction in industry.[3] But by this time large-scale projects which would take several years to complete increasingly dominated the industrial scene ; physical controls were supplementing financial levers as a method of transferring resources to major schemes ; inflation in a price-controlled economy undermined traditional methods of financial calculation ; the scale and speed with which Soviet industry was to be transformed meant that present calculations of future costs could be no more than rough guesses. It was inconceivable that in the atmosphere of 1929 important projects would have been stopped because the repayment of their capital costs out of future profits was not guaranteed ; and the use of a rate of return even to measure the

the practice of the socialist sector of our economy " ; for Shtern and Mantsev see pp. 279, 377 above.

[1] *Sobranie Zakonov, 1928*, No. 42, art. 377. See also A. Z. Arnold, *Banks, Credit and Money in Soviet Russia* (N.Y., 1937), pp. 292-296; M. Atlas, *Razvitie Gosudarstvennogo Banka SSSR* (1958), pp. 67-68.

[2] The number of branches of Prombank actually fell from 88 on October 1, 1926 to 33 on October 1, 1927, and 6 on October 1, 1928 (A. Z. Arnold, *Banks, Credit and Money in Soviet Russia* (N.Y , 1937), p. 284).

[3] One commentator prematurely observed at the end of 1928 that " in the struggle between two methods of financing — budgetary and banking — victory has been on the side of the latter " (*Ekonomicheskoe Obozrenie*, No. 12, 1928, p. 38).

efficiency of investment met with increasing opposition.[1]   In practice, the main task of Prombank was the disbursement of non-returnable budgetary allocations.[2]

The years from 1926 to 1929 saw the progressive eclipse of the policies for which Narkomfin had stood and of its own rôle in the administration of finance. The original conception had been that the budget would constitute the key economic plan of the state, and would be designed primarily to maintain financial stability, and that the key rôle in the formation of the budget would be played by Narkomfin. The banking system would work on commercial principles within this framework ; and the issue of credit and currency would be limited to what the economy could support without inflation. These aims proved wholly incompatible with the determination of the party leaders, strongly supported in Vesenkha, to press forward policies of industrialization designed to promote self-sufficiency on the basis of modern technology. The financial and budgetary powers previously exercised by Narkomfin were subordinated to an economic plan inspired by these purposes. Capital investment in industry was centrally planned by the state ; and the credit plan was geared to the requirements of industry and not to the dictates of financial orthodoxy as interpreted by Narkomfin. The investment programme led to almost continuous inflation ; the stability of the currency — meaning the stability of prices at home and of the exchange value of the ruble abroad — was sacrificed. The contribution of the financial system to the rapid industrialization of the country now became the criterion of its efficiency ; finance was subordinate to planning.

[1] For an account of the debates on this question see J.-M. Collette, *Politique des Investissements et Calcul Économique* (1964), pp. 51-65.

[2] A decree of May 23, 1930, ruled that all allocations from the unified budget to investment in state industry, trade, transport and agriculture were in future to be made as non-returnable grants (*Sobranie Zakonov, 1930*, No. 28, art. 316).

F: *Planning*

*

CHAPTER 32

PRINCIPLES OF PLANNING

I F the word " planning " is held merely to mean the exercise of
state authority to regulate the economy, then planning, and an
effective machinery of planning, existed almost from the beginning of NEP. In the state sector of the economy, which included
most of industry and transport and a large part of wholesale trade,
the central authorities provided finance and exercised control over
wholesale prices, tariffs and wages ; the private sector of the
economy was also strongly influenced by the fiscal, credit and price
policies of the state. State control of the economy was, however,
severely limited. While some physical controls existed, notably
in the producer goods industries and in foreign trade, planning
authority was in the main financial authority, exercised through
the budget and the credit system, in which Narkomfin called the
tune. The economy remained fundamentally a market economy ;
the connexion between the state sector and individual agriculture through the market dominated all other economic relations ;
most of the transactions of state industry were conducted
through the market, which dictated the pace and shape of the
recovery of the consumer goods industries between 1921 and
1924.

Once the restoration of the economy was well under way, the
state began to make an increasing effort to direct economic development.[1] In the economic year 1925–1926, substantial resources were channelled into capital investment by the state, and
fixed capital expanded more rapidly in industry than in any other
major sector of the economy.[2] This first victory of the policy of
industrialization marked the defeat of Narkomfin and the hard
core of the anti-planning group ; opposition to planning was
closely correlated with opposition to industrialization. By the

[1] For the first stages in this process see *Socialism in One Country, 1924–1926*,
Vol. 1, pp. 490-499.   [2] See Table No. 48, p. 980 below.

summer of 1926, the " dictatorship of finance ", in the sense of the dictation by Narkomfin of the terms and rate of economic expansion, had come to an end ; the issue had become not *whether* to industrialize, and to plan the allocation of resources to that end, but *how* to industrialize ; the prestige of planning in official circles had increased very considerably.

But what did " planning " mean ? On this question, party members and non-party experts in Gosplan and Vesenkha were at first more or less united, in practical terms at least ; in Gosplan, Groman and Bazarov advocated industrialization and stood together with Strumilin in defence of the control figures for 1925–1926 both against Narkomfin and against many prominent party leaders, including Rykov and Kamenev.[1] But in 1927 and 1928, radically new approaches to planning were developed in the party, and the earlier agreement on the major practical problems of planning was replaced by a wide cleavage of views about the methods and pace of industrialization. Planning, in the conception formulated in the party in the later nineteen-twenties, involved the fundamental reshaping of the economy ; through planning, resources were to be directed towards the fuel and power, iron and steel and engineering industries in order to transform the Soviet Union as rapidly as possible into a self-sufficient economy based on advanced technology.[2] These objectives, persistently advocated even in the early years of NEP by Krzhizhanovsky in Gosplan, and strongly supported in Vesenkha, came to be regarded as an essential part of the drive to overtake the advanced capitalist countries and to establish socialism in one country. It was inherent in this approach that the creation of a socialist order was the goal of planning. In 1925, Strumilin had commented that " the Struvian idea of developing the forces of production irrespective of where the development is going in no way allures us ".[3] The notion that the supreme criterion of economic policy should be the development of productive forces and that socialization should be regarded as a means subordinate to this end was persistently advocated by

[1] See *Socialism in One Country, 1924–1926*, Vol. 1, pp. 501-508, and p. 810 below.
[2] See pp. 413-415, 419, note 1 above.
[3] *Planovoe Khozyaistvo*, No. 1, 1926, p. 35 ; the Marxist Struve had gone over to the liberal movement in 1901, contending that the strengthening of the Russian bourgeoisie would facilitate the growth of productive forces.

Bazarov ;[1] and at a discussion in the Communist Academy in January 1928 Strumilin specifically accused Bazarov of a " Struvian approach ". He added a striking admission :

We are not children ; we are well aware that, if we move towards a social revolution, we *ipso facto* move for a number of years towards the reduction and destruction of productive forces.

The development of productive forces was " only a means, not an end " ; if it were an end in itself, the monopoly of foreign trade would have been relinquished.[2] The new approach to planning carried with it a more independent attitude to the market economy. Strumilin and Krzhizhanovsky in Gosplan, and the leading industrialists in Vesenkha, accepted the prevailing assumption that the market would continue to exist over a long period, and that a fully planned economy, which presupposed the socialization of agriculture, should be achieved by persuasion and economic incentive and not by administrative pressure. But they emphasized the need to overcome the market forces ; for them, as for Trotsky and Preobrazhensky, the restrictions imposed on planning by the market economy were obstacles in the way of the larger goal ; their eyes were on the road to full state planning which lay ahead.[3]

In March 1927, Strumilin gave classic expression to the new approach to planning in his report to the second Gosplan congress on the five-year plan.[4] He formulated the aim of the plan as being to achieve " such a *redistribution* of the existing productive forces of society, including both labour power and the material resources of the country, as would secure to the *optimum* extent the expanded and crisis-free reproduction of these productive forces *at the most rapid possible rate*, with the aim of *maximum* satisfaction of the current needs of the working masses and of bringing them *very rapidly* to the full reconstruction of society on the principles of

[1] See *ibid*. No. 7, 1926, p. 12 ; *Informatsionnyi Byulleten' Gosplana SSSR*, No. 2-3, 1927, pp. 49-50 ; No. 4, 1927, pp. 27-28.
[2] *O Pyatiletnem Plane Razvitiya Narodnogo Khozyaistva SSSR : Diskussiya v Kommunisticheskoi Akademii* (1928), pp. 37-38, 111-115. Krzhizhanovsky tried to be conciliatory, and said that Strumilin had been sharper about the question than he would have been ; there was no contradiction between the development of productive forces and reliance on socialist construction (*ibid*. pp. 68, 70).   [3] See pp. 626-628 above.
[4] For the congress and Strumilin's report see pp. 855-858 below.

socialism and communism ". This transformation would be brought about through " engineering projects ", involving a system of realistic and inter-connected quantitative targets which strictly corresponded to available resources, and were built up by combining, in " successive approximations ", the draft plans of each industry or economic sector. To integrate the plans, it was necessary to begin with industry, which he characterized as " the progressive and *leading* link of our economy " ; the growth-rate of industry must be more rapid than that of agriculture or of capitalist industry, but with a ceiling imposed by the resources available for capital investment. The plans for the other sectors of the economy such as agriculture should then be fitted into this in sequence : " the later plans rest on the earlier ", and were partly predetermined by them.[1] In practice, the result of this procedure was that the level of investment was not determined by the situation on the market, but by " engineering projects " in which the needs of industry were the determining factor. Strumilin tried to argue that the proposed rate of industrialization was consistent with non-coercion of the peasantry and with a continued increase in living standards in both town and country, and that the plans would not involve inflation. Whatever the validity of these contentions, his method rested on the assumption that the market and finance would follow the plan. In effect, it confronted the central authorities with proposals for industrial expansion which could not be reconciled with the presuppositions of NEP, and was thus an important step towards bursting the bounds of the market system. At a time when economic thinking in the USSR as well as in the west was dominated by belief in the gold standard and the need for deflation and budget surpluses, this was a revolutionary approach.

Much theoretical discussion among the planners turned on the rival merits of the " teleological " and the " genetic " approaches to planning.[2] At first, " teleology " and " genetics " seemed to be two aspects of a single system. Smilga, an enthusiastic planner, criticized at the first Gosplan congress in March 1926 those who " bow down before blind processes ", but also attacked the " hyper-

[1] S. Strumilin, *Ocherki Sovetskoi Ekonomiki* (1928), pp. 422-434.
[2] On the earlier stages of this controversy see *Socialism in One Country, 1924–1926*, Vol. 1, pp. 496-498, 500.

trophy of the plan " by some " planning maximalists " who
" treat the plan as entirely a matter of free discretion ".[1] Bazarov
in the summer of 1926 argued that the genetic and teleological
approach must be combined, and that, whereas agriculture was
" an area where genetic research plays the predominant part ", the
state sector of the economy was " an area of predominantly teleological constructs ".[2] Kondratiev conceded that all planning
necessarily involved perspectives based on possibilities, so that
even agricultural planning must make some use of the teleological
method.[3] From 1926 onwards, however, a distinctive teleological
approach to planning emerged. Its adherents differed from Kondratiev, Bazarov and Groman in two major respects. First, they
attached less importance to the peasantry and the market as constraints on planning ; they tended to talk in terms not so much of
market limitations as of physical limitations in general. Their
underlying attitude was expressed in an extreme form by Feldman,
a Gosplan economist who strongly supported the teleological
approach :

> The *opposition* of petty-bourgeois spontaneity *cannot and
> must not restrict* the rate of industrialization of the country ;
> this must be limited only by what all the working people of the
> USSR are physically able to achieve when strained to the
> margin of their physical and psychological capabilities.[4]

Secondly, they unambiguously took the objectives of the plan as
the pivot of planning. Here Pyatakov, Kuibyshev and Strumilin
were all in agreement. Pyatakov wrote in March 1926 :

> We are setting ourselves a task, we deliberately depict a
> model of industry to ourselves as we want it, so that it may
> be brought into existence ; in other words, we set ourselves a
> definite purpose and a task dictated by our will (volevaya
> zadacha) ; we free ourselves to a considerable extent in the given
> circumstances from the clutches of what is given by history ;
> we break the old bounds and gain a considerably greater creative

---

[1] *Problemy Planirovaniya (Itogi i Perspektivy)* (1926), p. 218 ; for Smilga
see pp. 277 and 286, note 1 above.
[2] *Planovoe Khozyaistvo*, No. 7, 1926, pp. 9-10.
[3] See his article in *Puti Sel'skogo Khozyaistva*, No. 2, 1927, pp. 3-36.
[4] *Planovoe Khozyaistvo*, No. 2, 1929, p. 192.

freedom. But not every task can be accomplished, and we must set ourselves *only tasks which can be accomplished*.[1]

In a similar vein, Strumilin in the spring of 1927 contrasted his own approach with that based on mere forecasting of tendencies, asserting that " not prediction, but targets (zadaniya) and advance directives (predukazaniya) are the central focus of any plan " ; the starting-point for planning must be " what can be indicated in advance by positing it as a goal ".[2] No unique solution existed to a planning problem ; planning " must be seen as a special kind of engineering art, and not as a science in the strict sense of the term ".[3] He emphasized the independent rôle of the planner : " armchair scholars " often neglected the " collective will of the producers " as a factor in the economy " ; the job of the planner was to mould this collective will.[4] A few months later, at the session of the TsIK of the USSR in October 1927, Kuibyshev spoke in similar terms :

> In America and elsewhere plans are usually an attempt to foresee how the further development of the economy is blindly forming itself as a result of the business management of economic units which are not interconnected by a unified will and leadership. With us it is a quite different matter. We can construct plans based not only on foreseeing what will happen, but also on a definite will to achieve specific tasks and purposes.[5]

As time went on the powers of the planner were increasingly emphasized, and the rôle of the market still further played down. At the beginning of 1928, Kuibyshev led the way with his insistence that the planners must not be deflected by *Konjunktur* trends.[6] Strumilin now regarded science as subordinate to the goals of the plan ; for him, " the purposive task set by our whole economic environment and our international and internal class position is for us an organizing and directing principle, in relation to which science, in spite of its high calling, and all other auxiliary

[1] *Materialy Osobogo Soveshchaniya po Vosstanovleniyu Osnovnogo Kapitala pri Prezidiume VSNKh SSSR*, Seriya II, i (1926), 4.

[2] S. Strumilin, *Ocherki Sovetskoi Ekonomiki* (1928), p. 479 ; *Planovoe Khozyaistvo*, No. 7, 1927, p. 14.

[3] S. Strumilin, *Ocherki Sovetskoi Ekonomiki* (1928), p. 422.

[4] *Planovoe Khozyaistvo*, No. 7, 1927, p. 11.

[5] *2 Sessiya Tsentral'nogo Ispolnitel'nogo Komiteta Soyuza SSR 4 Sozyva* (n.d. [1927]), p. 246.   [6] See p. 632 above.

means are only servants ".[1] Strumilin's enthusiastic supporter Vaisberg argued that the genetic approach implied acceptance of the " genetical inheritance " of 300 years of Tsarism, and resoundingly declared that " our plan lags behind reality " :

We can plan only by coming out against things and against people, by overcoming the limits of resistance.[2]

Bazarov condemned Strumilin's approach as that of the mediaeval church :

All the " teleology " of that time had religious dogmatics — theology — as its source. And science was a servant of theology. . . . The directives of theology were based not on human reason, but on a much higher source of cognition, on God's revelation. . . . And in our transition period the attempt to attach to Marxism the slave-like epistemology of the Christian church is of course profoundly reactionary.[3]

Some attempts at compromise were still made. Groman, the most stubborn defender of " the priority of the genetic standpoint ", conceded that " in the plan the genetical and teleological points of view represent a dialectical unity ", though he claimed " logical priority " for the genetic.[4] Gukhman, the Gosplan statistician, suggested that the quarrel about the " metaphysics " of planning should be ended :

No one will suspect that R. E. Vaisberg wants to replace " teleology " by " theology ". . . . I and other comrades working in planning can testify that on more than one occasion the " teleologist " Vaisberg was in practice no less a " geneticist " than Groman, and the latter often produced involuntary alarm in Vaisberg with his ready-made " purposive " proposals and constructs.[5]

But this was already an attempt to bridge the unbridgeable. Though accusations of aiming at counter-revolution were not yet

[1] O Pyatiletnem Plane Razvitiya Narodnogo Khozyaistva SSSR : Diskussiya v Kommunisticheskoi Akademii (1928), p. 39.
[2] Planovoe Khozyaistvo, No. 4, 1928, p. 167.
[3] O Pyatiletnem Plane Razvitiya Narodnogo Khozyaistva SSSR : Diskussiya v Kommunisticheskoi Akademii (1928), pp. 78-79.
[4] Planovoe Khozyaistvo, No. 6, 1928, pp. 159, 181.
[5] Ibid. No. 6, 1928, pp. 170-171.

made, "teleology" was already a term of praise for those who
tacitly wished to go beyond the market framework, and "genetics" a derogatory term for those who did not.

Closely associated with the discussion about the teleological
and genetic approaches to planning was a parallel discussion about
equilibrium (ravnovesie). Notions of equilibrium were a commonplace in western economic thought from the beginning of the
twentieth century; and the concept was extremely popular
among Soviet economists and officials in the nineteen-twenties. In
the Soviet Union it was particularly associated with the name of
Bukharin.[1] According to this concept, the crises of capitalism
were caused by breakdowns in equilibrium. Socialism would
avoid these breakdowns by maintaining equilibrium between
different factors and sectors in the economy — in the short term
between supply and demand on the market, in the long term
between agriculture and industry, between production and consumption. The positive concept of equilibrium was coupled with
the negative concept of "disproportions" (disproportsii). Bazarov expressed a characteristic view when he observed that temporary disproportions were inevitable in spontaneous or unplanned economic development, but intolerable in a planned
economy.[2] The word "disproportions" was used to refer both to

[1] Bukharin had long adhered to equilibrium theories. In *Ekonomika
Perekhodnogo Perioda*, i (1920), 127-129, he described the "*postulate of
equilibrium*" as the foundation of economic theory. His main theoretical work
on historical materialism, first published in 1921, revolved round the concept
of equilibrium, which included equilibrium between nature and society and
between different elements in society; he defined the concept as follows:
"*The equilibrium which we observe in nature and in society is not absolute, not
static equilibrium, but a dynamic equilibrium.* What does this mean? It means
that equilibrium is established, and is at once destroyed, and is established
anew on *a new basis*, and is again destroyed, and so on." This process was the
expression of the dialectic: thesis, antithesis, synthesis (*Teoriya Istoricheskogo
Materializma* (2nd ed. [n.d.] pp. 75-78, 270-272). Unstable equilibrium
could be positive, when productive forces were increasing, or negative, when
they were declining (*ibid.* p. 160, where Bukharin quoted a statement of Marx
in *Wage-Labour and Capital* that a social organization was in "unstable equilibrium" when productive forces were increasing). This theory exposed
Bukharin after 1929 to a charge of mechanistic materialism, which he was said
to have borrowed from Bogdanov; at the seventeenth party congress in
December 1934 he named "the so-called theory of equilibrium" as one of
"the theoretical presuppositions of the Right deviation" (*XVII S"ezd Vsesoyuznoi Kommunisticheskoi Partii (B)* (1934), p. 125).
[2] *Planovoe Khozyaistvo*, No. 7, 1926, p. 11.

short-term shortages or crises on the market such as occurred in
the autumn of 1925, and to long-term lack of correspondence in
the development of separate sectors of the economy such as
industry and agriculture.[1] The resolution of the fifteenth party
congress in December 1927 appeared to use the word in a long-
term sense when it listed four " basic disproportions " which must
be taken into account in constructing the five-year plan : between
industry and agriculture ; between industrial and agricultural
prices ; between the demand from industry for raw materials and
their supply from agriculture ; and between the availability of
labour in the countryside and the real possibility of its economic
utilization.[2] Narkomfin officials particularly emphasized short-
term or market aspects of equilibrium and disproportion : " equilibrium must be attained as the equilibrium of a commodity-
money economy ", wrote Yurovsky, adding that, while the state
could influence prices, its objectives " are realized on the market,
on which equilibrium must be achieved for the uninterrupted
flow of economic life ".[3] The long-term and short-term senses
of the words were often confused ; and until 1927 the situation
on the market was universally treated as the ultimate test of
the correctness of the proportions established in the economy.
Both the advocates of industrialization and the defenders of agriculture would point to the goods famine as a disproportion or disequilibrium indicating a fundamental disproportion in the basic
structure of the economy. But the former argued that the fundamental disproportion in the economy was the insufficient development of industry in relation to agriculture, and the latter that the
fundamental disproportion was the insufficient development of
agriculture in relation to industry.

The drive for industrialization in the summer and autumn of
1927, followed by the fiasco of the grain collections, produced
an alarmed recognition of the threat which industrialization
offered to the theory and practice of equilibrium and to the presuppositions of NEP. Doctrines of rapid industrialization were

---

[1] Kritsman pointed to a further distinction between *technical* disproportion
in the ratios of output of coal, cotton, metal, and so on, and the more important
social disproportion (*Vestnik Kommunisticheskoi Akademii*, xvi (1926), 251-252).

[2] *KPSS v Rezolyutsiyakh* (1954), ii, 455.

[3] L. Yurovsky, *Denezhnaya Politika Sovetskoi Vlasti (1917–1927)* (1928),
pp. 376-377 ; for Yurovsky see pp. 723, 727 above.

always difficult to reconcile with the theory of equilibrium. There was obviously a sense in which Preobrazhensky, with his theory of non-equivalent exchange, was suggesting a permanent disruption of equilibrium ; and the defence of such policies on the ground that they aimed at " dynamic " rather than " static " equilibrium was uneasy.[1] The party in its official statements at first reacted to the crisis by reasserting the importance of equilibrium. The fifteenth party congress in December 1927 denounced " the demand for a maximum transfer of resources from the sphere of the peasant economy to the sphere of industry " as " a violation of the equilibrium of the whole national economic system ", and stressed the importance of establishing equilibrium and eliminating disproportions.[2] The central committee in its resolution of April 1928 pronounced it " indispensable in the first instance to achieve a more correct proportion between the different elements in the national economy " ;[3] and in July 1928 the committee still deplored " the breakdown of market equilibrium and the aggravation of that breakdown by a growth of the purchasing power of the peasantry more rapid than that of the supply of industrial goods ".[4] About the same time Vaisberg, although a strong supporter of industrialization, used the notion of equilibrium to condemn Sabsovich's even bolder proposals from Vesenkha :

> Comrade Sabsovich completely ignores the element of equilibrium in the very development of the economy. In starting from a basic teleological approach, it was wrong to forget at the same time the conditions for the equilibrium of the whole economic system.[5]

But, as the year went on and the crisis became more acute, positions shifted sharply within the party, and a clear division appeared. The diagnosis of the crisis as " a violation of the conditions of

[1] Preobrazhensky's last major published article early in 1927 was significantly entitled *Economic Equilibrium in the Soviet System*, and advanced his characteristic policies in the form of seven " conditions for equilibrium " (*Vestnik Kommunisticheskoi Akademii*, xxii (1927), 19-71) ; Preobrazhensky posited an unstable equilibrium between three elements — the state economy, the private capitalist economy, and simple commodity production. This was criticized on Bukharinite lines in *Bol'shevik*, No. 12, June 30, 1928, pp. 11-25.
[2] *KPSS v Rezolyutsiyakh* (1954), ii, 453, 455-456, 463.
[3] *Ibid.* ii, 497.   [4] *Ibid.* ii, 514.
[5] *Informatsionnyi Byulleten' Gosplana SSSR*, No. 8-9, 1928, p. 8 ; for Sabsovich see p. 309 above.

economic equilibrium" found its most complete expression in Bukharin's *Notes of an Economist* of September 30, 1928. Bukharin argued that the "basic violation" of equilibrium which had occurred was an avoidable error. Industry must be planned not " in itself " but in relation to the peasant market : " the violation of necessary *economic* relations has as its other side the violation of *political* equilibrium in the country ".

> *It is necessary* [he concluded] *to obtain combinations of the main elements of the economy which are.as correct as possible (to " balance " them, allocate them in the most expedient fashion, actively influencing the course of economic life and the class struggle).*[1]

The association of " equilibrium " with the Right wing in the party now made the whole conception suspect in the eyes of official party opinion. Kuibyshev, in a speech delivered in Leningrad some days before the appearance of Bukharin's article, observed caustically that " the most serious disproportion, the one which does most harm to our economy, is the one between the production of means of production and the needs of the country ".[2] An editorial in the journal of the presidium of Vesenkha roundly declared, with obvious reference to Bukharin's article :

> To impose on the *annual* plans of our economic development the task of *getting rid* of the disproportions by the simple "balancing" of separate elements of the economy . . . means *not to understand anything* in the whole complex of our economy . . .
>
> A number of years will be required before these disproportions are finally resolved in the course of a *consciously* directed process of economic development and socialist construction. Until this time, disproportions will accompany our economic development, will inevitably intrude and make our forward movement difficult.[3]

But even this was not yet a clear condemnation of the theory of equilibrium ; and Stalin, speaking in the party central committee

---

[1] *Pravda*, September 30, 1928 ; for Bukharin's article see pp. 89-90, 317-319 above.

[2] *Pravda*, September 25, 1928 ; for other aspects of this speech see pp. 316-317 above.

[3] *Puti Industrializatsii*, No. 18, 1928, p. 7 ; for an altercation in November 1928 between Rykov and Kuibyshev about equilibrium see p. 325 above.

in November 1928, confined himself to sweeping away an underlying assumption of equilibrium without explicitly mentioning it :

> Agriculture has always lagged, and will always lag, behind industry.[1]

The discussion about equilibrium and disproportion overlapped with a discussion about the rôle of balances in planning. Balances were accounts or budgets of receipts and outgoings expressed in physical or monetary terms. At the Gosplan congress in March 1926, Groman defended their use, and argued that the method of balances should have been listed in the 1925–1926 control figures as one of the major methods used in compiling them.[2] The control figures for 1926–1927 spoke of " the recognition, as a basic method of preparing and realizing the control figures, of a system of balanced accounts which . . . should be finally combined in a single balance of the national economy of the USSR ".[3] The major function of the method, as it was practised in the middle nineteen-twenties, was to facilitate coordination between the different parts of the economy and to reduce, and if possible eliminate, disequilibrium or disproportion. Bazarov declared that " the movement of the economy from its present state to the final point indicated in the general plan must take place smoothly, *without interruptions*, and this in its turn presupposes the presence of definite economic reserves ".[4] Vaisberg conceded that the " balanced interconnexion of the separate elements of the economy is a completely necessary condition for guaranteeing the five-year plan against arbitrary targets ", and must be used to discover " limiting factors " (limity) or " bottlenecks " (uzkie mesta), and to calculate approximately the amount of savings and investment, export and import, and so on.[5] While the principle of equilibrium, once it had been invoked as an obstacle to the industrialization drive, was simply rejected, the " method of balances "

[1] Stalin, *Sochineniya*, xi, 258 ; it was not till December 1929 that Stalin directly denounced " the so-called theory of the ' equilibrium ' of the sectors of our national economy " (*ibid.* xii, 143).
[2] *Problemy Planirovaniya (Itogi i Perspektivy)* (1926), pp. 225-227, 255-256.
[3] *Kontrol'nye Tsifry Narodnogo Khozyaistva na 1926–1927 god* (1926), p. 14. [4] *Planovoe Khozyaistvo*, No. 7, 1926, p. 9.
[5] R. Vaisberg, *Printsipy i Metodologiya Perspektivnogo Planirovaniya* (n.d. [1928]), p. 20.

was adapted to the new needs of planning. The issue between the supporters of rapid industrialization and their opponents was what to do when confronted with a deficiency on one side of a planned balance. The traditional view, based on the experience of war communism, was that the bottlenecks should be taken as the key to the possible scope of the plan. Thus, even Pyatakov commented in April 1926 that a factory or group " must adapt itself to (ravnyat'sya po) the narrowest bottleneck, or the whole process of production will be held up ". He added, however, that bottlenecks could be " widened " with a relatively small amount of technical re-equipment.[1] Narkomzem, on the other hand, argued that " it is these factors and their movement which determine in the last resort the limits of possible development of other elements of the economy ".[2] Bukharin in his *Notes of an Economist* argued that plans for industry should be cut back owing to the shortages revealed in the planned balances for 1928–1929.[3] The industrial newspaper condemned this as a " reactionary " demand, insisting that a balance must not be a fetish, but a method of checking ; a balance must not be a means of cutting back to the bottlenecks, but a method of overcoming them, of " pressing actively on them and getting rid of them ".[4] What this meant in practice was that plans were increased to enable the bottlenecks to be eliminated. The planned supply of materials was recalculated upwards to enable production targets to be met ; the level of savings was adjusted in the savings-investment balance to the given level of investment. When handled in this manner, the method of balances ceased to be a means of establishing equilibrium, and contributed to the pressure for an increased rate of industrialization.[5]

In these new conditions, the methods of planning developed in the middle nineteen-twenties were obviously no longer appropriate.

[1] *Torgovo-Promyshlennaya Gazeta*, April 16, 1926.
[2] *Informatsionnyi Byulleten' Gosplana SSSR*, No. 7, 1927, p. 23.
[3] See pp. 317–319 above.
[4] *Torgovo-Promyshlennaya Gazeta*, October 12, 1928. At the Menshevik trial in 1931, Groman denounced as false the principle that " we should adapt ourselves to the bottlenecks instead of overcoming them and using accumulated forces " ; he and his colleagues had derived the principle from the " law of economic life " enunciated by Proudhon that " the weak link determines the opposition of the environment at a given moment " (*Protsess Kontrrevolyutsionnoi Organizatsii Men'shevikov* (1931), pp. 378–379).
[5] For " material balances " see pp. 830–831 below.

These methods had been designed to serve the needs of planning
in a basically market economy. The new approach assumed that
plans should not be restricted by conditions on the market or even
by the physical resources which were immediately available, and
repudiated plans derived from the study of the regularities of the
market economy. The use of comparative data drawn from
capitalist countries or from pre-war Russia to establish limits to
the planned growth of the Soviet Union was emphatically rejected.
Already by the spring of 1927 Strumilin treated the rates of growth
of capitalist countries not as an upper but as a lower limit in the
construction of Soviet plans ; [1] in October 1927 Kuibyshev
rejected " the method of comparison with the time before the war,
of comparison with last year or with previous years " ; [2] and in
January 1929 he firmly asserted that " to draw conclusions about
the realism or lack of realism of our planned rates of growth from
the evidence of the practice of capitalism is possible only if one
has the limited outlook of a bourgeois economist ".[3] By this time,
comparisons were made with other countries only to contrast the
rapidity of Soviet expansion with the slower rates of growth of
capitalism, and to measure the closing of the gap between the
USSR and the capitalist world. Another planning method
favoured in the middle nineteen-twenties, the use of " static and
dynamic coefficients " to extrapolate existing economic trends,
which was closely connected with the genetic approach to planning, was also speedily rejected.[4] None of the existing methods
of planning could lay any claim to precision. All schools of thought
agreed that, in view of the complexity of planning problems and
the inadequacy of available statistics, the development of a
" science of planning " using mathematical methods was a rather

[1] See p. 790 above.
[2] 2 Sessiya Tsentral'nogo Ispolnitel'nogo Soveta Soyuza SSR 4 Sozyva
(n.d. [1927]), p. 250.
[3] Puti Industrializatsii, No. 1, 1929, pp. 9-10.
[4] For these methods see Socialism in One Country, 1924–1926, Vol. 1, p. 501.
In February 1926 it was pointed out in Gosplan that the method of " static and
dynamic coefficients " failed to anticipate the rapidity of expansion and could
not take account of socio-economic and technical change ;   a speaker at the
first Gosplan congress a month later criticized the use of dynamic coefficients
as " economic astrology " (Informatsionnyi Byulleten' Gosplana SSSR, No.
2, 1926, pp. 29-31 ;   Problemy Planirovaniya (Itogi i Perspektivy) (1926), p.
248).

remote prospect.[1] All planners used "fairly crude devices";[2] and even plans couched in the form of elaborate statistical tables often reflected the beliefs of their authors rather than the objective possibilities of the situation.[3] From 1928 onwards, adherents of the teleological approach to planning were no longer limited by the need to show that their plans were compatible with the market situation, and both enthusiasts and sceptics about the use of mathematical methods freely and even rashly manipulated statistics and coefficients in order to justify their plans.[4] An increasing impatience was shown with what were seen as the narrow-minded objections of non-party experts ; at the sixteenth party conference in April 1929 Larin expressed what was by then a common view when he attacked Gosplan for relying too much on its own professional statisticians and engineers rather than consulting party economists, and for failing to keep abreast of " party economic thought ".[5] While planning at all levels remained crude and imprecise, the expanding industrialization programme carried with it much more detailed control of all sectors of the economy, and particularly of industry ; side by side with the rejection of market economics and traditional methods of planning a new and elaborate system of physical planning emerged.

---

[1] See for example Groman, *ibid.* pp. 225-226 ; Vaisberg in *Informatsionnyi Byulleten' Gosplana SSSR*, No. 5-6, 1927, pp. 61-62.

[2] *Planovoe Khozyaistvo*, No. 7, 1926, p. 13.

[3] Strumilin was easily able to point out statistical errors and wrong predictions in Kondratiev's writings (S. Strumilin, *Ocherki Sovetskoi Ekonomiki* (1928), pp. 486-492) ; Lyashchenko equally easily convicted Strumilin of "unjustified and unanalysed calculations " (*O Pyatiletnem Plane Razvitiya Narodnogo Khozyaistva SSSR : Diskussiya v Kommunisticheskoi Akademii* (1928), pp. 47-51). For the " statistical deviation " in planning see p. 872 below.

[4] For examples see pp. 841, 866-867 below.

[5] *Shestnadtsataya Konferentsiya VKP(B)* (1962), p. 148.

2 D

CHAPTER 33

AGENCIES OF PLANNING

GOSPLAN ranked, side by side with Vesenkha, Narkomfin and Narkomput', as an economic organ directly subordinate to STO and Sovnarkom. It was the only government agency explicitly and exclusively concerned with planning. As early as 1924, Gosplan possessed a skeleton structure which contained most of the elements of its future organization. It included sections (sektsii) for industry, transport, agriculture, and the budget and finance ; a council for *Konjunktur*, established in 1923, resembling the rival *Konjunktur* institute of Narkomfin, provided Gosplan with a source of current economic information independent of other government agencies.[1] Unlike Vesenkha, Gosplan did not acquire the status of a People's Commissariat and had no executive powers.[2] It started from small beginnings ; Strumilin reported in 1925 that it had " one or two dozen economists and approximately the same number of statisticians at its disposal ".[3] By the beginning of 1927, it already had a staff of 500.[4] The machinery of Gosplan developed mainly by enlarging and subdividing the existing sections rather than by introducing any new principle of organization. The most elaborately organized section was Promsektsiya, the industrial section, which was divided into production " groups " concerned with metals, building materials, textiles and so on ; in addition, presumably owing to the influence

[1] *Ekonomicheskaya Zhizn'*, January 13, 1924 ; for the structure of Gosplan in 1926 see *Informatsionnyi Byulleten' Gosplana SSSR*, No. 2, 1926, pp. 36-37.
[2] Sovnarkom ruled that in status Gosplan was only a commission of Sovnarkom and could not speak in its own name in other government organs (such as the budget commission of TsIK) without the preliminary approval of Sovnarkom (*Plenum Byudzhetnoi Komissii TsIK Soyuza SSR* (1927), p. 404).
[3] *Planovoe Khozyaistvo*, No. 10, 1925, p. 9.
[4] *Plenum Byudzhetnoi Komissii TsIK Soyuza SSR* (1927), p. 400 ; this figure excluded the section (sektor) of world economy.

of Krzhizhanovsky and the concept of *energetika*,[1] separate sections, independent of the industrial section, were in charge of fuel and electrification. Each group was responsible for advice to Gosplan on its industry ; the principal function of the groups was to prepare or scrutinize drafts of the annual control figures and of the five-year plan for their industries. Non-party experts played a major part in the work of Gosplan : these included economists such as Groman and Bazarov, and engineers such as Kalinnikov, president of the industrial section, Gartvan and Taube from the Urals, who were responsible for the metals group of Gosplan, and Ramzin, in the fuel section.[2] At first only a handful of party members worked in Gosplan ; by April 1929, 100 of the staff of 500 were party members.[3]

While Gosplan was devoted exclusively to planning, it never had a monopoly of planning or anything like complete control over all planning activities, annual or long-term. Planning had begun in the form of plans compiled by particular commissariats and for particular industries.[4] These practices continued throughout the nineteen-twenties. The work of Gosplan was duplicated and elaborated in greater detail in the commissariats. Each People's Commissariat had its own planning department which

---

[1] Gosplan was the child of Goelro, the commission on electrification presided over by Krzhizhanovsky (see *The Bolshevik Revolution, 1917–1923*, Vol. 2, p. 372), whose conviction of the primary importance of *energetika* or power dated from that time : *energetika* was the symbol of man's victorious struggle against nature (G. Krzhizhanovsky, *Sochineniya*, ii (1934), 231-236, 259-261). The second Gosplan congress in March 1927 described *energetika* as " the backbone of the whole programme of reconstruction " (*Informatsionnyi Byulleten' Gosplana SSSR*, No. 4, 1927, p. 2 ; cf. *ibid.* No. 3-4, 1928, p. 27) ; and the preface to the five-year plan observed that " the genuine triumph of the notion of *energetika* in the planning and construction of the national economy . . . has run like a red thread through the whole period of discussion of the five-year plan " (*Pyatiletnii Plan Narodno-Khozyaistvennogo Stroitel'stva SSSR* (1929), i, 5). But the term was used ambiguously. In the narrower sense, it was " a purely technical factor — mechanical power . . . and thermal power " ; in the wider sense, it covered " all forms of power, including living human labour and the work of animals " (*ibid.* ii, i, 7). For a table showing the utilization of different forms of power in different countries see p. 485, note 1 above.

[2] In February 1927 Ryazanov complained at the budget commission of TsIK that 47 specialists on the staff of Gosplan were receiving personal salaries ranging from 250 to 500 rubles a month (*Plenum Byudzhetnoi Komissii TsIK Soyuza SSR* (1927), p. 401) ; for the remuneration of specialists see pp. 601-604 above.   [3] *Shestnadtsataya Konferentsiya VKP(B)* (1962), p. 258.

[4] See *Socialism in One Country, 1924–1926*, Vol. 1, pp. 491, 499.

drew up five-year and annual plans or control figures to supplement or challenge the plans and control figures of Gosplan. Local authorities also drew up their own plans ; control figures for Moscow province were submitted to the Moscow party committee in October 1927.[1] Independent plans were prepared for the most varied activities.[2] The detailed plans of particular sectors or areas lay beyond the scope of Gosplan. In 1925 Strumilin poked fun at the idea that Gosplan could " take on itself the function of an all-Union nurse or guardian angel for every trust in the backwoods " ;[3] Vesenkha on its side insisted that Gosplan should examine only the " main data " of its plan for industry.[4] At the same time Vesenkha encroached seriously on the functions of Gosplan by establishing its own machinery for preparing plans for other sectors of the economy such as agriculture and transport, and coordinating them with those of industry ; in the summer of 1927, a Rabkrin commission complained that " Vesenkha duplicates the work of Gosplan ".[5]

Attempts continued to give Gosplan directive powers over the planning departments of all the commissariats, and to establish it as the supreme controller of the whole Soviet planning process. But these attempts were ineffective. Between 1924 and 1926, each commissariat expanded its planning department ; in Vesenkha planning departments were established in every *glavk* or directorate and eventually in every trust ; and these departments were in practice kept fully under commissariat control.[6] In the spring of 1927, a Rabkrin investigation recommended " the strengthening of the leading rôle of the Gosplan of the USSR " ; Rabkrin proposed that the Gosplan of the USSR should become the directive organ for the Gosplans of the republics, and reiterated that the planning departments of industry, while administratively controlled by Vesenkha, should be under dual subordination, with the duty to carry out Gosplan directives.[7] On June 8, 1927, a decree

---

[1] *Pravda*, October 6, 1927.
[2] In January 1928 STO approved a five-year plan for the dairy industry, and a ten-year plan for sheep-breeding (*Sobranie Zakonov, 1928*, No. 9, art. 81 ; No. 12, art. 108).
[3] *Planovoe Khozyaistvo*, No. 10, 1925, p. 9.
[4] *Torgovo-Promyshlennaya Gazeta*, August 29, 1926.
[5] *Ibid.* July 16, August 14, 1927.
[6] A. Gordon, *Sistema Planovykh Organov SSSR* (1929), p. 50 ; *Torgovo-Promyshlennaya Gazeta*, September 18, 1926.   [7] *Pravda*, May 10, 1927.

of Sovnarkom ruled that while the planning departments of the Vesenkha of the USSR and of other commissariats were to remain subordinate to their own commissariats, Gosplan had authority over them in matters of " procedure, programme of work, and dates ". The presidium of the Gosplan of the USSR was also authorized to call periodic conferences which included representatives of the planning departments of the commissariats.[1] In a subsequent article in *Pravda*, Gosplan was optimistically said to have acquired " approximately the same powers " over the planning organs of the commissariats as over the republican Gosplans ; and the decree was hailed as crowning a long process of " *continuous and unwavering growth from year to year of the authority and priority of the Gosplan of the USSR over other planning and controlling bodies* ".[2] But the commissariats continued to assert their independence ; and a year later, on June 14, 1928, when Gosplan was losing the initiative to Vesenkha in the preparation of the five-year plan,[3] a further decree once more reversed the balance in favour of the commissariats. It was now laid down that every People's Commissariat, except Narkomindel and Rabkrin, should set up its own planning department (this in most cases merely registered an existing situation), and that, while these departments might communicate directly with Gosplan, they were subordinate to their own commissariats, and instead of being guided solely by Gosplan in matters of procedure and dates they were henceforth to be guided by Gosplan and their commissariats jointly. Moreover, the planning departments of republican commissariats were to receive directives not from Gosplan, but from the planning organs of the Union commissariats.[4]

What therefore emerged from this struggle between Gosplan and the commissariats was the recognition of Gosplan as a co-ordinating, but not a directing, organ. The right of Gosplan to examine and comment on all draft plans before they were discussed by Sovnarkom and STO was never seriously challenged ; and from 1926 onwards Gosplan paid increasing attention to the

---

[1] *Sobranie Zakonov, 1927*, No. 37, art. 373 ; for this decree see also p. 807 below.
[2] *Pravda*, June 28, 1927.
[3] See pp. 877-878 below.
[4] *Sobranie Zakonov, 1928*, No. 37, art. 342 ; A. Gordon, *Sistema Planovykh Organov SSSR* (1929), p. 57.

problems of coordination. In 1926 Groman spoke of the importance of " examining the connexion between different sectors of the
economy and creating a conception of the conditions of development of the national economy as a whole " ; he described this as
" synthetic " (sinteticheskii) work which would be carried out
through close collaboration between the research and operational
sections of Gosplan.[1] The term " synthetic " became a fashion-
able term for describing the work of reconciling plans from different sectors of the economy ; and such Gosplan departments as the
budgetary and financial section and the section for regionalization
became known as " synthetic " sections.[2] By 1928, the constella-
tions of experts in Gosplan reproduced in miniature the structure of
economic administration in the country as a whole ; the budgetary
and financial section corresponded to Narkomfin, the industrial
section to Vesenkha, the transport section to Narkomput', and so
on, systematic informal contact being maintained between the
Gosplan sections and groups and the corresponding officials in the
commissariats. The work of all the Gosplan sections was itself
coordinated by commissions for the annual control figures, for the
five-year perspective plan, and for the general plan ; these commissions, which became a more or less permanent part of the
structure, were fused into a single central commission for perspective planning in 1928, when concentration of all efforts in Gosplan
on preparing the first five-year plan led to a switch of its personnel
away from short-term planning.[3] All major proposals were considered by the presidium of Gosplan, which included the expert
presidents of its principal sections as well as prominent party men
such as Krzhizhanovsky and Grinko.

While the attempt of Gosplan to establish its control over the
planning departments of the commissariats failed, the increasing
importance of central planning enabled it to extend its influence
over the Gosplans of the republics and the planning commissions
which had been established in many provincial Soviets.[4] These

---

[1] *Informatsionnyi Byulleten' Gosplana SSSR*, No. 11-12, 1926, pp. 42-43.
[2] See Krzhizhanovsky's article in *Ekonomicheskaya Zhizn'*, June 29, 1927.
[3] See pp. 874-875 below.
[4] Within the RSFSR, as part of an economy drive, the planning departments which had been formed in the territories of the future regions in advance
of regionalization were abolished in May 1926 in all those areas in which
regionalization had not yet been carried out (A. Gordon, *Sistema Planovykh*

CH. XXXIII   AGENCIES OF PLANNING   807

at first operated with a considerable amount of independence from the Gosplan of the USSR. The Gosplan of the RSFSR, for example, insisted, in violation of the decision of the first Gosplan congress, that it should work only on the general plan.[1] Uralplan, the planning commission for the Ural region, prepared a draft fifteen-year plan based largely on its own assumptions about the general growth of the economy and the part to be played by the Urals in this growth; in its turn, the planning commission for the Irbit department (okrug) rejected the proposals about the level wages made by Uralplan.[2] But neither the local planning commissions nor even the republican Gosplans were powerful bodies. They were usually ignored by Vesenkha and the *glavki* when plans for particular industries were compiled; [3] and they were brought fairly easily under Gosplan control. From 1927 onwards, republican Gosplans and local planning commissions were required to conform to the procedures adopted by Sovnarkom for the preparation and scrutiny of the annual control figures and the five-year plan; [4] the decree of June 8, 1927, which cautiously attempted to strengthen the powers of Gosplan over the planning departments of the commissariats, stipulated much more bluntly that the republican Gosplans were " subordinate to the directive authority of the Gosplan of the USSR ".[5] These changes placed the Gosplan of the USSR in a commanding position. By 1929, republican Gosplans and local planning commissions were in all major matters firmly under the control of the Gosplan of the USSR and its section for regionalization.

Organov SSSR (1928), p. 54; *Kontrol'nye Tsifry Narodnogo Khozyaistva na 1926–1927 god* (1926), p. 223); Gosplan complained that as a result the small " regional *Konjunktur* bureaus " of the Gosplan of the USSR were the only local planning organs above the provincial level in the non-regionalized areas, which included two-thirds of the population of the European part of the RSFSR (*Kontrol'nye Tsifry Narodnogo Khozyaistva SSSR na 1927–1928 god* (1928), p. 410). The position was rectified with the rapid development of regionalization in 1928 and 1929
[1] See p. 838 below.
[2] *General'nyi Plan Khozyaistva Urala v Period 1917–1941 gg. i Perspektivy Pervogo Pyatiletiya* (Sverdlovsk, 1927); *Khozyaistvo Urala*, No. 13-14, 1926, pp. 161-162.
[3] *Problemy Planirovaniya (Itogi i Perspektivy)* (1926), pp. 122-123.
[4] *Kontrol'nye Tsifry Narodnogo Khozyaistva SSSR na 1927–1928 god* (1928), pp. 410-411; *Informatsionnyi Byulleten' Gosplana SSSR*, No. 4, 1927, pp. 2, 30-31.   [5] For this decree see p. 805 above.

The influence of Gosplan over the collection of statistical information also increased with the advent of central planning. The responsibility for the collection and processing of primary statistics was divided between the Central Statistical Administration (TsSU), which like Gosplan was a separate agency subordinate to Sovnarkom, the provincial statistical departments, which were closely under the control of the Central Statistical Administration, and the statistical departments of the commissariats. Gosplan lacked any machinery of its own for collecting statistics, and apparently failed to influence the work of the statistical departments of the commissariats.[1]   But Gosplan persuaded the Central Statistical Administration, after a long period of conflict, to collect data in forms corresponding more closely to the needs of planning ; in May 1927, with the approval of Gosplan, a commission named Statplan was established within the Central Statistical Administration with the responsibility for planning the collection of statistics throughout the economy.[2]   This was to prove to be merely the prelude to the administrative subordination of the central and local statistical organs to Gosplan at the beginning of 1930.

[1] The organization of industrial statistics is discussed in relation to the position of Gosplan in Note D, p. 936 below ; for the *Konjunktur* council of Gosplan see p. 802 above.
[2] For the conflict between Gosplan and the Central Statistical Administration see *Informatsionnyi Byulleten' Gosplana SSSR*, No. 2, 1926, pp. 26-28 ; this conflict was partly due to the influence within the latter body of " neo-*narodnik* " statisticians, who had close ties with the experts of Narkomzem and Narkomfin (for the neo-*narodniks* see p. 20 and p. 29, note 2 above).   For the new arrangements see *Informatsionnyi Byulleten' Gosplana SSSR*, No. 10, 1926, pp. 17-19 ; *Sobranie Zakonov, 1927*, No. 33, art. 340 (dated May 11, 1927).

CHAPTER 34

THE CONTROL FIGURES

B Y the middle nineteen-twenties, the standard concept in
Gosplan envisaged three main levels of national economic
planning : the general plan (general'nyi plan, or *genplan*),
covering ten or fifteen years ; the five-year or " perspective "
plan ; and the annual control figures, which were to be a specific
segment of the longer-term plans, set out in operational detail.[1]
Between 1926 and 1929, strenuous efforts were made to realize
this programme. But no *genplan* was ever approved, and the five-
year plan was not approved until the spring of 1929. The annual
control figures, prepared more or less independently of the five-
year plan, were in this period the main means of directing economic
policy.

The first control figures, prepared by Gosplan in the summer of
1925, and covering the year 1925–1926, had been a bold attempt to
take over the central rôle in economic policy-making from Narkomfin and the budget. The sequel was paradoxical. For, while
the figures themselves suffered neglect or rejection at the hands of
higher authorities,[2] this apparent defeat was redeemed by acceptance in principle of annual control figures as a method of guiding
economic policy. In December 1925 a Gosplan commission, of
which Smilga was president and which included Strumilin,
Groman and Bazarov, set to work on the control figures for 1926–
1927.[3] At the first Gosplan congress in March 1926, Grinko, then
working in the Ukrainian Gosplan, spoke of the " new stage " in
the work of Gosplan, in which " government organs cannot take a
step without asking advice and comment from us on both major

---

[1] See *Socialism in One Country, 1924–1926*, Vol. 1, pp. 511-512 ; *Problemy Planirovaniya (Itogi i Perspektivy)* (1926), p. 324 ; *Planovoe Khozyaistvo*, No. 7, 1926, p. 9.
[2] See *Socialism in One Country, 1924–1926*, Vol. 1, pp. 503-508.
[3] *Kontrol'nye Tsifry Narodnogo Khozyaistva na 1926–1927 god* (1926), p. v.

and minor questions " ; the Soviet public (obshchestvennost')
was becoming accustomed to the fact that Gosplan gave guidance
on all aspects of economic development.[1] Smilga summarized the
ultimate significance of the labours of Gosplan in the previous
twelve months :

> Within a few years, and perhaps within a year, the control
> figures will become the main method of planning and managing the
> national economy. . . . Much more work must be done before we
> create fully realistic control figures. But it is now already im-
> possible to imagine the position without control figures. Every-
> one recognizes this, both the friends and the enemies of the first
> control figures.[2]

And Groman drew attention to the shift in the relative influence of
different organs of government which was the outcome of the
struggles of the autumn and winter of 1925–1926 :

> The volume of capital expenditure already being undertaken
> shows that the control figures have already won a certain victory ;
> for the attack from Narkomfin and Gosbank and Narkomzem
> on the control figures was resisted not only by Vesenkha, but
> also by Gosplan, armed with the revised control figures.[3]

Even Vainshtein was prepared half-heartedly to accept the use
of control figures in principle, though he still objected to the
methods used by Gosplan in compiling them ; he suggested that
it would be more accurate to call them " basic planning figures ",
and that they should be treated as " directives " rather than as
mere " prognosis ", in view of the fact that they incorporated
" our desires and purposes (volevye ustremleniya) ".[4]

The growing prestige and importance of the control figures as
an instrument for framing national economic policy became clear
as the preparation of the control figures proceeded. The importance attached by the party to the forthcoming 1926–1927 control
figures was indicated when a report on them from Gosplan
scheduled for September 1926 occupied first place in the " plan
of work " of the party central committee and the Politburo for
1926 approved by the committee at its April session.[5] The princi-

[1] *Problemy Planirovaniya* (*Itogi i Perspektivy*) (1926), p. 87.
[2] *Ibid.* pp. 217-218.   [3] *Ibid.* p. 232.
[4] *Sotsialisticheskoe Khozyaistvo*, No. 4, 1926, pp. 5-7 ; for Vainshtein see
p. 733 above.   [5] *VKP(B) v Rezolyutsiyakh* (1941), ii, 100.

pal People's Commissariats, including Vesenkha, now all had a regular procedure and machinery for preparing annual control figures and plans for their own sector of the economy.[1] Gosplan was careful to prepare a set of preliminary directives for 1926–1927 well in advance, and called a conference to discuss them as early as May 1926. This was important, for it meant that the commissariats were aware of the proposals of Gosplan when they prepared their own plans and policies ; once the views of Gosplan were taken into account in the plans of the commissariats, annual planning could begin to become an integrated process involving all the special interests of the economy, both sectional and regional, and the expert knowledge of the commissariats could be brought to bear on a single national plan. Smilga, presiding at the conference, which opened on May 19, 1926, declared, with more confidence than he had shown at the planning congress in March, that " the system of planning the national economy by means of compiling control figures has been accepted by the Union government, by the republics and by government departments ".[2]

On June 28, 1926, a further significant step was taken in the formal arrangements for annual planning : the preliminary directives of Gosplan were considered by a joint meeting of STO and Sovnarkom. On the surface the resulting resolution was cautious. The Gosplan figures were described as " preliminary and for orientation only, to be adjusted in accordance with the prospects of the harvest as these become clear, and in the process of the work of compilation ". But STO and Sovnarkom did " note " the proposals as the basis on which Gosplan should draw up the control figures.[3] This decision, and the appearance of the figures on the agenda of Sovnarkom at this early stage in the year, were revolutionary in their implication : plans of individual commissariats, including the state budget prepared by Narkomfin and the annual *promfinplan* and control figures for industry prepared by Vesenkha, were to be drawn up in the light of the view of the whole economy taken by Gosplan.[4] Gosplan and its control figures were now central, at least in form, to the annual economic policy deci-

[1] See pp. 803-804 above and 825 below.
[2] *Pravda*, May 21, 1926 ; for other aspects of the work of this conference see pp. 277-278 above.
[3] *Sobranie Zakonov, 1926*, No. 54, art. 396 ; for a further reference to this resolution see pp. 4-5 above.   [4] For the *promfinplan* see pp. 823-827 below.

sions of the Soviet Government. On July 23, 1926, the presidium of Gosplan heard reports of all the commissariats concerned and of the sections of Gosplan. After feverish activity in Gosplan, the control figures for 1926–1927 were finally approved by its presidium on August 18, 1926, and presented two days later to Sovnarkom and STO.[1] The rebuffs encountered by the control figures for 1925–1926 led the principal officials of Gosplan to exercise some caution in their work during the spring and summer of 1926 on the control figures for 1926–1927. The volume of control figures published in August 1926 claimed that the figures for the year 1925–1926 had contained no " substantial mistakes in the quantitative expression of the material processes taking place in our country " ; it admitted, however, that difficulties arising out of the 1925 harvest had been under-estimated, and exports and imports consequently over-estimated.[2] It was emphasized that Gosplan, schooled by this experience, had observed an exemplary restraint in planning the expansion of industry for 1926–1927 :

> When several variants were prepared during the work, the commission, bearing in mind the experience of last year, has given preference to the one which — if not the optimum — proposes a movement from a minimum to an optimum, and not the reverse movement from a maximum to an optimum.
>
> The process of cutting back is too onerous to risk repeating the circumstances of last year's work.[3]

The restraint exercised by Gosplan may also have been encouraged by the personal attitude of the authors of the control figures. Strumilin had been appointed president of the Gosplan commission to prepare the five-year plan ;[4] and, as the plan grew in

---

[1] *Kontrol'nye Tsifry Narodnogo Khozyaistva na 1926–1927 god* (1926), p. vi ; for the discussion of the control figures in relation to industry see pp. 277-283 above.

[2] *Kontrol'nye Tsifry Narodnogo Khozyaistva na 1926–1927 god* (1926), pp. 4-5. For subsequent comments in Gosplan circles blaming the control figures for the " autumn speculation " of 1925, and describing them as having " diverged from reality ", see *Informatsionnyi Byulleten' Gosplana SSSR*, No. 2-3, 1927, pp. 2-4 ; No. 4, 1927, p. 29 ; a Narkomfin writer declared that " the extremely optimistic outlook of our economic circles " had " brought our economy to the verge of an economic crisis " (*Vestnik Finansov*, No. 10, 1926, p. 11).

[3] *Kontrol'nye Tsifry Narodnogo Khozyaistva na 1926–1927 god* (1926), p. 32.

[4] See p. 854 below.

dimensions and prestige, and began to eclipse the less spectacular control figures, work on the latter was increasingly left in the hands of the more cautious Groman and Bazarov.[1]

The control figures submitted to Sovnarkom in August 1926 estimated that the combined production of the industrial and agricultural sectors would increase by 8 per cent in 1926–1927, the production of industry as a whole increasing by 13 per cent and of agriculture by 5 per cent ; the volume of capital investment in the socialized sector would increase by 19 per cent. In the current year 1925–1926, with the economy still in process of regaining its pre-war level, the combined production of industry and agriculture was expected to increase by as much as 25 per cent, and the volume of capital investment in the socialized sector to be double the low level of 1924–1925.[2] The plans for the expansion of industry were said to have been restrained by two " limiting factors " : the total of imports and the " possibilities of budget finance and short-term credit ".[3] In September 1926, when the control figures were discussed at a joint session of Sovnarkom and STO, Strumilin frankly admitted that their proposals for prices, exports, and currency and credit issues were " extremely modest ", and attributed this caution to the fact that the estimates for 1925–1926 had proved to be exaggerated.[4] The control figures for 1926–1927, like those for 1925–1926, had in any case no final or authoritative character. They were not intended to be approved in detail by the central authorities as a plan with the operational status of the budget, the credit plan or the *promfinplan*, but were simply to provide guide-lines for government departments and Gosplan when preparing and examining these sectional plans.[5] Further discussion in the autumn of 1926 underlined both the importance now attached to Gosplan and its control figures and the circumspection displayed by Gosplan in preparing them. The joint

[1] Smilga was replaced in November 1926 after joining the united opposition (see p. 286, note 1 above).

[2] *Kontrol'nye Tsifry Narodnogo Khozyaistva na 1926–1927 god* (1926), pp. 290–293, 316–317 ; the calculations were made in pre-war prices. The figures for agricultural production included forestry and fishing ; the figures for industrial production included both census and small-scale industry (excluding flour-milling). [3] *Ibid.* p. 19.

[4] *Torgovo-Promyshlennaya Gazeta*, September 21, 1926.

[5] *SSSR : God Raboty Pravitel'stva (Materialy k Otchetu za 1926–27 Byudzhetnyi god)* (1928), col. 67.

session of Sovnarkom and STO which discussed the control figures eventually issued on September 8, 1926, a directive specifically requiring larger capital investments than Gosplan had proposed.[1] In the following month, the sources and distribution of capital investment in industry were discussed at a joint meeting of the presidium of Gosplan and the presidium of Vesenkha.[2] The main features of the state budget itself were thrashed out at meetings between Narkomfin and Gosplan officials, and the head of the budgetary and financial section of Gosplan made a report on the budget to Sovnarkom. But Gosplan maintained its caution ; in December 1926 its representatives were persuaded by Narkomfin only after much discussion to abandon the estimate for budgetary revenue in the control figures, and to accept a higher Narkomfin figure.[3]

The restraint which had marked the work of Gosplan on the control figures of 1926–1927 was continued in the following year. Early in 1927 Bazarov advocated a cautious approach to the control figures for 1927–1928 ; and at the beginning of April 1927 a conference of planning organs, called to discuss the figures, passed a resolution, on a report by Bazarov, stressing the unhealthiness of the " *speculation which is poisoning industry and the trading atmosphere* ", and emphasizing the need to deal with agricultural overpopulation, to increase capital investment in transport, to improve the housing situation, and to give more attention to small-scale industry and to the training of labour.[4] On June 8, 1927, Sovnarkom passed an important resolution on the procedure for compiling the annual control figures, which were to provide " the principal foundations (numerical ceilings and main directives) for compiling operational economic plans ". While Sovnarkom would " note " that part of the control figures which dealt with general economic prospects, it would in future " approve and recommend

---

[1] For this directive see p. 742 above ; for the discussion at this session in relation to industry see pp. 284-285 above.

[2] *Torgovo-Promyshlennaya Gazeta*, October 13, 1926.

[3] *Ibid.* December 28, 1926.

[4] *Informatsionnyi Byulleten' Gosplana SSSR*, No. 2-3, 1927, pp. 49-52 ; No. 4, 1927, pp. 28-29 ; the atmosphere at the conference differed widely from that prevailing at the fourth Union Congress of Soviets in the same month (see pp. 293-295 above).

to the commissariats of the USSR and the governments of the Union republics for fulfilment " the part containing the " numerical ceilings and main directives ". The " preliminary indicators " distributed by Gosplan by July 1 of each year would include a statement about the possible size of capital investment, and would be used as the basis for constructing the plans of the commissariats and the republics, which would be examined by Gosplan and incorporated in the control figures by September 1. The government would still examine and approve the state budget and the export-import plan, and in addition it would approve the capital construction plan. But these would be fitted into the approved control figures.[1]

While the growing importance of the control figures in Soviet economic policy was thus made apparent, Gosplan continued to sound a cautious and indecisive note. At a further Gosplan conference which opened on June 29, 1927, Groman stressed the importance of maintaining " the dynamic equilibrium of the economy, which requires due proportion in the development of its separate elements " :

> We should plan an economy which develops progressively as a whole ; but its probable rate of development can be determined scientifically. Any attempts to overstep this rate will lead to a fruitless waste of efforts, and on the other hand can create for us an unexpected bottleneck which paralyses all other achievements. . . . We must have a system of control figures which guarantees us from ideas of genius and from arbitrary constructions.

Groman repeated the emphasis on the key rôle of the state budget which had been an important feature of the control figures for 1926–1927, and proposed that the budget should expand only in proportion to the value of goods in circulation : " this fixes one of the central quantities in our prognosis for the future ".[2] After the conference, on July 5, 1927, the presidium of Gosplan approved preliminary directives for compiling the control figures which reflected the tone and emphasis of Groman's report. The

---

[1] Sobranie Zakonov, 1927, No. 37, art. 373 ; Informatsionnyi Byulleten' Gosplana SSSR, No. 7, 1927, pp. 1-5.
[2] Planovoe Khozyaistvo, No. 7, 1927, pp. 131, 137-140.

year 1927–1928 was referred to as one of an " inevitable and completely regular slowing down " of rates of growth ; relations with
the capitalist world economy were " slowly deteriorating " ; pre-
cautions needed to be taken against the possibility of a bad harvest
in 1928 ; stocks must be increased ; the market equilibrium must
be maintained, and industrial prices must be further reduced. All
this meant that " special caution " was required in planning rates
of economic growth for the coming year.[1] The divisions of
opinion in Gosplan were by now becoming more marked. In the
tense international situation of the summer of 1927, Krzhizhanovsky, while not objecting to the proposed control figures, urgently
pressed the claims of planning ; in an article in the economic
newspaper, full of forebodings of war, he urged that " planned
discipline " rather than finance would be the artery of war in the
Soviet Union, pointing out that capitalist countries were greatly
assisted by planning during the war of 1914.[2]

The enhanced status of planning was further recognized in
August 1927 when the session of the party central committee for
the first time discussed the annual control figures as a separate
item on its agenda. But policy at the centre was still fluid and un-
decided. Pyatakov complained at the session with some justification that " we are offered not control figures, but only general
economic directives " couched " in so vague a quantitative form "
that " literally nothing remains in one's hands ".[3] The committee
issued a long but inconclusive set of directives. The introduction
referred to the dangers of the international crisis, and the importance of defence and heavy industry ; but the directives themselves were vague and imprecise, insisting at length on the need
to reduce costs of production and construction, promising increases in real wages, and warning of the possibility of a bad
harvest.[4] During the course of the next few weeks, however,
partly owing to pressure from Vesenkha, official support was given
to an increased rate of industrialization.[5] The final version of the

---

[1] *Informatsionnyi Byulleten' Gosplana SSSR*, No. 7, 1927, pp. 5-12 ; a
tantalizing note on page 12 states : " We omit the detailed directives and ceilings
for particular sectors of the economy owing to lack of space".

[2] *Ekonomicheskaya Zhizn'*, July 10, 1927.

[3] Cited in *Partiya i Oppozitsiya Nakakune XV S"ezda VKP(B)*, ii (1928),
139.   [4] *KPSS v Rezolyutsiyakh* (1954), ii, 372-381.

[5] See pp. 300-302 above.

control figures for 1927–1928, prepared in September 1927, but not actually published till the following year, reflected the new atmosphere at the centre. Like the resolution of the central committee, it referred to the possibility of a bad harvest in 1928 as a factor influencing the control figures, and to the deterioration in world economic relations due both to political and to market factors. But it also stressed the needs of defence due to the worsening international situation ; and the emphasis placed by Groman earlier in the summer on " equilibrium " gave way to stern injunctions : " *while carefully and soberly taking into account the needs of defence to the maximum, and preparing for a possible bad harvest, to secure the maximum rate of forced industrial development of the country* "; " *to secure the continuation of the forced rate of industrialization which has been adopted, while further strengthening the worker and peasant bloc and increasing as much as possible the defence capacity of the country* ".[1] The control figures proposed that total industrial production should increase by 13·4 per cent, as against the 13·7 per cent which was expected to be achieved in 1926–1927, and agricultural production by 3·2 as against 4·1 per cent ; the combined production of agriculture and industry would increase by 7·1 per cent as against 7·6 per cent expected in 1926–1927. Total capital investment by the socialized sector, including state investments in agriculture, would increase by more than 20 per cent, a higher rate of increase than in 1926–1927, the increase in industry being greater than the increase in agriculture ; the control figures incorporated proposals for capital investment in industry which had been described by Groman as too high.[2] In all the main indicators, the quantitative shift from the proposals made by Groman in June 1927 was not large ; but the change in approach was significant. From the summer of 1927 onwards the importance attached to financial stability and market equilibrium in the preparation of the control figures declined. The published version of the control figures predicted excess demand on the market in the first six months of 1927–1928, with textiles in particularly short supply, and concluded somewhat complacently that

[1] *Kontrol'nye Tsifry Narodnogo Khozyaistva SSSR na 1927–1928 god* (1928), pp. 11, 15.
[2] *Ibid.* pp. 20-21, 30, 464-465 ; the figures were based on calculations in pre-war prices.

" there may be somewhat more strain than in 1926–1927 ".[1]
Grinko, who had replaced Smilga as president of the commission
on the control figures, more frankly admitted that " the first six
months will be very strained ", but argued that neither industrial
prices nor taxes could be increased to reduce the strain.[2] A
Pravda editorial entitled " *Control Figures* " *of Growing Socialism*
declared that they would involve " material and financial strain ",
but praised the policy of allocating the lion's share of investment
to heavy industry :

> This is an absolutely right policy, guaranteeing us economic
> independence ; and it is being carried out by us in spite of the
> fact that it postpones somewhat the abolition of the shortage of
> consumer goods.

The control figures, it concluded, would involve a " *ferocious
straining of effort* " ; the outcome would be " decided by struggle ".[3]
Early in October 1927, a joint sitting of Sovnarkom and STO for
the first time formally approved the control figures.[4] The fifteenth
party congress in December 1927 was preoccupied by the five-year
plan to the exclusion of the control figures.[5] But this shift in emphasis to longer-term planning was the prelude to an even greater
concern for comprehensive planning and rapid industrialization.

When work began in the summer of 1928 on the control figures
for the following year, it was placed under the general direction of
the central commission on perspective planning of which Grinko
was also president ; and Groman and Bazarov remained in the
background.[6] With the concentration of effort on the five-year
plan, the lengthy procedures of consultation followed in preparing
the control figures in 1926 and 1927 were omitted ; Gosplan later
pointed out that its work had been made more difficult because
" the government did not examine preliminary directives about the

---

[1] *Kontrol'nye Tsifry Narodnogo Khozyaistva SSSR na 1927–1928 god* (1928),
pp. 24-25.
[2] *Pravda*, September 14, 1927.   [3] *Ibid.* September 16, 1927.
[4] See p. 302 above; the decision of Sovnarkom and STO does not appear
to have been published, though its main provisions are known.
[5] See pp. 872-873 below.
[6] *Kontrol'nye Tsifry Narodnogo Khozyaistva SSSR na 1928–1929 god*
(1929), p. 7 ; the names of Groman and Bazarov did not appear in the preface of this volume.

preparation of the control figures ".[1]   The completion of the
figures themselves was delayed.   Gosplan was under great pressure
to find additional resources.   After the crisis of the grain collections in the previous winter, the problem facing the party was
to find ways of meeting the needs of agriculture while simultaneously increasing capital investment in industry.   The pressure to
increase investment in industry was very strong ; in September
1928 one prominent official even proposed at the presidium of
Vesenkha that, in order to enable the claims of industry to be met,
" construction in other sectors of the economy, which constitutes
two-thirds of all construction ", should be stabilized " at the level
of last year ".[2]   On the other wing, Bukharin in his *Notes of an
Economist* of September 30, 1928, pressed for greater attention to
the needs of agriculture.[3]   When Gosplan presented the draft
control figures to STO and Sovnarkom at the time of the fourth
Gosplan congress in October 1928, it proposed a combined
increase in agricultural and industrial production by 9·6 per cent
in 1928–1929 as against the increase of 7·1 per cent expected in
1927–1928 ; industrial production would increase by 15·6 per
cent as against 16·5 per cent, and agricultural production by 4·2
per cent as against a reduction of 0·3 per cent.[4]   To achieve these
increases, and to lay the foundations for future growth, capital
investment in industry was to rise from 1306 million rubles in
1927–1928 to 1650 million rubles in 1928–1929, and state allocations to agriculture from the budget and credit system from 534 to
734 million rubles.   Investment in socialized agriculture was to
increase almost as rapidly as investment in industry ; this was the
inescapable corollary of the decision to force up agricultural
production in 1929.   Gosplan also yielded to pressure from the

[1] *Kontrol'nye Tsifry Narodnogo Khozyaistva SSSR na 1928–1929 god*
(1929), p. 22 ; see also p. 874 below.
[2] For this meeting see pp. 315-316 above ; in his reply Kuibyshev evasively
commented that questions of the relation of industry to other sectors of the
economy should be left in abeyance until Gosplan examined the figures for the
whole economy.   [3] See pp. 89-90, 317-319 above.
[4] *Ekonomicheskaya Zhizn'*, October 16, 1928 ; the figures are based on
calculations in 1926–1927 prices.   The annual volume of control figures
entitled *Kontrol'nye Tsifry Narodnogo Khozyaistva SSSR na 1928–1929 god*
was not published until 1929, but the figures in its tables (*ibid.* pp. 398-401)
are very close to the original proposals of Gosplan in October ; some major
amendments made later by the central authorities are specifically listed.

railways, which had been kept very short of funds in the middle nineteen-twenties, and from the education and health services, for larger allocations. These competing claims of different sectors made a formidable list. Investment in fixed and working capital in the socialized sector was planned to increase in real terms by about 30 per cent.[1]

How was so large an increase in total investment to be financed ? Grinko later put the matter frankly :

> It must be very firmly emphasized that in the course of the work on the control figures the dilemma clearly arose : either to achieve decisive improvements in the qualitative indicators of national economic production . . ., or reduce the rate of expansion of capital construction. All work on the control figures was based on the necessity of obtaining the first solution, i.e. the solution of reaching a high rate of development of the national economy by means of a high quality of work.[2]

In its draft proposals to the Gosplan congress, Gosplan exemplified this principle by endeavouring to impose on industry an extremely optimistic programme for reducing production costs, which would increase the profits available to industry and lessen the strain on the budget. In spite of strong resistance from Vesenkha on this point, the congress endorsed the main Gosplan proposals.[3] The control figures were a major item in the discussions preceding the session of the party central committee in November 1928.[4] The resolution adopted at this session, unlike the weak directives of August 1927,[5] incorporated major indicators for all sectors of the economy, including the state budget, which had now altogether lost its former commanding status. It was declared " indispensable *to guarantee in its entirety* the rate of growth adopted for the development of Group A industry (heavy industry, engineering, chemical industry, etc.) " ; and " *the economic plan* for 1928–1929 set out in the control figures " was described as " practicable, but *extremely strained* ". The resolution included a compromise target

---

[1] *Ekonomicheskaya Zhizn'*, October 16, 1928 ; *Kontrol'nye Tsifry Narodnogo Khozyaistva SSSR na 1928–1929 god* (1929), pp. 426-429.

[2] *Pravda*, October 30, 1928 ; " qualitative indicators " refer to economies leading to cost reduction as distinct from " quantitative indicators " of greater output.   [3] For these proceedings see pp. 321-322, 346-347 above.

[4] For these discussions see pp. 90-93, 324-325 above.

[5] See p. 816 above.

for reduction of costs in industry, but upheld the full capital investment plan proposed by Vesenkha.[1] The resolution thus marked another noteworthy stage in the process by which planning became the focus of economic policy. Grinko described the control figures for 1928–1929 as a " unified national economic plan ", and stated that " all the partial economic plans, however important in themselves, were this year in practice made directly and fully dependent on the unified economic plan ".[2] The published volume of the control figures pointed out that the budget and other sectional plans were much more closely tied in with the control figures, and that questions of defence and wage levels had been brought within their scope to a greater extent, than in previous years.[3]

In consequence of the decision to maintain the full capital investment plan for industry while adopting a less stringent target for cost reduction, the allocation to industry from the state budget was further increased. Sovnarkom decided early in December 1928 to obtain the extra 105 million rubles required by reducing allocations to agriculture, transport, trade and housing.[4] This solution did not escape the dilemmas resulting from the decision to undertake a very high level of investment in industry. It had the advantage of avoiding further inflation ; but it endangered the plans for other sectors of the economy, particularly agriculture. The original Gosplan proposals had already made very optimistic assumptions : throughout the discussions on the control figures in 1928 the party leaders demonstrated a readiness to risk further shortages of food and industrial consumer goods at a time when the peasant was already extremely reluctant to part with his grain. At a meeting of the presidium of Gosplan in March 1929, Mendelson reported the existence of " very substantial difficulties in particular sectors of the economy," but claimed that major changes

---

[1] KPSS v Rezolyutsiyakh (1954), ii, 525-540 ; for this resolution see also pp. 94, 325 above.

[2] G. Krzhizhanovsky and others, Osnovnye Problemy Kontrol'nykh Tsifr Narodnogo Khozyaistva na 1928/29 god (1929), p. 158.

[3] Kontrol'nye Tsifry Narodnogo Khozyaistva SSSR na 1928–1929 god (1929), p. 21.

[4] Ibid. pp. 506-507 ; the Sovnarkom decision, which does not appear to have been published, is presumably the decree of December 4, 1928, referred to ibid. p. 336, note 1 ; these decisions must certainly have been taken by Sovnarkom before TsIK approved the state budget on December 15, 1928.

in the plan were not required ; Kviring firmly rebuffed Groman's assertion in the course of the discussion that improved food supplies were " the prime necessity ".[1]   In the course of the implementation of the control figures of 1928–1929, allocations to industry in fact took precedence over allocations to other sectors ; [2] and at the same time, partly owing to the failure of industry to reduce costs as much as had been planned, further issues of currency were permitted.[3]   At the end of the economic year, the volume of control figures for the following year reported that the plans for industrial production in 1928–1929 had been exceeded, and that capital investment in industry was likely to exceed the plan.[4]   On the other hand, the output of almost every agricultural product was substantially less than had been projected ; [5] although investment in the state and cooperative sector of agriculture was substantially in excess of the plan, owing primarily to the expansion of Sovkhozy and kolkhozy, total capital investment in agriculture, including that carried out by the individual peasant, was estimated to have actually declined in 1928–1929.[6]   The rise of the control figures to the status of an annual plan of the national economy was accompanied by the subordination of all other sectors of the economy to the requirements of industry.

[1]   *Torgovo-Promyshlennaya Gazeta*, March 8, 1929.
[2]   See figures in *Kontrol'nye Tsifry Narodnogo Khozyaistva SSSR na 1929/30 god* (1930), pp. 592-595.   [3]   See p. 777 above.
[4]   *Kontrol'nye Tsifry Narodnogo Khozyaistva SSSR na 1929/30 god* (1930), pp. 4, 28.   [5]   *Ibid.* p. 118.
[6]   *Ibid.* pp. 448-449 ; for the investment figures see Table No. 47, p. 979 below.

CHAPTER 35

OPERATIONAL PLANS

THE practical planning and detailed guidance of economic activity was provided for in the sectional plans of the commissariats, the republics and the regions, which became known as " operational (operatsionnye) plans ". While the control figures were an important instrument for shaping the main decisions about the allocation of resources, they were not an exclusive or all-embracing instrument of economic planning ; their function was to coordinate and reconcile the sectional or operational plans and direct them towards the implementation of the major policy decisions of the party. The control figures were an annual document, and were aptly described by Grinko as " a programme of work for the year ahead " ; [1] in each year they were a long time in the making, and were not normally revised in the course of the year. Soviet economic policy, on the other hand, consisted of a continuous stream of decisions, spread over the whole year ; the wage increase of the autumn of 1926, the price reduction campaign launched in February 1927, the decision in October 1927 to introduce a seven-hour day, and the extraordinary measures of January and February 1928 were all examples of policies not anticipated by Gosplan or Sovnarkom when the control figures for the year concerned were first compiled. All these decisions were put into effect, not by revising the control figures, but by adjusting the operational plans.

Industry was the sector of the economy over which the central authorities exercised most control. The cardinal purpose of planning was to direct resources into industry and to mould its development ; an elaborate and formalized structure of plans was first developed in industry. As early as 1923, a procedure was adopted

---

[1] *Kontrol'nye Tsifry Narodnogo Khozyaistva SSSR na 1928–1929 god* (1929), p. 7.

823

by which each trust submitted an annual plan to its *glavk* or directorate, so that a plan for each industry could be prepared by the central staff of Vesenkha. These annual plans, which included both production and financial targets, became known as *promfinplans*, or " production and financial plans," and from 1924 onwards *promfinplans* for individual industries were examined by Gosplan and Narkomfin and belatedly approved by STO.[1] At this time, the only " plan " for the national economy as a whole was the state budget ; and it was as financial plans working within the framework set by the budget that the *promfinplans* were at first effective. As plans for the positive guidance of production they were at that time more formal than real. In 1923 and 1924, neither Vesenkha nor its directorates provided the trusts with advance directives for preparing their plans ; the final plans were an aggregation of the expectations and the desires of the trusts, trimmed to the available finance, rather than an instrument for moulding the behaviour of individual industries and factories to the will of the central administrators in Vesenkha ; and little evidence exists of effective action by the directorates to enforce production plans once approved.[2] All this corresponded to a situation in which the activities of industry were still in large part controlled by the profit motive and the market mechanism. But in 1925, simultaneously with the compilation by Gosplan of its first control figures for the national economy, the system began to undergo a fundamental change. By deciding to draw up a *promfinplan* for industry as a whole for the economic year 1925-1926, Vesenkha assumed for the first time a central guiding rôle. In a clear state-

---

[1] *Byulleten' Gosplana*, No. 5, 1923, pp. 35-37 ; *Ekonomicheskaya Zhizn'*, June 24, 1925 ; *Informatsionnyi Byulleten' Gosplana SSSR*, No. 9, 1926, pp. 14-16. STO approved the 1925-1926 " financial and production programmes " of the coal, oil, metal and sugar industries in January-March 1926 (*SSSR : Svodnye Materialy o Deyatel'nosti Soveta Narodnykh Komissarov i Soveta Truda i Oborony za II Kvartal (Yanvar'-Mart) 1925-26 g.* (1926), pp. 78-94), and of the electrical, basic chemical, aniline-dye and timber industries in April-June 1926 (*SSSR : Svodnye Materialy o Deyatel'nosti Soveta Narodnykh Komissarov i Soveta Truda i Oborony za III Kvartal (Aprel'-Iyun') 1925-26 g.* (1926), pp. 110-115). A similar procedure was followed in 1926-1927.

[2] *Perspektivy Promyshlennosti na 1925-26 Operatsionnyi god* (1925), p. 9 ; *Informatsionnyi Byulleten' Gosplana SSSR*, No. 9, 1926, pp. 14-16. In May 1923, Krzhizhanovsky commented on the industrial plans which were submitted to Gosplan that they were " not a plan, but mere spontaneity, in which there is no controlling will at work " (*Byulleten' Gosplana*, No. 5, 1923, p. 37).

ment of intent, it summarized its view of the new form which the
planning process in industry should take :

Inasmuch as the work of every trust, and even more of a
whole industry, will be almost entirely determined by the state,
which will provide it with a specific amount of supplementary
resources, the industrial plan can no longer be constructed by
adding up the proposals of the trusts. The proposals of the
trusts are moving into the background : into the foreground
move the proposals and intentions of the state, which is becoming the real master of its industry. Therefore, it is only
the state economic agencies which can construct the industrial
plan : the industrial plan must be constructed not from below,
but from above.[1]

In 1925, the *promfinplans* of industry were prepared independently of the first Gosplan control figures for the national
economy ; but their absorption into the general framework of
planning was not long delayed. On August 14, 1925, STO belatedly instructed Vesenkha to prepare the *promfinplans* for 1925–
1926 on the basis of the control figures of Gosplan, and to assist
Gosplan in preparing its control figures for the following year
1926–1927 by presenting it with preliminary information by July
5, 1926.[2] Vesenkha took its duties seriously. An elaborate order
of April 29, 1926, set out the procedures by which industrial plans
for 1926–1927 were to be prepared. A special commission, of
which Pyatakov was appointed president, was placed in charge of
preparing draft control figures for industry before July 1, 1926 ;
once these draft Vesenkha control figures had been coordinated in
the Gosplan control figures with the plans for transport and foreign
trade and with the state budget, the main industries were to prepare their *promfinplans* under the guidance of the commission.[3]

---

[1] *Perspektivy Promyshlennosti na 1925–26 Operatsionnyi god* (1925), p.
11 ; the arrangements were approved by the presidium of Vesenkha on a
proposal from Pyatakov (*ibid.* p. 13). In 1924 Gosplan, on the proposal of
Kalinnikov, had already attempted unsuccessfully to secure the introduction
of a procedure by which trust plans would be prepared within the framework of
" orientative statements " from Vesenkha, which would in their turn be based
on directives drawn up by Gosplan under government guidance (*Ekonomicheskaya Zhizn'*, June 24, 1925).

[2] For these decrees see *Socialism in One Country, 1924–1926*, Vol. 1, p. 500.

[3] *Torgovo-Promyshlennaya Gazeta*, April 30, 1926 ; for a supplementary
order see *ibid.* June 13, 1926.

The subordinate position in planning which the trusts were now
to occupy was indicated in a set of " basic directives " published
on July 1, 1926, which instructed the trusts how to prepare their
promfinplans.[1] Krzhizhanovsky later noted with pride that the
preparation of the 1926–1927 control figures was the first occasion
on which Gosplan had " heard a report from Vesenkha ".[2] Gosplan described the work of Vesenkha on its control figures as " a
model in the degree of its detail and in its meticulousness ".[3] In
both 1926 and 1927 Vesenkha prepared in the summer preliminary
control figures for the forthcoming economic year which coordinated the claims of its trusts and *glavki*, and then in the autumn
compiled both a " comprehensive (svodnyi) *promfinplan* " and a
series of *promfinplans* for particular industries, based on the
control figures of Gosplan as revised by Sovnarkom.[4] The comprehensive *promfinplans* for the years 1926–1927 and 1927–1928
were scrutinized by Gosplan and Narkomfin and submitted for
approval to a joint sitting of STO and Sovnarkom. While the comprehensive *promfinplan* thus ranked with the state budget and the
control figures of the national economy as one of the major annual
acts of economic policy, its dependence on the budget as well as
on the control figures was emphasized by the fact that it was not
examined by Sovnarkom till some time after the budget had been
considered. The 1926–1927 plan was not considered by Sovnarkom
till February 1927 and the 1927–1928 plan till March 20, 1928.[5]

During 1928, the future of the comprehensive *promfinplan*
was the subject of a protracted and confused debate, which was
resolved on September 5, 1928, when Sovnarkom, with the support of Vesenkha, Gosplan and Rabkrin, decided that the comprehensive *promfinplan* would no longer be considered by Sovnarkom ; instead, " production and financial targets (zadaniya) ",
on which the *promfinplans* of industries and enterprises were to be
based, would be approved by Vesenkha itself within the terms of
the control figures of the national economy as adopted by the

[1] *Torgovo-Promyshlennaya Gazeta*, July 1, 1926.
[2] *Pyatnadtsatyi S"ezd VKP(B)*, ii (1962), 892.
[3] *Kontrol'nye Tsifry Narodnogo Khozyaistva na 1926–1927 god* (1926), p. 15.
[4] A STO decree dated September 15, 1926, set out procedures and dates
for preparing the *promfinplans* for 1926–1927 (*Sobranie Zakonov, 1926*, No. 67,
art. 516).
[5] *Pravda*, February 2, 1927 ; *Sobranie Zakonov, 1928*, No. 20, art. 180.

government.[1] This move, ostensibly aimed at speeding up the whole process of industrial planning, had the effect of reducing the dependence of the comprehensive *promfinplan* on the budget and strengthening its connexion with the control figures prepared by Gosplan, while also enhancing the authority of Vesenkha.[2] Meanwhile, the subordinate position of the trusts in the planning process was increasingly marked. What one writer described as the " top to bottom " system of preparing the *promfinplans* was firmly established.[3] The central authorities were increasingly successful in enforcing obedience to the plans. Birman, president of Yugostal, complained that his trust was expected to carry out plans unconditionally even though they were frequently modified by the centre.[4] Behind this change in relations between Vesenkha and the trusts lay the growing importance, as capital investment expanded, of the state sector as a consumer and distributor of the products of industry.

Once industrialization got under way, the section of the *promfinplan* concerned with capital investment was increasingly singled out for attention. The comprehensive *promfinplan* and the *promfinplans* for each industry showed the resources which would be available for capital investment from the budget, from the credit system, and from industry itself, and how they would be spent. How far these plans were successfully enforced in Union industry in the middle nineteen-twenties is difficult to determine. In republican and local industry, trusts often undertook investment without central approval, and the investment plans of regional Sovnarkhozy and republican Vesenkhas were frequently not coordinated with the Vesenkha of the USSR. At the seventh trade union congress in December 1926, Kuibyshev insisted that " we must introduce a strict foundation of planning into capital expenditure " ; surplus profits should not be reinvested in the industry in which they were made, but should be redirected to investment

[1] *Sobranie Zakonov, 1928*, No. 20, arts. 504-505, 508.
[2] For the simplification of budgetary procedures undertaken at this time see pp. 721-722 above.
[3] *Torgovo-Promyshlennaya Gazeta*, April 14-15, 1928 ; proposals that the control figures of Vesenkha should be based on the claims of the trusts were brusquely rejected in favour of continuing the procedure by which the draft plans of the trusts were prepared in accordance with the directives of Vesenkha (*ibid.* October 23, November 25, 1928).
[4] *Ibid.* June 17, December 1, 1928.

in the " decisive industries ".[1] The importance now attached to the central planning of capital investment was stressed in a Sovnarkom decree of February 15, 1927, which belatedly regulated the amount of capital expenditure to be undertaken by industry during the current economic year.[2] On June 8, 1927, Sovnarkom further resolved that in future a plan of capital construction for the whole economy should be examined annually by the central government and should include an " itemized list " of major projects.[3] While a plan of capital construction for the whole economy separate from the control figures never apparently materialized, a plan of capital construction in Vesenkha-planned industry for 1927-1928 was approved on March 20, 1928, simultaneously with the comprehensive *promfinplan* ; [4] and the practice of specific approval of major construction projects by STO was regularly observed. These arrangements, and more elaborate procedures adopted within Vesenkha, soon placed the detailed planning of investment firmly in the hands of the central authorities.[5] As early as December 1927, at the fifteenth party congress, Chubar complained, with perhaps some exaggeration, of the over-centralization of investment planning :

> When planning here at the centre deals with as small a sum as 73 thousand [rubles], it loses the character of planning and becomes minute and unnecessary tutelage, while the millions escape control (Voices : " hear! hear! ") . . . .
> A rule existed that capital construction costing up to one million rubles could be undertaken in a republic or a region without approval from the centre. Gradually and little by little that has been whittled down, and now our republics and our local trusts rarely succeed in undertaking construction costing a mere thousand rubles, because everything is " planned " right to the bottom.[6]

[1] *Sed'moi S"ezd Professional'nykh Soyuzov SSSR* (1927), p. 515.

[2] *Sobranie Zakonov, 1927*, No. 10, art. 98.

[3] *Sobranie Zakonov, 1927*, No. 37, art. 373 ; for other aspects of this decree see pp. 814-815 above. On November 30, 1926, STO had already strengthened its control over investment in sectors of the economy other than industry by providing that any investment in these sectors valued at more than one million rubles should be submitted to it for approval (*Sobranie Zakonov, 1926*, No. 76, art. 610).   [4] *Sobranie Zakonov, 1928*, No. 20, art. 180.

[5] For the arrangements within Vesenkha see pp. 357-358 above.

[6] *Pyatnadtsatyi S"ezd VKP(B)*, ii (1962), 1000-1001.

Major new projects were discussed in some detail, sometimes on many occasions, by the Politburo as well as STO ; and the supply of the men, money and materials required was the special concern of Gosplan and Vesenkha. The planning of major projects became an increasingly important element in the whole planning process.[1]

During the second half of the nineteen-twenties, the central planning of the production, investment and finance of industry through the *promfinplan* was supplemented and reinforced by the rise of physical planning. Some physical controls had existed even in the early years of NEP : supplies to major state consumers, especially to Narkomput' and the armed forces, had always been subject to close central control, this arrangement being rendered necessary both by the scarcity of many goods and by the reluctance of industry to sell its production at the privileged prices which had been fixed for state consumers. By 1924 these arrangements were regular and systematic ; if the budget estimates of Narkomfin provided the model for the " control figures " of Gosplan, the planning of the orders placed by Narkomput' with Vesenkha provided the model for the physical planning system which later predominated throughout the economy. People's Commissariats such as Narkomput' and the Commissariat of War negotiated their major orders either with the *glavk* or directorate of Vesenkha or with the syndicate for the industry concerned ; these issued orders to, or negotiated with, the producer trusts, which in turn passed on the orders to the factories, the arrangements being enforced through the use by Vesenkha of its administrative powers.[2] The whole procedure was under the general control of the committee of state orders, formed in 1923, on which all the main commissariats were represented. The jurisdiction of the committee, as laid down in a statute of January 20, 1926, covered all orders placed by institutions and enterprises of the USSR with Union industrial enterprises subordinate to commissariats other than their own, although in practice its work seems to have been confined to orders

---

[1] See pp. 431-452 above and 898-915 below.
[2] Narkomput' orders were if necessary allocated compulsorily to trusts by Glavmetall (*Ekonomicheskaya Zhizn'*, July 25, 1926).

financed from the state budget. It was responsible for preparing a preliminary annual plan for state orders, which had to conform to the *promfinplan* of each industry concerned.[1]

As the industrialization drive gained momentum, the urgent requirements of the plan were met by inflationary spending, which in turn, in view of the fairly stringent price controls which operated in industry, resulted in worsening shortages of goods. In order to maintain the priorities of the plan in face of these shortages, planned distribution through centrally determined physical allocations was introduced for a rapidly increasing number of products, and, from 1925 onwards, was extended to the whole production of certain major industries. The first to be affected was iron and steel. In November 1925, a Vesenkha order instructed all consumers of metal in Vesenkha to submit claims through their directorates or the republican Vesenkhas on the basis of which Glavmetall would compile a balance of production and consumption of iron and steel. During the course of the next twelve months the system was extended to all consumers of metal, including the retail trade network, and served as the basis for the preparation of the annual metals balance which was approved by Vesenkha and STO, and for the more detailed quarterly balance.[2] This became something of a precedent for the preparation in other industries of what became known as " material balances ", and were really budgets of production and consumption in physical terms.[3] A fuel crisis led to similar arrangements being introduced in the same year for the fuel industries ; [4] and on March 11, 1927, STO issued an instruction that the plans of industry should include what was called an " energy " plan — a plan showing the fuel and power consumption of all enterprises in each

---

[1] *Sobranie Zakonov, 1926*, No. 9, art. 76. For the earlier history of the committee on state orders see *Socialism in One Country, 1924–1926*, Vol. 1, p. 344.

[2] *Protokol Zasedaniya Prezidiuma VSNKh SSSR, 1925–1926*, No. 2, art. 30 (order of November 23, 1925) ; *Torgovo-Promyshlennaya Gazeta*, April 26, May 8, September 17, 1926 ; P. Konnov, *Organizatsiya i Planirovanie Sbyta Chernykh Metallov* (1955), pp. 49–50.

[3] For the " method of balances " see pp. 798–799 above.

[4] *Torgovo-Promyshlennaya Gazeta*, May 16, September 19, October 1, 1926 ; the claims for fuel were at first negotiated directly between consuming trusts and regional fuel agents attached to Vesenkha, but were later submitted to Glavgortop, the *glavk* for the fuel industry, through the *glavk* to which the trust belonged.

region.[1] On June 15, 1928, when the shortage of building materials had become acute, Gosplan was instructed to include a balance of supply and demand for the major building materials in its annual control figures.[2] The distribution of industrial consumer goods was planned by similar procedures. In the spring of 1924, a first attempt was made by Narkomtorg to draw up a quarterly " delivery plan " (plan zavoza) for state industry, which fixed quotas of cotton cloth to be delivered to particular grain-producing regions. This early and crude attempt at physical planning foundered on the opposition of Vesenkha ; but in the summer of 1925 Narkomtorg secured the approval by STO of a quarterly delivery plan of limited scope. These early plans rested on no more solid basis than " empirical estimates of the minimum necessary to ensure the successful operation of the grain collections ". But the techniques of planning gradually improved. The first plan covering the whole country was drawn up early in 1926, being expressed in terms both of value and of railway wagon loads ; and in the economic year 1926–1927 a plan of reserves, to be switched from one destination to another on orders of Narkomtorg, was approved by STO.[3]

The introduction of the physical planning of distribution brought about important developments in the planning of production. The material balances showed the amount of production planned for the given period as well as the principal consumers to whom this production was to be allocated; the very broad production targets or indicators in the control figures of the national economy and in the *promfinplans*, and the more specific production figures of the material balances, were supposed to correspond. To assist the coordination of the *promfinplan* and the material balance for iron and steel, claims for an allocation of iron and steel had to be submitted sufficiently early for them to be known by Glavmetall when it prepared the production targets of the *promfinplan* ; [4]

---

[1] *Sobranie Zakonov, 1927*, No. 20, art. 234 ; a year later Sovnarkom complained that the *promfinplan* for 1927–1928 had failed to work out the " plan for the energy balance " in sufficient detail (*Sobranie Zakonov, 1928*, No. 20, art. 180) ; for the notion of energy (*energetika*) see p. 803, note 1 above.

[2] *Sobranie Zakonov, 1928*, No. 37, art. 337.

[3] *Voprosy Torgovli*, No. 2-3, November–December 1927, pp. 64-65 ; *Planovoe Khozyaistvo*, No. 5, 1928, pp. 129, 132 ; *Torgovo-Promyshlennaya Gazeta*, June 30, 1926 ; Yu. Moshinsky, *Ekonomika i Organizatsiya Obrashcheniya Sredstv Proizvodstva v SSSR* (1936), pp. 110-112 ; see also pp. 641-642 above.   [4] *Torgovo-Promyshlennaya Gazeta*, September 24, 1926.

this arrangement became standard in many industries. The material balances and delivery plans, although more detailed than the *promfinplan*, constituted only a general framework of decisions, which required detailed implementation. They normally related to a long period, a year or at least a quarter, and to broad groups of products ; [1] in the material balances allocations were normally made not to specific trusts or regional trading agencies, but to commissariats or other national organizations such as Narkomput' or Tsentrosoyuz, or, in the case of consumption by industry, to the *glavki* of Vesenkha. The work of turning the broad annual or quarterly production targets of the *promfinplan* and the allocations of the material balances into specific orders, usually covering a month's output, and addressed to specific producers and consumers, was primarily the responsibility of the syndicates ; and the rise of the syndicates was intimately associated with the rise of physical planning.[2] Vesenkha was also impelled to resort to *ad hoc* priorities and " shock " programmes, over-riding the provisions of the material balances, in order to push through the most urgent items of the plan.[3]

In 1926–1929 this attempt to introduce a novel and complex system was still at a preliminary and experimental stage. At a meeting of the presidium of Vesenkha in August 1928, Kuibyshev and Mezhlauk both complained that the balance of supply and demand for industrial consumer goods, the fuel and power balance, and the balance of building materials had not been properly completed.[4] In his evidence at the " industrial party " trial in 1930, Kalinnikov remarked of the metal balances that " those who know these balances will say they are only preliminary attempts to compile a balance ", and claimed that " so far we have not seen properly prepared material balances in Gosplan on one single occasion ".[5] At this time the prerequisites for central physical planning existed

[1] The " nomenclature " for iron and steel, for example, contained 53 groups, plus various sub-groups (*ibid*. May 8, 1926).
[2] For the syndicates, and the methods used by them in particular industries, see pp. 373-378, 636-650 above.
[3] At the second Gosplan congress in 1927, A. M. Ginzburg, reverting to a term much used during war communism, defended the use of the " shock principle " (printsip udarnosti) in planning (S. Strumilin, *Ocherki Sovetskoi Ekonomiki* (1928), p. 497).
[4] *Torgovo-Promyshlennaya Gazeta*, August 15, 1928.
[5] *Le Procès des Industriels de Moscou* (1931), p. 132.

only in part.   Statistical information necessary for the construction of the plans became available only gradually.   One commentator claimed that, owing to the absence of adequate information, the fuel distribution plans were ineffective :

> The plans did not really control anything ;   they merely made ends meet.   The fuel supply of the country drifted along, or, to be more precise, controlled itself.[1]

Even by 1929, standard " norms " for consumption of materials and fuel and for stocks, which were an essential prerequisite for drawing up an accurate plan of production and distribution in physical terms, were still in the process of being constructed.[2] Indicators for planning production in physical terms were also still in their infancy.[3]

The new system of physical planning, created amid the shortages endemic in the first stages of the industrialization drive, had certain characteristic defects.   Because planned orders were placed late, were often changed afterwards, and, when placed, were imperfectly executed, factories did not necessarily receive the materials and machinery allocated to them at the time or in the quantities specified :   " this question ", Tolokontsev remarked at the fourth Union Congress of Soviets in April 1927, " runs through our whole economy ".[4]   The danger of running short of supplies in its turn led factories to place excessive orders and to increase their stocks of materials.[5]   On the other hand, all industrial products sold quickly because they were in short supply, so that stocks of finished goods in the producing factories and in the warehouses of the syndicates tended to be low.[6]   In 1926 Grinko stigmatized as " direct disorganizers " of industry " a large

---

[1] *Fabrichno-Zavodskaya Promyshlennost' SSSR i ego Ekonomicheskikh Raionov*, ii (1928), 83.   [2] *Vestnik Finansov*, No. 4, 1929, pp. 14-15.
[3] See for example *Predpriyatie*, No. 1, 1928, pp. 17-20.
[4] *SSSR : 4 S"ezd Sovetov* (1927), p. 347 ;   see also the results of surveys of factories reported in *Torgovo-Promyshlennaya Gazeta*, September 21, 1927, July 26, 1928 ;   for Tolokontsev see p. 427 above.
[5] *Torgovo-Promyshlennaya Gazeta*, October 30, December 16, 1926 ;   a decree of STO of March 8, 1929, calling for a reduction of surplus stocks, identified " one of the main causes of stock-piling " as " the tendency of certain enterprises in the circumstances of the goods famine to protect themselves against shortages of materials " (*Direktivy KPSS i Sovetskogo Pravitel'-stva po Khozyaistvennym Voprosam*, ii (1957), 20).
[6] For an example see *Ekonomicheskoe Obozrenie*, No. 12, 1928, p. 82.

2 E

number of directors of trusts, factories, etc." who, " guided by
the short-sighted provincial slogan ' a victor is not judged ' ",
failed to keep within the plan and piled up stocks of materials.[1] A
Vesenkha survey of the spring of 1929 reported that " supply
workers of some enterprises have more or less permanent contacts
for mutual aid by borrowing materials and helping one another out
of trouble ".[2] But, in spite of these shortcomings, the system of
physical planning was increasingly effective in directing scarce
materials and products towards the key sectors of the economy [3]
and in securing that priority was given to the needs of major projects
like Dnieprostroi.

By 1929, industry was thus controlled by a combination of
physical and financial plans ; the individual industry and its
trusts and factories received allocations of both materials and
money, and were expected to meet both their production targets,
couched primarily in physical terms, and their financial targets,
primarily the target for costs reduction. The degree of control
exercised by the central authorities varied considerably between
industries and even between products : while the production and
distribution of important producer goods such as iron and steel
were closely controlled by Vesenkha and Gosplan, and even by
Sovnarkom, central controls over local and artisan industry were
much more rudimentary.

The processes of central planning, which had developed
farthest and fastest in industry, were also gradually extended to
the major sectors of the economy in which market forces had pre-

---

[1] *Khozyaistvo Ukrainy*, No. 7, 1926, p. 13.

[2] See Yu. Moshinsky, *Ekonomika i Organizatsiya Obrashcheniya Sredstv
Proizvodstva v SSSR* (1936), pp. 129-131. In both 1926 and 1927 campaigns
to eliminate official and unofficial agents (predstaviteli) and " fixers " (tolkachi)
proved unsuccessful (*Torgovo-Promyshlennaya Gazeta*, May 7, 8, 29, July 7,
1926 ; July 23, August 23, 1927). In March 1927, 645 out of 893 offices in
Moscow of such agents of trusts and other organizations were closed ; the
Donugol office alone employed a staff of 109. It was reported that the agent
of the Kharkov preserved foods trust, a former timber industrialist, confessed
to the GPU that his total earnings were 40,000 rubles a year ; the president
of the Ukrainian agricultural machinery trust Ukrselmash was said to have paid
a 20-year rent of 15,000 rubles to a private owner for a Moscow flat for his
agent (*Pravda*, March 30, 1927).

[3] See the figures for rolled steel in *Metall*, No. 7, 1929, pp. 71-73.

viously been predominant, notably to the consumer market and to peasant agriculture. Since the abolition of the direction of labour and of rationing at the beginning of NEP, the urban worker and the state employee had been free to choose his job (subject to the constraints of unemployment) and to spend his income on consumer goods of his own choosing (subject to goods shortages) ; and his income was itself the result of an elaborate bargaining process in which the trade unions enjoyed some autonomy. While no attempt was made to introduce direction of labour, between 1926 and 1929 much tighter central planning and control of wages were introduced in an attempt to limit urban consumption, and to reduce the costs, and hence the claims for financial resources, of state institutions and enterprises.[1] In spite of these controls, the rise in personal incomes far outstripped the supply of consumer goods, primarily as a result of the increase in the number of persons employed in the producer goods industries and the building industry ; the subsequent rationing of bread and other foodstuffs in the major towns marked the extension of the system of physical allocation to the individual urban consumer.[2]

The agricultural sector of the economy was least subject to central planning. In its control figures for 1927–1928, Gosplan commented :

> Up to and including the present no unified plan of measures carried out by the Narkomzems for the whole Union has existed. There are 25 Narkomzems of Union and autonomous republics on the territory of the USSR. Each of these republics compiles its own plan in the sphere of agriculture, and this plan does not coincide in time or method of compilation with the plans of other republics. Reports for previous years are also absent. Such a position with the planning of agriculture cannot continue in the future.

Gosplan added that " the fact that agriculture is scattered does not lessen, but increases, the need for a planned system of measures, closely interconnected with each other and taking into account the special features of each republic ".[3] The grain collections, designed to meet the assessed needs of the urban and factory

---

[1] See pp. 504-507, 520-529 above.   [2] See pp. 698-704 above.

[3] *Kontrol'nye Tsifry Narodnogo Khozyaistva SSSR na 1927–1928 god* (1928), p. 115.

population, the Red Army, the grain-deficit agricultural areas and the cotton-growing regions of Central Asia, together with the collections of " technical " crops used as raw material by industry, were a rudimentary form of the planning of distribution ; and the " extraordinary measures " of the first months of 1928 coincided with increased planning pressure in other sectors of the economy. But the production of more than 20 million individual peasant households was governed in the main by what was ironically called the " peasants' plan " (krestplan) or " heaven's plan " (neboplan). In 1928–1929 *kontraktatsiya* and mechanization were still in their infancy, and collectivization on any significant scale still lay in the future. It was through these instruments that some measure of planning control was eventually established over agriculture.

CHAPTER 36

THE GENERAL PLAN

THE Goelro plan, prepared in 1920, was the first major attempt to construct a 10-15-year plan for the economy as a whole; although its central theme was electrification, it included production targets and outline plans for the major industries.[1] The plan suffered from the major deficiency that it did not cover those parts of the USSR which were not in Soviet hands in the early months of 1920; it therefore excluded most of the Ukraine. By 1925 many of its detailed provisions were obviously out-of-date, and early in that year Gosplan charged Krzhizhanovsky with the revision of the Goelro plan and the preparation in its place both of a regional plan and of a comprehensive plan of the national economy; the latter was in turn to be divided into a five-year and a fifteen-year plan. This work was to be completed in time for the tenth anniversary of the revolution in October 1927.[2] The first Gosplan congress in March 1926 established two parallel commissions for long-term planning: a commission on the five-year plan under the presidency of Strumilin, and a commission on the 10-15-year general plan or *genplan* under the presidency of Osadchy, a non-party specialist.[3]

The Osadchy commission was instructed to make the assumption, which was to seem ludicrously modest within a few years, that real national income or product per head of population would double over the period of 10-15 years.[4] Even in Gosplan the work of the Osadchy commission seems to have been regarded with some scepticism. This was not because its proposals were felt to underestimate the possibilities of the future: condemnation of

[1] For Goelro see *The Bolshevik Revolution, 1917–1923*, Vol. 2, pp. 371-373.
[2] *Perspektivy Razvertyvaniya Narodnogo Khozyaistva SSSR na 1926/27–1930/31 gg.* (1927), pp. 55-56.
[3] *Informatsionnyi Byulleten' Gosplana SSSR*, No. 5, 1926, p. 7.
[4] *Ibid.* No. 6, 1926, p. 18.

Osadchy's plan as the work of a wrecker did not come till several years later. It was rather because the future was uncertain, and because neither Gosplan nor anyone else possessed the data, experience or ability to look so far ahead. The planners concentrated on the more feasible, if still difficult, five-year plan. In presenting the second Gosplan draft of the five-year plan in the spring of 1927, Krzhizhanovsky explained that, although final decisions about the main proposals of the *genplan* should really precede the five-year plan, this was impossible because the re-examination of the Goelro plan had been delayed.[1] Among the general plans for particular sectors of the economy, the plan for electrification was sufficiently far advanced at this time to be used in preparing the Gosplan draft of the five-year plan ;[2] but Vesenkha apparently prepared its own draft five-year plan in 1927 entirely without reference to the work of Gosplan on the *genplan*. Some general plans for particular regions were, however, more advanced. At the second Gosplan congress in March 1927 the Gosplan of the RSFSR reported that the preparation of the *genplan* had been made the pivot of all its work,[3] and was reproved by Strumilin for concentrating on the *genplan* to the neglect of the five-year plan.[4] The general plan for the Ural region published in the summer of 1927[5] was a large volume containing an elaborate programme for all sectors of the Ural economy. It followed the standard assumption that national income per head would approximately double over fifteen years, and estimated that only 73,000 peasant households out of a total of nearly two million would belong to some form of producer cooperative by 1941. Its plans for particular industries were also extremely cautious ; it assumed, for example, that total Soviet pig-iron production in 1940–1941 would not exceed 11 million tons.[6] Nevertheless, it was firmly a plan of industrialization, proposing that industrial production in 1940–1941 should be more than six times as large as in 1926–1927, while agricultural production would approximately double in the

[1] *Planovoe Khozyaistvo*, No. 3, 1927, pp. 8-9.
[2] See pp. 419-420 above ; for this draft of the five-year plan see pp. 855-856 below.
[3] *Ekonomicheskaya Zhizn'*, April 2, 1927.
[4] S. Strumilin, *Ocherki Sovetskoi Ekonomiki* (1928), pp. 477-478.
[5] See p. 807 above.
[6] For the actual production of pig-iron in 1941 see p. 888, note 2 below.

same period.[1]   A fifteen-year plan for Central Asia was completed a few months later.[2]   But the original intention of completing the *genplan* for the economy as a whole by October 1927 proved quite unrealizable.   The celebration meeting of TsIK in that month and the fifteenth party congress in December 1927 were entirely taken up with the problems of the five-year plan, and the *genplan* played little part in these discussions.

The new year 1928 did not begin auspiciously for the *genplan*. Gosplan established a new central commission on perspective planning, the prime function of which was to prepare the five-year plan, placed the commission on the *genplan* under its authority, and temporarily reduced the *genplan* staff.[3]   In the course of 1928, however, interest in the *genplan* revived, partly because of problems which arose in constructing the five-year plan.   All the targets and prospects for the five-year plan were in the melting-pot ; [4] and the provision of a long-term framework within which it could be prepared seemed urgently desirable.   Capital construction carried out in the next five years would greatly influence the subsequent pattern of development ; and projects which were to be completed in the middle nineteen-thirties would have to be started during the course of the first five-year plan.   In January 1928, Strumilin stressed at a discussion in the Communist Academy the difficulties caused for five-year planning by the absence of the *genplan*, which should have provided " the structural model of the social formation towards which we should progress " ; and Krzhizhanovsky looked forward to the publication of the *genplan* as an occasion which would be " a festival of the working people of the whole world, a tremendous transition from necessity to freedom ", adding, however, that the plan would not be ready for some years.[5]   In March 1928, Kovalevsky, who had replaced Osadchy, reported on the *genplan* to the third Gosplan congress ; an article which appeared after the congress explained that Gosplan had prepared detailed studies of the fifteen-year prospects for transport and for the fuel, textile and metal industries as well as for electrification, and

[1] *General'nyi Plan Khozyaistva Urala na Period 1927–1941 gg. i Perspektivy Pervogo Pyatiletiya* (Sverdlovsk, 1927), pp. 79-81, 513-517.
[2] *Planovoe Khozyaistvo*, No. 4, 1928, p. 7.
[3] See pp. 874-875 below.   [4] See pp. 876-888 below.
[5] *O Pyatiletnem Plane Razvitiya Narodnogo Khozyaistva SSSR : Diskussiya v Kommunisticheskoi Akademii* (1928), pp. 28, 66.

stressed that " *statistical calculations should have in this plan a strictly auxiliary rôle, subsidiary to political, economic and technical requirements* ".[1] Discussion about the *genplan*, being concerned with broad trends in social and economic development over a long period, tended to reveal clearly the widening gulf between the sceptics and the supporters of rapid industrialization. At a discussion held in the planning workers' club soon after the congress, Bazarov dismissed the proposal of Vesenkha to take 18–20 per cent a year as the " normal rate of growth " for industrial production, pointing out that such a rate of growth would mean that production would be 30 times as great within 15 years and 160 times as great within 30 years. Groman condemned " fantastic constructs ", stressed the influence of the peasant on economic development, and insisted that Soviet planners would not be full masters of the economy even by the end of the *genplan*.[2] Some general plans for particular sectors continued to reflect the conservative approach of non-party experts ; a special commission of the Gosplan of the USSR working on the *genplan* for the metal industry still proposed in the summer of 1928 that the output of pig-iron should reach only 8·5 million tons in 1935–1936 and only 11·5 million tons in 1940–1941 ; the latter figure was only a little above the figure already proposed in Vesenkha for the last year of the first five-year plan.[3] A Vesenkha planner ironically remarked a few months later that, " if the authors of this general plan had come out of this dispute as victors, the USSR in 1941 would have been on the same national economic level as Germany at the beginning of the twentieth century ", and would have been doomed to defeat in its struggle with the capitalist world.[4]

Meanwhile the more extreme enthusiasts among the supporters of industrialization were seized with enthusiasm for the construction of a new *genplan* which would clearly demonstrate the possibility of overtaking the capitalist world within a fairly short period.

---

[1] *Planovoe Khozyaistvo*, No. 4, 1928, pp. 7, 9 ; for the congress see pp. 877-878 below.   [2] *Planovoe Khozyaistvo*, No. 6, 1928, pp. 152, 159-160.

[3] The general plan for metals, prepared under the supervision of Gartvan, was published in *Vestnik Metallopromyshlennosti*, Nos. 7-8, 9-10, 1928 ; see also *Materialy k Pyatiletnemu Planu Promyshlennosti VSNKh SSSR* (1929), iii, 768-769.   For the five-year plan for metals see pp. 887-888 below.

[4] *Materialy k Pyatiletnemu Planu Promyshlennosti VSNKh SSSR* (1929), iii, p. xxvi.

In the spring of 1928, Motylev insisted that " we see nothing impossible in reaching the level of the United States in 20-25 years ".[1] Sabsovich, who rapidly became the most prominent figure in the campaign for a more optimistic *genplan*, argued in August 1928 that the rate of growth of industrial production must continue to increase throughout the fifteen years ; [2] three months later he condemned " realists " who thought that it would take many decades to close the gap between the USSR and the capitalist world.[3] In his own version of the *genplan*, put forward towards the end of 1928, Sabsovich proposed that the rate of growth of industrial production should rise to as much as 29 per cent a year by 1947–1948 ; Soviet industrial production would considerably exceed that of the United States within the fifteen years, and by 1947–1948 it would be one hundred times as large as in 1927–1928, even though the working-day would by then have been reduced to five hours.[4] Feldman, a Gosplan economist, put forward a theoretical model for a 10-20 year *genplan* which was similarly optimistic.[5] He reiterated this optimism in a further article in the Gosplan journal :

> Ten — at most fifteen — years is the time-limit within which we must re-construct all our relations of production in the country. The rate of growth must be such that the movement can be seen by every proletarian and peasant with eyes to see, inside and outside our country.[6]

These proposals had far outdistanced the original postulate that national income or product per head would double over 10-15 years. The difficulties of achieving this high rate of growth, while at the same time raising the standard of living in both town and country and maintaining the market relation with the peasantry, were overcome by heroic assumptions about improvements in the productivity of industrial labour or in the efficiency with

---

[1] V. Motylev, *Problema Tempa Razvitiya SSSR* (1929), p. 133.
[2] *Torgovo-Promyshlennaya Gazeta*, August 19, 1928 ; for Sabsovich see p. 309 above.   [3] *Torgovo-Promyshlennaya Gazeta*, November 29, 1928.
[4] *Planovoe Khozyaistvo*, No. 1, 1929, pp. 54-103. These proposals were re-published in what became a very popular pamphlet, L. Sabsovich, *SSSR cherez 15 Let* (1929) ; they are further discussed in E. Zaleski, *Planification de la Croissance et Fluctuations Économiques en U.R.S.S.*, i (1962), 108-109.
[5] *Planovoe Khozyaistvo*, No. 11, 1928, pp. 146-170 ; No. 12, 1928, pp. 151-178.   [6] *Ibid.* No. 2, 1929, p. 190.

which capital would be used.   At this time these schemes did not apparently receive much official encouragement.   The *genplan* was not mentioned in the final version of the five-year plan prepared by Gosplan, or in the resolution of the sixteenth party conference in April 1929 which approved the plan.   But the desire and the need to construct a plan covering a period of ten or fifteen years long continued to allure and to frustrate the Soviet planner.

CHAPTER 37

THE FIVE-YEAR PLAN

THE period of five years as the unit of time for planning was held to be convenient for several reasons. In the course of five years, large factories and electric power stations, major railway lines and important irrigation works could be begun and completed. In the course of five years, a cycle of good and bad harvests was likely to occur, so that the planners could assume an average yield.[1] All shades of opinion in Gosplan agreed that the preparation of a five-year, or " perspective ", plan was urgently necessary. In industry, Kuibyshev maintained that a five-year plan was essential to obviate " mistakes and zigzags " : without it, decisions about the allocations of resources between different areas were reached on the basis of " completely accidental indicators ", while " real economic need " remained unsatisfied.[2] In the first years of NEP many experiments in five-year planning had already been made. As early as 1923, a five-year plan for industry as a whole was prepared in Gosplan, covering the years from 1923–1924 to 1927–1928, and in Vesenkha in the same year Glavmetall prepared a five-year plan for the metal industry. In 1924, Narkomzem compiled a five-year plan for the agriculture of the RSFSR, and Narkomput' approved one for railway transport.[3] These plans were all basically concerned with the restoration of their sector of the economy to its pre-war level, and assumed that this would take many years. All of them, even the plan for agriculture, proved to have been unduly pessimistic. In the event, industrial production expanded so rapidly in 1924–1925 that during 1925 both Gosplan and Vesenkha embarked on the much more complex work of preparing five-year plans which would reshape the economic, and in particular

[1] *Planovoe Khozyaistvo*, No. 3, 1927, p. 8.
[2] *SSSR : 4 S"ezd Sovetov* (1927), p. 261.
[3] See *Socialism in One Country, 1924–1926*, Vol. 1, pp. 491, 499 S. Strumilin, *Na Planovom Fronte* (1958), pp. 273-300.

THE ECONOMIC ORDER

the industrial, structure inherited from pre-revolutionary Russia. On March 24, 1926, STO decided that the perspective plans for individual sectors of the economy should as a rule cover a five-year period, and should also take account of general prospects of development after the end of that period.[1] During the next three years, every People's Commissariat became involved in the business of five-year planning.

(a) The Osvok "Hypotheses" (1926)

On March 21, 1925, some months before Gosplan began work on its own draft of the five-year plan, the presidium of Vesenkha established Osvok, the " special conference on the restoration of fixed capital in industry ", with Pyatakov as its president.[2] For the next eighteen months, party members of all shades of opinion worked in Osvok with ex-Menshevik economists and non-party scientists and engineers on a five-year plan covering the years 1925 –1926 to 1929–1930 (October 1, 1925, to September 30, 1930). The core of the work was an attempt to examine the prospects of each industry concretely and in detail, and to reach precise conclusions about the location and capacity of the new works and factories which were required : Pyatakov commented that the preparation of such a list of new factories was " the soul of five-year plans ".[3] Osvok established 32 " production " sections, each dealing with a major industry, and five " functional " or general sections dealing with agriculture, transport, regionalization, technical training, and finance. Committees to prepare republican Osvok plans were established in the Vesenkhas of the RSFSR, the White Russian SSR and the Ukrainian SSR.[4] The existing staff of Promplan, the planning department of Vesenkha, and of its various sub-departments was available to Osvok, together with specialists from elsewhere in Vesenkha ; A. M. Ginzburg, who was primarily responsible for coordinating the plans of individual industries, later

---

[1] Informatsionnyi Byulleten' Gosplana SSSR, No. 5, 1926, pp. 8-9 ; the decision was adopted in connexion with a proposed three-year plan for the metal industry (see Socialism in One Country, 1924–1926, Vol. 1, p. 341).

[2] See Socialism in One Country, 1924–1926, Vol. 1, pp. 339-340.

[3] Torgovo-Promyshlennaya Gazeta, April 16, 1926.

[4] Materialy Osobogo Soveshchaniya po Vosstanovleniyu Osnovnogo Kapitala pri Prezidiume VSNKh SSSR, Seriya II, i (1926), 43-45.

claimed that " the work was done by a well-coordinated machine, which was accustomed to joint work ".[1] From April to December 1925, 1228 sittings of sections discussed 592 reports from experts.[2] In November 1925, a special commission was established to bring together the plans for individual industries into a " comprehensive five-year hypothesis " for industry as a whole.[3] The results of the work of Osvok and its various sections were published during 1926 and 1927 in a large number of volumes concerned both with individual industries and with different aspects of the general " hypothesis " for industry.[4]

In April 1926, an industrial conference was held under the auspices of Vesenkha in Moscow ; it was hailed by the industrial newspaper as " one of those conferences which coincide with turning-points in the development of the state economy ".[5] Pyatakov, in his report on " the perspective plan and new industrial construction ", placed the work of Osvok firmly in the context of the problem not of restoring, but of expanding, fixed capital, " the most important, the most difficult, the central problem of industrial policy and of all our economic policy ", but dealt with it fairly uncontroversially. He emphasized that existing capital was almost completely utilized, that much of it was worn out and more of it out-of-date, citing the example of an American glass works which had achieved with 800-850 workers a level of production that would require 18,000 men using Russian methods. But he admitted that American methods would be possible only if the standard of living and the resources available for investment were

[1] *Ibid.* Seriya III, i (1927), 5 ; for Promplan see pp. 354-356 above ; for Ginzburg see p. 296 above.
[2] *Materialy Osobogo Soveshchaniya po Vosstanovleniyu Osnovnogo Kapitala pri Prezidiume VSNKh SSSR,* Seriya II, i (1926), 45, 52-53.
[3] *Torgovo-Promyshlennaya Gazeta,* October 1, 1926.
[4] These had the general title *Materialy Osobogo Soveshchaniya po Vosstanovleniyu Osnovnogo Kapitala pri Prezidiume VSNKh SSSR.* The papers were published in three series : Series I, " Five-year Hypotheses for Branches of Industry ", contained 29 volumes on different industries varying in size from pamphlet to large book ; Series II, " Materials on the Criticism of Hypotheses ", consisted of a single volume, a detailed survey of the work of Osvok in 1925 and 1926 ; Series III, " Perspective of the Development of Industry in 1925-1926 to 1929-1930 ", included a brief general survey by Ginsburg and eight volumes on general questions such as agriculture, finance and territorial organization, normally prepared by the responsible section of Osvok.
[5] *Torgovo-Promyshlennaya Gazeta,* April 17, 1926.

higher. The Soviet Union was still a poor country ; its existing capital must therefore be used more intensively ; and " very strict discipline " must be observed in planning.[1] The conference resolved that " Osvok has in general moved correctly along the road to constructing a perspective plan for the industry of the USSR " ; perspective plans for economic areas should now be given priority and should be integrated with the " comprehensive hypothesis ", about which Osvok was to call a special conference. But the resolution also pointed out that the hypotheses relating to new construction were " non-obligatory " and " only proposals ".[2] Dzerzhinsky cautiously ruled a few weeks later that no official of Vesenkha should discuss the Osvok hypotheses with Gosplan or other authorities without his written permission ;[3] this may suggest incipient mistrust of Pyatakov's enthusiasm for industrialization, or scepticism about the more optimistic proposals of Osvok.[4]

During the next few months, work on the plans continued. In July 1926 a special commission of Vesenkha discussed the financial plan[5] and the planning department of Vesenkha, with Pyatakov in the chair, heard a report from Ginzburg on the preliminary attempt to construct the comprehensive hypothesis covering the whole of industry and all aspects of the plan.[6] The main weakness which emerged in the process of putting together the separate plans of Osvok was the lack of coordination inherent in the method of leaving each industry to prepare its own hypothesis more or less independently and without guiding directives from the centre. In fact, the hypotheses prepared for individual industries made assumptions about the future state of the market which were so contradictory as to defy coordination. In different consumer goods industries, the estimated production for 1929–1930 varied from 100 per cent to 200 per cent of the pre-war level. In the producer goods industries, less arbitrary estimates of demand could be made owing to the presence of large centralized con-

---

[1] *Torgovo-Promyshlennaya Gazeta*, April 16, 1926.
[2] *Ibid.* April 22, 1926 ; the resolution was endorsed by the presidium of Vesenkha on May 6, 1926 (*Protokol Zasedaniya Prezidiuma VSNKh SSSR, 1925–1926*, No. 8). [3] *Torgovo-Promyshlennaya Gazeta*, June 3, 1926.
[4] For Dzerzhinsky's similar ruling in the following month about the control figures of Vesenkha for 1926–1927 see p. 281 above.
[5] *Torgovo-Promyshlennaya Gazeta*, July 18, 1926.
[6] *Ibid.* July 31, 1926.

sumers, though here too assumptions about future demand were based at best on questioning industrial consumers or on guesses by each industry as to the rate of growth of the rest of the economy; the coal industry did not even make an estimate of future demand, but simply calculated its own production possibilities.[1] The estimates of capital investment required by each industry during the five years were based on these independent and usually optimistic guesses rather than on any common assumption about what resources could be made available in the rest of the economy for industrial development.[2] The plans for individual industries also made varying assumptions about the sources from which the proposed investment would be drawn. Some assumed that prices would be cut drastically, and investment financed by loans and budget subsidies; others that prices would remain high and that investment would be financed from profits.[3] The agricultural section of Osvok provided for a decline of 22·5 per cent in industrial prices on the peasant market, while delivery prices of agricultural products would fall by at most 5 per cent; [4] the implication of this for the plans of industry itself was that industry could not expect to obtain any major additional resources from agriculture, but would rather be expected to strengthen incentives for agriculture by lowering industrial prices.

When the production plans for different industries were combined into the comprehensive hypothesis, the resulting plan for industry as a whole involved an increase in the production of state industry by 109 per cent in the four-year period from 1926–1927 to 1929–1930, with the annual rate of growth declining from 31·6 per cent in the first year to 15·0 per cent in the last.[5] In the discussions in Vesenkha, the planned decline in the rate of growth, which

---

[1] *Materialy Osobogo Soveshchaniya po Vosstanovleniyu Osnovnogo Kapitala pri Prezidiume VSNKh SSSR*, Seriya II, i (1926), 17-22. Some of the programmes for the chemical industry were later said by a leading chemist to have been " highly fantastic, and obviously the work of individuals with more imagination than experience "; while they gave birth to " the idea of the five-year plan ", they had " no influence on the development of the chemical industry " (V. Ipatieff, *Life of a Chemist* (Stanford, 1946), p. 422).

[2] *Sotsialisticheskoe Khozyaistvo*, No. 4, 1926, p. 29.

[3] *Materialy Osobogo Soveshchaniya po Vosstanovleniyu Osnovnogo Kapitala pri Prezidiume VSNKh SSSR*, Seriya II, i (1926), 37-38.

[4] *Id.* Seriya III, ii (1927), 16-24.

[5] See Table No. 49, p. 981 below.

became known as an "attenuating curve" (zatukhayushchaya krivaya), was not seriously challenged;[1] it was taken for granted that this decline was inevitable as the pre-war level of production was approached and all spare industrial capacity was taken up.[2] The discussion in Vesenkha was mainly concerned with the question whether the general rate of growth proposed was too high; in the annual control figures which were being prepared simultaneously in Vesenkha, industrial production in 1926–1927 was to rise by only 16–17 per cent as compared with the proposed rise of 31·6 per cent in the Osvok comprehensive hypothesis.[3] The Osvok proposal for that year was obviously exaggerated; whether the proposals for the remaining years of the plan were feasible depended primarily on whether the proposed figure for capital investment in industry, amounting to 5300 million rubles over the remaining four years of the plan, could be achieved.

The comprehensive hypothesis solved the problem of the sources of industrial investment by assuming, as did all subsequent drafts of the plan, a substantial improvement in the efficiency of industry, resulting in a reduction of its costs. In the Osvok draft, the planned reduction in costs over the five-year period was 22 per cent: the most important single factor here was a planned increase in labour productivity by as much as 60 per cent, while nominal wages were to rise by only 26 per cent.[4] Part of the gain from the fall in costs was to accrue to industry in the form of increased profits; the remainder would be used to achieve the reduction in prices of industrial goods proposed by the agricultural section of Osvok. This would raise the real earnings both of the urban worker and of the peasant, and provide an increased incentive to the peasant to sell his products.[5] The reduction in costs would

---

[1] According to one account, Pyatakov criticized the "attenuating curve' of production (*Materialy Osobogo Soveshchaniya po Vosstanovleniyu Osnovnogo Kapitala pri Prezidiume VSNKh SSSR*, Seriya III, i (1927), 7); if this is true, he must have been almost alone in doing so at this time.
[2] At the fourteenth party congress in December 1925, Stalin stated that, in view of the shortage of capital, "the expansion of our industry in future will probably not be as rapid as it has been so far", and even predicted that over a number of years industry would grow less rapidly than agriculture (Stalin, *Sochineniya*, vii, 315-316).   [3] See p. 279 above.
[4] See Table No. 51, p. 983 below; for the ambiguities of the term " labour productivity " see pp. 484-485 above.
[5] *Torgovo-Promyshlennaya Gazeta*, July 18, 1926.

thus simultaneously contribute to solving both the problem of providing resources for industry itself and the problem of the " scissors " between industrial and agricultural prices.   The authors of the comprehensive hypothesis estimated, however, that it would be impossible to find sufficient resources within industry to finance the whole of its investment programme :   the state would have to allocate 2 milliard rubles to industry over the five years to make up the total of 7 milliard rubles required by the plan.   The difficulties were aggravated by the proposal of the comprehensive hypothesis to increase investment in industry very sharply in the second year of the plan, 1926–1927, and then reduce it in each of the subsequent years up to 1929–1930.[1]   This decline in the absolute annual amount of investment in the later years of the plan, which became known as the " attenuating curve " of investment, was much less defensible than the attenuating curve in the rate of growth of industrial production.   It was strongly criticized by Vesenkha officials, and Shtern summed up its obvious deficiency :

> In our conditions, there are no grounds for constructing an attenuating curve [of investment]; on the contrary, we must base ourselves on the view that, with the increase in accumulation and in the mobilization of a considerable part of it for the needs of industrialization, we shall follow an accelerating curve.[2]

The proposed decline in investment was due not to any point of principle, but to a technical shortcoming in the conception of the plans.   Individual industries included in their plans only those projects which would reach the production stage during the five years of the plan itself ;   insufficient provision was made in the last years of the plan to start construction of new factories which would come into operation after September 1930.   The effect was that the whole of the 2 milliard rubles supplied by the state would be required in the first three years of the plan.[3]   This requirement naturally cast doubts on the feasibility of the proposed level of investment in industry, particularly for the years 1926–1927 and 1927–1928.   Although the total sum for the whole five years was no larger than that proposed by Gosplan in its own first draft, the

---

[1] See Table No. 50, p. 982 below.
[2] *Torgovo-Promyshlennaya Gazeta*, July 18, 1926 ;   *Materialy Osobogo Soveshchaniya po Vosstanovleniyu Osnovnogo Kapitala pri Prezidiume VSNKh SSSR*, Seriya III, i (1927), 8.
[3] *Torgovo-Promyshlennaya Gazeta*, July 18, 1926.

main provisions of which had now become available, the financial section of Osvok, headed by S. D. Abramovich, an ex-Menshevik, concluded that the sum required was " evidently unrealizable for the five-year period under consideration ".[1]

Behind this issue lurked major differences of opinion, both about the rate of industrialization and about the sources of industrial investment, which were only just coming into the open, and which Pyatakov had evaded in his report to the conference of April 1926. Sabsovich wrote two years later of " two influences " on the Osvok plan, " one from the presidium of Osvok headed by Pyatakov, which gave a directive for the maximum development of industry ", and the other from the " large number " of specialists who suffered from " a certain narrowness of economic outlook (mainly basing themselves on what happened before the war) " and a " lack of confidence in the growth of the well-being of the population at a more rapid rate than before the war ".[2] When the financial proposals were discussed in Vesenkha in July 1926, Ginzburg, while insisting that " we must not fall into pessimism ", and that the plan was basically on the right lines, nevertheless considered the proposed rate of growth, with its heavy demands on the state budget, as " *beyond the limits of potential accumulation in the economy* ".[3] In the same month, Vainshtein scathingly criticized the high rate of investment planned for the first three years as " easily explained by psychological factors " but " irrational and unnecessary " ;[4] and Dvolaitsky of Narkomtorg at a discussion in the Communist Academy in September 1926 ridiculed the proposal to double industrial production in five years, referring amid laughter to a suggestion that industrial production could be trebled by 1931 and raised to twenty times the pre-war level by 1939.[5] Only the opposition was prepared at this time to press for a rate of industrialization higher than that advocated by Osvok. In an unpublished memorandum of September 1926 Trotsky attacked

[1] *Materialy Osobogo Soveshchaniya po Vosstanovleniyu Osnovnogo Kapitala pri Prezidiume VSNKh SSSR*, Seriya III, v (1927), 81 ; for the Gosplan draft see pp. 851-854 below.
[2] *Puti Industrializatsii*, No. 2, 1928, pp. 47-48 ; he described the Osvok plan in general as " a grandiose and interesting work " (*ibid.* No. 4, 1928, p. 59). [3] *Torgovo-Promyshlennaya Gazeta*, July 18, 1926.
[4] *Sotsialisticheskoe Khozyaistvo*, No. 4, 1926, p. 12.
[5] *Vestnik Kommunisticheskoi Akademii*, xvii (1926), 221-222.

all the estimates of Osvok as hopelessly inadequate. Consumption of industrial consumer goods per head of population would be less in 1929–1930 than in 1913 ; agricultural production would rise by only 6 per cent ; producer goods would amount to only 46 per cent of total industrial production in 1929–1930 as against 44 per cent in 1913 ; the proletariat would increase by only 100,000 a year. Trotsky dismissed this as a virtual renunciation of the industrialization programme.[1] About the same time Pyatakov, whose dismissal from Vesenkha a few weeks previously was closely connected with the controversy about the rate of industrialization, declared that the Osvok plan " requires serious corrections, not a reduction but an increase ".[2]

By this time Osvok had been dissolved in the course of the reorganization of Vesenkha.[3] At the beginning of September 1926, its central staff was incorporated in the new planning department of Vesenkha, and its production sections were attached to the appropriate *glavki*, which thus became directly concerned in long-term as well as in annual planning.[4] In the same month the planning department of Vesenkha established a special commission on perspective planning under the presidency of Ginzburg — an appointment which assured continuity with the work of Osvok.[5]

(b) First Gosplan Draft (1926)

Gosplan began to prepare its first version of the five-year plan during the winter of 1925–1926 ; like the Osvok draft, it covered

[1] An undated version of this memorandum is in the Trotsky archives, T 3004 ; a first draft (T 3005) is dated September 7, 1926.

[2] *Vestnik Kommunisticheskoi Akademii*, xvii (1926), p. 211. A year later, at the July 1927 session of the party central committee, Kuibyshev criticized the Osvok plan for " lack of confidence in the possibility of developing our industry " (A. Khavin, *U Rulya Promyshlennosti (Dokumental'nye Ocherki)* (1968), pp. 60-61) ; in 1930 Stalin attacked the Osvok proposals as " constructed on the principles of Trotskyism ", contrasting their " *attenuating* Trotskyite curve " for industrial investment and for the rate of growth of industrial production with the " *rising* Bolshevik curve " which had in fact been achieved (Stalin, *Sochineniya*, xii, 350-351).

[3] For the reorganization of Vesenkha see pp. 355-356 above.

[4] *Torgovo-Promyshlennaya Gazeta*, September 5, 1926 ; the inclusion of Osvok in the planning department had been proposed by Pyatakov and agreed by the presidium of Vesenkha on January 20, 1926 (*Protokol Zasedaniya Prezidiuma VSNKh SSSR, 1925–1926*, No. 4, art. 108).

[5] *Materialy k Pyatiletnemu Planu Razvitiya Promyshlennosti SSSR (1927/28–1931/32 gg.)* (1927), p. 9.

the economic years 1925-1926 to 1929-1930. On February 11, 1926, a special Gosplan commission was formed to analyse all existing perspective plans and to prepare an initial working hypothesis.[1] In a long report to the first Gosplan congress, which met from March 10 to 17, 1926, Strumilin presented an interim " outline sketch " for a five-year plan.[2] This first Gosplan draft lacked the detailed studies and proposals relating to particular sectors of the economy and particular industries which were an impressive feature of the work of Osvok. Like the Osvok draft, it was basically a plan for the state sector : investments in agriculture by the individual peasant were cited merely as estimates, and not included in the plan, on the ground that they were outside the control of the planners. Strumilin, describing state industry in his report as " the sector which interests us most ", explained that the proposals of Osvok had been utilized " in so far as they are already known to Gosplan ". The Gosplan draft proposed that the productive capacity of state industry should be approximately doubled by 1929-1930, while agricultural capital would increase by only 20-25 per cent.[3] Over the five years, capital investment in industry was to increase in each year ; and while the rate of increase in industrial production followed the standard " attenuating curve ", Gosplan still planned an increase of 15 per cent a year for the last two years of the plan, by which time prewar capacity would have been fully taken up. In its proposals as a whole, both for industrial production and for capital investment in industry, Gosplan was, however, less optimistic than Osvok, particularly for the years 1926-1927 and 1927-1928.[4] The proposals of Gosplan for agriculture were similar to those of Osvok.[5] Strumilin spoke enthusiastically of what he described as a " conclusion of colossal economic and political significance " :

> The problem of accumulation of the resources necessary to us for the regeneration of our economy on new foundations can

---

[1] *Informatsionnyi Byulleten' Gosplana SSSR*, No. 2, 1926, p. 2.
[2] For the congress see *Socialism in One Country, 1924-1926*, Vol. 1, pp. 510-512.
[3] *Problemy Planirovaniya (Itogi i Perspektivy)* (1926), pp. 24-25 ; this volume was the stenographic record of the congress.
[4] See Tables No. 49, 50, pp. 981, 981 below.
[5] *Problemy Planirovaniya (Itogi i Perspektivy)* (1926), pp. 34-36.

be solved quite satisfactorily even without assistance to us from outside — on the basis of the internal resources of the country alone.

To achieve this objective, he proposed that 10·8 milliards of the 16·3 milliard rubles to be invested by the state in all sectors of the economy during the five years should be met by profits and depreciation charges in the state sector itself.[1] Most of the investment would be in industry ; and the increase in industrial profits needed to finance it would require a substantial reduction of industrial costs, achieved as a result of a steep increase in labour productivity. The increase in investment would be accompanied by an improvement in the standard of living in town and country. Like the Osvok proposals, the draft assumed that the reduction in industrial costs would be sufficient to finance both the required increase in profits and a reduction in the retail prices of industrial goods ; at the same time, in contrast to the Osvok proposals, it optimistically assumed that, in spite of the reduction in costs, nominal wages in industry would rise almost as rapidly as labour productivity.[2] Strumilin admitted that the plan might in the end fail to secure the necessary resources and have to be spread over six or even seven years. But, in spite of the " great disillusionment and economic difficulties " which this delay might cause, " the general economic effect of such a plan would in the last resort undoubtedly be greater than if we miscalculated in the other direction ; for, if the labour resources of the country were completely unutilized due to lack of planning initiative, this would cause losses which could not be replaced ".[3]

In the discussion which followed Strumilin's report, Sokolnikov, now a deputy president of Gosplan, strongly criticized the underlying concept of the plan on the familiar grounds that it paid too much attention to industry in general and industrial self-sufficiency in particular, and did not allocate sufficient resources to agriculture to increase production and exports : " if we develop agriculture not by 20 but by 50–60 per cent ", Sokolnikov claimed,

---

[1] *Ibid.* pp. 74-75.   [2] See Table No. 51, p. 983 below.

[3] *Problemy Planirovaniya (Itogi i Perspektivy)* (1926), pp. 85-86 ; the opposite approach, that it was too onerous to cut back in the course of fulfilment of a plan which had proved over-optimistic, was adopted by Gosplan in the preparation of the annual control figures a few months later (see pp. 812-813 above).

" then industry will possibly develop more " than was planned.[1] Volf, an agricultural expert who was at that time an official of the Ukrainian Gosplan, also criticized Strumilin's assumption that " the state should make no investment or almost no investment in agriculture ".[2] But the discussion was desultory. The resolutions of the congress claimed that these " control figures " for a five-year plan, like the annual control figures for 1925–1926, were " a significant achievement ", and that improved control figures for a five-year plan, which would be sufficiently precise to be used in practice, could be elaborated within from six to twelve months ; nevertheless, the congress cautiously emphasized that Strumilin's proposals were " an outline sketch " which " could serve only as material for further work ".[3] On April 10, 1926, after the conclusion of the congress, Gosplan established a " central commission for perspective plans ", once more under the presidency of Strumilin, to prepare a revised plan. The commission, which was supposed to work on parallel lines to the Osadchy commission on the *genplan*, included representatives from the sections of the Gosplan of the USSR, from the Gosplans of the republics, and from Rabkrin and the Central Statistical Administration ; and other commissariats were invited to participate in the work as it affected them.[4]

(c) Second Gosplan and Vesenkha Drafts (Spring 1927)

The Gosplan commission under Strumilin set up in April 1926 worked during the rest of the year and the first weeks of 1927 on the preparation of a five-year plan which would cover the period October 1, 1926, to September 30, 1931, one year later than the Osvok hypotheses or the first Gosplan draft.[5] At the fifteenth

---

[1] For this speech and Sokolnikov's appointment see *Socialism in One Country, 1924–1926*, Vol. 1, p. 510 ; the speech was not included in the published stenographic report of the congress.

[2] *Problemy Planirovaniya (Itogi i Perspektivy)* (1926), p. 90 ; Volf prepared the agricultural section of the final draft of the five-year plan for the USSR (*Pyatiletnii Plan Narodno-Khozyaistvennogo Stroitel'stva SSSR* (1929), ii, i, 6).

[3] *Problemy Planirovaniya (Itogi i Perspektivy)* (1926), pp. 315-318.

[4] *Informatsionnyi Byulleten' Gosplana SSSR*, No. 5, 1926, p. 7 ; *Perspektivy Razvertyvaniya Narodnogo Khozyaistva SSSR na 1926/27–1930/31 gg.* (1927), p. xiii.

[5] At this time it was generally considered that the plan should not have a fixed time-span, but should be reconsidered every year and extended for a year

party conference in October 1926, Rykov reported that the plan
was not yet available because of pressure of work on the annual
control figures ; [1] the party central committee at its session of
February 1927, in the course of a resolution on capital construction in industry, for the first time drew specific attention to the
urgency and importance of long-term planning :

> The Politburo should accelerate the elaboration of the
> orientative five-year plan for the development of the national
> economy, and particularly of industry and transport, so that all
> economic plans for the forthcoming economic year may be
> properly coordinated and based on the perspectives established
> for the development of separate areas and sectors of the
> economy.[2]

The new draft by the Strumilin commission was ready in time for
the second Gosplan congress, which assembled on March 25,
1927, and was attended by central and local planning officials and
by prominent experts employed in Vesenkha, Narkomzem and
Narkomfin. In an article about the five-year plan which appeared
in the planning journal shortly before the congress, Krzhizhanovsky emphasized the novelty of the work ; the planners " are sailing
away from the old shores, and the features of the new shores are
depicted for them only in very vague outlines ". He insisted that
the plan could not yet be very accurate, and might be accomplished
in three years, or might take six years or more ; on the whole,
however, the potentialities of a rationalized economy were probably under-estimated.[3] The plan was eventually published as a
volume of 800 pages. Like the annual control figures, and the
later versions of the five-year plan, it contained chapters both on
sectors of the economy, such as industry and transport, and on
aspects of the plan affecting all sectors of the economy, such as

---

in the light of experience, so that an up-to-date perspective for five years ahead
would always be available (*Materialy Osobogo Soveshchaniya po Vosstanovleniyu
Osnovnogo Kapitala pri Prezidiume VSNKh SSSR*, Seriya III, i (1926), 14 ;
*Perspektivy Razvertyvaniya Narodnogo Khozyaistva SSSR na 1926/27–1930/31
gg.* (1927), p. xiv).

   [1] *XV Konferentsiya Vsesoyuznoi Kommunisticheskoi Partii (B)* (1927),
pp. 112-113.

   [2] *KPSS v Rezolyutsiyakh* (1954), ii, 344 ; a five-year electrification plan
was approved by Sovnarkom a few days after the session ended (see pp. 419-420
above).   [3] *Planovoe Khozyaistvo*, No. 3, 1927, pp. 7-8, 12-13.

credit and currency ; but the regional break-down was still extremely sketchy.[1]

The new draft was prepared on the basis of several variants for each sector of the economy ; the final estimates, presented as a single set of figures, were said to be those which were most likely to be achieved.[2] The draft was much more modest about the prospects for the growth of industrial production than the previous Osvok or Gosplan proposals : industrial production, which had been planned in the first Gosplan draft to increase by some 82 per cent in the four years 1926–1927 to 1929–1930, was now planned to increase by only 79·5 per cent in the five years to 1930–1931.[3] In most respects the draft differed little from that of the previous year.[4] As in previous drafts, the reduction of industrial costs was to be the key factor in financing the plan. The new proposals fell into line with the view that labour productivity should rise more rapidly than nominal wages : it proposed that the former should increase by 50 per cent and the latter by only 33 per cent.[5] In view of the planned reduction in retail prices of industrial goods, however, real wages were expected to rise almost as rapidly as productivity. The proposed reduction in industrial costs and in the retail prices of industrial goods sold to the peasant led the authors of the plan to stress that no burden would be placed on the peasantry :

> In the last resort all provision of finance for our economy, whether it comes out of the profits of our state enterprises or out of the budget, falls with its whole weight on working incomes and primarily on the urban proletariat.[6]

The second Gosplan congress of March 1927 provided the occasion for an open clash between opposing schools of thought

[1] *Perspektivy Razvertyvaniya Narodnogo Khozyaistva SSSR na 1926/27–1930/31 gg.* (1927). The preface was dated March 21, 1927 ; the volume itself was not actually available at the congress (*Planovoe Khozyaistvo*, No. 4, 1927, p. 1).
[2] *Perspektivy Razvertyvaniya Narodnogo Khozyaistva SSSR na 1926/27–1930/31 gg.* (1927), p. xiii.
[3] See Table No. 49, p. 981 below.
[4] For its proposals about the industrial labour force see p. 466, note 2 above.
[5] See Table No. 51, p. 983 below.
[6] *Perspektivy Razvertyvaniya Narodnogo Khozyaistva na 1926/27–1930/31 gg.* (1927), p. 28.

about planning.[1] After making his report on the plan, Strumilin
was subjected to a frontal assault from the representatives of
Narkomfin and Narkomzem : his most bitter opponents were
Kondratiev and Makarov, the latter waving his papers and shout-
ing, " Such plans *must not* be produced ".[2] Strumilin's proposals
were also criticized within Gosplan : the first public arguments
between its party members and its ex-Menshevik experts apparently occurred on this occasion. The issue which preoccupied the
experts was the fundamental relation between the village and the
town. At the congress, Groman claimed that on Strumilin's own
figures the rural standard of living would rise only by 20 per cent,
not by 30 per cent as Strumilin had claimed, and that this improvement was too small ; Groman also objected to the proposal that
the real wages of the industrial worker should rise as rapidly as his
productivity :

> I always agreed with Marx that the growth of labour pro-
> ductivity should accrue to the benefit of the whole of society,
> including the village.[3]

The critics did not have it all their own way. The brief report
of the congress in the press claimed that the majority of those
present accepted the principles of the draft.[4] Ginzburg, now
actively engaged in the preparation of a perspective plan for
Vesenkha,[5] agreed that the Gosplan and Vesenkha plans could be
easily reconciled ; Sabsovich suggested that both Vesenkha and
Gosplan should have planned for still greater achievements. In
his reply to the discussion Strumilin readily agreed that there was

[1] Apart from Strumilin's report and reply to the discussion, which appear
in S. Strumilin, *Ocherki Sovetskoi Ekonomiki* (1928), pp. 422-475, 476-498,
only brief records of the debate appear to have been published ; Strumilin's
report also appeared as the preface to the published volume of the plan and in
Planovoe Khozyaistvo, No. 3, 1927, pp. 17-54.

[2] S. Strumilin, *Ocherki Sovetskoi Ekonomiki* (1928), p. 494 ; for Kondratiev
and Makarov see pp. 20-21, 733 above. The first Gosplan draft had already
provoked a vehement attack on Strumilin by Kondratiev in the journal of
Narkomzem : " Most of Strumilin's calculations, for all their apparent con-
vincingness, are based on what is really shifting sand. Even if, contrary to
expectations, his calculations proved near to reality, it would simply be an
accident, and not the result of a properly grounded prognosis " ; for Kondratiev's article see p. 791 above.

[3] See S. Strumilin, *Ocherki Sovetskoi Ekonomiki* (1928), pp. 481-483 ;
Planovoe Khozyaistvo, No. 5, 1927, p. 35.

[4] *Ekonomicheskaya Zhizn'*, April 2, 1927.   [5] See p. 862 below.

THE ECONOMIC ORDER PT. I

a considerable " safety margin " (zapas prochnosti) in the draft,
but claimed that it was better to keep this in reserve.[1] Krzhizhanovsky, in his concluding remarks, assured the critics that " the
five-year plan consists of control figures which are still subject to
great changes ".[2]

The congress, in a fairly cautious resolution, described the draft
as an economic programme which " in the main correctly indicates
the most important main lines of our economic construction ", but
referred to the detailed figures as " illustrative data for orientation,
outlining the possible scale of development, rates of growth and
proportions ". A number of concessions were made to the critics.
The resolution proposed that all the circumstances should be re-
examined with a view to increasing the rate of growth of agriculture.
It claimed that more efficient use of investment, higher productivity
of labour, and lower industrial costs could be achieved ; these
improvements would make it possible both to increase living
standards more rapidly and to narrow the gap between town and
country. New proposals should be prepared, showing a maximum
and a minimum variant in addition to a middle-range variant.[3] The
new proposals should incorporate more of the ideas and assumptions of the *genplan*, particularly its emphasis on *energetika* and its
regional approach.[4] Neither the resolution nor the draft plan itself
satisfied the more enthusiastic protagonists of industrialization. At
the fourth Union Congress of Soviets in April 1927 Kuibyshev
concluded that the results which the Gosplan draft proposed to
achieve in the five years would " not be very significant ", and
suggested that " methodological errors " had been committed.

[1] S. Strumilin, *Ocherki Sovetskoi Ekonomiki* (1928), pp. 496-497.
[2] *Ekonomicheskaya Zhizn'*, April 2, 1927.
[3] Krzhizhanovsky suggested that the " minimum " figures in future drafts
should show " the economic limits which cannot be departed from without a
fundamental disturbance of our whole economic organism " ; the " maximum "
figures should show what could be achieved with strain but without overstrain, assuming favourable conditions such as good organization and the
receipt of credits from abroad (*Planovoe Khozyaistvo*, No. 3, 1927, pp.
14-15).
[4] *Informatsionnyi Byulleten' Gosplana SSSR*, No. 4, 1927, pp. 1-4 ;
Bol'shevik, No. 10, May 31, 1927, pp. 46-51 ; for *energetika* see p. 803, note 1
above. Later in the year, when this draft was criticized for excessive caution,
the point was made that it had never been formally approved by Gosplan —
and much less by the party (*Bol'shevik*, No. 17, September 15, 1927,
p. 81).

While this did not mean that " the work done by Gosplan and especially by Professor Strumilin is of little value and that attention should not be paid to it ", it did show that the creative processes which were taking place in industry had been underestimated ; the prognosis of a reduction in prices and costs by only 17 per cent was " pessimistic ".[1] A bolder plan was also supported by the labour economics department of the central council of trade unions, which called for an increase in industrial production, not by 79 per cent, but by 112 per cent, to be achieved by using the same amount of investment more efficiently, and argued that the revised plan should involve the introduction of 700-800,000 workers into state industry instead of only half that number, as well as a greater increase in labour productivity than Gosplan had proposed.[2]

The concessions made at the Gosplan congress did not silence the critics from the Right. The controversies between Strumilin and his adversaries in Narkomzem and Narkomfin were pursued in the journals of Gosplan and Narkomfin. In the issue of the Gosplan journal for April 1927 Kondratiev, presumably repeating arguments which he had already used at the congress, claimed that the plan offered no proper justification for its estimates ; everything in it was deduced from everything else. When no proper economic justification was presented, " a neat row of figures is just a row of figures, nothing more ". The proposal in the plan that the proportion of total national income annually invested in the state sector alone should increase during the five years from 8·7 per cent to 12·6 per cent was too high ; total capital investment before the war amounted to only 8·5 per cent of national income. Strumilin failed to realize that planning involved an assessment of such economic factors as the availability of resources and the size of the market in the period of the plan ; by ignoring such questions, he was making a step towards " completely arbitrary planning constructs ".[3] But the major fault of the plan was that it did not allocate enough resources to agriculture. To achieve the agricultural production proposed, either state investment in agriculture must be increased, with a consequent slower growth in

[1] SSSR: 4 S"ezd Sovetov (1927), pp. 260-261.
[2] Pravda, July 9, 1927.
[3] Planovoe Khozyaistvo, No. 4, 1927, pp. 1-17.

general consumption, or investment by the peasants themselves must be larger :

> The main mistake is that the compilers wanted to solve a number of tasks simultaneously to the maximum extent (maximum crisis-free growth of the productive forces and maximum satisfaction of current needs etc.) without sufficiently taking into account the fact that these particular tasks in their extreme expression come into collision with each other.[1]

In the following issue of the journal, Makarov proposed that the volume of state investment in agriculture should be increased from 2·3 to 3·3 milliard rubles, the allocation to industry and trade being reduced accordingly, and that industrial prices should be reduced by 25–30 per cent instead of 17 per cent; these changes would increase the income of the peasant, and the amount which he could set aside for the development of his own holding. The proposed reduction in industrial prices would also mean a reduction in the planned increase of urban incomes. Without such amendments, Makarov contended, the increase in agricultural production proposed by Strumilin, which was essential to the balance of the whole plan, could not be achieved.[2] In reply to Kondratiev and Makarov, Strumilin claimed that the proportion of the national income invested before the war had been higher than 8·5 per cent, and that the level of investment envisaged by the draft was " more than modest " : the draft had not proposed a large amount of new construction, but had concentrated on investment which would improve efficiency. He rejected Makarov's argument that the standard of living of the industrial worker should rise more slowly in order to promote capital accumulation in the countryside, commenting that " the policy of *sacrifices* by the proletariat in the name of capital accumulation by the *kulak* upper strata in the village is not our policy " ; the proletariat might be called upon to make even greater sacrifices, but these would be " in the name of other higher objectives ". Strumilin claimed that his draft already took account of the interests of the peasant :

> Not only will we not take a single million for industrialization from the village, but we shall not charge to the village a

[1] *Planovoe Khozyaistvo*, No. 4, 1927, pp. 31, 33.
[2] *Ibid.* No. 5, 1927, pp. 56-58.

farthing of expenditure on such general state needs as defence and administration.[1]

Kondratiev and Makarov were supported both by Narkomzem [2] and by the experts in Narkomfin; a writer in the Narkomfin journal claimed that the draft lacked " an objective analysis of the real economic situation " and had within it the danger of " a break in the link with the peasantry ".[3] What alarmed all these critics was the belief that Gosplan had in effect ceased to think in terms compatible with the link with the peasantry. The planners had calculated the rise in agricultural production to fit in with what appeared to be an arbitrarily determined level of industrial investment, instead of limiting the level of investment to what the market would bear.

At the opposite pole of opinion, the united opposition was placed in something of a quandary by the official enthusiasm for planning and by Kondratiev's charge against Gosplan of aiming at " super-industrialization " [4] — the imputation hitherto always levelled at Trotsky. When the party central committee met in April 1927 after the publication of the proposals of Gosplan, the most serious complaint of the opposition was that, owing to the dilatoriness of the majority, a year had been lost, so that no integrated plan yet existed : the capital investment plan was still merely " a variegated series of annual columns on paper for separate industries ".[5]   At the session of the committee in July 1927 Pyatakov again complained that no complete five-year plan yet existed by which the annual control figures could be evaluated, and that the plan did not go far enough to promote industrialization ; he claimed that the Osvok plan had been " more optimistic ".[6]

[1] *Ibid.* No. 8, 1927, pp. 10-12, 16-18.
[2] For Narkomzem objections to the plan see *Informatsionnyi Byulleten' Gosplana SSSR*, No. 7, 1927, pp. 23-26.
[3] *Vestnik Finansov*, No. 6, 1927, pp. 259, 263 ; a further article *ibid.* No. 7, 1927, p. 55, also condemned the plan as too ambitious ; see also a report of the financial and economic department of Narkomfin *ibid.* No. 9, 1927, pp. 31-56.
[4] Quoted in *Planovoe Khozyaistvo*, No. 5, 1927, p. 33.
[5] Trotsky archives, T 942, p. 3 ; this unpublished memorandum dated April 11, 1927, may have been circulated to the committee, or have been the brief for Trotsky's remarks at the session. On June 10, 1927, a *Pravda* editorial admitted — without referring to the opposition — that " it must be recognized that we were at least a year behind in compiling the perspective plan ".
[6] Quoted in *Bol'shevik*, No. 14, July 31, 1927, p. 26.

The committee, which issued directives on the control figures for 1927–1928,[1] took no specific decision on the five-year plan. But, in deciding to convene the fifteenth party congress for the following December, it placed the question of the five-year plan on the agenda.[2] This ensured that it would remain well in the limelight.

Meanwhile, though the Gosplan variant was in the centre of the picture and drew most of the criticism, Vesenkha continued to make a significant independent contribution to the work of long-term planning. The Vesenkha commission presided over by Ginzburg,[3] which began work in September 1926, followed Osvok in making its own assessments of the prospects for all sectors of the economy, including agriculture and finance, and in the light of these worked out the main " ceilings " within which industry would develop.[4] These were approved by the planning department of Vesenkha in January 1927 and by a conference of planning workers from the republican Vesenkhas in February. Since 1925 annual plans had been compiled in Vesenkha in the light of limits set centrally ; [5] and the same practice was followed when five-year plans were drafted. The sectional plans, which included 61 plans for particular industries, were coordinated into a comprehensive plan ; in June 1927 this was discussed by the planning department of Vesenkha and by a conference of industrial planning agencies. The published proposals covered the years 1927–1928 to 1931–1932, two years beyond the Osvok hypotheses and one year beyond the second Gosplan draft of March 1927.[6] Like the Gosplan proposals, the Vesenkha proposals contained only one set of figures, which it called the " optimum " variant, but included variants for particular industries : the commission of Vesenkha explained that " we consider it superfluous to work out the plan as a whole in two or three variants depending on worst and best conditions, because the number of deviations from the

[1] See p. 816 above.
[2] KPSS v Rezolyutsiyakh (1954), ii, 394.
[3] See p. 851 above.
[4] For transport it took as a basis one of the variants worked out in Narkomput' (Torgovo-Promyshlennaya Gazeta, November 3, 1926).
[5] See pp. 824–825 above.
[6] Materialy k Pyatiletnemu Planu Razvitiya Promyshlennosti SSSR (1927/28–1931/32 gg.) (1927) ; the procedures by which the proposals were compiled are described ibid. p. 9. See also Torgovo-Promyshlennaya Gazeta, November 6, 1926 ; Pravda, June 21, 24, 1927.

optimum, and their range, can be very extensive ".[1]

Compared with the second Gosplan draft, the second Vesenkha draft of June 1927 was not a polished or well integrated document : the published version consisted of little more than a series of essays on different aspects of economic and industrial development, tied together by certain basic quantitative targets or assumptions.   But, unlike the Gosplan draft, in which discussion of individual industries was slight, it included plans for each main industry, and proposals for the main industrial regions.   It was somewhat more ambitious than the Gosplan draft.   Capital investment in Vesenkha-planned industry was planned to be higher in each year than Gosplan had proposed.[2]   The attenuating curve in capital investment of the Osvok plan was duly corrected : describing the investment plan as " constructed on the principle of the rising curve ", the authors argued that investment in new factories must be pressed forward as resources became available.[3]   The attenuating curve in the rate of growth of industrial production was retained, but the total increase in production over the five years was to be 82·5 per cent, a slightly higher figure than that of the second Gosplan draft.[4]   A combined increase of 45 per cent was planned in the gross production of industry and agriculture over the five years : the authors of the plan commented that " few examples of such rapid growth can be found in economic history ", and that it was " very possible " that development might in fact be slower.[5]

Like previous drafts, the new Vesenkha proposals assumed that investment in industry would be financed, in part from the budget, but in major part from resources accumulated by industry itself.[6]

---

[1] *Materialy k Pyatiletnemu Planu Razvitiya Promyshlennosti SSSR (1927/28–1931/32 gg.)* (1927), p. 13.
[2] See Table No. 50, p. 982 below.
[3] *Materialy k Pyatiletnemu Planu Razvitiya Promyshlennosti SSSR (1927/28–1931/32 gg.)* (1927), p. 59.
[4] For the rate of growth for each year, see Table No. 49, p. 981 below.
[5] *Materialy k Pyatiletnemu Planu Razvitiya Promyshlennosti SSSR (1927/28–1931/32 gg.)* (1927), p. 48.
[6] An interesting analysis showed that a large part of industrial investment, including part of the investment financed from the budget, was in effect to be financed by transfers of profit from Group B industries to Group A industries ; under the plan, profits in the textile industries in particular would be much higher than investment, while profits in the metal industries would be much lower than investment.   The deficit in Group A industries was partly due to the fact that the prices of producer goods tended to be more tightly controlled by

Industrial costs were discussed in far greater detail than in the Gosplan draft ; Vesenkha concluded that a 16·6 per cent reduction, approximately the same as that proposed by Gosplan, was " the maximum amount of reduction ", even though in the Vesenkha proposals nominal wages were to rise more slowly than in the Gosplan draft ; the reduction of industrial costs was, however, to be supplemented by an even more drastic reduction in trading costs which would permit a cut in industrial retail prices by as much as 25 per cent.[1] Since agricultural prices would remain stable, the net result would be a greater improvement in the terms of trade for the peasantry than was expected by Gosplan. Nevertheless, the Vesenkha draft admitted, with more frankness than Strumilin had shown, that the ultimate effect of the plan was to bring about " an inevitable redistribution of accumulation from agriculture to industry ".[2]

By the time this second draft was completed in June 1927, it was already regarded in Vesenkha as too cautious. In April 1927, Kuibyshev had criticized the second Gosplan draft as inadequate and pessimistic.[3] This criticism could not fail to be reflected in Vesenkha. On June 25, 1927, its planning department proposed that the Vesenkha draft should be revised ; and a " commission for the re-examination of the five-year plan " was established. Kuibyshev was appointed president of the commission ; Mezhlauk was appointed president of a small bureau or subcommittee which organized the detailed work.[4]

the state and hence to be lower than those of consumer goods (on May 1, 1927 wholesale prices were 72 per cent above the 1913 level in Group A industries and 105 per cent above it in Group B industries), and partly to the higher level of investment planned for Group A. The proportion of total investment financed by credit or from the budget was, however, expected to decline during the course of the five years in all the deficit industries (*ibid.* pp. 57, 70-72, 114-121, 612-613).   [1] See Table No. 51, p. 983 below.

[2] *Materialy k Pyatiletnemu Planu Razvitiya Promyshlennosti SSSR (1927/28-1931/32 gg.)* (1927), pp. 28, 52-57, 605.   [3] See pp. 858-859 above.

[4] *Kontrol'nye Tsifry Pyatiletnogo Plana Razvitiya Promyshlennosti (1927/8-1931/2)* (1927), pp. xiii-xiv. Ginzburg was sent to the United States as the member responsible for finance in a Vesenkha commission (*Pravda*, August 20, 1927), remaining there for about five months (*Protsess Kontrrevolyutsionnoi Organizatsii Men'shevikov* (1931), p. 77). According to *Sotsialisticheskii Vestnik* (Berlin), No. 1, January 12, 1928, p. 11, his departure was connected with the rejection of the second Vesenkha draft, for which he had been largely responsible, and the volume was withdrawn from public sale ; Ginzburg re-emerged, however, in the spring of 1928 (see p. 878 below).

(d) Third Gosplan and Vesenkha Drafts (Autumn 1927)

In the autumn of 1927, with the approach of the tenth anniversary of the revolution at the beginning of November and the party congress in the following month, the controversy about the five-year plan reached a critical stage. The opposition platform of September 1927 attacked the second Gosplan draft of the plan as pessimistic and niggardly. The proposed rate of growth of industrial investment and production was too small ; so was the planned growth of consumption. Furthermore, the socialist sector would not receive adequate reinforcement. In the Gosplan proposals, the proportion of investment in industry financed by the budget was to decline over the five years ; the platform proposed that the rôle of the budget should increase, additional revenue being made available through taxes on kulaks and on the excess profits of nepmen.[1]

In official circles the climate of opinion was changing, especially in Vesenkha, which showed signs of taking over the lead in perspective planning from Gosplan. When the proposals of the Ginzburg commission were at length published at the beginning of September 1927, they carried a vigorous preface by Kuibyshev. Kuibyshev praised the " tremendous and conscientious work of the best Vesenkha experts ", but commented that the draft had been overtaken by events. The " first hypothesis compiled by Pyatakov's commission reflected all the defects of the restoration period " (the phrase carried a hint of later attacks on Osvok as unduly cautious) ; the second Vesenkha draft was based only on the experience of 1925–1926 which had involved little reconstruction. Kuibyshev contended that capital investment could be more effective than had been contemplated in the earlier drafts, and that in consequence the plan should allow for a further increase in labour productivity and a further reduction in costs. More accumulation would be possible ; investment would be more wisely allocated ; reorganization would bring results which had previously been thought to require new investment.[2] When the

---

[1] L. Trotsky, The Real Situation in Russia (n.d. [1928]), pp. 79-82, 87-93.
[2] Materialy k Pyatiletnemu Planu Promyshlennosti SSSR (1927/28–1931/32 gg.) (1927), preface ; the preface was also printed in full in Torgovo-Promyshlennaya Gazeta, September 2, 1927.

2 F

Vesenkha commission for the re-examination of the five-year plan [1] met on September 9, 1927, a week after the publication of Kuibyshev's preface to the previous draft, Mezhlauk referred to a governmental decision that the plan should be revised " within a short time ". He admitted that the commission would not have time to draft a fresh five-year plan ; it could, however, provide " a new conception for compiling the five-year plan ".[2] In the discussion which followed, Mezhlauk received the powerful backing of the engineer Khrennikov, who spoke of the need to cut out unnecessary slack in the plan. In a rather verbose summing-up Kuibyshev roundly told the commission that it was impossible to present the existing plan at the October celebrations, and made the significant remark that the way to proceed was by using " correction coefficients " to revise the original plan.[3]

To carry out the revision, sub-commissions or working groups of the Mezhlauk commission were established, each concerned with a different aspect of the plan. The assumptions of the Ginzburg commission were believed in Vesenkha to have been pessimistic partly because it consisted mainly of economists, and lacked engineers ; the working groups of the Mezhlauk commission included engineers, who were to make an expert examination of the provisions of the draft in order to decide on improvements. Shein, the president of the group concerned with capital equipment, explained that the technical experts for each aspect of the work would not concern themselves with " small detailed corrections, requiring detailed elaboration ", but would use the " correction coefficients " already mentioned by Kuibyshev.[4] The capital equipment group, sometimes referred to more grandly as the " commission for the expert examination of capital expenditure ", set up sub-groups under Khrennikov, Charnovsky and Shein himself. These names were significant, for they were non-party engineers, and Khrennikov and Charnovsky had some reputation

[1] See p. 864 above.

[2] *Torgovo-Promyshlennaya Gazeta*, September 13, 1927 ; he explained later that " orientative data " must be ready by October 15 for the TsIK session convened to celebrate the tenth anniversary of the revolution (*ibid.* October 2, 1927).

[3] *Ibid.* September 13, 1927.

[4] *Torgovo-Promyshlennaya Gazeta*, September 14, 1927.

for independence.[1] During the second half of September 1927, these sub-groups met representatives of each industry, and tried to persuade them to accept increases in their production plans and reductions in their investment allocations, and to work towards lower production costs than had been proposed in the previous draft.[2]

At the beginning of October 1927, the Mezhlauk commission established a further commission, including the presidents of all the groups, with the object of preparing a few overall tables of a still incomplete draft to submit to Gosplan by October 6, so that they could be considered before TsIK met on October 15.[3] What happened in the first fortnight in October is not recorded. Two days before TsIK assembled, a strong editorial in the industrial newspaper referred to past shortcomings in perspective planning and to the unutilized potentialities of the Soviet system. By the end of the five-year period, the Soviet Union must produce at least half her own machine-tools, and develop new lines of production, especially in the chemical industry : at the same time the standard of living must be gradually improved. The five-year plan must not treat these tasks as controversial ; it must aim at finding ways of tackling them.[4]

Meanwhile Gosplan revised its own proposals. On October 14–16, 1927, a meeting of the presidium of Gosplan, attended by representatives of the main commissariats, heard reports on the third Gosplan draft from Strumilin, Kalinnikov and others. Strumilin explained that the new Gosplan proposals, which like the third Vesenkha draft covered the years from 1927–1928 to 1931–1932, were based on the second Gosplan draft, but assumed

---

[1] For Shein see pp. 583, 585 above ; Khrennikov was prominent in Vesenkha ; Charnovsky was a professor in the iron and steel institute and head of the scientific and technical council for the metal industries. Shein was accused of being a wrecker and disappeared in 1930 ; Charnovsky was one of the accused in the " industrial party " trial ; Khrennikov died while under arrest (*Le Procès des Industriels de Moscou* (1931), p. 4).

[2] See reports of discussions with the oil, coal, cotton textiles, electricity, brick and engineering industries in *Torgovo-Promyshlennaya Gazeta*, September 20, 21, 24, 27, 28, 29, 1927. The cuts were not put through without resistance : the coal industry claimed that no substantial change in its production or investment plan was possible, and its report was accepted by the sub-group concerned.

[3] *Ibid.* October 2, 1927.   [4] *Ibid.* October 13, 1927.

higher rates of growth of industrial production. The proposals
were submitted in both a " basic " and an " optimum " variant,
corresponding to the " minimum " and " maximum " variants
proposed earlier in the year ; the basic variant planned an increase
in industrial production by 63 per cent over the five years, the
optimum variant by 79 per cent, while agricultural production
would increase by 24 or 31 per cent.[1] The presidium also heard a
preliminary report from Mezhlauk on the third Vesenkha draft.
Vesenkha had evidently decided that the economies proposed by
the various groups of its commission on the five-year plan should
be used to bring about substantial increases in production plans.
Production costs were now planned to fall by as much as 24 per
cent, and industrial production in 1931–1932 was planned to reach
203 per cent of the 1926–1927 level ; these were substantially
higher figures than those in the second Vesenkha draft or in the
current proposals of Gosplan.[2] The presidium of Gosplan does
not appear to have made a choice between the two sets of proposals
at this stage.

　　Simultaneously with the meeting of the presidium of Gosplan,
the anniversary session of TsIK met from October 15 to 20, 1927.
Kuibyshev, in his report to the session delivered on October 18,
affirmed that the Soviet economy was entering " a new phase of
development which has no precedent in our history or in the history
of other countries, . . . a period of the re-shaping and reconstruction of our whole social order on a new technical basis with new
social and economic relations ".[3] He admitted, however, that work
on the five-year plan was still at a preliminary stage, and that
several sets of proposals existed. According to Kuibyshev, the
basic variant of Gosplan assumed an insufficient improvement of
the state machinery, while its optimum variant took account of
the achievements possible through effort and economy ; a third
variant was also needed in case the war danger turned into an

　　[1] *Torgovo-Promyshlennaya Gazeta*, October 25, 1927 ; for the annual
figures for industry in the optimum variant see Table No. 49, p. 981 below.
The third Gosplan draft of October 1927 was eventually published as a pamphlet : *Perspektivnaya Orientirovka na 1927/28–1931/32 gg.* (1928).
　　[2] *Torgovo-Promyshlennaya Gazeta*, October 29, 1927 ; see Tables No. 51
and 49, pp. 983 and 981 below.
　　[3] *2 Sessiya Tsentral'nogo Ispolnitel'nogo Komiteta Soyuza SSR 4 Sozyva*
(n.d. [1927]), pp. 249-250.

actual attack.[1] He also presented a list of what he described as
" optimum " figures, which were in fact higher than those of
the optimum variant of Gosplan and were virtually identical with
those presented by Mezhlauk to the presidium of Gosplan at its
recent meeting. Kuibyshev strongly argued that the optimum
variant should be accepted as the national goal.[2] An editorial in
the industrial newspaper, stressing that the objective should be
to attain " *the maximum possible limit in economic expansion* ",
commented :

> Comrade Kuibyshev acted completely correctly when he
> emphasized in his report, and cited in a large number of cases,
> the *maximum* figures of the perspective proposals.[3]

This was a significant moment in the history of Soviet planning.
Vesenkha was now openly prepared to go much further and faster
in its proposals for the five-year plan than the earlier Gosplan and
Vesenkha drafts ; and its new proposals far outstripped those
current in Gosplan. Moreover, Kuibyshev, a member of the
Politburo as well as president of Vesenkha, felt strong enough to
advocate the new pace of development in a major report to this
much-publicized session of TsIK. The new proposals were,
however, neither accepted nor rejected by the party and the
government as a whole. The session of TsIK took the preparation
of the plan a stage further by resolving that the five-year plan was
to be presented to the next congress of Soviets, but was vague
about the content of the plan itself :

> The five-year economic plan which is being worked out at
> present must be constructed in conformity with the funda-
> mental objective of strengthening the socialist nucleus of our
> economy, based on the industrialization of the country and on a
> rate of economic development which will allow us in the shortest
> possible time to catch up and overtake the capitalist countries.
> Industrialization is the hub of all our economic policy.[4]

[1] *Ibid.* pp. 250-252 ; according to another source, an independent variant
for the contingency of an armed attack was actually in preparation (*Promyshlennost' za 10 Let (1917–1927)*, ed. V. Kuibyshev (1927), p. 90).
   [2] *2 Sessiya Tsentral'nogo Ispolnitel'nogo Komiteta Soyuza SSR 4 Sozyva*
(n.d. [1927]), pp. 253-258, 265.
   [3] *Torgovo-Promyshlennaya Gazeta*, October 19, 1927.
   [4] *2 Sessiya Tsentral'nogo Ispolnitel'nogo Komiteta Soyuza SSR 4 Sozyva:
Postanovleniya* (n.d. [1927]), p. 19.

When the party central committee met on October 21, 1927, the day after the session of TsIK ended, Rykov submitted the theses on the five-year plan agreed by the Politburo for presentation to the forthcoming party congress.[1] According to Bukharin, the Politburo had already decided that, since war and foreign intervention were very probable during the five-year period and future harvests were uncertain, a five-year plan could not be presented to the fifteenth party congress ; the congress would be supplied with new material, but not required to commit itself to specific figures.[2] No figures were included in the theses, which were described as " directives for compiling " the five-year plan ; and no attempt was made to choose between the new Vesenkha draft and the basic or optimum variants of Gosplan. The three major objectives of the five-year plan were uncontroversially listed as increased consumption, increased investment, and a rapid development of the whole economy, especially its socialist sector. The theses, in line with the procedure laid down by TsIK, instructed the party central committee to arrange that the five-year plan should be ready for the next congress of Soviets, and that there should be " a detailed and comprehensive discussion of the draft of the plan by all local Soviet, trade union, party and other organizations ". But on every specific point the terms were wide enough to cover a variety of solutions, and confirmed the impression of caution and hesitation still prevailing in economic policy.[3] At the session, this vagueness was bitterly criticized by the opposition. Smilga complained that the theses were not available until two or three hours before the central committee assembled, and that he had been prevented from obtaining official figures, and asserted that the platform of the opposition " formulates the problems far better, more clearly and more correctly " :

We are to discuss a five-year plan which contains not a single figure, but only comments on various subjects, strung together, badly inter-connected, and providing no perspective for five years or one year ahead, or for the present quarter.

[1] For the theses, and for the general atmosphere of the session, see pp. 34-35 above.
[2] *Partiya i Oppozitsiya Nakanune XV S"ezda VKP(B)*, ii (1928), 85-87.
[3] *KPSS v Rezolyutsiyakh*, ii (1954), 395-413 ; for the ambiguous handling of the problem of consumer goods in the theses see pp. 303-305 above.

His main theme was that the current economic situation was serious and dangerous, and was being ignored by the central committee :

> A discussion of the economic situation will offer the party more than to discuss a five-year plan compiled without a single figure.

Other opposition speakers were constantly interrupted.[1] On October 23, 1927, the theses, with only minor amendments, were approved by the central committee for submission to the congress. A week later, on November 1, 1927, the Mezhlauk proposals for the third Vesenkha draft, which became known as the " control figures " of Vesenkha, were approved by the presidium of Vesenkha as a basis for the five-year plan of industry, and the planning department of Vesenkha was instructed to prepare the plan within six months.[2] Thus challenged, Gosplan now moved some distance towards the Vesenkha proposals. At a Gosplan conference which met on November 11, 1927, to discuss the republican drafts of the plan, Strumilin reported that the adjustment of the third Gosplan draft to allow for a rise in the number of shifts worked would make possible a growth in the production of state census industry of 87 per cent ; this compared with the figure of 79 per cent in the optimum variant of a few weeks previously.[3]

The counter-theses of the opposition on the five-year plan, addressed to the fifteenth party congress, and published in *Pravda* on November 17, 1927, were a reply to the theses approved by the October session of the party central committee, and repeated the criticisms of the five-year plan and the proposals for financing industry which had been made in the September platform.[4] The party majority denounced the proposal to obtain the requisite

---

[1] For these proceedings see p. 35 above.

[2] *Torgovo-Promyshlennaya Gazeta*, November 2, 1927. The Mezhlauk draft later appeared as a pamphlet *Kontrol'nye Tsifry Pyatiletnego Plana Promyshlennosti (1927/8–1931/2)* (1927) ; it admitted (p. 120) that the allocation from the budget required by industry in 1928–1929 " evokes some doubts as to its realism ".

[3] *Informatsionnyi Byulleten' Gosplana SSSR*, No. 11-12, 1927, pp. 4, 6.

[4] See p. 36 above. The opposition now suggested that the net budgetary allocation to industry should be raised over the five years from 500 to 1000 million rubles a year ; in the third Vesenkha draft of the plan the net budgetary allocation to industry was to amount to only 290 million rubles in the final year 1931–1932 (*Torgovo-Promyshlennaya Gazeta*, November 4, 1927).

resources by taxing private entrepreneurs as demagogic and unrealistic. But the majority were themselves equally unrealistic
about the possibility of financing industrial development without
some sacrifice in the standard of living of the peasant or the urban
worker ; Mezhlauk strongly defended the feasibility of the proposal to finance the major part of capital investment from the
profits and other financial resources of industry rather than from
the budget, and claimed that " the rôle of the state budget is not
the main one in redistributing the national income ".[1] Strumilin
pointed out to the critics that the rate of increase in industrial
production actually achieved had already exceeded that envisaged
by Pyatakov in the Osvok plan or by Smilga in 1926 ; the latest
Gosplan proposals for the five-year plan proposed a rate of expansion even higher than that laid down in the Goelro plan.[2]

The cardinal importance of the plan was now accepted by all ;
the fifteenth party congress, which met from December 2 to 19,
1927, devoted to it seven of its 29 sittings. The Gosplan variants
and the more ambitious Vesenkha proposals were all distributed to
the delegates for information. The joint *rapporteurs*, Rykov and
Krzhizhanovsky, both explained that the plan was not yet nearly
ready. Rykov pointed out that seven drafts of the plan had
already been prepared ; the latest Gosplan draft had not yet been
discussed, as it had been prepared only just before the congress.[3]
He argued that all these drafts suffered from two main weaknesses.
First, they suffered from what he termed " a statistical deviation
in planning " ; the figures lacked sufficient economic foundation,
and did not take account of the technical requirements of production. Secondly, all the drafts lacked an adequate regional break-
down. Work on the plan had " not yet gone further than half-
way ".[4] Krzhizhanovsky enumerated three tasks of the five-year
plan : to speed up industrialization, to press on with the socialization not only of production but also of distribution, and " to
guarantee our military strength, the defence of our country ". He
introduced the basic and optimum variants of Gosplan, but

[1] For Mezhlauk's article see p. 750 above.

[2] *Pravda*, November 30, 1927.

[3] *Pyatnadtsatyi S"ezd VKP(B)*, ii (1962), 864 ; this draft was presumably
the revised version of the third draft which was discussed by the Gosplan
conference on November 11, 1927 (see p. 871 above).

[4] *Pyatnadtsatyi S"ezd VKP(B)*, ii (1962), 864-865.

eventually declared his preference for the Vesenkha draft :

At my request the control figures of the Vesenkha five-year plan have also been distributed to you. Without any departmental pride, we consider that what is proposed in the Vesenkha five-year plan is acceptable to Gosplan as the most favourable variant.[1]

In the debate which followed, one or two speakers hinted that the proposed pace of development was too fast : thus Lomov expressed doubts about the investment plan for the coal trust Donugol, of which he was president, and added :

I fear that for other industries also we have adopted a scale which would prove beyond our strength ; and before starting on this, it is necessary to reconsider, precisely from this angle, the whole five-year plan.[2]

Sokolnikov, now precariously returned to the ranks of the majority, suggested that provisional but firm two- or three-year investment programmes should be prepared for the main sectors of the economy, and reminded the congress that a limit was placed on growth by the availability of food and raw materials. The population must be protected from the most primitive effects of hunger and insufficient food ; the growth of industry and the growth of agriculture were intimately connected :

If we constructed our plan without being able to secure this obligatory and correct connexion, we should get a fanciful plan, which might give a very high growth coefficient, but would also show a very high percentage of failures and defeats.[3]

But in a party audience these were isolated voices. Kuibyshev, with some support from Rykov, firmly defended the policy of priority for producer goods.[4]   Strong support was given to planning and to heavy industry by Voroshilov, People's Commissar for War and a member of the Politburo, who emphasized the importance of the five-year plan for the strengthening of Soviet defence capacity.[5]   From the controversies of 1927, in which Vesenkha and Gosplan had been in a single camp against Narkomfin and Narkomzem, Vesenkha had emerged as the author of a five-year plan considerably more ambitious than any of the Gosplan drafts.

---

[1] *Ibid.* ii, 887, 892, 895, 909.
[2] *Ibid.* ii, 1059-1060.   [3] *Ibid.* ii, 1128-1129.
[4] See pp. 303-304 above.   [5] See pp. 426-427, 429-430 above.

2 F 2

The impression that the voice of Vesenkha was more influential than that of Gosplan was reinforced by a number of sharp criticisms of Gosplan and of Krzhizhanovsky from strong supporters of industrialization. Petrovsky blamed Gosplan for dreaming of electrification while the peasant could not even be supplied with cheap kerosene, and declared that " fantasy and poesy " should be replaced by a practical approach ; [1] Sukhomlin thought that Krzhizhanovsky's report " distracted us by posing a number of big problems which do not come into the five-year plan ".[2] For the time being, the congress was asked to endorse nothing more definite than the directives for the plan approved by the central committee in October ; it did not commit itself to any specific figures or to any of the available drafts or variants.[3]

(e) The Plan Takes Shape (January 1928–February 1929)

The discussions at the fifteenth party congress in December 1927 focused attention on the five-year plan ; shortly afterwards Sovnarkom set out in a detailed decree the stages by which the plan should be drawn up. The decree instructed Gosplan to issue " the most important targets " to republics and commissariats by February 20, 1928, and then to hold two Union conferences, one in March and one by the beginning of August 1928 ; the second of these was to issue directives for compiling the final plan, the draft of which, incorporating sectional drafts, was to be submitted to Sovnarkom and STO by February 1, 1929. In view of the work which this would involve, the Gosplan programme of work on the control figures for 1928–1929 was to be substantially reduced, and the procedure in Vesenkha for compiling the annual promfinplans was also to be simplified as much as possible.[4] The responsibilities which devolved on Gosplan were described by one of its officials as being " to compile the perspective plan and to direct all the organs preparing constituent parts of this plan ".[5] In order to accomplish this task, Gosplan strengthened its central commission for perspective planning by appointing Grinko as its

---

[1] Pyatnadtsatyi S"ezd VKP(B), ii (1962), 1018-1019.
[2] Ibid. ii, 1108-1109.
[3] KPSS v Rezolyutsiyakh (1954), ii, 450-469.
[4] Informatsionnyi Byulleten' Gosplana SSSR, No. 1-2, 1928, pp. 1-2.
[5] Ibid. No. 3-4, 1928, p. 4.

president, by placing the commission on the *genplan* under its authority, and by transferring to it many of the staff concerned with annual and general planning.[1]   Meanwhile the planning department of Vesenkha met towards the end of December 1927 to make arrangements for the preparation of a new draft to meet the requirements laid down at the fifteenth party congress.[2]

The rift with the non-party experts which led to the ejection of Kondratiev and his followers from the *Konjunktur* institute of Narkomfin early in 1928 [3] also had its repercussions in Gosplan. During a discussion about the five-year plan at the Communist Academy in January 1928, Strumilin, in a strong attack on his critics, coupled Groman and Bazarov with Kondratiev, and declared even more bluntly than before that attempts to balance capital expenditure with capital accumulation and demand with supply were " merely adjuncts " to " the fundamental objective of the five-year plan, the plan of capital construction ".[4]   Krzhizhanovsky tried later in the discussion to perform his traditional function of building a bridge between party and non-party experts. He referred to Lenin's strategy of putting everyone in his appropriate place and getting the best out of him, and spoke optimistically of the future movement of the intelligentsia to the side of Soviet power.   On Groman Krzhizhanovsky commented that, while his " impressionability exceeds his Marxist training ", he was one of the longest-established planning officials and " was not on the other side of the barricades " ; when Groman had criticized Krzhizhanovsky in 1921 as both " opponent and ally ", Krzhizhanovsky had recruited him to the staff.[5]   Bazarov, speaking at a session held three weeks after Strumilin's original speech, declared that " in the past three weeks we have managed to find a common Gosplan platform for re-examining the five-year plan " ; individual opinions, including his own, had been taken into account.[6]   But this was wishful thinking.   The time for reconciliation

[1] *Ibid.* No. 1-2, 1928, pp. 1-2 ; *Kontrol'nye Tsifry Narodnogo Khozyaistva SSSR na 1928–1929 god* (1929), p. 7 ; for Grinko see pp. 278-279, 321 above.

[2] *Torgovo-Promyshlennaya Gazeta*, December 24-25, 1927.

[3] See pp. 735-736 above.

[4] *O Pyatiletnem Plane Razvitiya Narodnogo Khozyaistva SSSR : Diskussiya v Kommunisticheskoi Akademii* (1928), pp. 29, 34-38 ; for Strumilin's criticisms of Bazarov see p. 789 above.

[5] *O Pyatiletnem Plane Razvitiya Narodnogo Khozyaistva SSSR : Diskussiya v Kommunisticheskoi Akademii* (1928), pp. 67-70.   [6] *Ibid.* p. 73.

was now past ; and the influence of the non-party economists was rapidly declining.

Meanwhile other voices were heard demanding more ambitious plans of industrialization. In an article in a Vesenkha journal early in 1928, Kuibyshev drew attention to the fact that the rate of growth of industrial production in the revised proposals for 1927–1928 was higher than the actual rate of growth in 1926–1927, and hailed this as " a break-through in the attenuating curve followed by the annual rate of growth since 1924–1925 ".[1] The successes in industrial production during 1927–1928, resulting in a growth of 26·3 per cent in Vesenkha-planned industry, exceeded previous records and expectations,[2] and undoubtedly played an important part in convincing the more enthusiastic supporters of industrialization that an annual growth-rate of 20 per cent, and a rising curve of growth, could become normal in Soviet conditions. The temptation was strong to believe that the difficulties with the peasantry which accompanied this growth could be surmounted by better management and without any relaxation of the pace of industrialization proposed in the plans. In the discussion on the five-year plan at the Communist Academy in January 1928, the economist Motylev, heralding an optimism which became more widespread in party circles later in the year, claimed that, in view of the level of capital investment in industry proposed for the first three years in both Vesenkha and Gosplan drafts, the attenuating curve of the rate of growth of industrial production in the later years of the plan could be replaced by a rising curve.[3] In his reply, Strumilin reviewed the history of the curve of the planned rate of growth of industrial production : the original *genplan* had proposed an attenuating curve in the whole of the first five years followed by a rising curve in the second five years ; Bazarov's counter-proposal that the curve should rise in the first five-year plan and attenuate in the second had been rejected. Gosplan now proposed that growth-rates would increase at first, while some remnants of the restoration period were still making themselves felt, and then slow down while new investment was being made ;

[1] *Puti Industrializatsii*, No. 1, 1928, pp. 12–13 ; another writer also used the word " break-through " (perelom) in this connexion (*ibid.* No. 2, 1928, p. 83).   [2] See p. 311 above, and Table No. 13, p. 947 below.

[3] *O Pyatiletnem Plane Razvitiya Narodnogo Khozyaistva SSSR : Diskussiya v Kommunisticheskoi Akademii* (1928), p. 57.

the rising curve would come into operation only during the second five-year plan or at the very end of the first.[1] Motylev continued his campaign against the attenuating curve in a controversy with Strumilin in the party journal.[2] He was joined by Sabsovich, who put forward early in 1928 an outline five-year plan in which the rate of growth of industrial production remained constant, at the high figure of 21 per cent a year, throughout the five years.[3]

Gosplan failed to carry out the Sovnarkom instruction to issue the most important targets of the plan by February 20, 1928.[4] But the third Gosplan congress met from March 6 to 14, 1928, only a few days behind schedule,[5] and devoted its main attention to preparations for the compilation of the plan. The congress resolution declared that central decisions on such major questions as rates of growth, price movements, wages and tax policy, were required to provide the framework for the five-year plan, and that the central rather than the republican or regional authorities should be responsible for planning to achieve equilibrium in the national economy and the proper proportions between economic sectors ; it also stressed, however, the importance of including in the central plan the " integrated plans for the development of Union republics and economic regions and of different sectors of the economy ". The congress resolved that Gosplan should issue the preliminary directives on the main contours of the plan by May 1, 1928.[6] This was the moment — if there was a moment — at which Gosplan could have taken control of the planning process. But a powerful

---

[1] *Ibid.* pp. 110-111.

[2] The main articles in this discussion were reprinted in V. Motylev, *Problema Tempa Razvitiya SSSR* (1929), which reproduces Motylev's side of the controversy, and in S. Strumilin, *Na Planovom Fronte* (1958), pp. 407-421, which sets out Strumilin's replies.

[3] *Puti Industrializatsii*, No. 2, 1928, pp. 48-50 ; No. 4, 1928, p. 61.

[4] See p. 874 above.

[5] The third Gosplan congress was described variously as a " Union planning congress " and as a " Union conference of planning workers " ; the first and second congresses, held in March 1926 and March–April 1927 (see pp. 852-854, 855-858 above), had been congresses of presidiums of Gosplans.

[6] *Ekonomicheskaya Zhizn'*, March 17, 1928 ; *Pravda*, March 6, 8, 16, 18, 1928 ; *Informatsionnyi Byulleten' Gosplana SSSR*, No. 3-4, 1928, pp. 4-5, 7. A Gosplan commentator pointed out that decisions about the major capital projects such as the Volga-Don canal and the Ural-Kuznetsk project could not be made " by individual commissariats, republics or areas independently ", even for the purpose of compiling the " preliminary control figures " of the five-year plan.

and independent machine for perspective planning was already working in Vesenkha, with the strong backing of Kuibyshev; Krzhizhanovsky complained rather wryly at the congress that " Vesenkha should become a People's Commissariat of Industry and not duplicate the work of Gosplan ".[1] The three new drafts prepared by Vesenkha in April, August and December 1928, rather than the Gosplan drafts, were the principal influence in forming official opinion.

In April 1928 Vesenkha issued a set of " directives on compiling the perspective plan " which proposed that industrial production should increase by 140 per cent by 1931–1932, Group A industries expanding by 150 per cent and Group B industries by 133 per cent: after 1928–1929, the rate of growth would not attenuate, but would remain more or less constant over the last three years of the plan.[2] To achieve the planned rate of industrial growth, the volume of industrial investment planned for each of the five years was increased as compared with the third Vesenkha draft.[3] The directives also gave a supplementary set of figures for the year 1932–1933 — the final year of the five-year plan as eventually adopted. The increases in targets were opposed by the ex-Menshevik and non-party experts in Vesenkha; when the April directives were discussed at an enlarged meeting of the planning department of Vesenkha on April 21, 1928, Shtern, Sokolovsky and Ginzburg[4] all complained that " insufficient economic justification " had been provided, and that the evidence produced did not permit the proposals to be analysed. But the enthusiastic industrializers in Vesenkha were more determined, more vigorously led and more numerous than their opposite numbers in Gosplan; the meeting resolved to accept " in principle " the main indicators of the directives.[5] The Vesenkha directives were discussed by the presidium of Gosplan on May 7, 1928, at a meeting which significantly had before it only a report from Vesenkha, with no report from Gosplan itself. On May 12, Gosplan issued its directives for the national economy as a whole. These did not attempt any independent assessment of the pros-

[1] *Informatsionnyi Byulleten' Gosplana SSSR*, No. 3-4, 1928, p. 29.
[2] See Table No. 49, p. 981 below.   [3] See Table No. 50, p. 982 below.
[4] For Shtern, Sokolovsky and Ginzburg see pp. 279, 339 and 296 above.
[5] *Torgovo-Promyshlennaya Gazeta*, April 24, 26, 1928.

pects for industry, but merely repeated the proposal for industrial production in the April directives of Vesenkha, pointing out that this would involve " a considerably greater rate of growth than the optimum variant of the five-year plan ". Gosplan instructed Union commissariats and republican planning organs to examine the possibility of such an industrial development " on the basis of the desirability and necessity of the maximum forced rate of development of industry ".[1]

The initiative remained in the hands of Vesenkha. In August 1928 Mezhlauk presented to a " permanent planning conference " which had been established under the presidium of Vesenkha, and to the presidium of Vesenkha itself, the next draft of the plan, which became known as the " August version ".[2] This version appears to have been a curious compromise between moderate and expansionist wings within Vesenkha. It provided for a further increase in investment in industry ;[3] but the increase of industrial production planned for the five years 1928–1929 to 1932–1933 was somewhat smaller than in the April directives, and the annual rate of growth was to follow an attenuating curve.[4] The August version was thus less optimistic than the April directives about the potential effectiveness of investment in industry. It was also somewhat less optimistic in its estimate of the reduction in industrial costs ;[5] since no additional industrial profits would therefore be available to meet the planned increase in investment in industry, the August version called for increased budgetary allocations to industry. These assumptions were realistic : while industrial costs had been falling since the spring of 1927, the planned rate of reduction had not been achieved, and the planning department of Vesenkha had already demanded a higher budgetary allocation for 1928–1929, the first year of the plan, than had been proposed in any previous draft.[6] But a version of the plan which proposed to increase investment in industry, and the claims of industry on the budget, without any compensating increase in productivity did not in any case commend itself to the authorities. Kuibyshev, in his

---

[1] *Informatsionnyi Byulleten' Gosplana SSSR*, No. 5, 1928, pp. 1-22 ; an article by Grinko based on his report to the presidium of Gosplan on May 12, 1928, appeared in *Planovoe Khozyaistvo*, No. 5, 1928, pp. 7-23.
[2] *Torgovo-Promyshlennaya Gazeta*, August 15, 1928.
[3] See Table No. 50, p. 982 below.   [4] See Table No. 49, p. 981 below.
[5] See Table No. 51, p. 983 below.   [6] See pp. 313-314, 345 above.

speech at the presidium of Vesenkha, firmly stated that the proposed budgetary allocations to industry must be reduced.[1] A further disquieting feature of the August version, and one less easy to justify, was that the annual increase proposed both in capital investment and in budgetary allocations in the first three years of the plan were particularly high, so that the investment curve became " hump-backed ". This was a repetition of the much criticized attenuating curve of investment of the Osvok proposals,[2] but at a far higher level of investment. In presenting the proposals to the presidium of Vesenkha, Mezhlauk drew attention to the " abnormal " investment curve and proposed that it should be levelled out to avoid strain on the budget. But the hump could also be eliminated by raising its right-hand side. In the discussion, Kuibyshev stressed that the investment planned in some industries, notably in the chemical industry, was insufficient.[3] While the presidium ambiguously resolved that the hump-backed curve should be eliminated by making investment increase regularly each year, the industrial newspaper concluded editorially that the curve must be corrected " not by a sharp cut in capital expenditure in the first years " of the plan, but principally by increasing the estimates for the later years.[4] During the next few weeks the Vesenkha planners revised the figures of the August version, and by the beginning of October new proposals combined a constant annual volume of investment, thus eliminating the attenuating curve of the last two years, with an increased investment total for the whole period.[5]

Though most of the non-party experts in Vesenkha and Gosplan still retained their posts, the fate of the August version indicated that effective resistance in Vesenkha to the pressure for increases in the five-year plan had ceased. The influence of the non-party experts was also distinctly weaker in Gosplan by September 1928.[6] The optimum variant in preparation in Gosplan at that time included a proposed increase in industrial production

[1] *Torgovo-Promyshlennaya Gazeta*, August 15, 1928.
[2] See p. 849 above.
[3] *Torgovo-Promyshlennaya Gazeta*, August 15, 1928.
[4] *Ibid.* August 17, 18, 1928.   [5] *Ibid.* October 7, 1928.
[6] The last of the periodical reviews of the economic situation which Groman regularly wrote for *Statisticheskoe Obozrenie*, the journal of the Central Statistical Administration, appeared in the number for August 1928.

even higher than Vesenkha had suggested in its August version.[1]
In the party itself, however, organized criticism from the Right
was becoming more vocal. At the meeting of the party central
committee in July 1928, many voices were raised against the
existing rate of industrialization ; [2] and in Bukharin's *Notes of an
Economist* at the end of September 1928 the August version of
Vesenkha was cited as a clear example of unwise and over-
ambitious planning. Bukharin's criticisms of the weaknesses in
the draft plan were made from a point of view opposite to that
prevalent in the leadership of Vesenkha. He argued that the
demands of the draft plan on the budget should be reduced by
rejecting its attempt to produce " a mad pressure on the rate in
the initial years, with a later inevitable decline ".[3] The struggle
against the Right, however, gave fresh encouragement to the advocates of more extreme policies of industrialization. Sabsovich,
who had by this time revised his own outline plan in order to provide for a rising annual rate of growth of industrial production
throughout the five years,[4] strongly criticized the August version
and the current Gosplan proposals in a series of articles and
speeches. He claimed that planners in Vesenkha had depended
too much on proposals collected from the *glavki*, and had accepted
" *a harmful and reactionary approach* " to rates of increase of
labour productivity. Costs must be reduced by as much as 32·3
per cent, and the rate of growth of production must increase
annually. All this would permit higher investments in each year
than the August version had proposed.[5]

The November session of the party central committee resulted
in a substantial defeat for the Right ; and in Vesenkha bolder
policies immediately became acceptable. During November and
early December 1928 what became known as the " December
variant " was prepared very intensively in the planning offices of
Vesenkha. The new draft met nearly all the prescriptions of the

[1] *Pravda*, September 2, 1928 ; a financial five-year plan prepared at this
time by Narkomfin included much higher planned capital investment in
industry than Narkomfin had previously regarded as feasible (*Informatsionnyi
Byulleten' Gosplana SSSR*, No. 8-9, 1928, pp. 30-36 ; *Torgovo-Promyshlennaya
Gazeta*, September 21, 1928).   [2] See pp. 76-78, 314-315 above.
[3] *Pravda*, September 30, 1928 ; for this article see also pp. 89-90, 317-319,
797 above.   [4] *Puti Industrializatsii*, No. 6, 1928, pp. 51-52.
[5] *Torgovo-Promyshlennaya Gazeta*, July 31, August 15, 19, 1928 ; *Pravda*,
September 2, 1928.

optimists. It increased the proposed capital investment in industry still further ; annual investment followed a rising curve throughout the five years, and the annual rate of growth of industrial production did not attenuate, but remained more or less constant ; over the five years industrial production was to increase by 168 per cent, with the production of Group A industries increasing by as much as 200 per cent.[1] In presenting preliminary proposals to a Vesenkha meeting on December 2, Zolotarev made it clear that in compiling the draft the method of " widening the bottleneck " had been used.[2] He explained that, when the production plans of the *glavki* had been put together in August 1928, supply had proved less than demand for a number of major products ; the December draft handled this deficiency by increasing production plans. To make such automatic increases was better than " to present a five-year plan defective in the sense that the most important needs of the national economy will not be satisfied." Critics from the Right in Vesenkha seem to have been silent. While Sabsovich pressed at the Vesenkha meeting for still higher targets, Kuibyshev felt that things had for the moment gone far enough ; he admitted in effect that some account had now to be taken of bottlenecks :

> It is technically impossible to increase further the work of existing factories, and it is also impossible to build still more new factories. In consequence, *it is necessary to cut back the requirements of other sectors of the economy in conformity with the state of ferrous metals* : . . . The financial position is hardly brilliant enough to permit further expansion.[3]

But the draft five-year plan on which Kuibyshev was prepared to take his stand marked an enormous increase in the proposed rate of industrialization as compared with the drafts of the previous year. During the course of 1928, the investment and production plans of industry had been rapidly increased in the successive drafts prepared in Vesenkha : investment in industry in 1930–1931, for example, was planned at 1500 million rubles in the Vesenkha draft of November 1927 ; at the end of 1928 the December variant proposed 2940 million rubles.[4] But official

[1] See Tables No. 49, 50, 51, pp. 981, 982, 983 below.
[2] *Torgovo-Promyshlennaya Gazeta*, December 4, 1928 ; for Zolotarev see p. 321 above ; for " widening the bottleneck " see pp. 798-799 above.
[3] *Torgovo-Promyshlennaya Gazeta*, December 4, 1928.
[4] See Table No. 50, p. 982 below.

policy continued to assert that industrialization would take place within the framework of the market and of the link with the peasantry ; increases in industrial investment, and the planned decline in the prices of industrial consumer goods, would be covered by huge reductions in industrial costs.[1] These were optimistic assumptions rather than realistic plans.

Details of the draft to be presented to the government were published in the industrial newspaper on December 15, 1928,[2] and on December 20 Kuibyshev delivered a report on the proposals to the eighth trade union congress, which had opened some days previously. The document circulated to congress delegates cautiously retained the conventional criticism of " super-industrialist " plans, and laid great stress on the importance of rapid increases in the production of tractors, agricultural implements and fertilizers.[3] Kuibyshev, in his report to the congress, was also circumspect. He made it clear that he was presenting a proposal for one important section of the plan, which had not yet been discussed in Gosplan, and conceded that " in Gosplan, our plan will have to undergo certain changes, so as to bring it into line with the requirements of the national economy " ; the final plan would not be ready till February or March 1929 for presentation to the congress of Soviets in April. But he obviously did not regard the main lines of the December draft as a matter for dispute. He made a strong attack on the " ' learned ' pessimism " of " professors of economics " in Narkomfin, and roundly rejected the hesitations within Vesenkha which had coloured the August version ; this had been " compiled without taking into account the resources existing in our economy and in industry as a whole ". The new draft did not meet with any coherent criticism at the trade union congress. Some uneasiness was expressed about the possibility of achieving the proposed level of wages and conditions of labour ; but speakers in the discussion proposed to increase

[1] See Table No. 51, p. 983 below.

[2] *Torgovo-Promyshlennaya Gazeta*, December 15, 1928. The draft was completed, unlike most of the earlier drafts, by the stipulated date, and part of it was even ready by December 8 ; in order to achieve this result, the office staff had to be paid overtime (*Protokol Zasedaniya Prezidiuma VSNKh SSSR, 1928–1929*, No. 7, Prilozhenie, art. 237).

[3] *Materialy k Dokladu V. V. Kuibysheva o Pyatiletnem Plane Razvitiya Promyshlennosti* (1928), pp. 5-6.

rather than reduce the targets for industry. On behalf of the
central council of trade unions, L. I. Ginzburg claimed that investment could be used more efficiently than Vesenkha proposed, and
that, with the same amount of capital investment in industry, production could treble during the five years.[1]

During 1927 and 1928, simultaneously with the increases in
the investment plans for industry in successive drafts of the five-
year plan, the investment plans of other sectors of the economy had
also been increased. By the end of October 1928, even before the
December draft of Vesenkha had been prepared, Gosplan estimated in its calculations for the economy as a whole that state
investment in agriculture and transport over five years would be
twice as large as had been proposed in the second Gosplan draft
of the spring of 1927.[2] The further increase in investment and
production in industry proposed in the December draft of Vesenkha seemed to Gosplan to put far too great a strain on the resources
which would be available. When the presidium of Gosplan discussed the Vesenkha draft on December 29, 1928, a number of
Gosplan officials drew attention to the " extraordinarily high and
strained rates of development proposed "; and every speaker
except Vaisberg criticized it, non-party experts and Strumilin
being for once united. Kalinnikov pointed out that Vesenkha now
proposed an investment in industry in the five-year period of
13,400 million rubles against the Gosplan figure of 10,900 millions,
and an increase, when measured in real terms, of over fifty per cent
in the single year 1929–1930. He commented :

[1] *Vos'moi S"ezd Professional'nykh Soyuzov* (1929), pp. 372-375, 410-411,
446-448 ; for Ginzburg see p. 525 above.
[2] The following totals of state capital investment in the three main sectors
were proposed by Gosplan (in million rubles at current prices) :

	Second Draft (1926–1927 to 1930–1931)	Autumn 1928 (1928–1929 to 1932–1933)
Industry	5,700	10,000–12,000
Agriculture	1,200	2,500– 3,500
Transport	5,000	8,000–10,000
Total	11,800	20,500–25,500

(*Perspektivy Razvertyvaniya Narodnogo Khozyaistva SSSR na 1926/27–1930/31
gg.* (1927), p. 32 ; *Pravda*, October 30, 1928.)

It may be seriously doubted whether Vesenkha will be able to undertake as early as next year an increase of more than 50 per cent in capital construction. It is a question not only of the shortage of building materials, but also of the capital equipment required.

Strumilin expressed doubt about the feasibility of the proposed jump in capital investment in 1929–1930, and pointed out that a lower rate of investment in industry would inevitably lengthen the five-year plan and turn it into a six- or even seven-year plan. In reply to these attacks, Zolotarev presented the Vesenkha proposals as being merely the larger of two variants of which the Gosplan draft was the smaller. He was concerned at the same time to show the interdependence of all the proposals : if agriculture was to grow by 30-35 per cent as planned, tractor production must increase drastically, and this implied increased production of iron and steel. He added that the proposals were so constructed as not to make " extensive requirements " of the state budget.[1]

Dissent in Gosplan was short-lived. On January 5, 1929, at a further meeting of the presidium of Gosplan, Grinko turned aside the criticisms made by his colleagues at the previous meeting by declaring that it was inappropriate to compare the Vesenkha proposals critically with those of Gosplan until the Vesenkha figures had been incorporated in an " optimum plan of the whole economy of the Soviet Union ", the basic elements of which were not yet known. The present task must simply be to " point out to Vesenkha controversial elements which should be further elaborated ". While Grinko made some criticisms of detail, he firmly declared that " the general framework of goals " in the Vesenkha draft was " completely correct " ; and most of the meeting as reported was taken up with speeches from Vesenkha officials, who seem to have turned up in strength, in favour of different aspects of their draft. Only Strumilin continued to strike a strongly critical note :

How far are these hypotheses of great rates of growth justified, and how are the separate parts of this optimum plan tied

[1] *Torgovo-Promyshlennaya Gazeta*, December 30, 1928. In September 1929, Kirov, apparently referring to this period, remarked in a speech to Leningrad textile workers : " When we had the draft of this five-year plan before us, it seemed to us, although we were responsible party leaders, that it was simply something unrealistic. I can tell you, it seemed to us that it went beyond the bounds of all possibilities " (*Istoricheskii Arkhiv*, No. 5, 1961, p. 109).

together ? . . . What sense is there in first making large jumps and then smoothly putting the brakes on one's movement ?

Kviring went further than Grinko in support of the Vesenkha draft ; he declared that those who had attacked it as exaggerated were " under the direct influence of the ' basic ' variant on which Gosplan continues to work ", and that the Vesenkha proposal to increase the amount of capital investment, particularly in Group A industries, should be supported.[1] The issue was for the moment unresolved ; the draft returned to Vesenkha and Gosplan for further work ; in February 1929, according to a statement by Kalinnikov, " the whole staff " of the industrial section of Gosplan still thought that the December draft of Vesenkha was unrealizable.[2] But effective resistance was no longer possible. In an article published at this time Strumilin conceded the presence of a " safety reserve (zapas prochnosti) " in the proposals of Gosplan, but added :

> Of course, I could easily have got rid of this reserve altogether by putting enough pressure on the specialists. Unfortunately it would hardly be rational to test the civil courage of those specialists who are already admitting in the corridors that they prefer to stand up (stoyat') for high rates of expansion rather than to sit in jail (sidet') for low ones.[3]

The general discussion of the five-year plan was accompanied by the preparation of more specific plans for every sector of the economy, every industry, and every region ; these plans were continuously revised to fit into successive drafts of the five-year plan of the national economy, and were extensively discussed both by the commissariat or region concerned and by Gosplan. During 1928, planning departments at every level became increasingly concerned with the relation between sectors and industries in physical as well as financial terms ; Vesenkha and Gosplan drew up material balances for each major group of products in an endeavour to bring the various sections of the plan into harmony.[4]

---

[1] *Torgovo-Promyshlennaya Gazeta*, January 6, 1929.
[2] Cited in *Le Procès des Industriels de Moscou* (1931), p. 647.
[3] *Planovoe Khozyaistvo*, No. 1, 1929, p. 109.
[4] For material balances see pp. 830-831 above.

The iron and steel industry, which had recovered much more slowly than other major industries,[1] provided the greatest difficulties, and may serve as an illustration of the general process. In the autumn of 1927, the Mezhlauk commission on the five-year plan increased the Glavmetall plan for the production of crude steel in 1931–1932 from 5·8 to 6·7 million tons ; but the increased figure, which was only 60 per cent greater than production in 1913, was hardly adequate to meet the level of production in industry as a whole, which was already planned to reach over twice the 1913 total by 1931–1932. With the further increases in the production plans of industry in the April draft of 1928, the planning department of Vesenkha proposed that the plan for crude steel production in 1932–1933 should be 8·5 million tons.[2] This proposal was strongly resisted by the leading specialists in Glavmetall on the grounds that it was physically and financially impossible to construct enough new capacity in the period.[3] After an acute shortage of pig-iron in the autumn of 1928 had threatened to hold back the development of industry, the presidium of Vesenkha ruled in favour of an even higher production target of 10 million tons of pig-iron by 1932–1933, which would enable approximately 10·5 million tons of crude steel to be produced in the same year.[4] Resistance continued from the experts in Gosplan ; but its presidium now accepted the higher figure.[5] According to Vesenkha calculations, even this level of production would be sufficient to meet the demands only of industry and transport ; less than half the demand from non-industrial building, the mass market and the artisan industries would be covered in the last year of the plan.[6] At a Gosplan conference on the five-year plan for the engineering

[1] See pp. 271-272, 435 above.

[2] *Torgovo-Promyshlennaya Gazeta*, April 20, 1928.

[3] *Ibid.* July 10, August 1, 4, 1928 ; *Materialy k Pyatiletnemu Planu Promyshlennosti VSNKh SSSR*, iii (1929), 769 ; the scientific and technical council of the industry less convincingly asserted that demand for steel would not be equal to the proposed supply.

[4] *Torgovo-Promyshlennaya Gazeta*, December 11, 1928 ; *Metall*, No. 1, 1929, pp. 37, 47-49.

[5] *Torgovo-Promyshlennaya Gazeta*, December 4, 30, 1928 ; January 6, 8, 9, 13, 1929.

[6] *Metall*, No. 1, 1929, pp. 37-46, 52-54 ; the authors of these calculations commented austerely that " the unproductive or secondary production requirements of our economy will again obtain their ' right to existence ' only when the new iron and steel giants begin production ".

industries held early in 1929, a speaker drew the lesson that in future the plans for engineering should not be cut to meet the possible supply of metal ; it was the problem of the metal industry to arrange the production of metal at a rate necessary for the development of engineering.[1] The proposed target of 10 million tons of pig-iron was incorporated in the optimum Gosplan variant of the plan.[2] This episode, repeated in different forms in every industry and every sector of the economy, made it clear that all the sectional plans were to be brought within the framework of rapid industrial growth established by the December draft of Vesenkha.

(f) The Adoption of the Plan (March–May 1929)

At the beginning of March 1929, the fifth Gosplan congress met to consider the five-year plan. The congress had before it a basic variant prepared in Gosplan and an optimum variant based on the December draft of Vesenkha, but now proposing an even more rapid rate of growth of industrial production, with the rate of growth increasing in each year.[3] Krzhizhanovsky reported at the outset a " *considerable coming together of the points of view of Gosplan and Vesenkha on a number of questions which were previously controversial* ".[4] The spokesmen of Vesenkha strongly argued that the optimum variant should become the basic one. Yurovsky made a half-hearted attempt to express the hesitations of Narkomfin, protesting that the plan provided for a rapid growth of both industry and agriculture, that requirements were concentrated on the first two years, and that the financial indicators did not reconcile the different parts of the plan ; the solution he proposed was not that rates of growth should be cut, but that " it is necessary to plan either less price reduction, or more cost reduction ". The congress marked a further stage in the relentless increase of the planned rate of industrialization : it resolved that " creative forces must be concentrated " on the optimum variant.[5]

---

[1] *Metall*, No. 3, 1929, pp. 31-32.
[2] Production of pig-iron was in fact 6·2 million tons in 1932 and 7·1 million tons in 1933 ; it reached 10 million tons in 1934 and 15 million tons in 1941 (*Promyshlennost' SSSR* (1964), p. 164).
[3] See Table No. 49, p. 981 below.
[4] *Torgovo-Promyshlennaya Gazeta*, March 8, 1929.
[5] *Ibid.* March 14, 15, 1929 ; *Pravda*, March 14, 15, 16, 1929.

The conclusion does not seem to have dissipated scepticism in Gosplan. Strumilin, writing at the end of March 1929, still treated the basic variant as the main plan.[1]

The issue now passed to Sovnarkom and STO, which discussed the five-year plan at a series of joint sittings at the end of March and beginning of April 1929. Mikoyan, Chubar, Yakovlev and Kuibyshev all defended the adoption of the optimum variant as the only one.[2] Rykov, still striving to avoid an open break, also declared that " *the optimum variant must be accepted in the decisive sectors of the economy* ", especially agriculture, though he added the rider that " for other less decisive sectors of the economy the fulfilment of the optimum variant must be recognized as less obligatory and much more dependent on the *Konjunktur* of each year ". But he also proposed that a two-year plan primarily concerned with agriculture should be introduced within the framework of the five-year plan. The main difficulty of the plan was " *in establishing correct relations between the development of different sectors of the economy* ". The " discrepancies " between different sectors in the first two or three years of the plan were the most serious, and had already produced the goods and food crisis. Rykov went on :

> Would it not be correct *to select from the five-year plan everything important that will ensure the elimination of this discrepancy, and compile a working plan for, say, the next two years to abolish the lack of correspondence of the development of agriculture and the requirements of the country,* and place the fulfilment of this part of the five-year plan in especially favourable conditions ?

He attributed current difficulties to the attenuating curve in agricultural production which had accompanied the rise in industrial production : " it is the relation between these two curves which has governed the economic difficulties of the past and present year, and may produce, if the directives of the government are not completely fulfilled, certain difficulties next year too ". But Rykov's suggestions were not taken up ; and Krzhizhanovsky in his reply to the discussion noted that no one had suggested that

[1] *Torgovo-Promyshlennaya Gazeta*, March 31, 1929.
[2] *Ibid.* April 2, 5, 1929 ; *Pravda*, April 3, 1929.

the five-year plan proposals should not be taken as a basis.[1]

Early in April 1929 Rykov presented to the Politburo, for sub-mission to the party central committee, draft theses on the five-year plan embodying the proposals which he had made at the meeting of Sovnarkom. A commission of the Politburo rejected Rykov's draft, and presented alternative theses to the session of the central committee, which lasted from April 16 to 23, 1929.[2] In the debate, Stalin strongly criticized Rykov's proposal for a " two-year plan for agriculture ", claiming that its motive was " to emphasize the unrealistic, paper character of the five-year plan ". According to Stalin, the majority of the Politburo had suggested that if Rykov wanted higher allocations for agriculture he should say so, and they would be willing to include them, either in the five-year plan or in the annual plans ; but he had had no such proposals to make :

> Rykov has brought the two-year plan on to the stage in order that later, when the five-year plan is being carried out in prac-tice, he could oppose the two-year plan to the five-year plan, reconstruct the five-year plan and adapt it to the two-year plan, cutting and squeezing the allocations for industrialization.[3]

The theses submitted by the Politburo for transmission to the sixteenth party conference were approved by the central committee ; they endorsed " the five-year plan of the state planning commis-sion in its optimum variant ", as " fully corresponding to the directives of the fifteenth congress of the party ". Unlike the reso-lution submitted to the fifteenth party congress, the new theses included a specific range of figures from this variant, which was more ambitious even than the December draft of Vesenkha. Invest-ment in industry was now to amount to 16·4 milliard rubles over the five years, and industrial production was to increase by 180 per cent. The new theses declared that capital " investment in industry is directed mainly to industries *producing means of pro-duction* (78 per cent of all capital investment in industry) " ; the gross production of means of production would increase by 230 per cent. The objectives of 10 million tons of pig-iron and 75 million tons of coal were specifically written into the resolution.

---

[1] *Torgovo-Promyshlennaya Gazeta*, April 6, 1929.
[2] For these events see pp. 248-252 above.
[3] Stalin, *Sochineniya*, xii, 81-82.

Agricultural production was to increase by as much as 55 per cent, and national income as a whole by 103 per cent. It was firmly stressed that this " programme of an extensive socialist offensive " would involve " tremendous internal and external difficulties " :

These difficulties result from the tension of the plan itself, due to the technical and economic backwardness of the country, from the complexity of the objective of reshaping many millions of scattered peasant farms on the basis of collective labour and, finally, from the circumstance of a capitalist encirclement of our country. These difficulties are made more profound by the sharpening of the class struggle and the resistance of the capitalist elements.

In spite of these stern warnings, the theses did not depart in principle from earlier assumptions about the way in which resources would be obtained for financing the plan. While there was a new stress on the rôle of the budget in financing the expansion of industry, the main emphasis was placed on an increase of labour productivity in industry by as much as 110 per cent ; this optimistic prognostication made it possible to reconcile a large increase in real wages with a fall in production costs of 35 per cent. The theses concluded, however, with further warnings ; they asserted that the Right deviation was the greatest danger within the party, and that the objectives posed by the plan could not be achieved without " a merciless rebuff to any vacillations in carrying out the general Bolshevik line ".[1] On April 23, 1929, the day on which the session of the central committee ended, Sovnarkom in its turn resolved " to approve the optimum variant of the plan as the programme of economic construction for the next five-year period ". Like the theses of the party central committee, the Sovnarkom decree endorsed some specific figures from the optimum variant ; at the same time it listed improvements which must be undertaken in the plan, and added the rider that Gosplan, Vesenkha and Narkomfin must correct the financial plan, basing it on " the need in the first place to secure in full the proposed programme of construction and production in state industry ".[2]

[1] *KPSS v Rezolyutsiyakh*, ii (1954), 569-575 ; for the agricultural provisions of the plan see pp. 181, 240, 253-254 above.

[2] *Sobranie Zakonov, 1929*, No. 29, art. 268 ; the decree was not published until after the sixteenth party conference (*Pravda*, May 9, 1929).

The five-year plan was the first item on the agenda of the sixteenth party conference which opened on the evening of April 23 ; the plan occupied five of its twelve sessions. An attempt was made to preserve the show of agreement among the leaders, and three reports were given on the five-year plan — by Rykov, president of Sovnarkom, by Krzhizhanovsky, president of Gosplan, and by Kuibyshev, president of Vesenkha. Rykov declared of the capital investment programme, " I think we are in a position to maintain such a rate ", and was critical of his own past attitude to growth-rates in industry.[1] But he also gave full weight to the weaknesses which had appeared during the first six months of the period of the five-year plan — the bread shortage, " the upward tendency in price movements ", failure to fulfil plans to reduce industrial costs and increase labour productivity.[2] Krzhizhanovsky and Kuibyshev — the one rhetorical, the other matter-of-fact — spoke in terms of unalloyed optimism.[3] During the debate Larin, now a champion of out-and-out industrialization, contrasted Rykov's " critical *étude* " and Krzhizhanovsky's " poem in prose " with the " business-like manner " adopted by Kuibyshev. He asserted that only pressure from public opinion in the party and from the corresponding organs, rather than the creative momentum of Gosplan itself, had led it to abandon the " attenuating curve " of industrial growth and adopt higher targets.[4] Skrypnik mildly reproached Rykov for his scepticism and drew attention to the inconsistency of his position. Another speaker cited disapprovingly the joke that the five-year plan had " planned a Right wing deviation for the whole five years ".[5] Krzhizhanovsky in his reply to the debate vigorously rebuffed Larin, pointing out that " certain minimalist features of our former long-term plans were present not only in the work of Gosplan, but also in our whole economic front ", and claiming that planning officials had done no more than " listen sensitively to party directives ".[6] This was a muted defence of the passive rôle of Gosplan in the winter of 1927–1928 and of its strong opposition to the December draft of Vesenkha in the winter of 1928–1929.

[1] See p. 330 above.
[2] *Shestnadtsataya Konferentsiya VKP(B)* (1962), pp. 20-21.
[3] *Ibid.* pp. 24-78 ; for Kuibyshev's speech see pp. 330-331 above.
[4] *Shestnadtsataya Konferentsiya VKP(B)* (1962), pp. 143-147.
[5] *Ibid.* pp. 169, 171.   [6] *Ibid.* pp. 259-260.

The debate brought out other important changes in planning work. First, the plan had now begun to take a definite regional shape. Much time was taken up at the conference with complaints about the inadequacy of the allocation to each area. As Ryazanov said amid laughter, " every speech from this platform ends with the conclusion : Give us a factory in the Urals, and to hell with the Rights! Give us a power station, and to hell with the Rights! ".[1] Some speakers complained that the regional division of the plan was inadequately developed. But behind the traditional quarrels about location between Leningrad, the Urals and the Ukraine, planning was assuming a new aspect. As one speaker put it :

> This five-year plan is sharply distinguished from the control figures of the national economy compiled in past years by its emphasis on the development of the productive forces of each separate region.[2]

Perhaps the most important change in the work of the planners since the first drafts of the plan were prepared in 1925 and 1926 was that new capital construction was no longer debated in the form of tentative or vague proposals. Kuibyshev was able to discuss each of the major industries in terms of the proposed capacity of each of the main factories, new and old, and to relate these capacities to proposed production targets ; he treated in this way the pig-iron target of 10 million tons, and the plans for tractor production.[3] The first five-year plan, as it stood in the spring of 1929, presented a paradox. It was heroically over-confident — a confidence which was to increase in the coming months. But this was not simply the blind confidence of overweening ambition ; the grandiose plans were taking specific shape in the form of construction projects. While these projects were not as a rule completed by the end of the first five-year plan, the heavy industries by the middle nineteen-thirties at least broadly resembled the intentions of Gosplan and Vesenkha in 1929. At the sixteenth party conference Krzhizhanovsky caught something of the mood of many party members at the time :

> In this plan the strain will not diminish but grow in comparison with the strain in the previous five-year period. In the

[1] *Ibid.* p. 214.   [2] *Ibid.* p. 224.   [3] *Ibid.* pp. 60-63.

discussions in Gosplan one speaker correctly pointed out why this was so, and why we cannot avoid such strain. What he said was something like this : This grandiose work of socialist economic construction can be thought of as resembling the job of lifting a huge load up a high mountain. We, as the haulers of socialism, will drag the heavy convoy to those distant shores, where another life can be envisaged, another way of living, different economic relations (Ryazanov : " Only the great-hearted will be borne there by the waves ").

If we began to feel the load was light, what would it mean ? It would mean we had broken out of our traces. If this work was made easy it would be disrupted.[1]

This was the atmosphere in which the conference resolved " to approve the five-year plan of the State Planning Commission in its optimum variant as approved by the Council of People's Commissars of the USSR as a plan fully corresponding to the directives of the fifteenth party congress ".[2] During May 1929, congresses of Soviets of the RSFSR and the Ukraine approved the five-year plans for their republics.[3] On May 28, 1929, a resolution of the fifth Union Congress of Soviets, more sober in its appraisal of the plan than the party conference or than the Sovnarkom decree a month earlier, ended with an appeal to all concerned to carry it into effect.[4]

The Five-Year Plan of National Economic Construction of the USSR, a set of three volumes of more than 1700 large pages, though it contained a preface from the presidium of Gosplan submitting it for consideration to the sixteenth party conference and the fifth Union Congress of Soviets, was in fact published after the conference and Sovnarkom had already approved the optimum variant.[5] It had evidently been completed at the time of the fifth

[1] *Shestnadtsataya Konferentsiya VKP(B)* (1962), p. 262.
[2] *KPSS v Rezolyutsiyakh* (1954), ii, 573.
[3] *S"ezdy Sovetov v Dokumentakh*, iv, i (1962), 118-120 ; v (1964), 217-227.
[4] *S"ezdy Sovetov v Dokumentakh*, iii (1960), 155-161 ; during his report to the congress, Krzhizhanovsky dramatically switched on coloured lights on a map depicting the power stations which were to be constructed during the five-year plan, showing that all the power-stations constructed in the USSR before 1929 had been " only pioneers " (*SSSR : 5 S"ezd Sovetov* (1929), No. 8, pp. 16-17) ; for the Sovnarkom decree see p. 891 above.
[5] *Pyatiletnii Plan Narodno-Khozyaistvennogo Stroitel'stva SSSR* (1929), i, 5 ; at the fifth Union Congress of Soviets on May 23, 1929, Krzhizhanovsky reported that the volumes had just been published (*SSSR : 5 S"ezd Sovetov* (1929), No. 8, p. 1).

Gosplan congress in March 1929. It still treated the optimum and basic variants as alternatives which would be applied according to circumstances, and put forward a number of qualifying conditions which would have to be fulfilled if the optimum variant were to be realized. These included freedom from harvest failure ; an increase in exports and in foreign trade credits ; a rapid improvement in industrial costs and in agricultural yield ; and no increase in the expenditure on armaments as compared with the basic variant.[1] None of these qualifications was cited in the resolution of the sixteenth party conference approving the optimum variant of the plan. While it might be said that the plan was already being revised at the time of its publication, it continued to be accepted as an authoritative programme, and was reprinted with only minor textual changes in three editions in 1929 and 1930. The first volume, entitled *Comprehensive Survey*, was stated to have been been compiled by Grinko under the general editorship of Krzhizhanovsky, Kviring and Strumilin. Its largest section was a survey of the " building programme of the five-year plan ". Shorter sections followed on skilled labour ; production and productivity ; labour problems ; problems of consumption, market equilibrium and price policy ; economic connexions with the world economy ; and the financial and social programme. The second volume was divided into two parts. Part one, " the building and production programme of the plan " was a detailed survey of each sector of the economy prepared by the specialized sections of Gosplan. Part two surveyed " social problems, problems of distribution, labour and culture ". Volume three was a detailed survey of " the regional breakdown of the plan ". A small volume entitled *Objects of New Construction of State Industry in the Five-Year Period*, and described as an appendix to the third volume, listed construction projects under the regions concerned ; a foreword explained that, unlike the other parts of the series, this list appertained to the optimum variant.[2] The list showed the year in which the construction of every new factory was planned to start and finish, its cost and the amount to be spent on it during the period of the plan. Although the whole plan was coloured by

[1] *Pyatiletnii Plan Narodno-Khozyaistvennogo Stroitel'stva SSSR* (1929), i, 11.
[2] *Ob"ekty Novogo Stroitel'stva Gosudarstvennoi Promyshlennosti na Pyatiletie* (1929), p. 5.

optimistic assumptions about costs, the productivity of industry and the behaviour of the peasant, and was influenced by such *a priori* principles as that of the rising curve, it gives a solid impression of competence and detail in its specific programmes.

The five-year plan for the economy as a whole was supplemented by a large number of special plans for republics, regions and sectors which appeared during the course of 1929. Of these the most important were three volumes of *Materials* published by the Vesenkha of the USSR and based on the optimum variant. The first, on " problems of *energetika* ", was prepared by a " commission on questions of *energetika* in the five-year plan of the national economy ", which was established under the presidium of Vesenkha and included representatives of Gosplan, and dealt with the fuel and power industries and their relevance to the rest of industry ; the second dealt with " the main lines of the technical reconstruction of industry " ; the third with the problem of " perspectives for the development of ferrous metals ".[1] The third volume set out plans for new iron and steel works in the light of the plan to produce 10 million tons of pig-iron in 1932–1933 ; new works would produce 2·4 million tons of the total output in that year, and would have an eventual capacity of 6·5 million tons as compared with the capacity of three million tons planned in the August version of 1928.[2] The authors of this volume, writing in June 1929, complained that in compiling the plan they were still suffering from a lack of detailed plans from the non-industrial commissariats which were consumers of metal, such as Narkomput' and Narkomzem ; a detailed transport plan, for instance, was available only for the basic variant. As a result, Vesenkha had once again been compelled to some extent to construct its own assumptions.[3] A characteristic footnote on the last page of the first volume of the *Materials* pointed out that, since the plan was drafted, the plan for power production in 1932–1933 had been increased from 19 to 22 milliard kilowatt-hours, so that the Soviet Union would then occupy fourth place in the world instead of the sixth place originally expected.[4] The five-year plan published by

[1] *Materialy k Pyatiletnemu Planu Promyshlennosti VSNKh SSSR na 1928/29–1932/33 gg.* (1929), i-iii ; for *energetika* see p. 803, note 1 above.

[2] *Materialy k Pyatiletnemu Planu Promyshlennosti VSNKh SSSR na 1928/29–1932/33 gg.* (1929), iii, pp. ix-xi.

[3] *Ibid.* iii, pp. xxviii-xxix, 771.   [4] *Ibid.* i, 511.

Gosplan did not become, as the planners had hoped, the firm document on the basis of which the more detailed annual control figures were compiled.   Nevertheless, the final plan as approved by the party and the government in April and May 1929 was of primary economic importance in setting out a thoroughly discussed and reasonably well inter-related scheme for the industrialization of the economy, and of political and social importance as a programme of socialist construction round which the industrialization effort could be concentrated.

2 G

CHAPTER 38

MAJOR PROJECTS

A VITAL part in the industrialization of the Soviet Union was played by the major construction schemes planned or started in the later nineteen-twenties. Most of these schemes were industrial in character, and their planning and execution was primarily the responsibility of Vesenkha,[1] just as most railway construction was handled by Narkomput'. But a number of the major schemes cut across departmental boundaries and were intended to have a transforming influence on the economy as a whole. These were treated as the special responsibility of central government ; and in the handling of them Gosplan, at least in the planning stage, played a very important part.

The most famous and ambitious of these schemes was Dnieprostroi,[2] the conception of which dated back to 1905, and which had as its central feature the construction of a dam and large hydro-electric station on the river Dnieper.[3] The construction of power stations, though it came within the administrative competence of Glavelektro in Vesenkha, had always been looked on as a special responsibility of Gosplan, which on its foundation in 1921 had taken over the work of Goelro.[4] The Dnieper scheme was particularly the child, or foster-child, of Gosplan. In 1920, the job of designing a single great dam and power station was entrusted to Aleksandrov, one of the principal members of Goelro.[5] As the scheme took shape at the beginning of 1926 it was intended not merely to provide cheap power, but

---

[1] See pp. 431-452 above.

[2] The term " Dnieprostroi " (short for " Dneprovskoe stroitel'stvo ", the " Dnieper construction ") referred to the construction job itself ; the hydro-electric station became known as " Dnieproges ".

[3] See *Socialism in One Country, 1924-1926*, Vol. 1, pp. 514-515.

[4] See *The Bolshevik Revolution, 1917–1923*, Vol. 2, pp. 375-376.

[5] For the early history of Dnieprostroi see Arzhanov and Mikhalevich, *Dneprostroi k XVI S"ezdu VKP(B)* (1930), pp. 5-6 ; V. Mazurin, *Kak Rodilsya*

also as a first step towards transforming the Dnieper into a major navigable waterway for oil, coal and wheat, partly for export; it would also promote land improvements in the vicinity of the dam. The power station, with a capacity of 230,000 kilowatts and an annual output of 1200-1300 million kilowatt-hours, would supply power both for existing factories and for a number of new ones, which would consume the energy of Dnieproges and utilize the new transport facilities.[1] Although in terms of output Dnieprostroi constituted only a small part of the total plan of power station construction, it involved a major effort for the underdeveloped Soviet economy : money, men and materials had to be concentrated on a single enterprise which was not expected to produce results for five or six years. Although the electricity eventually produced would be cheap, the capital cost of Dnieprostroi, as of other hydro-electric projects, would be high ; estimates in the summer of 1926 ranged from 120 to 200 million rubles, the lowest of which was twice as high as the cost of constructing a typical fuel-burning station of the same capacity.[2] Moreover, the construction of the power station implied a major future commitment to build the new factories which would consume its power ; estimates of the additional investment required ranged at this time from 200 to 1500 million rubles. The scheme was at first viewed with scepticism in Vesenkha ; [3] and as late as March 1926 the head of the power department of Gosplan spoke of the " negative attitude to the Dnieper [scheme] noticeable in certain economic organs ".[4] The main objections were neatly summarized in Stalin's simile

---

Dneprostroi (1929), pp. 17-20 ; B. Viktorov, *Dneprostroi* (1926) ; *Dneprostroi,* No. 1, 1927, pp. 35-39 ; *Bol'shaya Sovetskaya Entsiklopediya,* xxii (1935), 767-771.

[1] The principal features of the Dnieper scheme were summarized in *Bol'shevik,* No. 3, February 15, 1926, pp. 67-68, and by Aleksandrov in *Torgovo-Promyshlennaya Gazeta,* November 9, 1926, and *Planovoe Khozyaistvo,* No. 12, 1926, pp. 171-187.

[2] For these estimates of the cost of Dnieprostroi see *Torgovo-Promyshlennaya Gazeta,* October 7, 1926 ; for the capital cost of fuel-burning stations at this time see *Pervye Shagi Industrializatsii SSSR 1926-1927 gg.* (1959), p. 82.

[3] At a discussion on Dnieprostroi in the presidium of Gosplan in the summer of 1925, Tsyurupa, then the president of Gosplan, and the non-party specialist, Osadchy, expressed surprise at the lack of interest shown by Vesenkha in a scheme in which it should be thoroughly involved (*Ekonomicheskaya Zhizn',* July 4, 1925).

[4] *Problemy Planirovaniya (Itogi i Perspektivy)* (1926), p. 190.

about the peasant and the gramophone ; [1] it would be very expensive, and the money involved, if available at all, would be more advantageously spent on less ambitious projects.

In the spring of 1926, a Dnieprostroi commission visited the United States ; and on June 11, 1926, a contract to vet the project was signed with Colonel Hugh Cooper, who had been responsible for building the Wilson dam and power station at Muscle Shoals in Tennessee after the first world war. Two of Cooper's assistants arrived in Moscow in July, and on August 24, 1926, Cooper himself reached Moscow.[2] On September 1, the press reported that he and Aleksandrov had gone to the site ; [3] and by September 16 his first favourable comments were reported.[4] Krzhizhanovsky remarked that " the dry and cautious American expert Cooper said that, since he had got to know about the Dnieper project, he had turned into a poet ".[5] His reports were particularly encouraging about the cost of the scheme : his estimate of between 123 and 134 million rubles, the exact amount depending on wage costs, was closer to the lower than to the higher of the earlier estimates ; and he agreed with the optimists that power could be supplied at 0·46 kopeks per kilowatt-hour, more cheaply than anywhere else in the world except at Niagara.[6] A German construction firm, Siemens-Bauunion, also examined the site and drew up an alternative project, some features of which were incorporated in the final scheme.[7]

A second major project was also in an advanced state of preparation by the autumn of 1926. This was the railway designed to link Central Asia, Kazakhstan and western Siberia, at first known as the " Semirechie " railway, and later as " Turksib ".[8] The construction of the railway would encourage the economic development of the underpopulated and underdeveloped regions

[1] See Socialism in One Country, 1924–1926, Vol. 1, p. 355.
[2] Torgovo-Promyshlennaya Gazeta, November 18, 1926.
[3] Ibid. September 1, 1926.
[4] Ibid. September 16, 1926.
[5] Ekonomicheskaya Zhizn', November 7, 1926.
[6] Planovoe Khozyaistvo, No. 6, 1926, pp. 182-183 ; Torgovo-Promyshlennaya Gazeta, October 7, 8, November 18, 1926 ; Ekonomicheskaya Zhizn', October 28, 1926 ; Dneprostroi, No. 1, 1927, pp. 44-47.
[7] Ekonomicheskaya Zhizn', October 13, 28, 1926 ; Pravda, June 12, 1927.
[8] It was officially renamed " the Turksib railway " by Narkomput' in May 1927 (Turkestano-Sibirskaya Magistral' (1929), p. 285).

of Kazakhstan and Siberia.[1] At the same time it would contribute to the goal of self-sufficiency by helping to free the Soviet textile industry from dependence on imported cotton. Production of cotton in Central Asia had developed rapidly after the completion in 1906 of the Tashkent railway which enabled grain from European Russia to be sent into Central Asia in exchange for cotton ; the Turksib line would provide a similar link between Central Asia, Kazakhstan and Siberia.[2] At the seventh congress of trade unions in December 1926, Kuibyshev explained :

> This line is being built particularly in order to join the grain of Siberia, the main product of this part of the country, with Turkestan cotton, on the one hand to facilitate the development of cotton-growing in Central Asia in order to create a stable basis for the textile industry, and on the other hand to give a powerful impetus to the industrialization of Siberia.[3]

The argument was elaborated in a decree of the Sovnarkom of the RSFSR dated February 28, 1927, which spoke of the line as of " tremendous significance for the economic development of Central Asia, Kazakhstan and Siberia, and of the whole USSR ", emphasizing its importance for the supply of Siberian grain, timber and cattle to the cotton-growing areas of Central Asia, the development of agriculture, cattle-breeding and mining in Kazakhstan and the improvement of trade relations with western China and Outer Mongolia ; the decree also stressed the important auxiliary advantage that grain and timber at present sent from European Russia to Central Asia would be freed for export and other uses.[4]

[1] According to the 1926 census, the urban population of Kazakhstan, northern Kirgizia and western Siberia was only 487,000 out of a total population of 5,540,000. There were only seven towns with a population of more than 20,000 near the proposed railway — these were (population in thousands in brackets) : Barnaul (74), Semipalatinsk (57), Biisk (46), Alma-Ata (45), Frunze (36), Aulia-ata (25), Chimkent (22) (*ibid.* p. 44).

[2] The five-year plan adopted in April 1929 proposed that by 1932–1933 nearly all the grain and 70 per cent of the timber supplied to Central Asia should come from Siberia and Kazakhstan ; sales of cotton fibre would increase to between 525,000 and 610,000 tons, while imports would fall to 100,000-120,000 tons, thus making the USSR largely self-sufficient in cotton (*Pyatiletnii Plan Narodno-Khozyaistvennogo Stroitel'stva SSSR* (1929), ii, i, 299 ; iii, 314-316).

[3] *Sed'moi S"ezd Professional'nykh Soyuzov SSSR* (1927), p. 586.

[4] *Sobranie Uzakonenii, 1927*, No. 23, art. 154 ; at this time, while there was some talk of constructing cotton textile factories in Siberia, the possibility of developing the factory production of cotton textiles in the climatic conditions

By the middle nineteen-twenties, a great deal had already been done towards the construction of the line. In the north, shortly before the first world war, a line had been constructed from Novosibirsk on the Trans-Siberian railway through Barnaul to Semipalatinsk 650 kilometres to the south. In the south, the Semirechie company had received permission in 1912 to construct a line which ran northeastward from Tashkent to Pishpek (later Frunze) and Vernyi (later Alma-Ata) ; only the first part of this line had been constructed before 1917. Work was resumed in 1921 and the line was opened as far as Frunze in 1924. But the most difficult problems of Turksib still remained : to construct some 1500 kilometres of track which would first negotiate the high mountains between Frunze and Alma-Ata, and then run north-wards across the deserts, hills, ravines and fast-flowing rivers of earthquake-prone eastern Kazakhstan to Semipalatinsk.[1] The main difficulty in the way of constructing the line was, however, that of finance. The control figures of Gosplan for the year 1926–1927, completed in August 1926, allocated only 30 million rubles to new railway construction, to be used exclusively on completing lines already begun.[2] The estimate at this time of the cost of constructing Turksib was 120 million rubles.[3]

A third major scheme in an advanced state of preparation was the Volga–Don canal. The canal was intended to facilitate transport between the Volga region and the Ukraine and at the same time to make possible the irrigation of the surrounding area for increased grain production. The scheme was said to have been as far advanced as the Dnieprostroi project.[4] The cost was estimated at 140 million rubles, which was about the same as the estimated cost of Dnieprostroi or Turksib. In 1925 it had been postponed in favour of Dnieprostroi ; [5] but by the autumn of 1926 there was strong pressure, particularly from the RSFSR, to start construction. One of the protagonists of the canal claimed that the pre-

of Central Asia itself was regarded with scepticism (*Turkestano-Sibirskaya Magistral'* (1929), p. 197).

    [1] Developments up to 1926 are outlined *ibid.* pp. 236-237.
    [2] *Kontrol'nye Tsifry Narodnogo Khozyaistva na 1926–1927 god* (1926), p. 74.
    [3] *Ekonomicheskaya Zhizn'*, November 20, 1926.
    [4] *Torgovo-Promyshlennaya Gazeta*, November 11, 1926.
    [5] See *Socialism in One Country, 1924–1926*, Vol. 1, p. 515.

vailing opinion among economists and specialists was that it should be given priority ; Osadchy was reported to have stated in a preliminary study of Dnieprostroi that priority should be given to the Volga–Don canal because it was simpler and less dependent on foreign technology.[1]

A fourth proposal, which offered on a modest scale some of the advantages both of Dnieprostroi and of the Volga–Don canal, was the Svir'–Neva project, in which the construction of a group of hydro-electric stations on the river Svir' to provide Leningrad with cheap electricity was combined with the construction of a deep waterway from the Gulf of Finland to Lake Ladoga and the improvement of the Mariinsky canal system. The case for the power station or stations was strong : the proposed capacity of 40 thousand kilowatts was less than that of the Volkhov station which was just being completed, and less than a fifth of the proposed capacity of Dnieproges ; the cost of construction, though high in terms of capacity, was estimated at only 65 million rubles, half the cost of Dnieprostroi. There would be no problem, as with Dnieprostroi, of finding consumers : the Leningrad consumers already existed, and, according to Leningrad calculations, would be short of power in a few years' time if work were not started immediately. Moreover, men, materials and equipment from nearby Volkhovstroi, which were already being dispersed, could be transferred to the Svir'.[2]

In the last few months of 1926, the fate of all these projects was determined. This was a period of general economic optimism : the harvest had been good and the market was stable.[3] Against this background, Sovnarkom decided in September 1926 to invest in industry in the year 1926–1927 a larger sum than Gosplan had proposed in its control figures.[4] At the beginning of October, Chubar informed a session of the Ukrainian TsIK that a start could be made on major projects in the year 1926–1927, but that the choice was still open between Dnieprostroi, another hydro-electric

---

[1] *Torgovo-Promyshlennaya Gazeta*, November 11, 1926.
[2] *Ibid.* October 15, 1926 ; *Ekonomicheskaya Zhizn'*, October 23, 1926. For Volkhovstroi see *Socialism in One Country, 1924–1926*, Vol. 1, p. 514.
[3] See pp. 7-8, 288-289, 684 above.   [4] See pp. 284-285, 742 above.

station and the Volga–Don canal, and that it was necessary to prove to the Union authorities the superiority of the Dnieper scheme.[1] On October 7, 1926, a day or two after Chubar's announcement, the presidium of Vesenkha discussed a report on Dnieprostroi by a representative of Glavelektro, who reminded the meeting that the industries in the area which would consume the power must also be planned. Kuibyshev was absent, and the meeting was divided. Kviring and Rukhimovich, the first and second deputy presidents of Vesenkha, supported an immediate start on the scheme. Dolgov, the non-party engineer in charge of capital investment questions in Vesenkha, and Lobov, head of Glavelektro and president of the Vesenkha of the RSFSR, advocated postponement, and canvassed alternative projects. Eventually, in spite of this formidable opposition, the presidium of Vesenkha recommended that building work on Dnieprostroi should begin " in the near future ", and called for " a sum to be made available for large-scale capital construction " in the estimates for the current year ; it added, however, that the destination of this sum should be settled in the second half of the economic year. The presidium observed that the " planning commission on Dnieprostroi " (of which Trotsky was the president) had " failed to carry out the tasks it was set " ; most sections of the commission were reported to be far from finishing their work, and the commission had failed to meet in plenary session during 1926.[2] Meanwhile a Leningrad campaign for an immediate start on the Svir' project received the powerful support of Kirov, but does not appear to have gone beyond a modest demand for 3 million rubles in 1926–1927.[3]

When the fifteenth party conference opened on October 26, 1926, no decision had been taken about these projects.[4] On November 6, a special meeting of the presidium of Gosplan was called to discuss " the question of possible large construction

[1] *Torgovo-Promyshlennaya Gazeta*, October 7, 1926.
[2] *Protokol Zasedaniya Prezidiuma VSNKh SSSR, 1926–1927*, No. 1, art. 1 ; *Torgovo-Promyshlennaya Gazeta*, October 8, 1926. For the commission see *Socialism in One Country, 1924–1926*, Vol. 1, p. 515. A few weeks later Trotsky was replaced by Rukhimovich " in accordance with his personal request " (*Ekonomicheskaya Zhizn'*, December 3, 1926).
[3] *Torgovo-Promyshlennaya Gazeta*, October 15, 1926.
[4] *XV Konferentsiya Vsesoyuznoi Kommunisticheskoi Partii (B)* (1927), p. 262.

undertakings, all-Union in scale, and capable of forcing the development of the national economy as a whole ".   The meeting was attended both by representatives of republics and local areas, who were still in Moscow after the party conference, and by Rykov, as president of Sovnarkom, Kuibyshev and Rukhimovich from Vesenkha, Rudzutak, as People's Commissar for Communications and vice-president of Sovnarkom, Chubar, as president of the Ukrainian Sovnarkom, and Lobov as president of the Vesenkha of the RSFSR and of Glavelektro.   The meeting was told by Krzhizhanovsky, who presided, that 200 million rubles would be available to industry and transport during the next five years for major schemes outside the normal capital investment plan, and that the first 40 million rubles would be available in the current year 1926–1927 :   this was presumably in response to the request made by the presidium of Vesenkha on October 7, 1926, for a " sum to be made available for large-scale capital construction ".   It then heard reports on the four projects already discussed, as well as on three others which were, however, easily dismissed.   It accepted the Ukrainian estimate of the cost of Dnieprostroi — 120 million rubles — and proposed to allocate this sum to the project over the next five years.   The 80 million rubles which remained out of the 200 millions were allocated to Turksib and also spread over five years :   since the estimated cost of Turksib was about the same as that of Dnieprostroi, the grant was not sufficient for its completion. The presidium, while postponing the construction of the Svir'– Neva waterway, agreed that the first Svir' power station should be constructed at once, and that others should be built later as Leningrad consumption increased.   The Volga–Don canal project was again postponed as it had been in 1925 :   the presidium recommended that 700,000 rubles should be allocated towards its further elaboration.   At the same time the alternative possibility of a railway from Stalingrad to Rostov-on-Don was to be studied further.[1]

[1] This account is pieced together from reports in *Torgovo-Promyshlennaya Gazeta*, November 7, 9, 1926.   In July 1927 Glavelektro proposed an allocation to the Svir' station to be taken out of the Dnieprostroi allocation :   this was rejected (*ibid.* July 29, 1927).   Work at Svir' began in October 1927 (*ibid.* October 20, 1927), receiving an allocation of 5 million rubles for 1927–1928 (*Kontrol'nye Tsifry Narodnogo Khozyaistva SSSR na 1927–1928 god* (1928), p. 142), and of 13 millions for 1928–1929 (*Kontrol'nye Tsifry Narodnogo Khozyaistva SSSR na 1928–1929 god* (1929), p. 464).   The Volga–Don canal was not lost sight of ;   the manifesto on the tenth anniversary of the October

The industrial newspaper enthusiastically welcomed the decisions of Gosplan in an editorial entitled " Dnieprostroi and the Semirechie Railway ".[1]

The battle was not yet quite won. At the session of the TsIK of the RSFSR in the same month a number of delegates strenuously opposed the recommendations of Gosplan, which Beloborodov, the spokesman of the People's Commissariat of Internal Affairs, described as " unexpected for the government ". One delegate from Stalingrad went so far as to allege that " the Americans, fearing the growing export of grain from the USSR, have deliberately tried to distract attention from the Volga–Don Canal project " by urging that priority should be given to Dnieprostroi.[2] On November 19, 1926, the session passed a special resolution urging that the construction of the Volga–Don canal should be treated as a " priority task", and that the final project for the whole scheme should be completed during the year 1926–1927.[3] The decision in favour of Dnieprostroi finally came on November 26, 1926, when a resolution of the party central committee " On Large-scale Construction in the Current Economic Year " stated that the Semirechie railway and Dnieprostroi should be given priority, and that work on the Volga–Don canal should be confined to completing the survey and continuing the work at the port of Azov.[4] On December 3, 1926, STO, on a report from Krzhizhanovsky, resolved that it was " necessary to begin in the current year, for completion within five years, the construction of the Semirechie railway," and that the Dnieper power-station should be constructed with a capacity of 150,000 horse-power (100,000 kilowatts) ; it instructed Gosplan and Vesenkha to submit a plan

---

revolution (see p. 33 above) referred to "the Semirechie line, the Volga–Don canal and other giant installations " ; and Krzhizhanovsky spoke in its favour at the presidium of Gosplan in December 1927 (*Informatsionnyi Byulleten' Gosplana SSSR*, No. 1-2, 1928, pp. 10-13). The five-year plan allocated 75 million rubles to its construction, and proposed that it should be completed during the second five-year plan (*Pyatiletnii Plan Narodno-Khozyaistvennogo Stroitel'stva SSSR* (1929), i, 68) ; it was in fact completed in 1952.

[1] *Torgovo-Promyshlennaya Gazeta*, November 9, 1926.
[2] *Ibid.* November 11, 1926.
[3] *III Sessiya Vserossiiskogo Tsentral'nogo Ispolnitel'nogo Komiteta XII Sozyva: Postanovleniya* (1926), pp. 256-258.
[4] *Resheniya Partii i Pravitel'stva po Khozyaistvennym Voprosam*, i (1967), 561.

for the organization of the work for Dnieprostroi to STO within a
month.[1]   On December 22, 1926, STO appointed a board of
administration for Dnieprostroi including both Aleksandrov and
Vinter, who was soon made chief engineer ; [2] early in 1927, the
allocation for the project was fixed at 7 million rubles for the year
1926–1927.[3]   The decision was formally endorsed, and linked
with the Goelro plan, by the fourth Union Congress of Soviets in
April 1927 :

> The congress approves the decision of the government to
> construct a powerful hydro-electric station on the Dnieper and
> the Semirechie railway ; it considers that these large installa-
> tions are a beginning of a reconstruction of the whole economy of
> the country in accordance with the general plan of electrification.[4]

The Dnieper project was approved by STO in June 1927.   Construction was to be undertaken in two stages, the first stage, which
would cost 140 million rubles, being completed by December
1931 ; total capacity would be 220,000 kilowatts.[5]   By this time
preliminary work had already begun ; at the end of August 1927,
it was reported that 10,500 workers were already employed on the
site instead of the projected 3000.[6]

    Dnieprostroi became a symbolical landmark in Soviet develop-
ment, a practical application of " socialism in one country ".   It
was a national effort with a strong appeal to national pride and with
a rich promise of further advance.   Dnieprostroi would provide
the cheapest power in the world — the pre-requisite for competition with world industry.   It was merely a first stage :

> *The building of the Dnieper power station predetermines the
> industrial type of future development for the southern part of the
> Soviet Union.*[7]

It was moreover a socialist achievement.   Under capitalism, Dnieprostroi would be " seen as an isolated enterprise ", and yield

[1] *Torgovo-Promyshlennaya Gazeta*, December 5, 10, 1926 ; *Pravda*,
December 5, 1926 ; *Turkestano-Sibirskaya Magistral'* (1929), p. 273.
[2] *Sobranie Zakonov, 1927*, No. 3, art. 37 ; see also No. 8, art. 51 (dated
February 3), No. 9, art. 90 (dated February 22).
[3] *Ibid.* No. 10, art. 98.   [4] *S"ezdy Sovetov v Dokumentakh*, iii (1960), 115.
[5] *Pravda*, June 12, 1927.   [6] *Ibid.* September 2, 1927.
[7] *Torgovo-Promyshlennaya Gazeta*, November 9, 1926.

little profit — the precedent of similar schemes for the Rhône valley was quoted ; under a planned socialist economy, it would promote the cooperation and expansion of several associated sectors of the economy.[1]   On the other hand, it represented a borrowing of the most advanced technical achievements of the west. Aleksandrov spoke of it as the first test of the feasibility of bringing American technology to Soviet Russia ; it was " an example of culture in building, an example proving the possibility of adapting American technology to our conditions ".[2]   Cooper stressed its importance for the training of the population in modern production methods, confidently arguing that, given this training, the USSR was in a position, in view of its abundant human and natural resources, to " conquer a commanding position in the world ".[3] The head of the electrification section of Gosplan later declared :

> The whole of Europe is watching the construction of Dnieprostroi. This is our examination in technology, and we must create the best possible atmosphere, so that we can pass it.[4]

In the first two years, the construction ran into serious difficulties, the most important of which was increasing costs. Between 1926 and the end of 1928 the official estimates rose from 120 to over 200 million rubles,[5] and the cost of producing the power was also expected to be higher than the original estimate.[6] From time to time doubts were expressed about the wisdom of the whole project.[7] But the sceptics were without serious influence on policy. The project was well financed, with planned allocations of 34 million rubles in 1927–1928 and 45 million rubles in 1928–1929,

---

[1] *Bol'shevik*, No. 3, February 15, 1926, pp. 67-68.   It was pointed out in 1929 that in the Tennessee Valley " the enormous power station built by engineer Cooper stands idle ; the water of a great river flows past it, because it is state property and American capitalists do not want to use it " (*Shestnadtsataya Konferentsiya VKP(B)* (1962), p. 35) ; this neglect continued till the creation of the T.V.A.   [2] *Torgovo-Promyshlennaya Gazeta*, November 18, 1926.
[3] *Dnieprostroi*, No. 1, 1927, pp. 84-85.
[4] *Ekonomicheskaya Zhizn'*, September 19, 1928.
[5] *Materialy po Istorii SSSR*, vii (1959), 188.
[6] *Torgovo-Promyshlennaya Gazeta*, July 4, 1928.
[7] See, for example, *Vestnik Finansov*, No. 2, 1927, pp. 110-111, No. 7, 1927, p. 54, and Osinsky's remarks at the session of the party central committee in July 1928 (Trotsky archives, T 1834 ; *Sotsialisticheskii Vestnik* (Berlin), No. 21, November 14, 1928 p. 15), summarized on pp. 314-315 above.

which were substantially larger than had been intended at the end of 1926.[1]   Although the builders had thus received more than two-thirds of the estimated cost by the end of 1928–1929, progress was slower than had at first been planned ; in December 1928 the date of completion of the first stage was postponed by a year to December 1932 ; [2] at the same time, however, the planned capacity of the power-station when both stages were completed was raised to the grandiose figure of 530,000 kilowatts, more than twice Aleksandrov's original estimate ; the new figure, which was eventually achieved, involved the provision of generators twice as large as those originally proposed.[3] By the spring of 1929, the auxiliary installations and the preparatory work were complete ; in the summer the dam began to rise from the banks.[4]

An ambivalent attitude prevailed towards the use of foreign technicians and foreign equipment in the Dnieper project. The Soviet government had decided to rely on its own financial resources ; [5] but it was heavily dependent on the advanced capitalist countries for know-how and equipment. Stalin's one published comment on a technological problem at Dnieprostroi, in a

[1] *Torgovo-Promyshlennaya Gazeta*, September 8, 1927 ; *Kontrol'nye Tsifry Narodnogo Khozyaistva SSSR na 1928–1929 god* (1929), p. 464 ; according to *SSSR: God Raboty Pravitel'stva* (*Materialy k Otchetu za 1928/29 g.*) (1930), p. 136, a total sum of 60·7 million rubles had been spent on the project by October 1, 1928, and a further 36·4 million rubles was spent in 1928–1929.

[2] *Materialy po Istorii SSSR*, vii (1959), 180.

[3] *Protokol Rasshirennogo Zasedaniya Prezidiuma VSNKh SSSR, 1928–1929*, No. 1, art. 99, dated December 5 ; *Pravda*, December 9, 1928. The total generating capacity would operate only at times of high water ; at times of year when water was low, capacity would fall to less than a third of peak.

[4] Arzhanov and Mikhalevich, *Dneprostroi k XVI S"ezdu VKP(B)* (1930), pp. 14-15.

[5] During the discussions in 1926 the use of foreign capital or of a foreign contractor was seriously considered. In June 1926, Grinko proposed that foreign capital should participate in the construction (*Planovoe Khozyaistvo*, No. 6, 1926, pp. 182-183) ; as late as October 1926, Chubar suggested that foreign capital might help to construct Dnieprostroi or the factories associated with it (*Ekonomicheskaya Zhizn'*, October 8, 1926) ; a meeting of specialists recommended that the construction should be placed in foreign hands (A. Khavin, *Kratkii Ocherk Istorii Industrializatsii SSSR* (1962), p. 69). The final decision not to attempt to obtain foreign capital or to assign the work to a foreign contractor, but to employ Cooper as an adviser, was taken at an enlarged meeting of the Politburo (*Sdelaem Rossiyu Elektricheskoi* (1961), p. 53) ; the date is not known but it was presumably held early in November 1926. Attempts were made to interest foreign firms in the associated factories (*Torgovo-Promyshlennaya Gazeta*, November 9, 1926) ; but these too were eventually dropped.

letter to Kuibyshev of August 31, 1928, ran : " It seems to me . . . that *Cooper is right* and Vinter is wrong. . . . Cooper's views must certainly be given a proper hearing ".[1] A Rabkrin report in June 1929 complained that " extremely useful " proposals from the American engineers had been rejected, and that Dnieprostroi was not paying sufficient attention to American advice.[2] On the other hand, in a famous incident in 1929, Cooper wanted to build the dam from one bank at a time, and the Soviet engineers and officials to speed the process up by building from both banks simultaneously ; Cooper was overruled, and the Soviet method apparently worked.[3] Even in the wake of this incident, those who attempted to praise Soviet engineers at the expense of the Americans met with official disapproval.[4] The same toleration was not extended to the recruitment of foreign workers. When Cooper proposed to bring in various American skilled workers, Vinter proved intransigent :

> We must ourselves learn to work on these machines. . . . I do not complain about such things as half-a-dozen broken points or cranes collapsing. This is dozens and hundreds of times cheaper than signing on workers in great quantities to do work we are capable of.[5]

The question of Soviet-manufactured versus foreign equipment was keenly debated; in the event, most of the main equipment was imported.[6]

During the first two years of construction, no firm decisions were taken on the uses to which the available power would be put. The commission on Dnieprostroi presided over by Trotsky in 1925 and 1926 considered several proposals for the construction of new factories. But, when STO authorized the construction of the

[1] For this letter see p. 554, note 2 above.
[2] *Materialy po Istorii SSSR*, vii (1959), 189-190.
[3] *Opyt Stroitel'stva Gidroelektricheskikh Stantsii SSSR*, ed. P. Osadchy, i (1930), 234, 250.
[4] *Bol'shaya Sovetskaya Entsiklopediya*, xxii (1935), 772-773 ; *Dneprostroi*, No. 2-3, 1928, pp. 86-89, 95 ; *Opyt Stroitel'stva Gidroelektricheskikh Stantsii SSSR*, ed. P. Osadchy, i (1930), 271-272, 294. A pamphlet, one of the authors of which was Vinter's deputy, described as " rather dangerous ", and as " an outlook of an hurrah-patriotic character ", the tendency of some engineers and technicians to say that the consultants were not much help (Arzhanov and Mikhalevich, *Dneprostroi k XVI S"ezdu VKP(B)* (1930), p. 27).
[5] *Opyt Stroitel'stva Gidroelektricheskikh Stantsii SSSR*, ed. P. Osadchy, i (1930), 291-292.　　　　　[6] See pp. 411-412 above.

power station at the end of 1926, it was not able to go beyond the general recommendation that Dnieproges should form the centre of " a unified industrial complex economically and technically inter-connected ".[1] On June 29, 1927, on the proposal of STO, Vesenkha established a commission under the presidency of Dolgov " for the elaboration of a general plan for organizing consumers to utilize the energy of the Dnieper hydro-electric station ".[2] At the fifteenth party congress in December 1927, the question was brought up by several speakers. Chubar reasonably complained that, while a programme for constructing new works in connexion with Dnieprostroi existed " in a *commission* of the presidium of the Vesenkha of the USSR ", higher planning bodies had no firm policy. Petrovsky suggested that investment in the power station was not proved to be economic so long as its consumers had not been decided on : " if we supply power from Dnieprostroi only for the Donbass and the nearby towns, no gain will be achieved ".[3] Throughout 1928 the uncertainty continued ; and it was only the victory, first in Vesenkha and then at higher levels, of proposals to increase the long-term targets for producer goods industries which secured the acceptance of the more ambitious plans for the Dnieper region. The presidium of Vesenkha resolved on December 5, 1928, that iron and steel works should be built both at Zaporozhie and at Krivoi Rog during the first five-year plan, and that the Zaporozhie works should consume Dnieper power. It also recommended the construction of aluminium, ferro-alloy and high-grade steel works ; the aluminium works was to have a capacity of 10,000 tons, with the possibility of expanding it to 15,000 tons. The presidium resolved that Dnieproges should be connected to the Donbass, and that a fuel-burning power station should be built in the Donbass as a reserve for the Dnieper station when the river was low.[4]

Resistance to these decisions was still not quite at an end. On

[1] *Dneprostroi*, No. 1, 1927, pp. 47, 74-82.
[2] *Torgovo-Promyshlennaya Gazeta*, July 22, 1927.
[3] *Pyatnadtsatyi S"ezd VKP(B)*, ii (1962), 997, 1016-1017.
[4] *Protokol Rasshirennogo Zasedeniya Prezidiuma VSNKh SSSR, 1928-1929*, No. 1, art. 99 ; for further aspects of this decree, see p. 909 above ; the Dolgov commission had earlier recommended that Dnieproges power should not be supplied to the Donbass because the cost of transmission would be too high (*Torgovo-Promyshlennaya Gazeta*, December 2, 1927).

February 11–12, 1929, a conference attended by 76 representatives of government, industrial and research organizations under the chairmanship of Rykov again suggested that the decision to build the Zaporozhie works should be deferred for two or three months in order to examine further the alternative proposal to expand existing works or works already planned. This proved to be the last attempt at procrastination. On April 12, 1929, Sovnarkom finally approved a list of consumers of power from Dnieprostroi, including the aluminium works, a chemical combine, the Zaporozhie, Dnieprostal and Dnieprosplav works, and the towns of Dniepropetrovsk and Zaporozhie ; the Dnieper basin was also to be irrigated. The factories were to be completed in step with the bringing of the power station into use. A Donbass–Dnieprostroi transmission line was to be built at a date to be settled by Vesenkha and Gosplan.[1] But a speaker at the sixteenth party conference in April 1929 still complained that Dnieproges would be completed two years before the factories which would consume its power.[2] On May 3, 1929, a board was established in Moscow with responsibility for building the whole industrial combine ; on the site itself, the work of Dnieproges and the consuming factories was integrated by placing Dnieprostroi in charge of all building.[3] Within the next five years both the power station and the factories planned to consume its output were brought into operation.[4] Dnieprostroi remained the most noteworthy single achievement of the first period of Soviet industrialization.

When the proposal to construct Turksib was approved by STO on December 3, 1926, the route had not yet been finally decided. At that time it was intended to run it direct from Frunze to Semipalatinsk, with a branch line to Alma-Ata ;[5] the variant

[1] The principal articles in the discussion of January and February 1929 were published in *Izvestiya*, January 27, 29, 1929, and *Ekonomicheskaya Zhizn'*, February 2, 3, 24, 1929. The discussion, the February conference and the Sovnarkom decision are summarized in *Dneprostroi*, No. 3, 1929, pp. 146-153.

[2] *Shestnadtsataya Konferentsiya VKP(B)* (1962), pp. 175-176.

[3] *Protokol Zasedaniya Prezidiuma VSNKh SSSR, 1928–1929*, No. 17, Prilozhenie, art. 476.

[4] For the progress made down to 1934 see *Bol'shaya Sovetskaya Entsiklopediya*, xxii (1935), 722-726.

[5] *Turkestano-Sibirskaya Magistral'* (1929), p. 237.

finally adopted, which was the cheapest, and was estimated to save a year in building time, did not run direct from Frunze but from Lugovoi on the Tashkent–Frunze line north-east to Alma-Ata.[1] An organization called Turksibstroi, headed by the Russian-American revolutionary Bill Shatov, was set up to supervise the work of construction. Two sub-administrations at Semipalatinsk and Alma-Ata were responsible for constructing the northern and the southern sections respectively; each sub-administration was divided into groups (sektory) and sub-groups (distantsii) responsible for a length of the track. The only work to be contracted out was the erection of the large metal bridges, which was the responsibility of the industrial trusts which supplied them.[2] Work began in April 1927 at the northern end of the route, and on November 21, 1927, on the southern section.[3] The initial progress seems to have been more rapid on the Turksib than at Dnieprostroi; this was work in which Russians already had experience. The planning and execution of Turksibstroi closely involved both the Sovnarkom of the RSFSR and the local authorities for the area covered by the railway. Early in 1927, within a few weeks of the decision to build the line, the Sovnarkom of the RSFSR established a " committee of assistance " to Turksibstroi of which Ryskulov, deputy president of the Sovnarkom of the RSFSR, was president, and which included nationally prominent as well as local figures.[4] The Sovnarkom of the RSFSR also adopted an elaborate working programme for its commissariats, covering the recruitment of labour and the supply of industrial goods, foodstuffs and building materials.[5] In the course of the construction many questions were dealt with by the Sovnarkom of the RSFSR rather than by STO; even major decisions such as the variant of the line to be selected and the size of the estimate were first discussed by the Sovnarkom of the RSFSR and ratified shortly afterwards by STO. Local authorities were concerned throughout with such

---

[1] *Ibid.* pp. 241-243, 274, 286 (decree of the Sovnarkom of the RSFSR dated October 27, 1927 ; decree of STO dated October 28, 1927).
[2] *Ibid.* p. 257. For Shatov see *The Bolshevik Revolution, 1917–1923*, Vol. 1, p. 356.   [3] *Turkestano-Sibirskaya Magistral'* (1929), p. 244.
[4] *Sobranie Uzakonenii, 1927*, No. 9, art. 67 ; No. 23, art. 152 (decrees of January 9, February 23, 1927).
[5] *Sobranie Uzakonenii, 1927*, No. 23, art. 154 (dated February 23, 1927) ; *Turkestano-Sibirskaya Magistral'* (1929), pp. 282-283.

matters as the supply of timber and cement and the recruitment and training of local labour, and were actively involved in the preparation, under the auspices of the Gosplan of the USSR, of plans to develop the economy of the area.[1] The contrast with the highly centralized arrangements for Dnieprostroi, where the consumers of the power were mainly to be Union enterprises under the Vesenkha of the USSR, was significant.

Financial provision increased rapidly. Expenditure in 1926–1927 had been only 8 million rubles. Narkomput' requested an allocation of 25 million rubles for 1927–1928 ; and in its control figures for 1927–1928 Gosplan, perhaps still working on the basis of the sum of 80 million rubles over five years which had been agreed in November 1926, proposed an allocation of only 18 million rubles.[2] But, according to the decree of December 1926, construction was to be completed " within five years ", that is by the end of the economic year 1930–1931 ; and by the summer of 1927 the estimate for the total job had risen from the original 120 to 140-160 million rubles.[3] In September 1927, at a meeting of the Sovnarkom of the RSFSR, Ryskulov complained that, with the allocations now proposed by Gosplan and Narkomput', Turksib would take seven years to build, and requested a grant of 40 million rubles.[4] STO eventually agreed to allocate a sum of 32 million rubles, which was increased by a further 2 million rubles in May 1928 ; at the same time, it approved a proposal setting out in advance a capital investment grant for Turksibstroi for each of the three years 1928–1929 to 1930–1931. The increase in the total estimate for Turksibstroi to 204 million rubles was also approved.[5] These arrangements indicated the priority now

[1] *Turkestano-Sibirskaya Magistral'* (1939), pp. 276-277, 304, 309.

[2] *Torgovo-Promyshlennaya Gazeta*, August 23, 1927 ; *Kontrol'nye Tsifry Narodnogo Khozyaistva SSSR na 1927–1928 god* (1928), p. 168.

[3] *British-Russian Gazette and Trade Outlook*, iii (1927), No. 10, p. 378, gives 140 million rubles ; a figure of 160 million rubles is implied in *Torgovo-Promyshlennaya Gazeta*, August 23, 1927.

[4] *Ibid.* September 16, 1927 ; this figure had already been mentioned *ibid.* August 23, 1927.

[5] *Turkestano-Sibirskaya Magistral'* (1929), p. 276 (decrees of May 18 and 25, 1928). The planned grants (in million rubles) were :

1928–1929	58
1929–1930	69
1930–1931	47·5

enjoyed by Turksibstroi ; an important factor in this may have been that, at a time when the question of the future consumers of Dnieproges power remained unresolved, the proposed function of Turksib as a carrier of Siberian grain to the cotton-growing areas was clearly defined, and derived added importance from the grain difficulties of 1928.   Ryskulov later commented, with some disparagement of Dnieprostroi, that, since no other major construction had yet begun, all resources could be concentrated on Turksib.[1] By the end of 1928, some 330 kilometres of track had been laid in the north and 180 in the south, over one-third — though the easiest third — of the finally agreed length of 1481 kilometres.[2] The completion date was gradually brought forward : eventually the northern and southern sections joined on April 25, 1930, over a year earlier than was originally planned, and the line began running normally on January 1, 1931.[3]

[1] *Ibid.* p. 21.   [2] *Ibid.* pp. 11, 244, 254.
[3] *Ibid.* pp. 20, 295-296 ; B. Orlov, *Razvitie Transporta SSSR 1917–1962* (1962), p. 107.

NOTE A

MARKETED GRAIN PRODUCTION AND THE GRAIN COLLECTIONS

THE first claim on the grain harvest was, of course, that made by the cultivator for his own consumption and that of his family and animals. No statistics were kept of the amounts so consumed ; a rough guess could be made by deducting the amount of the crop marketed from the total amount produced. Difficulty arose, however, over the meaning of the term " marketed production " or " marketed part of the harvest ". The peasant who had produced in excess of his own needs habitually sold a substantial part of the surplus to other peasants, sometimes to those of his own village or locality, sometimes to those of more distant regions which were suffering from a shortage. These sales " on the peasant market " were normally, though not invariably, excluded from statistics of " marketed production ", partly perhaps because the compilers of the statistics were concerned primarily with the problem of supplying towns and factories, but mainly because accurate figures of this trade were impossible to obtain. Some sales on the peasant market were not paid for in cash, but were exchanges in kind, or payments for services. Some were direct sales by producers to other peasants in local booths or markets. Some were sales to private traders for re-sale to other rural areas. Apart from these uncertainties, most of these statistics were compiled on the basis of a limited number of perhaps unrepresentative peasant budgets. It was estimated by Groman that sales on the peasant market accounted in 1925–1926 for rather more than half the total of marketed production.[1] A similar estimate in terms of value appeared in the Gosplan control figures for 1927–1928.[2] Sales on the peasant market remained an uncertain and disturbing factor in any calculation of the distribution of agricultural products.

What, however, principally interested Soviet policy-makers and Soviet statisticians was what became of agricultural products after the needs of the peasant producer, and of other peasants to whom he trans-

[1] *Ekonomicheskaya Zhizn'*, April 2, 1927.
[2] *Kontrol'nye Tsifry Narodnogo Khozyaistva SSSR na 1927–1928 god* (1928), p. 477.

ferred part of his surplus production, had been catered for. The original conception of the Soviet authorities was that the part of the harvest not actually consumed on the farm would be disposed of in two different ways : by " sales on the peasant market " which could be neither controlled nor accurately computed, and by sales on what was called " the extra-rural (vnederevenskii) market ", which constituted " marketed production " or " the marketed part of the harvest " in the narrower sense. These were defined as " sales of products to satisfy the needs of the army, of the foreign market, of large-scale industry as a whole and of that part of small-scale industry which lies outside rural areas, and to satisfy the needs of that part of the urban population which is not covered by its own agricultural production ".[1]

On this basis, the " marketed part " of the grain harvest for 1926–1927 consisted of the " planned consumption " of the armed forces and industry, the consumption of other sectors of the urban population, and grain for export, amounting in all to almost exactly 10 million tons. To this was added (though not included in the " marketed part " in the strict sense) grain sold back to the agricultural population " from visible stocks " (i.e. not within the same village) amounting to 2·9 million tons, and certain minor items such as purchases of seed through seed loans or the seed fund. These additions brought up the total of sales " on the extra-rural market " to 13·2 million tons.[2] The picture was still further complicated by an upward revision, due to more extensive study of peasant budgets, from 2·9 to 5·9 millions in the figure for grain sold back to the agricultural population : this increase brought up the total grain turnover in 1926–1927 from 13·2 to more than 16 million tons.[3] The Central Statistical Administration handbook published in 1929 put the " marketed part " of the grain harvest in 1926–1927 at 16·2 million tons ; [4] the higher figure was evidently the result of this re-assessment of the total of " sales back " to the countryside " from visible stocks ". The revision did not, however, affect the total of approximately 10 million tons for the army and industry, for the urban population and for export (the " marketed part " in the narrower sense). This was the figure quoted by Stalin, on the authority of the statistician Nemchinov, in May 1928.[5]

Different estimates of total marketed production of grain were

[1] *Na Agrarnom Fronte*, No. 9, 1926, p. 133.
[2] *Statisticheskoe Obozrenie*, No. 9, 1927, pp. 62-63.
[3] *Ibid.* No. 12, 1929, pp. 58-59.
[4] *Statisticheskii Spravochnik SSSR za 1928 god* (1929), p. 280.
[5] Stalin, *Sochineniya*, xi, 85 ; V. Nemchinov, *Sel'skokhozyaistvennaya Statistika* (1945), p. 58. A later Soviet writer, struck by the discrepancy between the Gosplan–Nemchinov–Stalin figure of 10 million tons and the

reflected in different calculations of the ratio of marketed to total production. The *Konjunktur* institute of Narkomfin put it at 16·9 per cent ; the Central Statistical Administration at 20·6 per cent; the Nemchinov–Stalin figures, based on the Gosplan statistics, at 13·3 per cent. The *Konjunktur* institute calculated that 24 per cent of average pre-1914 grain production had been marketed, and that the " marketability " of grain in 1926–1927 had reached 72·4 per cent of the pre-1914 level ; the Nemchinov–Stalin figures put the pre-1914 percentage at 26, and calculated that the 1926–1927 percentage was barely more than half of this.[1] The absence of precise information about the basis of the pre-1914 figures makes it difficult to judge how far these were comparable. The evidence suggests, however, that a pre-war total of 18-19 million tons is roughly comparable with the 1926–1927 figure of 10 millions ; it is noteworthy that the substantial grain exports of the pre-1914 period had been drastically reduced in the nineteen-twenties. The multiplication of the number, and the reduction of size, of the units of production makes it certain that a substantially lower proportion of the grain harvest was brought to the market. But the statistical material available does not justify any precise estimate of the extent of the decline.

Statistics of the grain collections carried out by state and cooperative organs were compiled separately from those of marketed production, being concerned not with the way in which grain was disposed of to the consumer, but with the way in which it was acquired from the producer. These collections were described as " planned " or " centralized ". But certain local authorities were also entitled to collect grain for local requirements ; these were described as " non-planned " collections. Such arrangements appear to have been standardized in 1928, when it was decided that the central grain collections would cover the needs of workers, public servants and the Red Army, and that " small towns with a mainly non-worker population, as well as the non-worker population of large towns and factory centres " were to supply themselves from non-centralized collections or through the medium of the private market.[2] Outside the system of official collections, central and local,

---

Central Statistical Administration figure of 16·2 millions, and unaware of the different senses in which the term " marketed production " was used, implausibly attributed the lower figure to " the influence of certain workers in Gosplan who cultivated Menshevik-bourgeois theories of planning " (*Istoriya Sovetskogo Krest'yanstva i Kolkhoznogo Stroitel'stva v SSSR* (1963), p. 258).

[1] For the figures of the *Konjunktur* institute see *Ekonomicheskii Byulleten' Kon"yunkturnogo Instituta*, No. 11-12, 1927, pp. 4, 52 ; for those of the Central Statistical Administration see *Statisticheskii Spravochnik SSSR za 1928 g.* (1929), p. 280 ; for the Nemchinov–Stalin figures see p. 917, note 5 above.

[2] *Ekonomicheskoe Obozrenie*, No. 11, 1929, p. 132.

planned and non-planned, private traders purchased agricultural products in competition with state and cooperative organs, and generally at higher prices. Statistics of the centralized state and cooperative collections are probably reliable, those of non-planned and private collections, which are available only in the form of percentages, certainly less so.[1] The lack of correspondence between the grain collection figures and the Gosplan figures of marketed production is explained by the different basis on which they were drawn up. The former excluded grain collected and brought to the urban market by private traders (which was included in marketed production), and included grain collected by central organs and delivered to rural areas, e.g. to the cotton-growing regions of Central Asia (which was excluded from the Gosplan figures of marketed production). Hence it was natural that the Gosplan total of marketed production should exceed the total of the grain collections when private trade was large and fall below it as private trade contracted.

[1] For these statistics see Table No. 7, p. 943 below.

NOTE B

LENIN'S COOPERATIVE PLAN

AFTER the introduction of NEP Lenin modified his initial mistrust of the cooperatives as instruments of capitalism.[1] In his pamphlet of April 1921 *On the Food Tax*, he observed that, whereas cooperation was " a form of state capitalism " and " inevitably breeds petty bourgeois capitalist relations ", it was in Soviet conditions " favourable and useful at the present moment — of course, in a certain degree ". Having bracketed concessions and cooperatives as " forms of state capitalism ", he continued :

> The transition from cooperative organization of small producers to socialism is a transition from small to large-scale production, i.e. a transition more complex, but more capable in the event of success of embracing broader masses of population, capable of eradicating deeper and more vital roots of old pre-socialist and even pre-capitalist relations, which are most obstinate in their resistance to any " innovation ". . . . The cooperative policy in the event of success will give us an increase in small-scale production and facilitate its transition, in an undefined period, to large-scale production on principles of voluntary union.[2]

A few months later, the ninth congress of Soviets in December 1921 offered strong support to the agricultural cooperatives, *inter alia* " in order to facilitate a transition from the small holding to the large-scale comradely holding ".[3] More than a year afterwards, Lenin, in two short articles written in January 1923,[4] expressed the view that, with the proletariat in control of political power and of the basic economic institutions, the cooperatives might be found to provide " everything essential for the building of a full socialist society ". The articles were the unrevised jottings of a sick man, and were devoid of the incisive clarity characteristic of Lenin's writings. Their most serious ambiguity arose from Lenin's apparent failure to draw the distinction between

[1] See *The Bolshevik Revolution, 1917–1923*, Vol. 2, p. 337.
[2] Lenin, *Sochineniya*, xxvi, 336-337.
[3] *S"ezdy Sovetov v Dokumentakh*, i (1959), 172-173.
[4] See *Socialism In One Country, 1924–1926*, Vol. 1, p. 277 ; the articles are in Lenin, *Sochineniya*, xxvii, 391-397.

trading and producer cooperatives. Trade, both formerly and under
NEP, was treated as the normal activity of the cooperatives. What was
required was to combine " revolutionary enthusiasm " with " such
capacity to be a practical and educated trader as is fully sufficient to
make a good cooperator ". In existing conditions, however, " cooperative enterprises, as collective enterprises, are distinguishable from
private capitalist enterprises, but are in the same category as socialist
enterprises, if they are based on land and other means of production
belonging to the state, i.e. the working class " ; in these cryptic phrases,
Lenin seemed to be thinking, at any rate in part, of producer cooperatives. In the light of these reflexions, the growth of the cooperatives
was declared to be " identical for us . . . with the growth of socialism ".
It might have been inferred, though nothing specific supported the
inference, that Lenin thought of the coming evolution as leading from
trading cooperatives to producer cooperatives and thence to socialism.[1]
Nothing here was precise or explicit enough to deserve the name of a
" plan ".

For three years these utterances excited no great attention. Preobrazhensky, in his famous address to the Communist Academy in
August 1924 on *The Fundamental Law of Socialist Accumulation*, referred
rather cursorily to " a new kind of cooperatives representing a special
type of the transition of the small producer to socialism ", and named
" peasant communes and artels " as " one of the channels " of this new
form of cooperation under the dictatorship of the proletariat.[2] Bukharin,
in his reply published in *Pravda* on December 12, 1924, described Lenin
as having put forward " a vast definite plan ", and taunted Preobrazhensky with having found " *no* place for the *Leninist* cooperatives leading
the peasantry to socialism ", which were concerned with " cooperation
in trade (obrashchenie) " ; Preobrazhensky had spoken only of the
relatively unimportant producer " communes ". Bukharin at this stage
took a low view of producer cooperatives, and made no attempt to bring
them within the scope of Lenin's articles of 1923 :

> Here we shall come to socialism through the *process of trade*, not
> directly through the process of production ; we shall come to it
> through the cooperatives.[3]

The same view was implicit in the resolution of the third Union Congress of Soviets in May 1925 :

---

[1] This was Preobrazhensky's interpretation (E. Preobrazhensky, *Novaya
Ekonomika* (1926), pp. 208-209).

[2] *Ibid.* p. 111 ; for Preobrazhensky's continued scepticism about producer
cooperatives see p. 147 above.

[3] N. Bukharin, *Kritika Ekonomicheskoi Platformy Oppozitsii* (1926), pp.
17-19 ; for this article see *Socialism in One Country, 1924-1926*, Vol. 1, p. 207.

By way of uniting in cooperatives, the small peasant holding can avoid exploitation by capital and take an active part in socialist construction.[1]

This explained Bukharin's lukewarm attitude at this period to the kolkhozy, and his desire to subordinate them to the agricultural cooperatives.[2]

What lay behind Bukharin's thinking was expressed more clearly in a work by Chayanov, the former SR agricultural expert, on *The Organization of the Peasant Economy* published in 1925. Chayanov contrasted the method of " horizontal concentration ", meaning " the concentration of peasant lands into large producer units " and leading to " the proletarianization of the peasantry ", which he rejected as incompatible with Soviet policy, and the method of " vertical concentration " through the agricultural cooperatives, which he described as " one of the foundations of the economic order of the new society ". The cooperatives, starting as unions for the acquisition of means of production and developing into unions for the sale of agricultural products, would bring about by degrees " the industrialization of agriculture " and " the concentration and organization of agricultural production in new and higher forms ". Emphasis was laid on the gradualness of the process, which required " a new economic psychology ".[3] Thus what was required was not to promote collective cultivation by creating independent kolkhozy (or, by implication, Sovkhozy), but to allow it to develop under the aegis of the agricultural cooperatives. In this conception cooperatives and kolkhozy were thought of as the embodiment of policies opposed to one another. Bukharin further developed his views in a long essay called *The Road to Socialism*, published in the summer of 1925, in which he described the cooperatives as " the main road to socialism in our country " — the organization through which the essential link between worker and peasant would be maintained, and the contradiction between individual peasant production and state industry resolved. In terms which echoed Chayanov (though no evidence of direct borrowing exists, and the ideas were no doubt widely current), he wrote of the " separate peasant household " which, " under the influence of its own private small-producer interests, comes to the formation of social organizations, i.e. of marketing cooperatives ". Bukharin evidently still thought of cooperatives primarily as agents of trade and distribution. But at the end of the section on the coopera-

[1] *S"ezdy Sovetov v Dokumentakh*, iii (1960), 87-88.
[2] See *Socialism in One Country, 1924–1926*, Vol. 1, p. 221 ; for Rykov's endorsement of this thesis see *ibid.* Vol. 1, p. 280.
[3] A. Chayanov, *Organizatsiya Krest'yanskogo Khozyaistva* (1925), pp. 208-212 ; for Chayanov see p. 20 above.

tives he appeared to broaden the outlook :

> Thus the organization of the peasant economy begins with the trading cooperatives, continues with the industrial working-up of agricultural products, and finally ends with production in common properly so-called.[1]

Throughout this section, Bukharin did not quote Lenin's articles, or indeed refer to Lenin at all. Lenin's " vast definite plan " had been forgotten.

What happened next is obscure. In the autumn of 1926 an attempt was made — apparently without much success — to encourage the development of agricultural producer cooperatives.[2] A resolution of the party central committee of February 1927 announced that " the Leninist plan of individual membership of the cooperatives for the whole population in town and countryside as the road to socialism has found its confirmation in the fact of the enormously rapid growth of the co-operatives ".[3] But this resolution related to trade ; and nobody seems to have been interested to pursue the argument about producer co-operatives till in September 1927 the opposition, always eager to make Bukharin its target, and recalling his tactical move of 1925 to use the agricultural cooperatives as a counter-weight to the kolkhozy, condemned " the attempt to oppose Lenin's ' cooperative plan ' to his plan of electrification ", and proposed to devote " a much larger sum " to the creation of Sovkhozy and kolkhozy.[4] The fifteenth party congress three months later, in its resolution on the five-year plan, denounced the opposition proposal to withdraw funds from the cooperatives for the benefit of kolkhozy and Sovkhozy as " a blow at the whole of Lenin's cooperative plan ", and in another passage of the same resolution described opposition policy as incompatible with " *Lenin's cooperative plan* " ; and the resolution on work in the countryside again described the attitude of the opposition as " a renunciation of Lenin's cooperative plan ".[5] These appear to have been the first appearances of the phrase in authoritative party pronouncements. But from this time onwards

---

[1] N. Bukharin, *Put' k Sotsializmu* (1925), pp. 29-39.

[2] See p. 146 above.

[3] *KPSS v Rezolyutsiyakh* (1954), ii, 352 ; Larin in a work published in 1927 also defined the aim of " Lenin's cooperative plan " in a wide sense : " To draw on to its [i.e. the proletarian dictatorship's] side as a firm ally the overwhelming majority of simple working producers of commodities, and to find ways acceptable to them to re-shape the economy in the direction of approximation to a socialist order " (Yu. Larin, *Chastnyi Kapital v SSSR* (1927), p. 301).

[4] L. Trotsky, *The Real Situation in Russia* (n.d. [1928]), pp. 62, 71.

[5] *KPSS v Rezolyutsiyakh* (1954), ii, 461-462, 468, 476.

the plan was constantly invoked, no longer in the context of trade, or with reference to the specific organization of agricultural cooperatives, but in support of the expansion of the kolkhozy and of collectivization in general : the authors of the first five-year plan referred to the kolkhozy and to " various types of socialized and cooperative farming " as a " realization of Lenin's great cooperative plan ".[1] The first edition of the standard Soviet text-book of economics, published in 1928, quoting Bukharin as an authority, continued to denounce Preobrazhensky's theory of primitive socialist accumulation as opposed to " Lenin's cooperative plan ".[2]

In effect, two diametrically opposed interpretations of Lenin's " plan " now confronted each other. Bukharin reverted to his position of 1924, and in his *Pravda* article of January 24, 1929, on *The Political Testament of Lenin*, referred to " Lenin's cooperative plan " as a plan to maintain the link between workers and peasants through " cooperative exchange of goods " ; [3] and official commentators accused the Right opposition of " an opportunist conception of Lenin's plan, according to which the nub of the plan consists in the cooperative organization of the exchange of goods, and socialism is automatically brought into being through the exchange of goods ".[4] The issue was clinched when Stalin, in his address to the Marxist agrarian congress in December 1929, boldly declared that Lenin's article of 1923 applied to " all forms of cooperatives, both in their lower (supply, marketing) and in their higher (kolkhozy) forms ", and was especially relevant to " the kolkhozy of our period ".[5] Thereafter " Lenin's cooperative plan " was unconditionally identified with the policy of collectivization. The summit of disingenuousness seems to have been reached when Lenin's injunction in his last article to include the whole population in the cooperatives was cited in the party journal as an argument for the admission of *kulaks* to the kolkhozy.[6]

[1] *Pyatiletnii Plan Narodno-Khozyaistvennogo Stroitel'stva SSSR* (1929), ii, i, 287.
[2] I. Lapidus and K. Ostrovityanov, *Politicheskaya Ekonomika* (1928), pp. 395-399 ; the setting of this section in smaller type suggests that it was enlarged or amended after the work had been originally set.
[3] For this article see p. 247 above.
[4] *Na Agrarnom Fronte*, No. 5, 1929, pp. 21-22.
[5] Stalin, *Sochineniya*, xii, 162-163.
[6] *Bol'shevik*, No. 11, June 15, 1929, p. 27. In 1934 N. Popov, a party historian, wrote a monograph on *Lenin's Cooperative Plan*, which traced three stages in the development of the " plan " : before 1917, from 1917 to 1920, and after the introduction of NEP ; this publication seems to have been the culminating point of the myth (*Voprosy Istorii*, No. 3, 1961, p. 39 ; the work itself has not been available).

NOTE C

MIGRATION AND COLONIZATION

In 1926, when the machinery for the control and encouragement of migration within the USSR had been established,[1] the problem of " over-population ", or " land-deficiency " (malozemel'e), became a frequent topic of discussion and controversy. This was natural, since the relative concept of " over-population " has no measurable or scientific meaning, and is comprehensible only as an element in a programme for the redistribution of human energies and resources ; [2] in the Soviet Union it entered into the general argument on economic policy and prospects in a period of expansion. At the fourth Union Congress of Soviets in April 1927, Shlikhter estimated that in the RSFSR 10 per cent of the rural population was redundant, in White Russia 16 per cent and in the Ukraine 18 per cent.[3] What seems in retrospect remarkable is that nobody at this period, when industrial unemployment was still rife, contemplated a development of industry sufficiently rapid and intensive to take up the surplus rural population.[4]

In the later nineteen-twenties only two ways of dealing with rural over-population seemed possible : by introducing labour-intensive crops and bringing improved tools of production to the peasant on the spot, or by transplanting the peasant to regions where virgin soil offered hitherto untapped resources. The former seemed at first sight the more humane and the more promising. Bukharin supported it at the Moscow provincial party conference in January 1927, referring in particular to the development of technical crops.[5] Rykov at the fifteenth party congress later in the year cautiously observed that, though the Soviet Union embraced " enormous regions suitable for the settlement of surplus population ", the magnitude of the resources required for such an operation made it impracticable in the near future, and

[1] See *Socialism in One Country, 1924–1926*, Vol. 1, pp. 523-528.
[2] Stalin in December 1929 observed that the problem in Russia had never been an absolute shortage of land ; what had been lacking were resources to bring it into cultivation (Stalin, *Sochineniya*, xii, 155).
[3] *SSSR: 4 S"ezd Sovetov* (1927), pp. 428-429 ; this was the prelude to a complaint that the Ukraine did not get a fair share of the facilities for migration.
[4] See pp. 462-467 above.   [5] For this speech see pp. 12-13 above.

thought that the remedy for agrarian over-population and unemployment was " the intensification of agriculture, the development of labour-
consuming agricultural crops and the development of industry ".[1] This
was also the main method of overcoming " so-called ' agrarian over-
population ' " recommended in the resolution of the congress on work
in the countryside, " a correct migration policy " being barely mentioned almost as an afterthought at the end of the paragraph.[2] More
than a year later, Chubar argued at the sixteenth party conference that
instead of sending workers to expand grain production on virgin soil in
Siberia it would be better to increase it on the spot by the introduction
of tractors.[3] But this method also was limited by the paucity of resources in a backward economy ; and the mechanization of agriculture,
far from giving employment on the land to surplus rural population,
reduced the number of peasants required in agricultural work.[4] Meanwhile population continued to increase, and Strumilin's prognostication, made when the five-year plan was in preparation, that in the next
five years, even after intensification of agriculture and expansion of
industry, the surplus of rural population would, " in the best event,
merely not grow beyond its present dimensions ", still seemed to hold
good.[5]

Generally speaking, therefore, the view came to prevail in these
years that the main outlet for surplus rural population must be found in
migration to new territories which would thus be opened for cultivation
and add to the sources of the natural supply of grain. The Karelian
ASSR was opened to migrants by a decree of the RSFSR of September
6, 1926 ; and mention was later made of " experiments by the Murmansk railway in the settlement of the Murmansk–Karelian region ".
But these openings came to little.[6] Gamarnik at the fifteenth party

[1] *Pyatnadtsatyi S"ezd VKP(B)*, ii (1962), 874.
[2] *KPSS v Rezolyutsiyakh* (1954), ii, 472-473 ; the question was dealt
with in similar terms in the resolution on the five-year plan (*ibid.* ii, 460-461).
[3] *Shestnadtsataya Konferentsiya VKP(B)* (1962), p. 103.
[4] See pp. 415-416 above.
[5] S. Strumilin, *Ocherki Sovetskoi Ekonomiki* (1928), p. 447 ; Strumilin also
pointed out that large-scale mechanization was conceivable only " side by side
with the absorption of the cadres of surplus rural population " (*ibid.* p. 438).
[6] *Sobranie Uzakonenii, 1926*, No. 70, art. 548 (this seems to have been the
first official pronouncement which contemplated the settlement of migrants as
industrial workers — a foretaste of the industrialization of new regions in the
east) ; *Ekonomicheskoe Obozrenie*, No. 4, 1929, p. 115. Subsequently, " the
north . . . completely fell out " of the original plan as an area of settlement
(*ibid.* No. 3, 1929, p. 147), though the Karelian–Murmansk region was still
included in a decree of January 18, 1928 (see p. 928 below) ; according to a
source quoted in G. von Mende, *Studien zur Kolonisation in der Sovetunion*
(1933), p. 94, 1300 persons had been settled there by 1928.

conference in October 1926 strongly pressed for migration from the
crowded areas of the Ukraine and White Russia to the empty spaces of
Siberia and the Far East ; [1] and A. P. Smirnov about the same time
declared that " the solution for land-deficiency will be found only by
way of migration ".[2] A study of the problem made at this time estimated the surplus rural population at from 10 to 15 millions — mainly
in the Ukraine, in White Russia, in the Central Black Earth region of
the RSFSR and in the Middle Volga region ; in the more northern
regions of the RSFSR pressure was less acute and non-agricultural
employment more easily available. Re-settlement was possible only in
" empty or thinly populated borderlands ". Most of the migrants came
from " the poorer middle peasant households with grown up families ",
which were faced with " the dilemma either of breaking up into small,
minute holdings or of throwing new groups of unemployed into the
towns ". Migration offered the only chance " to maintain the unity of
the household in new places ".[3] Of migrants from 1925 to 1928 10·3
per cent had held no land, 39 per cent had less than 0·55 hectares (0·5
desyatins), 36·5 per cent from 0·55 to 1·09 hectares (0·5 to 1 desyatins) ;
the proportion taking animals or tools with them was insignificant.[4]
Under the agrarian code of 1922 (arts. 18 and 34) migrants had no right
to lease land left by them, and could therefore obtain no compensation
for it. By amendments to the code of December 1925 and February
1926 the right of leasing was allowed up to two or three years ; and in
1928 the limit was extended to six years.[5] This right was increasingly
exercised from 1926 onwards.[6] But 40 per cent of migrants simply
abandoned their holdings to the *mir* for redistribution, the rest leaving
them to members of the *dvor* who remained behind, or disposing of
them in some other way.[7] Later in the year, at the fifteenth party
congress, at which Rykov administered a cold douche to plans for large-
scale migration,[8] a delegate from the Far East embarked on a vigorous
plea for organized migration to Siberia and the Far Eastern region. A
commission which had been sent to investigate the situation had

[1] *XV Konferentsiya Vsesoyuznoi Kommunisticheskoi Partii (B)* (1927), pp.
253-254.   [2] *Na Agrarnom Fronte*, No. 11-12, 1926, p. 141.
[3] *Ibid.* No. 4, 1927, pp. 158-159.
[4] *Statisticheskoe Obozrenie*, No. 12, 1928, pp. 107, 109. By way of exception,
most of the small number migrating to the Volga region were middle or comparatively well-to-do peasants ; on the other hand those who went to the Far
East were poor peasants dependent on state subventions (*Ekonomicheskoe
Obozrenie*, No. 3, 1929, pp. 148, 155, 160).
[5] *Sobranie Uzakonenii, 1925*, No. 93, art. 674 ; *Sobranie Uzakonenii, 1926*,
No. 11, art. 89 ; *Sobranie Zakonov, 1928*, No. 8, art. 63.
[6] *Statisticheskoe Obozrenie*, No. 5, 1930, p. 88.
[7] *Ibid.* No. 12, 1928, p. 109.   [8] See p. 925 above.

reported that the organization was in confusion, and was two years behind the movement itself. A decision taken by Sovnarkom on October 4, 1927, presumably as a result of this report, and said to be awaiting confirmation by TsIK, to maintain the subordination of all organs concerned with migration to Narkomzem, and to ignore the regional executive committees in the receiving areas, would only make things worse.[1]

By this time, however, a certain change of emphasis had occurred in defining the purposes of migration. The Gosplan control figures for 1927–1928 observed, with the air of propounding a paradox, that " migration plays a significantly larger rôle from the economic point of view for the regions of settlement than for those from which the migrants come, though it has some effect in diminishing agrarian over-population ".[2] In spite of the slender encouragement derived from the fifteenth party congress, considerably more attention was paid in 1928 to the problems of migration — partly because the grain crisis had made the opening up of new sources of supply imperative, and partly because the machinery had begun to work more effectively. A major decree on migration of January 18, 1928,[3] named " the permanent economic integration of uninhabited or scarcely inhabited territories " as the primary purpose of migration policy ; its " chief task " was the settlement of the Far Eastern region, including Sakhalin and Kamchatka, the Siberian region, together with the adjacent parts of the Ural region, and the Karelian–Murmansk region : attention was also directed to the areas of Central Asia through which the projected Turksib railway would pass.[4] Funds made available to the Kazakh, Bashkir, Buryat–Mongolian and other autonomous republics were to be used

---

[1] *Pyatnadtsatyi S"ezd VKP(B)*, ii (1962), 937-941 ; the decision of October 4, 1927, was probably the foundation of the decree of January 18, 1928 (see below).

[2] *Kontrol'nye Tsifry Narodnogo Khozyaistva SSSR na 1927–1928 god* (1928), p. 118.

[3] *Sobranie Zakonov, 1928*, No. 8, art. 63.

[4] The Turksib project inspired in 1928 a far-reaching discussion of the possibilities of extensive grain cultivation in the virgin lands of Kazakhstan : such plans involved large-scale Russian immigration and the settlement of the nomadic local population (*Ekonomicheskoe Obozrenie*, No. 1, 1928, pp. 31-43) ; a critic of the scheme argued (*ibid.* No. 4, 1928, pp. 98-106) that only the northern sector of Kazakhstan had sufficient rainfall for grain cultivation, and that this was already well populated) ; see also G. von Mende, *Studien zur Kolonisation in der Sovetunion* (1933), pp. 76-77. On the other hand, a decree of the RSFSR of March 16, 1928, instructed Narkomtrud and Turksib to do their best to prevent a " spontaneous flow " of labour from the central regions seeking employment on the construction of the Turksib railway in competition with native labour (*Turkestano-Sibirskaya Magistral'* (1929), pp. 291-292).

primarily for migration and re-settlement within those republics, and secondarily for immigrants from other parts of the USSR. Authority at the centre continued to be exercised by the All-Union Migration Committee (VPK) attached to the TsIK of the USSR,[1] which was also instructed to prepare a plan of migration for the next 10-15 years. But measures to be taken in the receiving areas were the responsibility of the organs of the Narkomzems of the republics (in practice, almost exclusively, the RSFSR). Most important of all, substantial funds were for the first time provided in the budgets of the USSR and the RSFSR. The total had risen from 1,562,000 rubles in 1924-1925 to 6,189,000 rubles in 1925-1926 ; in 1926-1927 it jumped to 22,610,000 rubles, and in 1927-1928 to 26,257,000.[2] The decree provided for credits to poor and middle peasants to enable them to purchase the property of migrants leaving the region.[3] Preparation of land for settlement in advance of the arrival of the migrants was undertaken for the first time in 1926-1927.[4] As the authorities became more active, other aspects of public policy began to impinge on migration. A resolution of the Union congress of kolkhozy in May–June 1928 demanded " the preferential organization of migrants on collective principles ".[5] Six months later the peasant newspaper suggested that individual migration, which had cost millions of rubles and led to poor results, should be abandoned in favour of the settlement of Sovkhozy, and appealed to migrants to organize themselves in kolkhozy.[6]

Statistics of migration for these years are probably not very accurate, since they cover a movement which largely evaded control ; but they are sufficient to provide a general picture. The number of migrants increased steadily from 120,008 in 1925-1926 to 195,692 in 1927-1928 and jumped to 320,987 in 1928-1929.[7] These totals evidently included

[1] See *Socialism in One Country, 1924–1926*, Vol. 1, p. 524.
[2] For the sources of these figures, which probably give only a rough approximation to what was actually spent, see G. von Mende, *Studien zur Kolonisation in der Sovetunion* (1933), p. 107.
[3] It was calculated that migrants were in this way enabled to realize an average of 400-500 rubles on property left by them ; for landless migrants the average was only 277 rubles (*Statisticheskoe Obozrenie*, No. 5, 1930, p. 90).
[4] *Ekonomicheskoe Obozrenie*, No. 3, 1929, p. 156.
[5] *Pravda*, May 6, 1928 ; for this congress see p. 168 above.
[6] *Bednota*, December 28, 1928, February 8, 1929. It was later claimed that in 1928–1929 " the principles of collectivization had already begun to penetrate the migration movement " (*Statisticheskoe Obozrenie*, No. 5, 1930, p. 84) ; but little evidence of achievement on these lines has been found.
[7] *Statisticheskii Spravochnik SSSR za 1928 g.* (1929), pp. 66-67 ; *Statisticheskoe Obozrenie*, No. 5, 1930, pp. 84-85. The following table, taken from the same sources, gives figures for the three republics from which the migrants

" unplanned " migrants, and it is reasonable to suppose that the large
increase in numbers in 1929 was due not primarily to better organization and larger credits, but to harvest failures or to strife in the villages
over the grain collections. The proportion of unplanned migrants
from the RSFSR decreased from 70 per cent in 1925 to 33 per cent in
1928 and rose again to 54 per cent in 1929.[1] By far the most important
receiving area throughout this period was the Siberian region which in
1929 accounted for 63 per cent of the migrants. Next came the Far
Eastern region which took nearly 30 per cent in 1927 and 1928, but fell
away to less than 12 per cent in 1929 ; and this was followed by the
Ural region (for these purposes an annex of the Siberian region),
Kazakhstan and the Volga region.[2] The ratio of " re-migrants " returning from the settlement areas to migrants proceeding to those areas,
though far lower than in the earlier years, was still put at 22·1 per cent
for 1926, 26·4 per cent for 1927 and 1928, and 19 per cent for 1929.[3]

---

came (the number of migrants from the other republics was negligible) :

	1925/26	1926/27	1927/28	1928/29
RSFSR	78,070	90,745	102,851	190,825
Ukrainian SSR	21,945	43,945	57,713	68,449
White Russian SSR	19,871	26,895	34,741	61,067

[1] *God Raboty Pravitel'stva RSFSR 1926–27* (1927), p. 62 ; *God Raboty Pravitel'stva RSFSR 1928–29* (1929), p. 182. Of two official press reports of the spring of 1927, one stated that of all migrants to Siberia at this time " about half " were unplanned, the other that of 2000 settlers recently passing through Novosibirsk 400 were unplanned (*Izvestiya*, April 27, 1927 ; *Ekonomicheskaya Zhizn'*, March 8, 1927) ; according to *Statisticheskoe Obozrenie*, No. 12, 1928, p. 107, only 31 per cent of the migrants in 1925–1926 and 1926–1927 enjoyed the preferential railway tariffs accorded to " legal " or " planned " migrants ; the remaining 69 per cent must have been " illegal " or " voluntary " ; the proportion of " voluntary " migrants to the Far East may well have been lower than to other destinations. In 1928, owing to better organization, only one-third of all migrants (though one-half of those from the RSFSR) were said to have been voluntary and unaided (*ibid.* No. 5, 1930, p. 87).

[2] The following table (in percentages) gives the complete picture for the receiving areas :

	1925/26	1926/27	1927/28	1928/29
Siberia	55·2	35·8	41·9	62·9
Far East	10·3	28·4	29·3	11·8
Kazakhstan	7·9	6·7	4·6	7·2
Ural region	5·1	14·0	9·9	10·6
North Caucasus	10·7	3·3	1·3	0·5
Volga regions	7·9	11·1	9·3	3·9
Others	2·9	0·7	0·7	3·1

(*Statisticheskoe Obozrenie*, No. 5, 1930, p. 87).

[3] G. von Mende, *Studien zur Kolonisation in der Sovetunion* (1933), p. 94. Lower totals of re-migrants in 1926–1928 are given in *Ekonomicheskoe Obozrenie*,

The last detailed official plan of migration before the whole issue
was transformed by mass collectivization was announced in a decree of
February 13, 1929. The settlement of 210,000 migrants already provided for was to be completed, and preparations made for a further
119,800 migrants in 1929–1930. Of these 61,500 were to go to the Far
East, 45,000 to Siberia and 10,000 to Kazakhstan ; migration to other
regions was to be abandoned or reduced to insignificant proportions.
Of the migrants 45 per cent were to be taken from the RSFSR, 40 per
cent from the Ukraine, 15 per cent from White Russia.[1] About the
same time a report from Rabkrin led to a review of the whole policy in
a decree of March 6, 1929. Among the points emphasized were the
desirability of occupying " empty lands along the line of railways "
(another reference to the Turksib railway) and the need to arrange
settlement in such a way as to " assure the possibility of the maximum
development of mechanization and the collectivization of agriculture " ;
another article of the decree instructed the VPK to coordinate its plans
for migration with plans for the expansion of collective cultivation.[2]
The first five-year plan approved in the spring of 1929 provided that 25
per cent of migration should be in the form of collectives, and that
1,720,000 migrants were to be settled during the five-year period (with
provision made for a further 400,000). Significantly, attention was also
drawn to the need for the settlement in the Far Eastern region not only
of agricultural workers, but of craftsmen, artisans and persons engaged
in mining, hunting and fishing. The development of new regions was
now a primary factor in migration policy.[3]

The settlement of Jewish workers on the land [4] continued intermittently in this period. The regions of the USSR where Jewish over-
population was most acute (though this was urban rather than rural
over-population) were the White Russian SSR and the Western region
of the RSFSR. In White Russia a number of Jewish kolkhozy were
established ; [5] in the Western region of the RSFSR, according to a
party report of 1929, 45 Jewish kolkhozy with a total membership of
3000 had at that time been established, while 2180 Jews from the same
region had been settled elsewhere in the Soviet Union.[6] The southern

No. 3, 1929, p. 152 ; on the other hand the very high figure there given for
1925 is not confirmed by other sources.
    [1] *Sobranie Zakonov, 1929*, No. 14, art. 115.   [2] *Ibid.* No. 24, art. 209.
    [3] *Pyatiletnii Plan Narodno-Khozyaistvennogo Stroitel'stva SSSR* (1929), i,
215; ii, 133.   [4] See *Socialism in One Country, 1924–1926*, Vol. 1, pp. 528-529.
    [5] *Na Agrarnom Fronte*, No. 5, 1928, pp. 115-122.
    [6] M. Fainsod, *Smolensk under Soviet Rule* (1958), p. 444.

Ukraine and the Crimea continued to be the favoured area for Jewish settlement. In December 1926 the " Azov flats " were allocated by decree of the RSFSR for the purpose, but the prohibitive cost of reclaiming the land, estimated at 11 million rubles, caused the scheme to be abandoned.[1] In January 1928, by agreement between Zernotrest and the Jewish-American Agro-Joint, which supplied foreign currency to purchase equipment, a Sovkhoz of 50,000 hectares in the Crimea was established by Jewish settlers.[2] Most Jewish settlers in the Crimea came from White Russia ; few of them had been previously engaged in agriculture, 50 per cent being traders, 20 per cent artisans or craftsmen, 10 per cent workers and 5 per cent intellectuals.[3] In spite of this handicap, the efficiency and initiative of Jewish settlers contrasted favourably with the helplessness of other immigrants, and their desire " to occupy themselves seriously with agriculture " was noted.[4] The number of Jews working on the land in various parts of the Soviet Union rose from 35,000 in 1920 and 92,000 in 1924 to 200,000 at the beginning of 1929 ;· and plans were on foot to settle a further 10,000 Jewish families on the land in White Russia and in the Ukraine. In 1926–1927 Jewish settlers were said to have occupied 51,000 desyatins of land in the Ukrainian SSR, 32,000 in the Crimea and smaller areas in the White Russian SSR and in the northern Caucasus.[5] By 1929 half-a-million hectares of land in various European regions of the USSR had been allocated for Jewish settlement.[6] These measures sometimes encountered resistance from the local population. A report of the presidium of the TsIK of the White Russian SSR in December 1926 declared that the peasantry had " become convinced of the usefulness of these measures and overcome its initial suspiciousness of the affair ".[7] But a White Russian delegate at the congress of agrarian Marxists in December 1929 alleged that those who occupied land allocated for Jewish settlement in White Russia were primarily " not poor peasants, but the well-to-do part of the Jewish population, . . . merchants, members of the rabbinate and other free professions, including even persons ' working ' on the black market ".[8]

Meanwhile an initiative had been undertaken of a kind vaguely

---

[1] Na Agrarnom Fronte, No. 3, 1929, pp. 77-78.

[2] Ibid. No. 3, 1929, p. 77 ; another article ibid. No. 6-7, 1928, p. 58, evidently referring to the same agreement, gives the area as 100,000 desyatins and the number of settlers as 15,000.   [3] Ibid. No. 3, 1929, p. 81.

[4] Ibid. No. 3, 1928, p. 122.

[5] Sovetskoe Stroitel'stvo, No. 5-6 (10-11), May–June 1927, p. 170.

[6] Na Agrarnom Fronte, No. 3, 1929, pp. 76-77.

[7] Sovetskoe Stroitel'stvo, No. 1 (6), January 1927, pp. 138-139.

[8] Trudy Pervoi Vsesoyuznoi Konferentsii Agrarnikov-Marksistov, i (1930), 139.

adumbrated as early as 1925 [1] — an attempt to create a specifically Jewish district or region — though the choice of so distant and unpropitious a territory for the experiment may have betokened divided counsels and grudging approval of the project. On March 21, 1928, a decree of the USSR was issued revising and elaborating the decree of 1925 on the powers of " the committee for the settlement on the land of Jewish toilers " (Komzet) ; [2] and a week later a decree of the RSFSR vested in Komzet an area of three-and-a-half million hectares in eastern Siberia on the Amur river, known as Birobijan, to be occupied by Jewish settlers.[3] The offer, which combined the desire to find a convenient solution of the Jewish national problem with the desire to plant new settlers in the Far East, seems to have evoked no enthusiasm in any quarter. Komzet drew up a plan to settle 10,000 families in the region within five years, but estimated the cost at 25 million rubles — a figure which made the project quite unrealistic. Larin described the region as unsuitable " for such human material as *townsmen going over for the first time to agriculture* ", and compared the plan with the notorious project of settling the Jews in Uganda.[4] In the summer of 1928 only 416 Jewish families were recruited to take up residence in Birobijan — all of them workers or artisans ; and, in spite of an extensive publicity campaign, and many inflated estimates, the number of settlers never appears to have exceeded a few thousand.[5]

[1] See *Socialism in One Country, 1924–1926*, Vol. 1, p. 529.
[2] *Sobranie Zakonov, 1928*, No. 21, art. 188.
[3] *Na Agrarnom Fronte*, No. 3, 1929, p. 84.
[4] *Ibid.* No. 3, 1929, pp. 85-86.
[5] *Pravda*, May 28, 1932, put the number at 12,000, *Izvestiya*, December 10, 1932, at 9000.

NOTE D

INDUSTRIAL STATISTICS

THE problem of collecting and classifying statistics from tens of thousands of industrial units scattered over the vast territory of the USSR was simplified by the device, already employed long before 1917, of dividing industry into two major categories for statistical purposes, " census " (tsenzovaya) or large-scale (krupnaya) industry, and " non-census " (netsenzovaya) or small-scale (melkaya) industry. " Census " industry included industrial units (zavedeniya) which had the qualification (tsenz) of employing 16 workers or more, in the case of units which used mechanical motive power, and 30 workers or more, in the case of those which did not ; all industry which did not fall within this qualification was classified as " small-scale ". Many exceptions to the general rule were introduced for the statistics of particular industries.[1] Over 13,000 industrial units fell within the qualification in 1926–1927, 9000 of these being in the state sector.[2] A further distribution was made for planning and statistical purposes by classifying industry directly subordinate to the Vesenkhas of the USSR and the republics, and some of the more important units subordinate to the local Soviets, as " planned " or " Vesenkha-planned " industry ; this category embraced industry responsible for 75 per cent of the output of census industry in 1925–1926 and 80 per cent in 1928–1929.[3] These distinctions were not always clearly maintained in Soviet publications, particularly those which themselves obtained their material from secondary sources.[4]

Soviet industry was divided for statistical purposes into a number of industrial groups (gruppy), such as " chemical industry " and " food, drink and tobacco industry " (pishchevkusovaya promyshlennost'), which were in turn divided into branches (otrasli) ; thus the chemical industry included such branches as " basic ", " chemical-pharma-

[1] For these definitions see *Fabrichno-Zavodskaya Promyshlennost' SSSR: Osnovnye Pokazateli ee Dinamiki za 1924/25, 1925/26 i 1926/27 gg.* (1929), p. 30.
[2] *Ibid.* p. 16, Tablitsy, p. 4.   [3] See Table No. 12, p. 947 below.
[4] Even the usually reliable *Pokazateli Kon"yunktury Narodnogo Khozyaistva SSSR za 1923/24–1928/29 gg.*, ed. A. Mendel'son (1930), a Gosplan publication, reproduced on pp. 17-20 figures obtained from Vesenkha which are described as being for " all large-scale state industry ", but are lower than the standard series for " Vesenkha-planned " industry alone.

ceutical " and " soap, fats and perfumes ".[1] Each industrial unit was
attached for statistical purposes to the branch of industry which predominated in its production, and its total activity appeared in the
statistics of that branch. The statistics for groups and branches of
industry were in turn combined into two major Groups, Group A, production of means of production (producer or capital goods), and
Group B, production of articles of consumption (consumer goods).[2]
Group A included the coal, oil, ore, silicate (excluding china and earthenware), metal, electro-technical, chemical A (basic chemical, products
from bones, paints and dyestuffs, wood-chemical and " other "),
timber and timber products, and " other " industries ; Group B
included the textile, clothing, toilet, leather, china and earthenware,
Chemical B (rubber, match, fats and perfumes, and chemical-pharma-
ceutical), food, printing and paper industries.[3] In most statistical series
all the industrial units in a particular branch were assigned to the same
Group, and all the production of each unit was recorded with its branch.
The result was that the published statistics include consumer goods
produced by Group A branches of industry under Group A and producer goods produced by Group B industries under Group B.[4]

[1] *Fabrichno-Zavodskaya Promyshlennost' SSSR : Osnovnye Pokazateli ee
Dinamiki za 1924/25, 1925/26 i 1926/27 gg.* (1929), Tablitsy, pp. 4, 6. Changes
in definitions of different branches of industry were frequent (see, for example,
ibid. p. 31) ; and these classifications are somewhat different from those used
by Vesenkha in *Promyshlennost' SSSR v 1926/27 godu* (1928).
[2] For the relation between Groups A and B and Marx's Departments I and
II, see p. 422 above.
[3] *Pokazateli Kon"yunktury Narodnogo Khozyaistva SSSR za 1923/24–
1928/29 gg.*, ed. A. Mendel'son (1930), p. xiii. This conventional division
between the two groups sometimes led to confusion. In July 1926 Vesenkha
officials explained to Dzerzhinsky that, though the current plan showed a higher
rate of increase in Group A than in Group B industries, the rate of growth of
production for the consumer market and of production for the needs of industry,
transport and construction would be approximately equal, since some heavy
industries in fact worked for the consumer (F. Dzerzhinsky, *Izbrannye Proiz-
vedeniya* (1957), ii, 351) ; conversely, an industrial planner claimed in February
1928 that a recalculation of the *promfinplan*, which showed a more rapid expansion of Group B industries, would indicate a more or less equal rate of growth of
consumer and producer industries (*Torgovo-Promyshlennaya Gazeta*, February
17, 1928).
[4] In the control figures of Gosplan for 1926–1927, industrial production
was classified into Group A and Group B by taking each commodity separately ;
from 1927–1928 onwards Gosplan followed the more usual method of placing the
production of a whole industry in either Group A or Group B (*Kontrol'nye Tsifry
Narodnogo Khozyaistva SSSR na 1927–1928 god* (1928), pp. 55–56, note). In
order to mitigate the defects of the latter method, it was modified by splitting
up certain industries between Group A and Group B (see, for example, *Kontrol'nye Tsifry Narodnogo Khozyaistva SSSR na 1929/30 god* (1930), p. 444).

Although the trust remained the legal entity, the individual factory in census industry was responsible for recording statistical information and transmitting it to the authorities; in 1927 the journal of Red directors reported that most factories had their own system of statistical records of production and costs.[1] In this procedure, the trust and the *glavk* were by-passed, and merely received copies of relevant forms; [2] primary information was sent by the factories to the central department of statistics (TsOS) of Vesenkha and, through the provincial statistical departments, to the Central Statistical Administration. The monthly report-cards and forms submitted by the factories were the ultimate source of most statistical information about industry.[3] Gosplan had no independent channels for collecting industrial statistics but utilized and reworked the information collected by Vesenkha and the Central Statistical Administration.[4] Narkomfin collected much of its own data on the finances of industry, but otherwise depended on information collected by other government agencies. Statistics of small-scale industry were much less readily available and much less reliable. The Central Statistical Administration carried out two censuses of small-scale industry relating to this period, an 8-9 per cent sample in 1926–1927 and a 25-50 per cent sample in 1928–1929.[5] For other years, Gosplan and other organizations relied on their own estimates; [6] the resulting discrepancies are illustrated in Table No. 12, p. 947 below.

The most well-established, and at this time probably the most reliable, statistical series were those for industrial production, which were collected both in physical terms (for 75 products) and in monetary terms. The statistics of production in value terms distinguish between " gross turnover " (valovoi oborot), which is the value of all goods, semi-manufactures, materials and repair work, including goods unfinished in the period in question, " gross production " (valovaya produktsiya),

[1] *Predpriyatie*, No. 10, 1927, pp. 44-47.

[2] See the complaint in *Torgovo-Promyshlennaya Gazeta*, May 19, 1928.

[3] The procedures for collecting industrial statistics are discussed in *Fabrichno-Zavodskaya Promyshlennost' SSSR: Osnovnye Pokazateli ee Dinamiki za 1924/25, 1925/26 i 1926/27 gg.* (1929), pp. 30-32 ; *Torgovo-Promyshlennaya Gazeta*, May 19, 1928 ; *Ocherki po Istorii Statistiki SSSR*, [i] (1955), p. 229; iv (1961), 176-177 ; *Istoriya Sovetskoi Gosudarstvennoi Statistiki* (1960), p. 88.

[4] Vesenkha was specifically enjoined to supply regular information to Gosplan by a decree of STO dated August 14, 1925 (*Sobranie Zakonov, 1925*, No. 56, art. 423 ; for other aspects of this decree, see p. 825 above).

[5] *Ocherki po Istorii Statistiki SSSR*, [i] (1955), pp. 229-230 ; see also p. 390 above.

[6] *Kontrol'nye Tsifry Narodnogo Khozyaistva SSSR na 1928-1929 god* (1929), p. 407.

which is gross turnover less semi-manufactures produced and consumed by the reporting unit, and " commodity production " (tovarnaya produktsiya), goods and semi-manufactures completed ready for sale (i.e. unfinished production is excluded).¹ All these statistics in value terms contained a certain amount of double-counting. Most series showed the total sum of the production of all the factories concerned, so that materials and semi-manufactures transferred between factories were counted as part of the output both of the factory which produced them and of the factory which used them.² For the purpose of calculating national income, however, the Central Statistical Administration made estimates of net production (chistaya produktsiya), to obtain which both the value of all raw materials and producer goods used within industry during the period concerned and an allowance for depreciation were deducted from the figures for gross production.³ In making comparisons of production measured in value terms over time, the complicated question arose of turning statistics in the current prices of different periods into prices of a standard year. At first, pre-war 1913 prices were always used ; and on their monthly report-card factories were required to show production in pre-war as well as in current prices.⁴ From the summer of 1927 onwards, submission of plans calculated in terms both of current prices and of 1926–1927 prices became a standard requirement ; and from 1928 onwards statistical reports were also submitted in 1926–1927 prices as well as in current prices.⁵ The published series on industrial production in 1926–1927 prices at this period were, however, normally obtained by applying price-indexes to the production figures in current prices which factories had supplied on their monthly report-cards.⁶

As the system of industrial planning developed, complaints about the complexity and unreliability of the system of statistical reporting were frequently voiced ; and factories complained of being over-burdened with forms and requests for information.⁷ For all its defects, however, the system of industrial statistics, already highly developed by the middle nineteen-twenties, undoubtedly facilitated the speedy introduction of centralized planning and control of the national economy.

¹ *Ocherki po Istorii Statistiki SSSR*, [i] (1955), 222-224.
² *Ibid.* [i] (1955), 224-225, 227, 230 ; *Pokazateli Kon"yunktury Narodnogo Khozyaistva SSSR za 1923/24–1928/29 gg.*, ed. A. Mendel'son (1930), p. xiii. This was the method of " factory evaluation " ; the methods of " trust evaluation " and " branch evaluation " were also used.
³ *Ocherki po Istorii Statistiki SSSR*, [i] (1955), 226-227.
⁴ *Torgovo-Promyshlennaya Gazeta*, May 19, 1928.
⁵ *Ocherki po Istorii Statistiki SSSR*, [i] (1955), 225, 233.
⁶ *Kontrol'nye Tsifry Narodnogo Khozyaistva SSSR na 1929/30 god* (1930), p. 444.   ⁷ See for example *Predpriyatie*, No. 7, 1927, pp. 22-23.

2 H 2

NOTE E

TRADE UNIONS AND PRIVATE ENTERPRISE

A CURIOUS anomaly arose from the relation of the trade unions to workers in private and concession enterprises, estimated in 1926 to number from 150,000 to 180,000 ; of these two-thirds were in petty concerns employing from one to three workers, mainly in the food industries, and most of the remaining one-third in timber concessions.[1] The problem was how " to combine the economic advantage of utilizing private capital with the conduct of trade union work in the spirit of the class struggle against capital ". In 1926, 88 per cent of workers in private enterprises belonged to the trade unions, and made up 4·2 per cent of union membership. In general, private enterprises were said to have abandoned their earlier attitude of open hostility and aloofness, and sought to assimilate themselves to Soviet and trade union procedures. Even in foreign concessions, directors, managers and administrators joined the trade union (as they would have done in a nationalized enterprise) : this had now been prohibited. Trade union circulars calling for production conferences to promote rationalization and reduce costs had been sent to private enterprises and concessions. " Attempts " were reported " on the part of the unions to participate in organizing the economy of private enterprises and even actually to participate in the administration of these enterprises ".[2] The party central committee, in a resolution of August 23, 1926, on workers in private and concession enterprises, issued the cryptic instruction " to struggle against breaches of party and trade union discipline by members of the [party] cell and against failure in class solidarity in mutual relations with employers " ;[3] and three months later a " directive

[1] *Izvestiya Tsentral'nogo Komiteta VKP(B)*, No. 35-36 (156-157), September 6, 1926, p. 1.

[2] *Professional'nye Soyuzy SSSR, 1924–1926: Otchet k VII S"ezdu* (1926), pp. xi, 84-91 ; the president of the Ukrainian trade union council alleged that in some private enterprises joint production conferences were held, and trade union members shared in the profits of enterprises (*Stenograficheskii Otchet 3ᵍᵒ Vseukrainskogo S"ezda Profsoyuzov* (1927), p. 38).

[3] *Izvestiya Tsentral'nogo Komiteta VKP(B)*, No. 37-38 (158-159), September 20, 1926, p. 4.

letter " from the trade union central council to such workers sought to reconcile " the practical utility of the conduct of these enterprises in the interests of the working class " with the need not to subject the worker to capitalist control and make him an instrument of capitalist gain.[1] But, so long as these enterprises existed, the dilemma remained. Two years later members of the technical and administrative staff of concessions and relatives of the owners of private enterprises disguised as workers in these enterprises were still enrolled in trade unions.[2] The unions, faced with the need at all costs to increase production, did little to interfere with these not very important instances of collaboration between labour and private capital. As late as the spring of 1929, the party central committee prohibited party members from occupying " administrative posts in concession or private enterprises ", but admitted exceptions to the rule with the sanction of a regional or higher party committee.[3]

[1] *Trud*, December 3, 1926.
[2] *Professional'nye Soyuzy SSSR, 1926–1928: Otchet k VIII S"ezdu* (1928), p. 85
[3] *Izvestiya Tsentral'nogo Komiteta VKP(B)*, No. 13 (272), May 14, 1929, p. 28.

TABLES

A: AGRICULTURE

Table No. 1

Sown Area
(in thousand hectares)

	1913	1925	1926	1927	1928	1929
Grain *	94,400	87,300	93,700	94,700	92,200	96,000
Cotton	688	591	654	802	971	1,056
Flax	1,398	1,576	1,566	1,581	1,736	2,054
Sugar-beet (for factory use)	649	534	538	665	770	771
Potatoes	3,064	5,023	5,205	5,462	5,678	5,692
Other crops †	4,801	9,276	8,637	9,190	11,645	12,427
Total *	105,000	104,300	110,300	112,400	113,000	118,000

* Rounded to nearest 100,000 in original table.
† Residual : includes sunflower, hemp and tobacco.

Source : *Sotsialisticheskoe Stroitel'stvo SSSR* (1935), pp. 322-323.

Table No. 2

Agricultural Production

	1925	1926	1927	1928	1929
Grain (million tons) [a]	72·5	76·8	72·3	73·3	71·7
All Products (million rubles at 1926–1927 prices) [b]	15,342	16,485	16,273	16,568	17,019 *
Including Grain [b]	3,608	3,881	3,592	3,551	3,650 *
All Products (million rubles at current prices) [b]	15,939	16,485	17,530	21,183	20,393 *
Including Grain [b]	4,743	3,881	3,913	5,392	5,236 *

* Planned figure.

Sources : [a] *Sotsialisticheskoe Stroitel'stvo SSSR* (1935), p. 361.
[b] *Kontrol'nye Tsifry Narodnogo Khozyaistva SSSR na 1929/30 god* (1930), pp. 532-537.

Table No. 3

Number of Animals
(in thousands)

	1925	1926	1927	1928	1929
Horses	26,147	28,428	31,193	33,205	33,969
Cattle	59,838	63,274	67,320	69,762	68,069
Sheep and Goats	115,300	123,531	137,386	145,086	147,158
Pigs	21,060	21,027	22,552	25,619	20,890

Source: *Kontrol'nye Tsifry Narodnogo Khozyaistva SSSR na 1929/30 god* (1930), pp. 530-531.

Table No. 4

Marketed Production * of Agriculture

	1925–1926	1926–1927	1927–1928	1928–1929 (Preliminary)
Grain (million tons)	9·4	9·8	8·3	8·3
All Products (in million rubles at 1926–1927 prices)	2523	2610	2794	3062
Including Grain	491	542	452	449
All Products (in million rubles at current prices)	2671	2609	2948	3168 †
Including Grain	626	538	493	529 †

* For a definition of " marketed production ", see Note A, pp. 916-918 above ; these figures refer to " extra-rural " sales only.
† Planned figure.

Sources: *Kontrol'nye Tsifry Narodnogo Khozyaistva SSSR na 1929/30 god* (1930), pp. 538-541 ; the figures in current prices are taken from *Kontrol'nye Tsifry Narodnogo Khozyaistva SSSR na 1928–1929 god* (1929), p. 479.

Table No. 5

Marketed Production of Agriculture by Method of Collection *
(in percentages of total)

		Planned †	Non-Planned ‡	Private	Total
All Agricultural	1926–1927	56·4	9·5	31·1	100·0
Products	1927–1928	65·1	8·7	26·2	100·0
Grain	1926–1927	79·3	8·8	11·0	100·0
	1927–1928	84·3	9·2	6·5	100·0
Animal Products	1926–1927	44·2		55·8	100·0
	1927–1928	56·4		43·6	100·0

* " Extra-rural " sales only (see Note A, pp. 916-919 above).
† Central state and cooperative collections.
‡ Local collections.

Source : *Na Agrarnom Fronte*, No. 5, 1929, p. 12.

Table No. 6

Marketed Production of Grain by Category of Producer

(a) Amount Supplied by Each Category
(in million tons with percentages in brackets)

	Total Marketed Production	Sovkhozy	Kolkhozy	Peasant Households
1927	8·7	0·50 (5·7)	0·17 (1·9)	8·1 (92·4)
1928	7·6	0·57 (7·5)	0·28 (3·8)	6·6 (88·7)
1929	10·7	0·60 (5·5)	0·91 (8·5)	9·2 (86·0)

(b) Marketed Production as Percentage of Total Production of each Category

	All Producers	Sovkhozy	Kolkhozy	Peasant Households
1927	17·7	63·6	35·4	16·8
1928	16·1	68·2	39·9	14·7
1929	21·7	62·4	42·8 *	19·9

* Kalinin in the spring of 1929 put the ratio of marketed production at 48 per cent for communes, 36 per cent for *artels* and 30 per cent for TOZy (*SSSR: 5 S"ezd Sovetov* (1929), No. 15, p. 29).

Source : *Sdvigi v Sel'skom Khozyaistve SSSR* (2nd ed. 1931), p. 14.

Table No. 7

Monthly Grain Collections by State and Cooperative Agencies
(in thousand tons)

(a) Total

	1925–1926	1926–1927	1927–1928	1928–1929
July	194	226	288	97
August	945	767	998	557
September	1212	1424	1382	1415
October	848	1540	1074	1714
November	682	1560	696	974
December	797	1505	696	973
January	737	952	1284	616
February	908	876	1881	498
March	771	694	1165	476
April	609	438	246	324
May	420	307	301	172
June	292	301	371	486
Total for Agricultural Year	8415	10,590	10,382	8302

(b) Wheat and Rye

	1925–1926	1926–1927	1927–1928	1928–1929
July	166	194	263	56
August	659	665	936	405
September	794	1152	1154	1024
October	617	1228	816	1157
November	467	1179	496	604
December	483	1097	510	607
January	445	695	986	362
February	527	642	1462	303
March	490	520	887	251
April	418	332	180	161
May	284	255	230	85
June	228	256	287	285
Total for Agricultural Year	5578	8215	8207	5300

Source: *Pokazateli Kon''yunktury Narodnogo Khozyaistva SSSR za 1923/24–1928/29 gg.*, ed. A. Mendel'son (1930), pp. 51, 56.

Table No. 8
Stocks of Wheat and Rye
(in thousand tons)

	In Countryside		In Towns	
	Stocks at Beginning of Year (October 1)	Net Increase (+) or Decrease (−) during Year	Stocks at Beginning of Year (October 1)	Net Increase (+) or Decrease (−) during Year
1925–1926	2416	+1919	905	+129
1926–1927	4335	+2409	1034	+220
1927–1928	6744	−678	1254	−87
1928–1929	6066	−230 *	1167	—

* Estimated figure.

Source : *Statisticheskii Spravochnik za 1928 g.* (1929), pp. 236-237.

Table No. 9
Kolkhozy
(a) Number and Membership of Kolkhozy

	No. of Kolkhozy *	No. of Households (in thousands)	No. of Persons (in thousands)
October 1, 1926	17,874	217·2	868·8
October 1, 1927	18,840	286·1	1185·9
October 1, 1928	38,139	595·5	2534·7
June 1, 1929	60,282	1094·3	4814·8

(b) Sown Area and Marketed Production of Kolkhozy

	Sown Area Collectivized (in thousand hectares)	Percentage of Total Sown Area in USSR	Marketed Production (in million rubles) †	Percentage of Total Marketed Production in USSR
1926–1927	994·3	0·9	90·0	1·0
1927–1928	1830·6	1·6	119·5	1·8
1928–1929	4857·4	4·0	423·5	5·7

* Figures for numbers and production of kolkhozy vary considerably in different sources. According to a Soviet critic, four figures were in circulation for the number of kolkhozy on October 1, 1926 — 15,207 (Narkomzem), 9385 (Narkomfin), 10,063 (Central Statistical Administration) and 11,851 (Kolkhoztsentr). Yet another figure — 12,147 — appeared in a report to the fifteenth party congress ; it has been suggested that this was arrived at by taking the mean of the other figures (*Voprosy Istorii*, No. 1, 1965, p. 14).

† A table in *Kontrol'nye Tsifry Narodnogo Khozyaistva SSSR na 1928–1929 god* (1929), p. 241, gives substantially lower figures of marketed production for 1926–1927 and 1927–1928.

[*continued*

Table No. 9 (*continued*)

(c) Types of Kolkhozy

	October 1, 1927		October 1, 1928		June 1, 1929	
	Number	Percent-age of Total	Number	Percent-age of Total	Number	Percent-age of Total
Communes	1,377	7·3	1,920	5·0	3,328	5·5
Artels	8,675	46·1	12,928	34·0	25,127	41·7
TOZy	8,788	46·6	23,391	61·0	31,827	52·8
Total	18,840	100·0	38,139	100·0	60,282	100·0

Source : *Kolhhozy SSSR: Statisticheskii Spravochnik* (1929), pp. 9, 13, 15.

Table No. 10

Tractors

(a) Total Number
(on October 1 of each year)

1926	19,541	1928	26,733
1927	24,504	1929	34,943

(b) Number Delivered in Each Year

	Total	Soviet-built	Imported	Soviet-built as Percentage of Total
1925–1926	13,000	732	12,368	5·6
1926–1927	5,680	660	5,020	11·6
1927–1928	3,334	850	2,484	25·5
1928–1929	9,466	2800	6,666	29·6

Source : *Sotsialisticheskoe Stroitel'stvo SSSR* (1934), p. 166.

Table No. 11

Area under *Kontraktatsiya*
(in thousand hectares)

	1927–1928	1928–1929 (Plan)	1928–1929 (Actual)
Grain	6060	10,000	19,131
Technical Crops	3190	5,104	4,609
Including :			
Oil-Seeds	1041	1,650	1,145 *
Cotton and Flax	1204	1,838	1,794
Sugar	594	659	630
Tobacco	45	68	69
(including Makhorka)			

* This figure appears to relate to sunflower seeds alone and may therefore not be comparable with those for 1927–1928 and 1928–1929 (Plan).

Source : *Kontrol'nye Tsifry Narodnogo Khozyaistva SSSR na 1928–1929 god* (1929), pp. 246-247 ; *Kontrol'nye Tsifry Narodnogo Khozyaistva SSSR na 1929/30 god* (1930), p. 543. For a table giving percentages of crops covered by *kontraktatsiya*, ranging in 1927–1928 from 13 per cent for grain to 80 per cent for tobacco and 100 per cent for cotton, and showing an almost five-fold increase for the whole area under *kontraktatsiya* in 1929, see *Na Agrarnom Fronte*, No. 5, 1929, pp. 15, 19.

B : INDUSTRY

Table No. 12

Gross Industrial Production
(in million rubles)

(a) in current prices

	Vesenkha-planned Industry	All Census Industry	Small-scale Industry	All Industry
1925–1926	7,517	9,965	4185	14,141
1926–1927	8,763	11,439	4603	16,042
1927–1928	10,632	13,566	4748	18,314
1928–1929 *	13,120	16,416	4985	22,292

Source : *Kontrol'nye Tsifry Narodnogo Khozyaistva SSSR na 1929/30 god* (1930), pp. 422-423.

(b) in 1913 prices

	All Census Industry	Small-scale Industry	All Industry
1913	6390	2040	8,430
1925–1926	5720	1860	7,580
1926–1927	6720	2040	8,760
1927–1928	8140	1940	10,080
1928–1929 *	9890	—	—

Source : *Ekonomicheskoe Obozrenie*, No. 9, 1929, p. 114 (Gukhman's calculations) ; the figure for 1928–1929 has been estimated from alternative calculations for census industry in 1913 prices in *Kontrol'nye Tsifry Narodnogo Khozyaistva SSSR na 1929/30 god* (1930), pp. 438-439. According to a western calculation, the production of civilian industry was 17 per cent higher in 1928–1929 than in 1913 (G. W. Nutter, *Growth of Industrial Production in the Soviet Union* (Princeton, 1962), p. 525).

* The figures for 1928–1929 are provisional ; they are the amount anticipated when the control figures for 1929–1930 were drawn up towards the end of 1928–1929.

Table No. 13

Gross Production of Group A and Group B Industries
(in million rubles at 1926–1927 prices)

	1925–1926	1926–1927		1927–1928		1928–1929 *	
	Total	Total	Percentage Increase over previous Year	Total	Percentage Increase over previous Year	Total	Percentage Increase over previous Year
1. Vesenkha-planned Industry							
Group A	2,966	3,762	26·8	4,663	23·9	6,053	29·8
Group B	4,347	5,000	14·9	6,404	28·1	7,641	19·3
Total	7,313	8,763	16·6	11,067	26·3	13,693	23·7
2. All Industry							
Group A	3,493	4,332	24·0	5,197	20·0	6,390	23·0
Group B	10,196	11,710	14·8	13,896	18·7	15,902	14·4
Total	13,689	16,042	17·2	19,093	19·0	22,292	16·8

* Provisional figures (see note to Table No. 12).

Source : *Kontrol'nye Tsifry Narodnogo Khozyaistva SSSR na 1929/30 god* (1930), pp. 422–423, 503.

Table No. 14

Quarterly Index of Gross Production of Census Industry
(Same period of previous year = 100)
(in current prices)

	Group A Industries				Group B Industries				All Census Industry			
	1925–1926	1926–1927	1927–1928	1928–1929	1925–1926	1926–1927	1927–1928	1928–1929	1925–1926	1926–1927	1927–1928	1928–1929
First Quarter (October–December)	155·0	131·4	111·0	120·3	162·9	115·8	111·2	116·7	160·3	121·0	111·1	118·0
Second Quarter (January–March)	148·0	123·4	122·3	115·3	152·1	104·2	128·1	113·8	150·5	111·2	125·7	114·4
Third Quarter (April–June)	149·0	114·0	119·9	—	136·7	109·8	124·5	—	141·4	111·5	121·6	—
Fourth Quarter (July–September)	146·3	109·5	119·8	—	131·9	113·2	119·0	—	137·9	111·6	119·3	—
Whole Year (October–September)	149·4	119·1	118·2	—	146·4	110·9	119·7	—	147·5	114·0	119·0	—

Source: *Pokazateli Kon''yunktury Narodnogo Khozyaistva SSSR za 1923/24–1928/29 gg.*, ed. A. Mendel'son (1930), p. 36.

Table No. 15

Gross Production of Census Industry by Sector

(in million rubles at current prices)

	1925–1926		1926–1927		1927–1928		1928–1929 *	
	Amount	Percentage	Amount	Percentage	Amount	Percentage	Amount	Percentage
State Industry	8918	89·6	10,447	91·3	12,374	90·8	[14,791]	90·1
Cooperative Industry	639	6·4	734	6·4	1,053	7·8	[1,477]	9·0
Private Industry	363	3·6	204	1·8	111	0·8	[49]	0·3
Concession Industry	35	0·4	54	0·5	79	0·6	[98]	0·6
Total Census Industry	9956	100·0	11,439	100·0	13,618	100·0	16,416	100·0

* Provisional figures; the absolute figures for each sector are approximate, calculated from the absolute total figure and the percentage breakdown given in the original sources.

Sources: *Promyshlennost' SSSR v 1927/28 godu* (1930), p. 64; G. Krzhizhanovsky and others, *Osnovnye Problemy Kontrol'nykh Tsifr Narodnogo Khozyaistva SSSR na 1929/30 god* (1930), appendix table 4.

Table No. 16

Major Industrial Products in Physical Terms

	1913	1925–1926	1926–1927	1927–1928	1928–1929 *
Coal (million tons)	28·9	25·4	32·1	35·4	40·6
Crude Oil (million tons)	9·3	8·5	10·3	11·8	13·7
Electric Power (milliard kilowatt-hours)	1·9	3·2	3·9	5·2	6·5
Pig-iron (million tons)	4·2	2·2	3·0	3·3	4·0
Crude Steel (million tons)	4·3	2·0	3·0	4·2	4·7
Rolled Steel (million tons)	3·5	2·2	2·8	3·3	3·8
Agricultural Implements (million rubles at pre-war list prices)	67	70	97	129	185
Metal-cutting Machine Tools (thousands)	1·5	1·1	1·9	1·9	3·8
Electric Light Bulbs (millions)	2·9	13·5	13·3	13·7	19·1
Cement (million barrels)	12·3	8·5	9·7	11·9	14·4
Superphosphate (thousand tons)	55	80	90	150	213
Cotton Yarn (thousand tons)	271	240	277	322	353
Sugar (thousand tons)	1290 †	1063	870	1340	1280

* Provisional figures, except those for metal-cutting machine-tools and electric light bulbs. † 1914.

Sources : All figures are from *Kontrol'nye Tsifry Narodnogo Khozyaistva SSSR na 1929/30 god* (1930), pp. 437-438, except those for metal-cutting machine tools and electric light bulbs, which are from *Dvadtsat' Let Sovetskoi Vlasti* (1937), p. 26; *Promyshlennost' SSSR v 1926/27 godu* (1928), pp. 208, 258; *Promyshlennost' SSSR v 1927/28 godu* (1930), pp. 261, 309; and *Sotsialisticheskoe Stroitel'stvo SSSR* (1936), p. 37.

Table No. 17

Capital Investment in Census Industry by Sector *
(in million rubles at current prices)

	1925–1926	1926–1927	1927–1928	1928–1929†
Vesenkha-planned Industry	811	1098	1325	1679
Other State Industry	105	144	259	329
Total State Industry	916	1242	1584	2008
Cooperative Industry	26	28	31	38
Private Industry	61	63	64	56
Total Census Industry	1003	1333	1679	2102

* These and other capital investment figures refer to gross investment without deduction of investment in capital repairs.
† Provisional figures.

Source : *Kontrol'nye Tsifry Narodnogo Khozyaistva SSSR na 1929/30 god* (1930), p. 454 ; minor differences will be found between the figures for Vesenkha-planned industry here and in Table No. 18.

Table No. 18

Capital Investment in Vesenkha-planned Industry *
(in million rubles at current prices)

	1925–1926	1926–1927	1927–1928	1928–1929 †
1. Coal Industry	77 [a]	139 [b]	135 [c]	161 [c]
2. Oil Industry	150 [a]	180 [b]	213 [c]	218 [c]
3. (a) Iron and Steel Industry	71 [a]	111 [a]	198 [c]	235 [c]
(b) General Engineering (Union Trusts)	26 [a]	49 [a]	48 [a]	69 [f]
(c) Other Metal and Metal-working Industries †	93	122	122	146
Total Metal Industries	190 [g]	282 [b]	367 [c]	450 [c]
4. Electrical Industry	12 [a]	20 [a]	20 [c]	28 [c]
5. Chemical Industry Group A	39 [h]	45 [h]	58 [c]	139 [c]
6. Chemical Industry Group B	10 [h]	16 [h]	17 [c]	22 [c]
7. Textile and Tailoring Industries	147 [g]	174 [b]	191 [c]	201 [c]
8. Food Industry	68 [g]	65 [b]	88 [c]	95 [c]
9. Building Materials Industry §	33 [g]	43 [b]	68 [c]	104 [c]
10. Timber Industry	17 [g]	30 [b]	46 [c]	75 [c]
11. Other Industries ‡	68	74	100	166
Total	811 [g]	1068 [b]	1304 [c]	1659 [c]

* As no consistent series is available covering all these years, this Table has been compiled from several different sources.
† Provisional figures.   ‡ Residuals.
§ This entry is listed as " silicates industry " in 1925–1926 and 1926–1927.

Sources : [a] *Pervye Shagi Industrializatsii SSSR 1926–1927 gg.* (1959), pp. 121, 145, 153 ; these figures are from a report of the Vesenkha of the USSR to STO dated August 2, 1928.
[b] *Promyshlennost' SSSR v 1926/27 godu* (1928), p. 90.
[c] *Pyatiletnii Plan Narodnogo-Khozyaistvennogo Stroitel'stva SSSR* (1929), ii, i, 264.
[f] *Metall,* No. 11, 1929, pp. 95-109.
[g] *Ekonomicheskoe Obozrenie,* No. 10, 1927, p. 125.
[h] *Promyshlennost' SSSR v 1927/28 godu* (1930), p. 39.

Table No. 19

Stock of Fixed Capital in Census Industry
(in million rubles at 1926–1927 prices)

	October 1, 1925		October 1, 1929	
Vesenkha-planned Industry		5577		9,281
of which, Group A	2842		5612	
Group B	2735		3499	
Other State Industry		356		1,128
Total State Industry		5933		10,409
Cooperative Industry		348		318
Private Industry		679		774
Total Census Industry		6860		11,501

Source : *Kontrol'nye Tsifry Narodnogo Khozyaistva SSSR na 1929/30 god* (1930), pp. 446-447.

Table No. 20

Costs of Production in Industry
(as percentage increase (+) or decrease (−) on costs of previous year)

	1925–1926	1926–1927	1927–1928	1928–1929
Plan for Year	−7·0	−5·0	−6·0	−7·0
Actual : First Six Months	—	+1·2	−5·3	−1·9
Actual : Second Six Months	—	−5·6	+0·2	—
Actual : Whole Year	+1·7	−1·8	−5·1	−4·0 to −4·5

Sources : *Kontrol'nye Tsifry Narodnogo Khozyaistva SSSR na 1928–1929 god* (1929), pp. 280-281, except for the actual figures for 1928–1929, which are from *Protokol Zasedaniya Prezidiuma VSNKh SSSR, 1928–1929*, No. 19, Prilozhenie, and *Ekonomicheskoe Obozrenie*, No. 12, 1929, p. 17. The final official figure for 1927–1928 was 6·2 per cent (see p. 345 above).

C: LABOUR

Table No. 21

Number of Employed Persons
(annual average in thousands)

	1925–1926	1926–1927	1927–1928	1928–1929
Census Industry	2,678	2,839	3,096	3,366
Building *	426	547	723	918
Transport	1,240	1,302	1,270	1,302
Agriculture (including Forestry, Fishing, etc.)	2,008	2,078	2,037	2,028
State Establishments	2,151	2,340	2,426	2,504
Other Employed Persons	1,671	1,839	2,047	2,050
Total	10,173	10,944	11,599	12,168

* The annual averages for building workers conceal large seasonal fluctuations ; monthly figures for numbers of workers in building will be found in *Trud v SSSR* (1936), p. 244.

Sources : *Trud v SSSR* (1936), pp. 10-11, except for figures for persons employed in state establishments, which are from *Ekonomicheskoe Obozrenie*, No. 9, 1929, p. 124 (for a more detailed break-down of employees in state establishments see Table No. 22).

Table No. 22

Number of Persons Employed in State Establishments by
Type of Establishment
(in thousands)

	1925–1926	1926–1927	1927–1928	1928–1929
Administrative and Judicial	663·1	674·4	650·8	646·8
Science, Education and Social Welfare	602·8	714·7	776·9	825·1
Health, Medical and Veterinary	323·7	365·1	406·4	429·2
Economic Management	195·2	139·9	168·7	159·3
Others	365·8	395·8	423·1	443·2
Total	2150·6	2339·9	2425·9	2503·6

Source : *Ekonomicheskoe Obozrenie*, No. 9, 1929, p. 124.

Table No. 23

Wage-earners in Agriculture
(in thousands)

	1927	1928	1929
Proletariat in the Socialized Sector (Sovkhozy, Kolkhozy)	526	547	591
Proletariat in the Private Sector (Peasant Holdings)	1841	1804	1660
Semi-proletariat	4643	4288	3694

Source : *Trudy Pervoi Vsesoyuznoi Konferentsii Agrarnikov-Marksistov*, i (1930), 305.

Table No. 24

Labour Productivity in Census Industry
(Previous year = 100 ; measured in pre-war prices)

	1925–1926	1926–1927	1927–1928	1928–1929 (Preliminary)
All Industry	112	109	112	116
Group A Industry	109	114	115	114
Group B Industry	116	107	109	115

Source : *Ekonomicheskoe Obozrenie*, No. 10, 1929, p. 143 ; these figures refer to output per man-day.

Table No. 25

Monthly Wages in State Census Industry
(in rubles at current prices)

(a) Average Monthly Wage in Each Year by Branch of Industry*

	1926–1927	1927–1928	1928–1929
All State Census Industry	58·5	64·4	70·9
All Group A Industries	62·3	69·0	75·9
All Group B Industries	54·0	59·8	65·4
Coal-mining	53·9	56·8	61·3
Metal Industries	69·1	77·6	86·3
Electrical Industry	92·6	102·2	110·7
Textiles	49·3	53·3	57·4

Source : *Ekonomicheskoe Obozrenie*, No. 12, 1929, p. 204.

(b) Average Monthly Wage in Each Quarter*

	October–December	January–March	April–June	July–September	Average for Year
1925–1926	49·9	49·7	52·7	56·4	52·2
1926–1927	57·1	55·9	58·8	62·1	58·5
1927–1928	62·3	64·0	63·8	67·8	64·5
1928–1929	67·9	67·8	72·0	76·1	71·0

Source : *Pokazateli Kon"yunktury Narodnogo Khozyaistva SSSR za 1923/24–1928/29 gg.*, ed. A. Mendel'son (1930), pp. xii, 20, 150.

* These figures refer only to state industry on which data was collected by TsOS of Vesenkha (see Note D, p. 934, note 4 and p. 936 above).

(c) Average Monthly Wage in Each Year by Category of Employment

	1926	1927	1928	1929
Workers	57	63	69	75
Technical and Office Staff	106	115	128	134
Service Personnel	37	42	47	51

Source : *Trud v SSSR* (1936), p. 96.

Table No. 26

Payments from Social Insurance Fund
(in million rubles)

	1925–1926	1926–1927	1927–1928 (Preliminary)	1928–1929 (Plan)
Permanent Disability Pensions	110·3	157·4	203·8	250·9
Temporary Sickness Benefit	196·8	216·8	239·7	264·8
Other Temporary Benefits (Maternity, etc.)	83·7	81·2	69·8	61·9
Medical Services	195·4	239·6	240·5	258·1
Rest-homes, etc.	31·8	41·3	35·8	36·5
Subvention to Housing Fund	22·6	33·1	34·9	37·4
Unemployment Benefit	47·8	69·6	112·7	129·1
Old Age Pensions	—	—	—	8·0
Costs of Administration	34·0	33·3	31·3	29·0
Reserve	—	—	0·6	50·0
Total	722·4	872·3	969·2	1125·7

Source : *Kontrol'nye Tsifry Narodnogo Khozyaistva SSSR na 1928–1929 god* (1929), p. 162.

Table No. 27

Internal Trade Turnover

	In Million Rubles			In Percentages		
	1925–1926	1926–1927	1927–1928 (Plan)	1925–1926	1926–1927	1927–1928 (Plan)
(a) Syndicates	2,772	3,800	4,400	11·8	13·2	13·2
(b) Torgi	1,272	1,340	1,450	5·4	4·7	4·3
(c) Share Companies	1,019	1,300	1,360	4·3	4·5	4·0
(d) Enterprises on *Khozraschet*	1,462	1,500	1,570	6·2	5·2	4·7
(e) Others	1,187	1,315	1,440	5·0	4·6	4·3
1. Total for State Organs	7,718	9,255	10,220	32·7	32·2	30·5
(a) Consumer Cooperatives	7,053	10,130	12,700	29·9	35·2	38·0
(b) Agricultural Cooperatives	2,133	3,050	3,870	9·0	10·6	11·6
(c) Industrial Cooperatives	440	600	880	1·9	2·1	2·6
2. Total for Cooperatives	9,624	13,780	17,450	40·8	47·9	52·2
3. Private Trade	6,262	5,740	5,770	26·5	19·9	17·3
Total	23,606	28,775	33,440	100·0	100·0	100·0

Source : *Kontrol'nye Tsifry Narodnogo Khozyaistva SSSR na 1927–1928 god* (1928), p. 246.

Table No. 28

Internal Wholesale Trade by Sector
(in million rubles)

	1925–1926		1926–1927		1927–1928 (Plan)	
	Amount	Percentage of Total	Amount	Percentage of Total	Amount	Percentage of Total
State Trade	6,234	55·1	7,640	50·2	8,460	44·8
Cooperative Trade	4,100	36·2	6,793	44·7	9,688	51·2
Private Trade	988	8·7	780	5·1	750	4·0
Total Trade	11,322	100·0	15,213	100·0	18,898	100·0

Source: *Kontrol'nye Tsifry Narodnogo Khozyaistva SSSR na 1927–1928 god* (1928), pp. 484-485; for earlier figures see *Socialism in One Country, 1924–1926*, Vol. I, p. 424. After 1927 private wholesale trade was "almost nil" (G. Neiman, *Vnutrennyaya Torgovlya SSSR* (1935), p. 119).

2 I

Table No. 29

Internal Retail Trade by Sector
(in million rubles)

	1923–1924		1924–1925		1925–1926		1926–1927		1928		1929	
	Amount	Percentage of Total	Amount	Percentage of Total	Amount	Percentage of Total	Amount	Percentage of Total	Amount	Percentage of Total	Amount	Percentage of Total
State Trade	846	15·7	1190	15·3	1,544	13·2	1,817	13·3	2,409	15·9	3,198	18·9
Cooperative Trade	1437	26·6	3284	42·2	5,224	44·5	6,838	49·8	9,341	61·6	11,396	67·6
Private Trade	3117	57·7	3300	42·5	4,963	42·3	5,064	36·9	3,407	22·5	2,273	13·5
Total Trade	5399	100·0	7773	100·0	11,732	100·0	13,718	100·0	15,157	100·0	16,867	100·0

Source: *Sotsialisticheskoe Stroitel'stvo SSSR* (1935), pp. 552-553; the figures for the earlier years do not correspond precisely with the percentages quoted in *Socialism in One Country, 1924-1926*, Vol. I, p. 424. Slightly different figures are given in *Sovetskaya Torgovlya: Statisticheskii Sbornik* (1956), p. 14, according to which private trade reached its maximum turnover in 1926.

Table No. 30

Index Numbers of Wholesale Prices *

(1913 prices = 100)

	All Products	Industrial Products	Agricultural Products
October 1, 1925	174	195	156
January 1, 1926	183	198	169
April 1, 1926	196	202	191
July 1, 1926	183	204	164
1925–1926 Annual Average †	186	201	171
October 1, 1926	178	204	157
January 1, 1927	177	203	155
April 1, 1927	177	196	160
July 1, 1927	173	191	157
1926–1927 Annual Average †	176	197	157
October 1, 1927	170	188	154
January 1, 1928	171	188	156
April 1, 1928	171	188	156
July 1, 1928	172	187	157
1927–1928 Annual Average †	172	188	157
October 1, 1928	176	187	166
January 1, 1929	177	187	167
April 1, 1929	179	188	170
July 1, 1929	180	187	174
1928–1929 Annual Average †	179	188	171

    * Index numbers of the Central Statistical Administration.
    † This is the average of the index for each of the twelve months of the economic year.

    Source : *Pokazateli Kon"yunktury Narodnogo Khozyaistva SSSR za 1923/24 –1928/29 gg.*, ed. A. Mendel'son (1930), pp. 95-97, 156.

Table No. 31

Index Numbers of Retail Prices *

(1913 prices = 100)

	All Products			Industrial Products			Agricultural Products		
	All Trade	Socialized Trade	Private Trade	All Trade	Socialized Trade	Private Trade	All Trade	Socialized Trade	Private Trade
October 1, 1925	201	197	209	215	208	231	180	178	183
January 1, 1926	207	200	219	219	200	239	188	183	195
April 1, 1926	215	207	231	222	212	243	205	198	216
July 1, 1926	213	205	229	223	212	247	198	191	208
1925–1926 Annual Average †	210	202	224	220	210	242	194	187	202
October 1, 1926	206	198	224	220	209	247	186	180	196
January 1, 1927	207	197	227	219	207	251	187	181	198
April 1, 1927	200	190	227	209	198	242	186	175	208
July 1, 1927	196	184	229	202	192	235	186	171	220
1926–1927 Annual Average †	201	191	226	210	199	242	186	176	207

October 1, 1927	193	183	226	198	189	235	185	173	215
January 1, 1928	195	184	234	199	188	240	189	175	225
April 1, 1928	195	185	239	198	189	242	190	177	233
July 1, 1928	200	185	264	198	188	243	204	180	293
1927–1928 Annual Average †	197	184	244	198	188	242	194	177	278
October 1, 1928	199	185	263	198	188	247	201	180	285
January 1, 1929	203	189	273	200	190	254	209	186	299
April 1, 1929	210	192	313	203	192	268	223	191	381
July 1, 1929	217	195	345	205	193	280	240	200	450
1928–1929 Annual Average †	210	192	308	203	191	269	222	192	367

* Index numbers of *Konjunktur* institute of Narkomfin. The figures reproduced here are the so-called "new" indices of the *Konjunktur* institute; the "old" index for private trade, which was compiled until October 1927, was somewhat higher (e.g. annual average was 232 in 1925–1926 and 237 in 1926–1927; for details, see *Pokazateli Kon"yunktury Narodnogo Khozyaistva SSSR za 1923/24–1928/29 gg.*, ed. A. Mendel'son (1930), pp. xvi, 107–109).

† This is the average of the index for each of the twelve months of the economic year.

Source: *Pokazateli Kon"yunktury Narodnogo Khozyaistva SSSR za 1923/24–1928/29 gg.*, ed. A. Mendel'son (1930), pp. 98–106, 156–157.

Table No. 32

Average Annual Market Prices of Agricultural Products
(in rubles per ton)

	1924–1925	1925–1926	1926–1927	1927–1928	1928–1929
Rye	71·8	76·3	89·1	119·0	284·9
Oats	69·3	67·1	72·6	94·6	118·1
Flax	446·8	354·1	294·3	349·6	445·5
Hemp	467·0	474·9	384·0	420·8	404·3
Potatoes	16·5	22·6	20·8	39·1	67·0
Meat	280·0	333·0	385·0	486·0	516·0
Milk	58·0	64·0	77·0	77·0	126·0

Source : Quoted from official archives in V. Yakovtsevsky, *Agrarnye Otnosheniya v SSSR* (1964), p. 173.

Table No. 33

Index Numbers of Average Annual Prices Paid to Producers for
Agricultural Products
(1910–1913 average prices = 100)

	Official Collections	Private Collections
1925–1926	146	159
1926–1927	134	149
1927–1928	141	156
1928–1929	157	183

Sources : *Kontrol'nye Tsifry Narodnogo Khozyaistva SSSR na 1929/30 god* (1930), pp. 578-580.

Table No. 34

Monthly Index Numbers of Prices Paid for Grain by State and
Cooperative Agencies *

(1909–1913 average prices = 100)

	1925–1926	1926–1927	1927–1928	1928–1929
July	143	106	113	122
August	134	107	117	137
September	134	116	115	138
October	126	107	114	139
November	125	107	114	137
December	134	108	115	137
January	142	108	116	138
February	150	107	114	139
March	151	111	114	138
April	145	110	115	137
May	134	111	114	138
June	118	113	114	—
Annual Average for Agricultural Year	132	108	115	136 †

* This index was calculated by the economic department of Narkomtorg, and refers to prices paid by "planned collection agencies" (*Pokazateli Kon"yunktury Narodnogo Khozyaistva SSSR za 1923/24–1928/29gg.*, ed. A. Mendel'son (1930), pp. xiv-xv).

† Average of eleven months.

Source : *Pokazateli Kon"yunktury Narodnogo Khozyaistva SSSR za 1923/24–1928/29 gg.*, ed. A. Mendel'son (1930), p. 70.

Table No. 35

The " Scissors " (Ratio of Index Number of Retail Prices of
Industrial Products to Index Number of Planned Delivery Prices
of Agricultural Products)
(Ratio in 1913 = 100)

October 1, 1925	154	October 1, 1927	138
January 1, 1926	149	January 1, 1928	135
April 1, 1926	150	April 1, 1928	138
July 1, 1926	167	July 1, 1928	137
1925–1926 Annual Average	156	1927–1928 Annual Average	137
October 1, 1926	162	October 1, 1928	127
January 1, 1927	155	January 1, 1929	127
April 1, 1927	145	April 1, 1929	128
July 1, 1927	143	July 1, 1929	131
1926–1927 Annual Average	151	1928–1929 Annual Average	128

Source : *Pokazateli Kon"yunktury Narodnogo Khozyaistva SSSR za
1923/24–1928/29 gg.*, ed. A. Mendel'son (1930), p. 111.

Table No. 36

Average Daily Consumption per Head of Population
(in grams)

(a) Rural Population

	1924	1925	1926	1927	1928
	Consuming Zone				
Rye Flour	513	475	466	457	453
Wheat Flour	27	35	47	45	39
Sugar	8	12	14	18	21
Meat	64	115	106	102	121
Milk and Dairy Products	349	303	334	351	316
Other Foodstuffs	1212	1090	1057	1043	1037
All Foodstuffs	2173	2029	2023	2016	1986
	Producing Zone				
Rye Flour	283	249	221	203	199
Wheat Flour	259	311	331	311	302
Sugar	5	10	11	16	18
Meat	79	102	97	102	105
Milk and Dairy Products	288	250	275	259	253
Other Foodstuffs	963	869	922	833	967
All Foodstuffs	1877	1791	1855	1725	1844

[continued

Table No. 36 (*continued*)

(b) Urban Population

	1924	1925	1926	1927	1928
	Workers' Families				
Rye Flour	211	170	157	147	158
Wheat Flour	264	316	305	307	313
Sugar	24	32	37	45	50
Meat	128	154	151	154	160
Milk and Dairy Products	171	177	179	190	176
Other Foodstuffs	757	586	630	584	583
All Foodstuffs	1555	1434	1458	1427	1440
	Employees' Families				
Rye Flour	153	122	119	115	123
Wheat Flour	270	300	295	280	295
Sugar	33	43	50	57	60
Meat	151	178	172	164	172
Milk and Dairy Products	247	234	240	236	213
Other Foodstuffs	681	545	592	511	561
All Foodstuffs	1535	1422	1469	1363	1425

Note. These figures, compiled by the Central Statistical Administration, are for October of each year.

Source : *Sel' skoe Khozyaistvo 1925–1928* (1929), pp. 402-405, 408-411.

Table No. 37

Exports and Imports
(in million rubles at current prices)

	1913	1925–1926	1926–1927	1928	1929
Exports					
Agricultural	1119·6	421·3	470·2	369·6	398·0
Industrial	400·5	255·3	300·2	430·0	525·7
Total	1520·1	676·6	770·5	799·5	923·7
Imports					
Producer Imports *	884·4	590·5	607·8	835·8	749·7
Consumer Imports	392·0	153·5	82·9	79·3	89·3
Other	97·6	12·3	22·0	38·0	41·6
Total Imports	1374·0	756·3	712·7	953·1	880·6
Balance	+146·1	−79·7	+57·8	−153·6	+43·1

* Raw materials and equipment.

Source : *Narodnoe Khozyaistvo SSSR* (1932), p. xlviii ; see also *ibid.* pp. 387-389, 395-397 for more detailed figures for 1928 and 1929.

Table No. 38

Major Exports in Physical Terms
(in thousand tons)

	1913	1925–1926	1926–1927	1928	1929
Grain	9647	2069	2161	89	262
Timber Products	7598	1922	2485	3410	5544
Oil	947	1473	2086	3005	3852

Source : *Narodnoe Khozyaistvo SSSR* (1932), p. xlviii.

Table No. 39

Imports by Type of Product
(in million rubles at current prices)

(a) Imports by Product Groups

	1925–1926	1926–1927	1927–1928
Raw Materials	262·6	319·5	371·5
Semi-Manufactures	161·8	117·9	140·0
Equipment	102·9	147·8	239·9
Automobiles etc.	14·5	7·9	9·9
Supplies for Agriculture	65·8	44·0	45·5
Total Producer Goods	607·8	637·1	806·8
Total Consumer Goods	148·6	75·4	137·7
Total Imports	756·4	712·5	944·5

(b) Imports of Raw Materials

	1925–1926	1926–1927	1927–1928
Cotton	117·8	131·5	154·2
Wool	41·4	51·1	62·1
Non-Ferrous Metals	29·7	45·4	57·7
Coal	3·8	5·8	0·6
Nitrates,	1·4	2·5	7·0
Other Raw Materials	68·5	83·2	89·9
Total Raw Materials	262·6	319·5	371·5

(c) Imports of Semi-Manufactured Goods

	1925–1926	1926–1927	1927–1928
Dyestuffs	15·7	10·6	11·1
Tanning Materials	11·4	12·2	15·7
Cotton and Woollen Yarn	30·3	15·5	26·0
Special Ferrous Metals	9·4	10·2	16·3
Paper	27·1	17·4	12·9
Hides	4·9	4·7	8·4
Other Semi-Manufactured Goods	63·0	47·3	49·6
Total Semi-Manufactured Goods	161·8	117·9	140·0

[continued

Table No. 39 (*continued*)

(d) Imports of Equipment

	1925–1926	1926–1927	1927–1928
Machines (other than Electrical)	67·9	95·6	136·3
Electrical Equipment	14·8	24·4	46·0
Technical Supplies	19·7	26·7	48·5
Transport Equipment	0·4	1·2	9·1
Total Equipment	102·8	147·9	239·9

Source : *Promyshlennyi Import*, ed. S. Aralov and A. Shatkhan (1930), pp. 174, 178-179, 198-199, 228-229.

Table No. 40

Trade with Principal Countries
(in percentages of total exports and imports)

	1913		1928		1929	
	Exports	Imports	Exports	Imports	Exports	Imports
Germany	29·9	47·5	23·6	24·9	23·4	22·1
Great Britain	17·8	12·6	20·4	4·4	21·9	6·2
France	6·7	4·1	5·5	3·7	4·6	3·6
Italy	4·8	1·2	3·3	1·1	3·6	0·9
Poland	—	—	1·8	1·0	1·4	2·2
U.S.A.	0·9	5·8	5·7	19·5	4·6	20·1
Other Countries	39·9	28·8	39·7	45·4	40·9	44·9
Total	100.0	100·0	100·0	100·0	100·0	100·0

Source : *Narodnoe Khozyaistvo SSSR* (1932), pp. 387, 394.

Table No. 41

Net Expenditure of State Budget
(in million rubles at current prices)

	1925–1926		1926–1927		1927–1928		1928–1929	
	Amount	Per cent of Total	Amount	Per cent of Total	Amount	Per cent of Total	Amount	Per cent of Total
National Economy	681	26·0	1199	32·5	1675	38·3	2246	41·7
Social and Cultural Measures	276	10·5	356	9·6	426	9·7	482	8·9
Defence	638	24·3	634	17·2	775	17·7	880	16·3
Administration	262	10·0	369	10·0	335	7·7	327	6·1
Transferred to Local Budgets	666	25·4	909	24·6	966	22·1	1264	23·5
Other Expenditure	100	3·8	226	6·1	199	4·5	186	3·5
Total	2623	100·0	3693	100·0	4376	100·0	5385	100·0

Sources: See R. W. Davies, *The Development of the Soviet Budgetary System* (1958), pp. 83, 296. The above table is reclassified from the original data; it excludes "self-balancing" expenditure on the transport and postal services (expenditure which was covered by the income of these sectors; at this time all the income of these sectors appeared in the budget), and also excludes expenditure on servicing state loans. Local additions to the industrial tax have been included here under "Transferred to Local Budgets" for the years 1925–1926, 1926–1927 and 1927–1928 in order to make these years comparable with 1928–1929 (see Sources to Table No. 42, p. 975 below).

Net Revenue of State Budget
(in million rubles at current prices)

	1925–1926		1926–1927		1927–1928		1928–1929	
	Amount	Per cent of Total	Amount	Per cent of Total	Amount	Per cent of Total	Amount	Per cent of Total
1. Personal Income Tax	86	3·3	114	3·0	153	3·3	166	3·0
2. Industrial Tax on Private Sector	94	3·6	109	2·9	86	1·9	170	3·1
3. Industrial Tax : Local Addition	252	9·6	327	8·7	331	7·2	—	—
4. Industrial Tax on Socialized Sector	135	5·1	240	6·4	288	6·3	886	15·9
5. Income Tax on Socialized Sector	65	2·5	78	2·1	78	1·7	120	2·2
6. Agricultural Tax	252	9·6	358	9·5	354	7·7	449	8·1
7. Excise Duties	842	31·9	1210	32·3	1491	32·6	1802	32·3
8. Customs Duties	151	5·7	190	5·1	260	5·7	258	4·6
9. Other Tax Revenue	167	6·3	192	5·1	252	5·5	152	2·7
10. Deductions from Profits	172	6·5	308	8·2	382	8·3	418	7·5
11. Other Non-Tax Revenue	360	13·7	382	10·2	418	9·1	505	9·1
12. Other Revenue	33	1·3	22	0·6	60	1·3	238	4·3
13. State Loans : Net Receipts	28	1·1	218	5·8	427	9·3	407	7·3
Total	2636	100·0	3759	100·0	4579	100·0	5572	100·0

Sources : See R. W. Davies, *The Development of the Soviet Budgetary System* (1958), pp. 82–83. The above table omits the "self-balancing" revenue from transport and the postal services, and that part of revenue from state loans which was expended each year on repayments and interest on existing loans. It includes "local additions" to industrial tax in 1925–1926, 1926–1927 and 1927–1928, in order to make these years comparable with the year 1928–1929, in which local additions were incorporated in the industrial tax (the figures for local additions were obtained from N. Bryukhanov, *Khozyaistvennyi Pod'yem Sovetskogo Soyuza i ego Finansovaya Baza* (1929), pp. 37–39 and K. Plotnikov, *Byudzhet Sotsialisticheskogo Gosudarstva* (1948), p. 21). An unexplained increase of "other revenue" in 1928–1929, amounting to 178 million rubles, was probably due to accounting procedures ; if so, total revenue in comparable terms was only 5400 million rubles in 1928–1929.

Table No. 43

Revenue from Excise Duties
(in million rubles at current prices)

	1913	1925–1926	1926–1927	1927–1928	1928–1929
Wines, Spirits and Beer	711	364	585	697	973
Tobacco	84	125	155	168	209
Sugar	149	178	245	245	302
Tea and Coffee	—	23	32	30	30
Matches	20	21	21	25	32
Kerosene, etc.	49	34	36	41	55
Textiles	—	72	100	109	134
Rubber Footwear	—	6	16	23	27
Other	—	19	12	13	34
Total	1012	842	1202	1351	1796

Sources : See R. W. Davies, *The Development of the Soviet Budgetary System* (1958), p. 123 ; *SSSR : Deyatel'nost' Sovnarkom i STO : Svodnye Materialy : IV Kvartal (Iyul'-Sentyabr') 1928–29 g.* (1929), p. 75.

Table No. 44

Currency in Circulation
(in million rubles)

	October 1	January 1	April 1	July 1
1925–1926	1074	1206	1147	1157
1926–1927	1291	1354	1284	1420
1927–1928	1628	1668	1518	1701
1928–1929	1971	2028	1998	2213

Note. The currency in circulation on October 1, 1929, reached 2642 million rubles (*Ekonomicheskoe Obozrenie*, No. 10, 1929, p. 190).

Source : *Pokazateli Kon''yunktury Narodnogo Khozyaistva SSSR za 1923/24–1928/29 gg.*, ed. A. Mendel'son (1930), p. 126.

Table No. 45

National Income *

(in million rubles at 1913 prices)

	1913		1925–1926		1926–1927		1927–1928		1928–1929 (Plan)	
	Amount	Per cent of Total	Amount	Per cent of Total	Amount	Per cent of Total	Amount	Per cent of Total	Amount	Per cent of Total
Agriculture †	7,620 ‡	51·2	7,908	55·8	8,145	54·1	8,149	50·3	8,529	48·1
Industry	3,920	26·3	3,387	23·9	3,994	26·5	4,732	29·2	5,395	30·4
Building §	730	5·1	578	4·1	610	4·0	701	4·3	882	5·0
Transport and Posts ‖	1,240	8·3	555	3·9	627	4·2	634	3·9	694	4·0
Trade	1,350	9·1	1,737	12·3	1,687	11·2	1,983	12·3	2,219	12·5
Total	14,860	100·0	14,165	100·0	15,063	100·0	16,198	100·0	17,719	100·0

* This table includes depreciation and in this respect corresponds to the gross national product of western statistics ; in Soviet national income figures, however, unlike western figures, services are not included.
† Includes forestry, fishing and hunting.
‡ This figure is based on the average harvest for several years, not the particular harvest in 1913.
§ Includes expenditure on rural farm buildings and dwellings.
‖ Passenger transport is excluded in accordance with the Soviet definition of the national income (see note * above).

Sources : 1913 : *Ekonomicheskoe Obozrenie*, No. 9, 1929, pp. 117–118. All other years : *Kontrol'nye Tsifry Narodnogo Khozyaistva SSSR na 1928–1929 god* (1929), pp. 435, 441–442.

Table No. 46

Index Numbers of Money Incomes of Population
(Preceding Year = 100)

	1926–1927	1927–1928	1928–1929 *
Rural Population			
Total Incomes (excluding earnings within the village)	108·6	112·0	116·6
Agricultural Incomes	103·9	113·0	119·4
Non-agricultural Incomes	111·7	111·7	115·9
Urban Population			
Total Incomes	116·7	109·5	110·0
Wages	118·2	113·6	114·3

* Provisional figures.

Source : *Kontrol'nye Tsifry Narodnogo Khozyaistva SSSR na 1929/30 god* (1930), pp. 476-479.

Table No. 47

Capital Investment in the National Economy *
(in million rubles at current prices)

	1925–1926	1926–1927	1927–1928	1928–1929 (Preliminary)
Industry	1003	1333	1679	2102
Electrification †	100	247	269	369
Private Agriculture ‡	2846	3147	3055	2699
State and Cooperative Agriculture ‡	88	119	181	245
Transport and Posts	550	729	981	1261
Trading, Warehousing and Primary Food Processing	129	148	176	263
Education	26	66	114	244
Health	42	80	89	92
Administration	44	53	61	59
Municipal Utilities	113	121	170	231
Urban Housing §	360	438	513	526
Other	5	8	13	13
Total	5306	6489	7301	8078

* These and other capital investment figures are for gross investment including investment in capital repair.

† Includes regional and municipal power stations, and rural electrification ; factory power stations are included under " industry " (investment amounting to 35 million rubles in 1925–1926 and 67 million rubles in 1928–1929).

‡ Includes investment in machinery and implements, buildings (including rural housing), and farm animals.

§ In addition to this figure, housing was financed under the heads " industry ", " transport " and " electrification " ; capital investment under these heads amounted to 126 million rubles in 1925–1926 and 233 million rubles in 1928–1929.

Source : *Kontrol'nye Tsifry Narodnogo Khozyaistva SSSR na 1929/30 god* (1930), pp. 458–461.

Table No. 48

Stock of Fixed Capital in the National Economy
(in million rubles at 1926-1927 prices)

	Oct. 1, 1925	Oct. 1, 1926	Oct. 1, 1927	Oct. 1, 1928	Oct. 1, 1929
Industry	6,860	7,462	8,395	9,686	11,501
Electrification	356	429	654	917	1,301
Agriculture	25,127	26,547	27,899	29,079	29,982
Transport and Posts	11,986	11,171	11,496	12,098	13,044
Trading, Warehousing and Primary Food Processing	285	396	524	698	950
Education	1,777	1,770	1,804	1,892	2,131
Health	848	872	935	1,012	1,097
Administration	481	507	544	591	641
Municipal Utilities	2,097	2,120	2,152	2,235	2,389
Housing	11,213	11,183	11,248	11,400	11,588
Total	59,951	62,375	65,548	69,483	74,501

Note. There is an unexplained discrepancy in the above table; the individual items in each column add up to more than the total given in the source.

Source: *Kontrol'nye Tsifry Narodnogo Khozyaistva SSSR na 1929/30 god* (1930), pp. 446-453.

Table No. 49

Planned Annual Increase in Gross Industrial Production in Drafts of the Five-Year Plan

(as a percentage of the previous year, calculated in fixed prices)

	1925–1926	1926–1927	1927–1928	1928–1929	1929–1930	1930–1931	1931–1932	1932–1933
Osvok Draft (July 1926) [a]	30·3	31·6	22·9	15·5	15·0	—	—	—
First Gosplan Draft (March 1926) [b]	40·8	22·6	18·8	15·5	14·7	—	—	—
Second Gosplan Draft (spring 1927)	—	19·1	13·2	10·6	9·9	9·2	—	—
Second Vesenkha Draft (spring 1927)	—	—	16·3	13·1	13·7	10·5	10·0	—
Third Gosplan Draft (autumn 1927)	—	—	16·5	12·4	10·9	10·6	10·0	—
Third Vesenkha Draft (autumn 1927)	—	—	18·0	16·4	17·4	13·7	12·9	—
Vesenkha Draft (April 1928)	—	—	23·1	18·3	18·3	18·4	18·4	(18·4)
Vesenkha Draft (August 1928)	—	—	—	19·7	17·3	17·5	17·0	14·9
Vesenkha Draft (December 1928)	—	—	—	21·9	20·2	21·8	22·6	22·4
Gosplan Basic Variant (April 1929)	—	—	—	21·4	18·8	17·5	18·1	17·4
Gosplan Optimum Variant (April 1929)	—	—	—	21·4	21·5	22·1	23·8	25·2

Sources: [a] *Torgovo-Promyshlennaya Gazeta*, July 18, 1926 (growth measured in pre-war prices).
[b] *Problemy Planirovaniya* (*Itogi i Perspektivy*) (1926), p. 28 (pre-war prices) ; an alternative lower set of figures, measured in chervonets rubles, was also given *ibid.* p. 26.
All other figures are taken from I. Gladkov, *Ot Plana Goelro k Planu Shestoi Pyatiletki* (1956), p. 164. These figures, which are in 1926–1927 prices, have been checked with the original draft plans where possible, and variations appear to be minor ; however, the original plans usually in fact refer to *state* census industry and not to all census industry as implied in the heading in Gladkov's table.

Table No. 50

Planned Capital Investment in Vesenkha-planned Industry in Drafts of the Five-Year Plan

(in million rubles at current prices)

	1925–1926	1926–1927	1927–1928	1928–1929	1929–1930	1930–1931	1931–1932	1932–1933
Osvok Draft (July 1926) [a]	937	1550	1450	1250	960	—	—	—
First Gosplan Draft (March 1926) [b]	750	900	1000	1100	1200	—	—	—
Second Gosplan Draft (spring 1927) [c]	—	918	1142	1183	1206	1205	—	—
Second Vesenkha Draft (spring 1927) [d]	—	—	1152	1318	1380	1394	1452	—
Third Vesenkha Draft (autumn 1927) [e]	—	1002	1193	1401	1488	1501	1506	—
Vesenkha Draft (April 1928) [f]	—	—	1250	1500	1700	1875	2019	(2200)
Vesenkha Draft (August 1928) [g]	—	—	—	1647	2300	2467	2442	2240
Vesenkha Draft (December 1928) [h]	—	—	—	1619	2265	2940	3103	3159
Gosplan Basic Variant (April 1929) [i]	—	—	—	1659	2077	2395	2687	2936
Gosplan Optimum Variant (April 1929) [j]	—	—	—	1659	2331	2880	3165	3465

Sources : [a] *Torgovo-Promyshlennaya Gazeta*, July 18, 1926.
[b] *Problemy Planirovaniya (Itogi i Perspektivy)* (1926), p. 26.
[c] S. Strumilin, *Ocherki Sovetskoi Ekonomiki* (1928), p. 472.
[d] *Materialy k Pyatiletnemu Planu Razvitiya Promyshlennosti SSSR (1927/28–1931/32 gg.)* (1927), p. 72.
[e] *Torgovo-Promyshlennaya Gazeta*, November 4, 1927.
[f] *Ibid.* April 26, 1928.
[g] *Ibid.* August 15, 1928.
[h] *Ibid.* December 15, 1928; slightly different figures are given *ibid.* December 4, 1928.
[i] *Pyatiletnii Plan Narodno-Khozyaistvennogo Stroitel'stva SSSR* (1929), i, 160–161.
[j] *Ibid.* i, 162–163.

Table No. 51

Planned Industrial Productivity, Wages, Costs and Prices in Drafts of the Five-Year Plan

(percentage increase (+) or decrease (−) in last year of the plan as compared with the year preceding the initial year)

	Productivity of Labour in Industry	Nominal Wages in Industry	Costs of Industrial Production	Retail Prices of Industrial Goods	Period Covered by Plan
Osvok Draft (July 1926) [a]	+60	+26	−22	−22	1925–1926 to 1929–1930
First Gosplan Draft (March 1926) [b]	+57	+54	−28	−20	1925–1926 to 1929–1930
Second Gosplan Draft (spring 1927) [c]	+50	+33	−17	−18*	1926–1927 to 1930–1931
Second Vesenkha Draft (spring 1927) [d]	+50	+20	−17	−25	1927–1928 to 1931–1932
Third Gosplan Draft (autumn 1927) [e]	+56 to +63	+26	?	−20 to −21*	1927–1928 to 1931–1932
Third Vesenkha Draft (autumn 1927) [f]	+63	+25	−24	−25	1927–1928 to 1931–1932
Vesenkha Draft (April 1928) [g]	+75	+25	−27	−21	1928–1929 to 1932–1933
Vesenkha Draft (August 1928) [h]	+76	+28	−25	−22*	1928–1929 to 1932–1933
Vesenkha Draft (December 1928) [i]	+95	+36	−32	−24*	1928–1929 to 1932–1933
Gosplan Basic Variant (April 1929) [j]	+85	+40	−30	−20	1928–1929 to 1932–1933
Gosplan Optimum Variant (April 1929) [j]	+110	+47	−35	−23	1928–1929 to 1932–1933

* Wholesale industrial prices.

Sources: [a] *Torgovo-Promyshlennaya Gazeta*, July 18, 1926.
[b] *Problemy Planirovaniya (Itogi i Perspektivy)* (1926), pp. 28-29.
[c] S. Strumilin, *Ocherki Sovetskoi Ekonomiki* (1928), pp. 441-442, 456; *Planovoe Khozyaistvo*, No. 5, 1927, p. 11.
[d] *Materialy k Pyatiletnemu Planu Razvitiya Promyshlennosti SSSR (1927/28–1931/32 gg.)* (1927), pp. 23, 53; *Pravda*, June 21, 1927.
[e] *Torgovo-Promyshlennaya Gazeta*, October 25, 1927.
[f] *2 Sessiya Tsentral'nogo Ispolnitel'nogo Komiteta Soyuza SSR 4 Sozyva SSSR 4 Sozyva* (n.d. [1927]), pp. 256-257; *Torgovo-Promyshlennaya Gazeta*, November 4, 1927.
[g] *Ibid.* April 24, 1928.
[h] *Ibid.* August 15, 1928; *Pravda*, September 2, 1928.
[i] *Torgovo-Promyshlennaya Gazeta*, December 15, 1928.
[j] *Pyatiletnii Plan Narodno-Khozyaistvennogo Stroitel'stva SSSR* (1929), i, 83, 95, 105.

LIST OF ABBREVIATIONS

Arcos	= Vserossiskoe Kooperativnoe Aktsionernoe Obshchestvo (All-Russian Cooperative Joint Stock Company).
ASSR	= Avtonomnaya Sovetskaya Sotsialisticheskaya Respublika (Autonomous Soviet Socialist Republic).
Azneft	= Azerbaizhanskoe Neftyanoe Upravlenie (Azerbaijan Oil Administration).
Comintern	= Kommunisticheskii Internatsional (Communist International).
Dnieproges	= Dneprovskaya Gidroelektricheskaya Stantsiya (Dnieper Hydro-electric Station).
Dnieprostroi	= Dneprovskoe Stroitel'stvo (Dnieper Construction).
Donbass	= Donetskii Bassein (Donets Basin).
Elektrobank	= Aktsionernyi Bank po Elektrifikatsii (Joint Stock Bank for Electrification).
GAZ	= Gor'kovskii Avtomobil'nii Zavod (Gorky Motor Works).
genplan	= general'nyi plan (general [10–15-year] plan)
GET	= Gosudarstvennyi Elektrotekhnicheskii Trest (State Electrical Engineering Trust).
GEU	= Glavnoe Ekonomicheskoe Upravlenie (Chief Economic Administration [of Vesenkha]).
Gipromez	= Gosudarstvennyi Institut po Proektirovaniyu Metallicheskikh Zavodov (State Institute for Projects of Metal Works).
Giproshakht	= Gosudarstvennyi Institut po Proektirovaniyu Shakhtnogo Stroitel'stva v Kamennougol'noi Promyshlennosti (State Institute for Projects of Mines in the Coal Industry).
Glavchermet	= Glavnoe Upravlenie po Chernoi Metallurgii (Chief Administration for the Ferrous Metals Industry).
Glavelektro	= Glavnoe Upravlenie Elektricheskoi Promyshlennosti (Chief Administration of the Electrical Industry).

Glavgortop	= Glavnoe Gorno-toplivnoe i Geologo-geodicheskoe Upravlenie (Chief Administration for Mining, Fuel, Geology and Geodesy).
Glavk	= Glavnoe Upravlenie (Chief Administration).
Glavmetall	= Glavnoe Upravlenie Metallicheskoi Promyshlennosti (Chief Administration of the Metal Industry).
Glavprofobr	= Glavnyi Komitet Professional'no-Tekhnicheskogo Obrazovaniya (Chief Committee for Professional and Technical Education).
Glavtekstil	= Glavnoe Upravlenie Tekstil'noi Promyshlennosti (Chief Administration of the Textile Industry).
Goelro	= Gosudarstvennaya Komissiya po Elektrifikatsii Rossii (State Commission for the Electrification of Russia).
Gomzy	= Gosudarstvennye Ob"edinennye Mashinostroitel'nye Zavody (State Unified Engineering Factories).
Gorpo	= Gorodskoe Potrebitel'skoe Obshchestvo (Urban Consumer Society).
Gosbank	= Gosudarstvennyi Bank (State Bank).
Gosplan	= Gosudarstvennaya Planovaya Komissiya (State Planning Commission).
Gossel'sindikat	= Gosudarstvennyi Selskokhozyaistvennyi Sindikat (State Agricultural Syndicate).
GOST	= Gosudarstvennyi Standart (State Standard).
GPU	= Gosudarstvennoe Politicheskoe Upravlenie (State Political Administration).
Gubsovnarkhoz	= Gubernskii Sovet Narodnogo Khozyaistva (Provincial Council of National Economy).
GUM	= Gosudarstvennyi Universal'nyi Magazin (State Universal Store).
IKKI	= Ispolnitel'nyi Komitet Kommunisticheskogo Internatsionala (Executive Committee of the Communist International).
Ispolkom	= Ispolnitel'nyi Komitet (Executive Committee).
ITS	= Inzhenerno-Tekhnicheskaya Sektsiya (Engineers' and Technicians' Section).
Khleboprodukt	= Aktsionernoe Obshchestvo Torgovli Khlebnymi i Drugimi Sel'skohozyaistvennymi Produktami (Joint Stock Company for Trade in Grain and Other Agricultural Products).
Khozraschet	= Khozyaistvennyi Raschet (Economic Accounting).

KIM	= Kommunisticheskii Internatsional Molodezhi (Communist Youth International).
Kolkhoz	= Kollektivnoe Khozyaistvo (Collective Farm).
Kolkhoztsentr	= Vserossiiskii Soyuz Sel'skokhozyaistvennykh Kollektivov (All-Russian Union of Agricultural Collectives).
Komnezamozhi	= Komiteti Nezamozhikh Selyan ([Ukrainian] Committees of Poor Peasants).
Komsomol	= Kommunisticheskii Soyuz Molodezhi (Communist League of Youth).
Komzet	= Komitet po Zemel'nomu Ustroistvu Trudyashchikhsya Evreev (Committee for the Settlement on the Land of Jewish Toilers).
Kozhsindikat	= Kozhevennyi Sindikat (Leather Syndicate).
Kuznetsktroi	= Kuznetskoe Stroitel'stvo (Kuznetsk Construction).
Lenmashtrest	= Leningradskii Mashinostroitel'nyi Trest (Leningrad Engineering Trust).
L'notsentr	= Tsentral'nyi Kooperativnyi Soyuz L'novodov i Konoplevodov (Central Cooperative Union of Flax and Hemp Growers).
Metallosindikat	= Metallurgicheskii Sindikat (Metals Syndicate).
Mosmashtrest	= Moskovskii Mashinostroitel'nii Trest (Moscow Engineering Trust).
MPU	= Mobilizatsionno-Planovoe Upravlenie (Mobilization Planning Administration [of Vesenkha]).
MTS	= Mashino-Traktornaya Stantsiya (Machine Tractor Station).
Narkomat	= Narodnyi Komissariat (People's Commissariat).
Narkomfin	= Narodnyi Komissariat Finansov (People's Commissariat of Finance).
Narkomindel	= Narodnyi Komissariat Inostrannykh Del (People's Commissariat of Foreign Affairs).
Narkompros	= Narodnyi Komissariat Prosveshcheniya (People's Commissariat of Education [of RSFSR]).
Narkomput'	= Narodnyi Komissariat Putei Soobshcheniya (People's Commissariat of Communications).
Narkomtorg	= Narodnyi Komissariat Vneshnei i Vnutrennoi Torgovli (People's Commissariat of External and Internal Trade).
Narkomtrud	= Narodnyi Komissariat Truda (People's Commissariat of Labour).

Narkomyust	= Narodnyi Komissariat Yustitsii (People's Commissariat of Justice [of RSFSR]).
Narkomzem	= Narodnyi Komissariat Zemledeliya (People's Commissariat of Agriculture [of RSFSR unless otherwise stated]).
NEP	= Novaya Ekonomicheskaya Politika (New Economic Policy).
NTS	= Nauchno-Tekhnicheskii Sovet (Scientific and Technical Council).
NTU	= Nauchno-Tekhnicheskoe Upravlenie (Scientific and Technical Administration [of Vesenkha]).
ODK	= Otdel Dolgosrochnogo Kredita (Department of Long-term Credit [of Prombank]).
OGPU	= Ob"edinennoe Gosudarstvennoe Politicheskoe Upravlenie (Unified State Political Administration).
Orgraspred	= Organizatsionno-Raspreditel'nyi Otdel (Organization and Distribution Department).
Ornitso	= Obshchestvo Rabotnikov Nauki i Tekhniki dlya Sodeistviya Sotsialisticheskomu Stroitel'stvu (Society of Scientific and Technical Workers to Assist Socialist Construction).
Osoaviakhim	= Obshchestvo Sodeistviya Oborone, Aviatsii i Khimii (Society for the Promotion of Defence, Aviation and Chemistry).
Osvok	= Osoboe Soveshchanie po Vosstanovleniyu Osnovnogo Kapitala (Special Conference [of Vesenkha] for the Restoration of Fixed Capital).
PEU	= Planovo-Ekonomicheskoe Upravlenie (Planning and Economic Administration, referred to in this volume as "planning department of Vesenkha").
Prodamet	= Prodazha Metallov (Metal Sales [Syndicate]).
Prodasilikat	= Obshchestvo po Prodazhe Stekla, Tsementa, Keramiki i Stroitel'nykh Materialov Mineral'nogo Proiskhozhdeniya (Company [Syndicate] for the Sale of Glass, Cement, Ceramics and Building Materials of Mineral Origin).
Prombank	= (to June 1928) Torgovo-Promyshlennyi Bank (Bank of Industry and Trade); (from June 1928) Bank Dolgosrochnogo Kreditovaniya Promyshlennosti i Elektrokhozyaistva (Bank for Long-term Credit to Industry and Electrification).
Promburo	= Promyshlennoe Byuro (Industrial Bureau).

Promfinplan	= Proizvodstvenno-Finansovyi plan ([industrial] production and financial plan).
Promplan	= (to August 1926) Promyshlenno-Planovaya Komissiya (Industrial Planning Commission [of Vesenkha]) ; (August 1926 to May 1927) Planovoe Upravlenie (Planning Administration [of Vesenkha]).
Rabkrin (RKI)	= Narodnyi Komissariat Raboche-Krest'yanskoi Inspektsii (People's Commissariat of Workers' and Peasants' Inspection).
RKK	= Rastsenochno-Konfliktnaya Komissiya (Assessment and Conflict Commission).
RSFSR	= Rossiskaya Sovetskaya Federativnaya Sotsialisticheskaya Respublika (Russian Soviet Federative Socialist Republic).
Sel'kor	= Sel'skii Korrespondent (Rural Correspondent).
Sel'mashsindikat	= Sindikat Sel'skokhozyaistvennykh Mashin (Syndicate for Agricultural Machines).
Sel'po	= Sel'skoe Potrebitel'skoe Obshchestvo (Village Consumer Society).
Sel'skosoyuz	= Vserossiiskii Soyuz Sel'skokhozyaistvennykh Obshchestv (All-Russian Union of Agricultural Societies).
Sevzappromburo	= Severo-zapadnoe Promyshlennoe Byuro (North-Western Industrial Bureau).
Sovkhoz	= Sovetskoe Khozyaistvo (Soviet Farm).
Sovnarkhoz	= Sovet Narodnogo Khozyaistva (Council of National Economy).
Sovnarkom	= Sovet Narodnykh Komissarov (Council of People's Commissars).
SR	= Sotsial-Revolyutsioner (Social-Revolutionary).
SSR	= Sovetskaya Sotsialisticheskaya Respublika (Soviet Socialist Republic).
STO	= Sovet Truda i Oborony (Council of Labour and Defence).
TOZ	= Tovarishchestvo dlya Obshchego Zemlepol'zovaniya (Association for Common Cultivation of Land).
TsAGI	= Tsentral'nyi Aero-Gidrodinamicheskii Institut (Central Aero-Hydrodynamic Institute).
Tsekombank	= Tsentral'nyi Bank dlya Kommunal'nogo Khozyaistva i Zhilishchnogo Stroitel'stva (Central Bank for Municipal Economy and Housing Construction).

Tsentrosel'bank	= Vsesoyuznyi Tsentral'nyi Sel'skokhozyaistvennyi Bank (All-Union Central Agricultural Bank).
Tsentrosoyuz	= Vserossiskii (*later* Vsesoyuznyi) Tsentral'nyi Soyuz Potrebitel'skikh Obshchestv (All-Russian (*later* All-Union) Central Union of Consumers' Societies).
Tsentrospirt	= Tsentral'noe Pravlenie Gosudarstvennoi Spirtovoi Monopolii (Central Administration of the State Spirit Monopoly).
TsIK	= Tsentral'nyi Ispolnitel'nyi Komitet (Central Executive Committee).
TsIT	= Tsentral'nyi Institut Truda (Central Institute of Labour).
TsOS	= Tsentral'nyi Otdel Statistiki (Central Department of Statistics [of Vesenkha]).
TsSU	= Tsentral'noe Statisticheskoe Upravlenie (Central Statistical Administration).
TsUGProm	= Tsentral'noe Upravlenie Gosudarstvennoi Promyshlennosti (Central Administration of State Industry [of Vesenkha]).
Turksib	= Turkestano-Sibirskaya Zheleznaya Doroga (Turkestan-Siberian Railway).
Turksibstroi	= Turkestano-Sibirskoe Stroitel'stvo (Turkestan-Siberian Construction).
UKK	= Uralo-Kuznetskii Kombinat (Ural-Kuznetsk Combine).
Uralmashzavod (Uralmash)	= Ural'skii Zavod Tyazhelogo Mashinostroeniya (Urals Heavy Engineering Works).
VAI	= Vserossiskaya Assotsiatsiya Inzhenerov (All-Russian Association of Engineers).
Varnitso	= Vsesoyuznaya Assotsiatsiya Rabotnikov Nauki i Tekhniki dlya Sodeistviya Sotsialisticheskomu Stroitel'stvu (All-Union Association of Scientific and Technical Workers to Assist Socialist Construction).
Vesenkha	= Vysshii Sovet Narodnogo Khozyaistva (Supreme Council of National Economy).
VKP(B)	= Vsesoyuznaya Kommunisticheskaya Partiya (Bol'shevikov) (All-Union Communist Party (Bolsheviks)).
VMBIT	= Vsesoyuznoe Mezhsektsionnoe Byuro Inzhenerov i Tekhnikov (All-Union Intersectional Bureau of Engineers and Technicians).
VMS	= Vsesoyuznyi Metallurgicheskii Sindikat (All-Union Metal Syndicate).

VMTS	= Vsesoyuznyi Mashino-Tekhnicheskii Sindikat (All-Union Machine Syndicate).
Voenprom (VPU, Glavvoenprom)	= Voenno-Promyshlennoe Upravlenie (War Industry Administration).
Volkhovstroi	= Volkhovoskoe Stroitel'stvo (Volkhov Construction).
VPK	= Vsesoyuznyi Pereselencheskii Komitet (All-Union Migration Committee).
VPU	= see Voenprom
Vsekopromsovet	= Vsesoyuznyi Sovet Respublikanskikh Tsentrov Promyslovoi Kooperatsii (All-Union Council of Republican Centres of Industrial Cooperatives).
Vsekompromsoyuz	= Vserossiskii Soyuz Promyslovykh Kooperativov (All-Russian Union of Industrial Cooperatives).
Vserabotzemles	= Vserossiskii Professional'nyi Soyuz Rabotnikov Zemli i Lesa (All-Russian Trade Union of Agricultural and Forestry Workers).
VTS	= Vsesoyuznyi Tekstil'nii Sindikat (All-Union Textile Syndicate).
VTUZ	= Vysshee Tekhnicheskoe Uchebnoe Zavedenie (Higher Technical Educational Establishment).
VUMBIT	= Vseukrainskoe Mezhsektsionnoe Byuro Inzhenerov i Tekhnikov (All-Ukrainian Intersectional Bureau of Engineers and Technicians).
VUZ	= Vysshee Uchebnoe Zavedenie (Higher Educational Establishment).
Yurt	= Yuzhno-Rudnyi Trest (Southern Ore Trust).

INDEX

INDEX

Kavkhleb, 14

Kazakhstan : and grain crisis, 49-50, 85, 100-101 ; and *kulaks*, 130 ; and kolkhozy, 174, 176n; and Sovkhozy, 187, 198-190 ; and mechanization, 209n ; and prices, 699 ; and Turksib railway, 900-902 ; and migration, 928, 930-931

Kharkov, 411, 432n, 448, 451, 546, 584, 614n, 703n, 834n

Khauke, O., 230

Khinchuk, L., 655, 661

Khleboprodukt, 14-15, 68, 221

Khlebotsentr, 15, 88, 146, 210-211, 215n, 220-222, 224, 709

Khozraschet, 362, 370, 372n-373n, 380-383, 542, 621, 636, 652, 724, 730

Khrennikov, S., 866-867n

Khutorok Sovkhoz, 213n

Khutors, 120n-124, 150, 229-235

Kiev, 514, 673, 703n

Kirgizia, 901n

Kirov, S., 12, 459, 885n, 904

Kirtorg, 645

Kolchak, A., 98

Kolkhoztsentr, 148n, 160, 168, 174, 180n, 210, 266n

Kolkhozy (Collective farms) : 17-18, 32, 41-42, 68, 158-160, 168, 191, 233 ; and hired labour, 136n, 140, 142 ; and cooperatives, 144-147, 149, 152-153, 159, 170-171 ; and *kulaks*, 159, 164, 166n, 168, 172, 175-179, 181 ; composition and numbers, 160, 162, 164-170, 173-180, 185, 944-945 ; women and, 164, 175 ; "bogus", 165-166, 177 ; and 1928 kolkhoz congresses, 167-172 ; group organization of, 172-174 ; and mechanization, 172, 197, 202-209, 212-213n, 215, 218 ; output of, 180-181, 241, 243, 246-247 ; and MTS, 214-217 ; and *kontraktatsiya*, 221 ; and land consolidation, 227, 230, 233, 235-236 ; and uncultivated lands, 240 ; and class struggle, 258, 264 ; and workers' brigades, 262n ; and collectivization, 266-269 ; and labour, 519, 957 ; and foreign trade, 709 ; and migration, 929, 931 ; *see also*

Agriculture ; *Artels* ; Communes ; Sovkhozy ; TOZy

Komarov, N., 305

Komsomol, *see* All-Union Communist League of Youth

Komzet, *see* Committee for the Settlement on the Land of Jewish Toilers

Kondratiev, N. : 733-737, 801n, 875 ; and peasantry, 20-22, 31, 58n, 128 ; and credit cooperatives, 156n ; and industrialization, 243, 306, 311, 402-403 ; and planning, 300, 791 ; and five-year plan, 857-861

Konjunktur institute, *see under* People's Commissariat of Finance

Kosior, I., 315-316, 322, 346, 377, 586

Kosior, S., 125, 250, 571

Kostroma, 453n

Kovalevsky, N., 839

Kozelev, 511, 556

Kozhsindikat, 639n

Kramatorsk works, 438, 444

Krasin, L., 406, 706

Krasnoe Sormovo works, 407n

Krasnyi Oktyabr works, 449

Kraval, I., 286, 487, 489, 492, 496, 505, 517, 523-524, 569, 580n, 594-595, 736, 753n

Kremenchug wagon works, 536n

Kritsman, L., 21, 44n, 265, 795n

Krivoi Rog, 296, 436-438, 441, 443-444, 449, 911

Krol, S., 289n, 492, 549-550, 557-558

Krumin, G., 687n, 777

Krupp works, 412

Krupskaya, N., 6n, 246, 264n, 537

Krylenko, N., 585

Krzhizhanovsky, G., and agriculture, 34, 107 ; and Sovkhozy, 186 ; and mechanization, 210, 213n ; and agricultural production, 237n, 249, 252 ; and industrialization, 290, 307, 322, 326, 414-415, 788-789 ; and planning, 307, 788-789, 802-803n, 806, 816, 824n, 826 ; and regionalization, 363n ; and electrification, 420, 803n, 837 ; and defence, 431, 816 ; and labour, 470 ; and housing, 619, 621 ; and market

VUMBIT, see All-Ukrainian Inter-
sectional Bureau of Engineers and
Technicians
Vyselki, 234

Wages, 282, 287-288, 333, 336-339,
345, 349, 466, 487-489, 494-498,
505, 507, 512, 519n-544, 857, 958,
983 ; see also Labour ; Trade
Unions
Ware, H., 190
Wheat, 8, 63, 70-71, 88, 103-105, 219,
238n, 694, 698, 701-702n, 706, 712,
943-944, 969-971
White Russian SSR ; and grain crisis,
49, 57 ; land policy, 106, 111, 120 ;
and kulaks, 130 ; and kolkhozy, 164,
172n, 174n, 185 ; and Sovkhozy,
182, 185 ; and kontraktatsiya, 220 ;
and agricultural output, 239 ; and
wages, 543 ; and housing, 616n ;
and cooperatives, 662 ; and planning, 844 ; and peasant migration,
925, 927, 930n-932
Wine, 139, 762-763, 976
Wool, 711, 972
World Economic Conference, 342,
714

Yaglom, Ya., 553
Yakovlev, Ya., 9, 168, 233, 236n, 239,
241, 347n, 689, 889
Yaroslavl, 445, 549
Yaroslavsky, E., 78
Yugostal, 272, 304, 333, 346, 363,
370, 377, 379-380, 382-383, 432n,
434, 439, 455, 469, 486, 508, 510,
554, 827
Yurovsky, L., 278n, 723, 733, 735n,
775, 795, 888
Yurt, see Southern Ore Trust
Yuzhmashtrest, see Southern Engi-
neering Trust

Zalkind, L., 628n
Zaporozhie, 437, 441, 444, 911-912
Zbarsky, B., 583-584
Zernotrest, 189-191, 193-194, 932
Zhdanov, I. P., 50, 480, 556-557
Zinoviev, G. : and grain crisis, 5-6n,
10-11, 22n ; and peasantry, 28, 30 ;
and Kondratiev group, 31, 735-736 ;
expelled from party, 35, 37; and
industrialization, 286-287; and shift
system, 497-498; and wages, 525 ;
and specialists, 590 ; and price
control, 683
Zolotarev, A., 321, 346, 369n, 882, 885